T0310910

Intravascular Imaging:

Current Applications and Research Developments

Vasilios D. Tsakanikas
University of Ioannina, Greece

Lampros K. Michalis
University of Ioannina, Greece

Dimitrios I. Fotiadis
University of Ioannina, Greece

Katerina K. Naka
University of Ioannina, Greece, and Michaelideion Cardiology Center, Greece

Christos V. Bourantas
University of Ioannina, Greece

A volume in the Advances in
Bioinformatics and Biomedical
Engineering (ABBE) Book Series

Medical Information Science
REFERENCE
An Imprint of IGI Global

Managing Director:	Lindsay Johnston
Senior Editorial Director:	Heather Probst
Book Production Manager:	Sean Woznicki
Development Manager:	Joel Gamon
Development Editor:	Hannah Abelbeck
Acquisitions Editor:	Erika Gallagher
Typesetters:	Lisandro Gonzalez
Print Coordinator:	Jamie Snavely
Cover Design:	Nick Newcomer

Published in the United States of America by
Medical Information Science Reference (an imprint of IGI Global)
701 E. Chocolate Avenue
Hershey PA 17033
Tel: 717-533-8845
Fax: 717-533-8661
E-mail: cust@igi-global.com
Web site: http://www.igi-global.com

Library of Congress Cataloging-in-Publication Data

Intravascular imaging: current applications and research developments / Vasilios D. Tsakanikas ... [et al.], editors.
     p. ; cm.
  Includes bibliographical references and index.
  Summary: This book presents available intravascular imaging techniques and analyzes their impact in clinical practice and research--Provided by publisher.
  ISBN 978-1-61350-095-8 (hardcover) -- ISBN 978-1-61350-096-5 (ebook) -- ISBN 978-1-61350-097-2 (print & perpetual access)
  I. Tsakanikas, Vasilios D., 1983-
  [DNLM: 1. Coronary Artery Disease--ultrasonography. 2. Ultrasonography, Interventional--methods. 3. Diagnostic Imaging--methods. WG 300]
  LC classification not assigned
  617.4'1207543--dc23
                         2011030000

This book is published in the IGI Global book series Advances in Bioinformatics and Biomedical Engineering (ABBE) (ISSN: 2327-7033; eISSN: 2327-7041)

British Cataloguing in Publication Data
A Cataloguing in Publication record for this book is available from the British Library.

Advances in Bioinformatics and Biomedical Engineering (ABBE) Book Series

Ahmad Taher Azar
Benha University, Egypt

ISSN: 2327-7033
EISSN: 2327-7041

MISSION

The fields of biology and medicine are constantly changing as research evolves and novel engineering applications and methods of data analysis are developed. Continued research in the areas of bioinformatics and biomedical engineering is essential to continuing to advance the available knowledge and tools available to medical and healthcare professionals.

The **Advances in Bioinformatics and Biomedical Engineering (ABBE) Book Series** publishes research on all areas of bioinformatics and bioengineering including the development and testing of new computational methods, the management and analysis of biological data, and the implementation of novel engineering applications in all areas of medicine and biology. Through showcasing the latest in bioinformatics and biomedical engineering research, ABBE aims to be an essential resource for healthcare and medical professionals.

COVERAGE

- Biomechanical Engineering
- Biostatistics
- Chemical Structures
- Computational Biology
- Dental Engineering
- DNA sequencing
- Drug Design
- Genomics
- Rehabilitation Engineering
- Robotics and Medicine

IGI Global is currently accepting manuscripts for publication within this series. To submit a proposal for a volume in this series, please contact our Acquisition Editors at Acquisitions@igi-global.com or visit: http://www.igi-global.com/publish/.

Titles in this Series

For a list of additional titles in this series, please visit: www.igi-global.com

Technological Advancements in Biomedicine for Healthcare Applications
Jinglong Wu (Okayama University, Japan)
Medical Information Science Reference • copyright 2013 • 382pp • H/C (ISBN: 9781466621961) • US $245.00 (our price)

Biomedical Engineering and Cognitive Neuroscience for Healthcare Interdisciplinary Applications
Jinglong Wu (Okayama University, Japan)
Medical Information Science Reference • copyright 2013 • 472pp • H/C (ISBN: 9781466621138) • US $245.00 (our price)

Pharmacoinformatics and Drug Discovery Technologies Theories and Applications
Tagelsir Mohamed Gasmelseid (King Faisal University, Kingdom of Saudi Arabia)
Medical Information Science Reference • copyright 2012 • 442pp • H/C (ISBN: 9781466603097) • US $245.00 (our price)

Machine Learning in Computer-Aided Diagnosis Medical Imaging Intelligence and Analysis
Kenji Suzuki (University of Chicago, USA)
Medical Information Science Reference • copyright 2012 • 524pp • H/C (ISBN: 9781466600591) • US $245.00 (our price)

Systemic Approaches in Bioinformatics and Computational Systems Biology Recent Advances
Paola Lecca (The Microsoft Research – University of Trento, Centre for Computational and Systems Biology, Italy)
Dan Tulpan (National Research Council of Canada, Canada) and Kanagasabai Rajaraman (Institute for Infocomm Research, Singapore)
Medical Information Science Reference • copyright 2012 • 471pp • H/C (ISBN: 9781613504352) • US $265.00 (our price)

Intravascular Imaging Current Applications and Research Developments
Vasilios D. Tsakanikas (University of Ioannina, Greece) Lampros K. Michalis (University of Ioannina, Greece)
Dimitrios I. Fotiadis (University of Ioannina, Greece) Katerina K. Naka (University of Ioannina, Greece, and Michaelideion Cardiology Center, Greece) and Christos V. Bourantas (University of Ioannina, Greece)
Medical Information Science Reference • copyright 2012 • 478pp • H/C (ISBN: 9781613500958) • US $245.00 (our price)

DISSEMINATOR of KNOWLEDGE

www.igi-global.com

701 E. Chocolate Ave., Hershey, PA 17033
Order online at www.igi-global.com or call 717-533-8845 x100
To place a standing order for titles released in this series, contact: cust@igi-global.com
Mon-Fri 8:00 am - 5:00 pm (est) or fax 24 hours a day 717-533-8661

Table of Contents

Section 2
Imaging by Angioscopy

Section 3
Thermography

Section 4
Optical Coherence Tomography

Section 5
Intracoronary Near-Infrared Spectroscopy

Section 6
Intracardiac Echocardiography

Section 7
Fusion Methodologies

Section 8
Current Status of Vascular Imaging

Section 9
Intravascular Imaging and Haemodynamics

Section 10
Future Trends in Intravascular Imaging

Detailed Table of Contents

Section 1
Intravascular Ultrasound

Chapter 1

Ourania Katsarou, National and Kapodistrian University of Athens Medical School, Greece
Manolis Vavuranakis, National and Kapodistrian University of Athens Medical School, Greece

Before proceeding with the clinical and research utility of Intravascular Imaging, it is important to examine in detail the principles that the acquisition of the IVUS signal is based on. This chapter provides an insight into the principles of the IVUS imaging, while describing the image quality factors. Additionally, the equipment for IVUS examination is described, and the acquisition and display techniques are detailed. Finally, a brief summary of the limitations of the IVUS signal is attempted.

Chapter 2

Katerina K. Naka, University of Ioannina, Greece
Nikolaos D. Papamichael, University of Ioannina, Greece

Intravascular ultrasound (IVUS) is an imaging modality often used as a supplement to coronary angiography and allows accurate assessment of the lumen, vessel wall, and atherosclerotic plaque. A coherent interpretation of the IVUS images requires identification of the image artefacts that emerge during IVUS interrogation and can often be quite difficult. This chapter describes the morphologic appearance of the structures seen in IVUS, presents the morphologic characteristics of the different types of plaque, and summarizes the nomenclature and definitions used during IVUS interpretation. Moreover, it focuses on the quantitative analysis and reports the measurements obtained during IVUS processing. Finally, it presents some of the clinical (e.g. assessment of the extent and severity of a lesion, treatment planning) and research (e.g. evaluation of atherosclerotic progression/regression, transplant vasculopathy, peripheral arterial disease) applications of this modality aiming to highlight its value in the clinical and research arena.

Chapter 3

Antonis A. Sakellarios, University of Ioannina, Greece

Christos V. Bourantas, Castle Hill Hospital, UK

Lambros S. Athanasiou, University of Ioannina, Greece

Dimitrios I. Fotiadis, University of Ioannina, Greece

Lampros K. Michalis, University of Ioannina, Greece

Intravascular Ultrasound (IVUS) is an invasive imaging technique that allows detailed visualization of the arterial lumen and outer vessel wall and permits characterization of the type of the plaque and quantification of its burden. Traditionally IVUS processing was performed manually. However, it became apparent that manual segmentation is time consuming, and the obtained results depend on the experience of the operators. To overcome these limitations and enhance the role of IVUS in clinical practice and research, several (semi-) automated methods have been developed that expedite detection of the regions of interest and/or characterization of the type of the plaque. In this chapter we review the available IVUS processing techniques and present the developed commercial solutions for IVUS segmentation and plaque characterization.

Chapter 4

Attila Thury, Erasmus MC, The Netherlands & University of Szeged, Hungary

Héctor M. Garcia-Garcia, Erasmus MC, The Netherlands

Evelyn Regar, Erasmus MC, The Netherlands

IVUS opened new perspectives in our understanding of human coronary atherosclerosis and triggers of ACS (especially plaque rupture as its most dominant cause). Throughout this chapter we list the shortcomings of conventional (greyscale) IVUS to characterize tissue components of plaques and the potentials of radiofrequency signal processing to overcome these. In recent years, the technology matured, and especially with VH and IB-IVUS, many clinical studies showed accurate plaque estimation. Results of a prospective, natural history study have just been presented and proved the ability of VH to predict ACS. Palpography derives compositional information from functional (strain) measurements. Assessing several characteristics of a given plaque could potentially enhance invasive risk stratification by identifying very high-risk plaques, thereby reducing the number of vulnerable plaques that need to be serially followed and ultimately treated. Moreover, if a safe prophylactic local treatment was available, a sophisticated IVUS procedure would be a part of a "one-stop-shop" in preventive cardiology.

Chapter 5

Christos V. Bourantas, Castle Hill Hospital, UK

Katerina K. Naka, University of Ioannina, Greece

Scot Garg, Castle Hill Hospital, UK

Farqad M. Alamgir, Castle Hill Hospital, UK

Angela Hoye, Castle Hill Hospital, UK

Lampros K. Michalis, University of Ioannina, Greece

Intracoronary ultrasound (ICUS) provides detailed microscopic imaging of coronary anatomy within a living patient. These images allow visualization of lumen, outer vessel wall, and plaque and give reliable information regarding the constitution of the plaque and the extent of the atherosclerotic disease.

However, although it provides supplementary information to coronary angiography which may be useful in diagnosis and treatment planning, its clinical application is limited due to the additional expense, procedure time, and the risk of complication that ICUS examination carries. In this chapter, we review the literature and summarize the clinical indications of ICUS imaging in diagnostic and therapeutic procedures.

Hector M. Garcia-Garcia, Erasmus MC, The Netherlands
Scot Garg, Royal Blackburn Hospital, UK
Salvatore Brugaletta, Erasmus MC, The Netherlands
Roberto Diletti, Erasmus MC, The Netherlands
Eun-Seok Shin, Erasmus MC, The Netherlands & University of Ulsan College of Medicine, Korea
Patrick W. Serruys, Erasmus MC, The Netherlands

Intravascular ultrasound was designed to overcome the limitations of angiography, and in the process it has helped greatly with our understanding of coronary artery disease. There is no doubt that it plays an important role in contemporary interventional cardiology. In this regard, this chapter reviews the most important uses of intravascular ultrasound in current research.

Section 2
Imaging by Angioscopy

Michael Rees, Bangor University, UK

Within this chapter, the basic clinical and research utilities of Angioscopy are described. Among its paragraphs, an attempt is made to outline the role of angioscopy to the understanding of cardiovascular disease as well as its contribution to the understanding of cardiovascular procedures. Additionally, the techniques, which combine stenting procedures with angioscopy, are detailed.

Section 3
Thermography

Konstantinos Toutouzas, Athens Medical School, Greece
Maria Drakopoulou, Athens Medical School, Greece
Christodoulos Stefanadis, Athens Medical School, Greece

This chapter is devoted to Thermography, and more specifically, to the basic principles and mechanisms of data acquisition. A detailed description of the potential mechanisms of increased heat generation by vulnerable plaques is provides, along with a list of Thermography devices. Additionally, a special subsection of the chapter deals with the limitation of intracoronary thermography, an extremely crucial issue for both the clinical and research utility of Thermography.

This chapter completes the description of the Thermography within this publication. While the previous chapter of this section dealt with principles of data acquisition, this chapter provides a detailed description of the research and clinical utility of thermography. Separate sections are devoted to the ex vivo thermography studies, to the role of thermography in experimental models and finally to the contribution of thermography in clinical studies.

Section 4
Optical Coherence Tomography

This chapter is devoted to the description of the basic principles of data acquisition of the Optical Coherence Tomography imaging technique. The physical mechanisms of the tissue optics are detailed, while the architecture of the OCT system is provided, emphasizing on both the TD-OCT and FD-OCT. Then, after discussing about the OCT image resolution, a parametric comparison of OCT with regard to IVUS imaging technique is attempted. Finally, the limitations of the technique are described, along with the safety of its application to the clinical practice.

Optical coherence tomography (OCT) is a light-based invasive imaging method allowing accurate evaluation of coronary luminal morphology and reliable characterization of plaque. Its high resolution (10-20μm) offers the unique possibility of identifying clinically important coronary plaque microstructures such as macrophages, the presence and type of thrombus, stent expansion and endothelization and provides accurate assessment of the fibrous cap thickness in high risk plaques. These attributes placed OCT in a unique position as useful tool in research and clinical practice. As a new image modality, many interventional cardiologists are not familiar with its interpretation. In addition, there are only few developed methodologies able to process the OCT data and give comprehensive vessel representation and reliable measurements. Thus, this chapter focuses on the interpretation of OCT images and discusses the available image processing methodologies.

Chapter 12

Francesco Prati, San Giovanni Hospital, Italy & CLI Foundation, Italy

Alessandro Di Giorgio, Ferrarotto Hospital, Italy, & ETNA Foundation, Italy

Vito Ramazzotti, San Giovanni Hospital, Italy

Maria Teresa Mallus, San Giovanni Hospital, Italy

This chapter provides a detailed description of the role of the OCT technique in the clinical practice. A review section on data from clinical studies is provided, underlining the extent usage of OCT during the last years. Finally, the capability of OCT to assess ambiguous lesions and deferral of interventions is discussed just before describing the role of the technique during the post procedural assessment.

Chapter 13

Konstantinos Toutouzas, Athens Medical School, Greece

Antonios Karanasos, Athens Medical School, Greece

Christodoulos Stefanadis, Athens Medical School, Greece

Within this chapter, the research utility of OCT is detailed. Issues like the potential of OCT for plaque characterization are covered. Additionally, a comparative evaluation of OCT with other invasive imaging techniques, as far as plaque components identification is concerned, is attempted. Finally, the role of OCT for the evaluation of plaque progression is discussed as well as its part in the future research arena.

Section 5
Intracoronary Near-Infrared Spectroscopy

Chapter 14

Emmanouil S. Brilakis, Dallas VA Medical Center, USA

Stephen T. Sum, InfraReDx, USA

Sean P. Madden, InfraReDx, USA

James E. Muller, InfraReDx, USA

Intracoronary near-infrared spectroscopy (NIRS) is a novel catheter-based technique that allows determination of the chemical composition of the coronary artery wall. This is accomplished by measuring the proportion of near-infrared light diffusely reflected by the arterial wall after scattering and absorption have occurred. Histology and clinical studies have validated that NIRS can detect with high accuracy the presence of coronary lipid core plaques, which form the substrate for most acute coronary syndromes and complicate stenting procedures. Coronary NIRS is currently being evaluated as a tool to: (Clarke, Figg, & Maguire, 2006) optimize the outcomes of percutaneous coronary interventions (PCI), (Ross, 1999) identify coronary lesions at risk for causing events and optimize the medical management of such patients, and (Kagan, Livsic, Sternby, & Vihert, 1968) allow evaluation of novel anti-atherosclerotic treatments.

Section 6
Intracardiac Echocardiography

Chapter 15

Rajesh K Nair, Rigshospitalet, Denmark

Poay Huan Loh, Rigshospitalet, Denmark

Lars Sondergaard, Rigshospitalet, Denmark

Intracardiac echocardiography (ICE) represents one of the major recent advancements in cardiovascular imaging that has directly widened the scope of structural heart disease intervention. It has replaced trans-esophageal echocardiography in many of the structural heart disease interventional procedures and hence, precluded the need for general anaesthetic and its associated clinical and logistic issues. Although ICE has been available for more than two decades, it is still not widely used, and many interventional cardiologists remain unfamiliar to this technology. It is the aim of this chapter to provide a comprehensive overview of the commercially available devices with specific reference to the AcuNav™ catheter (Biosense Webster, California, USA), the procedural steps, and clinical applications of this imaging technique.

Section 7
Fusion Methodologies

Chapter 16

Panagiotis Siogkas, University of Ioannina, Greece

Dimitrios I. Fotiadis, University of Ioannina, Greece

Christos V. Bourantas, Castle Hill Hospital, UK & East Yorkshire NHS Trust, UK

Ann C. Tweddel, Castle Hill Hospital, UK & East Yorkshire NHS Trust, UK

Scot Garg, Royal Blackburn Hospital, UK

Lampros K. Michalis, University of Ioannina, Greece

Dimitris Koutsouris, National Technical University of Athens, Greece

New developments in the treatment of coronary artery disease have increased the demand for a more detailed, accurate, and comprehensive evaluation of coronary artery functional anatomy. Though there are a multitude of modalities available for the study of coronary anatomy, each has significant limitations, and thus, do not permit a complete functional assessment of coronary anatomy. To overcome these drawbacks, fusion of different imaging modalities has been proposed. The aim of this chapter is to describe the most prevalent and emerging of these fused imaging modalities and present their current and potential applications, highlighting their impact in the clinical and research arena.

Section 8
Current Status of Vascular Imaging

Chapter 17

Angela Hoye, Castle Hill Hospital, UK

When undertaking coronary intervention, the use of intravascular imaging is an important adjunct to gain additional information regarding the procedure and help to optimise the results. Intra-vascular ultrasound (IVUS) is a familiar modality that is particularly useful at assessing the vessel both prior to and following intervention with stent implantation. Optical coherence tomography (OCT) has been introduced more recently and provides highly detailed images enabling assessment of features such as tissue coverage of individual stent struts. However, OCT has only limited tissue penetration as compared with IVUS. The following chapter aims to provide an overview as to the strengths and weaknesses of both imaging techniques, which should be seen as complementary, and discusses the implications of these modalities in current clinical practice.

Chapter 18

Rupture of high risk atherosclerotic plaque is responsible for acute vascular events such as myocardial infarction and sudden cardiac death. Several non-invasive vascular imaging methods have been developed to identify and characterise atherosclerotic plaques at risk of rupture. In this chapter we will discuss the background, rationale, and current state of non-invasive vascular imaging.

Section 9
Intravascular Imaging and Haemodynamics

Chapter 19

Shear stress on the endothelial surface has been implicated in atherosclerosis localization, plaque vulnerability, and remodeling behavior of the arterial wall, as well as in-stent restenosis following percutaneous coronary interventions. The purposes of this chapter are to introduce haemodynamic shear stress, briefly explain the methodology for measuring and imaging shear stress in vivo, present the role of shear stress in the atherosclerotic disease process, and cite the evidence highlighting the effects of stent implantation on local blood flow patterns and linking shear stress at the stent surface to neointimal hyperplasia following coronary artery stenting.

Section 10
Future Trends in Intravascular Imaging

Chapter 20

Vulnerable plaques have certain histopathologic and regional characteristics. The advent of novel invasive and non-invasive imaging modalities aim to identify the histopathologic and regional characteristics of vulnerable plaque, thereby enabling the early diagnosis and potential application of treatments strategies to avert future acute coronary events.

Recent advances in geometrically correct 3D IVUS reconstruction enable the depiction of the true coronary anatomy by combining IVUS data with biplane angiographic images. Further development of the existing 3D IVUS reconstruction software, in conjunction with advancing hardware capabilities, is expected to allow the implementation of real-time 3D IVUS reconstruction within the catheterization laboratories.

Coronary computed tomography angiography (CCTA) is surrounded by the safety non-invasive methods offer and the advantages of high speed that multislice CT is associated with. While calcium score and recognition of anomalous coronary arteries are acceptable applications, CCTA reveals new fields of research on coronary artery disease, including lumen, bypass grafts, and stents patency, as well as endothelial shear stress and coronary stiffness measurements.

Beyond structural information obtained by traditional imaging modalities, molecular imaging can now visualize inflammation and proteolytic activity in the atheroma in-vivo. In addition, visualization of plaque neovascularization, and measurement of the plaque's mechanical properties may enhance the identification of rupture-prone lesions. While limited mainly at the pre-clinical level, these novel imaging methods show promise for clinical translation.

Preface

Over the last century there was a global increase in cardiovascular disease, and today, it is regarded as the leading cause of death in the developed world. This has been attributed to the raised proportion of older adults, as well as to the modern life style and type of diet. Among the cardiovascular causes of death, coronary artery disease is the main cause of mortality, and accounts for one in five deaths in men and women in Europe. To address this major problem, over the last year, a great effort was made in developing new effective treatments which will reduce the mortality and morbidity, and improve the quality of life of the patients who are known to have coronary atherosclerosis. Recent advances in coronary artery bypass surgery (CABG) (e.g. minimally invasive CABG), and especially in interventional cardiology (e.g. drug eluting stents, rotablator, aspiration devices), have made feasible the revascularization of high risk patients.

The augmented number of the available devices and treatment options has also created a need for a better and more detailed imaging of coronary artery pathology. Medical imaging has made a substantial progress over the last years, and nowadays, there are a multitude of imaging modalities available for the evaluation of the extent and the severity of coronary artery disease. New developments of signal processing have enabled non-invasive imaging modalities (e.g. computed tomographic coronary angiography [CTCA], magnetic resonance imaging [MRI] coronary angiography) to be used to study the coronary anatomy and detect the presence of atherosclerotic lesions. CTCA nowadays constitutes a useful alternative for the identification of luminal stenosis and the characterization of the type of the plaque, but on the other hand it has limited capability in quantifying the plaque burden especially in small caliper and stented coronaries and thus quite often adjunctive coronary angiography is required to assess the severity of a lesion and plan treatment. Similarly, MRI is not able yet to examine with accuracy the coronary pathology as its poor resolution limits coronary visualization, and hence, further development is required before being implemented in clinical and research arena.

The limitations of the non-invasive imaging modalities have been successfully addressed by invasive imaging. X-ray angiography continues to constitute the most popular imaging modality for evaluating the severity of coronary artery disease and planning treatment as it is able to provide a holistic visualization of vessel silhouette and geometry and allows direct assessment of luminal lesions. However, coronary angiography does not give information regarding the plaque composition and burden, while often it is unable to estimate accurately the severity of a stenosis as it has limited resolution. These drawbacks were overcome by intravascular imaging. Recently, the miniaturization of medical devices and advances in signal processing have allowed the development of numerous alternative invasive imaging modalities, which permit detailed imaging of coronary artery morphology from inside. The breakthrough in intravascular imaging started approximately 20 years ago with the introduction of intravascular ultrasound

(IVUS). IVUS has the unique ability to provide high resolution cross sectional images that portray the luminal morphology, as well as the type of the plaque and its burden. Initially, IVUS had limited utility, mainly in research in the study of the effect of invasive and non-invasive treatments on atherosclerotic process. However, as the complexity of interventions increased there was an increased interest towards the clinical applications of IVUS and today it constitutes a valuable tool in clinical practice.

Another clinically useful intravascular modality is optical coherence tomography (OCT), which, similar to IVUS, provides cross sectional images of the coronary artery. OCT has evolved over the last decade and is based on the analysis of reflected light. A unique advantage of OCT is its increased axial resolution that permits visualization of intra-coronary features which are unseen by IVUS (e.g. thrombus) and reliable detection of the vulnerable plaque. The third intravascular imaging modality, which also allows visualization of the lumen, is angioscopy. This uses illumination fibers to assess vessel wall morphology. Another relatively new invasive imaging modality is near infrared spectroscopy (NIRS), which, in contrast to the previous techniques, cannot portray morphological features of the studied vessel, but uses infrared light to detect the type of the plaque. Finally, thermography is the last intracoronary imaging modality, which was introduced to measure the vessel wall temperature. This information has been proven useful in the detection of the plaques which are prone to rupture and cause acute coronary events as in these there is increased inflammation, and thus, they tend to have higher temperatures comparing to the stable plaques.

Intracardiac echocardiography (ICE) is the last invasive imaging technique, recently introduced to visualize in great detail the cardiac chambers and the major blood vessels. It is similar to intravascular ultrasound, and in contrast to transesophageal echocardiography, it does not requires intubation. This advantage, as well as its unique ability to provide high quality diagnostic images in real time, has rendered it a unique tool in structural interventions and in electrophysiology.

Though the abovementioned imaging modalities only emerged over the last two decades, they already have a recognized role in research and clinical arena. They have been used to understand the atherosclerotic process, to assess the extent and severity of the coronary artery disease, to evaluate the effect of pharmacological and invasive treatments, to estimate prognosis, and guide complex percutaneous coronary and structural intervention. The augmented use of these techniques and the increased amount of the diagnostic information provided has created the need for the development of automated methodologies which will allow fast and accurate analysis of the acquired data. Furthermore, advances in image processing and miniaturization devices have permitted the combination of the information given by two or more different imaging techniques. These data fusion methodologies provide hybrid models that allow a more thorough representation of vessel anatomy and pathology, and have an already established value in clinical practice and research. However, although there is a real revolution in invasive cardiac imaging, many doctors insist on using the traditional and old-fashioned diagnostic tools to assess coronary pathology and guide treatment. This is at least partially due to the fact that many medical doctors are not familiar with the newly developed intravascular modalities and ignore the data which support their clinical and research utility.

This objective of this book is to inform the readers and give a thorough and complete description of all the available intravascular imaging modalities. More specifically, it presents the technical aspects of each methodology aiming to demonstrate their advantages and indigenous limitations. A major scope of this manuscript is to familiarize the clinicians with these new intravascular modalities and to provide guidance about the interpretation of the obtained data. This book also summarizes the applications of the available imaging modalities, reviews the literature, and informs the readers about how to use these methodologies in clinical practice and research. It also includes a complete and detailed description of the existing processing methodologies and systems currently used to analyze the provided data. Finally, it aims to address future trends in intravascular imaging and discuss their potential value.

This book is intended to a broad spectrum of scientists working in the field of cardiovascular imaging. Cardiologists and interventional radiologists can greatly benefit from this as it provides valuable clinical information. It also refers to biomedical engineers and researchers as it presents an overview of the available knowledge in the field of image processing, which provides not only the background for further research, but also highlights the current limitations that need to be addressed in the future. Finally, the book can be used as a textbook in graduate courses for medical schools or engineering schools focusing on biomedical aspects.

This book is an edited volume, which received contributions from many scientists and researchers in the field. Part of the work, as well as its organization, has been performed within the framework of the ARTREAT project (ARTREAT: Multi-level patient-specific artery and atherogenesis model for outcome prediction, decision support treatment, and virtual hand-on training, FP7-224297), whose aim was to integrate different imaging modalities in order to provide reliable and comprehensive coronary representation and study the effect of blood flow on the atherosclerotic evolution. The contributors kindly offered their knowledge, and the editors assigned them different parts of this book. All chapters passed through a review process and they have been resubmitted in their final form.

The book is organized in ten sections. The first six present the available intravascular imaging techniques, namely: IVUS, angioscopy, thermography, OCT, NIRS, and ICE. The other four are divided as follows: section seven focuses on the current applications of invasive and non-invasive imaging, which rapidly evolves and nowadays challenges intravascular imaging, section eight on the hybrid cardiovascular imaging; section nine highlights the role of intravascular imaging in the understanding of the impact of rheology on plaque development, and the book finishes with section ten, which presents the future trends in cardiovascular imaging.

Section one is devoted to IVUS and includes six chapters. The first chapter describes the basic principles of IVUS image acquisition. Issues like the physical phenomena behind IVUS are discussed, as well as the artifacts that can affect IVUS image quality. Chapter two focuses on the interpretation and limitations of IVUS images, while chapter three presents the available image processing methodologies. This provides an overview of the methods developed for the segmentation of the IVUS sequence and the identification of the type of the plaque in grayscale IVUS frames, and presents the commercially available systems that incorporate these algorithms. Chapter four describes the plaque characterization techniques that are based on the analysis of the IVUS radiofrequency backscatter signal, while the last two chapters review the literature and present the current clinical and research applications of IVUS.

Section two focuses on the clinical and research utility of angioscopy. Initially, we present the historic evolution of this imaging technique and its limitations. In the main part of the section we stress the value of angioscopy in the study of the atherosclerotic evolution, discuss its role in the understanding of the mechanism of action of different interventional devices (e.g. stent, atherectomy, laser, etc.), and compare this modality with other invasive imaging techniques.

Section three is devoted to thermography and is divided in two chapters. In the fist we analyze the basic principles of thermography, discuss its limitations, and present the available devices used to measure *in vivo* the temperature of the coronary atherosclerotic plaques. This chapter is completed with the description of microwave radiometry, an alternative technique that provides non-invasive measurements of the heating of the plaque, and is currently under clinical evaluation. In the second chapter we review the literature and present data from *in vitro* and *in vivo* studies that implemented thermography to measure the coronary wall temperature. These studies have improved our knowledge about the association between arterial wall inflammation and plaque vulnerability helped us to identify morphological characteristics associated with high risk plaques, and allowed us to assess their prevalence in different populations and the anti-inflammatory efficacy of various pharmacological treatments.

Section four deals with OCT and is divided in four chapters. The first chapter describes the engineering behind OCT image acquisition, while the second chapter focuses on the interpretation of OCT images and presents the available techniques developed for automated OCT processing. The third and the fourth chapter discuss the utility of this imaging technique in the current clinical practice and research arena.

NIRS is described in section five. Initially, we present the physical principles of NIRS and highlight its advantages in analyzing coronary wall tissue. In the main focus of the chapter we describe the NIRS system and present the results of the most important *in vitro* and *in vivo* validation studies. Finally, we discuss the clinical value of NIRS in assessing outcome after pharmaceutical or percutaneous coronary interventions and in detecting high risk patients who would be benefit by aggressive medical treatment.

Section six focuses on ICE. It describes the available devices and presents an overview of the typical images obtained during ICE examination. In addition, it discusses the current clinical applications of ICE in electrophysiology and structural interventional cardiology, and concludes with its limitations.

Section seven summarizes the current status of cardiovascular imaging. The first chapter of this section is devoted to the intravascular imaging techniques and particularly, IVUS and OCT, which are mainly used in clinical settings. The book focuses on their value in the assessment of the extent and the severity of coronary atherosclerosis and their utility in treatment planning during complex percutaneous coronary interventions. The second chapter deals with the non invasive imaging. It presents the current applications of non invasive imaging in portraying and assessing coronary atherosclerosis discusses its potentialities in the detection of vulnerable plaques and concludes with its current limitations.

Hybrid imaging is based on the integration of data provided by different imaging techniques and provides models which allow a more comprehensive and complete representation of coronary artery morphology. Today there are numerous data fusion methodologies with an evidenced based role in the diagnosis of coronary artery disease and have enriched our understanding about the atherosclerotic evolution. In section eight the available data fusion techniques are reviewed, and their clinical and research potentialities are discussed.

Blood flow haemodynamics appear to play a significant role in plaque development and destabilization. The current developments in intravascular imaging have allowed reliable representation of vessel's morphology and geometry and permitted *in vivo* study of the role of local haemodynamics in the atherosclerotic evolution. Section nine provides the definition regarding the haemodynamic forces and flow patterns, reviews the literature, and cites the evidence concerning the effect of blood flow on atherosclerotic process.

Finally, the last section is devoted to the future trends in cardiovascular imaging. In the first chapter we analyze the necessity in developing new invasive imaging techniques, which will allow more accurate assessment of the anatomical and histopathological characteristics associated with increased plaque vulnerability. The second chapter discusses the potentialities of non invasive imaging modalities, and particularly, of multi slice computed tomography. It summarizes the current clinical utility of this promising imaging technique and attempts to foresee its future clinical and research applications. The last chapter is devoted to imaging techniques applied not to assess coronary morphology and anatomy but mainly to detect other features associated with increased vulnerability, such as the biomechanical profile of the plaque, or the presence of inflammation and increased neo-vascularization, and aims to highlight the variety of the imaging options and the need to invest in the early detection of vulnerable plaques.

We would like to thank all authors for their valuable contributions, the reviewers for the careful review, as well as the advisory editorial board for its valuable comments and suggestions.

Lampros K. Michalis
University of Ioannina, Greece

Dimtrios I. Fotiadis
University of Ioannina, Greece

Katerina K. Naka
University of Ioannina, Greece

Christos V. Bourantas
Castle Hill Hospital, UK

Vasilios D. Tsakanikas
University of Ioannina, Greece

July 2011

Section 1
Intravascular Ultrasound

Chapter 1
Basic Principles of Image Acquisition

Ourania Katsarou
National and Kapodistrian University of Athens Medical School, Greece

Manolis Vavuranakis
National and Kapodistrian University of Athens Medical School, Greece

ABSTRACT

Before proceeding with the clinical and research utility of Intravascular Imaging, it is important to examine in detail the principles that the acquisition of the IVUS signal is based on. This chapter provides an insight into the principles of the IVUS imaging, while describing the image quality factors. Additionally, the equipment for IVUS examination is described, and the acquisition and display techniques are detailed. Finally, a brief summary of the limitations of the IVUS signal is attempted.

INSIGHTS INTO THE PRINCIPLES OF IVUS IMAGING

In order to understand the physics that governs image acquisition by intravascular ultrasound several fundamental principles of ultrasound wave transmission needs to be understood. We know that when ultrasound waves travel they have a frequency ≥ 20000 cycles per second. This is clearly above the human audible range, therefore ultrasound waves are not detected by the operators or other bystanders. A unique feature of the ultrasound waves is that, the velocity at which

sound travels through human soft tissue is fairly constant at approximately 1540 m/s. The production of these waves is created by transducers which are devices that convert one type of energy into another. In brief, the electrical current passes through a piezoelectric (pressure-electric) crystalline material (usually a ceramic) that expands and contracts to produce sound waves as it is excited by electrical current. Following emission of an ultrasound pulse, the ultrasound wave travels away from the transducer. When it encounters a boundary between two tissues - fat and muscle, for example - the beam will be partially reflected and partially transmitted. The degree of reflection depends on the difference between the mechanical

DOI: 10.4018/978-1-61350-095-8.ch001

impedance of the two materials. A characteristic illustration of the ultrasound wave reflection is the case of imaging of highly calcified structures where acoustic shadowing, a nearly complete reflection of the signal at the soft tissue/calcium interface, occurs. In situation where the wave passes through many tissue interfaces, its energy is *attenuated* (reduced). Thus, only a small percentage of the emitted signal returns to the transducer, which produces an electrical impulse that is converted into the image. Actually, the received signal is converted to electrical energy and sent to an external signal processing system for amplification, filtering, scan-conversion, user-controlled modification, and finally, graphic presentation. As we mentioned, ultrasound wave travels through all tissues at a fixed speed, thus the time that it takes for the transmitted ultrasound impulse to be backscattered and returned to the transducer is a measure of distance. Penetration depends on a number of factors including the power output of the transducer (which is in part related to transducer design and aperture) and imaging frequency. Penetration is inversely related to frequency – the higher the frequency the less the penetration. Larger transducers with lower frequencies are used for examination of large vessels because they create a deeper near field and have greater penetration.

The intensity of the backscattered signal depends on a number of factors. These include:

1. The distance from the transducer to the target (intensity is inversely related to distance);
2. The angle of the signal relative to the target (the closer the angle is to 90°, the more intense is the reflected signal); and
3. The density (or reflectivity) of the tissue (which determines how much ultrasound energy passes through the tissue and how much is backscattered).
4. The intensity of the transmitted signal;
5. The attenuation (reduction) of the signal as it passes through tissue (all tissue attenuates ultrasound energy);

All these factors not only affect the overall appearance of an image, but also the relative appearance of different sectors of the image throughout its 360° circumference.

Additionally, transmission of the ultrasound beam has some other limitation that we should keep in mind. The ultrasound beam remains fairly parallel for a certain distance (*near field*) and then it starts to diverge (*far field*). In the near field, as the beam is narrower and more parallel, the quality of ultrasound images and the resolution is greater, and a more accurate detection of the characteristic backscatter (reflection of ultrasound energy) from a given tissue can be achieved. The equation $L 5 r^2 / Y$, where L is the length of the near field, r is the radius of the transducer, and Y is the wave length can be used to define the length of the near field. Therefore, larger transducers with lower frequencies are used for examination of large vessels to extend the near field into the region of diagnostic interest. The consequences of increasing the distance of the imaging object, is that far field structures appear less distinct, their borders are less clear, and the interpretation is less certain.

Interpretation of the IVUS Image

The tendency of tissue to reflect ultrasound is reflected by the echogenicity of that area. The higher the echogenicity, the brighter the tissue appearance. However the algorithms that are used to form the IVUS gray scale image is derived from the envelope of the amplitude of the reflected signal. Obviously, this is a limitation when we want to obtain information regarding the composition of the tissue that reflects the ultrasound beam since its radiofrequency signature is totally ignored. Indeed it is well appreciated that much of the information in the reflected signal is not used.

The accuracy of the measurements performed in 2 dimensional IVUS gray scale images depends on several factors including correction for transducer, catheter, and sheath design) and estimation of the average speed of sound in blood and tissue which are all incorporated into the scan converting algorithm. In daily practice IVUS quantification should not require routine calibration.

One fundamental assumption of the currently available imaging techniques is that vessels are circular, that the catheter is located in the center of the artery, and that the transducer is parallel to the long axis of the vessel. However, both transducer obliquity and vessel curvature can produce an image that incorrectly suggests that the vessel is elliptical. Transducer obliquity maybe more of an issue in large vessels imaged with small catheters; it can result in an overestimation of dimensions and a reduction in image quality. However, in routine clinical coronary imaging, this error is relatively small. Importantly, it is not possible to underestimate dimensions.

Factors That Describe and Define Image Quality

Resolution is defined as the ability to discriminate two closely adjacent objects. Ultrasound cannot reliably detect or measure a structure that is smaller than the resolution of the device or differentiate between structures that are closer than the resolution of the device. The impact of low resolution would be obvious on the obtained images and manifested mainly on the sharpness of the image, the distinctness of the borders, and, the reproducibility of the IVUS measurements. In brief two important factors describe image quality: spatial resolution and contrast resolution.

Spatial Resolution

Any image that is created by IVUS is the representation of a three dimensional structure. Therefore, there are three spatial resolutions in each image slice: 1) axial resolution (the ability to discriminate two closely adjacent objects located along the axis of the ultrasound beam); 2) lateral resolution (the ability to discriminate two closely adjacent objects located along the length of the ultrasound catheter); and 3) angular or circum-ferential resolution (the ability to discriminate two closely adjacent objects located along the circumferential sweep of the ultrasound beam as it generates a planar image). Axial resolution is typically 80-120μm, and lateral resolution is typically 200-250μm. Axial resolution is primarily a function of wavelength while lateral is a function of wavelength and transducer size, or *aperture*. Circumferential resolution is highly dependent on imaging artifacts such as NURD (non–uniform rotational distortion) and has not been quantified.

Some basic principles that we should keep in mind when attempting IVUS imaging is that the frequency of an ultrasound wave is the number of sound cycles in a given time period, typically one second. We should all remember that wavelength is inversely related to frequency.

Ultrasound waves with higher frequency (shorter wavelengths) are reflected from smaller objects. A higher-frequency beam has greater resolution; however, because a larger percentage of higher-frequency ultrasound is reflected, penetration decreases. Therefore, in general, the greater is the required resolution, the higher the frequency of the ultrasound wave should be; and for a given frequency, the larger the size of the transducer aperture, the better the lateral resolution (the aperture is the face of the transducer that emits and/or receives ultrasound waves).

Contrast Resolution

Contrast resolution is the distribution of the gray scale of the reflected signal and is often referred to as dynamic range. Dynamic range is the number of gray scales that can be differentiated between the weakest and the strongest targets. It is usually expressed in decibels (dB). The dynamic range for IVUS is typically 17-55 dB. The greater the dynamic range, the broader the range of reflected signals (from weakest to strongest) that can be detected, displayed and differentiated, and the greater the number shades of gray that are used to display the image. Indeed, as the number of gray scale levels is a measure of the dynamic range, therefore, a large or broad dynamic range gives to the image a favorable characteristic and an image with a wide dynamic range has many shades of gray. An image with a poor dynamic range has an exaggerated contrast and is mostly black and white. While a contrast image may appear to be easier to interpret because borders are more distinct, in reality details are lost. Therefore an image of low dynamic range appears as black and white with a few in-between gray scale levels; images at high *dynamic range* are often softer, with preserved subtleties in the image presentation.

One should note that control of the actual and the displayed gray scale can be done through a variety of gray-scale curves, also called gamma curves that can be selected depending on operator preference, if they are available in the imaging system. These control the relationship between the actual and the displayed gray scale, and are used primarily to present a more pleasing image. However, they also affect dynamic range and qualitative and quantitative characteristics of the image, may result in measurement inaccuracies.

EQUIPMENT FOR IVUS EXAMINATION

The available IVUS transducers are of two different types: the mechanically rotating transducer and the electronically switched multi-element array system. The first design is referred to as a "mechanical IVUS system," and the latter a "solid-state design IVUS system."

A. Mechanical Systems

The mechanical system is based on a single rotating transducer is driven by a flexible drive cable at 1,800 rpm (30 revolutions per second) to sweep a beam almost perpendicular to the catheter. The transducer sends and receives ultrasound signals at approximately 1° increments. The time delay and amplitude of these pulses provide 256 individual radial scans for each image. In most mechanical systems, the transducer spins within a protective sheath while the imaging transducer is moved proximally and distally. This facilitates smooth and uniform mechanical pullback.

In the mechanical transducer catheters the absence of even a small air bubble in the IVUS sheath is crucial for the image creation. Flushing with saline is required in order to provide a fluid pathway for the ultrasound beam and avoid image degradation.

B. Electronic Systems

The electronic systems are characterized by, multiple transducer elements (currently up to 64) arranged in an annular array, which are activated sequentially to generate the image. The array can be programmed so that one set of elements transmits while a second set receives simultaneously. The coordinated beam generated by groups of elements is known as a synthetic aperture array. The image can be manipulated to focus optimally at a broad range of depths. Currently available electronic systems can also provide simultaneous coloration of blood flow using the Doppler effect.

Imaging Artifacts

Imaging artifacts can occur during IVUS acquisition and may lead to image misinterpretation. Their recognition is critical and prompt detection and correction is a prerequisite during IVUS image.

One of the well-recognized artifacts is the Ring-down effect. It refers to disorganization of the image closest to the face of the transducer or the surface of the catheter. Ring-down artifacts are usually observed as bright haloes of variable thickness surrounding the catheter that obscure the area immediately adjacent to the catheter. Ring down artifacts are present in all medical ultrasound devices and create a zone of uncertainty adjacent to the transducer surface. Ring-down can be minimized by optimal transducer and/or sheath design, but suppression of ring-down using system controls can also eliminate tissue in the near field. Among the available ultrasound transducers electronic-array systems tend to have more ring-down; ring-down can be partially reduced by digital subtraction of a reference mask as well as by blanking out the extreme near field. Since, this ring-down subtraction does not remain stable it may need to be repeated if IVUS is again performed later in the procedure. Although reduction of the near field ring down is warranted, it may limit the ability of electronic array systems to image right up to the surface of the catheter.

Another well described artifact is the NURD. It is an artifact unique to mechanical IVUS imaging systems; it stands for non-uniform rotational distortion. For optimal imaging, there must be a constant rotational velocity of the mechanical transducer. NURD is the consequence of asymmetric friction along any part of the drive- shaft mechanism, causing the transducer to lag during one part of its rotation and whip through the other part of its 360° course, resulting in geometric distortion of the image.

NURD affects angular (circumferential) resolution, precludes accurate cross- sectional measurements, and, for example, can distort the geometry of an implanted stent. It is beyond the scope of this chapter to describe all the mechanics beyond the creation of the non-uniform rotation distortion, but some of the reason it may occur includes the presence of acute bends in the artery, tortuous guiding catheter shapes, variance in manufacturing of the hub or driveshaft, excessive tightening of a haemostatic valve, kinking of the imaging sheath, or an excessive small guide catheter lumen. In an extreme situation, fracture of the drive cable can occur because of the friction. A distinct motion artifact can result from an unstable catheter position. The vessel moves before a complete circumferential image can be created. This results in cyclic deformation of the image. Recognizing NURD is particularly important when quantifying information from mechanical IVUS imaging systems.

Regardless of the type of the transducer we use they can both move as much as 5mm longitudinally between diastole and systole. This can preclude accurate assessment of arterial phenomena that depend on comparing systolic and diastolic images (i.e. arterial pulsation and compliance).

PRINCIPLES OF IVUS EXAMINATION

As every invasive procedure IVUS requires that the patient is anticoagulated, usually with heparin, before inserting the guidewire into the coronary artery. Unless it is contraindicated, image acquisition should be performed after administrating intra- coronary nitroglycerin to avoid catheter-induced spasm.

Using routine interventional techniques IVUS coronary catheter is advanced over a guide- wire beyond the target lesion. Subsequently, a pullback of the transducer tip through the lesion or segment of interest is performed. IVUS provides a series of tomographic, cross sectional images of the vessel. In most of the times a pullback device is used in order to obtain a steady speed pullback of 0.5mm/s and a frame rate of 30 images/sec will be obtained while, 60 images will be available from a pullback speed of 1mm segment. Typically, a subsample of these images is analysed, depending on the clinical indication. However, for volumetric analysis in research studies, multiple sequential IVUS images are obtained in a segment at constant intervals.

In cases where IVUS is used for guidance in interventional procedures, the worst lesion site where the luminal diameter is minimal, MLD) and a relatively normal, adjacent reference site is selected.

The currently ultrasound catheters currently available for intracoronary application have an outer diameter of between 2.9 and 3.5 French at the distal end.

Imaging Console

All IVUS systems are equipped with an imaging console which includes the hard and software which are necessary to convert the IVUS signal to the image, the monitor and the recording devices. The systems permit digital recording and permanent archiving on a recordable CD-ROM.

ACQUISITION AND DISPLAY TECHNIQUES

Image Acquisition

Handling of intracoronary ultrasound probes is similar to the handling of over the wire or monorail PTCA catheters, although additional caution is required. A stable guiding catheter position is more than desirable since intracoronary ultrasound catheters still have less tractability and a larger profile than most balloon catheters. All the short monorail catheters are prone to prolapse, so that the tip of the guide wire must be placed distal in the target vessel and the intracoronary ultra-sound catheter should never be advanced over the floppy end of the guide wire. In negotiating tortuous vessels, long monorail or over the wire intracoronary ultrasound catheters should be selected.

On the other hand, when interrogating an aorto-ostial lesion of the left main coronary artery, it is important to disengage the guiding catheter from the ostium before the pullback. Otherwise, the true aorto-ostial lumen may be masked by the guiding catheter and significant ostial lesions may be missed.

Although the damage to the vessel wall from modern flexible intracoronary ultrasound catheters is rare, in order to avoid such complications the IVUS catheters should not be advanced to the smallest distal coronary vessels and caution must be used in crossing stents immediately after deployment. The operator should keep in mind that intracoronary ultrasound catheters are larger and have less tapering than PTCA balloons, so that disruption of fragile coil stents can be induced by forceful pushing of the intracoronary ultrasound catheter. One way to avoid resistance is to adjust the guiding catheter and guidewire position in order to obtain a more central orientation of the intracoronary ultrasound catheter which may facilitate crossing of the stented segment.

There are two approaches on how to manipulate the IVUS catheter in order to image the segment of interest to: 1) motorized or 2) manual interrogation. Regardless of which method we use, imaging should include careful uninterrupted imaging of the target segment, generally including at least 10 mm of distal vessel, the lesion site(s), and the entire proximal vessel back to the aorta. Some advocate that *motorized transducer pullback* is performed at a speed of 0.5 mm/sec while faster pullback speeds have the disadvantage of imaging focal pathology too quickly, but they are commonly employed for longer extra- cardiac vessels in order to minimize imaging times. The advantages of motorized interrogation are that it provides a steady catheter withdrawal to avoid imaging any segment too quickly and the ability to concentrate on the images without having to pay attention to catheter manipulation. A major advantage of motorized pullbacks is that they permit length and volumetric measurements and provide uniform and reproducible image acquisition for multicenter and serial studies. However, inadequate examination of important regions of interest can occur because the transducer does not remain for long at any specific site in the vessel.

If the manual transducer pullback is used, it should be performed slowly, at a rate similar to motorized pullback. The advantage of this method is the ability to concentrate on specific regions of interest by pausing the transducer motion at a specific location in the vessel. Disadvantages include the possibility of skipping over significant pathology by pulling the transducer too quickly or unevenly and the inability to perform precise length and volume measurements. In addition, when the study is reviewed at a later date, antegrade and retrograde manual catheter movement can be confusing. Special care should be taken when interrogating aorto-ostial lesions it is important that the guiding catheter be disengaged from the ostium. If it is not, the true aorto-ostial lumen may be masked by the catheter and, therefore, not identified.

All IVUS systems usually display are cross sectional individual images which maybe, reviewed individually and as a video sequence.

Scrolling through adjacent cross-sectional images allows the experienced IVUS operator to obtain a three- dimensional impression of a vessel segment. Motorized transducer pullback and digital storage of cross- sectional images are necessary for longitudinal imaging. In a longitudinal imaging display, computerized image reconstruction techniques display a series of evenly spaced IVUS images along a single cut plane to approximate the longitudinal appearance of the artery (Figure 1).

There are some limitations to the longitudinal display of the image, including the obligate straight reconstruction of the artery and the display of only a single cut plane. The changes of vessel size during the cardiac cycle result in a characteristic artifact described as the saw tooth appearance. ECG-triggered image acquisition of image frames in the same cardiac phase can eliminate these artifacts.

Recently, automated, three- dimensional reconstruction of IVUS data has become available and involves the use of advanced computer rendering techniques to display a shaded or wireframe image of the vessel, giving the operator a view of the vessel in its entirety. However, true three-dimensional techniques require registration of the catheter path during the pullback.

IVUS Signals Beyond Conventional Imaging

In the gray scale images the raw IVUS signal is converted through filtering process in order to obtain the conventional image presentation on the standard display. Several investigators have managed to perform additional analysis of the reflected ultrasound signal, analyzing several characteristics of the digitized ultrasound signal with integrated radiofrequency analysis, backscatter analysis, and elastography. These techniques allow advanced tissue characterization and more objective and reproducible methods of categorizing wall morphology and plaque components.

Indeed, there is renewed interest in radiofrequency signal analysis for the purposes of tissue characterization. Frequency domain analysis may allow detailed assessment of plaque composition.

Currently, algorithms that permit the identification of tissue composition by in vivo analysis of the radiofrequency signals have been incorporated into the IVUS console and 'Virtual histology' has been adapted into clinical and research setting.

Despite all these new technological advancements and the appearance of several publications in relation to these new modalities, the clinical value of these advanced image analysis is not completely defined.

Undoubtedly, the invasive character of IVUS explains its preferential use in interventional cardiology and limits, in particular, the application in asymptomatic patients.

Figure 1. Gray scale IVUS image which represents a concentric atheromatic plaque of a coronary artery

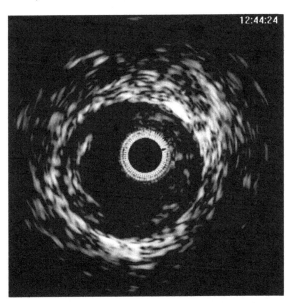

Figure 2. Left: Gray scale IVUS image of a coronary artery representing a concentric atheromatic plaque, Right: In vivo analysis of the gray scale radiofrequency signal (Virtual Histology). Notice the variety of colors which represent the different characteristics of the atheromatic plaque (red: necrotic core, green: fibrosis, white: calcification)

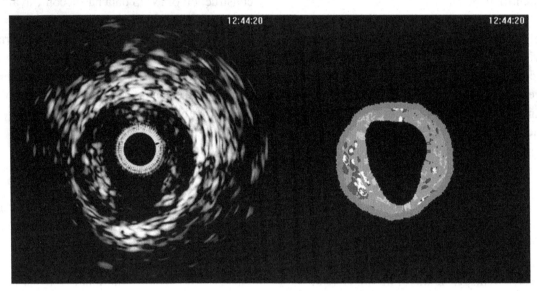

Limitations of IVUS

The limitations of the IVUS system emerge from the intrinsic restriction of the ultrasound beam. The characteristic signal drop-out behind calcium, which prohibits the visualization of deep vessel structures, is a commonly encountered problem. The physical size of ultrasound catheters (currently ≈ 1.0mm) constitutes an important limitation in imaging severe stenosis and small vessels. In such vessels, the introduction of the catheter may cause dilatation of the vessel (Dotter effect) and may limit exact measurements. Although spatial resolution of IVUS (≥150μm) allows detailed analysis of vessel wall structures, important structures of "vulnerable" atherosclerotic plaques, in particular the fibrous cap (60-100μm) cannot be reliably analyzed.

Safety of Coronary Ultrasound

Several studies have documented the safety of intracoronary ultrasound is well documented.

Complications, including dissection or vessel closure, are uncommon (less than ≤ 0.5%) and typically occur in patients undergoing coronary intervention rather than diagnostic imaging. Coronary spasm, occur in 1-3% of examinations, but it is transient and usually responds rapidly to intracoronary nitroglycerin. Transient ischemia, caused by introduction of the catheter in a small vessel or tight stenosis, is frequent in interventional procedures. Examination of vessels previously imaged by IVUS compared with non - instrumented vessels shows no accelerated progression of atheroma at 1 year of follow up. However, as every interventional procedure, selective coronary instrumentation always carries a potential risk of significant vessel injury and should only be performed by operators experienced in diagnostic and interventional therapeutic intracoronary catheter manipulation.

REFERENCES

Carlier, S., Kakadiaris, I., Dib, N., Vavuranakis, M., O'Malley, S., & Gul, K. (2005). Vasa vasorum imaging: A new window to the clinical detection of vulnerable atherosclerotic plaques. *Current Atherosclerosis Reports, 7*(4).

Di Mario, C., Gorge, G., Peters, R., & Kearney, P., F., P., Hausmann, D., et al. (1998). Clinical application and image interpretation in intracoronary ultrasound. *European Heart Journal, 19*, 207–229. doi:10.1053/euhj.1996.0433

Jim, M., Hau, W., Ko, R., Siu, C., Ho, H., & Yiu, K. (2010). Virtual histology by intravascular ultrasound study on degenerative aortocoronary saphenous vein grafts. *Heart and Vessels, 25*(3), 175–181. doi:10.1007/s00380-009-1185-7

Mintz, G. S., Nissen, S. E., Anderson, W. D., Bailey, S., Erbel, R., & Winters, W. L. Jr. (2001). ACC clinical expert consensus document, American College of Cardiology. Clinical expert consensus document on standards for acquisition, measurement and reporting of intravascular ultrasound studies (IVUS). A report of the American College of Cardiology. *Journal of the American College of Cardiology, 37*(5). doi:10.1016/S0735-1097(01)01175-5

Nair, A., Kuban, B., Tuzcu, E., Schoenhagen, P., Nissen, S., & Vince, D. (2002). Coronary plaque classification with intravascular ultrasound radiofrequency data analysis. *Circulation, 106*, 2200–2206. doi:10.1161/01.CIR.0000035654.18341.5E

Nishimura, R., Edwards, W., Warnes, C., Reeder, G., Holmes, D. Jr, & Tajik, A. (1990). Intravascular ultrasound imaging: in vitro validation and pathologic correlation. *Journal of the American College of Cardiology, 16*, 145–154. doi:10.1016/0735-1097(90)90472-2

Steinberg, D., Mintz, G., Mandinov, L., Yu, A., Ellis, S., & Grube, E. (2010). Long-term impact of routinely detected early and late incomplete stent apposition: an integrated intravascular ultrasound analysis of the TAXUS IV, V, and VI and TAXUS ATLAS workhorse, long lesion, and direct stent studies. *JACC: Cardiovascular Interventions, 3*(5), 486–494. doi:10.1016/j.jcin.2010.03.007

Wu, X., Maehara, A., Mintz, G., Kubo, T., Xu, K., & Choi, S. (2010). Virtual histology intravascular ultrasound analysis of non-culprit attenuated plaques detected by grayscale intravascular ultrasound in patients with acute coronary syndromes. *The American Journal of Cardiology, 105*(1), 48–53. doi:10.1016/j.amjcard.2009.08.649

Chapter 2
Intravascular Image Interpretation

Katerina K. Naka
University of Ioannina, Greece

Nikolaos D. Papamichael
University of Ioannina, Greece

ABSTRACT

Intravascular ultrasound (IVUS) is an imaging modality often used as a supplement to coronary angiography and allows accurate assessment of the lumen, vessel wall, and atherosclerotic plaque. A coherent interpretation of the IVUS images requires identification of the image artefacts that emerge during IVUS interrogation and can often be quite difficult. This chapter describes the morphologic appearance of the structures seen in IVUS, presents the morphologic characteristics of the different types of plaque, and summarizes the nomenclature and definitions used during IVUS interpretation. Moreover, it focuses on the quantitative analysis and reports the measurements obtained during IVUS processing. Finally, it presents some of the clinical (e.g. assessment of the extent and severity of a lesion, treatment planning) and research (e.g. evaluation of atherosclerotic progression/regression, transplant vasculopathy, peripheral arterial disease) applications of this modality aiming to highlight its value in the clinical and research arena.

INTRODUCTION

Coronary angiography is the principal imaging modality used to assess coronary vessel anatomy and morphology. However, despite the broad implementation and the unanimous acceptance of this technique for the evaluation of the extent and severity of coronary artery disease, it is well known that it has limited ability in assessing the atherosclerotic disease process as the obtained two-dimensional images cannot accurately depict the complex three-dimensional anatomy of the vessel and cannot give any information regarding the type of the plaque and its burden (Mintz et al., 2001). To address these limitations, Intravascular

DOI: 10.4018/978-1-61350-095-8.ch002

Ultrasound (IVUS) was introduced that provides high resolution cross-sectional imaging of the vessel which permits identification of the lumen, the plaque and the outer vessel wall and accurate evaluation of the plaque burden. Several studies have confirmed that IVUS is safe and thus today it is often used in clinical practice as a complementary to coronary angiography tool (Di Mario et al., 1998; Hausmann et al., 1995). IVUS appears to be useful in assessing the severity of ambiguous lesions and guiding complex percutaneous coronary interventions (PCIs). In addition, is it also valuable in research and has been implemented in a number of studies that examined the impact of several interventional and non-interventional treatments on the evolution of the atherosclerotic process (Schoenhagen et al., 2006). The present chapter focuses on the interpretation of IVUS images and discusses some of the clinical and research applications of this technique.

BACKGROUND

Normal Arterial Anatomy

In a normal coronary artery the following structures are identified: the vessel lumen (blood), the vessel wall and the adjacent structures (Mintz et al., 2001; Schoenhagen et al., 2006).

The Lumen

At frequencies >20 MHz, flowing blood presents a specific echogenic pattern called speckle. The blood speckle may be described as finely textured echoes moving in a swirling pattern in video loops/sequences. The blood speckle can provide valuable help in image interpretation as its typical morphology may facilitate differentiation between lumen and vessel wall and identification of vessel dissection which appears as a communication between the lumen and the dissected vascular wall. However, problems may arise in

a substantial proportion of cases and diagnosis may elude. Blood speckle can be much more prominent in higher imaging frequencies and might interfere with the delineation of the wall tissue rendering image interpretation a demanding process. Interrogating video sequences rather than frozen images and flushing the vessel with saline or contrast medium during IVUS imaging may help this differentiation, especially in cases of dissections.

The Vessel Wall

Previous IVUS studies performed on pressure-distended coronary arteries have provided the characteristic appearance of normal coronary arteries (Nissen et al., 1991; Potkin et al., 1990; Schoenhagen et al., 2006) (Figure 1). There are two distinct changes in acoustic impedance as ultrasound waves are reflected on vessel wall tissues. The first is created at the border between blood and the leading edge of the vessel intima and this trailing edge can be used reliably for measurements. The second is sited at the external elastic membrane (EEM) that is located at the media-adventitia interface. The outer border of the adventitia cannot be easily differentiated from the surrounding tissue. In high-quality images, the tunica media can be possibly visualized as an echolucent, lower density, layer. In young healthy subjects the intima thickness is normally reported to be 0.15±0.07 mm, while a thickness of 0.25-0.50 mm is usually considered as the upper reference limit for intima (Schoenhagen et al., 2006).

The Adjacent Structures

Arterial side branches, cardiac veins and the pericardium constitute the adjacent structures that can be recognized during pull-back of the IVUS catheter. Vessel bifurcations are frequently identified as the sites of early and eccentric plaque development which is due to the unique hemodynamic patterns seen in these areas. As the IVUS

Figure 1. a) Normal coronary artery (the echolucent round zone is the media, the black circle inside the lumen is the IVUS catheter, the shadow inside the lumen is due to the guidewire – obvious in most of the figures); b) Minimal intimal thickening (from 6 to 10 o'clock); c) Normal coronary artery (distal part of the vessel). Note that the media is not very obvious here; d) Normal coronary artery. Note the veins outside the adventitia.

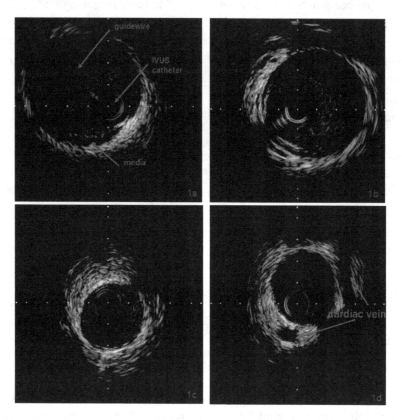

catheter is withdrawn the arterial side branches appear at the peripheral parts of the screen and gradually join the main vessel (Figure 2). In most cases, IVUS imaging allows partial assessment of the ostium of the branch. However a complete evaluation of the proximal segment is often not feasible as the IVUS catheter is moving at an angle compared to the side branch axis.

Cardiac veins are typically seen as vessels which run parallel or cross the coronary artery and can be recognized by their characteristic compression during systole (Figures 1d and 3). Arterial side branches and cardiac veins are frequently used as landmarks to match coronary arterial segments interrogated in serial examinations.

Coronary Venous Grafts

The wall morphology of venous bypass grafts is different from the native coronaries. The venous grafts have no surrounding tissue, no side branches and no EEM. The outer echolucent zone surrounding the intima corresponds to the 'EEM area' of the venous graft. Venous grafts gradually undergo characteristic morphological changes: intimal fibrous thickening, medial hypertrophy and lipid deposition that represent a distinct process leading to 'arterialization' of the grafts. The plaque burden and atheroma characterization are assessed in a similar to native coronary arteries manner.

Figure 2. a) Eccentric fibrofatty plaque (extending from 3 to 8 o'clock). Side-branch about to enter the main vessel at 9 o'clock; b) Eccentric fibrofatty plaque (extending from 3 to 9 o'clock). Large side branch entering the vessel from 12 to 2 o'clock. The site of entry could be confused with plaque rupture in this frozen image; c) Concentric fibrous plaque. Side branch at 12 o'clock; d) Side branch at 11-12 o'clock.

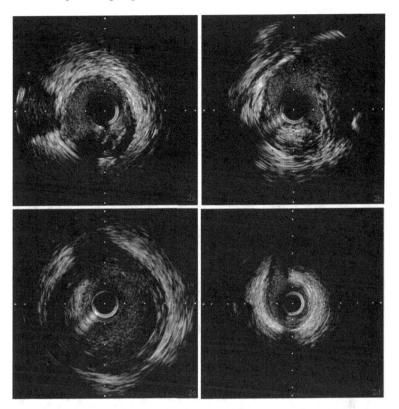

Image Artifacts

Several artifacts often seen in IVUS can impair the quality of the acquired images (Mintz et al., 2001; Schoenhagen et al., 2006). Some of them depends on the catheter design (mechanical or solid state transducer) while others are seen in IVUS images regardless of the catheter that was used for image acquisition.

Guidewire Artifact

When monorail catheter technology is used, the guidewire is situated outside the transducer and produces a "linear" or narrow-angled artifact that disturbs visualization behind its (shadow) (Figure 1a). Nevertheless, retraction of the guidewire is generally not recommended so that a secure access to the coronary vessel may be preserved.

Non-Uniform Rotational Distortion

Non-uniform rotational distortion (NURD) may be observed only when mechanical transducers are used. This artefact is caused by an uneven drag of the drive cable of the mechanical catheter. This results to cyclic oscillations that are observed as a severe distortion of the image. This particular artifact appears in several occasions such as: acute bends of the coronary artery, tortuous guide catheter shape or small lumen of the guide catheter, excessive tightening of the hemostatic valve, variance in manufacturing the driveshaft, or kinking of the image sheath.

Figure 3. a) Concentric fibrous plaque with a 45 degrees arc of superficial calcium (10-12 o'clock). Outside the artery note the longitudinal view of a vein extending from 5 to 8 o'clock; b) Normal coronary artery. Outside the artery note the large cardiac vein with branches extending from 11 to 3 o'clock; C) Cardiac vein 8-9 o'clock uncompressed - during diastole (arrow); d) Same cardiac vein as in Figure 3c compressed – during systole (arrow).

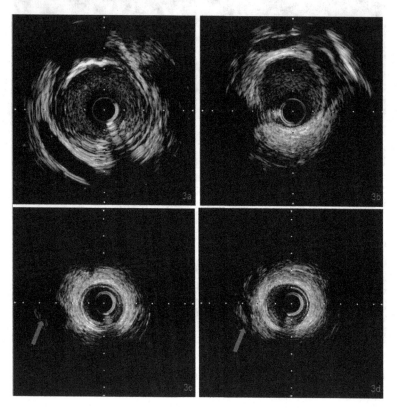

Ring-Down and Near Field Artifacts

Ring-down artifacts usually appear as bright halos of various thicknesses that surround the IVUS catheter. They are caused by acoustic oscillations of the transducer resulting in high-amplitude signals which mask the area surrounding the catheter. These artifacts are present in all types of catheters and create an obscure zone adjacent to the catheter surface. They can be reduced or eliminated by appropriate adjustment of the time gain compensation. However, excessive signal suppression can reduce signals from true targets. In electronic systems ring-down artifacts are partially decreased by digital subtraction of a reference mask. Digital subtraction though, can potentially remove true targets or introduce false ones, if it is not properly performed.

Slow Flow

The intensity of blood speckle increases exponentially as blood flow velocity decreases and transducer frequency increases. This can cause serious problems in differentiating vessel lumen from tissue (especially thrombus, neointima or echolucent plaques). This artifact can be accentuated with blood flow cessation or stagnation that is more evident when the catheter is advanced across a tight stenosis. Adjustment of time gain compensation can reduce blood speckle signals but it also reduces signals from real targets. In order to be able to differentiate the tissue borders from vessel lumen, some operators flush contrast or saline through the guiding catheter.

Coronary Pulsation and Motion Artifacts

In normal coronary vessels the maximal lumen diameter occurs in systole while the maximal blood flow occurs in diastole when myocardial capillary resistance is minimal. In contrast, at the site of myocardial bridges the lumen reaches its minimal diameter during systole when surrounding myocardium contracts. During each cardiac cycle the IVUS catheter can move up to 5 mm axially between systole and diastole. This can cause problems in the assessment of normal phenomena that emerge during the cardiac cycle (arterial pulsation or compliance as described above). Characteristic motion artifacts may also appear in cases of unstable position of the catheter, or movement of the vessel before a complete circumferential image is created, resulting thus in a cyclic deformation of the created image.

Catheter Obliquity, Eccentricity, and Vessel Curvature

Contemporary image reconstruction technologies assume that the vessel is circular and that the IVUS catheter is located in the center of the lumen, parallel to the long axis of the artery. In everyday clinical practice, this occurs rarely; transducer obliquity and vessel curvature may result in an elliptical image distortion of the vessel. The former is very common in large vessels and it is of great significance as it can cause overestimation of vessel dimensions and reduction in image quality. The reduction of image quality occurs because the amplitude of the echo signal reflected from an interface depends on the angle at which the echo beam strikes the interface. The strongest signals are obtained when the catheter is parallel to the vessel's long axis and the beam strikes the target with a 90° angle. On the other

hand when the catheter is not parallel to the vessel long axis the reflected signal is weak and this may affect the quality of the obtained images and their interpretation.

Spatial Orientation

Current IVUS catheters do not have a constant orientation and thus there is no anterior, posterior, medial or lateral direction in the acquired images. Nevertheless, some IVUS systems can provide a constant orientation by rotating the acquired images. For example, the images obtained during IVUS interrogation of a left anterior descending artery can be rotated so that the left circumflex artery to be positioned at 9 o'clock. In this setting, the diagonal branches appear on the left side of the image and the septal branches perpendicular to the diagonal branches. In everyday clinical practice, the spatial orientation of IVUS images can be extracted using anatomical markers such as of side branches, the pericardium, cardiac veins or muscle strands. These landmarks can also be used to identify correspondence in serial IVUS examinations and facilitate comparison.

Calcium Shadow

When the IVUS echo beam strikes on a calcified tissue, the signal is totally reflected. This reflection causes a characteristic signal drop-out (shadow) or multiple reflections of concentric arcs behind the calcified tissue (Figure 4).

MAIN FOCUS

Atheromatous Plaques: Morphology and Complications

In contrast to angiography which can only assess the degree of a luminal stenosis by comparing the lesion with an apparently 'normal' segment (reference segment), IVUS provides additional

Figure 4. a) Calcific plaque with acoustic shadowing – 90 degrees arc (3-6 o'clock); b) Eccentric fibrous plaque with deep calcium causing acoustic shadowing (7-8 o'clock); c) Calcific plaque 'egg shell' – 360 degrees arc of calcium surrounding the lumen; d) Calcific plaque in the left main coronary artery (extending from 3 to 9 o'clock). Note the calcium protruding in the lumen at 3-4 o'clock.

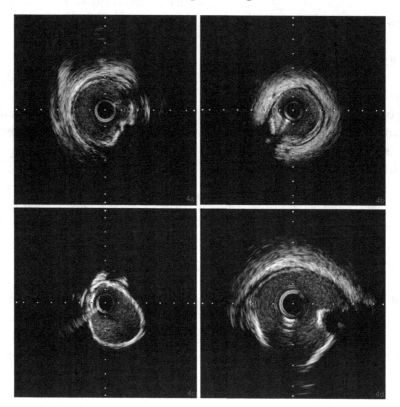

information regarding the vessel wall and is able to evaluate the atheromatous plaque burden, the extent of the atheroma (i.e. focal or diffuse) and the morphology of the plaque (i.e. concentric or eccentric). The plaque burden observed using IVUS does not appear to be always related to the luminal dimensions (Berry et al., 2007). This paradox is mainly attributed to vessel wall remodeling noted in the diseased segment; this can be classified as expansive or constrictive. In the expansive remodeling the diseased vessel enlarges so as to maintain its luminal size (Glagov et al., 1987) while in the constrictive remodeling there is an increased fibroprolifative process in the vessel wall resulting in a vascular constriction (Mintz et al., 1997).

IVUS imaging not only allows evaluation of plaque burden but also provides important information regarding its composition (Palmer et al., 1999; Potkin et al., 1990). For many years IVUS has been regarded as the gold standard for the *in vivo* characterization of plaque type; however, today it is evident that grayscale IVUS imaging has a moderate sensitivity and specificity in assessing the composition of the plaque (range: 67-100% and 61-95% respectively) (Kawasaki et al., 2006). To overcome these drawback, radio-frequency analysis of backscatter IVUS signal (RF-IVUS) (Nair et al., 2002) and elastography (de Korte et al., 2000) have been developed. These IVUS-based processing techniques have been validated against histology. The obtained results demonstrated that RF-IVUS is superior and provides reliable characterization of the type of the plaque and identification of vulnerable plaque characteristics (Mehta et al., 2007). Nevertheless, although grayscale IVUS is not the gold standard it is still useful and provides information regarding the composition of the plaque. In the obtained images the following plaque types can be seen.

Echolucent (Soft) Plaques

The term 'soft' is used to describe the acoustic properties of an anatomical structure (Figure 5a). From studies comparing IVUS to histological data, it is known that low echogenicity signal is seen in lipid-rich lesions (Palmer et al., 1999; Potkin et al., 1990; Yamagishi et al., 2000). Plaques with a large lipid pool result in echo attenuation and are considered to be vulnerable and prone to rupture. However, lower intensity hypoechoic zones can also be seen in other plaque components such as necrotizing tissue within the plaque, intramural hemorrhage or thrombus. Therefore, the term 'soft', that has also been implemented to describe 'vulnerable' or unstable plaques, should be avoided. In IVUS imaging, the term 'soft' refers to the reduced echodensity and not to specific mechanical or structural characteristics of the plaque.

Figure 5. a) Eccentric soft (echolucent) plaque (extending from 3 to 7 o'clock) with thin fibrous cap and some superficial calcifications; b) Mixed plaque with an echolucent zone (probably lipid core) and fibrous cap (extending from 12 to 3 o'clock) and a calcium arc with acoustic shadowing (from 9 to 12 o'clock); c) Concentric fibrous plaque. Note that the acoustic shadow produced by the guidewire should not be confused with a lipid core echolucent area; d) Eccentric fibrofatty plaque (extending from 2 to 8 o'clock).

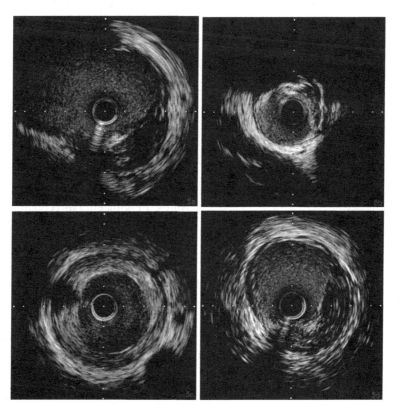

Echodense (Hard or Fibrous) Plaques

These plaques demonstrate an intermediate echogenicity between the echolucent (soft) and the highly echogenic calcific plaques (Figure 5) and they have been shown to have a high content of fibrous tissue (Palmer et al., 1999; Potkin et al., 1990). The greater the fibrous content, the more echogenic the appearance of the atheroma. In some cases when the atherosclerotic plaque consists of very dense fibrous tissue, this can cause acoustic shadowing and the plaque can be misclassified as calcified. Echodense and mixed plaques represent the majority of the atherosclerotic plaques seen in IVUS.

Calcific Plaques

IVUS imaging has exhibited a significantly higher sensitivity in detecting the presence of calcium compared to fluoroscopy (Tuzcu et al., 1996). Calcific deposits appear as bright echoes that obstruct the penetration of ultrasound waves resulting in an 'acoustic shadowing' that do not allow visualization of the underlying structures and accurate evaluation of plaque burden (Figure 4). The presence of calcium can also produce reverberations or multiple reflections. Extensive calcification usually indicates plaque stability whereas microcalcifications are frequently located within lipid-rich and vulnerable plaques (Ehara et al., 2004; Wang, Lu, Chen, Zhao, & Xia, 2008). Of note, these microcalcifications cannot be well reflected in IVUS images.

Mixed Plaques

Coronary atheromatous plaques often consist of components with different echogenic properties (Figure 5). Various zones of diverse morphology are usually identified within these mixed plaques. Depending on their content, several terms are used for their description: 'fibrofatty', 'fibrocalcific', etc.

Unstable (Vulnerable) Plaque and Plaque Rupture

Plaque fissure, superficial erosion, ulceration or rupture with subsequent formation of occlusive or non-occlusive thrombus, are key elements in the pathophysiology of acute coronary syndromes. The majority of coronary plaques are stable, while most vulnerable plaques do not lead to acute syndromes but stabilize either without rupture or following clinically silent rupture and resulting fibrosis. Only in few cases do vulnerable plaques rupture leading to thrombosis and manifestation of acute coronary syndromes. The mechanisms involved in plaque destabilization are complex and not fully understood. A very important factor for the evolution of an atheromatous plaque to a 'vulnerable' state is the balance between inflammation and fibrosis; increased inflammation increases plaque vulnerability while fibrosis is associated with greater plaque stability. Systemic triggering factors appear to play a significant role which becomes particularly evident in patients presenting with an acute coronary syndrome where multiple vulnerable lesions are often noted (Goldstein et al., 2000; Maehara et al., 2002).

Since most acute coronary events are caused by a rupture of mildly stenotic plaques (Maehara et al., 2002), the identification of specific structural characteristics that are associated with increased vulnerability has been considered to be of great clinical importance. Grayscale IVUS appears to have limited capability in identifying these features. Echolucent (soft) plaques described above are believed to represent potentially unstable coronary lesions. These plaques are seen more frequently in high risk patients and are associated with positive (expansive) remodeling and have an increased lipid-rich component. Histology has showed that a thin cap, macrophage infiltration, cholesterol clefts, thrombus, and microcalcifications are features associated with increased vulnerability (Kimura et al., 2009). Unfortunately, the fibrous cap, seen as an echogenic border at the lumen-intima interface, is expected to be so thin in unstable plaques (< 65 μm) that cannot be detected with IVUS. Studies using RF-IVUS recently showed that grayscale IVUS attenuated plaques are associated with a large amount of necrotic core and are markers of fibroatheromas that are associated with significant plaque progression compared to fibrous or fibrocalcific plaques (Wu et al., 2010). However, acute events associated with plaque rupture cannot be predicted using only grayscale IVUS characteristics. The PROSPECT trial that studiedpatients who presented with an acute coronary syndrome and underwent PCI, recently showed that combination of gray-scale and RF-IVUS can predict unanticipated adverse cardiac events from non-culprit lesions. Features associated with increased risk are: presence of thin-cap fibroatheromas, a large plaque burden, and a small luminal area (Stone et al., 2011).

There is no definite appearance of plaque rupture in IVUS. Frequently a ruptured plaque or ulceration appears as a 'cavity' in the vessel wall with a ruptured intima and remnants of the ruptured fibrous cap. Key point in the identification of these plaques is the presence of flow within the plaque cavity (Figure 6) especially in moving images, e.g. video loops To detect the communication point contrast injections may be necessary. In contrast, the development of thrombus may mask the site of rupture and impede correct diagnosis.

Figure 6. a) Eccentric, mostly fibrous plaque (extending from 10 to 3 o'clock). Rupture at 12 o'clock (arrow); b) Concentric mixed plaque with calcium (extending from 11 to 1 o'clock) and a rupture extending from 1 to 3 o'clock (arrow); c) Rupture of the fibrous cap (7 o'clock) and blood entry inside the plaque (from 3 to 9 o'clock); d) Intraplaque hematoma following plaque rupture (frame distal to 6c).

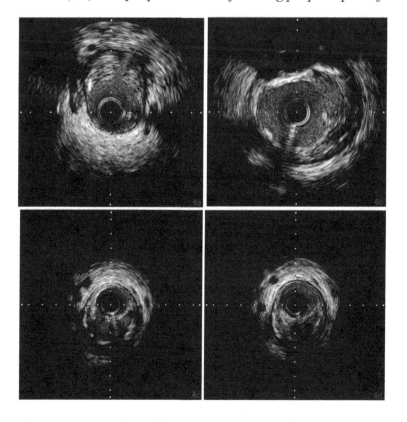

Thrombus

Thrombus may be recognized as a layered, lobular or peduncular mass usually located within the vessel's lumen. Thrombi are frequently echolucent but they may also have variable echogenicities with speckles or oscillations. Stasis of blood flow can be confused with thrombus with gray-white specular echoes located within the lumen. In this case, flushes with contrast medium or saline can disperse blood flow stagnation and differentiate stasis from thrombosis. It is very important to note that there is no morphologic feature pathognomonic for thrombus and thus IVUS has limited capability in differentiating thrombi from echolucent lipid-rich (soft) plaques, loose connective tissue or blood flow stasis (Figure 7a-7b). Therefore the diagnosis of thrombus by IVUS should always be considered presumptive.

Unusual and Ambiguous Lesions

Unusual and ambiguous lesions that are commonly assessed with IVUS may involve: lesions of uncertain stenotic severity, ostial lesions, aneurysmal lesions, left main stenoses, tortuous lesions, side branch ostial stenoses, sites of coronary spasm, filling defects and hazy lesions observed by angiography or dissections after PCI.

Figure 7. a) Eccentric complex plaque (extending from 3 to 9 o'clock) with double layer appearance that can be attributed to a lipid core within the plaque, or to the presence of thrombus in the lumen; b) Complex plaque causing severe stenosis of the lumen (annotated area). The double layer appearance (1 to 3 o'clock) could be due to the presence of thrombus in the lumen. c) Stent struts. The stent is well expanded and apposed to the vessel wall; d) Stent struts (visible from 3 to 9 o'clock). Intimal hyperplasia inside the stent struts is evident all around the vessel.

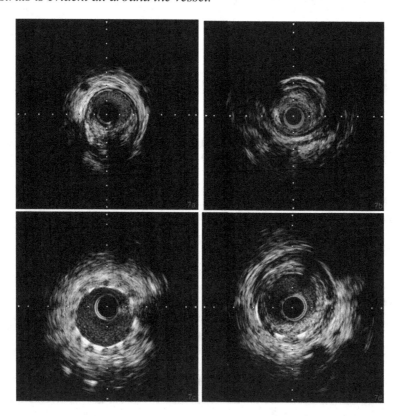

IVUS is considered to be the gold standard for the differentiation of a true aneurysm from a pseudoaneurysm. A *true aneurysm* is defined as a lesion that includes all vessel wall layers with a luminal and EEM diameter that are >50% larger than the proximal reference segment, while a *pseudoaneurysm* appears as a disruption of the EEM and usually observed after PCIs. The discrimination is of great clinical importance as true aneurysms have a favorable prognosis and do not mandate treatment while pseudoaneurysms need treatment to prevent thrombosis, distal emboli, enlargement or even wall rupture.

There are certain IVUS characteristics that allow the differentiation between *true* and *false lumen* (observed after a dissection). A false lumen is a channel that is parallel to the true lumen and does not communicate with the true lumen over a great portion of its length. The true lumen is surrounded by the three layers of the vascular wall (intima, media and adventitia) and communicates with the side branches.

IVUS is also used to determine whether ambiguous lesions of intermediate severity observed with angiography are clinically significant (angiographic stenosis of 40-70%). Previous IVUS studies with clinical follow-up (Abizaid et al., 1999a; Abizaid et al., 1999b; Jasti, Ivan, Yalamanchili, Wongpraparut, & Leesar, 2004; Nishioka et al., 1999; Takagi et al., 1999) have helped to establish criteria based on quantitative IVUS measurements that allow to assess whether an intermediate lesion has a favorable prognosis and thus can be treated conservatively with a low event rate or whether it is associated with a high event rate and hence revascularization is required in addition to medical treatment to improve clinical outcomes. However, it is important to note that IVUS cannot provide information on the physiology of the studied lesions. The hemodynamic significance of a lesion is usually assessed with the coronary pressure wire-derived fractional flow reserve (FFR). There are currently no randomized studies to compare IVUS and FFR and there is no indication of which methodology may be considered superior (Maluenda et al., 2010).

Intimal Hyperplasia

Intimal hyperplasia occurs in stented segments (Figure 7c-d). Histological studies suggest that neointimal tissue consists of extracellular matrix and proliferating cells that contribute to the development of in-stent restenosis. Their contribution varies with time with cell proliferation being more prominent early after intervention while the extracellular matrix accumulation is more significant in later stages (Chung et al., 2002). This phenomenon explains the appearance of the neointimal tissue using IVUS. In early in-stent restenosis, the intimal hyperplasia has low echogenicity which occasionally is lower than the blood speckle. Inappropriate system settings can potentially suppress ultrasound reflections of this low-echogenic material and render diagnosis difficult. In contrast, intimal hyperplasia in cases of late in-stent restenosis appears more echogenic than early in-stent restenosis.

Dissections

IVUS is often used to guide treatment during PCI and detect dissections that may occur during the procedure. The recommended classification of dissections is: a) *Intimal* that is limited to the intimal area or the atheroma and does not extend to the media; b) *Medial* that involves the media; c) *Adventitial* that involves the EEM; d) *Intramural hematoma* that represents accumulation of blood that is located at the medial space and pushes the internal elastic membrane inwards and the EEM outwards (on several occasions the entry and/or exit points of the dissection cannot be detected); and e) *Intra-stent dissection* that separates the neointima from the stent struts and is usually detected after in-stent restenosis treatment (Mintz et al., 2001). IVUS is also used to assess the dissection's severity on the basis of the following characteristics: 1) depth (e.g. into plaque or media); 2) circumferential extent (in degrees of an arc); 3) length (when using a motorized transducer); 4) size of the true lumen [cross sectional area, (CSA)]; and 5) CSA of the pseudo-lumen. Rarely, the dissection may be masked because it is located behind calcium or because of the scaffolding by the imaging catheter. Usually, such dissections that cannot be detected by IVUS can be demonstrated by angiography. Most non-flow limiting residual dissections occurring after a successful PCI are associated with a good long-term prognosis and additional stenting is not advised. In contrast, dissections associated with significant stenosis (>60%) are generally associated with increased major adverse cardiac events (Maluenda et al., 2010).

Intravascular Ultrasound Nomenclature and Definitions

IVUS studies usually reveal diffuse and more extensive coronary artery disease than coronary angiography. The diffuse nature of atherosclerosis causes several problems in the definition, the qualitative and quantitative characterization of lesions. There are cases in which the vessel segment presents diffuse disease but no focal narrowings and others where the coronary artery has discrete focal plaques causing severe luminal obstruction. Descriptions for lesions and reference segments require different nomenclature definitions when IVUS is implemented compared to the terms used in coronary angiography. Such definitions have been previously recommended by Mintz et al. (2001):

Proximal and Distal reference is the site of the largest luminal dimensions located proximally and distally to a stenosis respectively (usually up to 10 mm of the stenosis with no major branches). The reference site (either proximally or distally to the stenosis) with the largest luminal dimensions is called *the largest reference,* whereas *the average reference lumen size* is the mean value of the proximal and distal reference sites.

Lesion is a site with atherosclerotic plaque accumulation compared with a predefined reference site. *Stenosis* is a lesion that causes at least a 50% luminal narrowing (as assessed by CSA) compared to a predefined reference segment. The stenosis with the smallest luminal size is *the worst stenosis*, whereas lesions that may be classified as stenoses but have lumen sizes greater than the worst stenosis are *secondary stenoses*. Although the worst stenosis should be the image slice with the smallest luminal dimensions, this is not necessarily the site with the largest plaque. In case of multiple lesions within the same segment, distinct lesions require at least 5 mm distances between the stenoses; if otherwise, it should be considered as a single lesion.

Uninterrupted IVUS imaging should always start at least 10 mm distally to the target segment, and include the lesion site and the whole proximal vessel till the aorta. If possible the pull-back of the IVUS catheter should be performed with the use of an automated pull-back-device which withdraws the IVUS catheter at a constant speed at 0.5-1 mm/sec. Thus, a sequence of evenly spaced cross-sectional images is obtained which allow longitudinal reconstruction of the studied vessel.

A complete analysis of the entire studied segment is necessary in order to evaluate the extent and severity of a lesion, while the analysis of serial IVUS examinations requires the identification of corresponding segments between them. This can be achieved with the detection of anatomical landmarks (side branches, calcific or fibrotic deposits or cardiac veins) seen in all pull-backs. Then the region of interest is selected and its 'location' is defined by measuring its axial distance from the detected anatomical landmark. When the second study is performed, these landmarks and the previously measured distance are used to detect the cross-sections that correspond to those examined in the first study.

Intravascular Ultrasound Measurements

In general, if artifacts such as ring-down and NURD are present or the IVUS catheter is located obliquely in relation to the vessel wall, measurements should not be performed.

Border Identification

In the coronary arteries, two borders and three distinct layers may be identified (Figure 1). The first border is the lumen-intima interface and the second is the EEM (between the media and the adventitia). As these borders separate tissues with different properties, they induce a strong signal that allows their tracing. The first inner layer that is more echogenic from the vessel lumen consists of the intima, the plaque (in diseased vessels) and the internal elastic membrane. The internal elastic membrane is located at the trailing edge of the intima and is not always clearly defined. The second medial layer corresponds to the media that is usually less echogenic than the intima. There are cases that the media appears falsely thin (intense reflections from the intima or the EEM) or thick (faint reflections from the EEM). The third layer consists of the adventitia and peri-adventitial tissue. There are no clear borders to clearly separate the adventitia from the surrounding tissue. All measurements should be performed at the leading edge borders and never at the trailing edge since the leading edge boundaries are accurately depicted and highly reproducible in almost all IVUS systems utilized in contemporary clinical practice.

Luminal Measurements

Luminal measurements are performed using the leading edge of the intima, at the lumen-intima interface. In normal coronary segments the intima can be easily delineated from the lumen. In these cases the leading edge of the innermost echogenic layer should be considered as the luminal border. Sometimes the vessel wall has a single-layer appearance as the intima cannot be distinguished from the other tissues. Then, the inner most echogenic border should be used for luminal measurements. It is possible that in such cases the lumen measured may include the intima, but the thickness of this layer is <160 μm and thus, it adds only an inconsiderable error. Once the luminal borders are defined the following measurements may be obtained (Mintz et al., 2001):

- **Luminal CSA:** Is the area delineated by the luminal borders.
- **Minimum and Maximum luminal diameter:** Is the smallest and largest luminal diameter respectively. From these, the eccentricity of the lumen may be calculated:
- **Eccentricity:** 100 x (maximum - minimum luminal diameter) / maximum luminal diameter.
- **Lumen area stenosis:** Is defined as: 100 x (reference luminal CSA - minimum luminal CSA)/ reference luminal CSA. The reference segment used for the calculation should be stated (proximal, distal, largest or average).

All measurements are obtained with regards to the center of the lumen and not to the center of the IVUS catheter.

External Elastic Membrane (EEM) Measurements

These are similar to luminal measurements:

- **EEM CSA:** Is the area located within the EEM borders.
- **Minimum and maximum EEM diameter:** Is the smallest and largest diameter respectively of the EEM area.

The EEM circumference cannot always be clearly defined at frames depicting extensive calcified plaques or at the origin of large side branches (Figure 2b) and (Figures 5c and 5d). If the calcium shadowing corresponds to an arc <90°, then the EEM circumference can be extrapolated from the closest recognized to the shadowing EEM borders. However, if the calcification extends to an arc >90°, then the EEM area cannot be measured. Similarly, shadowing seen behind stent struts may often render unreliable the delineation of the EEM.

Atheroma Measurements

IVUS cannot determine the exact area that corresponds to the 'true atheroma' as it does not allow detection of the internal elastic membrane. Thus, the measured plaque is defined from the EEM and luminal CSAs. However, since the media represents only a small fraction of the true atheroma, the inclusion of media area to atheroma does not induce significant errors to the calculations performed. The following measurements of the atheroma have been recommended in clinical practice (Mintz et al., 2001):

- **Plaque CSA:** Is defined as: EEM CSA - luminal CSA.
- **Plaque burden:** Is given as plaque CSA / EEM CSA (e.g. the fraction of the EEM area occupied by the plaque).
- **Maximum and Minimum Plaque Thickness:** Is the longest and shortest distance from the intimal leading edge to the EEM along any line that passes through the center of the lumen. From these, the plaque eccentricity can be calculated as: 100 x (maximum plaque thickness - minimum plaque thickness) / maximum plaque thickness.

Several studies validate the ability of IVUS to discriminate clinically significant from non-significant coronary disease, and thus guide treatment (conservative vs. invasive treatment). It appears that for lesions located in the left main stem a CSA≥5.9 mm^2 and a MLD ≥2.8 mm on IVUS are associated with a low event rate and a favorable prognosis without an intervention (Abizaid et al., 1999a). In addition, for the proximal and middle segments of the large epicardial vessels, a minimal CSA <4 mm^2 indicates a hemodynamically significant stenosis as it is associated with ischaemia in myocardial perfusion imaging (Nishioka et al., 1999) and a pressure-derived fractional flow reserve (FFR) <0.75 (Abizaid et al., 1999b; Takagi et al., 1999). Furthermore, other criteria that have been associated with a significant stenosis are: a MLD <1.8 mm and a percent CSA stenosis >70% (Briguori et al., 2001). In small coronary arteries with a reference diameter <3 mm, IVUS-derived anatomic criteria have been recently introduced to predict significant stenoses (FFR <0.75). These are: a minimal CSA ≤2.0 mm^2, a plaque burden ≥80%, and a lesion length ≥20 mm (Lee et al., 2010). Which of the two techniques IVUS or FFR is superior in improving clinical outcomes has not been investigated yet. Both techniques are believed to be complementary providing very useful anatomical/structural and functional information respectively that guide clinical decision-making in the catheterization laboratory.

Calcium Measurements

Calcified deposits appear as bright echoes that do not allow the penetration of the ultrasound beam, resulting in the phenomenon known as 'acoustic shadow'. Hence, IVUS can identify only the leading edge of the calcium deposit but not its thickness. Other artifacts produced by calcium are reverberations and multiple reflections from the ultrasound oscillations that appear as concentric arcs in the image.

A qualitative characterization of calcium deposits that has been previously recommended (Mintz et al., 2001) is the *location/depth inside the plaque:* if the leading edge of the calcium shadowing is situated at the outer 50% side of the plaque then it is regarded as *superficial*; on the other hand if it is seen in the inner 50% part of the plaque then it is called *deep* (including the media).

Recommended quantitative measurements of calcium deposits (Mintz et al., 2001) are: 1) *The arc of calcium* that can be measured by using an electronic protractor centered in the lumen. This measurement is usually reliable only to ±15° due to beam-spread variability at given depths within the transmitted beam. Semi-quantitative methods have been also described classifying calcium as absent or occupying 1, 2, 3, 4 quadrants. 2) *The length of the calcific deposit* that can be measured only when a motorized pull-back device has been used to withdraw the IVUS catheter.

Stent Measurements

Stent struts strongly reflect the ultrasound waves and thus they appear as highly echogenic segments along the vessel's circumference. Each stent has a different acoustic appearance depending on its design (Figures 7c-d and Figure 8). Multicellular or slotted-tube stents appear as focal echogenic (metallic) points, while coiled stents appear as echogenic arcs that occupy entire sections of the vessel wall.

The stent apposition refers to the deployment of the stent struts in relation to the vessel wall. Good apposition is defined as a sufficient contact of the struts against the vessel wall that does not allow blood flow between them (Figure 7c). Stent

Figure 8. a) Overlapping stents (2 stents visible mostly from 3 to 5 o'clock); b) Stent at the ostium of a large vessel (side branch from 1 to 5 o'clock); c) Stent not apposed to the greatest part of the vessel wall (from 9 to 3 o'clock) due to late stent malapposition (the stent was placed 6 months ago with good apposition at the time of implantation); d) Longitudinal view of the same vessel as in Figure 8c. Both the stent malapposition and the vessel enlargement are evident (square).

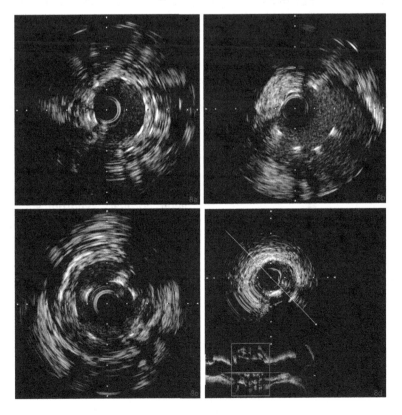

apposition can be examined by flushing contrast or saline through the guiding catheter. In case of malapposition, flow is present behind the struts. The arc and length of the malapposed segment should be reported. Appropriate gain settings are of paramount importance in assessing stent deployment. High gain settings should be avoided as the metallic struts create side lobes that obscure the stent and the true lumen borders and make the assessment of the lumen or stent's apposition difficult. The stent area is smaller than the luminal area when the stent is malapposed. On the other hand, in case of previous stent implantation, the stent area may be larger than the luminal area if there is neointimal proliferation. The stent-related measurements recommended to be used in IVUS studies (Mintz et al., 2001) are:

- **Stent CSA:** Is the area delineated by the stent borders.
- **Minimum and Maximum Stent Diameter:** Is the smallest and largest diameter through the center of mass of the stent respectively. Stent symmetry can be calculated as: 100 x (maximum stent diameter - minimum stent diameter) / maximum stent diameter.
- **Stent Expansion:** Is the minimum stent CSA compared to a predefined reference area (proximal, distal, largest or average area).

Remodeling

Vascular remodeling refers to the changes in the EEM area that take place during the atherosclerotic process. The remodeling is considered as 'positive' or expansive when the EEM increases during plaque development and 'negative' or constrictive when it decreases. The positive remodeling can: a) over-compensate for increasing plaque burden resulting in an absolute increase in luminal dimensions; b) exactly compensate for increasing plaque area resulting in no change in luminal dimensions;

and c) under-compensate for increasing plaque area; and then it is called inadequate remodeling. Based on IVUS measurements, several indices have been proposed to assess remodeling. An index ratio that can provide information about the extent and direction of the remodeling process is the ratio: lesion EEM CSA / reference EEM CSA, provided that large side branches are not included. Expansive (or constrictive) remodeling is defined when lesion EEM area is greater (or smaller) than the reference EEM area, i.e. the index will be >1.0 in case of expansive remodeling and <1.0 in case of constrictive remodeling. However, this index defines remodeling in relation to a reference segment that may have already undergone atherosclerotic changes and thus the results may be inaccurate. Serial measurements of the EEM CSA of the same segments obtained at different times can provide direct evidence of expansive or constrictive remodeling. Then, if the slope of the line that correlates the change in the EEM area to the change in the atheroma (plaque plus media) is >1.0 expansive remodeling has occurred, if it is <1.0 inadequate remodeling has taken place, while slope values <0 indicate constrictive remodeling.

Remodeling has been associated with other IVUS characteristics of coronary atherosclerosis as well as with the clinical presentation of coronary artery disease. Expansive (or positive) remodeling is often seen in plaques that have features associated with increased vulnerability such as a large atherosclerotic burden, echolucent plaques, presence of thrombus, etc. It is very common in acute coronary syndromes and has been related to worse prognosis. A higher incidence of major adverse cardiac events in both stable and unstable patients (Hong et al., 2007; Okura et al., 2009) and also an increased risk of PCI-related complications (no reflow during PCI and in-stent restenosis) (Okura et al., 2001) has been reported in lesions with expansive remodeling.

Length Measurements

Length measurements can be obtained only when the pull-back has been performed with the use of a motorized pull-back device. The length or distance can be calculated as the number of seconds multiplied by the pull-back speed. The length of a stenotic lesion, of a calcium deposit or of any other longitudinal structure as well as the distance between the plaque and an anatomical landmark can be measured in the longitudinal view of the reconstructed by the IVUS vessel.

Volumetric Measurements

IVUS can be used for quantitative volumetric analysis of the atheroma. Initially, a segment is selected between two landmarks (e.g. two side branches). Starting from the distal landmark, single frames at intervals of 0.5-1.0 mm are selected and for each of the selected intervals the EEM and luminal CSAs are measured. The Simpson's rule is then applied to calculated plaque volume by multiplying plaque area by the distance between the two adjacent images. Another approach includes ECG-gated selection of the frames in predefined relation to the cardiac cycle. The presence of calcium deposits or side branches is an important limitation of this method as the EEM cannot be measured reliably at those sites. To overcome this drawback specific recommendations have been proposed for the volumetric analysis to avoid caveats and to ensure homogeneity between studies: 1) If side branches exist extrapolation of the EEM measurements has been suggested 2) In case of calcification deposits which results in a acoustic shadowing involving a relatively small arc ($<90°$), the planimetry of the EEM circumference can be extrapolated from the closest identifiable EEM border (reduced accuracy and reproducibility), whereas if the calcifications extent to more than $90°$, the EEM measurements should not be reported; and 3) In case of in-stent restenosis the volumetric analysis of the neointimal tissue should

be the primary endpoint. In these studies the total plaque volume should not be reported because most stent designs obscure the EEM borders.

Intravascular Ultrasound Imaging in Specific Cases

Progression/Regression of Atherosclerosis

Given its known limitations, serial coronary angiography is regarded as an unreliable method for the detection of atherosclerosis progression/ regression and for the evaluation of the effect of anti-atherosclerotic treatments (Hong et al., 1994). On the other hand, IVUS, as a more sensitive method in detecting diffuse atherosclerosis and more accurate in quantifying the extent of disease compared with conventional angiography, appears to provide a valuable tool and is able to assess the progression or regression of the plaque burden and examine the effectiveness of several anti-athero-sclerotic treatments (Nissen, 2002). A significant advantage of IVUS is its high reproducibility regarding the plaque burden which allows detection of minor changes in the atheroma volume (Nissen, 2002; Schoenhagen et al., 2003). Over the last 15 years several randomized IVUS-based trials have been performed to determine changes in plaque volume and assess the effectiveness of different invasive or non-invasive therapies (Bourantas et al., 2011; Nissen et al., 2006; Nissen et al., 2008; Nissen et al., 2004). Recently, RF-IVUS has also been used to examine the evolution of coronary atherosclerosis and has provided useful insights in the prediction of coronary events (Stone et al., 2011; Wu et al., 2010).

Transplant Vasculopathy

Coronary artery disease developing following heart transplantation, or coronary transplant vas-culopathy, is the leading cause of death in the first year after heart transplantation and it is often silent due to the denervated transplanted heart. Ischemia becomes evident in stress testing only in advanced disease and therefore coronary angiography on an annual basis is suggested to assess the extent and the severity of atherosclerosis. However, the diffuse nature of coronary vasculopathy often hampers its detection on angiography and thus IVUS has been recommended for early detection (Kass & Haddad, 2006). Intimal thickening after heart transplantation should be differentiated from potential donor coronary atherosclerosis that may be present even in young donors. The cut-off values for the diagnosis of transplant vasculopathy remain controversial. Using intimal thickness of >0.5 mm as threshold, coronary transplant vasculopathy is seen in 50% of the patients at 1 year (Rickenbacher et al., 1995). As the severity of the arteriopathy is a poor prognostic indicator for early death and cardiac events, serial IVUS examinations are recommended to evaluate its evolution and estimate outcomes.

Aortic, Carotid and Peripheral Vascular Disease

Classic angiography has various limitations in assessing the anatomy of peripheral arteries since in many occasions it is impossible to acquire orthogonal or angulated views, while the presence of calcifications in the thoracic and abdominal arteries often render impossible the delineation of the luminal borders. Thus, it is not uncommon to detect severe stenoses with IVUS in segments which appear disease free on angiography. IVUS image interpretation and analysis of peripheral vessels is similar to that of coronary arteries. However, the limitations of IVUS imaging described above are more prominent in the peripheral arteries with the catheter obliquity being the more frequent. In addition, the shadowing artefact of calcified plaques is quite common while the presence of diffuse peripheral artery disease may conceal the identification of a 'normal' reference segment.

Assessment of the Target Lesion During Percutaneous Coronary Intervention

IVUS is often used to re–evaluate the target lesions pre-intervention, during the procedure, post-intervention and at the follow-up. Analysis of the smallest target site alone can result in false impression of plaque compression and reduction after a coronary intervention as the axial location of the smallest target site is likely to shift in any of these stages. On the other hand volumetric analysis can compensate for the shifting of the minimum luminal area and provide a more reliable assessment of plaque progression.

Qualitative assessment of the target lesion may help in the selection of the most appropriate treatment. Lesion-related features that are important to assess are usually the depth and extent of calcification, the presence of arterial remodeling, dissections or thrombus. Thus, the presence of a heavily calcified plaque may indicate the use of cutting balloons or of a rotablator while increased thrombus burden the use of aspiration thrombus devices. In addition, IVUS allows identification of several PCI related complications (e.g. dissections, intramural hematomas, pseudoaneurysms) that cannot be seen in coronary angiography.

IVUS offers important guidance for the feasibility of direct stenting, as well as for the optimization of stent deployment and apposition with post-dilation. Incomplete stent apposition, stent underexpansion, residual luminal stenosis, inadequate lesion coverage and significant coronary dissection have been considered to be the predictors of the main complications of stenting such as stent thrombosis and restenosis in both bare metal and drug-eluting stents leading to major adverse cardiac events (Bourantas et al., 2010).

Several IVUS studies have provided important information about the role of IVUS in the optimization of bare metal stent (BMS) implantation (Maluenda et al., 2010). The minimal CSA is the most important predictor for clinical, angiographic or IVUS BMS restenosis (Mintz & Weissman, 2006), while incomplete stent apposition is believed to contribute to stent thrombosis (Maluenda et al., 2010). Criteria of optimal stent deployment that have been associated with a low event rate after BMS are: 1) satisfactory stent apposition, 2) symmetric stent expansion, 3) acceptable stent CSA, (e.g. ≥80-90% of the average reference CSA or ≥100% of the reference CSA with lowest lumen area or CSA ≥90-100% of the distal reference area) and 4) absence of dissections. However, the risk of PCI-related complications has significantly decreased after the introduction of modern dual antiplatelet therapy, and thus IVUS is recommended only in the treatment of complex lesions or in cases where there is evidence of inadequate expansion or dissection on coronary angiography (Bourantas et al., 2010).

IVUS has also been proven useful in the drug eluting stent (DES) era. Although the use of DES has reduced the rate of restenosis, DES underexpansion is an important predictor of stent failure and thrombosis (Maluenda et al., 2010). It appears that there is an inverse relationship between the size of minimal stent CSA and the rate of restenosis while on the other hand complete stent apposition does not appear to predict outcomes. A minimal stent CSA of >5-5.5 mm^2 has been associated with a favorable outcome at follow-up and absence of angiographic restenosis. Of note this is derived mainly from studies on sirolimus-eluting stents, while data on paclitaxel stents are limited (Mintz & Weissman, 2006). Finally complete coverage of the lesion is also associated with improved prognosis and IVUS can be implemented to select the correct length of the stent.

Although IVUS guidance during DES implantation has shown to reduce DES thrombosis and the need for repeat revascularization (Mintz & Weissman, 2006; Roy et al., 2008), the superiority of the systematic use of IVUS during DES implantation is still controversial (Bourantas et al., 2010; Park et al., 2009; Roy et al., 2008) Today IVUS is recommended only in high-risk patients (patients with diabetes mellitus, heart or renal failure, and those who have contraindications for dual antiplatelet therapy) or high-risk lesions (left main lesions, ostial lesions, bifurcations, long lesions, in-stent restenosis and small vessels) (Bourantas et al., 2010; Maluenda et al., 2010; Mintz & Weissman, 2006).

Assessment of Restenosis

IVUS allows accurate assessment of the reference vessel, the stented segment, the restenotic lesion (the site of the smallest luminal area within the previously treated lesion) and identification of the mechanism involved. Serial stent studies have provided information for the in-stent restenosis, detected its predictors (mainly stent underexpansion) and clarified the role of neointimal hyperplasia and chronic stent recoil (Hoffmann et al., 1996; Post et al., 1997; Weissman et al., 2005).

During the assessment of a stented artery not only the stent but also the non stented segments located in the inflow and outflow of the stent should be examined as in many cases the site of the minimum luminal area lies outside the stent. In contrast to non-stented segments where the absolute values and changes in EEM, lumen and plaque areas/volumes should be measured, in stented segments only the absolute values and changes in luminal and stent dimensions should be recorded. IVUS allows volumetric analysis and computation of the entire stent, lumen and intimal hyperplasia (stent minus lumen) post-intervention and at follow-up as well as assessment of the distribution of the neointima hyperplasia within the vessel. Late luminal loss can be calculated by comparing the minimum CSA post-intervention and at follow-up. Similarly, chronic stent recoil can be calculated from the minimum stent CSA post-implantation and at follow-up.

In cases of restenosis after DES implantation, IVUS is very useful in the assessment of the mechanism of failure and the identification of the most appropriate treatment (Mintz & Weissman, 2006). The most common mechanism involved is stent underexpansion. In cases of neointimal hyperplasia, the pattern of in-stent restenosis is critical in decision-making. A focal restenosis (<10-20 mm) could be treated with high-pressure balloon dilatation or implantation of another DES, while diffuse DES restenosis (> 20 mm) suggesting an exaggerated neointimal response to stent, often may require a different treatment modality such as brachytherapy or even surgical revascularization (Maluenda et al., 2010). In cases of late stent malapposition that may be seen after DES implantation (Figure 8c-d), treatment is not recommended as it remains stable or may even regress.

IVUS has also been used to study the effects of brachytherapy that has been implemented in the past to treat in-stent restenosis (Hansen et al., 2001; Sabate et al., 1999). In brachytherapy studies, serial assessment (post-radiation and at follow-up) should include the non-stented and stented segments as mentioned above, while changes and absolute volumes of EEM, lumen and plaque of the non-treated segments should be calculated since radiation may also affect the neighboring non -treated segment. Characteristic examples of such effects are arterial remodeling (e.g. increase in luminal volume due to an adaptive increase of EEM volume) (Sabate et al., 1999) and the candy-wrapper effect (e.g. accelerated restenosis at the edges of the treated segment, where the radiation dose falls off) (Hansen et al., 2001). It should be mentioned that similar effects of arterial remodeling (Aoki et al., 2008; Jensen et al., 2009) and stent edge plaque progression leading to edge restenosis (Aoki et al., 2008) have also been described with the use of DES.

CONCLUSION

IVUS has become indispensable in everyday clinical practice. The supplementary information provided has rendered it valuable in guiding complex percutaneous coronary interventions and its use has significantly limited intervention-related complications. In addition, its increased radial resolution has rendered it a useful research tool that allows accurate evaluation of the plaque burden and estimation of the atherosclerotic evolution. In this chapter we focused on the interpretation of IVUS images and presented the current nomenclature and definitions as it is believed that its use is still restricted by the fact that many interventional cardiologists are not familiar with this modality. Finnaly, this chapter also discusses some of the applications of IVUS aiming to highlight its role in current clinical practice and patient management.

REFERENCES

Abizaid, A. S., Mintz, G. S., Abizaid, A., Mehran, R., Lansky, A. J., & Pichard, A. D. (1999a). One-year follow-up after intravascular ultrasound assessment of moderate left main coronary artery disease in patients with ambiguous angiograms. *Journal of the American College of Cardiology, 34*(3), 707–715. doi:10.1016/S0735-1097(99)00261-2

Abizaid, A. S., Mintz, G. S., Mehran, R., Abizaid, A., Lansky, A. J., & Pichard, A. D. (1999b). Long-term follow-up after percutaneous transluminal coronary angioplasty was not performed based on intravascular ultrasound findings: importance of lumen dimensions. *Circulation, 100*(3), 256–261.

Aoki, J., Mintz, G. S., Weissman, N. J., Mann, J. T., Cannon, L., & Greenberg, J. (2008). Chronic arterial responses to overlapping paclitaxel-eluting stents: Insights from serial intravascular ultrasound analyses in the TAXUS-V and -VI trials. *JACC: Cardiovascular Interventions, 1*(2), 161–167. doi:10.1016/j.jcin.2007.12.005

Berry, C., L'Allier, P. L., Gregoire, J., Lesperance, J., Levesque, S., & Ibrahim, R. (2007). Comparison of intravascular ultrasound and quantitative coronary angiography for the assessment of coronary artery disease progression. *Circulation, 115*(14), 1851–1857. doi:10.1161/CIRCULATIONAHA.106.655654

Bourantas, C. V., Garg, S., Naka, K. K., Thury, A., Hoye, A., & Michalis, L. K. (2011). Focus on the research utility of intravascular ultrasound - Comparison with other invasive modalities. *Cardiovascular Ultrasound*, *9*(1), 2. doi:10.1186/1476-7120-9-2

Bourantas, C. V., Naka, K. K., Garg, S., Thackray, S., Papadopoulos, D., & Alamgir, F. M. (2010). Clinical indications for intravascular ultrasound imaging. *Echocardiography (Mount Kisco, N.Y.)*, *27*(10), 1282–1290. doi:10.1111/j.1540-8175.2010.01259.x

Briguori, C., Anzuini, A., Airoldi, F., Gimelli, G., Nishida, T., & Adamian, M. (2001). Intravascular ultrasound criteria for the assessment of the functional significance of intermediate coronary artery stenoses and comparison with fractional flow reserve. *The American Journal of Cardiology*, *87*(2), 136–141. doi:10.1016/S0002-9149(00)01304-7

Chung, I. M., Gold, H. K., Schwartz, S. M., Ikari, Y., Reidy, M. A., & Wight, T. N. (2002). Enhanced extracellular matrix accumulation in restenosis of coronary arteries after stent deployment. *Journal of the American College of Cardiology*, *40*(12), 2072–2081. doi:10.1016/S0735-1097(02)02598-6

de Korte, C. L., Pasterkamp, G., van der Steen, A. F., Woutman, H. A., & Bom, N. (2000). Characterization of plaque components with intravascular ultrasound elastography in human femoral and coronary arteries in vitro. *Circulation*, *102*(6), 617–623.

Di Mario, C., Gorge, G., Peters, R., Kearney, P., Pinto, F., & Hausmann, D. (1998). Clinical application and image interpretation in intracoronary ultrasound. Study Group on Intracoronary Imaging of the Working Group of Coronary Circulation and of the Subgroup on Intravascular Ultrasound of the Working Group of Echocardiography of the European Society of Cardiology. *European Heart Journal*, *19*(2), 207–229. doi:10.1053/euhj.1996.0433

Ehara, S., Kobayashi, Y., Yoshiyama, M., Shimada, K., Shimada, Y., & Fukuda, D. (2004). Spotty calcification typifies the culprit plaque in patients with acute myocardial infarction: An intravascular ultrasound study. *Circulation*, *110*(22), 3424–3429. doi:10.1161/01.CIR.0000148131.41425.E9

Glagov, S., Weisenberg, E., Zarins, C. K., Stankunavicius, R., & Kolettis, G. J. (1987). Compensatory enlargement of human atherosclerotic coronary arteries. *The New England Journal of Medicine*, *316*(22), 1371–1375. doi:10.1056/NEJM198705283162204

Goldstein, J. A., Demetriou, D., Grines, C. L., Pica, M., Shoukfeh, M., & O'Neill, W. W. (2000). Multiple complex coronary plaques in patients with acute myocardial infarction. *The New England Journal of Medicine*, *343*(13), 915–922. doi:10.1056/NEJM200009283431303

Hansen, A., Hehrlein, C., Hardt, S., Bekeredjian, R., Brachmann, J., & Kubler, W. (2001). Is the "candy-wrapper" effect of (32)P radioactive beta-emitting stents due to remodeling or neointimal hyperplasia? Insights from intravascular ultrasound. *Catheterization and Cardiovascular Interventions*, *54*(1), 41–48. doi:10.1002/ccd.1235

Hausmann, D., Erbel, R., Alibelli-Chemarin, M. J., Boksch, W., Caracciolo, E., & Cohn, J. M. (1995). The safety of intracoronary ultrasound. A multicenter survey of 2207 examinations. *Circulation*, *91*(3), 623–630.

Hoffmann, R., Mintz, G. S., Dussaillant, G. R., Popma, J. J., Pichard, A. D., & Satler, L. F. (1996). Patterns and mechanisms of in-stent restenosis. A serial intravascular ultrasound study. *Circulation*, *94*(6), 1247–1254.

Hong, M. K., Mintz, G. S., Popma, J. J., Kent, K. M., Pichard, A. D., & Satler, L. F. (1994). Limitations of angiography for analyzing coronary atherosclerosis progression or regression. *Annals of Internal Medicine*, *121*(5), 348–354.

Hong, Y. J., Mintz, G. S., Kim, S. W., Lu, L., Bui, A. B., & Pichard, A. D. (2007). Impact of remodeling on cardiac events in patients with angiographically mild left main coronary artery disease. *The Journal of Invasive Cardiology, 19*(12), 500–505.

Jasti, V., Ivan, E., Yalamanchili, V., Wongpraparut, N., & Leesar, M. A. (2004). Correlations between fractional flow reserve and intravascular ultrasound in patients with an ambiguous left main coronary artery stenosis. *Circulation, 110*(18), 2831–2836. doi:10.1161/01.CIR.0000146338.62813.E7

Jensen, L. O., Maeng, M., Mintz, G. S., Christiansen, E. H., Hansen, K. N., & Galloe, A. (2009). Serial intravascular ultrasound analysis of peri-stent remodeling and proximal and distal edge effects after sirolimus-eluting or paclitaxel-eluting stent implantation in patients with diabetes mellitus. *The American Journal of Cardiology, 103*(8), 1083–1088. doi:10.1016/j.amjcard.2008.12.035

Kass, M., & Haddad, H. (2006). Cardiac allograft vasculopathy: Pathology, prevention and treatment. *Current Opinion in Cardiology, 21*(2), 132–137. doi:10.1097/01.hco.0000203184.89158.16

Kawasaki, M., Bouma, B. E., Bressner, J., Houser, S. L., Nadkarni, S. K., & MacNeill, B. D. (2006). Diagnostic accuracy of optical coherence tomography and integrated backscatter intravascular ultrasound images for tissue characterization of human coronary plaques. *Journal of the American College of Cardiology, 48*(1), 81–88. doi:10.1016/j.jacc.2006.02.062

Kimura, S., Kakuta, T., Yonetsu, T., Suzuki, A., Iesaka, Y., & Fujiwara, H. (2009). Clinical significance of echo signal attenuation on intravascular ultrasound in patients with coronary artery disease. *Circ Cardiovasc Interv, 2*(5), 444–454. doi:10.1161/CIRCINTERVENTIONS.108.821124

Lee, C. H., Tai, B. C., Soon, C. Y., Low, A. F., Poh, K. K., & Yeo, T. C. (2010). New set of intravascular ultrasound-derived anatomic criteria for defining functionally significant stenoses in small coronary arteries (results from Intravascular Ultrasound Diagnostic Evaluation of Atherosclerosis in Singapore [IDEAS] study). *The American Journal of Cardiology, 105*(10), 1378–1384. doi:10.1016/j.amjcard.2010.01.002

Maehara, A., Mintz, G. S., Bui, A. B., Walter, O. R., Castagna, M. T., & Canos, D. (2002). Morphologic and angiographic features of coronary plaque rupture detected by intravascular ultrasound. *Journal of the American College of Cardiology, 40*(5), 904–910. doi:10.1016/S0735-1097(02)02047-8

Maluenda, G., Pichard, A. D., & Waksman, R. (2010). Is there still a role for intravascular ultrasound in the current practice era? *EuroIntervention, 6 Suppl G,* G139-144.

Mehta, S. K., McCrary, J. R., Frutkin, A. D., Dolla, W. J., & Marso, S. P. (2007). Intravascular ultrasound radiofrequency analysis of coronary atherosclerosis: An emerging technology for the assessment of vulnerable plaque. *European Heart Journal, 28*(11), 1283–1288. doi:10.1093/eurheartj/ehm112

Mintz, G. S., Kent, K. M., Pichard, A. D., Satler, L. F., Popma, J. J., & Leon, M. B. (1997). Contribution of inadequate arterial remodeling to the development of focal coronary artery stenoses. An intravascular ultrasound study. *Circulation, 95*(7), 1791–1798.

Mintz, G. S., Nissen, S. E., Anderson, W. D., Bailey, S. R., Erbel, R., & Fitzgerald, P. J. (2001). American College of Cardiology clinical expert consensus document on standards for acquisition, measurement and reporting of intravascular ultrasound studies (IVUS). A report of the American College of Cardiology Task Force on Clinical Expert Consensus Documents. *Journal of the American College of Cardiology, 37*(5), 1478–1492. doi:10.1016/S0735-1097(01)01175-5

Mintz, G. S., & Weissman, N. J. (2006). Intravascular ultrasound in the drug-eluting stent era. *Journal of the American College of Cardiology, 48*(3), 421–429. doi:10.1016/j.jacc.2006.04.068

Nair, A., Kuban, B. D., Tuzcu, E. M., Schoenhagen, P., Nissen, S. E., & Vince, D. G. (2002). Coronary plaque classification with intravascular ultrasound radiofrequency data analysis. *Circulation, 106*(17), 2200–2206. doi:10.1161/01. CIR.0000035654.18341.5E

Nishioka, T., Amanullah, A. M., Luo, H., Berglund, H., Kim, C. J., & Nagai, T. (1999). Clinical validation of intravascular ultrasound imaging for assessment of coronary stenosis severity: Comparison with stress myocardial perfusion imaging. *Journal of the American College of Cardiology, 33*(7), 1870–1878. doi:10.1016/S0735-1097(99)00100-X

Nissen, S. E. (2002). Application of intravascular ultrasound to characterize coronary artery disease and assess the progression or regression of atherosclerosis. *The American Journal of Cardiology, 89*(4A), 24B–31B. doi:10.1016/S0002-9149(02)02217-8

Nissen, S. E., Gurley, J. C., Grines, C. L., Booth, D. C., McClure, R., & Berk, M. (1991). Intravascular ultrasound assessment of lumen size and wall morphology in normal subjects and patients with coronary artery disease. *Circulation, 84*(3), 1087–1099.

Nissen, S. E., Nicholls, S. J., Sipahi, I., Libby, P., Raichlen, J. S., & Ballantyne, C. M. (2006). Effect of very high-intensity statin therapy on regression of coronary atherosclerosis: The ASTEROID trial. *Journal of the American Medical Association, 295*(13), 1556–1565. doi:10.1001/jama.295.13.jpc60002

Nissen, S. E., Nicholls, S. J., Wolski, K., Nesto, R., Kupfer, S., & Perez, A. (2008). Comparison of pioglitazone vs glimepiride on progression of coronary atherosclerosis in patients with type 2 diabetes: The PERISCOPE randomized controlled trial. *Journal of the American Medical Association, 299*(13), 1561–1573. doi:10.1001/jama.299.13.1561

Nissen, S. E., Tuzcu, E. M., Schoenhagen, P., Brown, B. G., Ganz, P., & Vogel, R. A. (2004). Effect of intensive compared with moderate lipid-lowering therapy on progression of coronary atherosclerosis: A randomized controlled trial. *Journal of the American Medical Association, 291*(9), 1071–1080. doi:10.1001/jama.291.9.1071

Okura, H., Kobayashi, Y., Sumitsuji, S., Terashima, M., Kataoka, T., & Masutani, M. (2009). Effect of culprit-lesion remodeling versus plaque rupture on three-year outcome in patients with acute coronary syndrome. *The American Journal of Cardiology, 103*(6), 791–795. doi:10.1016/j.amjcard.2008.11.030

Okura, H., Morino, Y., Oshima, A., Hayase, M., Ward, M. R., & Popma, J. J. (2001). Preintervention arterial remodeling affects clinical outcome following stenting: an intravascular ultrasound study. *Journal of the American College of Cardiology, 37*(4), 1031–1035. doi:10.1016/S0735-1097(01)01145-7

Palmer, N. D., Northridge, D., Lessells, A., McDicken, W. N., & Fox, K. A. (1999). In vitro analysis of coronary atheromatous lesions by intravascular ultrasound; reproducibility and histological correlation of lesion morphology. *European Heart Journal, 20*(23), 1701–1706. doi:10.1053/euhj.1999.1627

Park, S. J., Kim, Y. H., Park, D. W., Lee, S. W., Kim, W. J., & Suh, J. (2009). Impact of intravascular ultrasound guidance on long-term mortality in stenting for unprotected left main coronary artery stenosis. *Circ Cardiovasc Interv, 2*(3), 167–177. doi:10.1161/CIRCINTERVENTIONS.108.799494

Post, M. J., de Smet, B. J., van der Helm, Y., Borst, C., & Kuntz, R. E. (1997). Arterial remodeling after balloon angioplasty or stenting in an atherosclerotic experimental model. *Circulation, 96*(3), 996–1003.

Potkin, B. N., Bartorelli, A. L., Gessert, J. M., Neville, R. F., Almagor, Y., & Roberts, W. C. (1990). Coronary artery imaging with intravascular high-frequency ultrasound. *Circulation, 81*(5), 1575–1585. doi:10.1161/01.CIR.81.5.1575

Rickenbacher, P. R., Pinto, F. J., Chenzbraun, A., Botas, J., Lewis, N. P., & Alderman, E. L. (1995). Incidence and severity of transplant coronary artery disease early and up to 15 years after transplantation as detected by intravascular ultrasound. *Journal of the American College of Cardiology, 25*(1), 171–177. doi:10.1016/0735-1097(94)00323-I

Roy, P., Steinberg, D. H., Sushinsky, S. J., Okabe, T., Pinto Slottow, T. L., & Kaneshige, K. (2008). The potential clinical utility of intravascular ultrasound guidance in patients undergoing percutaneous coronary intervention with drug-eluting stents. *European Heart Journal, 29*(15), 1851–1857. doi:10.1093/eurheartj/ehn249

Sabate, M., Serruys, P. W., van der Giessen, W. J., Ligthart, J. M., Coen, V. L., & Kay, I. P. (1999). Geometric vascular remodeling after balloon angioplasty and beta-radiation therapy: A three-dimensional intravascular ultrasound study. *Circulation, 100*(11), 1182–1188.

Schoenhagen, P., DeFranco, A., Nissen, S. E., & Tuzcu, E. M. (2006). *IVUS made easy*. Informa Healthcare.

Schoenhagen, P., Sapp, S. K., Tuzcu, E. M., Magyar, W. A., Popovich, J., & Boumitri, M. (2003). Variability of area measurements obtained with different intravascular ultrasound catheter systems: Impact on clinical trials and a method for accurate calibration. *Journal of the American Society of Echocardiography, 16*(3), 277–284. doi:10.1067/mje.2003.45

Stone, G. W., Maehara, A., Lansky, A. J., de Bruyne, B., Cristea, E., & Mintz, G. S. (2011). A prospective natural-history study of coronary atherosclerosis. *The New England Journal of Medicine, 364*(3), 226–235. doi:10.1056/NEJMoa1002358

Takagi, A., Tsurumi, Y., Ishii, Y., Suzuki, K., Kawana, M., & Kasanuki, H. (1999). Clinical potential of intravascular ultrasound for physiological assessment of coronary stenosis: Relationship between quantitative ultrasound tomography and pressure-derived fractional flow reserve. *Circulation, 100*(3), 250–255.

Tuzcu, E. M., Berkalp, B., De Franco, A. C., Ellis, S. G., Goormastic, M., & Whitlow, P. L. (1996). The dilemma of diagnosing coronary calcification: Angiography versus intravascular ultrasound. *Journal of the American College of Cardiology, 27*(4), 832–838. doi:10.1016/0735-1097(95)00537-4

Wang, X., Lu, C., Chen, X., Zhao, X., & Xia, D. (2008). A new method to quantify coronary calcification by intravascular ultrasound - The different patterns of calcification of acute myocardial infarction, unstable angina pectoris and stable angina pectoris. *The Journal of Invasive Cardiology, 20*(11), 587–590.

Weissman, N. J., Koglin, J., Cox, D. A., Hermiller, J., O'Shaughnessy, C., & Mann, J. T. (2005). Polymer-based paclitaxel-eluting stents reduce in-stent neointimal tissue proliferation: A serial volumetric intravascular ultrasound analysis from the TAXUS-IV trial. *Journal of the American College of Cardiology, 45*(8), 1201–1205. doi:10.1016/j.jacc.2004.10.078

Wu, X., Maehara, A., Mintz, G. S., Kubo, T., Xu, K., & Choi, S. Y. (2010). Virtual histology intravascular ultrasound analysis of non-culprit attenuated plaques detected by grayscale intravascular ultrasound in patients with acute coronary syndromes. *The American Journal of Cardiology, 105*(1), 48–53. doi:10.1016/j.amjcard.2009.08.649

Yamagishi, M., Terashima, M., Awano, K., Kijima, M., Nakatani, S., & Daikoku, S. (2000). Morphology of vulnerable coronary plaque: insights from follow-up of patients examined by intravascular ultrasound before an acute coronary syndrome. *Journal of the American College of Cardiology, 35*(1), 106–111. doi:10.1016/S0735-1097(99)00533-1

KEY TERMS AND DEFINITIONS

Balloon Angioplasty: a revascularization procedure that uses a catheter with a deflated balloon at its tip that is inserted into the narrowed part of the coronary artery. Then, the balloon is inflated, causing luminal dilation.

Elastography: an IVUS based technique that measures the local strain of the plaque tissue which is related to the mechanical properties of plaque components (e.g. the lipid plaque is strained more easily compared to the fibrous or calcified plaque) and has been used to identify high risk plaques.

Intravascular Ultrasound: an invasive imaging modality that provides intra-luminal visualization of the coronary artery using a specially designed catheter which contains a miniaturized ultrasound probe attached to its distal end. The probe is able to submit signals perpendicular to its axis and receive the scatter signal. Processing of the scatter signal generates cross-sectional images of the arterial segment which portray in detail the lumen, outer vessel wall and plaque.

Restenosis: literally means the re-occurrence of stenosis, a narrowing of a blood vessel, leading to restricted blood flow. In coronary artery disease, restenosis usually pertains to a coronary artery that has become narrowed after having received treatment to clear the blockage (with angioplasty or stenting).

Rotablator: an atherectomy technique in which a rotating bur is inserted over a guide wire through a catheter into an artery and then the burr rotates and debulks the atherosclerotic plaque.

Stent (Bare Netal and Drug Eluting): A metal mesh attached onto a deflated balloon. This is inserted and implanted into a diseased coronary artery to improve myocardial perfusion and keep the vessel open. In case of drug eluting stents, the stent struts are covered with a drug that is slowly released to block cellular proliferation.

Vulnerable Plaque: a type of atheromatous plaque that is unstable, prone to rupture and cause major adverse cardiac events including myocardial infarction or sudden death.

Chapter 3
IVUS Image Processing Methodologies

Antonis A. Sakellarios
University of Ioannina, Greece

Christos V. Bourantas
Castle Hill Hospital, UK

Lambros S. Athanasiou
University of Ioannina, Greece

Dimitrios I. Fotiadis
University of Ioannina, Greece

Lampros K. Michalis
University of Ioannina, Greece

ABSTRACT

Intravascular Ultrasound (IVUS) is an invasive imaging technique that allows detailed visualization of the arterial lumen and outer vessel wall and permits characterization of the type of the plaque and quantification of its burden. Traditionally IVUS processing was performed manually. However, it became apparent that manual segmentation is time consuming, and the obtained results depend on the experience of the operators. To overcome these limitations and enhance the role of IVUS in clinical practice and research, several (semi-) automated methods have been developed that expedite detection of the regions of interest and/or characterization of the type of the plaque. In this chapter we review the available IVUS processing techniques and present the developed commercial solutions for IVUS segmentation and plaque characterization.

DOI: 10.4018/978-1-61350-095-8.ch003

INTRODUCTION

Accurate evaluation of coronary artery pathology and reliable assessment of plaque burden requires visualization of the vessel wall with increased distinctness. Several invasive [intravascular ultrasound (IVUS), optical coherence tomography (OCT), angioscopy] and non-invasive imaging modalities [computed tomographic coronary angiography (CTCA) and magnetic resonance imaging (MRI)] are nowadays available that allows assessment of luminal pathology, quantification of plaque burden and characterization of the type of the plaque. Although invasive, IVUS remains the method of choice for the evaluation of the atherosclerotic process as it provides in real time two dimensional (2-D) cross-sectional images which portray in detail the lumen, outer vessel wall and the stent morphology and give information regarding the composition and the extent of the atheroma. The fact that IVUS is reliable and quick to use has allowed its extensive utilization over the last two decades in assessing vessel wall pathology and understanding the atherosclerotic process.

At the beginning of IVUS imaging, the segmentation of the obtained sequence was performed manually. However, it became apparent that this procedure is laborious, time consuming and the accuracy of the obtained results depends on the operators' expertise. To address these limitations, several methodologies have been developed which allow (semi)-automated segmentation of the IVUS sequence and computation of plaque volume and its composition. Some of these have been incorporated in commercially available systems that operate in a user-friendly environment and provide border detection and plaque characterization in almost real time. These features have rendered them useful in clinical practice and allowed their extensive use in the catheterization laboratory.

The present chapter discusses the available methodologies, developed for automated IVUS processing, and is organized as follows: in the background section we present the artefacts seen in IVUS highlighting the difficulties noted in IVUS processing. In the main focus section we analyze the developed IVUS border detection methodologies and the methods that allow characterization of the type of the plaque in grayscale IVUS images. In addition, we present the existing approaches for the automated identification of the end-diastolic IVUS frames and conclude with an overview of the available commercial systems which are currently available for IVUS processing.

BACKGROUND

Apart from the regions of interest (lumen, media-adventitia and stent border) and the plaque [which depending on its echogenisity can be classified as echolucent/soft (lipid rich) plaque, intermediate (fibrous) plaque, echo dense (calcific) plaque and mixed if it includes more than one acoustic subtypes] (Mintz *et al.* 2001) various artefacts are often seen in IVUS images which should be taken into consideration during the segmentation process (Figure 1). Some of these depend on the type of the catheter (mechanical or solid state) used, while others can be detected in all IVUS sequences. For example, the non-uniform rotational artefacts can be seen only in mechanical IVUS imaging and are due to asymmetric friction which leads the transducer to lag during one part of the rotation and whip through the other part of its 360° rotation resulting in geometrical distortion of the image. On the other hand the ring down artefact, the shadowing artefact, the reverberations and the blood speckles are seen in both mechanical and solid state IVUS imaging. The ring down artefact is due to signal disorganization and appears as a bright halo of variable thickness around the catheter while the shadowing artefact occurs when a structure with a marked difference in acoustic impedance (e.g. calcific plaque) blocks the transmission of the ultrasound beyond that point resulting in a shadow behind the echoreflective structure, which

Figure 1. Structures and artefacts seen in IVUS images

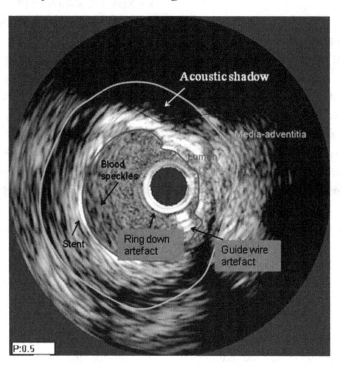

follows the ultrasound signal. The reverberations are artefacts caused by secondary false echoes of the same structure and are more common in strong echoreflectors such as calcium, stent or the guidewire. Finally, the blood speckles are spots that are moving with a characteristic pattern and are due to the reflection of the signal by the red blood cells (Nissen *et al.* 1998). From the above it is obvious that there is a variety of artefacts which renders the automated segmentation of the IVUS images a challenging process.

MAIN FOCUS

Primitive IVUS Processing Methodologies

The first IVUS processing methodology was developed by Rosenfiled *et al.* (1991) who stacked the acquired IVUS frames to form a cylinder – shaped object. This simplistic approach is still useful in research and clinical practice as it allows visualization of the vessel's morphology and quantification of the plaque burden with the implementation of Simpson's rule. Two years later Dhawale *et al.* (1993) presented the first semi-automated method for IVUS border detection. Their approach required an expert observer to approximate the regions of interest in each frame and then these estimations were used to guide a 1-D dynamic search algorithm. In contrast to the method developed by Rosenfiled *et al.* (1991) the methodology proposed by Dhawale *et al.* (1993) didn't appear useful since it was time consuming as it required manual guidance in each IVUS frame. However, the latter method was the first which demonstrated that the segmentation of the IVUS frames is feasible and opened new horizons in IVUS processing.

Since then a number of methodologies have been developed aiming to overcome previous limitations and provide fast and reliable IVUS border detection. Based on the implemented algorithms these approaches can be classified in four main categories: active contours, level sets, fast marching methods and others.

Automated Segmentation of IVUS Images

Active Contours

The active contour (snake or deformable model) method is the prevalent technique in IVUS segmentation. The snake is a parametrical curve which is described by an energy function (Kass *et al.* 1987):

$$E_{snake} = \int_0^1 (E_{int}(\nu(s)) + E_{image}(\nu(s)) + E_{con}(\nu(s)))ds$$

(1)

where, E_{con} is the energy due to external restrictions, E_{int} is the internal energy of the snake and E_{image} is the image energy. In an IVUS image these models have the ability to be attracted by the regions of interest as these minimize their energy function. This desirable feature renders them useful in IVUS processing. Hence, over the last two decades several methodologies have incorporated active contour models for border detection (Lobregt and Viergever 1995; Shekhar *et al.* 1999; Kovalski, *et al.* 2000; Klingensmith, *et al.* 2000; Luo *et al.* 2003; Brusseau, *et al.* 2004; Parissi, *et al.* 2006; Giannoglou, *et al.* 2007; Sun *et al.* 2009). The first who implemented these models were Lobregt and Viergever (1995) while few years later Shekhar *et al.* (1999) modeled the IVUS sequence into a 3-D cylinder – like object and then used for the first time a 3-D deformable model. Soon after, Kovalski *et al.* (2000) proposed a modification in the energy function of the 3-D model (adding a variable which tended to inflate the snake) introducing the balloon snakes.

Sonka *et al.* (1995) presented unique segmentation approach for the detection of media-adventitia and luminal border. Global image information and heuristic graph searching were implemented for IVUS segmentation. Using graph searching, an optimal 2-D path representing the border was identified over each IVUS frame and then cost functions were applied to re-format the initial path and match to the luminal/media-adventitia border. Thirty eight IVUS images were used for the validation of the method. The obtained results demonstrated that the detected by this approach borders correlated well with those detected by the experts (r = 0.96, y=1.02x+0.52mm² for the luminal area and r=0.95, y=1.07x−0.48mm² for the plaque area). A considerable limitation of this approach is that the authors assumed that the distance between media-adventitia and luminal border is at least 0.3mm which is not correct for the IVUS images portraying healthy segments.

Another interesting approach was proposed by Plissiti *et al.* (2004) who utilized a Hopfield neural network to expedite the minimization of the deformable model's energy function. They also incorporated techniques to overcome common artefacts observed in IVUS images (e.g. the blood speckle artefact and the guide wire artefact) and to address ordinary problems in IVUS segmentation such as the increased noise and the extraction of the media-adventitia border in images where calcified lesions are present.

Sanz-Requena *et al.* (2007) took into consideration different sets of parameters (e.g. rigidity, elasticity and viscosity) in the determination of snake's internal energy and implemented a knowledge-based technique to assign different levels of gray to the three regions of interest (media-adventitia plaque and lumen). The external force for the snakes was calculated by the gradient vector flow (GVF), which is a vector field that minimizes an energy function. The proposed method was validated using estimations of expert observers as gold standard. An average error was noted (<1mm²) for the luminal and media-adventitia areas (inter-observer variability above 10%), while the volume error for the plaque and lumen was >0.5mm^3 (inter-observer variability varied from 10-20%).

Giannoglou *et al.* (2007), proposed the first fully automated segmentation methodology. In this approach the initialization of the active contour was performed via an analysis mechanism that took into consideration the inherent morphologic characteristics of the IVUS images. This methodology was validated in 50 randomly selected images obtained from IVUS examinations performed in 9 patients. The obtained results showed a good agreement between the proposed method and the experts (mean differences: 0.70±2.68mm^2, 0.17±4.58mm^2, −0.53±3.50mm^2 for the luminal, media-adventitia and plaque cross-sectional areas, respectively). This approach was optimized a year

later by the same research team (Papadogiorgaki *et al.* 2008) with the implementation of a texture based technique.

Finally, Unal *et al.* (2008) used a dataset to train the active contour model and suggested a statistical shape-driven approach to detect the regions of interest. The validation of this approach showed a good agreement between the detected by the proposed method borders and the estimations of experts as the observed difference error was 0.65±1.27mm^2 for the luminal and 0.98±1.78mm^2 for the media-adventitia area.

Table 1 summarizes the most important methodologies that incorporate active contours for IVUS border detection. Though some of them appear to be stable and provide accurate results

Table 1. Summary of the most important snake based segmentation methodologies

Method	Approach	Advantages	Disadvantages	Validation
Sonka *et al.* (1995)	Knowledge based approach	Accurate border detection Fast	Is based on *a priori* knowledge which in some cases is not available	*Linear regression analysis for the luminal area:* $y=1.02x+0.52mm2$, $r=0.96$, *and for the plaque area:* $y=1.07x−0.48mm2$, $r=0.95$
Plissiti *et al.* (2004)	A Hopfield neural network is utilized to expedite border detection	Able to overcome common artefacts seen in IVUS images Fast	Requires the pull-back of the IVUS catheter to be performed by an automated pull-back device	*Linear regression analysis for the luminal area:* $y=0.97x+6.13mm2$, $r=0.99$ *and the plaque area:* $y=1.01x-5.47mm2$, $r=0.99$
Sanz-Requena *et al.* (2007)	Implementation of the GVF as an external force for the snakes	GVF can be used for more accurate results	Semi-automated Increased average error in the detection of media-adventitia border in low quality images Slow	Mean difference <1mm^2 for the luminal and media-adventitia area
Papadiorgakaki *et al.* (2008)	Implementation of a texture based technique	Fully automated Fast	Unreliable in heavily calcified segments. Threshold adjustments are necessary in different IVUS sequences	Mean difference 0.13± 1.21 mm^2 for the luminal and 0.06±1.59mm^2 for the media-adventitia area
Unal *et al.* (2008)	A statistical shape-driven approach	Reliable	Very slow	Mean difference: 0.65±1.27mm^2 for the luminal and 0.98±1.78mm^2 for the media-adventitia area

they require increased computational effort and time. However, these limitations are likely to be addressed by the rapid improvement of computer technology.

Level Sets

Though level sets have been widely used in medical imaging and particularly in the segmentation of MRI only recently they have been implemented in IVUS processing. The level sets are based on the principles that the shape of an object is embedded as a zero level set of a higher dimensional surface. During the evolution of the surface the zero level set contour deforms in order to find the desired boundaries. The morphological changes of the contour depend on the image features and it is governed by the principle to produce smooth boundaries. Considering two contours: the luminal (c_1) and the media-adventitia (c_2), then:

$$s(x) = \begin{cases} 0, & if \ x \in C \\ -d(x), & if \ x \ is \ outside \ c_1(0) \ but \ inside \ c_2(0) \\ d(x), & otherwise \end{cases} \quad (2)$$

where $d(x)$ is the shortest distance to C from point x. Then the following surface function is defined:

$$\varphi(x, t = 0) = G(a|s(x)|) * s(x) \quad (3)$$

The first approach which used level sets was presented by Iskurt *et al.* (2006) and incorporated a technique called min/max flow for faster border detection. The validation of this methodology demonstrated an inter-observer variability of 5.5% and 7% for the media-adventitia and luminal borders, respectively.

Najafi *et al.* (2007) proposed the combination of non-parametric deformable models and the level set method for IVUS segmentation. The results from the validation of this method showed a poor sensitivity and specificity for the detection of the media-adventitia and luminal (72% and 78%, respectively) borders. In order to improve the performance of this approach Wang *et al.* (2009) combined the level set method with B-spline models. Although this method appears promising, it lacks detailed validation which is necessary before its broad implementation.

The methodologies based on the level set models are fast and they do not require increased computational effort. However, significant disadvantages of the level set methods are the weak noise resistance and the large errors in edge detection as they involve multidimensional curved surfaces evolvement. These limitations render them less useful in IVUS segmentation than the active contour models which do not require parameterization, provide good numerical stability and topological flexibility and can be straightforward extended from the 2-D formulation to n-D. However, the fact that the level set models have been recently introduced in IVUS processing leaves plenty of space for improvement.

Fast Marching Methods

The fast marching method is a subclass of the level-set technique. In particular, in this case the surface function must satisfy the equation:

$$|\nabla T| F = 1 \quad (4)$$

stating that the arrival time difference between two adjacent voxels increases as the velocity of the contour F decreases as a function of time T. A time function map is constructed to evolve the interface. Godbout *et al.* (2005) was the first who used these models in IVUS processing while a year later Cardinal *et al.* (2006) presented a 3-D IVUS segmentation model that combined a fast marching method and gray level probability density functions (PDFs) of the vessel structures. This reliability of this approach was tested in both simulated and *in vivo* IVUS images. The mean distance, between the estimations of the method and the manually detected borders was <0.16mm, while the measured Hausdorff distance – which is the longest distance between two estimations – ranged from 0.31-0.40mm suggesting that the proposed methodology provides reliable results. Significant limitation of these techniques is the increased manual interaction required to segment the images obtained in complex lesions.

Finally, in a recently published work Wennogle *et al.* (2009) combined the fast marching methodologies proposed by Cardinal *et al.* (2006) with the level sets technique and obtained more reliable segmentation since after the implementation of level sets algorithm the non-overlapping volume error decreased from 7.6% to 5.9% for the luminal and from 5.5% to 4.5% for the media-adventitia borders.

Fast marching methods can handle the topological changes in IVUS images and furthermore by implementing an exhaustive analysis decrease the variability in IVUS segmentation. On the other hand, the first applications of this approach which are based basically on pixel intensity and other texture-based morphological features do not take into account statistical information underlying the IVUS data (Cardinal *et al.* 2006).

Other Approaches

Apart from the abovementioned methodologies several other segmentation techniques have been proposed such as radial gradient searching (Meier *et al.* 1997), region growing (Bouma *et al.* 1997), texture-based (Mojsilovic *et al.* 1997) as well as knowledge-based methods (Takagi *et al.* 2000). Most of these alternatives had significant limitations which restricted their clinical applicability. For example the methodology developed by Bouma *et al.* (1997) was able to identify only the luminal borders and not the media-adventitia, while the approaches developed by Mojsilovic *et al.* (1997) and Takagi *et al.* (2000) failed to detect the media-adventitia border in calcified lesions.

Haas *et al.* (2000) suggested an automated segmentation technique which implemented an optimized maximum *a posteriori* estimator for border detection. The concept of the method was based on the assumption that the pixels of the images follow a Rayleigh distribution. The initialization of the segmentation utilised also the information provided by the blood flow. The proposed approach has been validated using the estimations of two expert observers as gold standard. The obtained results demonstrated that the method overestimates the luminal and media-adventitia contour by 0.01±5.99% and 0.51±4.73%, respectively.

Hammers *et al.* (2001) introduced a clinically useful approach for analysis of the IVUS images. In particular 3-D reconstruction of the IVUS sequence was performed and then longitudinal cross-sections were obtained in which a semi-automated border detection algorithm was applied. A digital Deriche filter was implemented for edge detection, which provided the advantage of fast border segmentation. Then, edge-thinning and edge-linking methods were utilized in order to detect in longitudinal view the luminal, media-adventitia and stent border. These borders were then mapped in each IVUS frame and used to define Bezier curves which corresponded to the final regions of interest. It appeared that 8-9 longitudinal cross-sections are adequate for reliable and expedite segmentation. This method-system was validated in 24 IVUS sequences using the estimations of two experts as gold standard. The obtained results showed a mean error of -3.8±12.34%, 9.11±7.12% and -3.95±4.06% for the luminal, stent and media-adventitia volume, respectively.

Koning *et al.* (2002) presented a fast system for segmentation and visualization of IVUS studies. Longitudinal cutplanes are processed first and the detected borders on them are used as estimations for the detection on the transversal frames. The method incorporates knowledge about the 2-D and 3-D anatomy of the coronary vessels and about ultrasound image physics. The borders are detected automatically using the model-guided Minimum Cost Approach (MCA). In particular, cost-functions are used, which utilize the knowledge derived from images. Gradient filters and local intensities of images are implemented for the detection of luminal border. The method was validated using the experts' estimations as gold standard. The radius difference for the lumen and media-adventitia area was -0.03±0.07mm and 0.06±0.04mm, respectively.

An interesting approach was presented by Weichert *et al.* (2003) who displayed the IVUS images in polar coordinates and used a Canny-Edge filter to detect the media-adventitia borders. A Gaussian operator was then implemented to smooth the images and then, the regions of the image that contained high spatial derivatives were highlighted with the use of a 2-D first derivative operator. Afterwards a non-maximal suppression algorithm was applied to locate the maximums of the derivatives and to set the rest of the pixels to zero. Artefacts (calcifications or catheter shadows) were addressed with the use of a parameterized elliptical curve which resembled the shape of a non-deformed by the atherosclerotic process artery. *In vitro* and *in vivo* validation was performed and the observed results show good agreement between the automated and the manually detected borders.

From the above it is obvious that there is a variety of segmentation approaches with most of them being based on the basic principles of deformable models which appear to provide good numerical stability and topological flexibility. However, none of the available methodologies can be regarded as the gold standard is IVUS processing. This is due to the increased noise and artefacts seen in IVUS which often distract the developed algorithms leading to false estimations. In addition most of the described methodologies operate in a semi-automated manner requiring an initial approximation of the regions of interest, while others appear time consuming or are unable to detect all the regions of interest focusing e.g. only in the luminal borders.

Plaque Characterization

It is well known that prognosis depends not only on the degree of the stenosis and plaque burden but also on its composition (Virmani *et al.* 2006). Thus, the characterization of the type of the plaque and the identification of the plaque features which are associated with increased vulnerability is useful for assessing the atherosclerotic evolution and estimate prognosis. Autopsy studies showed that a vulnerable plaque consists of a lipid rich core and has a thin fibrous cap which may be disrupted. These plaques are mainly found in segments with positive remodelling, are infiltrated by macrophages and often have intraplaque hemorrhage (Naghavi *et al.* 2003). Radiofrequency backscatter analysis of the IVUS signal has been recently introduced for plaque characterization and is regarded as the gold standard (Mehta *et al.* 2007). However, this technology is not always available and thus often the cardiologist acquires this information by analyzing the grayscale IVUS. In order to overcome the limitations of manual processing (increased processing time and inter- and intra-observer variability) several methodologies have been developed for automated characterization of the type of the plaque.

The first approach was presented by Zhang *et al.* (1998). In this pioneer study several imaging features were tested including gray-level-based texture descriptors, co-occurrence matrices, run-length measures and fractal based measures with the best results being obtained with the radial profile, the long run emphasis and fractal based features. Subsequently, a classifier with linear discrimination functions was used to characterize the soft (lipid rich) and hard plaques (fibrotic and calcified). Then, the hard plaques were further divided to hard (fibrotic) and calcified hard plaques based on plaque's gray level intensity. The classifier was trained and tested in IVUS images obtained *in vivo*. The obtained results confirming the reliability of the proposed approach showing 89.2% and 90.2% accuracy for the hard and soft plaque respectively. The major limitation of this methodology was the fact that it requires an expert observer to manually delineate the regions of interest in each frame.

In another study, Vince *et al.* (2000) utilized the law's texture energy, the Haralick's, the neighborhood gray-tone different matrix (NGTDM), the first order statistics and the texture spectrum technique to identify the type of the plaque. More specifically, a pattern recognition approach was used where these methods were part of the training set. The most accurate results were obtained using the Haralick's method, with a resubstitution and cross-validation error 0.00 and 14.76%, respectively. Discriminant analysis was also performed in order to optimize the method. However, the limited number of IVUS frames restricted the use of only three texture features at most for the discrimination process, in order to claim statistical significance.

Pujol *et al.* (2004) proposed another approach to evaluate the composition of the plaque. In this study two different kinds of texture descriptors were implemented to optimally describe the plaque appearance. The former consisted of co-occurrence matrices and statistical descriptors and the latter of local binary patterns and cumulative moments. Then, an advanced classification scheme based on multiple classifiers named Adaptive boosting (AdaBoost) was applied to classify the type of the plaque (i.e. soft, mixed, calcium and fibrous). The results of the AdaBoost were compared to those derived by the Fisher linear discrimination which was assumed to be the gold standard. The AdaBoost provided reliable identification of the fibrous and calcified plaques with an average recognition rate of 88% and 95%, respectively but had a relatively limited capability (only 70%) in detecting the mixed plaques.

Stop & Go Snakes were implemented for first time by Brunenberg *et al.* (2006) for automatic tissue characterization. Features such as local binary patterns and Gabor filters were extracted and AdaBoost was used for the classification scheme. These results were then processed using a snake algorithm. To validate their approach Brunenberg *et al.* (2006) compared the estimations of their method with the annotations of experts. A good agreement was found for the calcified plaques (mean error: 1.86±1.49pixels), but on the other hand the performance of their approach was weak in the soft plaques (mean error: 5.71±5.40pixels).

Caballero *et al.* (2007) presented a classification scheme which used texture analysis and the AdaBoost. As before, Gabor filters, co-occurrence matrices and local binary patterns were extracted as features. Plaque classification was performed using decision stumps and AdaBoost. The method was validated using the annotations of two experts as gold standard. The classification accuracy rate was: 80.06% for the fibrotic, 94.72% for the soft and 99.38% for the calcified plaques (Figure 2). However, the obtained results may overestimate

Figure 2. Segmented image by (a) the physician and by (b) the classification algorithm. (Caballero, 2007 © 2008 IEEE)

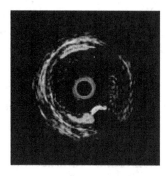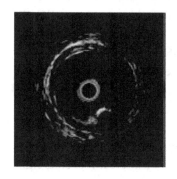

the performance of their approach as the validation was performed on normalized data and not on images obtained *in vivo*. Thus, further validation in clinical setting is necessary.

Moreover Filho *et al.* (2008) implemented adaptive thresholding and the Otsu's method to identify calcified plaques while Katouzian *et al.* (2008) compared and examined the usefulness of various image characteristics such as the integrated backscatter coefficient, the slope, the midband-fit (MBF), the intercept and the maximum and minimum powers in detecting the type of the plaque. As the ROC curves show in Figure 3 both a full spectrum classifier and a 7-parameter classifier provided more accurate results for the calcium and lipid than for the fibrotic and fibrolipidic plaque (Figure 3).

Zhang *et al.* (2010) implemented active contours and contourlet transform to detect calcifications in grayscale IVUS images. Initially, they used a technique which was based on the anisotropic diffusion to suppress the speckles and enhance the calcification edges and then they implemented contourlet transform to decompose the image in low and high pass bands. In a next step they incorporated adaptive thresholding on the low pass bands using the 2-D Reny's entropy to detect the regions of interest. Calcifications in 86 images were annotated manually by experienced physicians to serve as the ground truth. The obtained results demonstrated that the proposed method provides reliable identification of the calcific plaques with an observed sensitivity and specificity 87.16% and 87.35%, respectively. However, this approach is limited only in the detection of the calcified plaques.

Considerable limitations of the abovementioned methodologies are the fact that they operate in semi-automated fashion as they require at least minimum user interaction for the definition of the region of interest. In addition, some of them cannot provide complete plaque characterization while all of them were validated using the estimations of expert observers as gold standard; though it has been demonstrated that these differ from histology.

To overcome these drawbacks a novel methodology has been developed for fully automated characterization of the type of the plaque. The overall approach is considered hybrid as it utilizes both image processing techniques and machine

Figure 3. ROC curves comparing the linear separability of full spectral features (left) with that of a reduced set of seven features (right); 1451, 475, 10668, and 382 volumes of 128 samples of fibrolipid, lipid, fibrotic, and calcified tissue signals were used, respectively. (Katouzian et al., 2008 © 2008 IEEE)

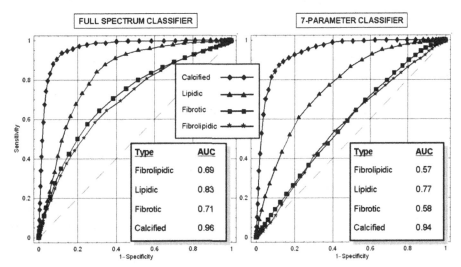

Figure 4. The application of the proposed method in two IVUS frames, (a,d) original IVUS images. (b-e) plaque characterization using virtual histology, and (c-f) our approach.

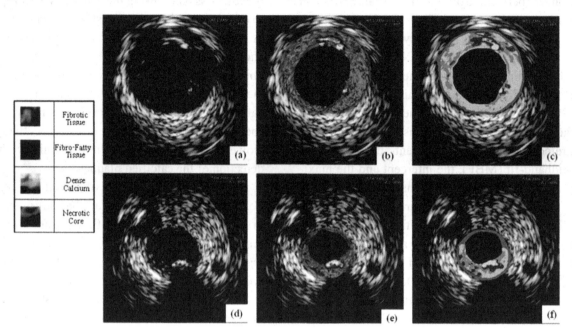

learning algorithms and was validated using integrated backscatter analysis as gold standard. Initially the plaque area was defined in each IVUS frame using the methodology developed by Plissiti *et al.* (2004). Then, the efficacy of several classification schemes (including co-occurrence matrix, local binary patterns, entropy and mean value) was tested and three classifiers (the 2–class Support Vector Machine, the Neural Network and the Random Forests) were used to characterize the type of the plaque. Among these classifiers the Random Forests appeared to be the most reliable with an overall accuracy of 83.95%. Our approach detected initially, two types of plaque the soft and the hard (fibrotic and calcified) and then the calcified plaque was differentiated from the fibrotic based on the presence or absence of acoustic shadow behind it. Finally, a color coded map was applied to annotate comprehensively the type of the plaque in the IVUS images with the green corresponding to the fibrotic, the red to the soft (lipid rich plaque) and the white to the calcific

plaque. The proposed approach was validated *in vivo* in 40 IVUS images using integrated backscatter analysis as gold standard. The accuracy of our algorithm was 87.81% for the calcified plaque, 88.32% for the fibrotic plaque and 84.05% for the soft plaque (Figure 4).

Automated Detection of End-Diastolic Frames in an IVUS Sequence

The 3-D reconstruction of the IVUS sequence proposed by Rosenfiled *et al.* (1991) does not take into account the changes noted in the luminal and outer vessel wall dimensions during the cardiac circle, resulting in a "sawtooth" artefact that is more prominent in normal vessels with increased diameter and preserved compliance. This problem was overcome by gating the image acquisition and selecting only the frames that corresponded to the same phase of the cardiac circle (e.g. to the end-diastolic phase) (Zhang *et al.*, 1998).

However, many IVUS systems do not allow simultaneous visualization of the IVUS frames and the electrocardiogram (ECG). To address this problem several investigators proposed methodologies that allows automated detection of the end-diastolic frames. Zhu *et al.* (2003) was the first who examined the feasibility of automated IVUS gating. More specifically two main techniques were studied: the first was based on the average intensity calculation while the second on the absolute intensity difference calculation. It was found that the first approach was better in phantoms where only pulsatile motion was assumed. On the other hand, the second method appeared more reliable *in vivo* but it has the disadvantage that it is time consuming and requires increased computational effort.

Nadkarni *et al.* (2005) presented an alternative approach which allows semi-automated gating of the IVUS images. They used a methodology based on discrete dynamic contours to identify the luminal borders which were changing during the cardiac cycle. The luminal border of the first frame was then used as a template and was compared with each border detected in the remained sequence. More specifically, they computed the average distance between the template border and each subsequent border and indentified the frames with the minimum average distance which were considered that they belonged to the same cardiac phase. This approach was validated using the ECG recordings (depicted on the IVUS sequence) as gold standard. An error <2% was noted in estimating the average cardiac cycle length demonstrating

that the proposed methodology provides accurate gating of the IVUS images. However limitation of the validation methodology was the fact that was performed in IVUS images obtained *in vitro* and not *in vivo* where the increased noise may affect the luminal segmentation.

O'Malley *et al.* (2007) introduced a methodology that imitated the ECG and permitted automated identification of the frame in each cardiac cycle at which the IVUS images were nearly motionless. The algorithm operated on a dissimilarity matrix which was constructed from pairwise comparisons of the frames of an IVUS sequence. Initially, a function was used to estimate the heart rate and then the proposed methodology searched for the frames that corresponded to the same phase of the cardiac circle. To achieve that, a path was traced on the dissimilarity matrix in which each frame was denoted by a point. The frames that corresponded to the points located onto the traced path were considered that they belonged to the same phase of the cardiac circle (Figure 5).

Finally, the methodology proposed by Hernandez *et al.* (2008) focused on the detection of the abrupt changes of the luminal position due to the cardiac motion. They implemented a Butterworth and Gabor filter to assess the cardiac motion profile. They proposed that the maximum and minimum of each filtered signal corresponded to the end-systolic and end-diastolic phase, respectively since maximum and minimum lumen areas correspond to the end- systolic and diastolic phase. In order to obtain smoother results and overcome the influence of various artefacts Hernandez *et*

Figure 5. Flowchart of the complete gating process. From left to right: the initial non-gated IVUS sequence, the dissimilarity matrix D with the traced path, the filtered matrix ^D with step-points indicating the gated frames, and the final gated sequence. (O'Malley, 2007, © 2007 IEEE)

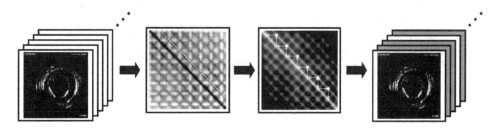

al. 2008 used the average from the two filter signals to estimate the end-diastolic/end-systolic frames.

COMMERCIALLY AVAILABLE SYSTEMS FOR AUTOMATED IVUS SEGMENTATION

Some of the previously described IVUS processing methodologies have been incorporated in user-friendly systems which are useful in clinical practice and research as they allows fast and reliable IVUS processing and quantification of the extent and the severity of coronary artery disease. The method developed by Hammers *et al.* (2001) was the first that integrated into a user-friendly system which allows fast segmentation of an IVUS sequence and direct inspection of the detected border. The system operates in a semi-automated fashion and provides the user with various measurements regarding the regions of interest (e.g. media-adventitia, luminal stent area etc) and plaque burden (e.g. plaque area/volume, in-stent restenosis area/volume etc).

The method proposed by Koning *et al.* (2002) has been also incorporated into a system called Quantitative Coronary Ultrasound – Clinical Measurement Solutions (QCU-CMS). Advantages of the proposed system are the user-friendly environment, the quantitative measurements provided (e.g. lumen and media-adventitia cross-sectional areas, the plaque burden, percentage of plaque burden etc) and the incorporation of a correction module which facilitates manual correction of false estimations.

Bourantas *et al.* (2005) presented a user-friendly system for 3-D coronary reconstruction using IVUS and angiographic data. One of the main components of this system is the integrated automate border detection module of the IVUS images. ANGIOCARE incorporates the methodology developed by Plisiti *et al.* (2004). It operates in a user-friendly environment and allows inspection of the segmentation process by an expert observer who can intervene and make the appropriate corrections if required. During the segmentation process it provides the user with a number of quantitative measurements including the minimum and mean luminal and media-adventitia cross-sectional area, the maximum % and length of the stenosis, the plaque area eccentricity and volume, etc which permit accurate evaluation of atherosclerotic burden (Figure 6). A significant advantage of this system is its speed as it needs only 3 minutes to process 1000 IVUS frames.

Figure 6. Snapshot of the user-interface showing the segmentation of the IVUS sequence process. The obtained measurements are displayed at the left side of the screen.

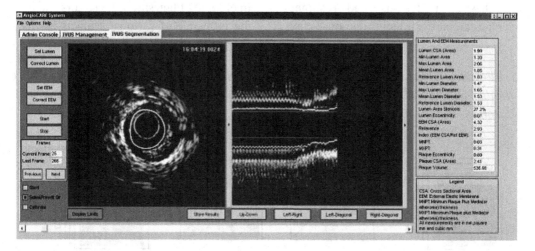

Figure 7. Snapshots of the Boston's Scientific iLab® Ultrasound Imaging System. Apart from the automated identification of the luminal and media-adventitia borders the system allows analysis of the backscatter signal and characterization of the type of the plaque which is comprehensively portrayed in IVUS images using in color coded map.

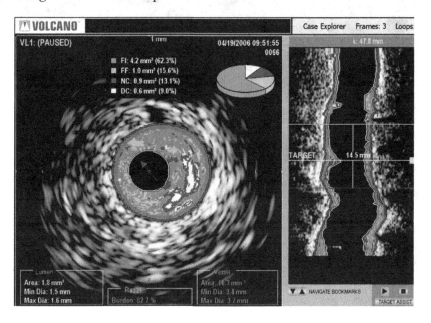

Volcano's 5™ Imaging System® incorporates the methodology proposed by Sonka *et al.* (1995) for the segmentation of the IVUS sequence while the characterization of the type of the plaque is based on the autoregressive modeling of the radiofrequency IVUS data. This approach allows identification of four plaque types which are comprehensively depicted in each IVUS frames using a color coded map (Figure 7). This system also offers plug and play simplicity for immediate imaging and implements an intuitive user-interface which facilitates training and workflow. Finally, in case that manual border detection is necessary a high fidelity user-friendly pressure sensor is attached which enables quick delineation of the regions of interest.

Finally, Boston's Scientific iLab® Ultrasound Imaging System has also implemented a segmentation methodology for expedite detection of the luminal and media-adventitia borders (Figure 8). It allows accurate quantification of the plaque burden and assessment of the % area stenosis. It

comes with a simplified user-friendly panel incorporating more monitors than previous versions and gives the opportunity of touch screen. It also allows zooming and coloring areas on the IVUS frames (e.g. the plaque, the lumen). The principal new feature of the system, is the implementation of a module, called iMap™, that allows fast Fourier transformation of the IVUS radiofrequency backscatter signal and identification four plaque types, namely fibrotic, lipid, necrotic and calcified, which are comprehensively portrayed in each frame using a color coded map.

CONCLUSION

IVUS is a valuable intravascular technique which allows detailed coronary visualization and assessment of plaque characteristics. Over the last years a multitude of methodologies have been developed which facilitated IVUS processing and reduced inter-observer variability. The proposed

Figure 8. IVUS images and border segmentation provided by Boston's system

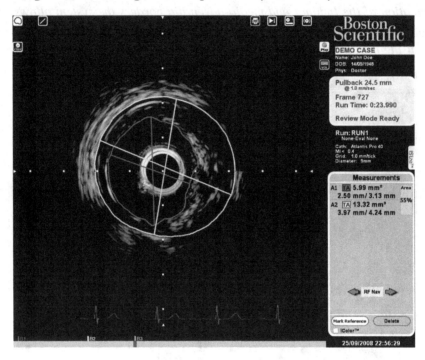

segmentation algorithms and plaque characterization techniques have been incorporated in efficient user-friendly commercially available systems that have been introduced in the catheterization laboratories and have enhanced the role of IVUS in clinical practice.

REFERENCES

Bouma, C., Niessen, W., Zuiderveld, K., Gussenhoven, E., & Viergever, M. (1997). Automated lumen definition from 30 MHz intravascular ultrasound images. *Medical Image Analysis, 1*(4), 363–377. doi:10.1016/S1361-8415(97)85007-4

Bourantas, C. V., Kalatzis, F. G., Papafaklis, M. I., Fotiadis, D. I., Tweddel, A. C., & Kourtis, I. C. (2008). Angiocare: An automated system for fast three-dimensional coronary reconstruction by integrating angiographic and intracoronary ultrasound data. *Catheterization and Cardiovascular Interventions, 72*(2), 166–175. doi:10.1002/ccd.21527

Bourantas, C. V., Kourtis, I. C., Plissiti, M. E., Fotiadis, D. I., Katsouras, C. S., Papafaklis, M. I., & Michalis, L. K. (2005). A method for 3D reconstruction of coronary arteries using biplane angiography and intravascular ultrasound images. *Computerized Medical Imaging and Graphics, 29*(8), 597–606. doi:10.1016/j.compmedimag.2005.07.001

Brunenberg, E., Pujol, O., Romeny, B., & Radeva, P. (2006). Automatic IVUS Segmentation of atherosclerotic plaque with Stop & Go Snake. *Proceedings of Medical Image Computing and Computer-Assisted Intervention: MICCAI, 9,* 9–16.

Brusseau, E., de Korte, C. L., Mastik, F., Schaar, J., & van der Steen, A. F. W. (2004). Fully automatic luminal contour segmentation in intracoronary ultrasound imaging – A statistical approach. *IEEE Transactions on Medical Imaging, 23*(5), 554–566. doi:10.1109/TMI.2004.825602

Caballero, K. L., Barajas, J., Pujol, O., Rodriguez, O., & Radeva, P. (2007). Using reconstructed IVUS images for coronary plaque classification. *Proceedings of Engineering in Medicine and Biology Society in 29th Annual International Conference of the IEEE,* (pp. 2167–2170).

Cardinal, M., Meunier, J., Soulez, G., Maurice, R., Therasse, E., & Cloutier, G. (2006). Intravascular ultrasound image segmentation: A three-dimensional fast-marching method based on gray level distributions. *IEEE Transactions on Medical Imaging, 25,* 590–601. doi:10.1109/TMI.2006.872142

Chalana, V., & Kim, Y. (1997). A methodology for evaluation of boundary detection algorithms on medical images. *IEEE Transactions on Medical Imaging, 16*(5), 642–652. doi:10.1109/42.640755

Dhawale, P., Rasheed, Q., Griffin, N., Wilson, D., & Hodgson, J. (1993). Intracoronary ultrasound plaque volume quantification. In *Proc Comput Cardiol* (pp. 121–124). Los Alamitos, CA: IEEE Computer Society Press.

Filho, E. S., Saijo, Y., Tanaka, A., & Yoshizawa, M. (2008). Detection and quantification of calcifications in intravascular ultrasound images by automatic thresholding. *Ultrasound in Medicine & Biology, 34*(1), 160–165. doi:10.1016/j.ultrasmedbio.2007.06.025

Filho, S., Saijo, Y., Tanaka, A., Yambe, T., Li, S., & Yoshizawa, M. (2007). Automated calcification detection and quantification in intravascular ultrasound images by adaptive thresholding. *Proceedings of World Congress on Medical Physics and Biomedical Engineering, 14,* 1421–1425. doi:10.1007/978-3-540-36841-0_348

Finet, G., Maurincomme, E., Reiber, J., Savalle, L., Magnin, I., & Beaune, J. (1998). Evaluation of an automatic intraluminal edge detection technique for intravascular ultrasound images. *Circulation Journal, 62*(2), 115–121. doi:10.1253/jcj.62.115

Giannoglou, G., Chatzizisis, Y., Koutkias, V., Kompatsiaris, I., Papadogiorgaki, M., & Mezaris, V. (2007). A novel active contour model for fully automated segmentation of intravascular ultrasound images: in vivo validation in human coronary arteries. *Computers in Biology and Medicine, 37*(9), 1292–1302. doi:10.1016/j.compbiomed.2006.12.003

Giannoglou, G., Chatzizisis, Y., Sianos, G., Tsikaderis, D., Matakos, A., & Koutkias, V. (2006). Integration of multi–modality imaging for accurate 3D reconstruction of human coronary arteries in vivo. *Nuclear Instruments and Methods in Physics Research, 569,* 310–313. doi:10.1016/j.nima.2006.08.057

Godbout, B., de Guise, J., Soulez, G., & Cloutier, G. (2005). 3D elastic registration of vessel structures from IVUS data on biplane angiography. *Academic Radiology, 12*(1), 10–16. doi:10.1016/j.acra.2004.10.058

Goshtasby, A., Turner, D. A., & Ackermann, L. V. (1992). Matching of tomographic slices for interpolation. *IEEE Transactions on Medical Imaging, 11,* 507–516. doi:10.1109/42.192686

Haas, C., Ermert, H., Holt, S., Grewe, P., Machraoui, A., & Barmeyer, J. (2000). Segmentation of 3D intravascular ultrasonic images based on a random field model. *Ultrasound in Medicine & Biology, 26*(2), 297–306. doi:10.1016/S0301-5629(99)00139-8

Hagenaars, T., Gussenhoven, E. J., Van Der Linden, E., & Bom, N. (2000). Reproducibility of calcified lesion quantification: A longitudinal intravascular ultrasound study. *Ultrasound in Medicine & Biology, 26,* 1075–1079. doi:10.1016/S0301-5629(00)00246-5

Hammers, R., Bruining, N., Knook, M., Sabate, M., & Roelandt, J. R. T. C. (2001). A novel approach to quantitative analysis of intravascular ultrasound images. *IEEE J, 28,* 589–592.

Hernandez, A., Rotger, D., & Gil, D. (2008). Image-based ECG sampling of IVUS sequences. *IEEE Ultrasonics Symposium*, (pp. 1330–1333).

Iskurt, A., Candemir, S., & Akgul, Y. S. (2006). Identification of luminal and medial adventitial borders in intravascular ultrasound images using level sets. *Lecture Notes in Computer Science, Lecture Notes in Artificial Intelligence, and Lecture Notes in Bioinformatics, 4263 LNCS*, (pp. 572-582).

Kass, M., Witkin, A., & Terzopoulos, D. (1987). Snakes: Active contour models. *International Journal of Computer Vision, 1*, 321–331. doi:10.1007/BF00133570

Katouzian, A., Sathyanarayana, S., Baseri, B., Konofagou, E., & Carlier, S. (2008). Challenges in atherosclerotic plaque characterization with intravascular ultrasound (IVUS): From data collection to classification. *Information Technology in Biomedicine. IEEE Transactions, 12*(3), 315–327.

Klingensmith, J. D., Shekhar, R., & Vince, D. G. (2000). Evaluation of three-dimensional segmentation algorithms for the identification of luminal and medial–adventitial borders in intravascular ultrasound images. *IEEE Transactions on Medical Imaging, 19*(10), 996–1011. doi:10.1109/42.887615

Koning, G., Dijkstra, J., Von Birgelen, C., Tuinenburg, J. C., Brunette, J., & Tardif, C. (2002). Advanced contour detection for three–dimensional intracoronary ultrasound: A validation in–vitro and in vivo. *The International Journal of Cardiovascular Imaging, 18*, 235–248. doi:10.1023/A:1015551920382

Kovalski, G., Beyar, R., Shofti, R., & Azhari, H. (2000). Three-dimensional automatic quantitative analysis of intravascular ultrasound images. *Ultrasound in Medicine & Biology, 26*(4), 527–537. doi:10.1016/S0301-5629(99)00167-2

Lobregt, S., & Viergever, M. A. (1995). Discrete dynamic control model. *IEEE Transactions on Medical Imaging, 14*, 12–24. doi:10.1109/42.370398

Matsumoto, M. S., Lemos, P. A., Yoneyama, T., & Furuie, S. S. (2009). Cardiac phase detection in intravascular ultrasound images, progress in biomedical optics and imaging. *Proceedings of the Society for Photo-Instrumentation Engineers, 6920*, 69200D.

Mehta, S. K., McCrary, J. R., Frutkin, A. D., Dolla, W. S., & Marso, S. P. (2007). Intravascular ultrasound radiofrequency analysis of coronary atherosclerosis: An emerging technology for the assessment of vulnerable plaque. *European Heart Journal, 28*, 1283–1288. doi:10.1093/eurheartj/ehm112

Meier, D., Cothren, R., Vince, D., & Cornhill, J. (1997). Automated morphometry of coronary arteries with digital image analysis of intravascular ultrasound. *American Heart Journal, 133*(6), 681–690. doi:10.1016/S0002-8703(97)70170-4

Mintz, G. S., Nissen, S. E., Anderson, W. D., Bailey, S. R., Elber, R., & Fitzgerald, P. J. (2001). American College of Cardiology clinical expert consensus document on standards for acquisition, measurement and reporting of intravascular ultrasound studies: A report of the American College of Cardiology task force on clinical expert consensus documents (committee to develop a clinical expert consensus on standards for acquisition, measurement and reporting of intravascular ultrasound studies [IVUS]). *Journal of the American College of Cardiology, 37*, 1478–1492. doi:10.1016/S0735-1097(01)01175-5

Mojsilović, A., Popović, M., Amodaj, N., Babić, R., & Ostojić, M. (1997). Automatic segmentation of intravascular ultrasound images: A texture-based approach. *Annals of Biomedical Engineering, 25*(6), 1059–1071.

Nadkarni, S. K., Boughner, D., & Fenster, A. (2005). Image-based cardiac gating for three-dimensional intravascular ultrasound imaging. *Ultrasound in Medicine & Biology, 31*(1), 53–63. doi:10.1016/j.ultrasmedbio.2004.08.025

Najafi, Z., Taki, A., Setarehdan, S. K., Zoroofi, R., Konig, A., & Navab, N. (2007). *A new method for automatic border detection in IVUS images and 3D visualization of segmented frames.* The 4th Visual Information Engineering Conference: VIE 2007, London, July 2007.

Nissen, S. E., Di Mario, C., & Tuzcu, E. M. (1998). Intravascular ultrasound angioscopy, doppler and pressure measurements. In Topol, E. J. (Ed.), *Comprehensive cardiovascular medicine* (pp. 2471–2501). Philadelphia, PA: Lippincott-Raven Publishers.

O'Malley, S. M., Carlier, S. G., Naghavi, M., & Kakadiaris, I. A. (2007). Image-based frame gating of IVUS pullbacks: A surrogate for ECG. *IEEE International Conference on Acoustics, Speech and Signal Processing, 1,* (pp. I-433-I-436).

O'Malley, S. M., Granada, J. F., Carlier, S., Naghavi, M., & Kakadiaris, I. A. (2008). Image-based gating of intravascular ultrasound pullback sequences. *IEEE Transactions on Information Technology in Biomedicine, 12,* 299–306. doi:10.1109/TITB.2008.921014

Papadogiorgaki, M., Mezaris, V., Chatzizisis, Y., Giannoglou, G., & Kompatsiaris, I. (2008). Image analysis techniques for automated IVUS contour detection. *Ultrasound in Medicine & Biology, 34*(9), 1482–1498. doi:10.1016/j.ultrasmedbio.2008.01.022

Parissi, E., Kompatsiaris, Y., Chatzizisis, Y. S., Koutkias, V., Maglaveras, N., Strintzis, M. G., & Giannoglou, G. D. (2006). An automated model for rapid and reliable segmentation of intravascular ultrasound images. *Proceedings Biological and Medical Data Analysis, 43*(45), 368–377. doi:10.1007/11946465_33

Plissiti, M. E., Fotiadis, D. I., Michalis, L. K., & Bozios, G. E. (2004). An automated method for lumen and media-adventitia border detection in a sequence of IVUS frames. *IEEE Transactions on Information Technology in Biomedicine, 8*(2), 131–141. doi:10.1109/TITB.2004.828889

Pujol, O., Radeva, P., Vitria, J., & Mauri, J. (2004). Adaboost to classify plaque appearance in IVUS images. *Lecture Notes in Computer Science, 3287,* 629–636. doi:10.1007/978-3-540-30463-0_79

Rosenfield, K., Losordo, D. W., Ramaswamy, K., Pastore, J. O., Langevin, R. E., & Razvi, S. (1991). Three dimensional reconstruction of human coronary and peripheral arteries from images recorded during two-dimensional intravascular ultrasound examination. *Circulation, 84*(5), 1938–1956.

Sanz-Requena, R., Moratal, D., García-Sánchez, D., Bodí, V., Rieta, J., & Sanchis, J. (2007). Automatic segmentation and 3D reconstruction of intravascular ultrasound images for a fast preliminary evaluation of vessel pathologies. *Computerized Medical Imaging and Graphics, 31*(2), 71–80. doi:10.1016/j.compmedimag.2006.11.004

Slager, C., Wentzel, J., Schuurbiers, J., Oomen, J., Kloet, J., & Krams, R. (2000). True 3 – Dimensional reconstruction of coronary arteries in patients by fusion of angiography and IVUS (ANGUS) and its quantitative validation. *Circulation, 102,* 511–516.

Sonka, M., Zhang, X., Siebes, M., Bissing, M., Dejong, S., Collins, S., & McKay, C. R. (1995). Segmentation of intravascular ultrasound images: A knowledge–based approach. *IEEE Transactions on Medical Imaging, 14*(4), 719–732. doi:10.1109/42.476113

Sun, F. R., Liu, Z., Li, Y. L., Babyn, P., Yao, G. H., & Zhang, Y. (2009). *Improved T-snake model based edge detection of the coronary arterial walls in intravascular ultrasound images.* iCBBE, Beijing, China, 2009.

Takagi, A., Hibi, K., Zhang, X., Teo, T., Bonneau, H., Yock, P., & Fitzgerald, P. (2000). Automated contour detection for high-frequency intravascular ultrasound imaging: A technique with blood noise reduction for edge enhancement. *Ultrasound in Medicine & Biology, 26*(6), 1033–1041. doi:10.1016/S0301-5629(00)00251-9

Unal, G., Bucher, S., Carlier, S., Slabaugh, G., Tong, F., & Tanaka, K. (2008). Shape-driven segmentation of the arterial wall in intravascular ultrasound images. *IEEE Transactions on Information Technology in Biomedicine, 12*(3), 335–347. doi:10.1109/TITB.2008.920620

Vince, D. G., Dixon, K. J., Cothren, R. M., & Cornhill, J. F. (2000). Comparison of texture analysis methods for the characterization of coronary plaques in intravascular ultrasound images. *Computerized Medical Imaging and Graphics, 24*(4), 221–229. doi:10.1016/S0895-6111(00)00011-2

Virmani, R., Burke, A. P., Farb, A., & Kolodgie, F. D. (2006). Pathology of the vulnerable plaque. *Journal of the American College of Cardiology, 47*(8), 13–18. doi:10.1016/j.jacc.2005.10.065

Wang, Y., Shu, Y., Hu, B., & Chen, J. (2009). *An improved level set method of ultrasound imaging to detect blood vessel walls.* International Conference on Image Analysis and Signal Processing, IASP 2009.

Weichert, F., Müller, H., Quast, U., Kraushaar, A., Spilles, P., & Heintz, M. (2003). Virtual 3D IVUS vessel model for intravascular brachytherapy planning. 3D segmentation, reconstruction and visualization of coronary artery architecture and orientation. *Medical Physics, 30*(9), 2530–2536. doi:10.1118/1.1603964

Wennogle, M., & Hoff, W. (2009). Three dimensional segmentation of intravascular ultrasound data. *Lecture Notes in Computer Science, 5627,* 772–781. doi:10.1007/978-3-642-02611-9_76

Zhang, Q., Wang, Y., Wang, W., Ma, J., Qian, J., & Ge, J. (2010). Automatic segmentation of calcifications in intravascular ultrasound images using snakes and the contourlet transform. *Ultrasound in Medicine & Biology, 36*(1), 111–129. doi:10.1016/j.ultrasmedbio.2009.06.1097

Zhang, X., McKay, C. R., & Sonka, M. (1998). Tissue characterization in intravascular ultrasound images. *IEEE Transactions on Medical Imaging, 17*(6), 889–899. doi:10.1109/42.746622

Zhu, H., Oakeson, K. D., & Friedman, M. H. (2003). Retrieval of cardiac phase from IVUS sequences. *Proc SPIE Medical Imaging, 5035,* 135–146.

KEY TERMS AND DEFINITIONS

Hopfield Neural Network: A recurrent artificial neural network invented by John Hopfield which serves as a content-addressable memory system with binary threshold units. It is guaranteed to converge to a local minimum.

Intravascular Ultrasound: An invasive imaging modality for the visualization of arterial morphology using a specially designed catheter with a miniaturized ultrasound probe attached to the distal end of its tip. This probe has the ability to transmit signal perpendicular to its axis and receive the reflected signal which after processing generates cr function is called edge map function. When the GVF is used in traditional snakes, it replaces the external energy term in order to formulate the GVF snake.

Otsu's Method: Used to automatically perform histogram shape-based image thresholding, or to transform a graylevel image to a binary image. It assumes that the image to be thresholded contains two classes of pixels and by calculating the optimum threshold separates those two classes so that their combined spread to be minimal. $f(x,y)$

Chapter 4
Analysis of Radiofrequency Ultrasound Signals:
Tissue Characterization With Virtual Histology and Palpography

Attila Thury
Erasmus MC, The Netherlands & University of Szeged, Hungary

Héctor M. Garcia-Garcia
Erasmus MC, The Netherlands

Evelyn Regar
Erasmus MC, The Netherlands

ABSTRACT

IVUS opened new perspectives in our understanding of human coronary atherosclerosis and triggers of ACS (especially plaque rupture as its most dominant cause). Throughout this chapter we list the shortcomings of conventional (greyscale) IVUS to characterize tissue components of plaques and the potentials of radiofrequency signal processing to overcome these. In recent years, the technology matured, and especially with VH and IB-IVUS, many clinical studies showed accurate plaque estimation. Results of a prospective, natural history study have just been presented and proved the ability of VH to predict ACS. Palpography derives compositional information from functional (strain) measurements. Assessing several characteristics of a given plaque could potentially enhance invasive risk stratification by identifying very high-risk plaques, thereby reducing the number of vulnerable plaques that need to be serially followed and ultimately treated. Moreover, if a safe prophylactic local treatment was available, a sophisticated IVUS procedure would be a part of a "one-stop-shop" in preventive cardiology.

DOI: 10.4018/978-1-61350-095-8.ch004

INTRODUCTION

Ischemic heart disease often presents as an acute coronary syndrome (ACS), even in patients with prior percutaneous treatment of a flow-limiting stenosis (Glaser *et al.*, 2005). Pathological substrate for an ACS is a (sub)occlusive thrombus filling the lumen which might stem from a segment of atherosclerotic coronary artery showing mild or borderline stenosis (often with complex morphological pattern) on a previous angiogram (Ambrose *et al.*, 1986; Goldstein *et al.*, 2000). These fragile (prone to rupture) foci of the coronary wall causing subsequent events(Falk, Shah, & Fuster, 1995) have been attributed as "vulnerable plaques" (VP)(Naghavi *et al.*, 2003) and identified as "thin-cap fibroatheromas" (TCFA) as a major substrate by pathologists(Virmani, Burke, Farb, & Kolodgie, 2006). Coronary artery disease (CAD) is a diffuse atheromatosus process of the epicardial coronary arteries (sometimes also with flow-limiting stenoses or multiple ruptures(Goldstein *et al.*, 2000)). Accordingly, the number of these VPs (manifesting in non-flow limiting stenosis) might be numerous(Rioufol *et al.*, 2002) and they present variable with time (as acute worsening is related to actual inflammatory alterations)(Goldstein *et al.*, 2000; Libby & Theroux, 2005). These notions may render efforts identification of a VP (before rupture!) in the catheterization laboratory a mission hard to accomplish(Ambrose, 2008). Pathological, imaging and clinical findings demonstrated that occlusive coronary thrombi tend to cluster in the proximal segments of coronary arteries(Wang, Normand, Mauri, & Kuntz, 2004) and pathology study showed TCFAs limited in number(Cheruvu *et al.*, 2007) make the hunt for VP timely identification justified. Moreover, traditional secondary preventive measures are limited in efficacy(Libby, 2005) and local treatment may well prove to be effective in the (near) future(Ramcharitar *et al.*, 2009).

GREYSCALE IVUS FOR VP DETECTION

Coronary Angiography Versus IVUS for VP Detection

Coronary angiography is the gold-standard for imaging CAD. Complex morphology pattern on prior angiogram can foresee instability of a specific lesion(Ambrose *et al.*, 1986; Goldstein *et al.*, 2000) but the severity of a stenosis is not predictive for subsequent myocardial infarction(Little *et al.*, 1988). This inability for identification of a VP is generally attributed to its restriction to visualize coronary lumen and not the vessel wall(Topol & Nissen, 1995).

In contrast, intravascular ultrasound (IVUS) can provide detailed morphologic view of alterations of the vessel wall in vivo, thus introduction of this tomogpraphic visualization to the catheterization laboratory as part of daily practice in interventional cardiology caused really a paradigm shift(Mintz *et al.*, 1995). At the tip of an IVUS catheter, a transducer emits an ultrasound signal and receives the reflected (backscattered) signal from tissue. Precise measurements of different types of atheroma and also the lumen (true extent of stenoses) became feasible(Garcia-Garcia, Costa, & Serruys, 2010; Mintz *et al.*, 2001). Possible indications for use include assessment of angiographically borderline lesions, sizing balloon or stent during of intracoronary procedure, exploring any damage to the vessel wall and others (e.g. optimization of stent expansion in order to avoid restenosis or stent thrombosis). We are not entitled to give details for these, instead refer to contemporary concise reviews(Bonello *et al.*, 2009; Nissen & Yock, 2001) and other chapters of this book.

IVUS has changed our conception about coronary atherosclerosis(Garcia-Garcia *et al.*, 2010; Topol & Nissen, 1995) and later it has been described as a tool for VP detection(DeMaria, Narula, Mahmud, & Tsimikas, 2006). In conventional (greyscale) IVUS the backscattered signal is processed in real-time into a two-dimensional video image. This modality has been extensively validated against pathology specimen: intensity of reflected ultrasound waves corresponded well with tissue components, especially when discriminating calcification from "soft" tissues(Nishimura *et al.*, 1990). However, analysis of "soft" tissues cannot be detailed, and despite of high-frequency conventional IVUS had been demonstrated to provide better (than previous 20 or 30 MHz catheters) accuracy for lipid assessment(Prati *et al.*, 2001), the overall precision for plaque characterization remained doubtful(Kimura, Bhargava, & DeMaria, 1995). Many publications described the specific IVUS characteristics of plaque rupture and differences of plaques in patients presenting with ACS than those of stable angina (Figure 1). Large echolucent areas of eccentric plaques and presence of positive remodeling has repeatedly been associated with vulnerability(Schoenhagen *et al.*, 2000). In addition, spotty calcification was found to be more prevalent in this patient subset(Ehara

et al., 2004). Recently, a new entity called "attenuated plaque" seen during greyscale IVUS has been identified as a special plaque type with large echolucent atheroma with some shadowing but without evident calcified content(Hara *et al.*, 2006). This has been associated with no-reflow phenomenon after stenting(Okura *et al.*, 2007) and found as part of more severe and complex lesions in ACS patients with high C-reactive protein level(S. Y. Lee *et al.*, 2009).

Limitations of Conventional IVUS for VP Detection

Our understanding of VP has substantially increased by pathologic observations(Virmani *et al.*, 2006) which resulted in identifying the most common cause of atherothrombosis as rupture-prone plaques i.e. TCFAs(Schaar, Muller, *et al.*, 2004). TCFAs have thin fibrous caps making them unable to withstand the circumferential stress exerted by pressure in the lumen(R. T. Lee & Libby, 1997), the thickness measured by pathologists was

Figure 1. Example of IVUS characteristics of plaque rupture in proximal segment of right coronary artery. This patient suffered a non-ST elevation myocardial infarction (NSTE-ACS) 1 day prior to cardiac catheterizastion and IVUS examination. Note the large echolucent plaque showing disruption of its fibrous cap and consequent lack of tissue at 9 to 11 o'clock (i.e. "emptied plaque"). This IVUS feature can accordingly reflect the clinical history of the patient.

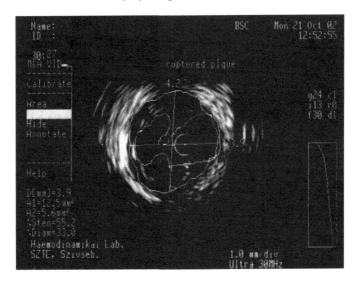

as small as 65 µm or less(Virmani *et al.*, 2006). The low resolution of IVUS (being 150 to 300 µm) rendering it ineligible to detect thin fibrous cap(DeMaria *et al.*, 2006). IVUS does not provide information on inflammation(Matter, Stuber, & Nahrendorf, 2009), which is a substantial player in the development of VPs(Virmani *et al.*, 2006). Plaque composition is a major determinant for plaque vulnerability but greyscale IVUS cannot precisely discriminate fibrous tissue from fatty plaque as latter one being mixture of low echogenic material and highly echogenic necrotic debris and microcalcifications(Peters *et al.*, 1994). Also, IVUS has limited value for quantifying the size of necrotic core which is a key component of VPs: risk of plaque rupture increases with necrotic core enlargement(Davies, Richardson, Woolf, Katz, & Mann, 1993). All these might be the underlying background that there is only 1 real prospective IVUS study to prove its ability for prediction of a subsequent event(Yamagishi *et al.*, 2000). Early attempts (computer-aided quantitative and videodensitometric analysis) to make compositional measurements more precise showed limited value (Nishimura *et al.*, 1990; Rasheed, Dhawale, Anderson, & Hodgson, 1995; Tobis *et al.*, 1991).

Apart from limitation of greyscale IVUS to qualitatively determine plaque composition, poor reproducibility is also a major problem. Crude estimation of plaque type (such as "echolucent") can be performed with good reproducibility(Palmer, Northridge, Lessells, McDicken, & Fox, 1999) but this can be misleading(Hiro *et al.*, 1997) since conventional IVUS cannot discriminate fibrous from fatty plaque(Peters *et al.*, 1994). When compared to histology low correlation was obtained for interobserver measurements of lipid pool areas ($r = 0.41$) even when improved transducer-type used(Prati *et al.*, 2001). Recently, very experienced experts in the field compared the ability of greyscale IVUS to detect fibrous or calcified tissue and necrotic core with that of virtual histology characterization (the main subject

of this chapter)(Gonzalo *et al.*, 2008). They found unacceptably high interobserver variability in the prediction of tissue type by visual assessment of greyscale IVUS(Gonzalo *et al.*, 2008).

Lack of accuracy of conventional IVUS may also derive from operator-dependent parameters such as brightness and gain, and the processing itself of the backscatter signal that distorts the relationship of the original acoustic data(Nishimura *et al.*, 1990). To overcome these, computer assisted greyscale analysis program ("echogenicity") was also developed(de Winter *et al.*, 2003) based on early tests suggesting quantitative analysis to be capable for acoustic tissue characterization(Okimoto *et al.*, 2002; Rasheed *et al.*, 1995). Echogenicity is based on discrimination of plaque components that have lower grey-level intensity (e.g. hypoechogenic tissue) than adventitia and/or tissue with a similar or higher grey-level intensity (e.g. hyperechogenic tissue). Hyperechogenic tissues accompanied with acoustic shadowing are identified as calcified areas. The method (for details see methodology article of the IBIS [Integrated Biomarker and Imaging Study]) trial(Van Mieghem *et al.*, 2005) has readily been used in the catheterization laboratory in human. However, this technique did not yield to have additional information in this study(Van Mieghem *et al.*, 2006).

General limitation of IVUS should also be mentioned: invasive, might cause spasm in smaller vessels, especially when crossing large bends, sometimes restricting the operator to image only proximal segments. However, overall major safety is ensured(Guedes *et al.*, 2005) and clustered location of VPs in proximal segments of coronary arteries(Wang *et al.*, 2004) justifies the use of IVUS in the catheterization laboratory since a more sensitive and specific method for VP detection is not available.

However, greyscale IVUS is overwhelmingly used as a detection tool of plaque volume presumed to be a surrogate marker for clinical events in plaque regression studies(Nicholls *et al.*, 2010).

Progression was indeed related to possible future acute ischemic events in 1 certain IVUS study(von Birgelen *et al.*, 2004), although its incremental value (over establishing angiographic progression) has repeatedly been questioned(Brown & Zhao, 2007) and experts call for the need of characterization of plaque structure(Finn, Chandrashekhar, & Narula, 2010).

RADIOFREQUENCY SIGNAL PROCESSING OF CONVENTIONAL IVUS: TECHNICAL BACKGROUND OF TISSUE CHARACTERIZATION

Virtual Histology™ IVUS: Image Generation and Validation Studies

It has long been established that in addition to the conventional greyscale visualization of the reflected (backscattered) ultrasound signals, there is much information buried inside (Figure 2). The theoretical framework for their analysis by spectral analysis was described early(Lizzi, Greenebaum, Feleppa, Elbaum, & Coleman, 1983) and first intracoronary applications showed that frequency based spectral analysis of unprocessed ultrasound signal might lead to accurate identification of atherosclerotic plaque morphology(Moore *et al.*, 1998). It was possible to differentiate among different densities of fibrosis, and lipid could be differentiated from other types of plaque by use of the y-axis intercept, spectral slope, or mean power (or some combination thereof)(Moore *et al.*, 1998). Later, against histopathological specimen Stahr *et al.* could prove that plaque compositional discrimination for early, "soft" lesions was more precise with radiofrequency (RF) analysis than conventional gray-scale IVUS (Stahr *et al.*, 2002).

Figure 2. Different imaging modalities based on signal post-processing of conventional IVUS (From: Garcia-Garcia HM et Eur Heart J. 2010 Oct;31(20):2456-69).

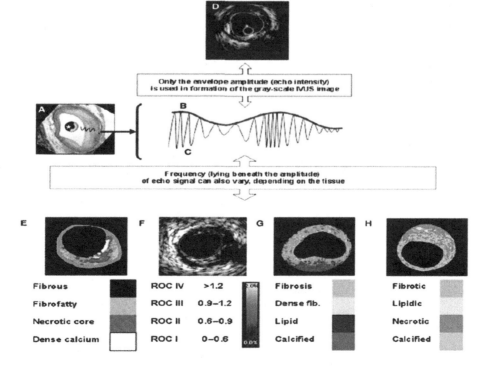

For technical details we refer to respective articles and a concise review(Carlier, Mintz, & Stone, 2006). In brief, a conventional gray-scale IVUS image is formed from the amplitude map encoding: the envelope of the received backscattered (reflected) RF signal. Low-amplitude signals are coded as dark gray or black; high-amplitude signals are coded as light gray or white. All frequency and phase information is lost during this process as illustrated in panel c (lower left-hand corner), where 2 very different reflected signal frequencies generate the same amplitude envelope. To capture the different signatures of backscattered ultrasound signals, it is necessary to perform a spectral analysis. For example, as simplified in Figure 3, the signal reflected from a lipid inclusion has more oscillations per second (ie, a higher frequency) than the signal reflected by the vessel wall, although their amplitudes are the same. This additional information can be calculated on the RF signal by use of tools such as fast Fourier

transformation or autoregressive modeling(Nair, Kuban, Obuchowski, & Vince, 2001). The frequency and power of the signal commonly differ between tissues, regardless of similarities in the amplitude.

Nair *et al.* explored whether autoregressive or classic Fourier spectra performed better for compositional analysis(Nair *et al.*, 2002). Accuracies of autoregressive classification schemes and classic Fourier spectra are of 90.4% for fibrous, 92.8% for fibrolipidic, 90.9% for calcified, and 89.5% for calcified-necrotic regions in the training data set and 79.7%, 81.2%, 92.8%, and 85.5% in the test data, respectively(Nair *et al.*, 2002). Tissue maps were reconstructed with the use of accurate predictions of plaque composition from the autoregressive classification scheme and further improvement of this technique was also described(Nair, Calvetti, & Vince, 2004). This method has been implemented clinically after introduction of the Volcano IVUS scanner (Ran-

Figure 3. Basics of intravascular tissue characterization (From: Carlier SG, Mintz GS, Stone GW. Imaging of atherosclerotic plaque using radiofrequency ultrasound signal processing. J Nucl Cardiol 2006; 13:831-40). Schematic representation of principle of plaque characterization from radiofrequency spectrum analysis. The backscattered signal from a lipid inclusion (yellow) demonstrates a higher frequency (pitch) than the signal received from the fibrotic tissue (green) (lower number of oscillations per second). This information cannot be derived solely from the amplitude envelope of the signal but may be extracted via spectral analysis tools such as fast Fourier transform or autoregressive modeling.

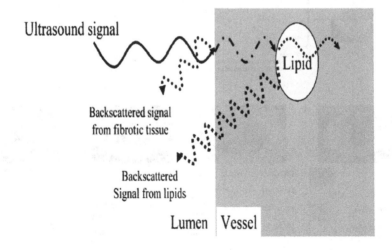

Figure 4. Color-coding of VH® IVUS – ex vivo validation (Modified from Nair A et al. Circulation 2002; 106: 2200-06)

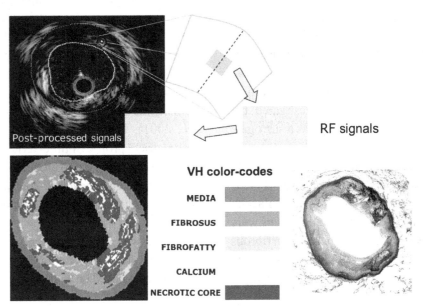

cho Cordova, Calif) as VH® IVUS, which constructs tissue maps that classify plaque into four major components: fibrous (green), fibbrofatty (light green), necrotic core (red), and dense calcium (white). Figure 4 shows the schema of color-coding of different signatures based on post-processed radiofrequency signals.

Nair *et al*. further validated VH by means of "training" the algorithm from human histology, with which it has been shown to highly correlate (93-97% accuracy)(Nair, Margolis, Kuban, & Vince, 2007). The kappa statistic was calculated to be 0.845, indicating very high agreement with histology(Nair *et al*., 2007). Moreover, high correlation also has been observed in vivo between human histology and VH plaque composition from both coronary atherectomy(Funada *et al*., 2009; Nasu *et al*., 2006) and carotid endarterectomy(Diethrich *et al*., 2007) specimens.

Integrated Backscatter Analysis

Integrated Backscatter (IB) IVUS (YD Corporation, Nara, Japan - http://www.yellow-dog.jp/

index.htm) is another mathematical technique being used in RF ultrasound backscatter analysis. This method (YFKO-1100 system is commercially available in Japan) utilizes IB values, calculated by Fourier transformation as the average power of the backscattered ultrasound signal from a sample tissue volume(Kawasaki *et al*., 2001). Fourier transformation extracts frequency components of a signal buried in the original IVUS signal. Similar to VH-IVUS, the IB-IVUS system constructs color-coded tissue maps, providing a quantitative visual readout as 4 types of plaque composition: calcification, fibrosis, dense fibrosis, and lipid pool(Kawasaki *et al*., 2002). A recent clinical study demonstrated that vulnerable plaques with subsequent ACS events within 3 years had distinct tissue characteristics from those of stable angina plaques at initial IB-IVUS examination(Sano *et al*., 2006). When a lipid area of >65% and a fibrous area of <25% were used as a cutoff, the positive predictive values for future ACS were 42% and 69%, respectively(Sano *et al*., 2006). In a recent study lipid-rich plaques measured by IB-IVUS proved to be an independent morphologic predictor of non-target ischemic events after PCI of the culprit lesion(Amano *et al.*, 2011). New autopsy study demonstrated that 43-MHz mode of the Terumo IVUS system is able to discriminate even thin fibrous caps, the correlation between IB-IVUS and histology and OCT derived thickness was very good(Kawasaki *et al.*). Another clinical study(Kawasaki *et al.*, 2005) investigated the potential utility of this technology as a surrogate endpoint of pharmacologic interventions, i.e. statin therapy resulted in a significant reduction in lipid component of coronary plaques, whereas no significant change was observed in the placebo group. The changes seen in the statin groups were accompanied with significant increases in fibrous component(Kawasaki *et al.*, 2005), indicating possible stabilization of lipid-rich plaque by lipid lowering therapies.

A direct qualitative comparison(Okubo *et al.*, 2008) has already been published with VH® IVUS, which showed the overall agreement between the histological and IB-IVUS diagnoses was higher (Cohen'sκ=0.81, 95% CI: 0.72–0.89) than between the histological and VH-IVUS diagnoses (Cohen'sκ=0.30, 95%CI: 0.14–0.41). Although the location of each tissue component depicted by VH-IVUS did not always accurately reflect the histological location, the overall agreement of VH-IVUS in the "quantitative" comparison (0.73) was better than that in the "qualitative" comparison (0.66), whereas the IB-IVUS values were similar (0.83 and 0.81)(Okubo *et al.*, 2008).

There is an alternative method for IVUS plaque characterization, namely wavelet analysis, which was first described by Hiro *et al*(Hiro *et al.*, 2001). This utilizes the local changes in a geometrical profile of time-series signals to map lipid-laden atherosclerotic plaques with good accuracy(Murashige *et al.*, 2005). However, this technology is not yet commercially available for clinical use.

Here, we give a comparative table (Table 1) of current available techniques for plaque characterization based on greyscale IVUS:

Spectral Similarity Method for Plaque Characterization (iMap™)

iMap™ (Boston Scientific Corporation, Natick, MA) has recently been introduced((News Release: Boston Scientific Announces Release of Next-Generation iLab® System Software Sep 21) as an up-to-date tissue characterization method that is compatible with the latest 40-MHz mechanical

Table 1. Current available techniques for plaque characterization based on greyscale IVUS

	VH-IVUS	iMap™	IB-IVUS	Palpography
Method of post-processing of RF signals	Autoregressive	Pattern recognition	Fast Fourier transformation	Cross-correlation at different time-points
Clinical studies	Extensive: necrotic core change in response to therapy and also for clinical outcome	Limited (case study and technical paper have only been published to date)	Extensive: compositional change after treatment and also for clinical outcome	Extensive validation studies for possible VPs. Outcome clinical results are pending.
Future perspectives	Extended clinical use (important further results from the "Global VH Registry" are anticipated)	Clinical results are awaited, (multi-frequency IVUS)	Current algorithm might be more precise qualitatively than VH-IVUS	Valuable adjunctive functional parameter to morphological characteristics
Limitations	Low resolution of grey-scale image of current catheter, thrombus	NA	Not widely available	Sensitive to technical errors, labour-intensive

RF = radiofrequency, NA = not applicable, VPs = vulnerable plaques

Figure 5. Visualization of calcified fibro-atheroma with iMapTM. Example of a motorized pullback in the left main trunk from our laboratory. IVUS pullback with a Atlantis® SR Pro catheter (Boston Scientific Corporation, Natick, MA) in proximal left coronary artery. On angiography (A) a calcified lesion is suspected in the very proximal part of the left main trunk. Conventional grey-scale IVUS (B) shows an extended superficial calcium in the lesion. On panel C the analysis with the iMapTM is shown: the fibrotic plaque along the left main turns into a lesion type of "calcified fibro-atheroma" according to tissue charactersiation. Necrotic areas behind calcium should be interpreted cautiosly.

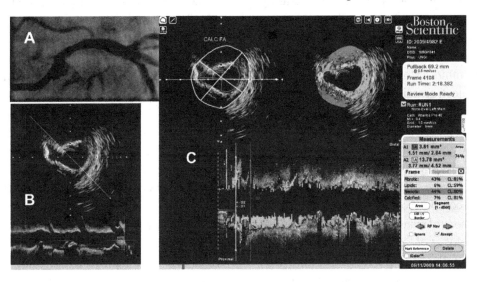

IVUS imaging system (as opposed to VH® IVUS with 20-MHz solid-state IVUS system). Also, a technical difference that this is not ECG-gated, instead, many frames/mm are captured. Thus, if the pullback speed at follow-up remains the same as at the index study, it will more likely result in the same length for volumetric analysis. Similar to other RF-based tissue characterization techniques, iMap allows identification and quantification of 4 different types of atherosclerotic plaque components: fibrotic, necrotic, lipidic, and calcified tissues (Figure 5). Ex-vivo validation using a swine animal model demonstrated accuracies at the highest level of confidence as: 97%, 98%, 95%, and 98% for necrotic, lipidic, fibrotic, and calcified tissues, respectively(Sathyanarayana, Carlier, Li, & Thomas, 2009). Unlike VH-IVUS utilizing a classification tree, iMap™ discriminates tissue types based upon the degree of spectral similarity between the received signals versus the reference library data obtained from known tissue types(Sathyanarayana *et al.*, 2009). This unique

approach provides a measure of the confidence for each region of interest characterized, along with a color-mapped presentation superimposed on the corresponding greyscale image. While the characterized tissue type is represented as color, the confidence is represented as transparency with high confidence characterizations shown with more solid color. Therefore, clinicians may use the reported confidence to estimate the probability of accurate classification on a pixel-by-pixel basis. However, clinical experiences with this new technology are preliminary: in a case with no-reflow phenomenon larger necrotic core was detected as opposed to other lesion of another ACS patient and that of a stable angina patient(Lin, Honye, & Saito, 2010). The authors note the advantage of high-resolution gray-scale images on which this algorithm (iMap™) is based on. There is also a unique novel technique under development, i.e. multi-frequency IVUS(Li, Carrillo, Jian, Tat-Jin, & Thomas, 2008).

VIRTUAL HISTOLOGY™ IVUS

Technique, Reproducibility and Interpretation

Data from VH-IVUS are currently acquired using a commercially available 64-element phased-array catheter (EagleEye™ 20 MHz catheter, Volcano Therapeutics). Using an automated pullback device, the transducer is withdrawn at a continuous speed of 0.5 mm/s up to the ostium. VH-IVUS acquisition is electrocardiogram (ECG)-gated at the R-wave peaks using a dedicated console. IVUS B-mode images are reconstructed using customized software, and contour detection is performed using cross-sectional views with semiautomatic contour detection software to provide quantitative geometrical and compositional measurements. Owing to the limitations of manual calibration(Rodriguez-Granillo, Aoki, *et al*., 2005), the radiofrequency data are normalized using a technique known as "blind deconvolution," an iterative algorithm that deconvolves the catheter transfer function from the backscatter, thus accounting for catheter-to-catheter variability(Kaaresen & Bolviken, 1999). The system (s5 for tower and s5i for the cath-lab integrated version) (http://volcanocorp.com/products/ivus-imaging/vh-ivus.asp) offers near–real-time tissue characterization in vivo via EagleEye™ series of catheters due to built-in automated characterisation algorithm(Nair *et al*., 2007).

A critical step in employing VH-IVUS in longitudinal studies or clinical trials is to establish the reproducibility of quantitation of vessel geometry and plaque composition. In one study(Rodriguez-Granillo, Bruining, *et al*., 2005), VH-IVUS data was acquired at 16 non-intervened lesions of 15 patients referred for elective percutaneous intervention (PCI). IVUS-VH interrogations were performed twice on each vessel and measurements were made by two blinded observers. Both inter-catheter and inter-observer differences were small (relative difference <1% intercatheter and <5%

inter-observer) for geometric measurements of vessel diameter and cross-sectional area (CSA). For measurements of plaque eccentricity, a value derived mathematically from plaque thickness, intra-observer and inter-observer differences were greater (relative difference of 5–10 and.50%, respectively). Inter-observer differences were, 10% for calcium CSA and necrotic core, while the inter-observer relative differences for fibrous and fibrolipidic CSA were greater (10 and 24%, respectively)(Rodriguez-Granillo, Bruining, *et al*., 2005). Following study confirmed the acceptable intraobserver reproducibilies; the volumetric measurement of the necrotic-core shows on average the highest reproducibility of the compositional RF-IVUS measurements(Hartmann *et al*., 2009). Another aspect of reproducibility(Huisman *et al*., 2010) is interobserver and intercenter (intraclass) variability. On 36 coronary segments in 4 different European centres the intraclass was tested here were significant but small differences for vessel, lumen, fibrous and calcified volumes, and there was no significant difference for plaque volume. Of the plaque components necrotic core and calcified volume showed on average the highest reproducibility (Huisman *et al*., 2010).

The technical details for acquisition and analysis of VH-IVUS examinations have recently been published as a recommendation of broad spectrum of experts in the field(Garcia-Garcia *et al*., 2009). We are not going to quote all of the very specific considerations regarding the "tips and tricks" of image acquisition. However, we emphasize the importance of clear and "large" R-wave to ensure on the ECG as a prerequisite for VH recording. Since every tomographic slice of VH images are created solely on the exact end-diastolic frame its computation can only be performed once per cardiac cycle, which significantly decreases the longitudinal resolution of VH. Although constant (ideally 0.5 mm/sec) pullback speed is recommended, it is obvious that higher heart rate will result in more data resulting in possible uncertainties of serial studies of atherosclerosis.

Figure 6. Different lesion types discriminated by VH-IVUS. (From: Garcia-Garcia HM et al. Euro-intervention 2009;5:177-189). Examples of VH-IVUS images classified by a two-dimensional lesion analysis. (IMT) intimal medial thickening; (PIT) pathological intimal thickening; (FT) fibrotic plaque; (FC) fibrocalcific plaque; (FA) fibroatheroma and (CaFA) calcified fibroatheroma; (VH-TCFA) Virtual Histology-thin cap fibroatheroma and (VH-CaTCFA) Virtual Histology-calcified thin cap fibroatheroma. Table gives the precise description different lesion types.

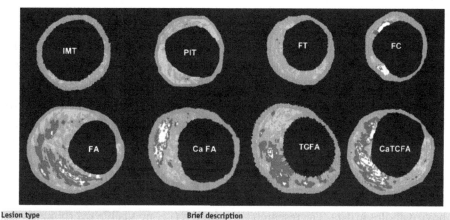

Lesion type	Brief description
Intimal Medial Thickening (IMT)	<600 μm of intima thickness
Pathological Intimal Thickening (PIT)	≥600 μm thickness for >20% of the circumference with FF >15%, and no confluent NC or DC
Fibrotic Plaque	Dominant FT and no confluent NC or DC
Fibrocalcific Plaque	>10% Confluent DC with no confluent NC
Fibroatheroma (FA)	>10% Confluent NC on three consecutive frames
Virtual Histology Thin Cap Fibroatheroma (VH-TCFA)	>10% Confluent NC on three consecutive frames and arc of NC in contact with the lumen for 36 degrees along lumen circumference

FT: fibrous tissue; FF: fibro-fatty tissue; ND: necrotic core; DC: dense calcium

Other technical limitations are also explained in this "white-paper" and suggestions for image analysis and reporting are given(Garcia-Garcia *et al.*, 2009). What is outstandingly important is that definitions of different VH-IVUS derived lesion types are also provided (Figure 6) (Garcia-Garcia *et al.*, 2009).

Improvements are already underway for volumetric measurements (including necrotic core): the Shin's method(Shin, Garcia-Garcia, & Serruys, 2010) might prevent uncertainty of volumetric measurements by delineating the IVUS catheter border rather than the lumen (also decreasing the impact of the usual "ring-down" artefact).

CLINICAL FINDINGS WITH VIRTUAL HISTOLOGY™

Results of Plaque Characterization in Relation to Patient Characteristics

Pathologic lesion classification is based on static images obtained from autopsy specimens(Virmani, Kolodgie, Burke, Farb, & Schwartz, 2000). The mechanism underlying lesion progression is the subject of continuous debate. Some believe that atherosclerotic lesion progression starts with pathologic intimal thickening in which lipid accumulates in areas rich in proteoglycans (lipid pools), but no trace of necrotic core. Others believe that the earliest change of atherosclerosis is the fatty streak, also called intimal xanthoma. The earliest lesion with a necrotic core is the fibroatheroma, and this is the precursor lesion that may give rise to symptomatic heart disease. Thin-capped fibroatheroma (TCFA) is a lesion characterized by a large necrotic core containing numerous cholesterol clefts(Virmani *et al.*, 2000). The overlying cap is thin and rich in inflammatory cells, macrophages and T-lymphocytes, with few smooth muscle cells. Plaques prone to rupture are those with thin cap thickness, large lipid–necrotic core, and severe inflammatory infiltrate. A study by Burke *et al.* identifed a cut-off value for cap thickness of <65 µm for vulnerable coronary plaque definition(Burke *et al.*, 1997).

VH-IVUS can potentially identify TCFAs. In addition, the progression of the disease can also be followed up. Figure 6 shows the plaque and lesion types defined by VH that are proposed based on the above pathologic data. The research group of Thoraxcenter, Rotterdam evaluated the incidence of IVUS-derived thin-cap fibroatheroma (ID-TCFA) using VH-IVUS(Rodriguez-Granillo, Garcia-Garcia, *et al.*, 2005). Two independent IVUS analysts defined ID-TCFA as a lesion fulfilling the following criteria in at least three consecutive cross-sectional areas: (1) necrotic core $\geq 10\%$ without evident overlying fibrous tissue, and (2) lumen obstruction $\geq 40\%$. In this study, 62% of patients had at least one ID-TCFA in the interrogated vessels. The number of ID-TCFAs per coronary artery was significantly higher in patients with acute coronary syndrome than in stable patients: 3.0 (interquartile range [IQR] 0.0 – 5.0) versus 1.0 (IQR 0.0 – 2.8) (P = 0.018). Finally, a clear clustering pattern was seen along the coronary arteries, with 66.7% of all ID-TCFAs located in the first 20 mm, whereas further along the vessels the incidence was significantly lower (33.3%, P = 0.008). This distribution of ID-TCFAs is consistent with previous ex vivo and clinical studies, with a clear clustering pattern from the ostium demonstrating a nonuniform distribution of vulnerable plaques along the coronary tree(Wang *et al.*, 2004). Patients presenting with acute coronary syndrome had a significantly higher prevalence of ID-TCFA

even in nonculprit vessels, supporting the concept of a multifocal process(Rioufol *et al.*, 2002). Of note, the proportion of the lesion area affected by stenosis and the mean area of necrotic core of the ID-TCFAs detected by VH-IVUS were also similar to previously reported histopathologic data (55.9% vs. 59.6% and 19% vs. 23%, respectively) (Virmani *et al.*, 2006).

Dedicated software has been developed to quantify the amount of necrotic core in contact with the lumen, enabling refinement of the analysis(Shin, Garcia-Garcia, & Serruys, 2010). The current definition of an IVUS-derived TCFA is a lesion fulfilling the following criteria in at least three consecutive cross-sectional areas (CSAs): (1) plaque burden of $\geq 40\%$ and (2) confluent necrotic core of $\geq 10\%$ in direct contact with the lumen (i.e. no visible overlying tissue) in the investigated CSA. All consecutive CSAs having the same morphologic characteristics are considered as part of the same ID-TCFA lesion(Garcia-Garcia *et al.*, 2006). In a study using this refined definition of TCFA, as assessed by VH-IVUS, in patients with acute coronary syndrome who underwent IVUS of all three epicardial coronaries, there were, on average, two IVUS-derived TCFAs per patient, with half of them showing outward remodeling(Garcia-Garcia *et al.*, 2006). The ratio of NC to calcification detected by VH-IVUS in diseased coronary segments is related to known risk factors for sudden coronary death (i.e. cigarette smoking and an increased total cholesterol-to-high-density lipoprotein cholesterol ratio), thus, may be associated with a worse prognosis(Missel *et al.*, 2008).

Identification of subclinical high-risk plaques is potentially important because they may be more likely to rupture and result in thrombosis. In 55 patients, a nonculprit vessel with < 50% diameter stenosis was studied with VH-IVUS. Mean necrotic core percentage was significantly higher in patients with acute coronary syndrome (ACS) than in stable patients (12.26%±7.0% vs. 7.40%±5.5%, p=0.006). In addition, stable patients showed more fibrotic vessels (70.97%±9.3% vs. 63.96%±9.1%, p=0.007)(Rodriguez-Granillo, McFadden, *et al.*, 2006). However, not only is the amount of necrotic core content larger in patients with acute coronary syndrome, but it appears that necrotic core is also unevenly distributed. In 51 consecutive patients, a nonculprit vessel was investigated using VH-IVUS. The overall length of the region of interest, subsequently divided into 10-mm segments, was 41.5±13 mm. No significant change was observed in terms of relative plaque composition along the vessel with respect to fibrous, fibrofatty, and calcified tissue, whereas the percentage of necrotic core was higher in the first (median 8.75%; IQR 5.7 –18) than in the third (median 6.1%; IQR 3.2 –12) (p=0.036) and fourth (median 4.5%; IQR 2.4 – 7.9) (p=0.006) segments. At multivariable regression analysis, distance from the ostium was an independent predictor of relative necrotic content (beta = −0.28 [95% CI −0.15 to −0.41]), together with older age, unstable presentation, no use of statins, and the presence of diabetes mellitus(Valgimigli *et al.*, 2006).

Although, ID-TCFAs are the most frequent cause of plaque rupture and consequent ACS, the around 20% of cases is linked to another pathological substrate, i.e. plaque erosion and focal superficial calcium(Virmani *et al.*, 2006). Calcium deposits were detected also with IVUS(Ehara *et al.*, 2004); but a direct relationship between this "spotty calcification" and coronary events (in line with pathological substrate of "calcified nodule") cannot be justified as yet. On a recent IB-IVUS analysis(Inaba *et al.*, 2009), the average degree of all the spotty calcifications negatively correlated with the percent lipid volume on IB-IVUS; somewhat pointing at the pathological process of lesion "aging" when lipids are replaced by necrotic then calcifying tissues. Plaque erosions are more common in young women and men <50 years of age and are associated with smoking, especially in premenopausal women(Virmani *et al.*, 2000). We have very limited knowledge on the substrate of plaque erosion in terms of IVUS

in vivo investigations, but a very recent interesting article proposes use of VH in clarification of mechanism of apical balloning syndrome for investigation plaque characteristics(Pawlowski, Mintz, Kulawik, & Gil, 2010). This syndrome is almost unique to women and its pathologic substrate might well be plaque erosion. However, in this report, VH found TCFAs and necrotic core in these patients(Pawlowski *et al.*, 2010). In somewhat contrast lesions in patients with variant angina (vasospasm) shows different pattern, ie. negative remodeling and less TCFA or necrotic core than patients with unstable angina(Young Joon *et al.*, 2009). Lesions at bifurcations are prone to have TCFAs(Gonzalo *et al.*, 2009).

Vulnerable Plaque Identification (PROSPECT)

The PROSPECT (Providing Regional Observations to Study Predictors of Events in the Coronary Tree) trial is a first-of-its-kind multicenter, natural history study of ACS patients(PROSPECT, Study., & ClinicalTrials.gov, 2006). All patients underwent PCI in their culprit lesion at baseline. Following the PCI procedure, an angiogram and a detailed IVUS (including virtual histology and palpography) image was captured in the three major coronary arteries. Patients were clinically followed up for three years(Stone *et al.*, 2011). Most untreated plaques (on angiography causing only mild stenosis) which become symptomatic have a large plaque burden and small lumen area (which are detectable by IVUS but not significantly stenosed on angiography). The highest risk PROSPECT plaque type being VH-TCFAs with a minimum lumen area of ≤ 4 mm^2 and a large plaque burden ($\geq 70\%$), had a 17.2% likelihood of causing an event within 3 years [HR 10.8 (95% CI 4.3–27.2), P<0.001] (Figure 7). If IVUS-detected luminal stenosis was extracted, the likelihood of event at lesion level(!) remained 15.3% if identified as VH-TCFA (in contrast to that of the type pathological intimal thickening), underlying the

Figure 7. Result of the Prospect study: presence of VH identified features of high-risk (i.e. VH-TCFA or TCFA on the figure) is a predictor of MACE rate at the lesion site. From: Stone GW et al. A prospective natural history study of coronary atherosclerosis. N Engl J Med. 2011 Jan 20;364(3):226-35.

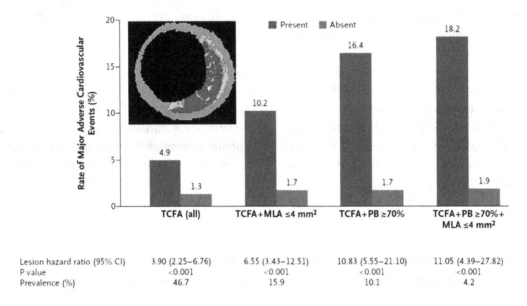

	TCFA (all)	TCFA+MLA ≤4 mm²	TCFA+PB ≥70%	TCFA+PB ≥70%+ MLA ≤4 mm²
Lesion hazard ratio (95% CI)	3.90 (2.25–6.76)	6.55 (3.43–12.51)	10.83 (5.55–21.10)	11.05 (4.39–27.82)
P value	<0.001	<0.001	<0.001	<0.001
Prevalence (%)	46.7	15.9	10.1	4.2

importance of plaque composition (Stone *et al.*, 2011). Thus, one can say that VH-IVUS is capable to detect this 3-fold increased hazard of resulting in future major adverse cardiovascular events, independent of clinical characteristics, biomarkers, and other greyscale IVUS characteristics. As we can see, luminal stenosis (as defined in miminal lumen area, but below the cut-off of angiographically significant diameter stenosis) is also predictive for future events. However, VH-TCFA appeared to be stronger predictor in PROSPECT in the multivariate analysis of independent predictors of lesion level events (Table 2) (Stone *et al.*, 2011).

Accordingly, in another in vivo human study showed that the site of minimal lumen area is rarely at the site of greatest instability (defined as largest NC and remodeling)(Kaple *et al.*, 2009). Additionally, in PROSPECT the prevalance of VH-TCFA among the examined ACS patients (considered as having multifoci plaque instability) was only 11%. Indeed, in an analysis of PROSPECT data showed that approximately half of patients presenting with ACS have no addi-tional VH-TCFAs (in detail 27.3% having 1 VH-TCFA, 12.0% having 2 VH-TCFAs, 6.2% having 3 VH-TCFAs)(McPherson, Maehara, Mintz, Serruys, & Stone, 2010). Thus, one can say that (in contrast to previous belief) TCFAs occur focally and are limited in extent which is reflecting the results of an important pathology study showing TCFAs limited in number(Cheruvu *et al.*, 2007).

As we earlier pointed out, cut-off value for cap thickness of <65 µm for vulnerable coronary plaque was found in pathological examinations(Burke *et al.*, 1997). Since IVUS has resolution beyont this threshold, its capability of identifying vulnerable plaques is restricted. Another newly developed intravascular imaging modality is optical coherence tomography (OCT; detailed in another chapter of this book), which can accurately measure the thickness of the fibrous cap(Cilingiroglu *et al.*, 2006). With its rapidly improving quality OCT offers a number of specific diagnostic features to study culprit lesions in patients suffering from ACS(Regar *et al.*, 2010). The Thoraxcentre group have introduced a new approach to study

Table 2. Independent correlates of major adverse cardiovascular events related to nonculprit lesions during follow-up*

Correlates	Hazard Ratio [95% CI]	P value
Predictors of patient-level events†		
Insulin-requiring diabetes	3.32 [1.43, 7.72]	0.005
Prior PCI	2.03 [1.15, 3.59]	0.02
Predictors of events at individual lesion sites‡		
Plaque-burden ≥70%	5.03 [2.51, 10.11]	<0.0001
VH-TCFA	3.35 [1.77, 6.36]	0.0002
MLA ≤4.0 mm2	3.21 [1.61, 6.42]	0.001

* Major adverse cardiovascular events comprised death from cardiac causes, cardiac arrest, myocardial infarction, and rehospitalization for unstable or progressive angina. MLA denotes minimal luminal area.

† Demographic, clinical, and laboratory-based variables were considered for entry into the patient-level multivariate regression model. The final variables entered were age, sex, hypertension, insulin-requiring diabetes, previous percutaneous coronary intervention, baseline C-reactive protein level, and family history of premature coronary artery disease.

‡ Angiographic and ultrasonographic variables, as well as the significant patient-level predictors, were considered for entry into the lesion-level multivariate regression model. The final variables entered were MLA, plaque burden at the MLA, external elastic membrane at the MLA, lesion length, distance from the coronary ostium to the MLA, remodeling index, thin-cap fibroatheroma, insulin-requiring diabetes, and previous percutaneous coronary intervention.

An MLA of 4.0 mm2 or less and a plaque burden of 70% or more were prespecified for use in this model, since they have been used frequently in previous studies. However, the same variables (plaque burden, MLA, and TCFA) were identified as the three independent determinants of future cardiac events associated with specific nonculprit lesions in post hoc multivariate models that incorporated MLA and plaque burden as continuous data or with cutoff points selected on the basis of receiver-operating-characteristic curves.

potentially vulnerable plaques by combination of VH-IVUS and OCT(Gonzalo *et al.*, 2010). Subsequently, they compared plaque classification by OCT, VH-IVUS, and a combination of both(Goderie *et al.*, 2010). The combined data yielded more correct classifications than either technique alone, although differences were small. VH-IVUS showed a high-false-negative rate for fibroatheroma, while in the OCT data, they found a large number of false positives for this plaque type(Goderie *et al.*, 2010). One can expect that, before development of a completely new imaging modality, this combinative approach will increase our understanding of the pathophysiology and the prevention of ACS.

Controlling Medical Therapy with VH-IVUS

Theoretically, medical interventions (especially the ones aiming at cholesterol lowering) that slow the progression of atherosclerotic disease should also improve clinical outcomes(Nicholls *et al.*). Previous studies using coronary angiography and carotid ultrasound have established a strong relationship between the extent of disease, its rate of progression, and subsequent cardiovascular morbidity and mortality(O'Leary *et al.*, 1999; Ringqvist *et al.*, 1983). These findings have even prompted regulatory authorities to permit labeling of therapies on the basis of their effects on atherosclerosis progression. However, from methodological(Brown & Zhao, 2007) and clinical(Finn, Chandrashekhar, & Narula) reasons grey-scale IVUS might not be the ideal modality to find appropriate surrogate endpoint for replacement large-scale clinical trials. Indeed by IB-IVUS a significant reduction in lipid volume and corresponding increase in fibrous lesion volume has been demonstrated in response to statins(Kawasaki *et al.*, 2005). The change in lipid volume occurred without significant changes in lumen area and diameter stenosis, indicating plaque stabilization and changes in plaque characteristics before geometric plaque regression. Similarly, wavelet analysis of radiofrequency IVUS signals allows mathematical assessment of focal differences within arterial walls. Color coding of the wavelet correlation coefficient detects changes in the geometric profile of time-series signals to derive an image of plaque components, as validated in necropsy or directional atherectomy specimens(Murashige *et al.*, 2005).

A recent elegant study of serial VH-IVUS aimed to investigate what type of lesions would show plaque regression or other signs of plaque stabilization(Hong, Jeong, Choi, *et al.*, 2010). Sixty-six patients who underwent baseline and 9-month follow-up virtual histology plus intravascular ultrasound for nonintervened intermediate coronary stenosis were grouped according to plaque progression (increase of plaque plus media area, n=22) or plaque regression (decrease of plaque plus media area, n=44) at baseline minimum lumen area (MLA) site at follow-up and compared the various parameters including baseline plaque components between the 2 groups. Baseline percent necrotic core (NC) area was significantly larger (26.1±10.9% vs 17.6±10.8%, p=0.004) and baseline percent fibrofatty area was significantly smaller (8.1±6.2% vs 14.2±12.1%, p=0.008) at the MLA site in the progression group compared to the regression group. TCFA was observed more frequently in the progression group compared to the regression group (32% vs 9%, p=0.02). Change of plaque plus media area from baseline to follow-up at the MLA site correlated with baseline percent NC area (r=0.375, p=0.002), baseline percent fibrofatty area (r=-0.388, p=0.001). Thus it seems that size of necrotic core is a strong predictor of plaque progression(Hong, Jeong, Choi, *et al.*, 2010). This is in line with observation by Nicholls *et al.* who reported that calcified plaques are more resistant to undergoing changes in size in response to systemic interventions targeting atherosclerotic risk factors(Nicholls *et al.*, 2007).

There are some studies on the effect of statins on VH-identified plaque changes. Nasu *et al.* detected significant regression of plaque volume and alterations in atherosclerotic plaque composition with a significant reduction of fibro-fatty volume after one-year lipid-lowering therapy by fluvastatin(Nasu *et al.*, 2009). As it is anticipated, higher doses of atorvastatin slowed down NC expansion more than low-dose at 6-month follow-up VH-IVUS in the VENUS study(S. W. Lee, Hau, Kong, & Chan, 2010). Interestingly, not only long-term but as early as 2-3 weeks of a potent statin administration resulted in plaque regression in a study by Japanese investigators(Toi *et al.*, 2009). After treatment, total cholesterol and low-density lipoprotein-cholesterol (LDL-C) showed significant decreases to similar levels in each group (p<0.001). But the pitavastatin group (2 mg/day), the plaque volume index and fibrofatty volume index (FFVI) also decreased significantly compared to baseline and no change in the atorvastatin (10 mg/day) group(Toi *et al.*, 2009). Other medication might also have a positive role in plaque stabilization/regression; studies are underway with VH-IVUS, first results with an angiotensin-receptor blocker has been reported(Inoue, Ueshima, Fujimoto, & Kihyon, 2010).

There is a recently reported specific concept targeting vulnerable plaques with a medication and its control by VH (Serruys *et al.*, 2008). Lipoprotein-associated phospholipase A2 (Lp-PLA2) is expressed abundantly in the necrotic core of coronary lesions and products of its enzymatic activity may contribute to inflammation and cell death, rendering plaque vulnerable to rupture(Bhatti, Hakeem, & Cilingiroglu, 2010). The IBIS 2 study (IBIS = Integrated Biomarker and Imaging Study) compared the effects of 12 months of treatment with darapladib (oral Lp-PLA2 inhibitor, 160 mg daily) or placebo on coronary atheroma deformability (IVUS-palpography) and plasma hsCRP in 330 patients with angiographically documented coronary disease. Secondary end-points included changes in necrotic core size (IVUS-VH), atheroma size (IVUS-greyscale), and blood biomarkers.

Background therapy was comparable between groups, with no difference in LDLcholesterol at 12 months (placebo: 88 ± 34 and darapladib: 84 ± 31 mg/dL, p=0.37). In contrast, Lp-PLA2 activity was inhibited by 59% with darapladib (p<0.001 versus placebo). After 12 months, there were no significant differences between groups in plaque deformability (p=0.22) or plasma hsCRP (p=0.35). In the placebo-treated group, however, necrotic core volume increased significantly, whereas darapladib halted this increase, resulting in a significant treatment difference of −5.2 mm3 (p=0.012). These intra-plaque compositional changes occurred without a significant treatment difference in total atheroma volume (p=0.95). Despite adherence to a high level of standard of care treatment, the necrotic core continued to expand among patients receiving placebo. In contrast, Lp-PLA2 inhibition with darapladib prevented necrotic core expansion(Serruys *et al.*, 2008).

Virtual Histology and Plaque Rupture

The Thoraxcenter group described(Rodriguez-Granillo, Garcia-Garcia, Valgimigli, Vaina, *et al.*, 2006) the ruptured plaque profile assessed by VH-IVUS in a prospective study of 40 patients referred for cardiac catheterization. There were 13 patients with stable angina, 12 with unstable angina, and 15 with acute myocardial infarction. The risk factors were fairly typical of patients with coronary artery disease: 10% of patients had diabetes, 73% were male, 38% were smokers, and 50% had elevated cholesterol. Of note, the impact of risk factors were subsequently analyzed in the frame of the large-scale international global virtual histology registry(Philipp *et al.*, 2010). Marked differences were detected in coronary plaque composition related to the risk factor profile: greater amounts of NC were associated with diabetes, hypertension, MI, and low HDL-C(Philipp *et al.*, 2010). In the above mentioned study ruptured plaque was identified in 26 patients and, as expected, was more frequent in patients

with acute myocardial infarction and unstable angina. Patients with ruptured plaques had a larger body mass index than those without plaque rupture and were more likely to be smokers, and patients with ruptures had more widespread calcification and a larger area of necrotic core. Of note, the location of plaque ruptures in this study mirrors the pathologic findings(Rodriguez-Granillo, Garcia-Garcia, Valgimigli, Vaina, *et al.*, 2006). In this study, the LAD was the most common site of plaque rupture, in which it was usually proximal, whereas in the RCA, rupture was as frequently found mid-artery as in the proximal segment. In a pathologic series of 79 ruptures, Burke *et al.*(Burke, Joner, & Virmani, 2006) found that, out of 34 ruptures in the LAD, 25 (74%) were in the proximal segment. In contrast, out of 28 ruptures in the RCA, only 10 (36%) were in the proximal segment, 12 in the mid-artery, and six in the distal segment. Similarly, in pathologic studies and in this study, in the LCx only one-fourth were located in the proximal part, with the rest located distally or in the obtuse marginal branches(Rodriguez-Granillo, Garcia-Garcia, Valgimigli, Vaina, *et al.*, 2006). We have to add that not only the VH-features above can point at possible rupture of the plaque but presence or absence of calcification and number of focal or layered calcific deposits (presumed evidence of previous rupture)(Garcia-Garcia *et al.*, 2009).

Originally plaque rupture was described occurring on very thin-capped TCFAs (Kolodgie *et al.*, 2001). Indeed, the preceding lesion type on the road to rupture resemble in morphology to rupture itself(Finn, Nakano, Narula, Kolodgie, & Virmani, 2010). Since the spatial resolution of VH-IVUS is well beyond this thin cap cut-off (65 µm), this might question its ability to prospectively detect the plaques which will really exhibit rupture in the future. At last, we do have a natural history study with VH-IVUS (i.e. the PROSPECT study) supporting its use. In turn, a new report by Virmani *et al.* stated that many plaques with "thin fibrous cap" do not present rupture and also emphasized the independent predictive value of NC size for impending rupture(Finn, Nakano, *et al.*, 2010), which notion further justify ongoing research with this technology for detecting high-risk plaque for rupture.

Virtual Histology and Coronary Stenting

Recently, two studies have evaluated the usefulness of VH-IVUS plaque composition to predict the risk of embolization during stenting(Kawaguchi *et al.*, 2007; Kawamoto *et al.*, 2007). One included 71 patients with ST-elevation myocardial infarction who underwent primary PCI within 12 h of onset of the symptoms. After crossing the lesion with a guidewire and performing thrombectomy with an aspiration catheter, VH-IVUS of the infarct-related vessel was performed. The stent was then deployed without embolic protection. During stenting, ST segment re-elevation was used as a marker of distal embolization. Eleven patients presented with ST segment re-elevation after stenting. Total plaque volume was similar in both groups, but the necrotic core volume was significantly higher in the group of patients with ST segment re-elevation (32.9 ± 14.1 mm^3 vs. 20.4 ± 19.1 mm^3, p<0.05). On receiver operating characteristic curves, necrotic core volume was a better predictor of ST re-elevation after stent deployment than fibrous, fibrofatty, dense calcium, and total plaque volumes. The cut-off point for necrotic core volume that was highly predictive for ST re-elevation was 33.4 mm^3, with a sensitivity of 81.7% and a specificity of 63.6%(Kawaguchi *et al.*, 2007). The second study(Kawamoto *et al.*, 2007) included 44 patients who underwent elective coronary stenting. Plaque composition was assessed with VH-IVUS, and small embolic particles liberated during stenting were detected as high-intensity transient signals (HITS) with a Doppler guidewire. Patients were divided into the tertiles according to the HITS counts. Dense calcium and necrotic core area were significantly

larger in the highest tertile. In the multivariate logistic regression analysis, only necrotic core area was an independent predictor of high HITS counts (odds ratio 4.41, P = 0.045)(Kawamoto *et al.*, 2007).

Risk of embolization during stenting was further studied in ACS patients; post-stenting no-reflow was associated with plaque components defined by VH-IVUS analysis with larger NC and more TCFAs(Hong *et al.*, 2009). As mentioned above patients presenting with ACS tend to have attenuated plaque on greyscale IVUS which have deleterious features also during PCI (e.g. predicting distal embolization following stent deployment)(Kawamoto *et al.*, 2007). On a recent VH retrospective analysis on PROSPECT patients (Figure 8) these plaques showed larger amount of necrotic core when compared to the ones at the minimum luminal sites of 65 control vessels(Wu *et al.*, 2010). The authors concluded that this feature being a marker of the presence of fibroatheromas (VH-TCFA or VH-ThFA) may explain the biologic instability of these lesions (Wu *et al.*, 2010). Indeed, VH analysis of culprit lesions in STEMI patients revealed necrotic core volume as predictive for ST-segment re-elevation (sign of distal embolization)(Kawaguchi *et al.*, 2007). The above mentioned Shin's method was tested to better characterize patients prone to post-PCI CK-elevation and since it is less time-consuming it might help "real-time" clinical decision making for stenting procedure(Shin, Garcia-Garcia, Garg, *et al.*, 2010). Plaque embolization during carotid stenting is also a potential area for utilization of this technology(Timaran *et al.*, 2010).

There is an emerging clinical application (often dubbed as the "culprit of the culprit") where VH-IVUS has the potential to help improve the technical success of treating culprit lesions in acute patients, especially STEMI. Because plaque rupture sites that lead to clinical events are often found proximal to the luminal narrowing, they can be missed up to 60% of the time if relying on angiography alone, resulting in stent edges land-

Figure 8. Example of an "attenuated plaque". (From: Wu X, Maehara A, Mintz GS, et al. Virtual histology intravascular ultrasound analysis of non-culprit attenuated plaques detected by grayscale intravascular ultrasound in patients with acute coronary syndromes. Am J Cardiol 2010; 105:48-53). Attenuated plaque versus nonattenuated plaque in grayscale IVUS and VH-IVUS. An attenuated plaque studied using grayscale IVUS (A) and VH-IVUS (B) and a nonattenuated plaque studied using grayscale IVUS (C) and VH-IVUS (D).

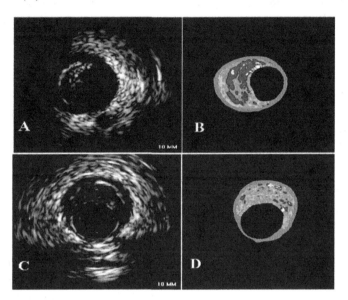

ing in or completely missing necrotic core. VH-IVUS can identify the necrotic core and plaque burden typical of ruptured atheromas responsible for thrombotic events. In stable patient, there has always been attempts to optimize stent implantation by IVUS but evidences were not substantial enough to raise the indication to a guideline level. There is a study (called ATHEROREMO) being conducted where after optimal PCI (by QCA <30% residual stenosis) VH-IVUS was performed in 100 patients to assess complete lesion coverage, i.e. plaque burden less then 40% and NC confluent to the lumen less then 10% should ideally remain only(Sarno, Garg, Gomez-Lara, & Serruys, 2010). Significantly more percent of patients has optimal stent placement when controlled by VH-IVUS than in those only with documentation with VH(Sarno *et al.*, 2010). Thus, VH-IVUS in the long-term might prove to be a valuable tool for stent optimization in most of our PCI practice.

Specifically, drug-eluting stent (DES) implantation is another field with some encouraging results already been published. Plaque prolapse might have an impact on failure of DES-therapy; a recent study showed that NC and fibrotic components were associated with development of plaque prolapse; and NC and fibrotic components in prolapsed plaque were associated with cardiac enzyme elevation after DES implantation(Hong, Jeong, Kim, *et al.*, 2010). To determine which VH-IVUS parameter is a predictor of stent thrombosis, the ADAPT-DES study(http://clinicaltrials.gov/ ct2/show/NCT00638794) has a VH-substudy in 3000 patients (according to a report of Volcano Corporation (http://volcanocorp.com/clinical/ clinical-studies-trials.asp)). However, there is already a published serial VH-IVUS analysis(Kubo *et al.*, 2010) of DES-treated lesions which showed a greater frequency of unstable lesion morphometry at follow-up compared with BMS. The apparent mechanism was a suppression of the protective neointimal hyperplasia layer coupled with a lack of vulnerable plaque resolution at reference segments in DES compared with BMS (Kubo *et al.*, 2010).

Another growing utilization of VH-IVUS is the examination of newly-developed bioabsorbable stents (or scaffolds)(Ormiston *et al.*, 2008). In a detailed analysis with multiple imaging methods, VH-IVUS assessments showed that the percentage of each plaque component did not differ significantly between 6 months and 2 years. The absolute fibrofatty area and fibrous plaque area decreased significantly between 6 months and 2 years. When compared with measurements taken immediately after the procedure, none of the 2-year parameters differed significantly, apart from necrotic core area(Serruys *et al.*, 2009). There temporal change in plaque behind the struts interestingly revealed a significant progression of necrotic core but the area contacting the lumen did not change(Brugaletta *et al.*).

LIMITATIONS OF VH-IVUS

As discussed above reproducibility (interobserver variability) is good (Rodriguez-Granillo, Bruining, *et al.*, 2005). However a study observed that between-center reproducibility was not really satisfying (Huisman *et al.*, 2010). This is of paramount importance taking into account that increasing number of multicenter studies are being launched with this technology. Here can be be listed technical imperfections (non-uniform pullback speed, border segmentation problems) or other, such as the classification tree does not recognize thrombus(Nasu *et al.*, 2008). Accordingly, for volume analysis conventional greyscale images obtained by mechanical high-frequency catheters might prove better. In this respect, iMap from Boston Scientific Corporation and 45-MHz catheter from Volcano Corporation is also being tested in humans for the use of VH software.

New finding using adult atherosclerosis-prone minipigs questioned the value of VH-derived necrotic core measurement(Thim *et al.*, 2010). However, this study was carried out by well-known researchers experienced in this field, its validity has been crutinized by the letter of Stone and Mintz(Stone & Mintz), with many points could be well taken, e.g. precision of matching the image sample to the autopsy sections and the scattered correlations points of the study's main finding. Moreover, there is also a concern on suitability of porcine model of atherosclerotic arteries for the assessment of human coronary artery disease, which is concordant with the finding of Granada *et al.* that complex lesions were not accurately analyized by VH software(Granada *et al.*, 2007). However, in a rabbit model VH-IVUS had a high sensitivity, specificity and positive predictive value for the detection of non-calcified thin cap fibroatheroma (88%, 96%, 87%, respectively) and calcified thin cap fibroatheroma (95%, 99%, 93%, respectively)(Van Herck *et al.*, 2009).

There is an ongoing controversy whether VH-IVUS can see behind calcium (example on Figure 9). If there is a solid "rock" of calcium, then VH-IVUS cannot see behind the calcium, in a porcine pathological investigation VH-IVUS often misidentified calcium in the absence of histological calcification(Granada *et al.*, 2007). Solid "rocks" of calcium can be superficial (near the lumen) or deep (near the adventitia). Conversely, if the calcium is non-confluent with gaps of approximately 100 microns (typical with speckled calcium that is present in a necrotic core), then some signal is present even if it is attenuated. On VH-IVUS imaging large confluent calcium deposits can be solid "rocks" of calcium or represent multiple, nearby, calcium deposits and it is described that dense calcium on the measurement of necrotic tissue causes overestimation its quantity(Sales *et al.*, 2010). It is also unclear how often there is a definable signal and how often there is mostly noise; the current hardware and software do not make this distinction. Therefore, in some cases, the signal behind calcium is mostly noise while in other cases it contains useful data. Studies are

Figure 9. "Plaque behind calcium". A non-significant stenosis in proximal LAD of a patients shows superficial calcium on grey-scale conventional IVUS (panel A shows the image of EagleEye Gold catheter, panel B shows image of Atlantis SR Pro catheter). On VH-IVUS "Calcified fibro-atheroma" can be identified. However fibrotic component behind the superficial calcified spot at 12 o'clock should be considered cautiously.

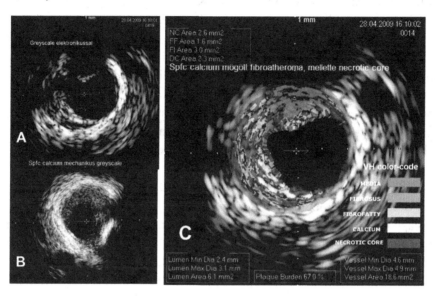

currently underway to determine when there is enough signal to accurately assess plaque composition behind calcium and when there is mostly noise and the signal ambiguous. Nevertheless, in the case of both solid and speckled (or multifocal) calcium, shadowing caused by the presence of calcifications necessitates extrapolation of the EEM contours(Garcia-Garcia *et al.*, 2009).

FROM ELASTOGRAPHY TO PALPOGRAPHY AND MODULOGRAPHY: TECHNIQUE AND CLINICAL RESULTS

Basics of the Technology

As already pictured on Figure 2, RF data can also be calculated in a different way, i.e. cross correlation analysis. Céspedes *et al.*(Cespedes, Ophir, Ponnekanti, & Maklad, 1993) and Ophir *et al.*(Ophir, Cespedes, Ponnekanti, Yazdi, & Li,

1991) developed an imaging technique called elastography, which was based on tissue deformation. The rate of deformation (strain) of the tissue is directly related to the mechanical properties. The tissue under inspection is deformed and the strain between pairs of ultrasound signals before and after deformation is determined(Cespedes, Huang, Ophir, & Spratt, 1995). For intravascular purposes, the compression can be obtained from the pressure difference in the artery. The principle of intravascular elastography is based on ultrasound images of a human coronary artery are acquired at different intracoronary pressures; the second acquisition at a slightly lower pressure (~3 mmHg) is performed. The strain is determined by estimating displacement of the RF signals of the two IVUS images(Schaar, de Korte, Mastik, Baldewsing, *et al.*, 2003). The local displacement of the tissue is determined using cross-correlation analysis of the depth-gated RF signals. A cross-correlation function between two shifted RF signals will have its maximum at the displacement that will align these signals. For each angle, starting from the lumen boundary, the displacement of a layer (225 µm) of tissue is determined. Then the displacement of the next (225 µm) layer of tissue is determined. The strain of the tissue can be calculated by dividing the differential displacement (displacement of proximal layer - displacement of distal layer) by the distance between these two layers. When the strain is determined for multiple layers in depth, a color-coded two-dimensional (2D) image of the strain can be constructed. The elastogram (image of the radial strain) is plotted as a complimentary image to the IVUS image. The elastogram shows the presence of an eccentric region with increased strain values at the shoulders of the eccentric plaque. Because the acting force of the blood pressure is applied on the lumen boundary a surface-based assessment of the mechanical properties - called palpography - was developed assessing the first 450 µm layer, in contrast to elastography, which assesses the entire plaque. This robust technique(Schaar, de Korte, Mastik, Baldewsing, *et al.*, 2003) is easier to interpret and is based on the same cross-correlation technique. Palpography derives mechanical information of the surface of the plaque, where the rupture may happen. This information is color-coded and superimposed on the IVUS image.

Intravascular ultrasound palpography was validated in vivo using an atherosclerotic Yucatan minipig(de Korte *et al.*, 2002). In total, 20 cross sections were investigated with a 20-MHz Visions catheter (Volcano). The tissue was strained by the pulsatile blood pressure. Two frames acquired at end-diastole with a pressure differential of ~3 mm Hg were taken to determine the elastograms. Strains were similar in the plaque-free arterial wall and the early and advanced fibrous plaques. Univariate analysis of variance revealed significantly higher strain values in cross-sections with early fatty lesions than with fibrous plaques (p=0.02) independently of the presence of macrophages. the presence of a high strain region had a high sensitivity (92%) and specificity (92%) to identify

the presence of macrophages. Therefore, it was concluded that the tissue type dominates the mean strain value. Localized high strain values are related to local phenomena such as inflammation(de Korte *et al.*, 2002). However, early during its development researchers tried to detect possible sources of error in elastography(Konofagou & Ophir, 1998). These errors result in potential inaccuracies in strain estimates due to out of plane motion, catheter eccentricity, and tilt(Konofagou & Ophir, 1998). Since then there has been several technical refinement to address these; some of them we give details hereof.

New Developments in Palpography

Geometry of the vessel and catheter position distorts the accuracy of the aquired elastogramm. The dependence and the correspondence of these can be quantified with a proper finite element model (FEM)(Baldewsing, de Korte, Schaar, Mastik, & van der Steen, 2004). This method demonstrated that the FEM can simulate elastograms measured from arteries. As such, the FEM may help in quantifying strain-dependencies and assist in tissue characterization by reconstructing a Young's modulus image from a measured elastogram(Baldewsing *et al.*, 2004). An addition to current strain measurement has been introduced also by the Thoraxcenter group called modulography(Baldewsing *et al.*, 2008). This implies an inverse method for imaging the local elasticity of atherosclerotic coronary plaques and is capable of reconstructing a heterogeneous Young's modulus distribution. Therefore it has the potential to correct for heterogeneous elastic material composition of complex plaques (Baldewsing *et al.*, 2008). Recently, another iteration of this approach was published aiming at precise measurement of peak cap stress amplitude which is considered a major indicator for future plaque rupture(Le Floc'h *et al.*, 2010). Also, peak radial and circumferential strain measured by velocity vector imaging is a novel index for detecting vulnerable plaques in a rabbit model of atherosclerosis(Zhang *et al.*, 2010).

In palpography, out-of-plane motion is considered one of the main sources for decorrelation (= lack of correlation) of the signals, thus decreasing the quality of the strain estimate(Kallel & Ophir, 1998; Konofagou & Ophir, 1998). However, if the pullback speed is only 1 mm/s and the strain is determined using two subsequent frames, the motion introduced by the pullback is minimal. Furthermore, it is known that due to the contraction of the heart, in diastole the catheter will move distally in the coronary if the catheter is kept in a steady position. Therefore, performing a pullback will decrease out-of-plane motion in this phase of the heart cycle. Since elastography uses data acquired in the diastolic phase, performing a pullback and thus obtaining 3-D data seems feasible. This technology was originally patented to the Biomedical Engineering group of the Thoraxcenter, Rotterdam(van der Steen, de Korte, Mastik, & Schaar, 2003). Preliminary experiments in rabbit aortas revealed that 3-D palpography is feasible in vivo. Despite the introduction of out-of-plane motion by the continuous pullback of the catheter, the similarity between successive frames acquired in the diastolic phase is high enough to calculate several palpograms per heart cycle. By combining these palpograms, one compound palpogram per heart cycle is determined (Doyley *et al.*, 2001). In a recent study(Schaar, Regar, *et al.*, 2004) in humans, 3-D palpograms were derived from continuous IVUS pullbacks of entire coronary arteries. Stable angina patients had significantly fewer deformable plaques per vessel (0.6±0.6) than did unstable angina patients (1.6±0.7, P<0.0019) or AMI patients (2.0±0.7, P <0.0001) (Schaar, Regar, *et al.*, 2004).

Both palpography and VH use IVUS radiofrequency analysis (RFA) and are acquired in the same IVUS pullback. A new combined imaging assessment(Rodriguez-Granillo, Garcia-Garcia, Valgimigli, Schaar, *et al.*, 2006) might allow a more accurate and complete characterization in vivo of allegedly high-risk plaques. Thereby, it may offer the opportunity to truly identify the number of high-risk plaques in vivo. The Thoraxcenter group has previously studied the relationship between them, analyzing 123 matched cross-sectional areas (CSAs) from two different transducers (20 MHz and 30 MHz) of the same vessel. In this preliminary study, the mean strain value was higher in CSAs with necrotic core in contact with the lumen (NCCL) than in CSAs with no NCCL (1.03±0.5 vs 0.86±0.4, *P*=0.06). The sensitivity, specificity, positive predictive value, and negative predictive value of IVUS-VH to detect high strain were 75.0%, 44.4%, 56.3%, and 65.1% respectively(Rodriguez-Granillo, Garcia-Garcia, Valgimigli, Schaar, *et al.*, 2006). This, as yet labour-intensive methodology holds great promise for future studies to reveal the relation of functional and compositional features of high-risk plaques.

Clinical Results with Palpography

Palpography allows the assessment of local mechanical tissue properties. At any given pressure, soft tissue (e.g., lipid-rich) components will deform more than hard tissue components (e.g., fibrous, calcified)(Schaar, De Korte, Mastik, Strijder, *et al.*, 2003; Schaar, Regar, *et al.*, 2004). RF data obtained at different pressure levels are compared to determine the local tissue deformation. Each palpogram represents the strain information for a certain cross-section over the full cardiac cycle. Palpograms are acquired using a 20-MHz phased-array IVUS catheter (Eagle Eye™ 20 MHz catheter, Volcano Therapeutics, Rancho Cordova, CA, USA). Digital radiofrequency data are acquired using the same console as for VH. With palpography, the local strain of the tissue is obtained. This

strain is directly related to the mechanical properties of plaque components: soft fatty tissue will be more strained than stiff fibrous tissue when equally stressed. Because the mechanical properties of fibrous and fatty plaque components are different(R. T. Lee *et al.*, 1992; Loree *et al.*, 1994), palpography has the potential to differentiate between different plaque components. An even more promising feature of palpography is the detection of high stress regions. Using computer simulations, concentrations of circumferential tensile stress were more frequently found in unstable plaque than in stable plaques(Cheng, Loree, Kamm, Fishbein, & Lee, 1993; Richardson, Davies, & Born, 1989). A local increase in circumferential stress in tissue is directly related to an increase in radial strain. The local strain is calculated from the gated radiofrequency traces, using cross-correlation analysis, and displayed in color coded form: blue for 0% strain to red to yellow for 2% strain(Schaar, de Korte, Mastik, Baldewsing, *et al.*, 2003). Plaque strain values are assigned a Rotterdam Classification (ROC) score ranging from 1 to 4 (ROC I, 0 to < 0.6%; ROC II, 0.6% to < 0.9%; ROC III, 0.9% to < 1.2%; ROC IV, ≥ 1.2%) (see Figure 2)(Van Mieghem *et al.*, 2005).

The Thoraxcenter group has demonstrated that palpography has a high sensitivity (88%) and specificity (89%) to detect vulnerable plaques in vitro(Schaar, De Korte, Mastik, Strijder, *et al.*, 2003). Postmortem coronary arteries were investigated with intravascular elastography, and were subsequently processed for histology. There was a positive correlation between the level of strain and the degree of macrophage infiltration ($p<0.006$), and an inverse relation between the number of smooth muscle cells and strain ($p<0.0001$). Vulnerable plaques identified by palpography had a thinner cap than nonvulnerable plaques ($p<0.0001$). In a subsequent study, 55 patients with either stable or unstable angina or acute myocardial infarction were analyzed. The prevalence of deformable plaques per vessel was significantly lower ($0.6±0.6$) among patients with stable angina than in patients presenting with unstable angina ($1.6±0.7$, $p=0.0019$) or with acute myocardial infarction ($2.0 ± 0.7$, $p<0.0001$). In the Integrated Biomarker and Imaging Study I

(IBIS-I) on palpography, both the absolute number of high-strain spots (grade III/IV) in the region of interest (ROI; $p=0.009$) and the density per centimeter ($p=0.012$) decreased significantly between baseline and follow-up. This decrease in the overall population was largely driven by changes in the subgroup of patients with STEMI; this group had both the highest number of high-strain spots at baseline and the most marked relative decrease during follow-up compared with patients with other clinical presentations(Van Mieghem *et al.*, 2006). Indeed, as proof-of-concept clinical comparative study of ACS and stable angina patients high-strain lesions were more often seen in ACS and correlated with C-reactive protein levels(Schaar, Regar, *et al.*, 2004).

Strain values of patients treated with a new plaque-stabilizing medication under development (darapladib) was used as primary endpoints in the placebo-controlled Integrated Biomarker and Imaging Study II (IBIS-II) trial (Serruys *et al.*, 2008). The IVUS palpography failed to detect(Serruys *et al.*, 2008) a significant effect on biomechanical properties of coronary plaques during darapladib treatment. Specifically, In the 10-mm subsegments with the highest baseline density of high strain per 10 mm (placebo, $1.22±1.56$; darapladib, $1.21±1.62$), both groups showed significant reductions after 12 months (placebo, 35%, $p=0.001$; darapladib, 33%, $p=0.002$), but the difference between groups was not significant ($p=0.87$). As an explanation for this lack of finding, the authors noted(Serruys *et al.*, 2008) that an unexpectedly high percentage of patients without high strain (37%) at baseline may have reduced the statistical power needed to demonstrate significant differences between treatment groups (Van Mieghem *et al.*, 2006). Supporting this hypothesis is the prespecified sensitivity analysis demonstrating a significant reduction in high strain in the darapladib group ($p=0.009$) when only patients with highly deformable plaque at baseline were analyzed(Serruys *et al.*, 2008).

Strain measurements give an indication of the mechanical properties of the plaque, without

Figure 10. Relationship of shear stress with local strain measurement in human coronary arteries in vivo. (From: Gijsen FJ, Wentzel JJ, Thury A, et al. Strain distribution over plaques in human coronary arteries relates to shear stress. Am J Physiol Heart Circ Physiol 2008; 295:H1608-14).

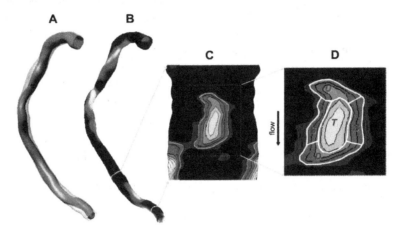

taking into account the shear forces that may be responsible for activation of biologic processes which induce instabilities. Assessment of shear stress is feasible by obtaining high-resolution reconstruction of 3D coronary lumen and wall morphology using a combination of angiography and IVUS(Slager *et al.*, 2000). Although from a mechanical point of view shear stress is of a very small magnitude compared with blood pressure induced tensile stress, it has a profound influence on vascular biology(Malek, Alper, & Izumo, 1999; Thury *et al.*, 2002), and explains the localization of atherosclerotic plaque in the presence of systemic risk factors(Malek *et al.*, 1999). Many of these biologic processes, including inflammation, thrombogenicity, vessel remodeling, intimal thickening or regression, and SMC proliferation, also influence the stability of the vulnerable plaque(Slager *et al.*, 2005). Therefore, the assessment of shear stress in combination with strain measurement would reveal significant pathophysiologic aspects of plaque vulnerability. Our group of the Thoraxcenter investigated this relationship in human coronary arteries(Gijsen *et al.*, 2008). We imaged 31 plaques in coronary arteries with angiography and intravascular ultrasound. Computational fluid dynamics was used to obtain shear stress. Palpography was applied

to measure strain. Each plaque was divided into four regions: upstream, throat, shoulder, and downstream (Figure 10). Average shear stress and strain were determined in each region. Shear stress in the upstream, shoulder, throat, and downstream region was 2.55±0.89, 2.07±0.98, 2.32±1.11, and 0.67±0.35 Pa, respectively. Shear stress in the downstream region was significantly lower. Strain in the downstream region was also significantly lower than the values in the other regions (0.23±0.08% vs. 0.48±0.15%, 0.43±0.17%, and 0.47±0.12%, for the upstream, shoulder, and throat regions, respectively). Thus, the findings from this study(Gijsen *et al.*, 2008) demonstrate for the first time a relationship between blood flow-induced shear stress and strain in human coronary arteries in vivo. Plaque regions downstream of plaques are exposed to low shear stress, and the low strain values found indicate that the plaque is stiffer there. Plaque regions, exposed to high shear stress, show high strain values, indicating weaker underlying wall material, and these regions might therefore be more prone to rupture. It can be speculated that the regions of a cap of a vulnerable plaque, exposed to high shear stress, will continue to weaken over time, eventually leading to the rupture of the cap(Gijsen *et al.*, 2008).

REFERENCES

Amano, T., Matsubara, T., Uetani, T., Kato, M., Kato, B., & Yoshida, T. (2011). Lipid-rich plaques predict non-target-lesion ischemic events in patients undergoing percutaneous coronary intervention: Insights from integrated backscatter intravascular ultrasound & ndash. *Circulation Journal*, *75*(1), 157–166. doi:10.1253/circj.CJ-10-0612

Ambrose, J. A. (2008). In search of the "vulnerable plaque": Can it be localized and will focal regional therapy ever be an option for cardiac prevention? *Journal of the American College of Cardiology*, *51*(16), 1539–1542. doi:10.1016/j.jacc.2007.12.041

Ambrose, J. A., Winters, S. L., Arora, R. R., Eng, A., Riccio, A., & Gorlin, R. (1986). Angiographic evolution of coronary artery morphology in unstable angina. *Journal of the American College of Cardiology*, *7*(3), 472–478. doi:10.1016/S0735-1097(86)80455-7

Baldewsing, R. A., Danilouchkine, M. G., Mastik, F., Schaar, J. A., Serruys, P. W., & van der Steen, A. F. (2008). An inverse method for imaging the local elasticity of atherosclerotic coronary plaques. *IEEE Transactions on Information Technology in Biomedicine*, *12*(3), 277–289. doi:10.1109/TITB.2007.907980

Baldewsing, R. A., de Korte, C. L., Schaar, J. A., Mastik, F., & van der Steen, A. F. (2004). A finite element model for performing intravascular ultrasound elastography of human atherosclerotic coronary arteries. *Ultrasound in Medicine & Biology*, *30*(6), 803–813. doi:10.1016/j.ultrasmedbio.2004.04.005

Bhatti, S., Hakeem, A., & Cilingiroglu, M. (2010). Lp-PLA(2) as a marker of cardiovascular diseases. *Current Atherosclerosis Reports*, *12*(2), 140–144. doi:10.1007/s11883-010-0095-6

Bonello, L., De Labriolle, A., Lemesle, G., Roy, P., Steinberg, D. H., & Pichard, A. D. (2009). Intravascular ultrasound-guided percutaneous coronary interventions in contemporary practice. *Arch Cardiovasc Dis*, *102*(2), 143–151. doi:10.1016/j.acvd.2008.11.002

Boston Scientific. (2009). News release: Boston Scientific announces release of next-generation iLab® system software. Retrieved from http://bostonscientific.mediaroom.com/index.php?s=43&item=864

Brown, B. G., & Zhao, X. Q. (2007). Is intravascular ultrasound the gold standard surrogate for clinically relevant atherosclerosis progression? *Journal of the American College of Cardiology*, *49*(9), 933–938. doi:10.1016/j.jacc.2006.12.014

Brugaletta, S., Garcia-Garcia, H. M., Garg, S., Gomez-Lara, J., Diletti, R., & Onuma, Y. (2010). Temporal changes of coronary artery plaque located behind the struts of the everolimus eluting bioresorbable vascular scaffold. *The International Journal of Cardiovascular Imaging*, *27*(6).

Burke, A. P., Farb, A., Malcom, G. T., Liang, Y. H., Smialek, J., & Virmani, R. (1997). Coronary risk factors and plaque morphology in men with coronary disease who died suddenly. *The New England Journal of Medicine*, *336*(18), 1276–1282. doi:10.1056/NEJM199705013361802

Burke, A. P., Joner, M., & Virmani, R. (2006). IVUS-VH: A predictor of plaque morphology? *European Heart Journal*, *27*(16), 1889–1890. doi:10.1093/eurheartj/ehl126

Carlier, S. G., Mintz, G. S., & Stone, G. W. (2006). Imaging of atherosclerotic plaque using radiofrequency ultrasound signal processing. *Journal of Nuclear Cardiology*, *13*(6), 831–840. doi:10.1016/j.nuclcard.2006.10.013

Cespedes, I., Huang, Y., Ophir, J., & Spratt, S. (1995). Methods for estimation of subsample time delays of digitized echo signals. *Ultrasonic Imaging*, *17*(2), 142–171. doi:10.1006/uimg.1995.1007

Cespedes, I., Ophir, J., Ponnekanti, H., & Maklad, N. (1993). Elastography: Elasticity imaging using ultrasound with application to muscle and breast in vivo. *Ultrasonic Imaging, 15*(2), 73–88. doi:10.1006/uimg.1993.1007

Cheng, G. C., Loree, H. M., Kamm, R. D., Fishbein, M. C., & Lee, R. T. (1993). Distribution of circumferential stress in ruptured and stable atherosclerotic lesions. A structural analysis with histopathological correlation. *Circulation, 87*(4), 1179–1187.

Cheruvu, P. K., Finn, A. V., Gardner, C., Caplan, J., Goldstein, J., & Stone, G. W. (2007). Frequency and distribution of thin-cap fibroatheroma and ruptured plaques in human coronary arteries: A pathologic study. *Journal of the American College of Cardiology, 50*(10), 940–949. doi:10.1016/j. jacc.2007.04.086

Cilingiroglu, M., Oh, J. H., Sugunan, B., Kemp, N. J., Kim, J., & Lee, S. (2006). Detection of vulnerable plaque in a murine model of atherosclerosis with optical coherence tomography. *Catheterization and Cardiovascular Interventions, 67*(6), 915–923. doi:10.1002/ccd.20717

ClinicalTrials.gov. (2006). *PROSPECT: An imaging study in patients with unstable atherosclerotic lesions.* Retrieved from http://www.clinicaltrials. gov/ct/gui/show/NCT00180466;jsessionid=732 C53C19413A1117791F0BE7FE99369?order=9

ClinicalTrials.gov. (2009). Assessment of dual antiplatelet therapy with drug eluting stents (ADAPT-DES). Retrieved from http://clinicaltrials.gov/ct2/show/NCT00638794

Davies, M. J., Richardson, P. D., Woolf, N., Katz, D. R., & Mann, J. (1993). Risk of thrombosis in human atherosclerotic plaques: Role of extracellular lipid, macrophage, and smooth muscle cell content. *British Heart Journal, 69*(5), 377–381. doi:10.1136/hrt.69.5.377

de Korte, C. L., Sierevogel, M. J., Mastik, F., Strijder, C., Schaar, J. A., & Velema, E. (2002). Identification of atherosclerotic plaque components with intravascular ultrasound elastography in vivo: A Yucatan pig study. *Circulation, 105*(14), 1627–1630. doi:10.1161/01.CIR.0000014988.66572.2E

de Winter, S., Heller, I., Hamers, R., de Feyter, P., Serruys, P., & Roelandt, J. (2003). Computer assisted three-dimensional plaque characterization in ultracoronary ultrasound studies. *Computers in Cardiology, 30*, 73–76.

DeMaria, A. N., Narula, J., Mahmud, E., & Tsimikas, S. (2006). Imaging vulnerable plaque by ultrasound. *Journal of the American College of Cardiology, 47*(8Suppl), C32–C39. doi:10.1016/j. jacc.2005.11.047

Diethrich, E. B., Pauliina Margolis, M., Reid, D. B., Burke, A., Ramaiah, V., & Rodriguez-Lopez, J. A. (2007). Virtual histology intravascular ultrasound assessment of carotid artery disease: the Carotid Artery Plaque Virtual Histology Evaluation (CAPITAL) study. *Journal of Endovascular Therapy, 14*(5), 676–686. doi:10.1583/1545-1550(2007)14[676:VHIUAO]2.0.CO;2

Doyley, M. M., Mastik, F., de Korte, C. L., Carlier, S. G., Cespedes, E. I., & Serruys, P. W. (2001). Advancing intravascular ultrasonic palpation toward clinical applications. *Ultrasound in Medicine & Biology, 27*(11), 1471–1480. doi:10.1016/S0301-5629(01)00457-4

Ehara, S., Kobayashi, Y., Yoshiyama, M., Shimada, K., Shimada, Y., & Fukuda, D. (2004). Spotty calcification typifies the culprit plaque in patients with acute myocardial infarction: An intravascular ultrasound study. *Circulation, 110*(22), 3424–3429. doi:10.1161/01.CIR.0000148131.41425.E9

Falk, E., Shah, P. K., & Fuster, V. (1995). Coronary plaque disruption. *Circulation, 92*(3), 657–671.

Finn, A. V., Chandrashekhar, Y., & Narula, J. (2010). Seeking alternatives to hard end points: Is imaging the best approach? *Circulation, 121*(10), 1165–1168. doi:10.1161/CIR.0b013e3181d83b4f

Finn, A. V., Nakano, M., Narula, J., Kolodgie, F. D., & Virmani, R. (2010). Concept of vulnerable/unstable plaque. *Arteriosclerosis, Thrombosis, and Vascular Biology, 30*(7), 1282–1292. doi:10.1161/ATVBAHA.108.179739

Funada, R., Oikawa, Y., Yajima, J., Kirigaya, H., Nagashima, K., & Ogasawara, K. (2009). The potential of RF backscattered IVUS data and multidetector-row computed tomography images for tissue characterization of human coronary atherosclerotic plaques. *The International Journal of Cardiovascular Imaging, 25*(5), 471–478. doi:10.1007/s10554-009-9446-1

Garcia-Garcia, H. M., Costa, M. A., & Serruys, P. W. (2010). Imaging of coronary atherosclerosis: Intravascular ultrasound. *European Heart Journal, 31*(20), 2456–2469. doi:10.1093/eurheartj/ehq280

Garcia-Garcia, H. M., Goedhart, D., Schuurbiers, J. C., Kukreja, N., Tanimoto, S., & Daemen, J. (2006). Virtual histology and remodelling index allow in vivo identification of allegedly high-risk coronary plaques in patients with acute coronary syndromes: A three vessel intravascular ultrasound radiofrequency data analysis. *EuroIntervention, 2*(3), 338–344.

Garcia-Garcia, H. M., Mintz, G. S., Lerman, A., Goedhart, D., Schuurbiers, J. C., & Kukreja, N. (2009). Tissue characterisation using intravascular radiofrequency data analysis: Recommendations for aquisition, analysis, interpretation and reporting. *EuroIntervention, 5*, 177–189. doi:10.4244/EIJV5I2A29

Gijsen, F. J., Wentzel, J. J., Thury, A., Mastik, F., Schaar, J. A., & Schuurbiers, J. C. (2008). Strain distribution over plaques in human coronary arteries relates to shear stress. *American Journal of Physiology. Heart and Circulatory Physiology, 295*(4), H1608–H1614. doi:10.1152/ajpheart.01081.2007

Glaser, R., Selzer, F., Faxon, D. P., Laskey, W. K., Cohen, H. A., & Slater, J. (2005). Clinical progression of incidental, asymptomatic lesions discovered during culprit vessel coronary intervention. *Circulation, 111*(2), 143–149. doi:10.1161/01.CIR.0000150335.01285.12

Goderie, T. P., van Soest, G., Garcia-Garcia, H. M., Gonzalo, N., Koljenovic, S., van Leenders, G. J., et al. (2010). Combined optical coherence tomography and intravascular ultrasound radio frequency data analysis for plaque characterization. Classification accuracy of human coronary plaques in vitro. *Int J Cardiovasc Imaging.*

Goldstein, J. A., Demetriou, D., Grines, C. L., Pica, M., Shoukfeh, M., & O'Neill, W. W. (2000). Multiple complex coronary plaques in patients with acute myocardial infarction. *The New England Journal of Medicine, 343*(13), 915–922. doi:10.1056/NEJM200009283431303

Gonzalo, N., Garcia-Garcia, H. M., Ligthart, J., Rodriguez-Granillo, G., Meliga, E., & Onuma, Y. (2008). Coronary plaque composition as assessed by greyscale intravascular ultrasound and radiofrequency spectral data analysis. *The International Journal of Cardiovascular Imaging, 24*(8), 811–818. doi:10.1007/s10554-008-9324-2

Gonzalo, N., Garcia-Garcia, H. M., Regar, E., Barlis, P., Wentzel, J., & Onuma, Y. (2009). In vivo assessment of high-risk coronary plaques at bifurcations with combined intravascular ultrasound and optical coherence tomography. *JACC: Cardiovascular Imaging, 2*(4), 473–482. doi:10.1016/j.jcmg.2008.11.016

Gonzalo, N., Serruys, P. W., Barlis, P., Ligthart, J., Garcia-Garcia, H. M., & Regar, E. (2010). Multi-modality intra-coronary plaque characterization: A pilot study. *International Journal of Cardiology*, *138*(1), 32–39. doi:10.1016/j.ijcard.2008.08.030

Granada, J. F., Wallace-Bradley, D., Win, H. K., Alviar, C. L., Builes, A., & Lev, E. I. (2007). In vivo plaque characterization using intravascular ultrasound-virtual histology in a porcine model of complex coronary lesions. *Arteriosclerosis, Thrombosis, and Vascular Biology*, *27*(2), 387–393. doi:10.1161/01.ATV.0000253907.51681.0e

Guedes, A., Keller, P. F., L'Allier, P. L., Lesperance, J., Gregoire, J., & Tardif, J. C. (2005). Long-term safety of intravascular ultrasound in nontransplant, nonintervened, atherosclerotic coronary arteries. *Journal of the American College of Cardiology*, *45*(4), 559–564. doi:10.1016/j.jacc.2004.10.063

Hara, H., Tsunoda, T., Moroi, M., Kubota, T., Kunimasa, T., & Shiba, M. (2006). Ultrasound attenuation behind coronary atheroma without calcification: Mechanism revealed by autopsy. *Acute Cardiac Care*, *8*(2), 110–112. doi:10.1080/14628840600637781

Hartmann, M., Mattern, E. S., Huisman, J., van Houwelingen, G. K., de Man, F. H., & Stoel, M. G. (2009). Reproducibility of volumetric intravascular ultrasound radiofrequency-based analysis of coronary plaque composition in vivo. *The International Journal of Cardiovascular Imaging*, *25*(1), 13–23. doi:10.1007/s10554-008-9338-9

Hiro, T., Fujii, T., Yasumoto, K., Murata, T., Murashige, A., & Matsuzaki, M. (2001). Detection of fibrous cap in atherosclerotic plaque by intravascular ultrasound by use of color mapping of angle-dependent echo-intensity variation. *Circulation*, *103*(9), 1206–1211.

Hiro, T., Leung, C. Y., De Guzman, S., Caiozzo, V. J., Farvid, A. R., & Karimi, H. (1997). Are soft echoes really soft? Intravascular ultrasound assessment of mechanical properties in human atherosclerotic tissue. *American Heart Journal*, *133*(1), 1–7. doi:10.1016/S0002-8703(97)70241-2

Hong, Y. J., Jeong, M. H., Choi, Y. H., Ko, J. S., Lee, M. G., & Kang, W. Y. (2009). Impact of plaque components on no-reflow phenomenon after stent deployment in patients with acute coronary syndrome: A virtual histology-intravascular ultrasound analysis. *European Heart Journal*, 32.

Hong, Y. J., Jeong, M. H., Choi, Y. H., Ma, E. H., Ko, J. S., & Lee, M. G. (2010). Impact of baseline plaque components on plaque progression in nonintervened coronary segments in patients with angina pectoris on rosuvastatin 10 mg/day. *The American Journal of Cardiology*, *106*(9), 1241–1247. doi:10.1016/j.amjcard.2010.06.046

Hong, Y. J., Jeong, M. H., Kim, S. W., Choi, Y. H., Ma, E. H., & Ko, J. S. (2010). Relation between plaque components and plaque prolapse after drug-eluting stent implantation--Virtual histology-intravascular ultrasound. *Circulation Journal*, *74*(6), 1142–1151. doi:10.1253/circj.CJ-09-0781

Huisman, J., Egede, R., Rdzanek, A., Bose, D., Erbel, R., & Kochman, J. (2010). Between-centre reproducibility of volumetric intravascular ultrasound radiofrequency-based analyses in mild-to-moderate coronary atherosclerosis: An international multicentre study. *EuroIntervention*, *5*(8), 925–931. doi:10.4244/EIJV5I8A156

Inaba, S., Okayama, H., Funada, J. I., Hashida, H., Hiasa, G., & Sumimoto, T. (2009). Relationship between smaller calcifications and lipid-rich plaques on integrated backscatter-intravascular ultrasound. *International Journal of Cardiology*, *145*(2).

Inoue, F., Ueshima, K., Fujimoto, T., & Kihyon, A. (2010). Effect of angiotensin receptor blockade on the coronary plaque component in patients with stable angina: Virtual histology intravascular ultrasound study. *Circulation, 122,* A13580.

Kaaresen, K. F., & Bolviken, E. (1999). Blind deconvolution of ultrasonic traces accounting for pulse variance. *IEEE Transactions on Ultrasonics, Ferroelectrics, and Frequency Control, 46*(3), 564–573. doi:10.1109/58.764843

Kallel, F., & Ophir, J. (1998). Limits on the contrast of strain concentrations in elastography. *Ultrasound in Medicine & Biology, 24*(8), 1215–1219. doi:10.1016/S0301-5629(98)00106-9

Kaple, R. K., Maehara, A., Sano, K., Missel, E., Castellanos, C., & Tsujita, K. (2009). The axial distribution of lesion-site atherosclerotic plaque components: An in vivo volumetric intravascular ultrasound radio-frequency analysis of lumen stenosis, necrotic core and vessel remodeling. *Ultrasound in Medicine & Biology, 35*(4), 550–557. doi:10.1016/j.ultrasmedbio.2008.09.024

Kawaguchi, R., Oshima, S., Jingu, M., Tsurugaya, H., Toyama, T., & Hoshizaki, H. (2007). Usefulness of virtual histology intravascular ultrasound to predict distal embolization for ST-segment elevation myocardial infarction. *Journal of the American College of Cardiology, 50*(17), 1641–1646. doi:10.1016/j.jacc.2007.06.051

Kawamoto, T., Okura, H., Koyama, Y., Toda, I., Taguchi, H., & Tamita, K. (2007). The relationship between coronary plaque characteristics and small embolic particles during coronary stent implantation. *Journal of the American College of Cardiology, 50*(17), 1635–1640. doi:10.1016/j.jacc.2007.05.050

Kawasaki, M., Hattori, A., Ishihara, Y., Okubo, M., Nishigaki, K., & Takemura, G. (2010). Tissue Characterization of coronary plaques and assessment of thickness of fibrous cap using integrated backscatter intravascular ultrasound. *Circulation Journal, 74*(12). doi:10.1253/circj.CJ-10-0547

Kawasaki, M., Sano, K., Okubo, M., Yokoyama, H., Ito, Y., & Murata, I. (2005). Volumetric quantitative analysis of tissue characteristics of coronary plaques after statin therapy using three-dimensional integrated backscatter intravascular ultrasound. *Journal of the American College of Cardiology, 45*(12), 1946–1953. doi:10.1016/j.jacc.2004.09.081

Kawasaki, M., Takatsu, H., Noda, T., Ito, Y., Kunishima, A., & Arai, M. (2001). Noninvasive quantitative tissue characterization and two-dimensional color-coded map of human atherosclerotic lesions using ultrasound integrated backscatter: Comparison between histology and integrated backscatter images. *Journal of the American College of Cardiology, 38*(2), 486–492. doi:10.1016/S0735-1097(01)01393-6

Kawasaki, M., Takatsu, H., Noda, T., Sano, K., Ito, Y., & Hayakawa, K. (2002). In vivo quantitative tissue characterization of human coronary arterial plaques by use of integrated backscatter intravascular ultrasound and comparison with angioscopic findings. *Circulation, 105*(21), 2487–2492. doi:10.1161/01.CIR.0000017200.47342.10

Kimura, B. J., Bhargava, V., & DeMaria, A. N. (1995). Value and limitations of intravascular ultrasound imaging in characterizing coronary atherosclerotic plaque. *American Heart Journal, 130*(2), 386–396. doi:10.1016/0002-8703(95)90457-3

Kolodgie, F. D., Burke, A. P., Farb, A., Gold, H. K., Yuan, J., & Narula, J. (2001). The thin-cap fibroatheroma: A type of vulnerable plaque: The major precursor lesion to acute coronary syndromes. *Current Opinion in Cardiology, 16*(5), 285–292. doi:10.1097/00001573-200109000-00006

Konofagou, E., & Ophir, J. (1998). A new elastographic method for estimation and imaging of lateral displacements, lateral strains, corrected axial strains and Poisson's ratios in tissues. *Ultrasound in Medicine & Biology, 24*(8), 1183–1199. doi:10.1016/S0301-5629(98)00109-4

Kubo, T., Maehara, A., Mintz, G. S., Garcia-Garcia, H. M., Serruys, P. W., & Suzuki, T. (2010). Analysis of the long-term effects of drug-eluting stents on coronary arterial wall morphology as assessed by virtual histology intravascular ultrasound. *American Heart Journal, 159*(2), 271–277. doi:10.1016/j.ahj.2009.11.008

Le Floc'h, S., Cloutier, G., Finet, G., Tracqui, P., Pettigrew, R. I., & Ohayon, J. (2010). On the potential of a new IVUS elasticity modulus imaging approach for detecting vulnerable atherosclerotic coronary plaques: In vitro vessel phantom study. *Physics in Medicine and Biology, 55*(19), 5701–5721. doi:10.1088/0031-9155/55/19/006

Lee, R. T., & Libby, P. (1997). The unstable atheroma. *Arteriosclerosis, Thrombosis, and Vascular Biology, 17*(10), 1859–1867. doi:10.1161/01.ATV.17.10.1859

Lee, R. T., Richardson, S. G., Loree, H. M., Grodzinsky, A. J., Gharib, S. A., & Schoen, F. J. (1992). Prediction of mechanical properties of human atherosclerotic tissue by high-frequency intravascular ultrasound imaging. An in vitro study. *Arteriosclerosis and Thrombosis, 12*(1), 1–5. doi:10.1161/01.ATV.12.1.1

Lee, S. W., Hau, W. K., Kong, S. L., & Chan, R. W. (2010). Virtual histology findings of the effects of atorvastatin treatment on coronary plaque volume and composition (the venus study): final results. *Circulation, 122*, a13301.

Lee, S. Y., Mintz, G. S., Kim, S. Y., Hong, Y. J., Kim, S. W., & Okabe, T. (2009). Attenuated plaque detected by intravascular ultrasound: clinical, angiographic, and morphologic features and post-percutaneous coronary intervention complications in patients with acute coronary syndromes. *JACC: Cardiovascular Interventions, 2*(1), 65–72. doi:10.1016/j.jcin.2008.08.022

Li, W., Carrillo, R., Jian, Y., Tat-Jin, T., & Thomas, L. (2008). Multi-frequency processing for lumen enhancement with wideband intravascular ultrasound. *IEEE Ultrasonics Symposium, 2-5 Nov. 2008*, (pp. 371–374).

Libby, P. (2005). The forgotten majority: Unfinished business in cardiovascular risk reduction. *Journal of the American College of Cardiology, 46*(7), 1225–1228. doi:10.1016/j.jacc.2005.07.006

Libby, P., & Theroux, P. (2005). Pathophysiology of coronary artery disease. *Circulation, 111*(25), 3481–3488. doi:10.1161/CIRCULATIONAHA.105.537878

Lin, C. P., Honye, J., & Saito, S. (2010). New modality for evaluating plaque characteristics of the culprit lesion in a patient with acute coronary syndrome and no reflow phenomenon. *International Heart Journal, 51*(3), 207–210. doi:10.1536/ihj.51.207

Little, W. C., Constantinescu, M., Applegate, R. J., Kutcher, M. A., Burrows, M. T., & Kahl, F. R. (1988). Can coronary angiography predict the site of a subsequent myocardial infarction in patients with mild-to-moderate coronary artery disease? *Circulation, 78*(5 Pt 1), 1157–1166. doi:10.1161/01.CIR.78.5.1157

Lizzi, F. L., Greenebaum, M., Feleppa, E. J., Elbaum, M., & Coleman, D. J. (1983). Theoretical framework for spectrum analysis in ultrasonic tissue characterization. *The Journal of the Acoustical Society of America, 73*(4), 1366–1373. doi:10.1121/1.389241

Loree, H. M., Tobias, B. J., Gibson, L. J., Kamm, R. D., Small, D. M., & Lee, R. T. (1994). Mechanical properties of model atherosclerotic lesion lipid pools. *Arteriosclerosis and Thrombosis, 14*(2), 230–234. doi:10.1161/01.ATV.14.2.230

Malek, A. M., Alper, S. L., & Izumo, S. (1999). Hemodynamic shear stress and its role in atherosclerosis. *Journal of the American Medical Association, 282*(21), 2035–2042. doi:10.1001/jama.282.21.2035

Matter, C. M., Stuber, M., & Nahrendorf, M. (2009). Imaging of the unstable plaque: How far have we got? *European Heart Journal, 30*(21), 2566–2574. doi:10.1093/eurheartj/ehp419

McPherson, J. A., Maehara, A., Mintz, G. S., Serruys, P. W., & Stone, P. H. (2010). Are vulnerable plaques widely disseminated or focal? A baseline 3-vessel IVUS analysis from the PROSPECT trial. *Journal of the American College of Cardiology, 55*(10A), A178. doi:10.1016/S0735-1097(10)61670-1

Mintz, G. S., Nissen, S. E., Anderson, W. D., Bailey, S. R., Erbel, R., & Fitzgerald, P. J. (2001). American College of Cardiology clinical expert consensus document on standards for acquisition, measurement and reporting of intravascular ultrasound studies (IVUS). A report of the American College of Cardiology Task Force on Clinical Expert Consensus Documents. *Journal of the American College of Cardiology, 37*(5), 1478–1492. doi:10.1016/S0735-1097(01)01175-5

Mintz, G. S., Painter, J. A., Pichard, A. D., Kent, K. M., Satler, L. F., & Popma, J. J. (1995). Atherosclerosis in angiographically "normal" coronary artery reference segments: An intravascular ultrasound study with clinical correlations. *Journal of the American College of Cardiology, 25*(7), 1479–1485. doi:10.1016/0735-1097(95)00088-L

Missel, E., Mintz, G. S., Carlier, S. G., Qian, J., Shan, S., & Castellanos, C. (2008). In vivo virtual histology intravascular ultrasound correlates of risk factors for sudden coronary death in men: Results from the prospective, multi-centre virtual histology intravascular ultrasound registry. *European Heart Journal, 29*(17), 2141–2147. doi:10.1093/eurheartj/ehn293

Moore, M. P., Spencer, T., Salter, D. M., Kearney, P. P., Shaw, T. R., & Starkey, I. R. (1998). Characterisation of coronary atherosclerotic morphology by spectral analysis of radiofrequency signal: In vitro intravascular ultrasound study with histological and radiological validation. *Heart (British Cardiac Society), 79*(5), 459–467.

Murashige, A., Hiro, T., Fujii, T., Imoto, K., Murata, T., & Fukumoto, Y. (2005). Detection of lipid-laden atherosclerotic plaque by wavelet analysis of radiofrequency intravascular ultrasound signals: In vitro validation and preliminary in vivo application. *Journal of the American College of Cardiology, 45*(12), 1954–1960. doi:10.1016/j.jacc.2004.10.080

Naghavi, M., Libby, P., Falk, E., Casscells, S. W., Litovsky, S., & Rumberger, J. (2003). From vulnerable plaque to vulnerable patient: A call for new definitions and risk assessment strategies: Part I. *Circulation, 108*(14), 1664–1672. doi:10.1161/01.CIR.0000087480.94275.97

Nair, A., Calvetti, D., & Vince, D. G. (2004). Regularized autoregressive analysis of intravascular ultrasound backscatter: Improvement in spatial accuracy of tissue maps. *IEEE Transactions on Ultrasonics, Ferroelectrics, and Frequency Control, 51*(4), 420–431. doi:10.1109/TUFFC.2004.1295427

Nair, A., Kuban, B. D., Obuchowski, N., & Vince, D. G. (2001). Assessing spectral algorithms to predict atherosclerotic plaque composition with normalized and raw intravascular ultrasound data. *Ultrasound in Medicine & Biology, 27*(10), 1319–1331. doi:10.1016/S0301-5629(01)00436-7

Nair, A., Kuban, B. D., Tuzcu, E. M., Schoenhagen, P., Nissen, S. E., & Vince, D. G. (2002). Coronary plaque classification with intravascular ultrasound radiofrequency data analysis. *Circulation, 106*(17), 2200–2206. doi:10.1161/01.CIR.0000035654.18341.5E

Nair, A., Margolis, M. P., Kuban, B. D., & Vince, D. G. (2007). Automated coronary plaque characterisation with intravascular ultrasound backscatter: Ex vivo validation. *EuroIntervention, 3*(1), 113–120.

Nasu, K., Tsuchikane, E., Katoh, O., Tanaka, N., Kimura, M., & Ehara, M. (2009). Effect of fluvastatin on progression of coronary atherosclerotic plaque evaluated by virtual histology intravascular ultrasound. *JACC: Cardiovascular Interventions*, *2*(7), 689–696. doi:10.1016/j.jcin.2009.04.016

Nasu, K., Tsuchikane, E., Katoh, O., Vince, D. G., Margolis, P. M., & Virmani, R. (2008). Impact of intramural thrombus in coronary arteries on the accuracy of tissue characterization by in vivo intravascular ultrasound radiofrequency data analysis. *The American Journal of Cardiology*, *101*(8), 1079–1083. doi:10.1016/j.amjcard.2007.11.064

Nasu, K., Tsuchikane, E., Katoh, O., Vince, D. G., Virmani, R., & Surmely, J. F. (2006). Accuracy of in vivo coronary plaque morphology assessment: A validation study of in vivo virtual histology compared with in vitro histopathology. *Journal of the American College of Cardiology*, *47*(12), 2405–2412. doi:10.1016/j.jacc.2006.02.044

Nicholls, S. J., Hsu, A., Wolski, K., Hu, B., Bayturan, O., & Lavoie, A. (2010). Intravascular ultrasound-derived measures of coronary atherosclerotic plaque burden and clinical outcome. *Journal of the American College of Cardiology*, *55*(21), 2399–2407. doi:10.1016/j.jacc.2010.02.026

Nicholls, S. J., Hsu, A., Wolski, K., Hu, B., Bayturan, O., & Lavoie, A.. Intravascular ultrasound-derived measures of coronary atherosclerotic plaque burden and clinical outcome. *Journal of the American College of Cardiology*, *55*(21), 2399–2407. doi:10.1016/j.jacc.2010.02.026

Nicholls, S. J., Tuzcu, E. M., Wolski, K., Sipahi, I., Schoenhagen, P., & Crowe, T. (2007). Coronary artery calcification and changes in atheroma burden in response to established medical therapies. *Journal of the American College of Cardiology*, *49*(2), 263–270. doi:10.1016/j.jacc.2006.10.038

Nishimura, R. A., Edwards, W. D., Warnes, C. A., Reeder, G. S., Holmes, D. R. Jr, & Tajik, A. J. (1990). Intravascular ultrasound imaging: in vitro validation and pathologic correlation. *Journal of the American College of Cardiology*, *16*(1), 145–154. doi:10.1016/0735-1097(90)90472-2

Nissen, S. E., & Yock, P. (2001). Intravascular ultrasound: Novel pathophysiological insights and current clinical applications. *Circulation*, *103*(4), 604–616.

O'Leary, D. H., Polak, J. F., Kronmal, R. A., Manolio, T. A., Burke, G. L., & Wolfson, S. K. Jr. (1999). Carotid-artery intima and media thickness as a risk factor for myocardial infarction and stroke in older adults. Cardiovascular Health Study Collaborative Research Group. *The New England Journal of Medicine*, *340*(1), 14–22. doi:10.1056/NEJM199901073400103

Okimoto, T., Imazu, M., Hayashi, Y., Fujiwara, H., Ueda, H., & Kohno, N. (2002). Atherosclerotic plaque characterization by quantitative analysis using intravascular ultrasound: Correlation with histological and immunohistochemical findings. *Circulation Journal*, *66*(2), 173–177. doi:10.1253/circj.66.173

Okubo, M., Kawasaki, M., Ishihara, Y., Takeyama, U., Yasuda, S., & Kubota, T. (2008). Tissue characterization of coronary plaques: Comparison of integrated backscatter intravascular ultrasound with virtual histology intravascular ultrasound. *Circulation Journal*, *72*(10), 1631–1639. doi:10.1253/circj.CJ-07-0936

Okura, H., Taguchi, H., Kubo, T., Toda, I., Yoshida, K., & Yoshiyama, M. (2007). Atherosclerotic plaque with ultrasonic attenuation affects coronary reflow and infarct size in patients with acute coronary syndrome: An intravascular ultrasound study. *Circulation Journal*, *71*(5), 648–653. doi:10.1253/circj.71.648

Ophir, J., Cespedes, I., Ponnekanti, H., Yazdi, Y., & Li, X. (1991). Elastography: A quantitative method for imaging the elasticity of biological tissues. *Ultrasonic Imaging, 13*(2), 111–134. doi:10.1016/0161-7346(91)90079-W

Ormiston, J. A., Serruys, P. W., Regar, E., Dudek, D., Thuesen, L., & Webster, M. W. (2008). A bioabsorbable everolimus-eluting coronary stent system for patients with single de-novo coronary artery lesions (ABSORB): A prospective open-label trial. *Lancet, 371*(9616), 899–907. doi:10.1016/S0140-6736(08)60415-8

Palmer, N. D., Northridge, D., Lessells, A., McDicken, W. N., & Fox, K. A. (1999). In vitro analysis of coronary atheromatous lesions by intravascular ultrasound: Reproducibility and histological correlation of lesion morphology. *European Heart Journal, 20*(23), 1701–1706. doi:10.1053/euhj.1999.1627

Pawlowski, T., Mintz, G. S., Kulawik, T., & Gil, R. J. (2010). Virtual histology intravascular ultrasound evaluation of the left anterior descending coronary artery in patients with transient left ventricular ballooning syndrome. *Kardiologia Polska, 68*(10), 1093–1098.

Peters, R. J., Kok, W. E., Havenith, M. G., Rijsterborgh, H., van der Wal, A. C., & Visser, C. A. (1994). Histopathologic validation of intracoronary ultrasound imaging. *Journal of the American Society of Echocardiography, 7*(3 Pt 1), 230–241.

Philipp, S., Bose, D., Wijns, W., Marso, S. P., Schwartz, R. S., & Konig, A. (2010). Do systemic risk factors impact invasive findings from virtual histology? Insights from the international virtual histology registry. *European Heart Journal, 31*(2), 196–202. doi:10.1093/eurheartj/ehp428

Prati, F., Arbustini, E., Labellarte, A., Dal Bello, B., Sommariva, L., & Mallus, M. T. (2001). Correlation between high frequency intravascular ultrasound and histomorphology in human coronary arteries. *Heart (British Cardiac Society), 85*(5), 567–570. doi:10.1136/heart.85.5.567

Ramcharitar, S., Gonzalo, N., van Geuns, R. J., Garcia-Garcia, H. M., Wykrzykowska, J. J., & Ligthart, J. M. (2009). First case of stenting of a vulnerable plaque in the SECRITT I trial-the dawn of a new era? *Nat Rev Cardiol, 6*(5), 374–378. doi:10.1038/nrcardio.2009.34

Rasheed, Q., Dhawale, P. J., Anderson, J., & Hodgson, J. M. (1995). Intracoronary ultrasound-defined plaque composition: Computer-aided plaque characterization and correlation with histologic samples obtained during directional coronary atherectomy. *American Heart Journal, 129*(4), 631–637. doi:10.1016/0002-8703(95)90307-0

Regar, E., van Soest, G., Bruining, N., Constantinescu, A. A., van Geuns, R. J., van der Giessen, W., et al. (2010). Optical coherence tomography in patients with acute coronary syndrome. *Euro-Intervention, 6 Suppl G*, G154-160.

Richardson, P. D., Davies, M. J., & Born, G. V. (1989). Influence of plaque configuration and stress distribution on fissuring of coronary atherosclerotic plaques. *Lancet, 2*(8669), 941–944. doi:10.1016/S0140-6736(89)90953-7

Ringqvist, I., Fisher, L. D., Mock, M., Davis, K. B., Wedel, H., & Chaitman, B. R. (1983). Prognostic value of angiographic indices of coronary artery disease from the Coronary Artery Surgery Study (CASS). *The Journal of Clinical Investigation, 71*(6), 1854–1866. doi:10.1172/JCI110941

Rioufol, G., Finet, G., Ginon, I., Andre-Fouet, X., Rossi, R., & Vialle, E. (2002). Multiple atherosclerotic plaque rupture in acute coronary syndrome: A three-vessel intravascular ultrasound study. *Circulation, 106*(7), 804–808. doi:10.1161/01.CIR.0000025609.13806.31

Rodriguez-Granillo, G. A., Aoki, J., Ong, A. T., Valgimigli, M., Van Mieghem, C. A., & Regar, E. (2005). Methodological considerations and approach to cross-technique comparisons using in vivo coronary plaque characterization based on intravascular ultrasound radiofrequency data analysis: Insights from the Integrated Biomarker and Imaging Study (IBIS). *International Journal of Cardiovascular Interventions, 7*(1), 52–58.

Rodriguez-Granillo, G. A., Bruining, N., Mc Fadden, E., Ligthart, J. M., Aoki, J., & Regar, E. (2005). Geometrical validation of intravascular ultrasound radiofrequency data analysis (virtual histology) acquired with a 30 MHz Boston Scientific corporation imaging catheter. *Catheterization and Cardiovascular Interventions, 66*(4), 514–518. doi:10.1002/ccd.20447

Rodriguez-Granillo, G. A., Garcia-Garcia, H. M., Mc Fadden, E. P., Valgimigli, M., Aoki, J., & de Feyter, P. (2005). In vivo intravascular ultrasound-derived thin-cap fibroatheroma detection using ultrasound radiofrequency data analysis. *Journal of the American College of Cardiology, 46*(11), 2038–2042. doi:10.1016/j.jacc.2005.07.064

Rodriguez-Granillo, G. A., Garcia-Garcia, H. M., Valgimigli, M., Schaar, J. A., Pawar, R., van der Giessen, W. J., et al. (2006). In vivo relationship between compositional and mechanical imaging of coronary arteries. Insights from intravascular ultrasound radiofrequency data analysis. *Am Heart J, 151*(5), 1025 e1021-1026.

Rodriguez-Granillo, G. A., Garcia-Garcia, H. M., Valgimigli, M., Vaina, S., van Mieghem, C., & van Geuns, R. J. (2006). Global characterization of coronary plaque rupture phenotype using three-vessel intravascular ultrasound radiofrequency data analysis. *European Heart Journal, 27*(16), 1921–1927. doi:10.1093/eurheartj/ehl104

Rodriguez-Granillo, G. A., McFadden, E. P., Valgimigli, M., van Mieghem, C. A., Regar, E., & de Feyter, P. J. (2006). Coronary plaque composition of nonculprit lesions, assessed by in vivo intracoronary ultrasound radio frequency data analysis, is related to clinical presentation. *American Heart Journal, 151*(5), 1020–1024. doi:10.1016/j.ahj.2005.06.040

Sales, F. J., Falcao, B. A., Falcao, J. L., Ribeiro, E. E., Perin, M. A., & Horta, P. E. (2010). Evaluation of plaque composition by intravascular ultrasound "virtual histology": The impact of dense calcium on the measurement of necrotic tissue. *EuroIntervention, 6*(3), 394–399. doi:10.4244/EIJV6I3A65

Sano, K., Kawasaki, M., Ishihara, Y., Okubo, M., Tsuchiya, K., & Nishigaki, K. (2006). Assessment of vulnerable plaques causing acute coronary syndrome using integrated backscatter intravascular ultrasound. *Journal of the American College of Cardiology, 47*(4), 734–741. doi:10.1016/j.jacc.2005.09.061

Sarno, G., Garg, S., Gomez-Lara, J., & Serruys, P. W. (2010). Intravascular ultrasound radiofrequency analysis after optimal coronary stenting with initial quantitative coronary angiography guidance: An ATHEROREMO sub-study. *EuroIntervention*(ahead of print, June 2010).

Sathyanarayana, S., Carlier, S., Li, W., & Thomas, L. (2009). Characterisation of atherosclerotic plaque by spectral similarity of radiofrequency intravascular ultrasound signals. *EuroIntervention, 5*(1), 133–139. doi:10.4244/EIJV5I1A21

Schaar, J. A., de Korte, C. L., Mastik, F., Baldewsing, R., Regar, E., & de Feyter, P. (2003). Intravascular palpography for high-risk vulnerable plaque assessment. *Herz, 28*(6), 488–495. doi:10.1007/s00059-003-2488-6

Schaar, J. A., De Korte, C. L., Mastik, F., Strijder, C., Pasterkamp, G., & Boersma, E. (2003). Characterizing vulnerable plaque features with intravascular elastography. *Circulation, 108*(21), 2636–2641. doi:10.1161/01.CIR.0000097067.96619.1F

Schaar, J. A., Muller, J. E., Falk, E., Virmani, R., Fuster, V., & Serruys, P. W. (2004). Terminology for high-risk and vulnerable coronary artery plaques. Report of a meeting on the vulnerable plaque, June 17 and 18, 2003, Santorini, Greece. *European Heart Journal, 25*(12), 1077–1082. doi:10.1016/j.ehj.2004.01.002

Schaar, J. A., Regar, E., Mastik, F., McFadden, E. P., Saia, F., & Disco, C. (2004). Incidence of high-strain patterns in human coronary arteries: Assessment with three-dimensional intravascular palpography and correlation with clinical presentation. *Circulation, 109*(22), 2716–2719. doi:10.1161/01.CIR.0000131887.65955.3B

Schoenhagen, P., Ziada, K. M., Kapadia, S. R., Crowe, T. D., Nissen, S. E., & Tuzcu, E. M. (2000). Extent and direction of arterial remodeling in stable versus unstable coronary syndromes: An intravascular ultrasound study. *Circulation, 101*(6), 598–603.

Serruys, P. W., Garcia-Garcia, H. M., Buszman, P., Erne, P., Verheye, S., & Aschermann, M. (2008). Effects of the direct lipoprotein-associated phospholipase A(2) inhibitor darapladib on human coronary atherosclerotic plaque. *Circulation, 118*(11), 1172–1182. doi:10.1161/CIRCULATIONAHA.108.771899

Serruys, P. W., Ormiston, J. A., Onuma, Y., Regar, E., Gonzalo, N., & Garcia-Garcia, H. M. (2009). A bioabsorbable everolimus-eluting coronary stent system (ABSORB): 2-year outcomes and results from multiple imaging methods. *Lancet, 373*(9667), 897–910. doi:10.1016/S0140-6736(09)60325-1

Shin, E. S., Garcia-Garcia, H. M., Garg, S., Park, J., Kim, S. J., & Serruys, P. W. (2010). The assessment of Shin's method for the prediction of creatinine kinase-MB elevation after percutaneous coronary intervention: an intravascular ultrasound study. *The International Journal of Cardiovascular Imaging, 27*(6).

Shin, E. S., Garcia-Garcia, H. M., & Serruys, P. W. (2010). A new method to measure necrotic core and calcium content in coronary plaques using intravascular ultrasound radiofrequency-based analysis. *The International Journal of Cardiovascular Imaging, 26*(4), 387–396. doi:10.1007/s10554-009-9567-6

Slager, C. J., Wentzel, J. J., Gijsen, F. J., Thury, A., van der Wal, A. C., & Schaar, J. A. (2005). The role of shear stress in the destabilization of vulnerable plaques and related therapeutic implications. *Nature Clinical Practice. Cardiovascular Medicine, 2*(9), 456–464. doi:10.1038/ncpcardio0298

Slager, C. J., Wentzel, J. J., Schuurbiers, J. C., Oomen, J. A., Kloet, J., & Krams, R. (2000). True 3-dimensional reconstruction of coronary arteries in patients by fusion of angiography and IVUS (ANGUS) and its quantitative validation. *Circulation, 102*(5), 511–516.

Stahr, P. M., Hofflinghaus, T., Voigtlander, T., Courtney, B. K., Victor, A., & Otto, M. (2002). Discrimination of early/intermediate and advanced/complicated coronary plaque types by radiofrequency intravascular ultrasound analysis. *The American Journal of Cardiology, 90*(1), 19–23. doi:10.1016/S0002-9149(02)02379-2

Stone, G. W., Maehara, A., Lansky, A. J., de Bruyne, B., Cristea, E., & Mintz, G. S. (2011). A prospective natural-history study of coronary atherosclerosis. *The New England Journal of Medicine, 364*(3), 226–235. doi:10.1056/NEJMoa1002358

Stone, G. W., & Mintz, G. S. Letter by Stone and Mintz regarding article, "unreliable assessment of necrotic core by virtual histology intravascular ultrasound in porcine coronary artery disease". *Circ Cardiovasc Imaging, 3*(5), e4; author reply e5.

Thim, T., Hagensen, M. K., Wallace-Bradley, D., Granada, J. F., Kaluza, G. L., & Drouet, L. (2010). Unreliable assessment of necrotic core by virtual histology intravascular ultrasound in porcine coronary artery disease. *Circ Cardiovasc Imaging, 3*(4), 384–391. doi:10.1161/CIRCIMAGING.109.919357

Thury, A., Wentzel, J. J., Vinke, R. V., Gijsen, F. J., Schuurbiers, J. C., & Krams, R. (2002). Images in cardiovascular medicine. Focal in-stent restenosis near step-up: Roles of low and oscillating shear stress? *Circulation, 105*(23), e185–e187. doi:10.1161/01.CIR.0000018282.32332.13

Timaran, C. H., Rosero, E. B., Martinez, A. E., Ilarraza, A., Modrall, J. G., & Clagett, G. P. (2010). Atherosclerotic plaque composition assessed by virtual histology intravascular ultrasound and cerebral embolization after carotid stenting. *Journal of Vascular Surgery, 52*(5). doi:10.1016/j.jvs.2010.05.101

Tobis, J. M., Mallery, J., Mahon, D., Lehmann, K., Zalesky, P., & Griffith, J. (1991). Intravascular ultrasound imaging of human coronary arteries in vivo. Analysis of tissue characterizations with comparison to in vitro histological specimens. *Circulation, 83*(3), 913–926.

Toi, T., Taguchi, I., Yoneda, S., Kageyama, M., Kikuchi, A., & Tokura, M. (2009). Early effect of lipid-lowering therapy with pitavastatin on regression of coronary atherosclerotic plaque. Comparison with atorvastatin. *Circulation Journal, 73*(8), 1466–1472. doi:10.1253/circj.CJ-08-1051

Topol, E. J., & Nissen, S. E. (1995). Our preoccupation with coronary luminology. The dissociation between clinical and angiographic findings in ischemic heart disease. *Circulation, 92*(8), 2333–2342.

Valgimigli, M., Rodriguez-Granillo, G. A., Garcia-Garcia, H. M., Malagutti, P., Regar, E., & de Jaegere, P. (2006). Distance from the ostium as an independent determinant of coronary plaque composition in vivo: An intravascular ultrasound study based radiofrequency data analysis in humans. *European Heart Journal, 27*(6), 655–663. doi:10.1093/eurheartj/ehi716

van der Steen, A., de Korte, C., Mastik, F., & Schaar, J. (2003). Three dimensional tissue hardness imaging. *World Patent, WO03*(017845), A1.

Van Herck, J., De Meyer, G., Ennekens, G., Van Herck, P., Herman, A., & Vrints, C. (2009). Validation of in vivo plaque characterisation by virtual histology in a rabbit model of atherosclerosis. *EuroIntervention, 5*(1), 149–156. doi:10.4244/EIJV5I1A23

Van Mieghem, C. A., Bruining, N., Schaar, J. A., McFadden, E., Mollet, N., & Cademartiri, F. (2005). Rationale and methods of the integrated biomarker and imaging study (IBIS): Combining invasive and non-invasive imaging with biomarkers to detect subclinical atherosclerosis and assess coronary lesion biology. *The International Journal of Cardiovascular Imaging, 21*(4), 425–441. doi:10.1007/s10554-004-7986-y

Van Mieghem, C. A., McFadden, E. P., de Feyter, P. J., Bruining, N., Schaar, J. A., & Mollet, N. R. (2006). Noninvasive detection of subclinical coronary atherosclerosis coupled with assessment of changes in plaque characteristics using novel invasive imaging modalities: The integrated biomarker and imaging study (IBIS). *Journal of the American College of Cardiology, 47*(6), 1134–1142. doi:10.1016/j.jacc.2005.09.075

Virmani, R., Burke, A. P., Farb, A., & Kolodgie, F. D. (2006). Pathology of the vulnerable plaque. *Journal of the American College of Cardiology, 47*(8Suppl), C13–C18. doi:10.1016/j.jacc.2005.10.065

Virmani, R., Kolodgie, F. D., Burke, A. P., Farb, A., & Schwartz, S. M. (2000). Lessons from sudden coronary death: A comprehensive morphological classification scheme for atherosclerotic lesions. *Arteriosclerosis, Thrombosis, and Vascular Biology, 20*(5), 1262–1275. doi:10.1161/01. ATV.20.5.1262

Volcano. (n.d.). *Clinical studies and trials*. Retrieved from http://volcanocorp.com/clinical/clinical-studies-trials.asp

Volcano. (n.d.). *Products: IVUS imaging*. Retrieved from http://volcanocorp.com/products/ivus-imaging/vh-ivus.asp

von Birgelen, C., Hartmann, M., Mintz, G. S., van Houwelingen, K. G., Deppermann, N., & Schmermund, A. (2004). Relationship between cardiovascular risk as predicted by established risk scores versus plaque progression as measured by serial intravascular ultrasound in left main coronary arteries. *Circulation, 110*(12), 1579–1585. doi:10.1161/01.CIR.0000142048.94084.CA

Wang, J. C., Normand, S. L., Mauri, L., & Kuntz, R. E. (2004). Coronary artery spatial distribution of acute myocardial infarction occlusions. *Circulation, 110*(3), 278–284. doi:10.1161/01. CIR.0000135468.67850.F4

Wu, X., Maehara, A., Mintz, G. S., Kubo, T., Xu, K., & Choi, S. Y. (2010). Virtual histology intravascular ultrasound analysis of non-culprit attenuated plaques detected by grayscale intravascular ultrasound in patients with acute coronary syndromes. *The American Journal of Cardiology, 105*(1), 48–53. doi:10.1016/j.amjcard.2009.08.649

Yamagishi, M., Terashima, M., Awano, K., Kijima, M., Nakatani, S., & Daikoku, S. (2000). Morphology of vulnerable coronary plaque: Insights from follow-up of patients examined by intravascular ultrasound before an acute coronary syndrome. *Journal of the American College of Cardiology, 35*(1), 106–111. doi:10.1016/S0735-1097(99)00533-1

Young Joon, H., Myung Ho, J., Yun Ha, C., Eun Hye, M., Jum Suk, K., Min Goo, L., et al. (2009). Plaque components at coronary sites with focal spasm in patients with variant angina: Virtual histology-intravascular ultrasound analysis. *Int J Cardiol.*

Zhang, L., Liu, Y., Zhang, P. F., Zhao, Y. X., Ji, X. P., & Lu, X. T. (2010). Peak radial and circumferential strain measured by velocity vector imaging is a novel index for detecting vulnerable plaques in a rabbit model of atherosclerosis. *Atherosclerosis, 211*(1), 146–152. doi:10.1016/j.atherosclerosis.2010.01.023

APPENDIX

ABBREVIATIONS

- **ACS:** Acute Coronary Syndrome
- **CAD:** Coronary Artery Disease
- **DES:** Drug-Eluting Stent
- **IB:** Integrated Backscatter
- **ID:** IVUS-Derived
- **IVUS:** Intravascular Ultrasound
- **NC:** Necrotic Core
- **OCT:** Optical Coherence Tomography
- **PCI:** Percuteneous Coronary Intervention
- **PROSPECT:** Providing Regional Observations to Study Predictors of Events in the Coronary Tree
- **QCA:** Quantitative Coronary Angiography
- **RF:** Radiofrequency
- **TCFA:** Thin-Cap Fibroatheroma
- **VH:** Virtual Histology
- **VP:** Vulnerable Plaque

Chapter 5
Implications of Intracoronary Ultrasound Imaging for Clinical Practice

Christos V. Bourantas
Castle Hill Hospital, UK

Katerina K. Naka
University of Ioannina, Greece

Scot Garg
Castle Hill Hospital, UK

Farqad M. Alamgir
Castle Hill Hospital, UK

Angela Hoye
Castle Hill Hospital, UK

Lampros K. Michalis
University of Ioannina, Greece

ABSTRACT

Intracoronary ultrasound (ICUS) provides detailed microscopic imaging of coronary anatomy within a living patient. These images allow visualization of lumen, outer vessel wall, and plaque and give reliable information regarding the constitution of the plaque and the extent of the atherosclerotic disease. However, although it provides supplementary information to coronary angiography which may be useful in diagnosis and treatment planning, its clinical application is limited due to the additional expense, procedure time, and the risk of complication that ICUS examination carries. In this chapter, we review the literature and summarize the clinical indications of ICUS imaging in diagnostic and therapeutic procedures.

DOI: 10.4018/978-1-61350-095-8.ch005

INTRODUCTION

Coronary angiography constitutes the predominant imaging modality for portraying coronary artery morphology and anatomy, and guiding interventions. Its ability to provide in two dimensions (2-D) a holistic visualization of vessels' silhouette and geometry allows direct assessment of the extent and severity of coronary atherosclerosis and provides valuable information for treatment planning. As the complexity of interventions has increased it has become apparent that coronary angiography has significant limitations. First of all due to its limited resolution coronary angiography cannot accurately estimate the severity of moderate lesions. In addition, it provides only 2-D images of the luminal silhouette and not the real 3-D anatomy of the vessel; a fact which renders it unreliable for assessing luminal narrowing in the cases of overlapping or foreshortened segments. Finally, it is unable to delineate the complex anatomy of a lesion and gives no data regarding the plaque load and the constitution of the atheroma information that are valuable to plan treatment and estimate prognosis (Kotani *et al.* 2003, Hong *et al.* 2004).

To overcome these limitations intracoronary ultrasound (ICUS) was introduced as a supplementary image modality to coronary angiography. This provides the interventional cardiologist with transverse cross sections of the lumen, stent and vessel wall and allows accurate assessment of plaque burden and identification of the constitution of the plaque. These additional data allow a more accurate assessment of coronary lesions and may offer potential advantages over coronary angiography for deciding appropriate therapy. This chapter focus on the clinical indications of ICUS imaging and is organized as follows: the background section discusses the controversies over the use of ICUS; the main section presents the current indications for ICUS in diagnostic angiography and in percutaneous coronary interventions (PCI) while in the future trends section,

we explore the potential role of systems, which will allow automated ICUS processing in clinical practice.

BACKGROUND

Although ICUS is regarded as the gold standard for assessing coronary dimensions and evaluating coronary pathology it has a limited clinical applicability. Recent data from British Cardiovascular Interventional Society indicates that ICUS imaging is only available in 60% of UK PCI's centers, and used in less than 2.5% of PCI procedures. This paradox has been attributed to the fact that ICUS examination is expensive, can be time consuming, requires additional radiation exposure and caries a small risk of complication such as coronary dissection or abrupt vessel closure (Hausmann *et al.* 1995). In addition, many interventional cardiologists avoid using ICUS since they are not familiar with it, and are unaware of the potential advantages of its use.

On the other hand, new developments in coronary intervention (e.g. drug eluting stents (DES), improved guidewires) have enabled more complex lesions to be amenable to PCI; a fact which has created a greater need for more detailed visualization of coronary pathology. Thus, over the recent past there has been an increased interest in the role of ICUS in clinical practice and a trend towards more frequent use.

Main Focus - Clinical Indications of ICUS Imaging

Utility of ICUS in Diagnostic Procedures

The conventional method for the evaluation of a lesion and for the quantification of coronary artery disease progress is quantitative coronary angiography (QCA). To validate the performance of QCA a number of studies have compared ICUS

Table 1. Studies which investigated the correlation between ICUS and QCA in native coronary segments

Study	Patients enrolled	Condition	Number of segments studied	Correlation between ICUS and QCA	Variable
Nissen *et al.*	8 43	Normal CAD	33 segments 162 diseased segments	High correlation High correlation	MLD (r=0.92) MLD (r=0.86)
Werner *et al.*	14	CAD	14 segments	High correlation	LA (r=0.86; p<0.001) LD (r=0.91; p<0.0001)
Hodgson *et al.*	65	CAD	65 diseased segments	Good correlation Moderate correlation	LA for the reference segment (r=0.70, p<0.001) LA for the lesions (r=0.63, p<0.05)
De Scheerder *et al.*	48	CAD	46 normal segments 80 with mild disease	High correlation Moderate correlation	LD (r=0.92, p<0.0001) LD (r=0.47, p<0.001)
Alfonso *et al.*	25	CAD	25 normal segments on X-ray angiogram	Moderate correlation	MLD (r=0.59; p<0.05) Maximum RLD (r=0.61; p<0.05)
Iwami *et al.*	21	CAD	46 diseased segments	High correlation	LA (r=0.93, p<0.001)
Ozaki *et al.*	150	CAD	41 diseased segments	Moderate correlation	LD (r=0.59, p<0.01)
Hoffman *et al.*	57	CAD	71 diseased segments	Moderate correlation	MLD (r=0.65; p<0.0001) RLD (r=0.67; p<0.0001)
			71 lesions after BA	Good correlation	MLD (r=0.79; p<0.0001) RLD (r=0.72; p<0.0001)
Bourantas *et al.*	23	CAD	24 diseased segments	Good correlation	LA (r=0.69, p<0.01)

r, correlation coefficient; p, significance of the differences; ICUS, intracoronary ultrasound; QCA, quantitative coronary angiography; CAD, coronary artery disease; MLD, minimal luminal diameter; BA, balloon angioplasty; LA, luminal area; RLD reference luminal diameter; LD, luminal diameter.

and QCA measurements in native and in treated segments, demonstrating that in most cases QCA correlates well with ICUS and provides a reliable assessment of the severity of a lesion (Table 1 and 2). However, there are occasions where ICUS imaging is necessary. More specifically in native segments ICUS should be used to study diffusely diseased segments with a large plaque burden as in these segments QCA maybe unreliable, since its accuracy depends on the assumption that the vessel segments neighboring the stenosed segment are healthy (Jensen *et al.* 2008). In addition, QCA may undervalue the severity of lesions located at the origin of a side branch due to the increased density of contrast agent in these areas (Bourantas et. al. 2008). Finally, ICUS examination (and fractional flow reserve ratio) can be used to assess the severity of a hazy or intermediate stenosis where coronary angiography cannot provide accurate

information. By ICUS, a minimum luminal area (MLA) of less than 4mm^2 suggests a significant stenosis, which requires further treatment as it is associated with reduced myocardial perfusion (Nishioka *et al.* 1999).

ICUS appears also useful in assessing lesions located in the left main coronary artery (LMCA) (Figure 1). Jasti *et al.* (2004) showed that a MLA less than 6mm^2 suggests a significant LMCA stenosis; while two studies (Sano et al. 2007, Abizaid *et al.* 1999) reported a poor association between ICUS and QCA measurements for the minimum luminal diameter (MLD) of an intermediate LMCA lesion. Finally, Sano *et al.* (2007) showed that almost half of intermediate LMCA lesions have an MLD <6mm^2 on ICUS, whilst Abizaid *et al.* (1999) demonstrated that in contrast to fractional flow reserve, ICUS measurements

Table 2. Studies which investigated the correlation between ICUS and QCA after percutaneous coronary intervention

Study	Patients enrolled	Number of studied segments	Procedure	Correlation between ICUS and QCA	Variable
Werner et al.	14	11	BA	Good Poor	LD (r=0.82; p<0.001) LA (r=0.48; p=0.10)
De Scheerder et al.	48	48	BA	Poor	LD (r=0.28, p<0.05)
Nakamura et al.	84	91	BA	Moderate	MLD in segments without injury (r=0.67, p=0.001);
				None	MLD in segments with deep injury
Ozaki et al.	150	100	BA	Low	LD (r=0.47, p<0.05)
		50	Rotational atherectomy	Low	LD (r=0.44, p<0.05)
Hoffman et al.	57	71	BA	High	MLD (r=0.79; p<0.0001) RLD (r=0.72; p<0.0001)
Prati et al.	131	151	Stent implantation	Moderate	QCA indexes of in-stent restenosis and ICUS measurements of neointimal hyperplasia (p=0.61-0.74; p<0.0001)
Blasini et al.	223	223	Stent implantation	Good	Reference luminal diameter (r=0.89; p<0.0001)
				Moderate	MLD (r=0.71; p<0.001)
Bourantas et al.	23	17	Stent implantation	Moderate	LA (r=0.55, p<0.01)

r, correlation coefficient; p, significance of the differences. ICUS, intracoronary ultrasound; QCA, quantitative coronary angiography; BA, balloon angioplasty; CAD, coronary heart disease; LD, luminal diameter; LA, luminal area; MLD, minimum luminal diameter; RLD, reference luminal diameter.

Figure 1. Angiographic images of left coronary system in right anterior oblique caudal (A) and postero-anterior caudal (C) projection, and ICUS image of the distal LMCA There appears to be only minor distal left main coronary artery plaque on angiography, however ICUS images demonstrate a significant distal LMCA lesion (B), with a minimum luminal area of 5.8mm².

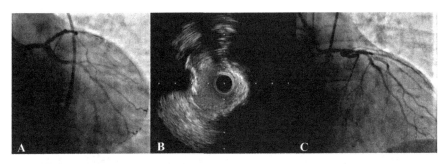

also provide valuable prognostic information in patients with an ambiguous LMCA lesion.

ICUS seems also to have a role in assessing the severity of a lesion located in segments treated with PCI. Trials examining the accuracy of QCA in segments treated with balloon angioplasty (BA) or directional coronary atherectomy (DCA), have shown that QCA estimations differs from the ICUS derived measurements (Table 2). This discrepancy has been attributed to the inability of QCA to evaluate the plaque injury, luminal damage and luminal complexity created from these procedures. Similar results have also been noted in stented segments. Three studies showed a moderate correlation between ICUS and QCA measurements in stented segments (Blasini *et al.* 1997, Prati *et al.* 2002, Bourantas *et al.* 2008) with the largest study showing a drop in the correlation coefficient between ICUS and QCA estimations for the luminal area in segments with in-stent restenosis (ISR) (from r = 0.55, *p* < 0.01 to r = 0.44, *p* < 0.01). These findings indicate that QCA may provide unreliable measurements in segments treated with any type of percutaneous intervention and thus whenever there is an increased suspicion of either a suboptimal result post BA, DCA or ISR, ICUS examination should be performed to assess luminal morphology and dimensions and guide further treatment (Figure 2).

Role of ICUS in Treatment Planning

Apart from the accurate assessment of luminal lesions ICUS imaging also offers potential advantages over coronary angiography for deciding the appropriate treatment. Mintz *et al.* (1994)

and Lee at al. (1995) reported that the additional information (plaque's morphology and composition) provided by ICUS may change therapy in up to 40% of treated lesions.

Plaque Morphology

Until recently there was a general agreement that coronary revascularization should be performed only in cases of significant luminal compromise. However, many acute coronary syndromes are provoked by a ruptured plaque which often originates in a non-obstructive lesion. Two studies have attempted to address the prognostic significance of ruptured plaques and both found that there is a low event rate long term, and this supports a conservative treatment (Rioufol *et al.* 2004, Ohlmann *et al.* 2005). However, these studies examined plaques which had already ruptured and contained no thrombus, and thus it was argued that these plaques were likely to be biological inactive and had lost their potential to form thrombus. Consequently, there is still a dilemma about how to treat a recently ruptured plaque, located in a non stenotic segment and containing thrombus, with some of the interventional cardiologists to argue that it is sensible to stent these lesions (Arampatzis *et al.* 2003). ICUS can be used to detect a newly

Figure 2. Left anterior oblique angiographic image of a right coronary artery (A). The arrow corresponds to the catheter's location at the point where the ICUS image (B) was obtained. ICUS demonstrates significant ISR (40% of the stent area) which cannot be seen on the coronary angiogram.

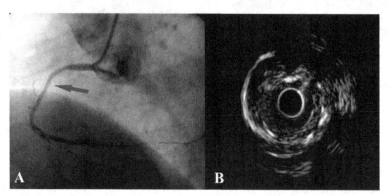

Figure 3. Angiographic images of the right coronary artery before (A) and after the injection of diluted contrast agent (C). There is non-flow limiting disease and haziness in the mid right coronary artery (arrow). ICUS examination (B) revealed a non-obstructive plaque with extensive calcium deposition that was not detected on coronary angiography.

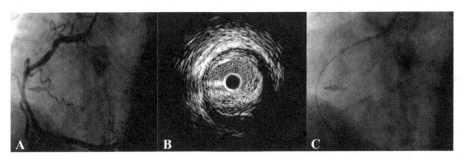

ruptured plaque with thrombus and potentially to modify the treatment strategy.

Plaque Composition

The histological characteristics of plaque play an important role in the natural evolvement of the atherosclerotic process and may be key in a lesion-specific treatment strategy. It has been demonstrated that the presence of calcium at the site of the stenosis is identified in only 15% cases using coronary angiography, whereas with the use of ICUS, calcium detection improves up to 85% (Figure 3). More importantly ICUS provides also information about the distribution of calcium throughout the length and the circumference of the vessel. Calcified coronary lesions result in a smaller final lumen diameter and less acute lumen gain after BA especially in cases where the calcium is located close to the luminal border. To achieve optimal treatment higher pressure balloon inflations or the use of cutting balloons or a rotablator is necessary before stent implantation (Henneke *et al.* 1999, Vavuranakis *et al.* 2001). Furthermore, stent implantation in this setting is associated with more frequent complications such as coronary dissection which increases the risk for ISR (Kawaguchi *et al.* 2008). Thus, whenever there is an increased suspicion of a calcified lesion, and especially in cases of unsuccessful balloon

dilation of a lesion, ICUS examination should be performed to assess plaque composition and guide treatment.

Utility of ICUS in Guiding Treatment

Balloon Angioplasty

Since the development of drug eluting stents (DES) coronary stenting constitutes the treatment of choice in the majority of PCIs. However, there are occasions where BA is preferred especially in cases of diffusely diseased vessels or when the stent cannot be advanced to the lesion (e.g. due to an increased tortuosity of the proximal segment) or in bifurcation lesions for the treatment of the side branch stenosis. In this setting ICUS imaging can be used to guide BA as it provides information regarding the reference diameter and the length of the lesion. In the CLOUT study (Stone *et al.* 1997) ICUS was implemented to assess plaque burden and vessel dimensions, and to select an appropriately sized balloon (balloon's diameter halfway between the lumen and external elastic membrane). This resulted in significant improvements in luminal dimensions post BA without increased rates of dissections or other major complications (Table 3). Similar results were reported in BEST study where ICUS guided BA

Table 3. Studies used to assess the value of ICUS during percutaneous coronary interventions

Study	No of patients	Aim	End points	Results
CLOYT	102 patients (104 lesions, ICUS guided angioplasty performed in 77 lesions)	To investigate whether the use of oversized balloons selected by ICUS would improve outcome after angioplasty	• Reduction in %DS and increase in MLD before and after ICUS guided balloon angioplasty as measured in ICUS and angiographic images • Clinical complications before and after ICUS guided angioplasty	• Improvement in %DS and MLD after ICUS guided balloon angioplasty in ICUS and angiographic images • Trend toward an increase in mild/moderate dissections but no difference in severe complications
BEST	254 (132 randomised to ICUS guided balloon angioplasty and 122 had stent implantation)	To assess whether an ICUS guided angioplasty would provide similar results to stent implantation.	• **Primary:** angiographic restenosis (>50% DS) at 6 months • **Secondary:** MACE (death, MI, unstable angina, TLR)	• No differences between the two groups in primary end points • Restenosis more frequent in the stent group
OARS	199 (213 lesions) underwent DCA under ICUS inspection	To examine whether a more aggressive DCA performed under ICUS guidance is safe and results in larger luminal diameters and lower restenosis	• **Primary:** angiographic restenosis (>50% DS) at 6 months. • **Secondary:** post procedural DS 50%, TVR, MI, and death.	• Reduction of angiographic restenosis (29% vs. 50% in CAVEAT study) • Compared to CAVEAT study increased procedural success (97% vs. 82%), and reduction in major complications (2.5% vs. 4.0%) and TVR (18% vs. 34%) was noted
OPTICUS	550 (275 assigned to ICUS guided, and 275 to angiographic based treatment)	To assess the effect of ICUS guidance during stent implantation on restenosis at follow up	• **Primary:** restenosis rate, MLD, %DS at 6 months • **Secondary:** MACE (death, MI, TVR) at 6 and 12 months follow-up	No differences between the two groups in primary and secondary end points
CRUISE	499 patients (270 in the ICUS guided and 229 patients in the angiographic guided group)	To compare ICUS and angiographic guided stenting in patients undergoing stent implantation at high pressures.	• **Primary:** Minimum luminal dimensions determined by angiography and ICUS • **Secondary:** MACE (death, Q-wave MI, TVR) at 9 months.	• The luminal dimensions were larger in the ICUS guided group • No differences in death and MI between the two groups but there was lower risk for TVR in the ICUS guided group.
TULIP	150 patients (74 randomized to ICUS and 76 to angiographic guided stenting	To examine whether ICUS guided stenting in long lesions (>20m) improves outcome	• **Primary:** MLD and MACE (cardiac death, MI and TLR) at 6months follow up • **Secondary:** angiographic success and restenosis, combined events at 12 months	• ICUS group has larger MLD at 6months follow up • Fewer MACE occurred at 6 and at 12 months in the ICUS group

CSA, cross sectional area; DS, diameter stenosis; ICUS, intravascular ultrasound; MACE, major adverse events; MI, myocardial infarction; MLD, minimal lumen diameter; TLR, target lesion revascularization; TVR, target vessel revascularization.

appeared to be non inferior to stent implantation (Schiele *et al.* 2003).

ICUS can also be used after a BA to detect vessel injury. In the past interventional cardiologists argued that coronary dissection post BA is a marker of abrupt closure; however recent data show that abrupt closure occurs in only 5% of dissected segments. Thus nowadays there is a general agreement that further treatment is required in cases where the dissection results in reduced Thrombolysis In Myocardial Infarction (TIMI) flow (less than III) while in cases where there is an angiographic suspicion of significant circumferential and longitudinal extent of the dissected plaque ICUS examination can be implemented to assess extent and decide on further treatment (Honye *et al.* 1992).

Directional Atherectomy and Rotational Atherectomy

Nowadays DCA is rarely used. However, when it is considered ICUS can be used to identify suitable lesions by demonstrating the presence of calcification which is a predictor of procedural failure. In addition, it can be implemented to reduce the risk of complications and improve the short and long term results as it can demonstrate the areas with the maximal plaque and thus direct DCA. The use of ICUS guidance during DCA can also allow a more aggressive plaque removal, improving the immediate results and reducing the frequency of ISR (from 50% in the CAVET study (Topol *et al.* 1993) to 29% in OARS study (Simonton *et al.* 1998)). Therefore, the authors suggest the implementation of ICUS in DCA since it contributes to higher success rates, reduced repeat revascularisation procedures and lower cardiac mortality.

In a similar manner ICUS imaging appears to be useful in the context of rotational atherectomy. Accurate measurement of the luminal dimensions before the procedure may allow the safe use of larger burrs and thus increased plaque removal resulting in a greater luminal gain (De Franco *et al.* 1996). In addition ICUS can be implemented after the end of the procedure to examine the final results and detect vessel injury.

Bare Metal Stent Implantation

When bare metal stents (BMS) were initially used, a high rate of sub-acute stent thrombosis (ST) and ISR was noted. The introduction of antiplatelet therapy and the development of more refined stents contributed to an improvement in both short and long term results while ICUS imaging helped to understand the mechanism involved in BMS failure. Colombo *et al.* (1995) implemented ICUS to show that the main cause of BMS throm-

bosis was incomplete stent strut apposition and asymmetrical stent expansion and suggested the concept of higher pressure inflation. The addition of antiplatelet treatment further decrease the risk of stent thrombosis (ST) to <1% while large randomized trials showed controversial results regarding the impact of ICUS on BMS ISR. Three studies (OPTICUS, CRUISE and RESIST) reported no difference in prognosis between the patients who had ICUS guided BMS implantation and those who had angiographically guided stenting while TULIP trial demonstrated improved prognosis in the ICUS guided group at 12-month follow-up (target lesion revascularization 10% vs. 23%; *p* = 0.02 and major adverse events 12% vs. 27%; *p* = 0.03 Table 3). In view of these results the routine use of ICUS is not recommended during BMS implantation. However, in complex cases or in cases where inadequate stent expansion is suspected ICUS can be used to assess the final results and guide further treatment. Finally, ICUS imaging is indicated in those patients with long coronary lesions who cannot be treated with DES (e.g. inability to receive treatment with aspirin and clopidogrel). In this setting the approach of ICUS guided BA with spot stenting appears to be associated with improved prognosis (Colombo *et al.* 2001).

Drug Eluting Stent Implantation

Since the first applications of DES a number of ICUS based studies have been performed to assess their efficacy and investigate the cause of early or late stent thrombosis (ST) and ISR. The obtained results were similar to those noted in the BMS. Thus, stent under-expansion (Mintz 2007), small stent areas (minimum stent area is >5mm^2; Fujii *et al.* 2004), increased length of the stent and DES struts disruption appeared to be associated with an increased risk for ISR while inadequate plaque coverage seemed to lead edge stenosis (Lemos *et al.* 2003). There are fewer data regarding the causes of ST but it seems that malapposition (Cook *et al.*

Figure 4. Angiographic images obtained after the implantation of a drug eluting stent in the LCx (A). In the fluoroscopic image showing the implanted stent (arrow) there was no evidence of stent malapposition. However, ICUS examination showed areas with where the stent struts were not fully apposed (*), (C).

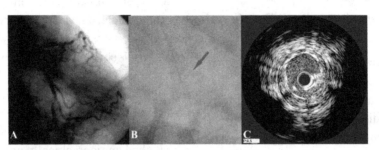

2007) and inadequate DES expansion (Fujii *et al.* 2005) may also be predictors of ST (Figure 4).

Three studies have examined the clinical utility of ICUS in patients treated with DES. Gil *et al.* (2007) showed that ICUS guided stenting is associated with a reduced risk of major adverse events (7.3% in ICUS group vs. 16.2% in the group who had DES implantation without ICUS guidance). However, on the other hand Fujimoto *et al.* (2008) showed that angiographically guided sirolimus-eluting stent implantation is safe, and provides a good mid-term outcome that compares well to ICUS guided treatment. Finally Roy *et al.* (2008) demonstrated that routine ICUS-guided DES deployment does not reduce the risk of major adverse events, or late ST at 1 year follow-up. Therefore, nowadays ICUS examination is not recommended during routine DES implantation. However, it has been suggested ICUS examination to be considered in high risk patients (e.g. diabetics, patients with renal failure or in those who cannot be treated with dual anti-platelet treatment) though, there is no randomised data to support this recommendation (Mintz and Weissman 2006).

ICUS Imaging in Complex Lesions

In 2008 Gerber and Colombo announced the commencement of the first trial (AVIO) which aims to investigate whether ICUS guided DES implantation is complex lesion results in increased

luminal diameter and improves prognosis (Gerber and Colombo 2008). Unfortunately, this study has not been completed yet and as there are no specific recommendations, the use of ICUS in this setting depends on operator judgment and experience.

Mintz and Weissman 2006 suggested the use of ICUS imaging for optimizing DES deployment in bifurcation lesions in long stenoses and in small vessels where the risk of ISR is high. Many interventionists also advocate the use of ICUS to plan LMCA PCI, assess the final result after DES implantation and optimize stent deployment. Recently Park *et al.* (2009) demonstrated that ICUS is indicated during LMCA DES implantation as it results to improved prognosis (3-year mortality: 4.7% for the ICUS guided group vs. 16% for the angiographically guided group, p=0.048) while it appears to not affect outcome in patients who receive BMS (3-year mortality: 8.6% vs. 10.8%, p=0.38 respectively).

ICUS has an emerging role in helping to identify sub-intimal position of the guide-wire in case of coronary dissections as it allows the visualization of contrast agent injection into the true lumen (Figure 5). Finally, it can also be used in chronic total occlusions to identify the entry site in cases where there is an abrupt stamp at the origin of a side branch (Ochiai *et al.* 2006).

Figure 5. Angiographic views during a PCI in a chronically occluded LAD. Right anterior oblique caudal view showing the blocked LAD.

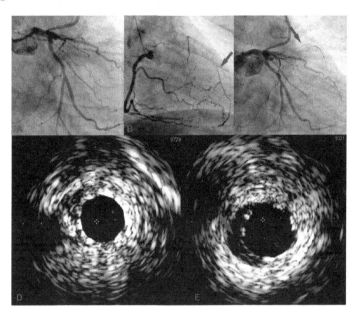

FUTURE TRENDS

Over the last years a number of (semi-) automated methodologies and softwares have been developed which allowed fast and reliable ICUS processing (Sonka *et al*. 1995, Koning *et al*. 2002). These systems operate in a user-friendly environment and provide accurate measurements regarding luminal, outer vessel wall and stent dimensions and thus have contributed to the broad use of ICUS in research and in the study of the atherosclerosis. Further processing of ICUS signal using radiofrequency integrated backscatter analysis provided expedite and reliable quantification of the type of the plaque and identification of vulnerable plaques. Although there are no data to support the implementation of these technologies in clinical practice it is possible in future clinical data from on-going studies to support their use in treatment planning.

Bourantas *et al*. recently reported the first user-friendly software which is able to provide in real time 3-D coronary artery reconstruction by fusing ICUS and angiographic data (Bourantas

et al. 2008). The described system allowed reliable and comprehensive representation of vessel morphology and plaque distribution and provides quantitative measurements which maybe useful in clinical practice and assist optimal treatment. However, randomized control trials are first required to test the efficacy and the utility of this system before its broad use in therapeutic procedures.

CONCLUSION

In this review we have attempted to summarize the clinical indications for ICUS imaging (Table 4). ICUS may be used to assess the severity of an ambiguous lesion and plaque burden and provide information regarding the composition of the plaque. During intervention, IVUS has several potential advantages, enabling accurate choice of stent or balloon diameter and length or the need for atherectomy. Thus, although ICUS adds to the cost and duration of the procedure, it is a useful tool in selective cases as it allows correct diagnosis and may improve prognosis.

Table 4. Clinical indications for ICUS imaging

Diagnostic procedure	Degree of evidence
Assessment of a lesion located in a diffusely diseased segment	++
Hazy lesion or lesion with intermediate severity	+
Lesions located at the origin of a side branch	++
Evaluation of a lesions located in the LMCA	++
Detection of restenosis in segments treated with BA, DCA or stent implantation	++
Treatment planning	
Identification of the morphology and constitution of the plaque	+
BA: Selection of balloon's dimensions and assessment of final result	+++
DCA: Identification of the type of the plaque of the areas with increased plaque	++
Rotational atherectomy: Selection of the appropriate burr	+
BMS: Routine use in clinical practice for optimal final results	-
Spot stenting	++
Inadequate stent expansion on coronary angiography	+
DES: Routine use in clinical practice for optimal final results	-
High risk patients (renal failure, diabetes mellitus, patients who cannot be treated with long term dual antiplatelet therapy)	+
Sub-optimal results in coronary angiography	+
Complex lesions: Coronary bifurcations	+
Small vessels	+
Long lesions	+
LMCA stenting	+++
Identification of the true lumen in dissected segments	+
Identification of optimal entry/true lumen in CTO	+

LMCA, left main coronary artery; POBA, balloon angioplasty; DCA, directional coronary atherectomy; CTO, chronic total occlusion; BMS, bare metal stent; DES, drug eluting stent.

Degree of evidence: (-): ICUS is not necessary; (+): ICUS is suggested but lack of clinical evidence to support its utility; (++): ICUS is recommended based on data from small observational studies; (+++): ICUS is indicated according to data from randomized control trials.

REFERENCES

Abizaid, A. S., Mintz, G. S., Abizaid, A., Mehran, R., Lansky, A. J., & Pichard, A. D. (1999). One-year follow-up after intravascular ultrasound assessment of moderate left main coronary artery disease in patients with ambiguous angiograms. *Journal of the American College of Cardiology, 34*(3), 707–715. doi:10.1016/S0735-1097(99)00261-2

Arampatzis, C. A., Ligthart, J. M., Schaar, J. A., Nieman, K., Serruys, P. W., & de Feyter, P. J. (2003). Images in cardiovascular medicine. Detection of a vulnerable coronary plaque: A treatment dilemma. *Circulation, 108*(5), e34–e35. doi:10.1161/01.CIR.0000075303.04340.EF

Blasini, R., Neumann, F. J., Schmitt, C., Böken-kamp, J., & Schömig, A. (1997). Comparison of angiography and intravascular ultrasound for the assessment of lumen size after coronary stent placement: Impact of dilation pressures. *Catheterization and Cardiovascular Diagnosis, 42*(2), 113–119. doi:10.1002/(SICI)1097-0304(199710)42:2<113::AID-CCD2>3.0.CO;2-G

Bourantas, C. V., Kalatzis, F. G., Papafaklis, M. I., Fotiadis, D. I., Tweddel, A. C., & Katsouras, C. S. (2008). ANGIOCARE: An automated system for fast three dimensional coronary reconstruction using angiographic and intracoronary ultrasound data. *Catheterization and Cardiovascular Interventions, 72*(2), 166–175. doi:10.1002/ccd.21527

Bourantas, C. V., Tweddel, A. C., Papafaklis, M. I., Karvelis, P. S., Fotiadis, D. I., & Katsouras, C. S. (2009). Comparison of quantitative coronary angiography with intracoronary ultrasound. Can quantitative coronary angiography accurately estimate the severity of a luminal stenosis? *Angiology, 60*(2), 169–179.

Colombo, A., De Gregorio, J., Moussa, I., Kobayashi, Y., Karvouni, E., & Di Mario, C. (2001). Intravascular ultrasound-guided percutaneous transluminal coronary angioplasty with provisional spot stenting for treatment of long coronary lesions. *Journal of the American College of Cardiology, 38*(5), 1427–1433. doi:10.1016/S0735-1097(01)01557-1

Colombo, A., Hall, P., Nakamura, S., Almagor, Y., Maiello, L., & Martini, G. (1995). Intracoronary stenting without anticoagulation accomplished with intravascular ultrasound guidance. *Circulation, 91*, 1676–1688.

Cook, S., Wenaweser, P., Togni, M., Billinger, M., Morger, C., & Seiler, C. (2007). Incomplete stent apposition and very late stent thrombosis after drug-eluting stent implantation. *Circulation, 115*(18), 2426–2434. doi:10.1161/CIRCULATIONAHA.106.658237

De Franco, A. C., Nissen, S. E., Tuzcu, E. M., & Whitlow, P. L. (1996). Incremental value of intravascular ultrasound during rotational coronary atherectomy. *Catheterization and Cardiovascular Diagnosis*, (Suppl), 23–33.

Fujii, K., Carlier, S. G., Mintz, G. S., Yang, Y. M., Moussa, I., & Weisz, G. (2005). Stent underexpansion and residual reference segment stenosis are related to stent thrombosis after sirolimus-eluting stent implantation: An intravascular ultrasound study. *Journal of the American College of Cardiology, 45*(7), 995–998. doi:10.1016/j.jacc.2004.12.066

Fujii, K., Mintz, G. S., Kobayashi, Y., Carlier, S. G., Takebayashi, H., & Yasuda, T. (2004). Contribution of stent underexpansion to recurrence after sirolimus-eluting stent implantation for in-stent restenosis. *Circulation, 109*(9), 1085–1088. doi:10.1161/01.CIR.0000121327.67756.19

Fujimoto, H., Tao, S., Dohi, T., Ito, S., Masuda, J., & Haruo, M. (2008). Primary and mid-term outcome of sirolimus-eluting stent implantation with angiographic guidance alone. *Journal of Cardiology, 51*(1), 18–24. doi:10.1016/j.jjcc.2007.09.002

Gerber, R., & Colombo, A. (2008). Does IVUS guidance of coronary interventions affect outcome? A prime example of the failure of randomized clinical trials. *Catheterization and Cardiovascular Interventions, 71*, 646–654. doi:10.1002/ccd.21489

Gil, R. J., Pawłowski, T., Dudek, D., Horszczaruk, G., Zmudka, K., & Lesiak, M. (2007). Investigators of direct stenting vs optimal angioplasty trial (DIPOL): Comparison of angiographically guided direct stenting technique with direct stenting and optimal balloon angioplasty guided with intravascular ultrasound. The multicenter, randomized trial results. *American Heart Journal, 154*(4), 669–675. doi:10.1016/j.ahj.2007.06.017

Hausmann, D., Erbel, R., Alibelli-Chemarin, M. J., Boksch, W., Caracciolo, E., & Cohn, J. M. (1995). The safety of intracoronary ultrasound. A multicenter survey of 2207 examinations. *Circulation, 91*(3), 623–630.

Henneke, K. H., Regar, E., König, A., Werner, F., Klauss, V., & Metz, J. (1999). Impact of target lesion calcification on coronary stent expansion after rotational atherectomy. *American Heart Journal, 137*(1), 93–99. doi:10.1016/S0002-8703(99)70463-1

Hong, M. K., Mintz, G. S., Lee, C. W., Kim, Y. H., Lee, S. W., & Song, J. M. (2004). Comparison of coronary plaque rupture between stable angina and acute myocardial infarction: A three-vessel intravascular ultrasound study in 235 patients. *Circulation*, *110*(8), 928–933. doi:10.1161/01. CIR.0000139858.69915.2E

Honye, J., Mahon, D. J., Jain, A., White, C. J., Ramee, S. R., & Wallis, J. B. (1992). Morphological effects of coronary balloon angioplasty in vivo assessed by intravascular ultrasound imaging. *Circulation*, *85*(3), 1012–1025.

Hu, F. B., Tamai, H., Kosuga, K., Kyo, E., Hata, T., & Okada, M. (2003). Intravascular ultrasound-guided directional coronary atherectomy for unprotected left main coronary stenoses with distal bifurcation involvement. *The American Journal of Cardiology*, *92*(8), 936–940. doi:10.1016/ S0002-9149(03)00973-1

Jasti, V., Ivan, E., Yalamanchili, V., Wongpraparut, N., & Leesar, M. A. (2004). Correlations between fractional flow reserve and intravascular ultrasound in patients with an ambiguous left main coronary artery stenosis. *Circulation*, *110*(18), 2831–2836. doi:10.1161/01.CIR.0000146338.62813.E7

Jensen, L. O., Thayssen, P., Mintz, G. S., Egede, R., Maeng, M., & Junker, A. (2008). Comparison of intravascular ultrasound and angiographic assessment of coronary reference segment size in patients with type 2 diabetes mellitus. *The American Journal of Cardiology*, *101*(5), 590–595. doi:10.1016/j.amjcard.2007.10.020

Kawaguchi, R., Tsurugaya, H., Hoshizaki, H., Toyama, T., Oshima, S., & Taniguchi, K. (2008). Impact of lesion calcification on clinical and angiographic outcome after sirolimus-eluting stent implantation in real-world patients. *Cardiovascular Revascularization Medicine; Including Molecular Interventions*, *9*(1), 2–8. doi:10.1016/j. carrev.2007.07.004

Kawasaki, M., Takatsu, H., Noda, T., Sano, K., Ito, Y., & Hayakawa, K. (2002). In vivo quantitative tissue characterization of human coronary arterial plaques by use of integrated backscatter intravascular ultrasound and comparison with angioscopic findings. *Circulation*, *105*(21), 2487–2492. doi:10.1161/01.CIR.0000017200.47342.10

Koning, G., Dijkstra, J., Von Birgelen, C., Tuinenburg, J. C., Brunette, J., & Tardif, J. C. (2002). Advanced contour detection for three – dimensional intracoronary ultrasound: A validation in – vitro and in vivo. *The International Journal of Cardiovascular Imaging*, *18*, 235–248. doi:10.1023/A:1015551920382

Kotani, J., Mintz, G. S., Castagna, M. T., Pinnow, E., Berzingi, C. O., & Bui, A. B. (2003). Intravascular ultrasound analysis of infarct-related and non-infarct-related arteries in patients who presented with an acute myocardial infarction. *Circulation*, *107*(23), 2889–2893. doi:10.1161/01. CIR.0000072768.80031.74

Lee, D. Y., Eigler, N., Luo, H., Nishioka, T., Tabak, S. W., & Forrester, J. S. (1995). Effect of intracoronary ultrasound imaging on clinical decision making. *American Heart Journal*, *129*(6), 1084–1093. doi:10.1016/0002-8703(95)90387-9

Lemos, P. A., Saia, F., Ligthart, J. M., Arampatzis, C. A., Sianos, G., & Tanabe, K. (2003). Coronary restenosis after sirolimus-eluting stent implantation: Morphological description and mechanistic analysis from a consecutive series of cases. *Circulation*, *108*(3), 257–260. doi:10.1161/01. CIR.0000083366.33686.11

Mintz, G. S. (2007). Features and parameters of drug-eluting stent deployment discoverable by intravascular ultrasound. *The American Journal of Cardiology*, *100*, 26M–35M. doi:10.1016/j. amjcard.2007.08.019

Mintz, G. S., Pichard, A. D., Kovach, J. A., Kent, K. M., Satler, L. F., & Javier, S. P. (1994). Impact of preintervention intravascular ultrasound imaging on transcatheter treatment strategies in coronary artery disease. *The American Journal of Cardiology*, *73*(7), 423–430. doi:10.1016/0002-9149(94)90670-X

Mintz, G. S., & Weissman, N. J. (2006). Intravascular ultrasound in the drug-eluting stent era. *Journal of the American College of Cardiology*, *48*(3), 421–429. doi:10.1016/j.jacc.2006.04.068

Nishioka, T., Amanullah, A. M., Luo, H., Berglund, H., Kim, C. J., & Nagai, T. (1999). Clinical validation of intravascular ultrasound imaging for assessment of coronary stenosis severity: Comparison with stress myocardial perfusion imaging. *Journal of the American College of Cardiology*, *33*(7), 1870–1878. doi:10.1016/S0735-1097(99)00100-X

Ochiai, M., Ogata, N., Araki, H., Ashida, K., Isomura, N., & Mikoshiba, Y. (2006). Intravascular ultrasound guided wiring for chronic total occlusions. *Indian Heart Journal*, *58*(1), 15–20.

Ohlmann, P., Kim, S. W., Mintz, G. S., Pregowski, J., Tyczynski, P., & Maehara, A. (2005). Cardiovascular events in patients with coronary plaque rupture and nonsignificant stenosis. *The American Journal of Cardiology*, *96*(12), 1631–1635. doi:10.1016/j.amjcard.2005.07.087

Park, S. J., Kim, Y. H., Park, D. W., Lee, S. W., Kim, W. J., & Suh, J. (2009). MAIN-COMPARE Investigators: Impact of intravascular ultrasound guidance on long-term mortality in stenting for unprotected left main coronary artery stenosis. *Circ Cardiovasc Interv*, *2*(3), 167–177. doi:10.1161/CIRCINTERVENTIONS.108.799494

Prati, F., Pawlowski, T., Sommariva, L., Labellarte, A., Manzoli, A., & Boccanelli, A. (2002). Intravascular ultrasound and quantitative coronary angiography assessment of late in-stent restenosis: In vivo human correlation and methodological implications. *Catheterization and Cardiovascular Interventions*, *57*(2), 155–160. doi:10.1002/ccd.10298

Rioufol, G., Gilard, M., Finet, G., Ginon, I., Boschat, J., & Andre-Fouet, X. (2004). Evolution of spontaneous atherosclerotic plaque rupture with medical therapy: Long-term follow-up with intravascular ultrasound. *Circulation*, *110*, 2875–2880. doi:10.1161/01.CIR.0000146337.05073.22

Roy, P., Steinberg, D. H., Sushinsky, S. J., Okabe, T., Pinto Slottow, T. L., & Kaneshige, K. (2008). The potential clinical utility of intravascular ultrasound guidance in patients undergoing percutaneous coronary intervention with drug-eluting stents. *European Heart Journal*, *29*(15), 1851–1857. doi:10.1093/eurheartj/ehn249

Sano, K., Mintz, G. S., Carlier, S. G., de Ribamar, C., Qian, J., & Missel, E. (2007). Assessing intermediate left main coronary lesions using intravascular ultrasound. *American Heart Journal*, *154*(5), 983–988. doi:10.1016/j.ahj.2007.07.001

Schiele, F., Meneveau, N., Gilard, M., Boschat, J., Commeau, P., & Ming, L. P. (2003). Intravascular ultrasound-guided balloon angioplasty compared with stent: immediate and 6-month results of the multicenter, randomized balloon equivalent to stent study (BEST). *Circulation*, *107*, 545–551. doi:10.1161/01.CIR.0000047212.94399.7E

Simonton, C. A., Leon, M. B., Baim, D. S., Hinohara, T., Kent, K. M., & Bersin, R. M. (1998). Optimal directional coronary atherectomy: Final results of the Optimal Atherectomy Restenosis Study (OARS). *Circulation*, *97*(4), 332–339.

Sonka, M., Zhang, X., Siebes, M., Bissing, M., DeJong, S., & Collins, S. (1995). Segmentation of intravascular ultrasound images: A knowledge-based approach. *IEEE Transactions on Medical Imaging, 14*(4), 719–732. doi:10.1109/42.476113

Stone, G. W., Hodgson, J. M., St Goar, F. G., Frey, A., Mudra, H., & Sheehan, H. (1997). Improved procedural results of coronary angioplasty with intravascular ultrasound-guided balloon sizing: The CLOUT pilot trial. Clinical outcomes with ultrasound trial (CLOUT) investigators. *Circulation, 95*(8), 2044–2052.

Topol, E. J., Leya, F., Pinkerton, C. A., Whitlow, P. L., Hofling, B., & Simonton, C. A. (1993). A comparison of directional atherectomy with coronary angioplasty in patients with coronary artery disease. The CAVEAT Study Group. *The New England Journal of Medicine, 329*(4), 221–227. doi:10.1056/NEJM199307223290401

Vavuranakis, M., Toutouzas, K., Stefanadis, C., Chrisohou, C., Markou, D., & Toutouzas, P. (2001). Stent deployment in calcified lesions: Can we overcome calcific restraint with high-pressure balloon inflations? *Catheterization and Cardiovascular Interventions, 52*(2), 164–172. doi:10.1002/1522-726X(200102)52:2<164::AID-CCD1041>3.0.CO;2-S

KEY TERMS AND DEFINITIONS

Balloon Angioplasty: Is a revascularization procedure that uses a catheter with a deflated balloon at the tip that is inserted into the narrowed part of the coronary artery. The balloon is then inflated, causing luminal dilation.

Directional Atherectomy: Is an adjunctive technique used in coronary revascularizations, which involves the selective excision and retrieval of an atherosclerotic plaque using a cutter on the end of a catheter that is directed under fluoroscopic guidance towards the plaque and is able to erase the atherosclerotic material.

Fractional Flow Reserve: Is a technique used in coronary interventions to assess the heaemodynamc significance of a stenosis by measuring the pressure differences across a coronary lesion at maximal hyperaemia.

Intracoronary Ultrasound: Is a medical imaging modality that provides intra-luminal visualisation visualization of the coronary artery using a specially designed catheter with contains a miniaturized ultrasound probe attached on its distal end. The probe is able to submit signals perpendicular to its axis and receive the scatter signal. Processing of the scatter signal generates cross-sectional images of the arterial segment which portray in detail the lumen, outer vessel wall and plaque.

Quantitative Coronary Angiography: Is a semi-automated method used to estimate the severity of a lesion. It involves the implementation of an edge detection algorithm which identifies the luminal borders in angiographic images and then assesses the severity of the lesion using the neighboring disease free segments as a reference.

Rotational Atherectomy: An adjunctive technique used in coronary revascularizations that utilizes a high-speed rotating diamond coated elliptically shaped burr to ablate atheroma in the coronary arteries.

Stent (Bare Metal and Drug Eluting): A metal tube, which is implanted into diseased coronary arteries to keep them open. In the case of drug eluting stents the tube is covered by a drug that is progressively released and blocks cellular proliferation.

Chapter 6
Research Utility of Intravascular Ultrasound

Hector M. Garcia-Garcia
Erasmus MC, The Netherlands

Scot Garg
Royal Blackburn Hospital, UK

Salvatore Brugaletta
Erasmus MC, The Netherlands

Roberto Diletti
Erasmus MC, The Netherlands

Eun-Seok Shin
Erasmus MC, The Netherlands
University of Ulsan, Korea

Patrick W. Serruys
Erasmus MC, The Netherlands

ABSTRACT

Intravascular ultrasound was designed to overcome the limitations of angiography, and in the process it has helped greatly with our understanding of coronary artery disease. There is no doubt that it plays an important role in contemporary interventional cardiology. In this regard, this chapter reviews the most important uses of intravascular ultrasound in current research.

INTRODUCTION / BACKGROUND

Intravascular ultrasound (IVUS) was designed to overcome the limitations of angiographic "luminography", and was the first intravascular coronary imaging technique to be developed. The technique has made significant contributions to our current understanding of coronary artery disease through its capacity to obtain *in vivo* images of the vessel wall and its interaction with coronary devices. In addition, IVUS has played a key role in the field of percutaneous coronary interventions (PCI), depicting the pitfalls of stent deployment and improving stenting techniques, a major step

DOI: 10.4018/978-1-61350-095-8.ch006

that has dramatically decreased peri-procedural complications, allowing the use of the simpler anti-thrombotic treatments used today. Of note, many modern trials assessing PCI are IVUS based. Knowledge of coronary vessel remodeling during atherogenesis is largely based on IVUS evidence, and many progression/regression studies of atherosclerosis are also IVUS-based. In 20 years of existence, IVUS has undergone major changes. In the last decade backscatter analysis was introduced, facilitating characterization of plaque components and its mechanical properties. Intracoronary multimodality imaging is therefore a promising technique in the study of vulnerable plaques. In complex subsets of PCI, IVUS is an indispensable tool, and new modalities for specific purposes, like forward-looking IVUS for chronic total occlusion recanalisation, are being developed. These trends will be reviewed in this chapter, along with a review of the most important uses of IVUS in current research.

DRUG EFFECTS ON ATHEROSCLEROSIS (TABLE 1)

The initial observations of a positive continuous relationship between coronary heart disease risk and blood cholesterol levels led to the conduction of a number of IVUS-based studies to evaluate the effect of different lipid lowering drugs on atheroma size. Changes in plaque characteristics may be a more relevant endpoint than plaque progression or regression in the prediction of the risk of vascular thrombosis, however imaging tools to accurately evaluate plaque characteristics have only recently become widely available. Other limitations of using conventional grayscale IVUS to assess the natural history of atherosclerosis which should be considered include: 1. catheterization is an invasive procedure and is required for serial imaging; 2. only a segment of the coronary tree can be studied; 3. plaque composition is not obtained; 4. there is no direct evi-

dence linking changes in coronary plaques and clinical events. Figure 1 shows two examples of serial assessment of plaque size changes.

Lipid Modifying Agents

The efficacy of lowering low density lipoprotein (LDL)-C with inhibitors of hydroxymethylglutaryl coenzyme A reductase (statins) is unequivocal; however the change in atheroma size by statins is not constant across all IVUS studies. There are many potential explanations for these discrepancies such as different drug properties, dose, and duration of treatment. In early studies, like the German Atorvastatin Intravascular Ultrasound (GAIN) study,(Schartl *et al.,* 2001) atheroma volume was not reduced by atorvastatin despite the reduction in LDL-C (86 vs. 140 mg/dL) at 12 months. In contrast, the Reversal of Atherosclerosis with Aggressive Lipid Lowering (REVERSAL) (Nissen, Tuzcu, Schoenhagen *et al.*, 2004) study showed that LDL-C levels were lowered by a greater extent with treatment with atorvastatin when compared to pravastatin (110 mg/dL vs. 79 mg/dL), which was subsequently associated with a 2.7% increase in atheroma volume in pravastatin-treated patients, and in a 0.4% reduction in atheroma volume in atorvastatin-treated patients. The clinical significance and the accuracy of IVUS for such measurements are still debated, but these results were "statistically significant". The Pravastatin or Atorvastatin Evaluation and Infection Therapy (PROVE-IT) study,(Cannon *et al.*, 2004) showed that the lower the LDL-C and C-reactive proteins (CRP) values, the greater the reduction in clinical events and atheroma progression.

One of the first studies showing regression of plaque size was the ASTEROID trial (A Study to Evaluate the Effect of Rosuvastatin on Intravascular Ultrasound-Derived Coronary Atheroma Burden) (Nissen *et al.*, 2006). At 24 months, treatment with rosuvastatin 40 mg daily resulted in a lowering of LDL-C to 60.8 mg/dL and an

Table 1. Intravascular ultrasound progression/regression studies

Statin trials Study	Design	Year	Treatment	n	FU	Primary endpoint†	Results (mean±SD)
GAIN (Schartl, et al., 2001)	RCT	2001	Atorvastatin	48	12 months	% change in plaque volume	2.5±24.9%
			Control	51			11.8±31.0%
ESTABLISH (Okazaki et al., 2004)	RCT	2004	Atorvastatin	24	6 months	% change in plaque volume	-13.1±12.8%*
			Control	24			-8.7±14.9%
REVERSAL (Nissen, Tuzcu, Schoenhagen, et al., 2004)	RCT	2004	Atorvastatin	253	18 months	% change in plaque volume	4.1±29.6%*
			Pravastatin	249			5.4±20.1%
Jensen (Jensen et al., 2004)	Observational	2004	Simvastatin	40	12 months	% change in plaque volume	-6.3%
Petronio (Petronio et al., 2005)	RCT	2005	Simvastatin	36	12 months	Plaque volume	-2.5±3.0 mm³/mm*
			Control	35			1.0±3.0 mm³/mm
Nishioka (Nishioka et al., 2004)	Observational	2004	Pravastatin, atorvastatin, simvastatin and fluvastatin	22	6 months	Plaque Volume	-35.5±12.7 mm³*
			Control	26			-30.9±15.6 mm³
Tani (Tani et al., 2005)	RCT	2005	Pravastatin	52	6 months	% change in plaque volume	-14.4±23%*
			Control	23			1.1±4.6%
ASTEROID (Nissen, Nicholls, et al., 2006)	Observational	2006	Rosuvastatin	349	24 months	Change in PAV	-0.98±3.15%‡
Takashima (Takashima et al., 2007)	Observational	2007	Pitavastatin	41	6 months	% change in plaque volume	-10.6±9.4%*
			Control	41			8.1±14.0%
COSMOS (Takayama et al., 2009)	Observational	2009	Rosuvastatin	126	18 months	Change in PAV	-5.1±14.1%‡
JAPAN-ACS (Hiro et al., 2009)	RCT	2009	Atorvastatin	127	8-12 months	% change in plaque volume	-18.1±14.2%
			Pitavastatin	125			-16.9±13.9%
ACAT (acyl coenzyme A:cholesterol acyltransferase) inhibitor trials							
A-PLUS (Tardif et al., 2004)	RCT	2004	Avasimibe 50 mg	108	24 months	Change in PAV	0.7±0.4%
			Avasimibe 250 mg	98			0.8±0.4%
			Avasimibe 750 mg	117			1.0±0.3%
			Placebo	109			0.4±0.4%
ACTIVATE (Nissen, Tuzcu, et al., 2006)	RCT	2006	Pactimibe	206	18 months	Change in PAV	0.69±0.25%
			Placebo	202			0.59±0.25%
Increasing high-density lipoprotein therapies							

continued on following page

Table 1. Continued

Statin trials Study	Design	Year	Treatment	n	FU	Primary endpoint†	Results (mean±SD)
ApoA-I Milano (Nissen et al., 2003)	RCT	2003	ApoA-I Milano 15mg/kg	21	5 weeks	Change in PAV	-1.29±3.5%
			ApoA-I Milano 45mg/kg	15			-0.73±2.8%
			Placebo	11			0.14±3.09%
ERASE (Tardif, et al., 2007)	RCT	2007	CSL-111 (re-constituted HDL infusion)	89	4 weeks	% change in plaque volume	-3.41 (IQR -6.55 to 2.25)‡
			Placebo	47			-1.62 (IQR -5.95 to 1.94)
CART-2 (Tardif et al., 2008)	RCT	2008	Succinobucol (AGI-1067)	183	12 months	Absolute change in plaque volume	-3.4±14.5 mm^3
			Placebo	49			-0.6±13.4 mm^3
Others Therapies							
CAMELOT (Nissen, Tuzcu, Libby, et al., 2004)	RCT	2004	Amlodipine	91	24 months	Change in PAV	0.5±3.9%
			Enalapril	88			0.8±3.7%
			Placebo	95			1.3±4.4%‡
ILLUSTRATE (Nissen, et al., 2007)	RCT	2007	Torcetrapib + Atorvastatin	464	24 months	Change in PAV	0.12±2.99%
			Atorvastatin	446			0.19±2.83%
PERSPECTIVE (Rodriguez-Granillo, et al., 2007)	RCT	2007	Perindopril	75	36 months	Change in plaque area	-0.2±1.6mm^2
			Placebo	69			-0.1±1.2mm^2
PERISCOPE (Nissen, Nicholls, Wolski, Nesto, et al., 2008)	RCT	2008	Pioglitazone,	179	18 months	Change in PAV	-0.16% (95% CI: −0.57% to 0.25%)*
			Glimepiride	181			0.73% (95%CI: 0.33% to 1.12%)
STRADIVARIUS (Nissen, Nicholls, Wolski, Rodes-Cabau et al., 2008)	RCT	2008	Rimonabant	335	18 months	Change in PAV	0.25% (95% CI: −0.04% to 0.54%)
			Placebo	341			0.51% (95% CI: 0.22% to 0.80%)
ENCORE II (Luscher et al., 2009)	RCT	2009	Nifedipine	97	18-24 months	% change in plaque volume	5.0 (95% CI: -1.3, 11.2)
			Placebo	96			3.2 (95% CI: -1.9, 8.3)
APPROACH (Gerstein et al., 2010)	RCT	2010	Rosiglitazone	233	18 months	Change in PAV	-0.21 (95% CI: -0.86, 0.44)
			Glipizide	229			0.43 (95% CI: -0.22, 1.08)
IVUS-based tissue characterization studies							

continued on following page

Table 1. Continued

Statin trials Study	Design	Year	Treatment	n	FU	Primary endpoint†	Results (mean±SD)
Yokoyama (Yokoyama et al., 2005)	RCT	2005	Atorvastatin	25	6 months	Overall plaque size and tissue characterization by IB IVUS	Atorvastatin reduced plaque size and changed plaque composition
			Control	25			
Kawasaki (Kawasaki et al., 2005)	RCT	2005	Pravastatin,	17	6 months	Overall tissue characterization by IB IVUS	Statins reduced lipid without changes in plaque size
			Atorvastatin	18			
			Diet	17			
IBIS 2 (Serruys, et al., 2008)	RCT	2008	Darapladib	175	12 months	Necrotic core volume by IVUS VH	Darapladid significantly reduced necrotic core
			Placebo	155			
Nasu (Nasu, et al., 2009)	Observational	2009	Fluvastatin	40	12 months	Overall tissue characterization by IVUS-VH	Fluvastatin reduced plaque and fibro-fatty volume
			Control	40			
Hong (Hong, et al., 2009)	RCT	2009	Simvastatin	50	12 months	Overall tissue characterization by IVUS-VH	Both reduced necrotic core and increased fibro-fatty volume
			Rosuvastatin	50			
Toi (Toi et al., 2009)	RCT	2009	Atorvastatin	80	2-3 weeks	Overall tissue characterization by IVUS-VH	Pitavastatin reduced plaque volume and fibro-fatty
			Pivastatin	80			
Miyagi (Miyagi et al., 2009)	Observational	2009	Statin (pravastatin, Pitavastatin, atorvastatin, fluvastatin, simvastatin)	44	6 months	Overall tissue characterization by IB IVUS	Statins reduced lipid and increased fibrous
			Non-statin	56			

RCT, randomised controlled trial; PAV, percent atheroma volume; IVUS, intravascular ultrasound; IB, integrated backscatter; VH, virtual histology.

*p<0.05 between groups ‡p<0.05 vs. Baseline

† *%Change in Plaque volume* = [Total plaque volume $_{FOLLOW-UP}$ − Total plaque volume $_{BASELINE}$] / [Total plaque volume $_{BASELINE}$]*100

Total plaque volume = [External elastic membrane (EEM) $_{cross\ sectional\ area\ (CSA)}$] − [Lumen$_{CSA}$]

PAV = (EEM$_{CSA}$ − Lumen$_{CSA}$) / (EEM$_{CSA}$) * 100

elevation of high-density lipoprotein cholesterol (HDL-C) by 14.7%. These lipid changes were associated with statistically significant, albeit small reductions in % atheroma volume (0.79%) and total atheroma volume (6.8%).

There are several recent reports showing serial changes of plaque composition in patients treated with various statin treatments. In one of them, patients with stable angina pectoris (n= 80) treated with fluvastatin for 1 year had significant regression of plaque volume, and changes in ath-

erosclerotic plaque composition with a significant reduction of fibrofatty volume (p < 0.0001). This change in fibrofatty volume had a significant correlation with change in LDL-cholesterol level (r = 0.703, p < 0.0001) and change in high sensitive-CRP level (r = 0.357, p = 0.006) (Nasu *et al.*, 2009). Of note, the necrotic core did not change significantly. In a second study, Hong *et al.* (2009), randomized 100 patients with stable angina pectoris (SAP) and acute coronary syndrome (ACS) to either rosuvastatin 10 mg or simvastatin 20 mg for

Figure 1. Serial assessment of progression/regression plaque size. At the top, two corresponding frames from a patient imaged at baseline and follow-up (1 year). In these frames a decrease in plaque burden can be observed (regression of 7%). In addition, negative remodeling of the vessel is present (reduction of vessel area of 2mm²). At the bottom, in contrast, two corresponding frames from a patient imaged at baseline and follow-up (1 year) are showing increase in plaque burden (progression of 4%).

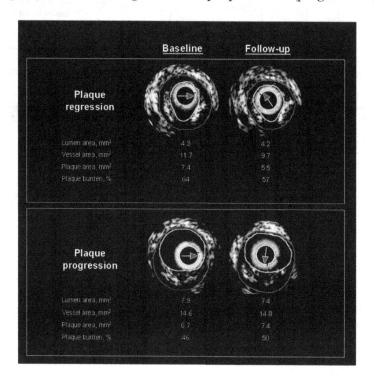

1 year. Overall necrotic core volume significantly decreased (p = 0.010) and fibrofatty plaque volume increased (p = 0.006) after statin treatment. Of note, there was a significant decrease in necrotic core volume (p = 0.015) in the rosuvastatin-treated subgroup. By multiple stepwise logistic regression analysis, the only independent clinical predictor of a decrease in necrotic core volume was baseline HDL-cholesterol level (p = 0.040, odds ratio: 1.044, 95% confidence interval (CI): 1.002 to 1.089) (Hong *et al.*, 2009).

IVUS studies have also demonstrated coronary plaque modification in HDL-treated patients. The infusion of synthetic HDL-C particles containing the variant apolipoprotein, apoA-I Milano, complexed with phospholipids (ETC-216) reduced the percent atheroma volume by -1.06% (3.17%

p = 0.02 compared with baseline) in the combined ETC-216 group at 5 weeks. On the contrary, in the placebo group, percent atheroma volume increased by 0.14% (3.09%; p = 0.97) compared with baseline. In the ERASE study, (Tardif *et al.*, 2007) 60 patients were randomly assigned to receive 4 weekly infusions of placebo (saline), 111 to receive 40 mg/kg of reconstituted HDL (CSL-111); and 12 to receive 80 mg/kg of CSL-111. The latter was discontinued due to liver function test abnormalities. Within the treated group, the percentage change in atheroma volume was -3.4% with CSL-111 (p<0.001 vs. baseline), whilst for the placebo group was -1.6% (p = 0.48 between groups). It is still unclear what the future holds for these therapeutic agents.

Patients with human deficiency of cholesteryl ester transfer protein (CETP) have elevated circulating levels of HDL-C. This has led to research on CETP inhibition as a novel and potentially effective approach to elevate HDL-C. In the ILLUSTRATE trial, the percent atheroma volume (the primary efficacy measure) increase was similarly low in patients receiving atorvastatin monotherapy versus those receiving the combined torcetrapib–atorvastatin therapy after 24 months (0.19% vs. 0.12%, respectively) (Nissen *et al.*, 2007).

The enzyme acyl–coenzyme A: cholesterol acyltransferase (ACAT) esterifies cholesterol in a variety of cells and tissues. Inhibition of ACAT1, by blocking the esterification of cholesterol, can prevent the transformation of macrophages into foam cells, and can slow the progression of atherosclerosis, while inhibition of ACAT2 would be expected to decrease serum lipid levels. However, in the ACTIVATE study, the change in percent atheroma volume was similar in the pactimibe (100 mg daily) and placebo groups (0.69 percent and 0.59 percent, respectively; p= 0.77) (Nissen, Tuzcu *et al.*, 2006).

Anti-hypertensive Agents

Systolic blood pressure has been shown to be an independent predictor of plaque progression by IVUS. A randomized study of patients with coronary artery disease and a diastolic blood pressure < 100 mmHg treated with placebo or antihypertensive therapy using either amlodipine 10 mg daily or enalapril 20 mg daily showed that patients treated with amlodipine had a reduction in plaque size and also a reduction in cardiovascular events as compared to placebo at 24 months.(Nissen, Tuzcu, Libby *et al.*, 2004) The PERSPECTIVE study (Rodriguez-Granillo *et al.*, 2007) a substudy of the EUROPA trial, evaluated the effect of perindopril on coronary plaque progression in 244 patients. There were no differences in the changes in IVUS plaque measurements detected between the perindopril and placebo groups.

Thiazolidinediones

Thiazolidinediones (TZDs) increase insulin sensitivity in peripheral tissues thereby lowering glucose. In addition, TZDs (i.e. rosiglitazone and pioglitazone) lower blood pressure, inflammatory markers, and improve lipid profile, endothelial function, and carotid intimal media thickness. TZDs may therefore reduce progression of coronary atherosclerosis compared to other antidiabetic drugs. Two studies have addressed this question. The APPROACH (Assessment on the Prevention of Progression by Rosiglitazone On Atherosclerosis in Diabetes Patients with Cardiovascular History) (Gerstein *et al.*, 2010) and the PERISCOPE (Comparison of Pioglitazone vs. Glimepiride on Progression of Coronary Atherosclerosis in Patients With Type 2 Diabetes) trials *(Nissen, Nicholls, Wolski, Nesto et al.*, 2008). Rosiglitazone significantly reduced normalized total atheroma volume (TAV) by 5.1 mm^3 (95% CI -10.0, -0.3; p=0.04) when compared to glipizide, whereas pioglitazone just failed to achieve a statistically significant in change in total atheroma volume (−5.5±1.6 vs. −1.5±1.5 mm^3, p=0.06) when compared to glimepiride. Changes in percentage atheroma volume (PAV) in the APPROACH study were not different in patients allocated to glipizide or rosiglitazone (-0.64%, 95% CI -1.46, 0.17; p=0.12), while in the PERISCOPE study pioglitazone was associated with favourable effects on the change of PAV compared to glimepiride (−0.16±0.21 vs. 0.73±0.20%, p=0.002). Pioglitazone resulted in a comparable plaque size reduction compared to rosiglitazone but this reduction was associated with an almost 50% reduction in vessel size so that the change in normalized lumen volume was quite comparable.

Darapladib

The IBIS 2 study compared the effects of 12 months of treatment with darapladib (oral Lp-PLA2 inhibitor, 160 mg daily) or placebo in 330 patients (Serruys *et al.*, 2008). Endpoints included changes in necrotic core size (assessed by IVUS-virtual histology [IVUS-VH]), and atheroma size (assessed by IVUS-grayscale). Background therapy was comparable between groups, with no difference in LDL-cholesterol at 12 months (placebo: 88±34 and darapladib: 84±31 mg/dL, p=0.37). In the placebo-treated group, however, necrotic core volume increased significantly, whereas darapladib halted this increase, resulting in a significant treatment difference of -5.2 mm^3 (p=0.012). These intra-plaque compositional changes occurred without a significant treatment difference in total atheroma volume.

PLAQUE TYPE CHARACTERIZATION

ACS is often the first manifestation of coronary atherosclerosis, making the identification of plaques at high-risk of complication an important component of strategies to reduce casualties associated with atherosclerosis. Our current understanding of plaque biology suggests that ~60% of clinically evident plaque rupture originates within an inflamed thin-capped fibroatheroma (TCFA) (Schaar *et al.*, 2004; Virmani *et al.*, 2006) Pathological studies demonstrated that ruptured plaques are mainly located in the proximal portions of the left anterior descending and circumflex arteries, and are more disperse in the right coronary artery. (Cheruvu *et al.*, 2007) This tendency of advanced plaques to develop preferentially in these locations has been explained by the low shear stress conditions generated in areas with tortuosity or many branches. Low shear stress may induce the migration of lipid and monocytes into the vessel wall leading to the progression of the lesion towards a plaque with high risk of rupture. (Cunningham & Gotlieb, 2005)

Several IVUS-based tissue characterisation imaging techniques are currently available (Table 2 and 3). These imaging modalities should be able to provide insights on the different phases of the development of plaque, as well as of the different key players (i.e. components of the plaque such as necrotic core). Although they may have different platforms and work using different information from the ultrasound signals, they aim at characterising the tissue types of the plaques. The most widely used is IVUS virtual histology (IVUS-VH). Using IVUS-VH, the definition of an IVUS-derived TCFA is a lesion fulfilling the following two criteria in at least 3 frames: (1) plaque burden $\geq$ 40%; and (2) confluent necrotic core $\geq$ 10% in direct contact with the lumen (i.e. no visible overlying tissue) (Garcia-Garcia *et al.*, 2006). Using this definition of IVUS-derived TCFA, on average in patients with ACS who underwent IVUS of all three epicardial coronaries, there were two IVUS-derived TCFAs per patient with half of them showing outward remodelling (Garcia-Garcia, *et al.*, 2006).

Hong *et al.* (2008), reported the frequency and distribution of TCFA in 105 ACS and 107 SAP patients in a 3-vessel IVUS-VH study (Hong *et al.*, 2008). There were 2.5 ± 1.5 in ACS and 1.7 ± 1.1 in SAP TCFAs per patient, p < 0.001. Presentation of ACS was the only independent predictor for multiple IVUS-VH derived TCFA (VH-TCFA) (p = 0.011). Eighty-three percent of VH-TCFAs were located within 40 mm of the coronary ostia.

The potential value of these IVUS-VH derived plaque types in the prediction of adverse coronary events was evaluated in an international multi-centre prospective study, the Providing Regional Observations to Study Predictors of Events in the Coronary Tree study (PROSPECT study) (Stone *et al.*, 2011).

Table 2. Similarities and differences of IVUS and IVUS-based imaging modalities

	IVUS	VH	i-MAP	Integrated Backscatter	Echogenicity
Type of device	Mechanical & electrical	Mechanical and Electrical	Mechanical	Mechanical	Mechanical and electrical
Transducer Frequency	20-40 MHz	20-40 MHz	40MHz	40 MHz	20-40 MHz
Color code	Gray-scale	Fibrous: Green / Necrotic Core: Red / Calcium: White / Fibrofatty: Light green	Fibrous: Light green / Necrotic Core: Pink / Calcium: Blue / Fibrofatty: Yellow	Fibrous: Green / Necrotic Core: Blue / Calcium: Red / Fibrofatty: Yellow	Red for hyperechogenic areas and green for hypoechogenic areas
Backscatter Radiofrequency signal analysis	Amplitude (dB)	Autoregressive model	Fast Fourier Transformation	Fast Fourier Transformation	It does not use backscatter radiofrequency but the amplitude of the signal

The PROSPECT trial was a multi-center, natural history study of ACS patients. All patients underwent PCI in their culprit lesion at baseline, followed by an angiogram and IVUS-VH of the three major coronary arteries. A TCFA with a minimum lumen area of ≤4mm² and a large plaque burden (≥70%), had a 17.2% likelihood of causing an event within three years (Stone, *et al.*, 2011). Interestingly, the anticipated high frequency of acute thrombotic cardiovascular events did not occur, with only a 1% rate of myocardial infarction and no deaths directly attributable to non-culprit vessels over 3 years of follow-up. These results suggest that non-culprit, yet obstructive coronary plaques are most likely to be associated with increasing symptoms rather than thrombotic acute events, with 8.5% of patients presenting with worsening angina and 3.3% with unstable angina.

VASCULAR RESPONSE TO ENDOVASCULAR DEVICES

IVUS has been used extensively as surrogate endpoint in stent trials, primarily to assess effectiveness of devices as it relates to neointimal proliferation. Moreover, IVUS was an essential investigational tool during the initial clinical testing of drug-eluting stents (DES), (Morice *et al.*, 2002; Sousa *et al.*, 2001) confirming the dramatic suppression of neointimal proliferation, revealing new patterns of restenosis and establishing intravascular imaging metrics of stent optimization. In all these studies there is a progressive reduction in neointima hyperplasia from paclitaxel eluting stents (PES) until the new drug-eluting devices. Importantly, factors influencing neointima proliferation include not only the drug eluted, but also the stent design and stent material used. It is also important to highlight that IVUS assessment of the vascular response to endovascular devices

Table 3. Validation studies of IVUS and IVUS based imaging modalities

Author	Study settings	Year	Primary objective	Results			
Grayscale IVUS							
Palmer (Palmer et al., 1999)	*In vitro*	1999	IVUS vs. histology	High inter- and intra-observer reproducibility for: Plaque-type (Kappa 0.87 and 0.89) Focal calcification (0.78 and 0.88) Agreement for overall plaque type between IVUS and histology occurred in 89% of sites (Kappa 0.73 [0.69-0.77]). Specificity ≥90%			
Prati (Prati et al., 2001)	*In vitro*	2001	IVUS vs. histomorphology	IVUS revealed the presence of lipid pools with a sensitivity 65%, and specificity ≥95%			
Virtual Histology IVUS							
Nasu (Nasu et al., 2006)	*In vivo*	2006	Virtual histology compared with in vitro histopathology	Predictive accuracies were NC 88.3%, FT 87.1%, FF 87.1%, DC 96.5% Sensitivities: NC 67.3%, FT 86%, FF 79.3%, DC 50%. Specificities: NC 92.9%, FT 90.5%, FF 100%, DC 98.9%			
Nair (Nair et al., 2007)	*Ex vivo*	2007	Automated coronary plaque characterization with IVUS IB	Predictive accuracies were NC 95.8%, FT 93.5%, FF 94.1%, DC 96.7% Sensitivities: NC 91.7%, FT 95.7%, FF 72.3%, DC 86.5%. Specificities: NC 96.6%, FT 90.9%, FF 97.9%, DC 98.9%			
Granada (Granada et al., 2007)	*Ex vivo*	2007	Plaque characterization using IVUS-VH in a porcine model of complex coronary lesions	IVUS-VH identified the presence of fibrous, fibro-fatty, and necrotic tissue in 58.33%, 38.33%, and 38.33% of lesions, respectively. Sensitivities: FT 76.1%, FF 46%, and NC 41.1%			
Van Herk (Van Herck et al., 2009)	*Ex vivo*	2009	Validation of plaque characterization by IVUS-VH in a rabbit model of atherosclerosis		IVUS-VH Sensitivity	IVUS-VH Specificity	IVUS-VH +ve predictive valve
				Non-calcified thin TCFA	88	96	87
				Calcified TCFA	95	99	93
				Non-calcified fibroatherom	78	98	84
				Calcified atheroma	74	92	70
				VH-IVUS had a kappa value of 0.79			
Thim (Thim et al., 2010)	*Ex vivo*	2010	Unreliable assessment of NC by IVUS-VH in porcine coronary arteries	No correlations were found between the size and/or presence of the NC determined by IVUS-VH and histology.			
Integrated Backscatter IVUS							
Kawasaki (Kawasaki et al., 2002)	*In vivo*	2002	Quantitative tissue characterization of human coronary arterial plaques by use of IB IVUS vs. angioscopic	r:0.954 for each category DC, FF, FT, NC			

continued on following page

Table 3. Continued

Author	Study settings	Year	Primary objective	Results
Kawasaki (Kawasaki et al., 2006)	*In vivo*	2006	Diagnostic accuracy of optical coherence tomography and IB IVUS images for tissue characterization of human coronary plaques	Sensitivities: DC:100% FT:94% Lipid pool:84% Specificities: DC:99% FT:84% Lipid pool:97%
Okubo (Okubo et al., 2008)	*Ex vivo*	2008	Development of IB IVUS for tissue characterization of coronary plaques	Fibrous, lipid-rich and fibrocalcific plaque components classified with accuracy of 93%, 90% and 96%, respectively
iMAP				
Sathyanarayana (Sathyanarayana et al., 2009)	*In vivo*	2009	Characterization of atherosclerotic plaque by spectral similarity of radio-frequency IVUS signals	Ex vivo validation demonstrated accuracies of: 97%, 98%, 95%, and 98% for necrotic, lipidic, fibrotic and calcified regions respectively
Echogenicity				
Bruining (Bruining et al., 2007)	*Ex vivo*	2007	Three-dimensional and quantitative analysis of atherosclerotic plaque composition by automated differential echogenicity	Areas of hypoechogenicity correlated with the presence of smooth muscle cells, and presence of collagen. Areas of hyperechogenicity with acoustic shadowing correlated with calcium

IVUS, intra-vascular ultrasound; DC, dense calcium; FF, fibrofatty tissue; FT, fibrous tissue; NC, necrotic core

can allow identification of the causes of stent restenosis (e.g. sub-optimal expansion of stent; stent fracture, etc) (Brugaletta *et al.,* 2011) and stent thrombosis (e.g. stent under-expansion, edge dissection, geographical miss, residual stenosis, incomplete stent apposition and aneurysms) (Garcia-Garcia et al, 2008).

One of the most common variables used to report restenosis is percentage intimal hyperplasia volume in the stent segment (Mintz, 2007) (Figure 2).

This variable normalizes the intimal hyperplasia to the stent length therefore allowing the comparison of different stent types (bare metal stents [BMS] vs. DES), as well as different drug types (i.e. sirolimus eluting stent –SES- vs.PES) (Table 4**).** This parameter, the percentage intimal

hyperplasia, however, minimizes the impact of focal restenosis. A meta-analysis of TAXUS IV, V and VI demonstrated that nearly half of the stent length was free of intimal hyperplasia in the Taxus group (48.8 ± 36.0% vs. 13.4 ± 22.1% in the control group, p <0.0001) (Escolar *et al.,* 2007). In another study comparing PES and SES, 46.1% and 5.4% of the stent length had neointimal covering, p < 0.001, respectively (Jensen *et al.,* 2008). A similar intimal hyperplasia distribution to the Taxus stent has been reported for the zotarolimus-eluting stent (Miyazawa *et al.,* 2008). It has been suggested that the "patchy" distribution of intimal growth associated with DES (i.e. lack of neointimal tissue in the mid portion of the stent) could be related to a higher concentration

Figure 2. Evaluation of in-stent restenosis by IVUS. These figures show a stent at implant (panels a and a') and 6 months afterwards (panels b and b').

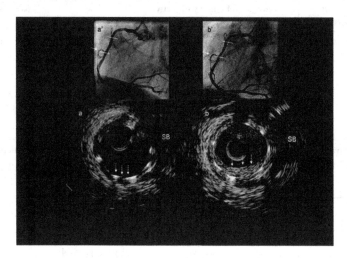

Table 4. Percentage of intimal hyperplasia volume in drug eluting stent trials assessed by intravascular ultrasound.

	Subgroup	Follow-Up (months)	%IH Volume (Mean ± SD)
Sirolimus Eluting Stent Trials			
RAVEL (Serruys et al., 2002)	SES (n= 48)	6	1 ± 3%*
	BMS (n= 47)		29 ± 20%
RAVEL (Abizaid et al., 2004)	SES, diabetes mellitus (n= 19)	6	0.82 ± 1.38%†*
	BMS, diabetes mellitus (n= 25)		30.2 ± 22.9%
SIRIUS (Moses et al., 2003)	SES (n= 23)	9	3.1%*
	BMS (n= 20)		33.4%
SICTO (Lotan et al., 2006)	SES in chronic total occlusions (n= 25)	6	4.9 ± 6.8%
Sao Paulo (Feres et al., 2005)	SES (n= 25)	12	6.6 ±3.0%*
	β radiation (n= 25)		38.0 ± 7.8%
DIABETES I (Jimenez-Queve-do et al., 2006)	SES for diabetics (n= 75)	9	1.31 ± 3.5%
	BMS for diabetics (n= 65)		28.4 ± 21.9%
RIBS II§ (Alfonso et al., 2006)	SES in in-stent restenosis(n= 76)	9	279 mm³ * [IQR 227 to 300]
	Balloon angioplasty in-stent restenosis (n= 74)		197 mm³ [IQR 177 to 230]
Paclitaxel Eluting Stent trials			
TAXUS II (Colombo et al., 2003)	PES slow release (n= 131)	6	7.8 ± 9.9%*
	BMS (n= 136)		23.2 ± 18.2%
TAXUS II (Colombo, et al., 2003)	PES moderate release (n= 135)	6	7.8 ± 9.7%*
	BMS (n= 134)		20.5 ± 16.7%

continued on following page

Table 4. Continued

	Subgroup	Follow-Up (months)	%IH Volume (Mean ± SD)
TAXUS IV (Weissman et al., 2005)	PES slow release (n= 88)	9	12.2 ± 12.4%*
	BMS (n= 82)		29.4 ± 14.1%
TAXUS V	PES (n= 149)	9	13.2 ± 12.0%*
	BMS (n= 135)		31.8 ± 15.1%
TAXUS VI	PES (n= 67)	9	10.7 ± 10.8%*
	BMS (n= 63)		33.0 ± 15.1%
Meta-analysis of TAXUS IV, TAXUS V, TAXUS VI (Weissman et al., 2007)	Overlapping	9	
	PES (n= 45)		9.8 ± 12.0%*
	BMS (n= 35)		39.0 ± 17.1%
	Non-overlapping		
	PES		11.3 ± 10.9%*
	BMS		33.4 ± 16.6%
Meta-analysis of TAXUS IV, TAXUS V, TAXUS VI (Kimura et al., 2008)	Patients with diabetes mellitus	9	
	PES (n= 84)		13.7%*
	BMS (n= 70)		34.9%
	Patients without diabetes mellitus	9	
	PES (n= 208)		11.9%*
	BMS (n= 204)		30.1%
Meta-analysis of TAXUS IV, TAXUS V, TAXUS VI (Doi et al., 2009)	Lesions >26 mm	9	
	PES (n= 38)		13.4 ± 9.2%*
	BMS (n= 29)		34.6 ± 15.7%
DiabeDES (Jensen, et al., 2008)	SES (n= 57)	8	1.0 ± 3.0%*
	PES (n= 51)		12.5 ± 13.4%
Other DES Trials			
ENDEAVOR II (Sakurai et al., 2007)	ZES (n= 178)	8	17.6 ± 10.1%*
	BMS (n= 165)		29.4 ± 17.2%
ENDEAVOR III (Miyazawa, et al., 2008)‡	ZES (n= 190)	8	1.1 ± 0.8 mm^3/mm
	SES (n= 68)		0.2 ± 0.1 mm^3/mm*
ENDEAVOR IV (Waseda et al., 2009)	ZES (n= 79)		16.6 ± 12.0%
	PES (n = 86)		9.9 ± 8.9%*
ENDEAVOR in real world(registry) (Feres et al., 2009)	ZES (n =100)	6	14.4±13.4%
RESOLUTE FIM (Meredith IT, 2007)	ZES (n=30)	4	2.23 ± 2.43%
RESOLUTE (Meredith et al., 2009)	ZES (n= 130)	9	3.73 ± 4.05%
NOBORI I (Chevalier et al., 2009)	Biolimus A9 (n= 43)	9	1.8 ± 5.2%*
	PES (n= 29)		5.5 ± 7.2%
AXXESS PLUS (Miyazawa et al., 2007)	Biolimus A9 (n= 49)	6	2.3 ± 2.2%

continued on following page

Table 4. Continued

	Subgroup	Follow-Up (months)	%IH Volume (Mean ± SD)
AXXENT (Hasegawa et al., 2009)	Biolimus A9 (n= 26)	6	3.0 ± 4.1%
SPIRIT I (Serruys et al., 2005)	EES (n= 21)	6	8.0 ± 10.4%*
	BMS (n= 24)		28.1 ± 14%
SPIRIT I (Tsuchida et al., 2005)	EES (n= 16)	12	10.0 ± 7.0%*
	BMS (n= 21)		28.0 ±12.0%
SPIRIT II (Serruys et al., 2006)	EES(n= 225)	6	2.5 ± 4.7%
	PES (n= 75)		7.4 ± 7.0%
	EES(n= 64)	24	5.2± 6.2%
	PES (n= 31)		5.8 ± 6.3%
SPIRIT III (Stone et al., 2008)	EES(n= 115)	8	6.9 ± 6.4%*
	PES (n= 45)		11.2 ± 9.9%
EXCELLA FIM (Costa et al., 2008)	Novolimus eluting stent (n= 15)	4	2.6 ± 2.6%
		8	6.0 ± 4.4%
GENESIS (Verheye et al., 2009)	Costar PES (n= 16)	6	16.6 ± 12%
	SymBio P and Pimecrolimus ES (n= 26)		27.1 ± 12.4%
	Corio Pimecrolimus ES (n= 16)		41.2 ± 11.5%
Non-polymer SES (Costa et al., 2009)	Non-polymer Vestasync SES (n=15)	9	4.0 ± 2.2%
ABSORB (Ormiston et al., 2008)	Bioresorbable vascular scaffold (n= 29)	6	5.5 ± 8.5%

*p<0.05 vs. control
† median (inter-quartile range)
‡ percentage of neointimal volume index
§ Lumen volume
Table modified from Mintz G (Mintz, 2007)

SES, sirolimus-eluting stents; PES, paclitaxel-eluting stents; ZES, zotarolimus-eluting stent; EES, everolimus-eluting stent; IH vol, intimial hyperplasia volume

of drug in that portion of the stent (Finn *et al.*, 2007).

Some have suggested that DES should be considered as "vulnerable stents" because they have a low but definitive long-term risk of thrombosis (Alfonso, 2008). A "vulnerability triangle" may be formed by 1) a predisposing underlying anatomical substrate (identifiable by IVUS) (Garcia-Garcia, *et al.*, 2008); 2) an unfavourable thrombogenic milieu and 3) the trigger (any potent stimulus for platelet aggregation). Clinical, angiographic and IVUS findings of "vulnerable" stents have been identified. The profound ability of DES to inhibit neointimal proliferation seems to be closely linked to a delayed endothelialization process which, in turn, may favour thrombus formation (Alfonso, 2008). DES deployed in or at the edges of vulnerable plaques may also have a higher risk for this complication (Garcia-Garcia, *et al.*, 2008).

IVUS provides a unique tool to visualize the underlying mechanical factors involved in stent thrombosis. (Cook *et al.*, 2009; Garcia-Garcia, *et al.*, 2008) In the BMS era, IVUS demonstrated that stent under-expansion, malapposition, significant residual plaque at the stent edges or residual dissections were predictive factors for stent thrombosis (Moreno *et al.*, 2004).

In the DES era, severe stent under-expansion appears to be the most important factor affecting most patients suffering from this catastrophic complication (Alfonso *et al.*, 2007; Cook *et al.*, 2007; Fujii *et al.*, 2005). Residual plaque at the edges of the stent have also been detected in most cases. (Cook, *et al.*, 2007; Fujii, *et al.*, 2005) However, residual edge dissections appear to be a more important aetiological factor for stent thrombosis after BMS than after SES implantation. (Alfonso *et al.*, 2004; Alfonso, *et al.*, 2007) As previously discussed, the role of stent malapposition is more controversial. When patients with late incomplete malapposition are followed-up, most of them have an uncomplicated clinical course even in the absence of dual anti-platelet therapy. However, when patients suffering episodes of DES thrombosis are examined during the acute episode, half of them show incomplete malapposition with relatively large areas of malapposition. (Alfonso, *et al.*, 2007; Cook, *et al.*, 2007).

The use of IVUS is highly recommended during coronary interventions performed to treat episodes of stent thrombosis. In a previous study, patients suffering episodes of DES thrombosis were imaged using 3-D IVUS (Alfonso, *et al.*, 2007). An occlusive thrombus within the stent (50% of total stent volume) was recognized in all patients. Most DES had severe under-expansion and all patients had inflow-outflow disease. Notably, malapposition was detected in 50% of cases. A major side-branch jailed by the stent struts was present in 67% of cases. Classic optimal criteria for stent deployment were not seen in any patient.

Following interventions using IVUS guided large balloons or higher pressures, stent expansion improved (minimum stent area 9 ± 3 vs. 12 ± 4 mm^2, p<0.08) and malappositon was resolved in all cases. However, 17% of total stent volume was occupied by residual "resistant" lining thrombus. (Alfonso, *et al.*, 2007) In the study by Cook *et al.*, (Cook, *et al.*, 2007) incomplete apposition was visualized in 77% of patients suffering from very late DES thrombosis.

Most studies suggest that despite early and aggressive treatment, stent thrombosis have dreadful consequences leading to large Q-waves myocardial infarctions and a high mortality rate (from 17% to 45%) (Alfonso, 2008). The large thrombus burden present in most cases of stent thrombosis explains the poorer clinical outcome compared with other patients requiring primary angioplasty (Alfonso, 2008). Treatment of patients with stent thrombosis represents a uniquely challenging procedure. (Alfonso, 2008; Alfonso, *et al.*, 2004; Alfonso, *et al.*, 2007) IVUS should be always used to identify any potential mechanical predisposing factors and to ensure an optimal final result. Whenever possible, implantation of a new stent to improve a suboptimal result should be avoided. In most of these cases, the underlying mechanism will be a resistant thrombus and aggressive pharmacological therapy may cause disappearance of residual thrombus within 1 week (Alfonso, *et al.*, 2007) It is important to keep in mind that in addition to addressing mechanical factors, other important factors (vulnerability triangle) (Alfonso, 2008) should be corrected in these patients and functional studies on platelet reactivity should also be considered (Alfonso, 2006). Two prospective IVUS studies of patients treated with primary angioplasty for episodes of stent thrombosis demonstrate that despite all optimization efforts (IVUS-guided high pressure balloon inflations and systematic intracoronary administration of glycoprotein IIb/IIIa platelet inhibitors and routine use of thrombectomy devices), there was still a significant amount of residual "resistant" thrombus within the stent at the end of the procedure (Alfonso, *et al.*, 2004; Alfonso, *et al.*, 2007). This residual thrombus detected by IVUS appears to explain why suboptimal angiographic results are frequently obtained despite aggressive interventions (Alfonso, *et al.*, 2007).

Recently, the feasibility and safety of an everolimus-eluting bioabsorbable vascular scaffold (BVS) has been assessed with intravascular imaging. The prospective, open-label ABSORB study, enrolled 30 patients with a single de-novo lesion that was suitable for treatment with a single BVS. Post-procedure a notable increase in "dense calcium" (DC) and "necrotic core" (NC) was observed by IVUS-VH, which was thought to reflect the polymeric struts of the BVS. Moreover, at 6-months follow-up, bioresoprtion of the BVS was associated with a corresponding reduction in DC and NC (Garcia-Garcia *et al.*, 2009) (Figure 3).

FUTURE DIRECTIONS

In the future, integration of multiple image technologies in a single catheter is likely to provide a more comprehensive assessment of the coronary vasculature. The combined use of IVUS-VH analysis and optical coherence tomography (OCT) seems to improve the accuracy for TCFA detection (Gonzalo *et al.*, 2009; Sawada *et al.*, 2008) (Figure 4).

Another imaging modality able to characterize coronary athereosclerosis (i.e. lipid core) invasively is near infra-red spectroscopy (NIRS) (Gardner *et al.*, 2008). The NIRS catheter is a 3.2F FDA approved catheter which is compatible with a conventional 0.014" guidewire, and contains a rotating (240Hz) NIRS light source at its tip which is pulled back by a motor drive unit at 0.5mm/s. The catheter's ability to detect lipid core

Figure 3. Imaging of a bioabsorbable scaffold. Patient was imaged with greyscale IVUS (left column) and IVUS-VH (middle column) before and after implantation of a bioabsorbable stent (BVS, Abbott Vascular, Santa Clara, CA, US) and at 6 months.

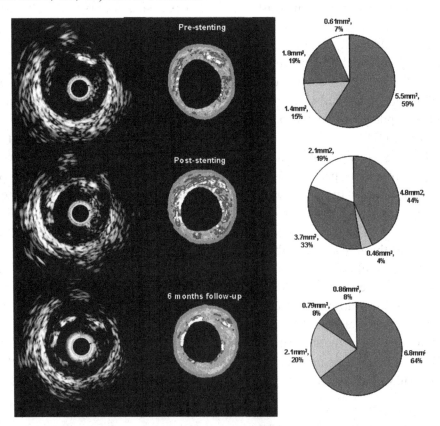

Figure 4. Multimodality assessment of coronary plaques. At the top, a patient was studied with greyscale IVUS (left), IVUS-VH (middle) and OCT (right).

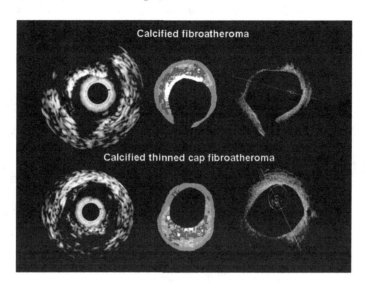

plaque (LCP) has been validated successfully in a human autopsy study, where the device algorithm prospectively identified LCP with a receiver-operator characteristic area of 0.80 (95% confidence interval: 0.76 to 0.85) (Gardner, *et al.*, 2008). A newer 3.2F rapid exchange catheter, the Apollo catheter, has recently been introduced, which combines a 40MHz real time IVUS catheter with a frame speed of 16 frames/second operating at a pullback speed of 0.5mm/sec, with a standard NIRS catheter (Garg *et al.*, 2010). The SPECTACL (SPECTroscopic Assessment of Coronary Lipid) trial, which was a parallel first-in-human multicenter study designed to demonstrate the applicability of the LCP detection algorithm in 106 living patients, confirmed that the intravascular NIRS system safely obtained spectral data in patients that were similar to those from autopsy specimens (Waxman *et al.*, 2009) Another potential combination is NIRS with OCT. Both imaging techniques are light-based which may facilitate their combination in one single catheter. Using NIRS, an accurate characterization of NC can be achieved, while OCT will provide morphological information about the relationship of the NC and lumen, as well as information on the fibrous cap overlying the pool of NC.

IVUS guidance during some interventional procedures may increase the likelihood of a greater success rate. Specifically, in the context of the treatment of chronic total occlusions, the most challenging component of the procedure is to enter the proximal part of the occlusion, and to keep the guidewire within the limits of the vessel to avoid coronary perforations. Forward-looking intravascular ultrasound (FL-IVUS) holds promise because it allows visualization of the vessel, plaque morphology, and true and false lumens in front of the imaging catheter (Figure 5).

The FL-IVUS (Preview catheter) is currently undergoing preclinical and early clinical evaluation. It is a single-use, over the-wire imaging catheter which is advanced over a conventional 0.014-inch guide-wire to the site of the occlusion. The current generation of this catheter has a 45-MHz transducer at the tip and is compatible with a 7-F guide.

CONCLUSION

IVUS has been, and still is, a very important imaging tool for the assessment of intact coronary plaques and the effect of local (i.e. stent) or sys-

Figure 5. Forward-looking intravascular ultrasound (FL-IVUS - Volcano Corporation) is a 45-MHz transducer oriented at a 45° angle at the tip of the catheter, which rotates providing a forward-looking cone of visualization (A). A 0.014-inch chronic total occlusion dedicated guidewire can be advanced through the catheter, and true lumen position can be maintained under FL-IVUS guidance in an antegrade manner. An FL-IVUS view of the proximal end of CTO phantom model (B). Pending permission of Eur Heart Journal.

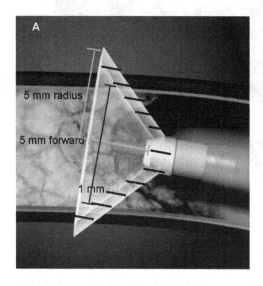
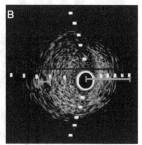

- 5 mm forward
- Tick marks are 1 mm in cross-sectional plane for easy diameter sizing
- This vessel is 9mm across

temic therapies. With the advent of IVUS-based tissue characterization, the use of these evolving imaging modalities will no doubt improve our understanding of coronary atherosclerosis.

REFERENCES

Abizaid, A., Costa, M. A., Blanchard, D., Albertal, M., Eltchaninoff, H., & Guagliumi, G. (2004). Sirolimus-eluting stents inhibit neointimal hyperplasia in diabetic patients. Insights from the RAVEL Trial. *European Heart Journal, 25*(2), 107–112. doi:10.1016/j.ehj.2003.11.002

Alfonso, F. (2006). Pathophysiology of stent thrombosis: platelet activation, mechanical factors, or both? *Journal of the American College of Cardiology, 47*(5), 1086–1087, author reply 1087. doi:10.1016/j.jacc.2005.12.008

Alfonso, F. (2008). The "vulnerable" stent: Why so dreadful? *Journal of the American College of Cardiology, 51*(25), 2403–2406. doi:10.1016/j.jacc.2008.03.029

Alfonso, F., Perez-Vizcayno, M. J., Hernandez, R., Bethencourt, A., Marti, V., & Lopez-Minguez, J. R. (2006). A randomized comparison of sirolimus-eluting stent with balloon angioplasty in patients with in-stent restenosis: Results of the Restenosis Intrastent: Balloon Angioplasty Versus Elective Sirolimus-Eluting Stenting (RIBS-II) trial. *Journal of the American College of Cardiology, 47*(11), 2152–2160. doi:10.1016/j.jacc.2005.10.078

Alfonso, F., Suarez, A., Angiolillo, D. J., Sabate, M., Escaned, J., & Moreno, R. (2004). Findings of intravascular ultrasound during acute stent thrombosis. *Heart (British Cardiac Society), 90*(12), 1455–1459. doi:10.1136/hrt.2003.026047

Alfonso, F., Suarez, A., Perez-Vizcayno, M. J., Moreno, R., Escaned, J., & Banuelos, C. (2007). Intravascular ultrasound findings during episodes of drug-eluting stent thrombosis. *Journal of the American College of Cardiology, 50*(21), 2095–2097. doi:10.1016/j.jacc.2007.08.015

Brugaletta, S., Ribamar Costa Jr, J., & Garcia-Garcia, H. M. (2011). (in press). Assessment of drug-eluting stents and bioresorbable stents by grayscale IVUS and IVUS-based imaging modalities. *The International Journal of Cardiovascular Imaging.* doi:10.1007/s10554-010-9788-8

Bruining, N., Verheye, S., Knaapen, M., Somers, P., Roelandt, J. R., & Regar, E. (2007). Three-dimensional and quantitative analysis of atherosclerotic plaque composition by automated differential echogenicity. *Catheterization and Cardiovascular Interventions, 70*(7), 968–978. doi:10.1002/ccd.21310

Cannon, C. P., Braunwald, E., McCabe, C. H., Rader, D. J., Rouleau, J. L., & Belder, R. (2004). Intensive versus moderate lipid lowering with statins after acute coronary syndromes. *The New England Journal of Medicine, 350*(15), 1495–1504. doi:10.1056/NEJMoa040583

Cheruvu, P. K., Finn, A. V., Gardner, C., Caplan, J., Goldstein, J., & Stone, G. W. (2007). Frequency and distribution of thin-cap fibroatheroma and ruptured plaques in human coronary arteries: A pathologic study. *Journal of the American College of Cardiology, 50*(10), 940–949. doi:10.1016/j.jacc.2007.04.086

Chevalier, B., Silber, S., Park, S. J., Garcia, E., Schuler, G., & Suryapranata, H. (2009). Randomized comparison of the Nobori Biolimus A9-eluting coronary stent with the Taxus Liberte paclitaxel-eluting coronary stent in patients with stenosis in native coronary arteries: The NOBORI 1 trial--Phase 2. *Circ Cardiovasc Interv, 2*(3), 188–195. doi:10.1161/CIRCINTERVENTIONS.108.823443

Colombo, A., Drzewiecki, J., Banning, A., Grube, E., Hauptmann, K., & Silber, S. (2003). Randomized study to assess the effectiveness of slow- and moderate-release polymer-based paclitaxel-eluting stents for coronary artery lesions. *Circulation, 108*(7), 788–794. doi:10.1161/01.CIR.0000086926.62288.A6

Cook, S., Ladich, E., Nakazawa, G., Eshtehardi, P., Neidhart, M., & Vogel, R. (2009). Correlation of intravascular ultrasound findings with histopathological analysis of thrombus aspirates in patients with very late drug-eluting stent thrombosis. *Circulation, 120*(5), 391–399. doi:10.1161/CIRCULATIONAHA.109.854398

Cook, S., Wenaweser, P., Togni, M., Billinger, M., Morger, C., & Seiler, C. (2007). Incomplete stent apposition and very late stent thrombosis after drug-eluting stent implantation. *Circulation, 115*(18), 2426–2434. doi:10.1161/CIRCULATIONAHA.106.658237

Costa, J. R. Jr, Abizaid, A., Costa, R., Feres, F., Tanajura, L. F., & Maldonado, G. (2009). 1-year results of the hydroxyapatite polymer-free sirolimus-eluting stent for the treatment of single de novo coronary lesions: The VESTASYNC I trial. *JACC: Cardiovascular Interventions, 2*(5), 422–427. doi:10.1016/j.jcin.2009.02.009

Costa, J. R. Jr, Abizaid, A., Feres, F., Costa, R., Seixas, A. C., & Maia, F. (2008). EXCELLA First-in-Man (FIM) study: Safety and efficacy of novolimus-eluting stent in de novo coronary lesions. *EuroIntervention, 4*(1), 53–58. doi:10.4244/EIJV4I1A10

Cunningham, K. S., & Gotlieb, A. I. (2005). The role of shear stress in the pathogenesis of atherosclerosis. *Laboratory Investigation, 85*(1), 9–23.

Doi, H., Maehara, A., Mintz, G. S., Yu, A., Wang, H., & Mandinov, L. (2009). Impact of post-intervention minimal stent area on 9-month follow-up patency of paclitaxel-eluting stents an integrated intravascular ultrasound analysis from the TAXUS IV, V, and VI and TAXUS ATLAS workhorse, long lesion, and direct stent trials. *JACC: Cardiovascular Interventions*, *2*(12), 1269–1275. doi:10.1016/j.jcin.2009.10.005

Escolar, E., Mintz, G. S., Popma, J., Michalek, A., Kim, S. W., & Mandinov, L. (2007). Meta-analysis of angiographic versus intravascular ultrasound parameters of drug-eluting stent efficacy (from TAXUS IV, V, and VI). *The American Journal of Cardiology*, *100*(4), 621–626. doi:10.1016/j. amjcard.2007.03.076

Feres, F., Andrade, P. B., Costa, R. A., de Ribamar Costa, J. Jr, Abizaid, A., & Staico, R. (2009). Angiographic and intravascular ultrasound findings following implantation of the Endeavor zotarolimus-eluting stents in patients from the real-world clinical practice. *EuroIntervention*, *5*(3), 355–362. doi:10.4244/V5I3A56

Feres, F., Munoz, J. S., Abizaid, A., Albertal, M., Mintz, G. S., & Staico, R. (2005). Comparison between sirolimus-eluting stents and intracoronary catheter-based beta radiation for the treatment of in-stent restenosis. *The American Journal of Cardiology*, *96*(12), 1656–1662. doi:10.1016/j. amjcard.2005.07.081

Finn, A. V., Nakazawa, G., Joner, M., Kolodgie, F. D., Mont, E. K., & Gold, H. K. (2007). Vascular responses to drug eluting stents: importance of delayed healing. *Arteriosclerosis, Thrombosis, and Vascular Biology*, *27*(7), 1500–1510. doi:10.1161/ ATVBAHA.107.144220

Fujii, K., Carlier, S. G., Mintz, G. S., Yang, Y. M., Moussa, I., & Weisz, G. (2005). Stent underexpansion and residual reference segment stenosis are related to stent thrombosis after sirolimus-eluting stent implantation: An intravascular ultrasound study. *Journal of the American College of Cardiology*, *45*(7), 995–998. doi:10.1016/j. jacc.2004.12.066

Garcia-Garcia, H. M., Goedhart, D., Schuurbiers, J. C., Kukreja, N., Tanimoto, S., & Daemen, J. (2006). Virtual histology and remodelling index allow in vivo identification of allegedly high-risk coronary plaques in patients with acute coronary syndromes: a three vessel intravascular ultrasound radiofrequency data analysis. *EuroIntervention*, *2*(3), 338–344.

Garcia-Garcia, H. M., Gonzalo, N., Kukreja, N., & Alfonso, F. (2008). Greyscale intravascular ultrasound and IVUS-radiofrequency tissue characterisation to improve understanding of the mechanisms of coronary stent thrombosis in drug-eluting stents. *EuroIntervention*, *4*(Suppl C), C33–C38.

Garcia-Garcia, H. M., Gonzalo, N., Pawar, R., Kukreja, N., Dudek, D., & Thuesen, L. (2009). Assessment of the absorption process following bioabsorbable everolimus-eluting stent implantation: Temporal changes in strain values and tissue composition using intravascular ultrasound radiofrequency data analysis. A substudy of the ABSORB clinical trial. *EuroIntervention*, *4*(4), 443–448. doi:10.4244/EIJV4I4A77

Gardner, C. M., Tan, H., Hull, E. L., Lisauskas, J. B., Sum, S. T., & Meese, T. M. (2008). Detection of lipid core coronary plaques in autopsy specimens with a novel catheter-based near-infrared spectroscopy system. *JACC: Cardiovascular Imaging*, *1*(5), 638–648. doi:10.1016/j.jcmg.2008.06.001

Garg, S., Serruys, P. W., van der Ent, M., Schultz, C., Mastik, F., & van Soest, G. (2010). First use in patients of a combined near infra-red spectroscopy and intra-vascular ultrasound catheter to identify composition and structure of coronary plaque. *EuroIntervention*, *5*(6), 755–756. doi:10.4244/EIJV5I6A126

Gerstein, H. C., Ratner, R. E., Cannon, C. P., Serruys, P. W., Garcia-Garcia, H. M., & van Es, G. A. (2010). Effect of rosiglitazone on progression of coronary atherosclerosis in patients with type 2 diabetes mellitus and coronary artery disease: The assessment on the prevention of progression by rosiglitazone on atherosclerosis in diabetes patients with cardiovascular history trial. *Circulation*, *121*(10), 1176–1187. doi:10.1161/CIRCULATIONAHA.109.881003

Gonzalo, N., Garcia-Garcia, H. M., Regar, E., Barlis, P., Wentzel, J., & Onuma, Y. (2009). In vivo assessment of high-risk coronary plaques at bifurcations with combined intravascular ultrasound and optical coherence tomography. *JACC: Cardiovascular Imaging*, *2*(4), 473–482. doi:10.1016/j.jcmg.2008.11.016

Granada, J. F., Wallace-Bradley, D., Win, H. K., Alviar, C. L., Builes, A., & Lev, E. I. (2007). In vivo plaque characterization using intravascular ultrasound-virtual histology in a porcine model of complex coronary lesions. *Arteriosclerosis, Thrombosis, and Vascular Biology*, *27*(2), 387–393. doi:10.1161/01.ATV.0000253907.51681.0e

Hasegawa, T., Ako, J., Koo, B. K., Miyazawa, A., Sakurai, R., & Chang, H. (2009). Analysis of left main coronary artery bifurcation lesions treated with biolimus-eluting DEVAX AXXESS plus nitinol self-expanding stent: intravascular ultrasound results of the AXXENT trial. *Catheterization and Cardiovascular Interventions*, *73*(1), 34–41. doi:10.1002/ccd.21765

Hiro, T., Kimura, T., Morimoto, T., Miyauchi, K., Nakagawa, Y., & Yamagishi, M. (2009). Effect of intensive statin therapy on regression of coronary atherosclerosis in patients with acute coronary syndrome: a multicenter randomized trial evaluated by volumetric intravascular ultrasound using pitavastatin versus atorvastatin (JAPAN-ACS [Japan assessment of pitavastatin and atorvastatin in acute coronary syndrome] study). *Journal of the American College of Cardiology*, *54*(4), 293–302. doi:10.1016/j.jacc.2009.04.033

Hong, M. K., Mintz, G. S., Lee, C. W., Lee, J. W., Park, J. H., & Park, D. W. (2008). A three-vessel virtual histology intravascular ultrasound analysis of frequency and distribution of thin-cap fibroatheromas in patients with acute coronary syndrome or stable angina pectoris. *The American Journal of Cardiology*, *101*(5), 568–572. doi:10.1016/j.amjcard.2007.09.113

Hong, M. K., Park, D. W., Lee, C. W., Lee, S. W., Kim, Y. H., & Kang, D. H. (2009). Effects of statin treatments on coronary plaques assessed by volumetric virtual histology intravascular ultrasound analysis. *JACC: Cardiovascular Interventions*, *2*(7), 679–688. doi:10.1016/j.jcin.2009.03.015

Jensen, L. O., Maeng, M., Thayssen, P., Christiansen, E. H., Hansen, K. N., & Galloe, A. (2008). Neointimal hyperplasia after sirolimus-eluting and paclitaxel-eluting stent implantation in diabetic patients: the Randomized Diabetes and Drug-Eluting Stent (DiabeDES) Intravascular Ultrasound Trial. *European Heart Journal*, *29*(22), 2733–2741. doi:10.1093/eurheartj/ehn434

Jensen, L. O., Thayssen, P., Pedersen, K. E., Stender, S., & Haghfelt, T. (2004). Regression of coronary atherosclerosis by simvastatin: a serial intravascular ultrasound study. *Circulation*, *110*(3), 265–270. doi:10.1161/01.CIR.0000135215.75876.41

Jimenez-Quevedo, P., Sabate, M., Angiolillo, D. J., Costa, M. A., Alfonso, F., & Gomez-Hospital, J. A. (2006). Vascular effects of sirolimus-eluting versus bare-metal stents in diabetic patients: three-dimensional ultrasound results of the Diabetes and Sirolimus-Eluting Stent (DIABETES) Trial. *Journal of the American College of Cardiology, 47*(11), 2172–2179.

Kawasaki, M., Bouma, B. E., Bressner, J., Houser, S. L., Nadkarni, S. K., & MacNeill, B. D. (2006). Diagnostic accuracy of optical coherence tomography and integrated backscatter intravascular ultrasound images for tissue characterization of human coronary plaques. *Journal of the American College of Cardiology, 48*(1), 81–88. doi:10.1016/j.jacc.2006.02.062

Kawasaki, M., Sano, K., Okubo, M., Yokoyama, H., Ito, Y., & Murata, I. (2005). Volumetric quantitative analysis of tissue characteristics of coronary plaques after statin therapy using three-dimensional integrated backscatter intravascular ultrasound. *Journal of the American College of Cardiology, 45*(12), 1946–1953. doi:10.1016/j.jacc.2004.09.081

Kawasaki, M., Takatsu, H., Noda, T., Sano, K., Ito, Y., & Hayakawa, K. (2002). In vivo quantitative tissue characterization of human coronary arterial plaques by use of integrated backscatter intravascular ultrasound and comparison with angioscopic findings. *Circulation, 105*(21), 2487–2492. doi:10.1161/01.CIR.0000017200.47342.10

Kimura, M., Mintz, G. S., Weissman, N. J., Dawkins, K. D., Grube, E., & Ellis, S. G. (2008). Meta-analysis of the effects of paclitaxel-eluting stents versus bare metal stents on volumetric intravascular ultrasound in patients with versus without diabetes mellitus. *The American Journal of Cardiology, 101*(9), 1263–1268. doi:10.1016/j.amjcard.2007.12.025

Lotan, C., Almagor, Y., Kuiper, K., Suttorp, M. J., & Wijns, W. (2006). Sirolimus-eluting stent in chronic total occlusion: the SICTO study. *Journal of Interventional Cardiology, 19*(4), 307–312. doi:10.1111/j.1540-8183.2006.00151.x

Luscher, T. F., Pieper, M., Tendera, M., Vrolix, M., Rutsch, W., & van den Branden, F. (2009). A randomized placebo-controlled study on the effect of nifedipine on coronary endothelial function and plaque formation in patients with coronary artery disease: the ENCORE II study. *European Heart Journal, 30*(13), 1590–1597. doi:10.1093/eurheartj/ehp151

Meredith, I. T., Whitbourn, R., Walters, D., Popma, J., Cutlip, D., & Fitzgerald, P. (2007). The next-generation Endeavor Resolute stent: 4-month clinical and angiographic results from the Endeavor Resolute first-in-man trial. *Euro-Intervention, 3*, 50–53.

Meredith, I. T., Worthley, S., Whitbourn, R., Walters, D. L., McClean, D., & Horrigan, M. (2009). Clinical and angiographic results with the next-generation resolute stent system: A prospective, multicenter, first-in-human trial. *JACC: Cardiovascular Interventions, 2*(10), 977–985. doi:10.1016/j.jcin.2009.07.007

Mintz, G. S. (2007). Features and parameters of drug-eluting stent deployment discoverable by intravascular ultrasound. *The American Journal of Cardiology, 100*(8B), 26M–35M. doi:10.1016/j.amjcard.2007.08.019

Miyagi, M., Ishii, H., Murakami, R., Isobe, S., Hayashi, M., & Amano, T. (2009). Impact of long-term statin treatment on coronary plaque composition at angiographically severe lesions: A nonrandomized study of the history of long-term statin treatment before coronary angioplasty. *Clinical Therapeutics, 31*(1), 64–73. doi:10.1016/j.clinthera.2009.01.002

Miyazawa, A., Ako, J., Hassan, A., Hasegawa, T., Abizaid, A., & Verheye, S. (2007). Analysis of bifurcation lesions treated with novel drug-eluting dedicated bifurcation stent system: Intravascular ultrasound results of the AXXESS PLUS trial. *Catheterization and Cardiovascular Interventions, 70*(7), 952–957. doi:10.1002/ccd.21269

Miyazawa, A., Ako, J., Hongo, Y., Hur, S. H., Tsujino, I., & Courtney, B. K. (2008). Comparison of vascular response to zotarolimus-eluting stent versus sirolimus-eluting stent: Intravascular ultrasound results from ENDEAVOR III. *American Heart Journal, 155*(1), 108–113. doi:10.1016/j.ahj.2007.08.008

Moreno, R., Fernandez, C., Alfonso, F., Hernandez, R., Perez-Vizcayno, M. J., & Escaned, J. (2004). Coronary stenting versus balloon angioplasty in small vessels: A meta-analysis from 11 randomized studies. *Journal of the American College of Cardiology, 43*(11), 1964–1972. doi:10.1016/j.jacc.2004.01.039

Morice, M. C., Serruys, P. W., Sousa, J. E., Fajadet, J., Ban Hayashi, E., & Perin, M. (2002). A randomized comparison of a sirolimus-eluting stent with a standard stent for coronary revascularization. *The New England Journal of Medicine, 346*(23), 1773–1780. doi:10.1056/NEJMoa012843

Moses, J. W., Leon, M. B., Popma, J. J., Fitzgerald, P. J., Holmes, D. R., O'Shaughnessy, C. (2003). Sirolimus-eluting stents versus standard stents in patients with stenosis in a native coronary artery. *N Engl J Med, 349*(14), 1315-1323.4

Nair, A., Margolis, M. P., Kuban, B. D., & Vince, D. G. (2007). Automated coronary plaque characterisation with intravascular ultrasound backscatter: Ex vivo validation. *EuroIntervention, 3*(1), 113–120.

Nasu, K., Tsuchikane, E., Katoh, O., Tanaka, N., Kimura, M., & Ehara, M. (2009). Effect of fluvastatin on progression of coronary atherosclerotic plaque evaluated by virtual histology intravascular ultrasound. *JACC: Cardiovascular Interventions, 2*(7), 689–696. doi:10.1016/j.jcin.2009.04.016

Nasu, K., Tsuchikane, E., Katoh, O., Vince, D. G., Virmani, R., & Surmely, J.-F. i. (2006). Accuracy of in vivo coronary plaque morphology assessment: A validation study of in vivo virtual histology compared with in vitro histopathology. *Journal of the American College of Cardiology, 47*(12), 2405–2412. doi:10.1016/j.jacc.2006.02.044

Nishioka, H., Shimada, K., Kataoka, T., Hirose, M., Asawa, K., & Hasegawa, T. (2004). Impact of HMG-CoA reductase inhibitors for non-treated coronary segments. *Osaka City Medical Journal, 50*(2), 61–68.

Nissen, S. E., Nicholls, S. J., Sipahi, I., Libby, P., Raichlen, J. S., & Ballantyne, C. M. (2006). Effect of very high-intensity statin therapy on regression of coronary atherosclerosis: The ASTEROID trial. *Journal of the American Medical Association, 295*(13), 1556–1565. doi:10.1001/jama.295.13.jpc60002

Nissen, S. E., Nicholls, S. J., Wolski, K., Nesto, R., Kupfer, S., & Perez, A. (2008). Comparison of pioglitazone vs glimepiride on progression of coronary atherosclerosis in patients with type 2 diabetes: The PERISCOPE randomized controlled trial. *Journal of the American Medical Association, 299*(13), 1561–1573. doi:10.1001/jama.299.13.1561

Nissen, S. E., Nicholls, S. J., Wolski, K., Rodes-Cabau, J., Cannon, C. P., & Deanfield, J. E. (2008). Effect of rimonabant on progression of atherosclerosis in patients with abdominal obesity and coronary artery disease: The STRADIVARIUS randomized controlled trial. *Journal of the American Medical Association, 299*(13), 1547–1560. doi:10.1001/jama.299.13.1547

Nissen, S. E., Tardif, J. C., Nicholls, S. J., Revkin, J. H., Shear, C. L., & Duggan, W. T. (2007). Effect of torcetrapib on the progression of coronary atherosclerosis. *The New England Journal of Medicine, 356*(13), 1304–1316. doi:10.1056/NEJMoa070635

Nissen, S. E., Tsunoda, T., Tuzcu, E. M., Schoenhagen, P., Cooper, C. J., & Yasin, M. (2003). Effect of recombinant ApoA-I Milano on coronary atherosclerosis in patients with acute coronary syndromes: A randomized controlled trial. *Journal of the American Medical Association, 290*(17), 2292–2300. doi:10.1001/jama.290.17.2292

Nissen, S. E., Tuzcu, E. M., Brewer, H. B., Sipahi, I., Nicholls, S. J., & Ganz, P. (2006). Effect of ACAT inhibition on the progression of coronary atherosclerosis. *The New England Journal of Medicine, 354*(12), 1253–1263. doi:10.1056/NEJMoa054699

Nissen, S. E., Tuzcu, E. M., Libby, P., Thompson, P. D., Ghali, M., & Garza, D. (2004). Effect of antihypertensive agents on cardiovascular events in patients with coronary disease and normal blood pressure: The CAMELOT study: a randomized controlled trial. *Journal of the American Medical Association, 292*(18), 2217–2225. doi:10.1001/jama.292.18.2217

Nissen, S. E., Tuzcu, E. M., Schoenhagen, P., Brown, B. G., Ganz, P., & Vogel, R. A. (2004). Effect of intensive compared with moderate lipid-lowering therapy on progression of coronary atherosclerosis: a randomized controlled trial. *Journal of the American Medical Association, 291*(9), 1071–1080. doi:10.1001/jama.291.9.1071

Okazaki, S., Yokoyama, T., Miyauchi, K., Shimada, K., Kurata, T., & Sato, H. (2004). Early statin treatment in patients with acute coronary syndrome: demonstration of the beneficial effect on atherosclerotic lesions by serial volumetric intravascular ultrasound analysis during half a year after coronary event: The ESTABLISH study. *Circulation, 110*(9), 1061–1068. doi:10.1161/01.CIR.0000140261.58966.A4

Okubo, M., Kawasaki, M., Ishihara, Y., Takeyama, U., Kubota, T., & Yamaki, T. (2008). Development of integrated backscatter intravascular ultrasound for tissue characterization of coronary plaques. *Ultrasound in Medicine & Biology, 34*(4), 655–663. doi:10.1016/j.ultrasmedbio.2007.09.015

Ormiston, J. A., Serruys, P. W., Regar, E., Dudek, D., Thuesen, L., & Webster, M. W. (2008). A bioabsorbable everolimus-eluting coronary stent system for patients with single de-novo coronary artery lesions (ABSORB): A prospective open-label trial. *Lancet, 371*(9616), 899–907. doi:10.1016/S0140-6736(08)60415-8

Palmer, N. D., Northridge, D., Lessells, A., McDicken, W. N., & Fox, K. A. (1999). In vitro analysis of coronary atheromatous lesions by intravascular ultrasound; reproducibility and histological correlation of lesion morphology. *European Heart Journal, 20*(23), 1701–1706. doi:10.1053/euhj.1999.1627

Petronio, A. S., Amoroso, G., Limbruno, U., Papini, B., De Carlo, M., & Micheli, A. (2005). Simvastatin does not inhibit intimal hyperplasia and restenosis but promotes plaque regression in normocholesterolemic patients undergoing coronary stenting: A randomized study with intravascular ultrasound. *American Heart Journal, 149*(3), 520–526. doi:10.1016/j.ahj.2004.10.032

Prati, F., Arbustini, E., Labellarte, A., Dal Bello, B., Sommariva, L., & Mallus, M. T. (2001). Correlation between high frequency intravascular ultrasound and histomorphology in human coronary arteries. *Heart (British Cardiac Society), 85*(5), 567–570. doi:10.1136/heart.85.5.567

Rodriguez-Granillo, G. A., Vos, J., Bruining, N., Garcia-Garcia, H. M., de Winter, S., & Ligthart, J. M. (2007). Long-term effect of perindopril on coronary atherosclerosis progression (from the perindopril's prospective effect on coronary atherosclerosis by angiography and intravascular ultrasound evaluation [PERSPECTIVE] study). *The American Journal of Cardiology, 100*(2), 159–163. doi:10.1016/j.amjcard.2007.02.073

Sakurai, R., Hongo, Y., Yamasaki, M., Honda, Y., Bonneau, H. N., & Yock, P. G. (2007). Detailed intravascular ultrasound analysis of Zotarolimus-eluting phosphorylcholine-coated cobalt-chromium alloy stent in de novo coronary lesions (results from the ENDEAVOR II trial). *The American Journal of Cardiology, 100*(5), 818–823. doi:10.1016/j.amjcard.2007.04.016

Sathyanarayana, S., Carlier, S., Li, W., & Thomas, L. (2009). Characterisation of atherosclerotic plaque by spectral similarity of radiofrequency intravascular ultrasound signals. *EuroIntervention, 5*(1), 133–139. doi:10.4244/EIJV5I1A21

Sawada, T., Shite, J., Garcia-Garcia, H. M., Shinke, T., Watanabe, S., & Otake, H. (2008). Feasibility of combined use of intravascular ultrasound radiofrequency data analysis and optical coherence tomography for detecting thin-cap fibroatheroma. *European Heart Journal, 29*(9), 1136–1146. doi:10.1093/eurheartj/ehn132

Schaar, J. A., Muller, J. E., Falk, E., Virmani, R., Fuster, V., & Serruys, P. W. (2004). Terminology for high-risk and vulnerable coronary artery plaques. Report of a meeting on the vulnerable plaque, June 17 and 18, 2003, Santorini, Greece. *European Heart Journal, 25*(12), 1077–1082. doi:10.1016/j.ehj.2004.01.002

Schartl, M., Bocksch, W., Koschyk, D. H., Voelker, W., Karsch, K. R., & Kreuzer, J. (2001). Use of intravascular ultrasound to compare effects of different strategies of lipid-lowering therapy on plaque volume and composition in patients with coronary artery disease. *Circulation, 104*(4), 387–392. doi:10.1161/hc2901.093188

Serruys, P. W., Degertekin, M., Tanabe, K., Abizaid, A., Sousa, J. E., & Colombo, A. (2002). Intravascular ultrasound findings in the multicenter, randomized, double-blind RAVEL (RAndomized study with the sirolimus-eluting VElocity balloon-expandable stent in the treatment of patients with de novo native coronary artery Lesions) trial. *Circulation, 106*(7), 798–803. doi:10.1161/01.CIR.0000025585.63486.59

Serruys, P. W., Garcia-Garcia, H. M., Buszman, P., Erne, P., Verheye, S., & Aschermann, M. (2008). Effects of the direct lipoprotein-associated phospholipase A(2) inhibitor darapladib on human coronary atherosclerotic plaque. *Circulation, 118*(11), 1172–1182. doi:10.1161/CIRCULATIONAHA.108.771899

Serruys, P. W., Ong, A. T., Piek, J. J., Neumann, F. J., van der Giessen, W. J., & Wiemer, M. (2005). A randomized comparison of a durable polymer Everolimus-eluting stent with a bare metal coronary stent: The SPIRIT first trial. *EuroIntervention, 1*(1), 58–65.

Serruys, P. W., Ruygrok, P., Neuzner, J., Piek, J. J., Seth, A., & Schofer, J. J. (2006). A randomised comparison of an everolimus-eluting coronary stent with a paclitaxel-eluting coronary stent:the SPIRIT II trial. *EuroIntervention, 2*(3), 286–294.

Sousa, J. E., Costa, M. A., Abizaid, A., Abizaid, A. S., Feres, F., & Pinto, I. M. (2001). Lack of neointimal proliferation after implantation of sirolimus-coated stents in human coronary arteries: a quantitative coronary angiography and three-dimensional intravascular ultrasound study. *Circulation, 103*(2), 192–195.

Stone, G. W., Maehara, A., Lansky, A. J., de Bruyne, B., Cristea, E., & Mintz, G. S. (2011). A prospective natural-history study of coronary atherosclerosis. *The New England Journal of Medicine, 364*(3), 226–235. doi:10.1056/NEJMoa1002358

Stone, G. W., Midei, M., Newman, W., Sanz, M., Hermiller, J. B., & Williams, J. (2008). Comparison of an everolimus-eluting stent and a paclitaxel-eluting stent in patients with coronary artery disease: A randomized trial. *Journal of the American Medical Association, 299*(16), 1903–1913. doi:10.1001/jama.299.16.1903

Takashima, H., Ozaki, Y., Yasukawa, T., Waseda, K., Asai, K., & Wakita, Y. (2007). Impact of lipid-lowering therapy with pitavastatin, a new HMG-CoA reductase inhibitor, on regression of coronary atherosclerotic plaque. *Circulation Journal*, *71*(11), 1678–1684. doi:10.1253/circj.71.1678

Takayama, T., Hiro, T., Yamagishi, M., Daida, H., Hirayama, A., & Saito, S. (2009). Effect of rosuvastatin on coronary atheroma in stable coronary artery disease: multicenter coronary atherosclerosis study measuring effects of rosuvastatin using intravascular ultrasound in Japanese subjects (COSMOS). *Circulation Journal*, *73*(11), 2110–2117. doi:10.1253/circj.CJ-09-0358

Tani, S., Watanabe, I., Anazawa, T., Kawamata, H., Tachibana, E., & Furukawa, K. (2005). Effect of pravastatin on malondialdehyde-modified low-density lipoprotein levels and coronary plaque regression as determined by three-dimensional intravascular ultrasound. *The American Journal of Cardiology*, *96*(8), 1089–1094. doi:10.1016/j.amjcard.2005.05.069

Tardif, J. C., Gregoire, J., L'Allier, P. L., Anderson, T. J., Bertrand, O., & Reeves, F. (2004). Effects of the acyl coenzyme A:cholesterol acyltransferase inhibitor avasimibe on human atherosclerotic lesions. *Circulation*, *110*(21), 3372–3377. doi:10.1161/01.CIR.0000147777.12010.EF

Tardif, J. C., Gregoire, J., L'Allier, P. L., Ibrahim, R., Anderson, T. J., & Reeves, F. (2008). Effects of the antioxidant succinobucol (AGI-1067) on human atherosclerosis in a randomized clinical trial. *Atherosclerosis*, *197*(1), 480–486. doi:10.1016/j.atherosclerosis.2006.11.039

Tardif, J. C., Gregoire, J., L'Allier, P. L., Ibrahim, R., Lesperance, J., & Heinonen, T. M. (2007). Effects of reconstituted high-density lipoprotein infusions on coronary atherosclerosis: A randomized controlled trial. *Journal of the American Medical Association*, *297*(15), 1675–1682. doi:10.1001/jama.297.15.jpc70004

Thim, T., Hagensen, M. K., Wallace-Bradley, D., Granada, J. F., Kaluza, G. L., & Drouet, L. (2010). *Unreliable assessment of necrotic core by VHTM IVUS in porcine coronary artery disease.* Circ Cardiovasc Imaging.

Toi, T., Taguchi, I., Yoneda, S., Kageyama, M., Kikuchi, A., & Tokura, M. (2009). Early effect of lipid-lowering therapy with pitavastatin on regression of coronary atherosclerotic plaque. Comparison with atorvastatin. *Circulation Journal*, *73*(8), 1466–1472. doi:10.1253/circj.CJ-08-1051

Tsuchida, K., Piek, J. J., Neumann, F. J., van der Giessen, W. J., Wiemer, M., & Zeiher, A. M. (2005). One-year results of a durable polymer everolimus-eluting stent in de novo coronary narrowings (The SPIRIT FIRST Trial). *EuroIntervention*, *1*(3), 266–272.

Van Herck, J., De Meyer, G., Ennekens, G., Van Herck, P., Herman, A., & Vrints, C. (2009). Validation of in vivo plaque characterisation by virtual histology in a rabbit model of atherosclerosis. *EuroIntervention*, *5*(1), 149–156. doi:10.4244/EIJV5I1A23

Verheye, S., Agostoni, P., Dawkins, K. D., Dens, J., Rutsch, W., & Carrie, D. (2009). The GENESIS (Randomized, Multicenter Study of the Pimecrolimus-Eluting and Pimecrolimus/Paclitaxel-Eluting Coronary stent system in patients with de novo lesions of the native coronary arteries) trial. *JACC: Cardiovascular Interventions*, *2*(3), 205–214. doi:10.1016/j.jcin.2008.12.011

Virmani, R., Burke, A. P., Farb, A., & Kolodgie, F. D. (2006). Pathology of the vulnerable plaque. *Journal of the American College of Cardiology*, *47*(8Suppl), C13–C18. doi:10.1016/j.jacc.2005.10.065

Waseda, K., Miyazawa, A., Ako, J., Hasegawa, T., Tsujino, I., & Sakurai, R. (2009). Intravascular ultrasound results from the ENDEAVOR IV trial: Randomized comparison between zotarolimus- and paclitaxel-eluting stents in patients with coronary artery disease. *JACC: Cardiovascular Interventions*, *2*(8), 779–784. doi:10.1016/j.jcin.2009.05.015

Waxman, S., Dixon, S. R., L'Allier, P., Moses, J. W., Petersen, J. L., & Cutlip, D. (2009). In vivo validation of a catheter-based near-infrared spectroscopy system for detection of lipid core coronary plaques: Initial results of the SPEC-TACL study. *JACC: Cardiovascular Imaging*, *2*(7), 858–868. doi:10.1016/j.jcmg.2009.05.001

Weissman, N. J., Ellis, S. G., Grube, E., Dawkins, K. D., Greenberg, J. D., & Mann, T. (2007). Effect of the polymer-based, paclitaxel-eluting TAXUS Express stent on vascular tissue responses: A volumetric intravascular ultrasound integrated analysis from the TAXUS IV, V, and VI trials. *European Heart Journal*, *28*(13), 1574–1582. doi:10.1093/eurheartj/ehm174

Weissman, N. J., Koglin, J., Cox, D. A., Hermiller, J., O'Shaughnessy, C., & Mann, J. T. (2005). Polymer-based paclitaxel-eluting stents reduce in-stent neointimal tissue proliferation: A serial volumetric intravascular ultrasound analysis from the TAXUS-IV trial. *Journal of the American College of Cardiology*, *45*(8), 1201–1205. doi:10.1016/j.jacc.2004.10.078

Yokoyama, M., Komiyama, N., Courtney, B. K., Nakayama, T., Namikawa, S., & Kuriyama, N. (2005). Plasma low-density lipoprotein reduction and structural effects on coronary atherosclerotic plaques by atorvastatin as clinically assessed with intravascular ultrasound radio-frequency signal analysis: A randomized prospective study. *American Heart Journal*, *150*(2), 287. doi:10.1016/j.ahj.2005.03.059

ADDITONAL READING

Alfonso, F., Suarez, A., Perez-Vizcayno, M. J., Moreno, R., Escaned, J., & Banuelos, C. (2007). Intravascular ultrasound findings during episodes of drug-eluting stent thrombosis. *Journal of the American College of Cardiology*, *50*(21), 2095–2097. doi:10.1016/j.jacc.2007.08.015

Cook, S., Ladich, E., Nakazawa, G., Eshtehardi, P., Neidhart, M., & Vogel, R. (2009). Correlation of intravascular ultrasound findings with histopathological analysis of thrombus aspirates in patients with very late drug-eluting stent thrombosis. *Circulation*, *120*(5), 391–399. doi:10.1161/CIRCULATIONAHA.109.854398

Garcia-Garcia, H. M., Mintz, G. S., Lerman, A., Vince, D. G., Margolis, M. P., & van Es, G. A. (2009). Tissue characterisation using intravascular radiofrequency data analysis: recommendations for acquisition, analysis, interpretation and reporting. *EuroIntervention*, *5*(2), 177–189. doi:10.4244/EIJV5I2A29

Mintz, G. S., Nissen, S. E., Anderson, W. D., Bailey, S. R., Erbel, R., & Fitzgerald, P. J. (2001). American College of Cardiology Clinical Expert Consensus Document on Standards for Acquisition, Measurement and Reporting of Intravascular Ultrasound Studies (IVUS). A report of the American College of Cardiology Task Force on Clinical Expert Consensus Documents. *Journal of the American College of Cardiology*, *37*(5), 1478–1492. doi:10.1016/S0735-1097(01)01175-5

Sawada, T., Shite, J., Garcia-Garcia, H. M., Shinke, T., Watanabe, S., & Otake, H. (2008). Feasibility of combined use of intravascular ultrasound radiofrequency data analysis and optical coherence tomography for detecting thin-cap fibroatheroma. *European Heart Journal*, *29*(9), 1136–1146. doi:10.1093/eurheartj/ehn132

Serruys, P. W., Garcia-Garcia, H. M., Buszman, P., Erne, P., Verheye, S., & Aschermann, M. (2008). Effects of the direct lipoprotein-associated phospholipase A(2) inhibitor darapladib on human coronary atherosclerotic plaque. *Circulation*, *118*(11), 1172–1182. doi:10.1161/CIRCULATIONAHA.108.771899

Serruys, P. W., Ormiston, J. A., Onuma, Y., Regar, E., Gonzalo, N., & Garcia-Garcia, H. M. (2009). A bioabsorbable everolimus-eluting coronary stent system (ABSORB): 2-year outcomes and results from multiple imaging methods. *Lancet*, *373*(9667), 897–910. doi:10.1016/S0140-6736(09)60325-1

Stone, G. W., Maehara, A., Lansky, A. J., de Bruyne, B., Cristea, E., & Mintz, G. S. (2011). A prospective natural-history study of coronary atherosclerosis. *The New England Journal of Medicine*, *364*(3), 226–235. doi:10.1056/NEJMoa1002358

KEY TERMS AND DEFINITIONS

Atherosclerosis: A condition in which fatty material collects along the walls of arteries. This fatty material thickens, hardens (forms calcium deposits), and may eventually block the arteries.

Incomplete Stent Apposition (ISA): Is the intravascular ultrasound finding of lack of contact between stent struts, not overlying a side branch, and the underlying arterial wall. Acute ISA occurs at the time of stent implantation, whilst late ISA may be due either to persistence of acute ISA or late-acquired ISA occurring between stent implantation and follow-up.

Intravascular Imaging: Imaging performed using catheters which are advanced within vascular structures to provide real-time images of the inside of the vessel.

Intravascular Ultrasound (IVUS): An imaging modality which utilizes a catheter which has an ultrasound transducer at its tip. The catheter is inserted into a vessel, and enables real-time ultrasound images of the vessel wall to be seen.

Restenosis: The reoccurrence of stenosis, a narrowing of a blood vessel, leading to restricted blood flow.

Stent: An artificial 'tube' usually made of metal which is inserted into a natural passage/conduit in the body to prevent, or counteract, a disease-induced, localized flow constriction.

Section 2
Imaging by Angioscopy

Chapter 7
Imaging by Angioscopy

Michael Rees
Bangor University, UK

ABSTRACT

Within this chapter, the basic clinical and research utilities of Angioscopy are described. Among its paragraphs, an attempt is made to outline the role of angioscopy to the understanding of cardiovascular disease as well as its contribution to the understanding of cardiovascular procedures. Additionally, the techniques, which combine stenting procedures with angioscopy, are detailed.

BACKGROUND: HISTORY OF ANGIOSCOPY

Angioscopy is a technique of direct visualisation of an artery that became commonly used as an intravascular imaging technique in the late 1980's and early 1990's (White, Ramee, Collins, Mesa, Jain, & Ventur, 1993). The introduction however, of angioscopy was much earlier and developed from a technique named cardioscopy which was prompted by the need to develop imaging within the heart to supplement or replace other diagnostic methods. The technique of cardioscopy was documented in 1924 (Cutler, Levine, & Beck, 1924). This reference describes that the technique was practised as far back as 1913 by Rhea and Walker who described a rigid cardioscope which had to be held against the mitral valve. These early attempts of visualisation were generally unsuccessful as there was no method for displacing blood from between the scope and the valve despite the fact that the scopes were illuminated with small light bulbs. Later attempts at cardioscopy during the 1930's used balloons inflated with saline to partially fill the cardiac chamber and displace blood away from the valves (Harken & Glidden, 1932). For the next decades significant research in this field was carried out in Japan where a number of techniques were developed to combine cutting devices with cardioscopes to perform valvotomy. Most of these devices used saline inflated balloons attached to the scopes to aid visualisation. Cardioscopy developed as a technique during this period as the majority of cardiac surgical procedures were closed heart rather than the later open heart techniques been developed after cardio-pulmonary by-pass. For this reason most of the cardioscopy devices incorporated a knife or other cardiotomy devices to cut the valve.

DOI: 10.4018/978-1-61350-095-8.ch007

Experimental devices in the 1950's were made of transparent plastic (Butterworth, 1951) but were primarily used as research devices and were not implemented in the clinical context. It was generally felt by most surgeons experimenting with these devices that transparent balloons to gain a visual field were more successful than direct viewing instruments or using saline flushing to visualise the heart.

A step forward was achieved in intra-cardiac imaging by the use of fibre-optic endoscopes which were first trialled in 1967 by Gamble and Ennis; they used a large inflatable balloon to displace the blood from the visual field (Gamble & Ennis, 1967). In experimental conditions in an animal model they reported good imaging of the left heart including the aortic valve. An alternative method of visualisation was the displacement of blood by clear fluid. This required a pressurised injection. This method was proved in animal experiments producing clear visualisation of the aortic valve however this was accompanied by drastic methods to reduce cardiac output which could not be reproduced in closed heart surgery in humans (Dee & Crosby, 1977). Pressurised injection of clear fluid in an animal model was also found to cause trauma, an experience which was repeated in early cases of peripheral angioscopy using flexible instruments where fluid irrigation caused rupture of a fragile arterial wall after atherectomy (Vollmar & Storz). Despite all of these early difficulties with technique and instrumentation, angioscopy did develop into a viable adjunct procedure to a significant number of surgical and interventional techniques particularly in peripheral vessels. This was achieved by developments in instrumentation which included the introduction of thin fibre scopes and angioscopes with balloons attached to the scopes and improvements in sterilisation and delivery of clear fluid.

In our laboratory we started work with angioscopy as a means to evaluate interventional and surgical techniques. Our centre started using early angioscopes which were modified fibre-

Figure 1. Coronary angioscope

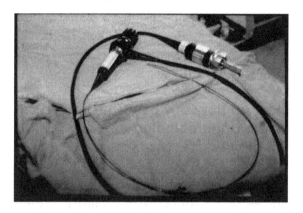

optic endoscopes manufactured by Olympus, but also experimented with instruments more specifically designed for intra vascular use manufactured by companies including Baxter (Spears, *et al.*, 1994) and Trimedyne (Cortis, Hussein, Khandekar, Principe, & Tkaczuk, 1984). These more specific devices suffered from restrictions in their optical resolution compared to multifibre endoscopes but could give reasonable clinical data. The Baxter Endoscope was particularly useful in percutaneous coronary use and was one of the first disposable instruments to be used. This was a 4.5 French diameter device with a low pressure balloon attached to the device which could be inflated to occlude the vessel. This devices required less irrigation of the vessel to obtain a clear view. Care was needed not to inflate the balloon for more than a minute to avoid inducing ischaemia (Gehani, Ashley, Brooks, Ball, & Rees, 1990). All other endoscopes had to be re-sterilised giving rise to all of the risks that are associated with re-sterilised instruments.

Our initial work in coronary arteries started with explanted or post mortem hearts where appearances visualised by angioscopy were compared to post mortem or explanted findings (Richens, Rees, & Watson, 1987) This early demonstration of direct coronary angioscopy demonstrated coronary angioscopy was useful and could document coronary atheroma accurately

(Rees & Richens, 1988) paved the way for the use of this technique intra-operatively during cardiac surgery (Richens, Renzulli, & Hilton, Dissection of the left main coronary artery: diagnosis by angioscopy, 1990)

How Angioscopy has Contributed to the Understanding of Cardiovascular Disease

Our early work with angioscopy of peripheral arteries started with work on occlusive disease. Investigation of this type of disease facilitated obtaining a clear view of the vessel under examination. This work demonstrated that atheroma in vivo was extremely varied and friable, with segments of atheromatous arteries having a varied appearance with material which was often partially attached to the arterial wall and could be easily detached by guide wire or catheter intervention. It is surprising that significant embolic events do not occur more in diagnostic and interventional procedures given these findings. Observation of these friable vessels was made easier by the use of video recording of the angioscopic procedure which allowed for more complete recording and documentation of the procedure (Rees, Gehani, Ashley, & Davies, 1989).

An early observation in peripheral occlusions was the presence of different types of plaque. We observed both yellow and white plaque, and these observations would be confirmed at a later date by observers who related the different appearance of plaque to plaque stability or vulnerability in coronary arteries (Masamichi, Kyoichi, Kentaro, Shinya, Takayoshi, & Shunta, 2001).

Another observation is the striking degree to which thrombus contributes to the makeup of stenoses and occlusions. The degree of thrombus in stenoses is a pointer to the need for anticoagulation from the onset of the angioplasty procedure even before the vessel is ballooned. The presence of thrombus in occlusions is helpful in the treatment of these lesions. Recent occlusions are largely

thrombotic however chronic occlusions contain a surprising degree of thrombus content. This seems to occur whether the occlusion is primarily white or yellow plaque in peripheral arteries. These findings contrast to the situation in coronary arteries where thrombus is more associated with yellow

Figure 2. Stenosis with yellow plaque

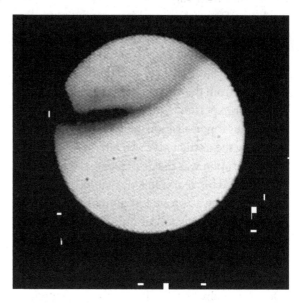

Figure 3. Stenosis with irregular plaque and thrombus

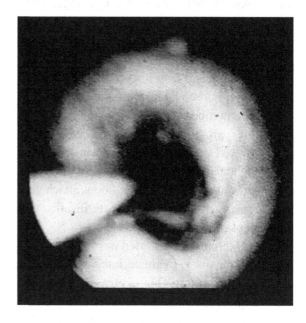

Figure 4. Thrombotic occlusion

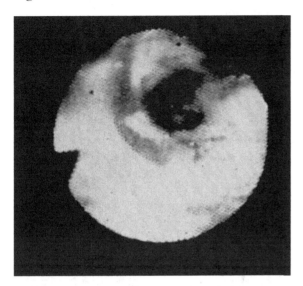

Figure 5. Sheath viewed via an angioscope showing thrombus formation

plaque. Ueda *et al.* (Ueda, Ohtani, Shimizu, Hirayama, & Kodama, 2004) examined 843 patients by catheter and angioscopy and determined that thrombus formation was much more frequent on yellow plaque (52%) than white plaque (15%). Further angioscopic studies have confirmed that plaque colour relates to characteristics including the thickness of the fibrous cap and the lipid core size (Isoda, Satomura, & Ohsuzu).

The appearance of thrombus in occlusive disease helped in the understanding of the mechanism of success or failure of several interventional techniques. The technique of 'vibrational' or 'activated guide wire' angioplasty was developed to take account of the observation that many occlusions have a thrombotic core. The concept behind activated guidewire angioplasty was that rapid fine random movements of a guide wire through a catheter would 'find' the path of least resistance through an occlusive vessel (Rees & Michalis, 1995). This technique was particularly successful in coronary arteries when there was thrombus present in the occlusion. Angioscopy was instrumental in demonstrating that thrombus could be present in even very chronic occlusions.

Another observation was that thrombus could form very quickly on instruments and sheaths. Although this is well understood in cardiovascular intervention, angioscopic demonstration of new thrombus formation in a vessel or a sheath during angioplasty was an aid to changing practice in our laboratory clearly indicating the need for monitoring the coagulation status of the patient.

The Contribution of Angioscopy to the Understanding of Interventional Cardiovascular Procedures

Angioscopy of Balloon Angioplasty

Before intravascular ultrasound became a more common procedure, angioscopy clearly demonstrated the striking degree with which balloon angioplasty of a vessel caused disruption to the intima and frequently to the media of the vessel. This preceded the introduction of stenting but clearly demonstrated that balloon induced dissections can result in thrombosis and near obstruction of the vessel even when it is thought that the flow

Figure 6. Post balloon angioplasty appearance

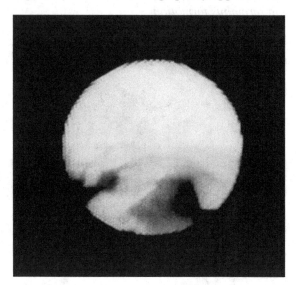

Figure 7. Angioscopy post laser angioplasty showing thermal effect

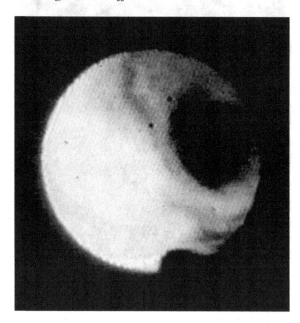

in the vessel has improved. This is because in contrast enhanced angiography the contrast may flow around and under the dissection giving the impression that the vessel is more patent than it really is (Rees, Gehani, & Feith, 1989).

Angioscopy of Laser Angioplasty

There was a rapid development of interventional devices in the decade from 1985-1995 with many different approaches to the treatment of the disease being promoted and researched. There were two broad approaches used a) laser therapy and b) mechanical devices. Laser vascular therapy started with the concept of lasers heating a bulbous wire tip termed laser thermal angioplasty (Sanborn, Faxon, & Kellett, 1986) and developed through a phase of using direct laser energy which was investigated in various forms from continuous wave to pulsed wave lasers and through various different wavelengths.

One of the important questions answered by angiocopy was the extent to which laser angioplasty was achieved or facilitated by mechanical means because of the shape of the angioplasty probe and the extent that laser application of the

atheroma took place. This could be seen directly by angioscopy particularly when laser energy was converted into thermal energy (Ashley, Brooks, Kester, & Rees, 1990). When the laser was inactive and the passage through the occlusion or stenosis was by mainly mechanical means the vessel appeared 'serrated' without any evidence of charring or thermal energy having been applied. When the laser energy was the effecter of the angioplasty procedure the vessel showed evidence of charring or carbonisation where the probe had passed. Angioscopy was used to study different types of lasers from continuous wave ND YAG lasers, pulsed holmium YAG, copper vapour (Ashley, Brooks, Wright, Gehani, & Rees, 1991) and Excimer lasers. An interesting use of laser angioplasty using Nd YAG energy was to 'seal' dissections resulting from balloon angioplasty this effect was clearly demonstrated by angioscopy (Gehan, Ashley, Brooks, Kester, Ball, & Rees, 1988).

Angioscopy of Mechanical Devices

Studying a range of mechanical devices proved more challenging. These devices were generally trialled in peripheral vessels before coronary intervention was attempted. This potentially introduced a number of variables since peripheral and coronary vessels differ in several important aspects. Atheroma tends to be more continuous in peripheral vessels and patients with peripheral disease tend to present later with a greater degree of calcification occurring in peripheral vessels with advanced disease. The size of the peripheral vessels meant that different calibre of device had to be used in the coronary vessels following peripheral trials. Peripheral vessels are more robust than coronary vessels and devices which are effective in peripheral vessels may be too forceful for coronary vessels. Angioscopy was a very valuable technique to monitor device mediated angioplasty to observe the effects of mechanical devices on atheroma and the vessels wall.

Atherectomy Devices

Atherectomy devices became popular for coronary and peripheral use in the decade from 1986. The first device to be widely used was the directional

Figure 8. Dissection following mechanical angioplasty

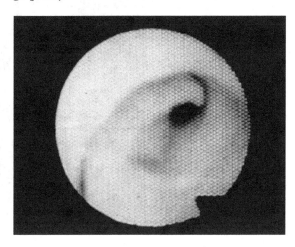

atherectomy device (Schwarten, Katzen, Simpson, & Cutcliff, 1988), (Adelman, *et al.*, 1993) while other devices to perform atherectomy were also investigated. In our laboratory we performed some of the earlier work on the Fischell pull-back atherectomy device (Fischell & Drexler, 1996).

The study on pullback atherectomy revealed that this device was particularly effective in cutting into atheroma; however it also revealed that overly aggressive use of the device could result in cutting deeply into the wall of the vessel and

Figure 9. Post atherectomy showing cut into media

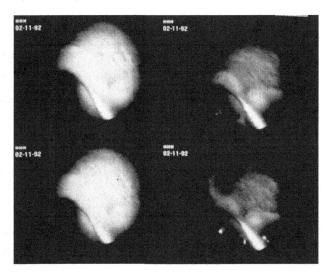

Figure 10. Comparison of IVUS and angioscopy showing greater detail with angioscopy

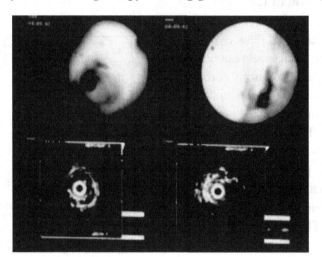

exposing the media. The inference of these results was that atherectomy required careful control and intravascular imaging techniques were a useful adjunct to safe operation of these devices (Rees, Wexler, Sivananthan, Fishcell, & Dake, 1993).

Drill Devices

A number of rotating devices were introduced from 1990 onwards which aimed to recanalise vessels by a rotating mechanism. Of these devices the most commonly used was the Rotablator. r Rival devices including the 'Kensey' catheter and the 'Rotacs' devices were also introduced during the same period. We investigated a number of these devices using angioscopy. In our laboratory the most studied device was the 'Kensey' catheter because we felt that this device had some unique properties that should be investigated. Among the properties were that the device would not cause trauma to the elastic tissue and could find a path through an occluded vessel without a guide wire. We investigated the use of the 8 French peripheral device and the 5 French coronary device. Angioscopic study revealed that the device had some self centring ability but that the operator control of the device was limited and that it tended to seek a pathway down a vessel that was not completely

controlled (Gehani, Davies, Stoodley, Ashley, Brooks, & Rees, 1991).

Angioscopy of Stents

Early studies of stents by angioscopy were very helpful in outlining how well stents expanded and were sited in relation to the vessel wall. Flow of blood around a stent could be observed as well as the process of forming endothelium within the vessel. Non formation of endothelium was observed more accurately by angioscopy rather

Figure 11. Stent viewed by angioscopy showing incomplete expansion

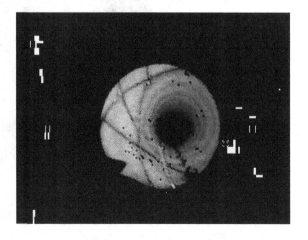

than by IVUS which is less sensitive to imaging of the endothelium.

CONCLUSION

Angioscopy has been instrumental in developing a greater understanding of cardiovascular disease and has been very helpful in developing and evaluating cardiovascular interventional techniques. Although it is not commonly used in current interventional practice as it is a difficult technique, the imaging of vessels pre and post intervention by angioscopy has been invaluable in developing modern cardiovascular intervention.

REFERENCES

Adelman, A., Cohen, E., Kimball, B., Bonan, R., Ricci, D., & Webb, J. (1993). A comparison of directional atherectomy with balloon angioplasty for lesions of the left anterior descending coronary artery. *The New England Journal of Medicine, 329,* 228–233. doi:10.1056/NEJM199307223290402

Ashley, S., Brooks, S., Kester, R., & Rees, M. (1990). Thermal characteristics of sapphire contact probe delivery systems for laser angioplasty. *Lasers in Surgery and Medicine,* 10.

Ashley, S., Brooks, S., Wright, H., Gehani, A., & Rees, M. (1991). Acute effects of a copper vapour laser on atheroma. *Lasers in Medical Science, 6*(1), 23–27. doi:10.1007/BF02042642

Butterworth, R. (1951). A new operating cardioscope. *The Journal of Thoracic and Cardiovascular Surgery, 22,* 319–322.

Cortis, B., Hussein, H., Khandekar, C., Principe, J., & Tkaczuk, R. (1984). Angioscopy in vivo. *Catheterization and Cardiovascular Diagnosis, 10*(5), 493–500. doi:10.1002/ccd.1810100513

Cutler, E., Levine, S., & Beck, C. (1924). The surgical treatment of mitral stenosis. *Experimental and Clinical Studies Arch Surg, 9,* 689–821.

Dee, P., & Crosby, I. (1977). Fibreoptic studies of the aortic valve in dogs. *British Heart Journal, 39,* 459–461. doi:10.1136/hrt.39.4.459

Fischell, T., & Drexler, H. (1996, Jun). Pullback atherectomy (PAC) for the treatment of complex bifurcation coronary artery disease. *Catheterization and Cardiovascular Diagnosis, 38*(2), 218–2. doi:10.1002/(SICI)1097-0304(199606)38:2<218::AID-CCD23>3.0.CO;2-D

Gamble, W., & Ennis, R. (1967). Experimental intracardiac visualisation. *The New England Journal of Medicine, 276,* 1397–1403. doi:10.1056/NEJM196706222762502

Gehan, I. A., Ashley, S., Brooks, S., Kester, R., Ball, S., & Rees, M. (1988). Percutaneous angioscopy and sapphire tip lasing of intimal flaps following angioplasty. *Heart and Vessels, 4*(1), 52.

Gehani, A., Ashley, S., Brooks, S., Ball, S., & Rees, M. (1990). Percutaneous angioscopy from peripheral to coronary arteries. *British Heart Journal, 64*(1), 63.

Gehani, A., Davies, A., Stoodley, K., Ashley, S., Brooks, S., & Rees, M. (1991). Does the Kensey catheter keep a coaxial position inside the arterial lumen? An in vitro angioscopic study. *Cardiovascular and Interventional Radiology, 14,* 222–229. doi:10.1007/BF02578463

Harken, D., & Glidden, E. (1932). Experiments in intra-cardiac surgery. *The Journal of Thoracic and Cardiovascular Surgery, 12,* 566–572.

Isoda, K., Satomura, K., & Ohsuzu, F. (n.d.). Pathological characterization of yellow and white plaques under angioscopy. *International Journal of Angiology, 10*(3), 183-187.

Masamichi, T., Kyoichi, M., Kentaro, O., Shinya, Y., Takayoshi, O., & Shunta, S. (2001). Mechanical and structural characteristics of vulnerable plaques: Analysis by coronary angioscopy and intravascular ultrasound. *Journal of the American College of Cardiology, 38,* 99–104. doi:10.1016/S0735-1097(01)01315-8

Rees, M., Gehani, A., Ashley, S., & Davies, A. (1989). Percutaneous video angioscopy. *Clinical Radiology, 40,* 347–351. doi:10.1016/S0009-9260(89)80116-3

Rees, M., Gehani, A., & Feith, F. (1989). Percutaneous angioscopy. *British Heart Journal, 61*(1), 86.

Rees, M., & Michalis, L. (1995). Activated guidewire technique for treating chronic coronary artery occlusion. *Lancet, 346,* 943–944. doi:10.1016/S0140-6736(95)91560-5

Rees, M., & Richens, D. (1988). Coronary angioscopy. *The British Journal of Radiology, 61,* 728.

Rees, M., Wexler, L., Sivananthan, U., Fishcell, T., & Dake, M. (1993, January). Treatment of peripheral vascular disease with the pullback atherectomy catheter - Assessment by intravascular ultrasound and angioscopy. Endovascular Interventions. *International Congress VI,* Scottsdale, (pp. 27-31).

Richens, D., Rees, M., & Watson, D. (1987, September 19). Laser coronary angioplasty under direct vision. *Lancet, 2*(8560), 683. doi:10.1016/S0140-6736(87)92462-7

Richens, D., Renzulli, A., & Hilton, C. (1990, March). Dissection of the left main coronary artery: Diagnosis by angioscopy. *The Annals of Thoracic Surgery, 49*(3), 469–470. doi:10.1016/0003-4975(90)90259-9

Sanborn, T., Faxon, D., & Kellett, M. E. (1986). Percutaneous coronary laser thermal angioplasty. *Journal of the American College of Cardiology, 8,* 1437–1440. doi:10.1016/S0735-1097(86)80320-5

Schwarten, D., Katzen, B., Simpson, J., & Cutcliff, W. (1988, Apr). Simpson catheter for percutaneous transluminal removal of atheroma. *AJR. American Journal of Roentgenology, 150*(4), 799–801.

Spears, J., Ali, M., Raza, S., Ayer, G., Ravi, S., & Crilly, R. (1994). Quantative angioscopy: A novel method of measurement of luminal dimensions during angioscopy with se of a lightwire. *Cardiovascular and Interventional Radiology, 17,* 197–203. doi:10.1007/BF00571534

Ueda, Y., Ohtani, T., Shimizu, M., Hirayama, A., & Kodama, K. (2004, Aug). Assessment of plaque vulnerability by angioscopic classification of plaque color. *American Heart Journal, 148*(2), 333–335. doi:10.1016/j.ahj.2004.03.047

Vollmar, J., & Storz, L. (n.d.). Vascular endoscopy: Possibilities and limits of its clinical application. *Surgical Clinics of North America, 54,* 111-112.

White, C., Ramee, S., Collins, T., Mesa, J., Jain, A., & Ventur, A. H. (1993, Mar). Percutaneous coronary angioscopy: Applications in interventional cardiology. *Journal of Interventional Cardiology, 6*(1), 61–67. doi:10.1111/j.1540-8183.1993.tb00442.x

Section 3
Thermography

Chapter 8
Thermography:
Basic Principles of Data Acquisition

Konstantinos Toutouzas
Athens Medical School, Greece

Maria Drakopoulou
Athens Medical School, Greece

Christodoulos Stefanadis
Athens Medical School, Greece

ABSTRACT

This chapter is devoted to Thermography, and more specifically, to the basic principles and mechanisms of data acquisition. A detailed description of the potential mechanisms of increased heat generation by vulnerable plaques is provides, along with a list of Thermography devices. Additionally, a special subsection of the chapter deals with the limitation of intracoronary thermography, an extremely crucial issue for both the clinical and research utility of Thermography.

INTRODUCTION

During the last decades, the scientific interest in interventional cardiology has been focused on the early detection of vulnerable lesions, which are ultimately responsible for a majority of acute coronary and cerebrovascular events (Hamdan, Assali, Fuchs, Battler, & Kornowski, 2007), (Corti, Hutter, Badimon, & Fuster, 2004). Novel diagnostic techniques have offered promise as methods of detecting vulnerable plaques (Honda & Fitzgerald, 2008), (Tan & Lip, 2008).

DOI: 10.4018/978-1-61350-095-8.ch008

It is by now well established that acute coronary syndromes are usually caused by plaques initially associated with <50% diameter luminal narrowing (Corti, Hutter, Badimon, & Fuster, 2004). Moreover, it seems that inflammatory processes play a key role in the initiation, progression and complications of atherosclerotic disease (Libby, Ridker, & Maseri, 2002), (Ross, 1999). Since atherosclerosis is an inflammatory process, vulnerable plaques characterized by an increased inflammatory infiltrate, generate heat. Based on this concept, intracoronary thermography has been introduced as a catheter-based technique for the functional imaging of atherosclerotic plaques, with the ability to identify potential vulnerable and culprit plaques in patients with coronary artery disease. After the first clinical application of intracoronary thermography, several thermography catheters have been designed. Intracoronary thermography is able to detect thermal heterogeneity, which has been shown to be present more often in unstable coronary plaques, and positively correlated to vulnerable plaque morphology characteristics and serum markers of systemic inflammation (Toutouzas, *et al.*, 2007), (Toutouzas, *et al.*, 2007), (Worthley, Farouque, Worthley, Baldi, Chew, & Meredith, 2006), (ten Have, Gijsen, Wentzel, Slager, Serruys, & van der Steen, 2006), (Rzeszutko, *et al.*, 2006), (Madjid, Willerson, & Casscells, 2006), (Toutouzas, *et al.*, 2005), (Toutouzas, Drakopoulou, Stefanadi, Siasos, & Stefanadis, 485-489), (Leborgne, *et al.*, 2005), (Dudek, *et al.*, 2005), (Stefanadis, *et al.*, 2003), (Schmermund, Rodermann, & Erbel, 2003). Heat produced, has also been shown to have a good predictive value for clinical events after percutaneous coronary intervention. However due to several technical shortcomings of current technology, the method is yet to be validated in large prospective trials and thus, the benefit of this method in current clinical practice still needs to be determined. However it still remains a tool that may be used in the future to direct local and/or systemic therapy in patients with coronary artery disease.

POTENTIAL MECHANISMS OF INCREASED HEAT GENERATION BY VULNERABLE PLAQUES

Vulnerable plaques are characterized by several pathologic features including: (1) a thin fibrous cap (<65 lm); (2) a large lipid pool; and (3) activated macrophages near the fibrous cap. a large lipid core, a thin fibrous cap, high neo-vessel formation, and infiltration by inflammatory cells. Several of these features (ie, presence and acti-

vation of inflammatory cells, neo-vessel formation, and fibrous cap thinning) can potentially lead to increased production and dissipation to heat the plaque surface (Naghavi, *et al.*, 2003). This concept is based on the hypothesis that if atherosclerotic lesions are inflamed by virtue of inflammatory cell infiltration, they will give off more heat than normal areas of the arterial system (ten Have, Gijsen, Wentzel, Slager, & van der Steen, Temperature distribution in atherosclerotic coronary arteries: influence of plaque geometry and flow (a numerical study), 2004), (Shah, 2003).

The possible reasons for this increased heat production are: 1) high metabolic rate of macrophages, 2) ineffective thermogenesis (indicated by increased expression of mitochondrial uncoupling protein 2 and 3), 3) increased neoangiogenesis and 4) infections. Macrophages, T-cells, and mast cells are very active cells with a high metabolic rate and high rate of energy consumption (Ten Have, Gijsen, Wentzel, Slager, Serruys, & van der Steen, 2005). Arterial foam cells that have been found in autopsy studies as constituents of the vulnerable plaque consume three times more oxygen than isolated smooth muscle cells. In specific, a study using numeric simulations has suggested that heat-producing macrophages at the shoulder region of vulnerable plaques contribute most to the higher temperature measurements. Moreover, in another study it was demonstrated that the final temperature of the plaque is determined by a balance of heat produced by the macrophages and the cooling effect of blood flow (ten Have, Gijsen, Wentzel, Slager, Serruys, & van der Steen, A numerical study on the influence of vulnerable plaque composition on intravascular thermography measurements, 2006), (ten Have, *et al.*, 2007). The ineffective thermogenesis may be attributed to the lack of oxygen and ischemia on vulnerable plaques that leads to ineffective metabolism of nutrients and greater loss of energy in the form of heat instead of ATP production. More interestingly, macrophages in atherosclerotic plaques show increased expression of mitochondrial uncoupling protein (UCP)-2 and UCP-3 that are both thermogenins and may contribute to heat production. Recent studies have shown increased neoangiogenesis in vulnerable plaques. Neovessel formation increases blood flow inside plaques, being thus another possible mechanism o heat production (Papaioannou, *et al.*, 2009), (Sanidas, *et al.*, 2008), (Carlier, *et al.*, 2005). Several infectious agents have been implicated in the pathogenesis of atherosclerosis (Chlamydia pneumoniae, herpes viruses, and influenza). The possible local infection and subsequent inflammation may contribute to plaque heat production.

Thus, it seems that the final measured surface temperature over the arterial wall will depend on: 1) the metabolic activity of cellular components of plaques (especially more superficial cells), 2) heat diffusion to and from adjacent tissues, and 3) blood tissue thermal diffusion.

Thermography Devices

The *in vivo* temperature measurement of coronary atherosclerotic plaque has become feasible by the use of specially designed thermography catheters. The local vessel wall temperature can be assessed by thermistor-, thermocouple- or infrared-based measurements. An additional method that has been recently applied in cardiology for the estimation of arterial wall temperature difference is microwave radiometry.

Several studies have been performed by thermistor-based devices. In early 1990, for the first time, Casscells *et al.* studied atherosclerotic plaques from the carotid arteries of patients undergoing endarterectomy and found marked temperature heterogeneity over the plaque surface (Casscells, *et al.*, 1996). Within 15 min of removal of a sample of artery, a thermistor (Cole-Parmer model 8402-20) with a 24-gauge needle tip (accuracy 0-1°C, time constant 0-15 s) was used to measure the temperature of the luminal surface in 20 locations. Temperature measurements at multiple spots over each plaque showed remarkable variations in surface temperature, ranging from 0.2°C to 2.2°C. Stefanadis *et al.* was the first to evaluated temperature differences along the coronary arterial wall by a dedicated thermography catheter (Epiphany; Medispes S. W., Zug, Switzerland) (Figure 1) (Stefanadis & Toutouzas, In vivo local thermography of coronary artery atherosclerotic plaques in humans, 1998),

Figure 1. Photograph of the thermography catheter of the Thermocore Medical Systems, illustrating the engaged distal end of the catheter, with the 4 thermistors widely expanded (each at 90°C). Scale bar is 1 cm. This thermography catheter is an over-the-wire system that consists of a functional end that can be engaged by retracting a covering sheath. The distal part with the 4 dedicated thermistors at the distal end of 4 flexible nitinol strips (each at 90-degrees) with an expansion width of 9 mm, ensures endoluminal surface contact of the aorta.

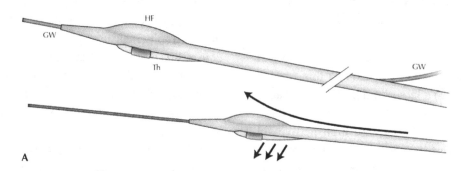

(Stefanadis, *et al.*, 1999). This intracoronary thermography catheter utilized in a number of clinical studies to date, uses a thermistor-based sensor and consists of two lumens (Toutouzas, *et al.*, 2007), (Toutouzas, *et al.*, 2005), (Stefanadis & Toutouzas, In vivo local thermography of coronary artery atherosclerotic plaques in humans, 1998), (Toutouzas, *et al.*, 2004), (Stefanadis C., *et al.*, Increased local temperature in human coronary atherosclerotic plaques: an independent predictor of clinical outcome in patients undergoing a percutaneous coronary intervention, 2001), (Stefanadis C., *et al.*, 2002), (Toutouzas, *et al.*, 2006), (Toutouzas, Markou, Drakopoulou, Mitropoulos, Tsiamis, & Stefanadis, Patients with type two diabetes mellitus: increased local inflammatory activation in culprit atheromatous plaques, 2005), (Toutouzas, *et al.*, 2007), (Toutouzas, *et al.*, 2009), (Toutouzas, Spanos, & Ribichini, A correlation of coronary plaque temperature with inflammatory markers obtained from atherectomy specimens in humans, 2003). The first runs through the distal 20 cm of the device and is used for insertion of a 0.014-inc guidewire that serves as a monorail provision system. The thermistor is positioned at the distal part of the thermography catheter in the second lumen. The technical characteristics of this particular polyamide thermistor include 1) temperature accuracy of $0.05°$ C; 2) time constant of 300 ms; 3) spatial resolution of 0.5 mm; and 4) linear correlation of resistance versus temperature over the range of $33°$ to $43°C$. This catheter is 3, 3.5, or 4 F in diameter, depending on the size of the vessel. A series of clinical studies by this catheter have shown that temperature difference between atherosclerotic plaque and healthy vessel wall increases progressively with clinical syndrome. Moreover increased temperature difference has been shown to correlate with C-reactive protein and systemic inflammation (Toutouzas, *et al.*, 2007), (Toutouzas, Spanos, & Ribichini, A correlation of coronary plaque temperature with inflammatory markers obtained from atherectomy specimens in humans, 2003), (Stefanadis, *et al.*,

2000), (Stefanadis C., *et al.*, Relation between local temperature and C-reactive protein levels in patients with coronary artery disease: effects of atorvastatin treatment, 2007), (Toutouzas, *et al.*, 2009). The same group has shown the beneficial effect of statins on thermal heterogeneity and the negative impact of diabetes mellitus (Toutouzas, *et al.*, 2007), (Toutouzas, *et al.*, Increased heat generation from atherosclerotic plaques in patients with type 2 diabetes: an increased local inflammatory activation, 2005), (Toutouzas, *et al.*, 2004), (Stefanadis C., *et al.*, 2002), (Toutouzas, *et al.*, 2009). Moreover, increased local temperature in atherosclerotic plaques was shown to be a strong predictor of an unfavorable clinical outcome in patients with coronary artery disease undergoing percutaneous interventions (Stefanadis C., *et al.*, Increased local temperature in human coronary atherosclerotic plaques: an independent predictor of clinical outcome in patients undergoing a percutaneous coronary intervention, 2001), (Toutouzas, Colombo, & Stefanadis, Inflammation and restenosis after percutaneous coronary interventions, 2004). Furthermore, for the first time a correlation of morphological and functional plaque characteristics has been performed. In specific in a study with thermography and intravascular ultrasound, a strong and positive correlation between the coronary remodelling index (defined as the ratio of the external elastic membrane area at the lesion, to that at the proximal site) and the temperature difference between the atherosclerotic plaque and healthy vascular wall was found (Toutouzas, *et al.*, 2007). Furthermore, a correlation of thermographic findings with optical coherence tomography findings has been recorded (Toutouzas, *et al.*, 2007), (Toutouzas, *et al.*, 2009), (Toutouzas, *et al.*, 2008), (Toutouzas K., *et al.*, 2007). Due to the possible cooling effect of blood flow during the thermographic measurements and the underestimation of the plaque temperature, the same group designed another catheter that possesses opposite to the thermistor a non-compliant semi-balloon (Stefanadis C., Toutouzas, Vavuranakis, Tsiamis,

Vaina, & Toutouzas, New balloon-thermography catheter for in vivo temperature measurements in human coronary atherosclerotic plaques: a novel approach for thermography?, 2003). Progressive inflation of the balloon at low pressures interrupts blood flow without dilatation of the arterial wall. Indeed, the study that was performed by the balloon thermography catheter showed higher temperature differences after complete interruption of blood flow by inflation of the balloon (Stefanadis C., Toutouzas, Vavuranakis, Tsiamis, Vaina, & Toutouzas, New balloon-thermography catheter for in vivo temperature measurements in human coronary atherosclerotic plaques: a novel approach for thermography?, 2003). Based on the concept that atherosclerosis is not a local phenomenon but rather affects the whole coronary arterial tree, temperature measurements were performed in the coronary sinus and right atrium, thus evaluating the diffuse coronary inflammation (Toutouzas, *et al.*, Increased coronary sinus blood temperature: correlation with systemic inflammation, 2006), (Toutouzas, *et al.*, 2006), (Stefanadis, *et al.*, 2004). The dedicated catheter has a steering arm with a connector for the thermistor lead wires that is attached to the proximal part of the catheter. The steering arm passes through the lumen of the catheter and is attached to its tip. The distal 7 cm of the catheter shaft consists of a soft non-thrombogenic material. The thermistor lead-wires end at the connector and pass through another lumen of the catheter. A thermistor probe is positioned at the centre of the catheter tip. Manipulation of the steering arm proximally enables the distal end of the catheter to be curved (0°to180°). The sensitivity of the thermistor is 0.05°C and time-constant is 300ms. Temperature difference between the coronary sinus and the right atrium was greater in patients with acute coronary syndrome and with stable angina compared to patients without angiographically significant coronary artery disease, independently of the severity and the site of the atherosclerotic lesions (Toutouzas, *et al.*, Increased coronary sinus blood temperature: correlation with systemic inflammation, 2006).

The A prototype *ThermoCoil System* (Imetrx, Mountain View, California) has been used for also for temperature measurements (Courtney, *et al.*, 2004), (Wainstein, Costa, Ribeiro, Zago, & Rogers, 2007). The system includes a 0.014_guidewire that is 175 cm long and contains a thermocouple at its most distal end within a polymeric sphere designed to contact the vessel surface. A localized bend in the tip of the guidewire approximately 10 mm from its most distal end causes the thermo-sensitive tip of the wire to contact the vessel wall. The thermocouple is specified to have a time constant of 30 msec. Electrical contacts at the proximal end allow the guidewire to be coupled to a motor drive unit and interface that records the temperature from the distal end. The motor drive unit was set to rotate the guidewire at a rate of approximately 25 rpm and included a pullback device that caused the tip of the wire to travel longitudinally within the vessel at a rate of 0.83 mm/sec. This particular combination of rotation and pullback motions is such that the distal tip of the catheter travels a spiral path along the vessel wall with an average pitch of 2 mm and travels a targeted distance of 50 mm in 60 sec. The recording and control interface is connected to a laptop computer for the display and archiving of thermographic data. The interface displayed a real-time temperature vs. distance plot during the pullback, allowing direct observation of the guidewire's ability to detect changes in temperature. Wainstein *et al.* studied a small number of patients with the ThermoCoil thermography catheter (Imetrx, Mountain View, Calif) and reported detecting intracoronary temperature differences ranging from 0.1°C to 0.3°C in 4 subjects (Wainstein, Costa, Ribeiro, Zago, & Rogers, 2007).

Other studies have been performed with a 3.5-F thermography catheter that has a self-expanding basket with five nitinol arms and a thermocouple on each arm (Volcano Therapeutics Inc., Rancho

Figure 2. Schematic of the distal part of the thermography catheter (Epiphany Medispes Systems). A thermistor probe (Th), is attached to the distal end of the catheter. Exactly opposite the probe is a hydrofoil that ensures contact with the vessel wall.

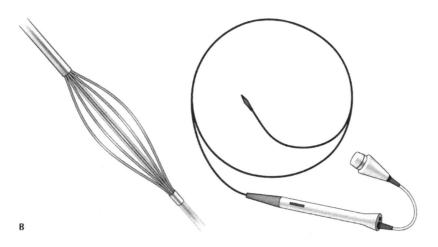

B

Cordova, CA). This intracoronary thermography system (Volcano Corporation, Rancho Cordova, Calif) is designed for the measurement and graphic recording of vessel wall and blood temperature (Figure 2). Measurements are taken using a 3.5-F catheter tipped with a 19.4-mm self-expanding basket with 5 nitinol arms. Nitinol has elastic properties ensuring that basket arms are in contact with all segments of the wall, if the vessel has a diameter of 2.5 to 4.0 mm. The catheter, compatible with guides 6-F or larger, is used to insert the folded basket over a long 0.014' guide wire. The basket can easily be expanded when positioned at the distal vessel segment. Five thermocouples placed on each nitinol arm to measure the vessel wall temperature and one central thermocouple measuring the blood temperature, transform the heat energy into electric signals. The signals are then analyzed within the computer based console providing absolute and relative temperatures, for 5 arms and blood temperature simultaneously. Measurements are taken along the vessel axis every 0.5 mm. By this method a thermal map of the scanned vessel segment can be obtained. The system is manufactured to detect temperature differences of 0.05°C. In animal studies, this

catheter could detect temperature heterogeneity over the atherosclerotic plaques in the femoral arteries of inbred atherosclerotic dogs and the aortas of Watanabe rabbits (Naghavi, *et al.*, 2003), (Naghavi, *et al.*, 2002). Rzeszutko *et al.* in Poland used the Volcano thermography system in 40 patients with ACS. The gradient between blood temperature and maximum wall temperature was 0.1°C or greater in 16 patients (40%) (Rzeszutko, *et al.*, 2006). There was a significant temperature difference between culprit and adjacent nonculprit segments when blood flow was interrupted during thermography but was marginally nonsignificant when the flow was preserved. In an another thermography study with this device the authors reported focal temperature increases ranging from 0.14°C to 0.36°C in 7 patients over the culprit lesions. Hot plaques were found in 4 patients with UA (50%) and 3 patients with SA (27%) (Schmermund, Rodermann, & Erbel, 2003). However, in study of Dudek *et al.*, thermography was unable to differentiate between lesions at risk, despite a selection of lesions that should appear most distinct to differentiate (Dudek, *et al.*, 2005).

The Thermocore thermography catheter (Thermocore Medical Systems Inc.) is an over the wire

Figure 3. The Volcano intravascular thermography catheter. It is a 3.5-F catheter tipped with a 19.4-mm self-expanding basket with 5 nitinol arms. Nitinol has elastic properties ensuring that basket arms are in contact with all segments of the wall, if the vessel has a diameter of 2.5 to 4.0 mm.

catheter that consists of four thermistors, touching the vessel wall. Accuracy of each of the thermistors is 0.0068°C. The thermography catheter is connected to a dedicated pull-back system, which allows a constant pull-back speed of 0.2 mm/s (Figure 3). The catheter has been applied in experimental and clinical studies. A study by Verheye *et al.* intracoronary thermography tested in both rabbit aortas and pig coronary arteries is safe and feasible and that temperature heterogeneity remains unchanged under normal physiologic flow conditions (Verheye, De Meyer, Van Langenhove, Knaapen, & Kockx, 2002). The same group demonstrated that in vivo temperature heterogeneity of rabbit atherosclerotic plaques is determined by plaque composition (Verheye, *et al.*, 2004). On the same study it was demonstrated that modification of atherosclerotic cell composition by dietary cholesterol lowering, influences temperature heterogeneity. By the clinical application of this catheter, Krams *et al.* showed that In vivo temperature measurements enable to detect plaques that contain more macrophages, less smooth muscle cells, and a higher MMP-9 activity (Krams, *et al.*, 2005).

Clinical studies have also been performed with the 0.014-inch Radi wire (Medical Systems, Uppsala, Sweden) equipped with a high-sensitivity thermistor (sensitivity 0.1° C) (Worthley, Farouque, Worthley, Baldi, Chew, & Meredith, 2006), (Cuisset, *et al.*, 2009), (Takumi, *et al.*, 2007), (Toutouzas, Tsiamis, & Stefanadis, The

Radi Pressure Wire thermistor for intracoronary thermography, 2007). This 0.014-inch pressure/temperature (P/T) guidewire (Pressure wire RADI 5, Radi Medical Systems, Uppsala, Sweden), can be used instead of a standard guidewire during percutaneous coronary intervention. The wire has a microsensor located 3 cm from the wire tip, which enables simultaneous recordings of coronary pressure and temperature measurement. The accuracy of pressure and temperature is 1 mm Hg and 0.02°C, respectively. Continuous signals of pressure and temperature were displayed and recorded on a suitable interface (Radi-Analyzer, Radi Medical Systems). Worthley *et al.* in a recent study showed that mean temperature differences measured in the culprit lesions was below the resolution of the thermistor and not significantly different from the baseline temperature difference (Worthley, Farouque, Worthley, Baldi, Chew, & Meredith, 2006). Accordingly, in a recent article Cuisset *et al.* by using the same system proposed that measurements by catheter-based devices may be affected by pressure and flow artefacts (Cuisset, *et al.*, 2009). This device is not designed for measuring the coronary plaque temperature, but rather for measuring the blood temperature within the lumen and its thermistor is not always in contact with the arterial wall. In a recent article, Takumi *et al.* demonstrated that the maximal temperature site is significantly distal to the angiographic occlusive site in patients with total occlusion (Takumi, *et al.*, 2007). Thus, although the angiographic evaluation of the culprit plaque showed limited utility, thermography identified accurately the culprit plaque in patients with acute myocardial infarction and coronary total occlusion.

Limitations of the Intracoronary Thermography

A discrepancy between the ex vivo and in vivo temperature measurements has been observed in several studies. This has been attributed to the "cooling" effects of blood flow, and the potential inability of the catheters to contact the vessel wall (Toutouzas, Tsiamis, Drakopoulou, & Stefanadis, Regarding the study In vitro and in vivo studies on thermistor-based intracoronary temperature measurements: effect of pressure and flow, 2009). This discrepancy raises concern about the accuracy of the method and the potential clinical utility (Toutouzas, Drakopoulou, Stefanadi, Siasos, & Stefanadis, 485-489). Further, despite the fact that only a single "culprit" or vulnerable plaque is clinically symptomatic, it has been demonstrated that coronary inflammation is not only a local phenomenon, but a widespread, "pancoronary" process in patients with acute coronary syndromes. However, the proposed intracoronary devices do not record temperature measurements along the coronary arteries but rather obtain spot measurements in the coronary arteries. All these shortcomings prohibit the performance of large prospective clinical trials with intravascular thermography. Improvement of technology is required targeting at ensuring accurate thermal scanning of the coronary arterial tree.

Non-invasive Assessment of Arterial Thermal Heterogeneity

Microwave radiometry (MR) is a non-invasive diagnostic method that provides accurate measurement of the temperature of tissues. MR measures natural electromagnetic radiation from a patient's internal tissue at microwave frequencies, based on the principle that the intensity of the radiation is proportional to the temperature of tissues (Williams & Springer, 1981). It has been applied in oncology for the detection of breast and thyroid cancers, and for monitoring of the treatment of benign tumors (Mizushina, Shimizu, & Sugiura, 1992), (Myers, Barrett, & Sadowsky, 1980), (Vetshev, Chilingaridi, Zolkin, Vesnin, Gabaidze, & Bannyi, 2006). The microwave radiometry antenna detects temperature from internal tissues at microwave frequencies. The system of MR possesses an antenna with a sensor that filters all possible microwaves or radiofrequency waves that may be present in the room vicinity and may cause interference with the sensor. The internal temperature sensor has an accuracy of 0.2 °C and is connected with a processing unit. The diameter of the antenna is 3.9 cm. The sensor of the antenna measures the 'volume under investigation' as a rectangular area of 3 cm in length and 2 cm in width and 3-7 cm in depth depending on the water content of the body. During measurements the microwave antenna of the device is placed in contact with the skin over the 'area under investigation', in position for 10sec, during which time the receiver integrates the microwave emission and a microprocessor converts the measured signal to temperature. The temperature data are displayed as a temperature field, that in which cool areas of the vessel are displayed by "cold" colours (i.e. blue) and hot ones are reflected by "warm" colours (red and orange). Theoretically, thermal scanning by microwave radiometry can be performed in all arterial segments in a depth of 1-7 cm from the skin. This proposal of thermal mapping in arterial segments has been already investigated in an experimental hypercholesterolemic rabbit model with promising results (Toutouzas, *et al.*). In specific, thermal heterogeneity of atherosclerotic aortas was evaluated by intravascular thermography and microwave radiometry. Temperature differences by the two methods correlated positively. Moreover atheroslclerotic aortas had higher temperature differences compared to control aortas. Moreover, histological analysis showed good correlates of temperature differences with histology and immunohistochemistry

The method is also currently under clinical evaluation in human carotid arteries (Toutouzas, *et al.*). It seems that carotid arteries with atherosclerosis show higher temperature differences compared to those detected to controls. Moreover, among atherosclerotic carotid arteries fatty plaques have higher temperature differences compared to mixed and calcified plaques as detected by ultrasound. To date, there is no other available non invasive method for in vivo detection of thermal heterogeneity. It seems that the technical characteristics of the device fulfill the criteria for the detection of heat production in solid organs, but up to now there is no experience in the vascular system. The potential improvement of the sensitivity and the dimensions of the antenna may provide more accurate measurements. The clinical value of microwave radiometry in the detection and prognosis of atherosclerotic disease needs to be evaluated in clinical studies.

CONCLUSION

Thermography is a catheter-based technique for the functional imaging of atherosclerotic plaques with the ability to identify potential vulnerable plaques and culprit plaques in patients with coronary artery disease. Intracoronary thermography has provided important information regarding the mechanisms involved in the pathophysiology of the vulnerable plaque. Moreover, it has been shown to have a good predictive value for clinical events in patients with increased temperature differences. However, although coronary thermography is a safe and feasible method for the functional evaluation of atherosclerotic plaques, it has certain technical limitations. The potential clinical utility of intracoronary thermography to identify vulnerable plaques and affect local and systemic treatment algorithms for patients with coronary artery disease remains to be validated in large prospective trials.

REFERENCES

Carlier, S., Kakadiaris, I., Dib, N., Vavuranakis, M., O'Malley, S., & Gul, K. (2005). Vasa vasorum imaging: A new window to the clinical detection of vulnerable atherosclerotic plaques. *Current Atherosclerosis Reports, 7*, 164–169. doi:10.1007/s11883-005-0040-2

Casscells, W., Hathorn, B., David, M., Krabach, T., Vaughn, W., & McAllister, H. (1996). Thermal detection of cellular infiltrates in living atherosclerotic plaques: Possible implications for plaque rupture and thrombosis. *Lancet, 347*, 1447–1451. doi:10.1016/S0140-6736(96)91684-0

Corti, R., Hutter, R., Badimon, J., & Fuster, V. (2004). Evolving concepts in the triad of atherosclerosis, inflammation and thrombosis. *Journal of Thrombosis and Thrombolysis, 17*, 35–44. doi:10.1023/B:THRO.0000036027.39353.70

Courtney, B., Nakamura, M., Tsugita, R., Lilly, R., Basisht, R., & Grube, E. (2004). Validation of a thermographic guidewire for endoluminal mapping of atherosclerotic disease: An in vitro study. *Catheterization and Cardiovascular Interventions, 62*, 221–229. doi:10.1002/ccd.10750

Cuisset, T., Beauloye, C., Melikian, N., Hamilos, M., Sarma, J., & Sarno, G. (2009). In vitro and in vivo studies on thermistor-based intracoronary temperature measurements: Effect of pressure and flow. *Catheterization and Cardiovascular Interventions, 73*, 224–230. doi:10.1002/ccd.21780

Dudek, D., Rzeszutko, L., Legutko, J., Wizimirski, M., Chyrchel, M., & Witanek, B. (2005). High-risk coronary artery plaques diagnosed by intracoronary thermography. *Kardiologia Polska, 62*, 383–389.

Hamdan, A., Assali, A., Fuchs, S., Battler, A., & Kornowski, R. (2007). Imaging of vulnerable coronary artery plaques. *Catheterization and Cardiovascular Interventions, 70*, 65–74. doi:10.1002/ccd.21117

Honda, Y., & Fitzgerald, P. (2008). Frontiers in intravascular imaging technologies. *Circulation*, *117*, 2024–2037. doi:10.1161/CIRCULATIONAHA.105.551804

Krams, R., Verheye, S., van Damme, L., Tempel, D., Mousavi Gourabi, B., & Boersma, E. (2005). In vivo temperature heterogeneity is associated with plaque regions of increased MMP-9 activity. *European Heart Journal*, *26*, 2200–2205. doi:10.1093/eurheartj/ehi461

Leborgne, L., Dascotte, O., Jarry, G., Levy, F., Kamel, S., & Maizel, J. (2005). *Multi-vessel coronary plaque temperature heterogeneity in patients with acute coronary syndromes. First study with the Radi Medical System wire*. In AHA.

Libby, P., Ridker, P., & Maseri, A. (2002). Inflammation and atherosclerosis. *Circulation*, *105*, 1135–1143. doi:10.1161/hc0902.104353

Madjid, M., Willerson, J., & Casscells, S. (2006). Intracoronary thermography for detection of high-risk vulnerable plaques. *Journal of the American College of Cardiology*, *47*, C80–C85. doi:10.1016/j.jacc.2005.11.050

Mizushina, S., Shimizu, T., & Sugiura, T. (1992). Non-invasive thermometry with multi-frequency microwave radiometry. *Frontiers of Medical and Biological Engineering*, *4*, 129–133.

Myers, P., Barrett, A., & Sadowsky, N. (1980). Microwave thermography of normal and cancerous breast tissue. *Annals of the New York Academy of Sciences*, *335*, 443–455. doi:10.1111/j.1749-6632.1980.tb50768.x

Naghavi, M., John, R., Naguib, S., Siadaty, M., Grasu, R., & Kurian, K. (2002). pH heterogeneity of human and rabbit atherosclerotic plaques: A new insight into detection of vulnerable plaque. *Atherosclerosis*, *164*, 27–35. doi:10.1016/S0021-9150(02)00018-7

Naghavi, M., Libby, P., Falk, E., Casscells, S., Litovsky, S., & Rumberger, J. (2003). From vulnerable plaque to vulnerable patient: a call for new definitions and risk assessment strategies: Part I. *Circulation*, *108*, 1664–1672. doi:10.1161/01.CIR.0000087480.94275.97

Naghavi, M., Madjid, M., Gul, K., Siadaty, M., Litovsky, S., & Willerson, J. (2003). Thermography basket catheter: in vivo measurement of the temperature of atherosclerotic plaques for detection of vulnerable plaques. *Catheterization and Cardiovascular Interventions*, *59*, 52–59. doi:10.1002/ccd.10486

Papaioannou, T., Vavuranakis, M., Androulakis, A., Lazaros, G., Kakadiaris, I., & Vlaseros, I. (2009). In-vivo imaging of carotid plaque neo-angiogenesis with contrast-enhanced harmonic ultrasound. *International Journal of Cardiology*, *134*, e110–e112. doi:10.1016/j.ijcard.2008.01.020

Ross, R. (1999). Atherosclerosis--an inflammatory disease. *The New England Journal of Medicine*, *340*, 115–126. doi:10.1056/NEJM199901143400207

Rzeszutko, L., Legutko, J., Kaluza, G., Wizimirski, M., Richter, A., & Chyrchel, M. (2006). Assessment of culprit plaque temperature by intracoronary thermography appears inconclusive in patients with acute coronary syndromes. *Arteriosclerosis, Thrombosis, and Vascular Biology*, *26*, 1889–1894. doi:10.1161/01.ATV.0000232500.93340.54

Sanidas, E., Vavuranakis, M., Papaioannou, T., Kakadiaris, I., Carlier, S., & Syros, G. (2008). Study of atheromatous plaque using intravascular ultrasound. *Hellenic Journal of Cardiology; HJC = Hellenike Kardiologike Epitheorese*, *49*, 415–421.

Schmermund, A., Rodermann, J., & Erbel, R. (2003). Intracoronary thermography. *Herz*, *28*, 505–512. doi:10.1007/s00059-003-2495-7

Shah, P. (2003). Mechanisms of plaque vulnerability and rupture. *Journal of the American College of Cardiology, 41,* 15S–22S. doi:10.1016/S0735-1097(02)02834-6

Stefanadis, C., Diamantopoulos, L., Dernellis, J., Economou, E., Tsiamis, E., & Toutouzas, K. (2000). Heat production of atherosclerotic plaques and inflammation assessed by the acute phase proteins in acute coronary syndromes. *Journal of Molecular and Cellular Cardiology, 32,* 43–52. doi:10.1006/jmcc.1999.1049

Stefanadis, C., Diamantopoulos, L., Vlachopoulos, C., Tsiamis, E., Dernellis, J., & Toutouzas, K. (1999). Thermal heterogeneity within human atherosclerotic coronary arteries detected in vivo: A new method of detection by application of a special thermography catheter. *Circulation, 99,* 1965–1971.

Stefanadis, C., Toutouzas, K., Tsiamis, E., Mitropoulos, I., Tsioufis, C., & Kallikazaros, I. (2003). Thermal heterogeneity in stable human coronary atherosclerotic plaques is underestimated in vivo: the "cooling effect" of blood flow. *Journal of the American College of Cardiology, 41,* 403–408. doi:10.1016/S0735-1097(02)02817-6

Stefanadis, C., Toutouzas, K., Tsiamis, E., Stratos, C., Vavuranakis, M., & Kallikazaros, I. (2001). Increased local temperature in human coronary atherosclerotic plaques: an independent predictor of clinical outcome in patients undergoing a percutaneous coronary intervention. *Journal of the American College of Cardiology, 37,* 1277–1283. doi:10.1016/S0735-1097(01)01137-8

Stefanadis, C., Toutouzas, K., Tsiamis, E., Vavuranakis, M., Tsioufis, C., & Stefanadi, E. (2007). Relation between local temperature and C-reactive protein levels in patients with coronary artery disease: effects of atorvastatin treatment. *Atherosclerosis, 192,* 396–400. doi:10.1016/j.atherosclerosis.2006.05.038

Stefanadis, C., Toutouzas, K., Vavuranakis, M., Tsiamis, E., Tousoulis, D., & Panagiotakos, D. (2002). Statin treatment is associated with reduced thermal heterogeneity in human atherosclerotic plaques. *European Heart Journal, 23,* 1664–1669.

Stefanadis, C., Toutouzas, K., Vavuranakis, M., Tsiamis, E., Vaina, S., & Toutouzas, P. (2003). New balloon-thermography catheter for in vivo temperature measurements in human coronary atherosclerotic plaques: A novel approach for thermography? *Catheterization and Cardiovascular Interventions, 58,* 344–350. doi:10.1002/ccd.10449

Stefanadis, C., & Toutouzas, P. (1998). In vivo local thermography of coronary artery atherosclerotic plaques in humans. *Annals of Internal Medicine, 129,* 1079–1080.

Stefanadis, C., Tsiamis, E., Vaina, S., Toutouzas, K., Boudoulas, H., & Gialafos, J. (2004). Temperature of blood in the coronary sinus and right atrium in patients with and without coronary artery disease. *The American Journal of Cardiology, 93,* 207–210. doi:10.1016/j.amjcard.2003.09.040

Takumi, T., Lee, S., Hamasaki, S., Toyonaga, K., Kanda, D., & Kusumoto, K. (2007). Limitation of angiography to identify the culprit plaque in acute myocardial infarction with coronary total occlusion utility of coronary plaque temperature measurement to identify the culprit plaque. *Journal of the American College of Cardiology, 50,* 2197–2203. doi:10.1016/j.jacc.2007.07.079

Tan, K., & Lip, G. (2008). Imaging of the unstable plaque. *International Journal of Cardiology, 127,* 157–165. doi:10.1016/j.ijcard.2007.11.054

ten Have, A., Draaijers, E., Gijsen, F., Wentzel, J., Slager, C., & Serruys, P. (2007). Influence of catheter design on lumen wall temperature distribution in intracoronary thermography. *Journal of Biomechanics, 40,* 281–288. doi:10.1016/j.jbiomech.2006.01.016

Ten Have, A., Gijsen, F., Wentzel, J., Slager, C., Serruys, P., & van der Steen, A. (2005). Intracoronary thermography: heat generation; transfer and detection. *EuroIntervention, 1*, 105–114.

ten Have, A., Gijsen, F., Wentzel, J., Slager, C., Serruys, P., & van der Steen, A. (2006). A numerical study on the influence of vulnerable plaque composition on intravascular thermography measurements. *Physics in Medicine and Biology, 51*, 5875–5887. doi:10.1088/0031-9155/51/22/010

ten Have, A., Gijsen, F., Wentzel, J., Slager, C., & van der Steen, A. (2004). Temperature distribution in atherosclerotic coronary arteries: Influence of plaque geometry and flow (a numerical study). *Physics in Medicine and Biology, 49*, 4447–4462. doi:10.1088/0031-9155/49/19/001

Toutouzas, K., Colombo, A., & Stefanadis, C. (2004). Inflammation and restenosis after percutaneous coronary interventions. *European Heart Journal, 25*, 1679–1687. doi:10.1016/j.ehj.2004.06.011

Toutouzas, K., Drakopoulou, M., Markou, V., Karabelas, I., Vaina, S., & Vavuranakis, M. (2007). Correlation of systemic inflammation with local inflammatory activity in non-culprit lesions: Beneficial effect of statins. *International Journal of Cardiology, 119*, 368–373. doi:10.1016/j.ijcard.2006.08.026

Toutouzas, K., Drakopoulou, M., Markou, V., Stougianos, P., Tsiamis, E., & Tousoulis, D. (2006). Increased coronary sinus blood temperature: Correlation with systemic inflammation. *European Journal of Clinical Investigation, 36*(4). doi:10.1111/j.1365-2362.2006.01625.x

Toutouzas, K., Drakopoulou, M., Mitropoulos, J., Tsiamis, E., Vaina, S., & Vavuranakis, M. (2006). Elevated plaque temperature in non-culprit de novo atheromatous lesions of patients with acute coronary syndromes. *Journal of the American College of Cardiology, 47*, 301–306. doi:10.1016/j.jacc.2005.07.069

Toutouzas, K., Drakopoulou, M., Stefanadi, E., Siasos, G., & Stefanadis, C. (2005). (485-489). Intracoronary thermography: Does it help us in clinical decision making? *Journal of Interventional Cardiology, 18*.

Toutouzas, K., Markou, V., Drakopoulou, M., Mitropoulos, I., Tsiamis, E., & Stefanadis, C. (2005). Patients with type two diabetes mellitus: increased local inflammatory activation in culprit atheromatous plaques. *Hellenic Journal of Cardiology; HJC = Hellenike Kardiologike Epitheorese, 46*, 283–288.

Toutouzas, K., Markou, V., Drakopoulou, M., Mitropoulos, I., Tsiamis, E., & Vavuranakis, M. (2005). Increased heat generation from atherosclerotic plaques in patients with type 2 diabetes: An increased local inflammatory activation. *Diabetes Care, 28*, 1656–1661. doi:10.2337/diacare.28.7.1656

Toutouzas, K., Riga, M., Patsa, C., Synetos, A., Vavuranakis, M., & Tsiamis, E. (2007). Thin fibrous cap and ruptured plaques are associated with increased local inflammatory activation: Insights from optical coherence tomography in patients with acute coronary syndromes. *European Heart Journal, 28*, 4041.

Toutouzas, K., Riga, M., Synetos, A., Karanasos, A., Tsiamis, E., & Tousoulis, D. (2009). Optical coherence tomography analysis of culprit lesions of patients with acute myocardial infarction in combination with intracoronary thermography: Excessive macrophage infiltration of thin fibrous caps are associated with increased local temperature. *Journal of the American College of Cardiology, 53*, 2523.

Toutouzas, K., Riga, M., Vaina, S., Patsa, C., Synetos, A., & Vavuranakis, M. (2008). In acute coronary syndromes thin fibrous cap and ruptured plaques are associated with increased local inflammatory activation: A combination of intravascular optical coherence tomography and intracoronary thermography study. *Journal of the American College of Cardiology, 51,* 1033.

Toutouzas, K., Riga, M., Vaina, S., Patsa, C., Synetos, A., & Vavuranakis, V. (2007). Optical coherence tomography in patients with acute coronary syndromes. Increased local inflammatory activation in ruptured plaques with thin fibrous cap. *Circulation, 116,* 1989.

Toutouzas, K., Spanos, V., & Ribichini, F. (2003). A correlation of coronary plaque temperature with inflammatory markers obtained from atherectomy specimens in humans. *The American Journal of Cardiology, 92,* 476.

Toutouzas, K., Stougianos, P., Drakopoulou, M., Mitropoulos, J., Bosinakou, E., & Markou, V. (2006). Coronary sinus thermography in idiopathic dilated cardiomyopathy: Correlation with systemic inflammation and left ventricular contractility. *European Journal of Heart Failure, 9*(2).

Toutouzas, K., Synetos, A., Drakopoulou, M., Moldovan, C., Siores, E., Grassos, C., *et al.* (n.d.). *A new non-invasive method for detection of local inflammatory activation in atheromatic plaques: Experimental evaluation of microwave thermography.* ESC2010.

Toutouzas, K., Synetos, A., Stefanadi, E., Vaina, S., Markou, V., & Vavuranakis, M. (2007). Correlation between morphologic characteristics and local temperature differences in culprit lesions of patients with symptomatic coronary artery disease. *Journal of the American College of Cardiology, 49,* 2264–2271. doi:10.1016/j.jacc.2007.03.026

Toutouzas, K., Tsiamis, E., Drakopoulou, M., & Stefanadis, C. (2009). Regarding the study in vitro and in vivo studies on thermistor-based intracoronary temperature measurements: Effect of pressure and flow. *Catheterization and Cardiovascular Interventions, 74,* 815–816. doi:10.1002/ccd.22083

Toutouzas, K., Tsiamis, E., Drakopoulou, M., Synetos, A., Karampelas, J., & Riga, M. (2009). Impact of type 2 diabetes mellitus on diffuse inflammatory activation of de novo atheromatous lesions: Implications for systemic inflammation. *Diabetes & Metabolism, 35,* 299–304. doi:10.1016/j.diabet.2009.01.005

Toutouzas, K., Tsiamis, E., & Stefanadis, C. (2007). The Radi PressureWire thermistor for intracoronary thermography. *The Journal of Invasive Cardiology, 19,* 152–154, author reply 152–154.

Toutouzas, K., Vaina, S., Tsiamis, E., Vavuranakis, M., Mitropoulos, J., & Bosinakou, E. (2004). Detection of increased temperature of the culprit lesion after recent myocardial infarction: The favorable effect of statins. *American Heart Journal, 148,* 783–788. doi:10.1016/j.ahj.2004.05.013

Verheye, S., De Meyer, G., Krams, R., Kockx, M., Van Damme, L., & Mousavi Gourabi, B. (2004). Intravascular thermography: Immediate functional and morphological vascular findings. *European Heart Journal, 25,* 158–165. doi:10.1016/j.ehj.2003.10.023

Verheye, S., De Meyer, G., Van Langenhove, G., Knaapen, M., & Kockx, M. (2002). In vivo temperature heterogeneity of atherosclerotic plaques is determined by plaque composition. *Circulation, 105,* 1596–1601. doi:10.1161/01.CIR.0000012527.94843.BF

Vetshev, P., Chilingaridi, K., Zolkin, A., Vesnin, S., Gabaidze, D., & Bannyi, D. (2006). Radiothermometry in diagnosis of thyroid diseases. *Khirurgiia,* 54–58.

Wainstein, M., Costa, M., Ribeiro, J., Zago, A., & Rogers, C. (2007). Vulnerable plaque detection by temperature heterogeneity measured with a guidewire system: Clinical, intravascular ultrasound and histopathologic correlates. *The Journal of Invasive Cardiology, 19*, 49–54.

Williams, L., & Springer, E. (1981). Microwave radiation: Environmental impact and medical application. *Minnesota Medicine, 64*, 593–599.

Worthley, S., Farouque, M., Worthley, M., Baldi, M., Chew, D., & Meredith, I. (2006). The RADI PressureWire high-sensitivity thermistor and culprit lesion temperature in patients with acute coronary syndromes. *The Journal of Invasive Cardiology, 18*, 528–531.

Chapter 9
Research and Clinical Utility of Thermography

Konstantinos Toutouzas
Athens Medical School, Greece

Eleftherios Tsiamis
Athens Medical School, Greece

Maria Drakopoulou
Athens Medical School, Greece

Christodoulos Stefanadis
Athens Medical School, Greece

ABSTRACT

This chapter completes the description of the Thermography within this publication. While the previous chapter of this section dealt with principles of data acquisition, this chapter provides a detailed description of the research and clinical utility of thermography. Separate sections are devoted to the ex vivo thermography studies, to the role of thermography in experimental models and finally to the contribution of thermography in clinical studies.

INTRODUCTION

Atherosclerosis is the underlying cause of acute coronary syndromes, the most important entity of cardiovascular diseases (Rosamond, *et al.*, 2008). Despite advances in current imaging modalities the ability to identify patients that are at high risk for an acute coronary event is still limited mostly because these events may occur as the first manifestation of coronary atherosclerosis in previously apparently asymptomatic individuals with non-flow-limiting vulnerable plaques (Honda & Fitzgerald, 2008). Thus, advances in the identification of vulnerable plaques can be an important step in preventing myocardial infarction and sudden cardiac death.

Several histological characteristics of plaques that are prone to rupture and cause an acute coronary event have been identified. These vulnerable plaques possess: (1) a thin fibrous cap (<65 lm); (2) a large lipid pool; and (3) activated macrophages near the fibrous cap (Naghavi, *et al.*, 2003). The

DOI: 10.4018/978-1-61350-095-8.ch009

Figure 1. Marked temperature heterogeneity was observed (in degrees Celsius) over the surface of endarterectomy samples from carotid plaques

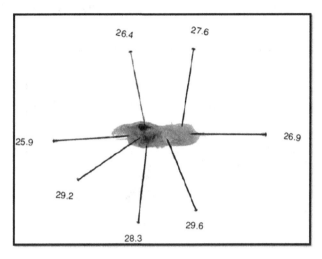

first prospective trial of the natural history of atherosclerosis using multimodality imaging to characterize the coronary tree (Providing Regional Observations to Study Predictors of Events Coronary Tree Trial- PROSPECT) showed that most non-culprit plaques which become symptomatic have a large plaque burden, a large lipid core and a small lumen area (Stone, 2009). However, the impact of other features of vulnerable plaques such as inflammation has not been studied in prospective studies. This intense inflammatory activation, a hallmark feature of vulnerable plaques, manifested by the local invasion of macrophages and lymphocytes and the activation of matrix metalloproteinases has been shown to degrade the supporting collagen and promote plaque fragility, playing thus, a crucial role not only in the first stages of atherosclerosis, but also in the development of its acute complications.

Given that inflammation has a central role in atherosclerosis, intracoronary thermography has been introduced as a technique for the identification of the local inflammatory activation of a vulnerable plaque (Hamdan, Assal, Fuchs, Battler, & Kornowski, 2007). The increased heat production from unstable plaques has been confirmed in several ex vivo human studies, in experimental models, and in clinical studies.

EX VIVO THERMOGRAPHY STUDIES

The concept that plaque temperature is a marker of local inflammation was originally proposed by Casscells *et al.* in 1996 (Figure 1) (Casscells, *et al.*, 1996). This was the first study demonstrating that heat is generated from inflamed atheromatous plaques in humans. In this study, carotid artery samples obtained by endarterectomy were probed with a thermistor (24-gauge needle tip; accuracy 0.1 °C; time contrast 0.15s). Plaques showed several regions in which the surface temperatures varied reproducibly by 0.2–0.3°C. Points with substantially different temperatures could not be distinguished from one another by the naked eye and were sometimes very close to one another (< 1mm apart). Temperature correlated positively with cell density (r = 0.68; p = 0.0001) and inversely with the distance of the cell clusters (mostly macrophages) from the luminal surface (r = –0.38; p= 0.000 (Figure 2) (Casscells, *et al.*, 1996). The thermal heterogeneity observed could also be confirmed using an infrared camera *in vivo*. In order to assess the possible contribution of infection to generation of heat, the genus-specific monoclonal antibody CF-2 against Chlamydia pneumonia was used (Madjid, Naghavi, Malik, Litovsky, Willerson, & Casscells, 2002). However,

Figure 2. The graph represents the correlation of surface temperature with cell density. Relative cell density was the ratio of cell density in an area of interest to that of a background area. Temperature measurements were made at room temperature (20° C) on 24 carotid endarterectomy samples from 22 patients 10–15 min after removal.

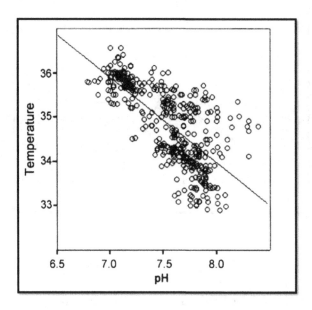

no significant association between temperature heterogeneity and C Pneumonia was found. After incubation of hot plaques with indomethacin, a gradual decrease in plaque heat production over 5 hours was observed, suggesting an inflammatory origin of heat production in atherosclerotic plaques.

Another study showed lower pH readings in vulnerable plaques of human carotid endarterectomised specimens and atherosclerotic rabbit aortas. Areas with lower pH had higher temperature, and areas with a large lipid core showed lower pH with higher temperature, whereas calcified regions had lower temperature and higher pH (Naghavi, et al., 2002). This finding is in accordance with the assumption that lipid-rich vulnerable areas may have a more acidic environment.

These observations were also confirmed in preliminary clinical studies combining temperature measurements with directional atherectomy of the respective specimens. In specific, a correlation between the serum matrix metalloproteinase -1, -3,

and -9 concentration with temperature differences in direct coronary atherectomy specimens has been reported (Toutouzas, Spanos, & Ribichini, 2003). However, the strength of the relationship between levels of serum matrix metalloproteinases and focal activity of such enzymes at the plaque level remains to be determined.

THERMOGRAPHY IN EXPERIMENTAL MODELS

The feasibility of intracoronary thermography for the assessment of thermal heterogeneity *in vivo* has been validated in multiple animal studies (Verheye, De Meyer, Van Langenhove, Knaapen, & Kockx, 2002), (Naghavi, *et al.*, 2003), (Verheye, *et al.*, 2004), (Krams, *et al.*, 2005). Although there are significant differences in the technological characteristics of the devices designed, important pathophysiological insights in the development of the unstable plaque have been obtained. Naghavi *et al.* developed a contact-based "thermobasket" catheter for measuring *in vivo* the temperature at several points on the vessel wall in the presence of blood flow (Zarrabi, Gul, Willerson, Casscell, & Naghavi, 2002), (Naghavi, *et al.*, 2003), (Krams, *et al.*, 2005), (Verheye, *et al.*, 2004). The system was applied in a canine and a rabbit model of atherosclerosis. In inbred cholesterol-fed dogs with femoral atherosclerosis, marked thermal heterogeneity was found on the surface of atherosclerotic regions, but not on disease-free regions. Marked temperature heterogeneity was also observed in the aortas of atherosclerotic Watanabe rabbits and not in normal rabbits. This device showed satisfactory accuracy, reproducibility, and safety.

In an *in vivo* setting, Verheye *et al.* examined temperature heterogeneity in the rabbit aorta. The animals received either a normal or cholesterol-rich (0.3%) diet for 6 months before undergoing thermography of the surface of aortic arch and descending aorta. In the animals receiving a normal diet, plaque formation and temperature heterogeneity were absent. In hypercholesterolemic rabbits, plaque formation was prominent in the thoracic aorta and showed markedly elevated temperature heterogeneity which increased with plaque thickness. Importantly, after 3 months of cholesterol lowering, plaque thickness remained unchanged, but temperature heterogeneity was significantly decreased. Thus, *in vivo* temperature heterogeneity of rabbit atherosclerotic plaques was determined by plaque composition (Verheye, De Meyer, Van Langenhove, Knaapen, & Kockx, 2002). In another study, *in vivo* temperature heterogeneity was found to be associated with plaque regions of increased inflammatory activity. The plaques were experimentally induced in rabbit aortas, and at the day of sacrifice, a pull-back was performed with a thermography catheter. *In vivo* temperature measurements showed increased temperature in plaques that contained higher density of macrophages, less smooth muscle cell concentration, and higher metalloproteinase -9 activity (Krams, *et al.*, 2005).

CLINICAL THERMOGRAPHY STUDIES

The first clinical study with intravascular thermography performed by Stefanadis *et al.* in 1999, demonstrated that the temperature difference between atherosclerotic plaques and adjacent healthy segments increased progressively from control subjects through the ACS spectrum, with acute myocardial infarction (AMI) patients recording the highest values (Stefanadis, *et al.*, 1999). Temperature was constant within the arteries of the control subjects, whereas most atherosclerotic plaques showed higher temperature difference compared with healthy vessel wall. Plaque temperature heterogeneity was present in 20%, 40%, and 67% of the patients with stable angina, unstable angina, and acute myocardial infarction, respectively, and did not correlate with the degree of stenosis. Thermal heterogeneity was absent in the control group. Another study including 55 patients showed increased plaque temperature for an extended period after myocardial infarction, indicating that the inflammatory process is sustained after plaque rupture (Toutouzas, *et al.*, 2004). Schmermund *et al.* recorded intracoronary temperature differences ranging from 0.14°C to 0.36°C. Focal temperature heterogeneity was observed in 50% of patients with unstable angina and in 27% of patients with stable angina. Although this study showed a difference between the two groups, there was still a considerable overlap (Schmermund, Rodermann, & Erbel, 2003). Wainstein *et al.* used a different thermography catheter (ThermoCoil Guidewire). Thirteen patients presenting with either acute or chronic coronary syndromes as indications for percutaneous coronary intervention were evaluated by intracoronary thermography, intravascular ultrasound, and angiography. In addition, directional atherectomy was performed in 2 patients and tissue was analyzed by histology. Intra-arterial temperature rises between 0.1°C and 0.3°C were noted in 4 subjects. Intravascular ultrasound findings and atherectomy tissue histology showed correlates of plaque vulnerability in plaques with elevated temperature (Wainstein, Costa, Ribeiro, Zago, & Rogers, 2007).

Worthley *et al.* measured by the 0.014-inch Radi PressureWire XT (Radi Medical Systems, Uppsala, Sweden) a mean temperature difference of 0.02±0.01°C in the culprit lesion, which was below the resolution of the thermistor and not significantly different from the baseline temperature difference of 0.00°C±0.01°C. In a recent article Cuisset *et al.* by using the same system assessed intracoronary pressure and temperature variations in 18 patients with acute myocardial infarction. In this study when the sensor was advanced across the lesion, an increase in the temperature signal (average 0.059±0.028°C) was uniformly observed in all patients. However, the increase in the temperature signal was proportional to the pressure drop across the stenosis (R= 0.72, p<0.001) (Cuisset, *et al.*, 2009). This study suggested that thermistor-based sensors may not be suited for assessing *in vivo* coronary thermal heterogeneity and that the data obtained so far in patients with acute coronary syndrome may be affected by pressure and flow artefacts. These studies however, may have been limited by the fact that the Radi wire is not designed for measuring the coronary

plaque temperature, but rather for measuring the blood temperature within the lumen and its thermistor is not always in contact with the arterial wall (Worthley, Farouque, Worthley, Baldi, Chew, & Meredith, 2006). However, the correct interpretation of intravascular thermographic measurements might require knowledge of the flow and the morphological characteristics of the atherosclerotic plaque that are not readily available at this stage. Takumi *et al* assessed the hypothesis that the maximal temperature site, as measured by thermal wire, coincides with the culprit plaque as detected by intravascular ultrasound in patients with acute myocardial infarction (Takumi, *et al.*, 2007). In this study of 45 consecutive patients with a first anterior myocardial infarction, temperature measurement with the pressure/temperature guidewire (Pressure Wire RADI 5; Radi Medical Systems, Uppsala, Sweden) demonstrated that the maximal temperature site was significantly distal to the angiographic occlusive site in patients with total occlusion. In the same study, the maximal temperature site as opposed to the angiographic occlusive site coincided with the ruptured "culprit" plaque as assessed by intravascular ultrasound in patients with total occlusion (Figure 3). Thus, although the angiographic evaluation of the cul-

Figure 3. Temperature difference between atherosclerotic plaque temperature and background temperature (ΔT) stratified by clinical syndrome and remodeling index

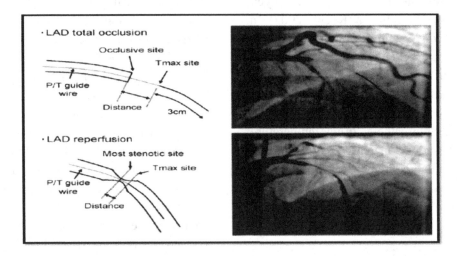

prit plaque showed limited utility, thermography identified accurately the culprit plaque in patients with AMI and coronary total occlusion.

Morphological Characteristics

Intravascular ultrasound has been widely used for detection of the morphological characteristics of the vulnerable plaque (Hamdan, Assal, Fuchs, Battler, & Kornowski, 2007). Distinct morphologic characteristics, including positive arterial wall remodeling and increased number of ruptured plaques have been detected in plaques of patients with acute coronary syndromes. In a study by intravascular ultrasound a strong and positive correlation between the coronary remodelling index (defined as the ratio of the external elastic (Hamdan, Assal, Fuchs, Battler, & Kornowski, 2007) membrane area at the lesion, to that at the proximal site) and the temperature difference between the atherosclerotic plaque and healthy vascular wall was found (Toutouzas, *et al.*, 2007). In specific, patients with acute coronary syndrome had greater remodeling index than patients with stable angina and increased atherosclerotic plaque temperature. Moreover, patients with positive remodeling had higher thermal heterogeneity than patients with negative remodeling. In patients with negative remodeling there was no difference in thermal heterogeneity between acute coronary syndrome and stable angina. Patients with plaque rupture had increased temperature difference compared to patients without rupture as determined by intravascular ultrasound. This study showed that culprit lesions with plaque rupture and positive arterial remodeling have increased thermal heterogeneity, although in certain patients a discrepancy was observed between morphologic and functional characteristics. These results confirm the concept that there is no ideal method for identification of unstable or high-risk lesions. However, this study showed that a combination of morphologic and functional examination may offer additional diagnostic information.

In recent preliminary studies, assessment of culprit lesions in patients with acute coronary syndrome has been performed both by intracoronary thermography and optical coherence tomography (OCT) (Toutouzas, *et al.*, 2008), (Toutouzas, *et al.*, 2009), (Riga, *et al.*, 2008). Plaques with increased thermal heterogeneity had thinner fibrous compared to plaques without temperature increase. Moreover, the incidence of intraluminal thrombus was not related to plaque temperature.

Impact of Diabetes Mellitus

Especially in patients with diabetes mellitus, inflammation is significantly pronounced and atherosclerotic lesions have increased infiltration of inflammatory cells. In a study including 45 patients with diabetes mellitus and 63 patients without, patients with diabetes mellitus had increased temperature difference compared to patients without (Toutouzas, *et al.*, 2009), (Toutouzas, *et al.*, 2005), (Toutouzas, Markou, Drakopoulou, Mitropoulos, Tsiamis, & Stefanadis, Patients with type two diabetes mellitus: increased local inflammatory activation in culprit atheromatous plaques, 2005). Moreover, patients with diabetes mellitus suffering from acute coronary syndrome or stable angina showed increased local inflammatory involvement compared to patients without diabetes mellitus. This finding is in accordance with previous observations that patients with diabetes mellitus have more severe inflammation in their coronary atherosclerotic plaques, suggesting that diabetes mellitus has a strong impact on plaque destabilization by inflammatory activation. The increased local inflammatory activation in patients with diabetes mellitus may explain the negative results of trials in lowering the cardiovascular events even in patients with intensive treatment to control blood glucose levels. Possibly the combination of strict control of glucose levels with stabilization of local inflammatory involvement could reduce the cardiovascular mortality in this high risk group of patients.

Impact on Prognosis

Another emerging application of thermography is its potential use in the prognosis of patients with coronary artery disease. The impact of intracoronary thermography on risk stratification of patients undergoing percutaneous coronary intervention has been also investigated. In a study population including 86 patients after successful percutaneous coronary intervention with bare metal stents at the culprit lesion, the association of temperature difference between the atherosclerotic plaque and the healthy vessel wall with the event-free survival has been studied (Stefanadis, *et al.*, 2001). The patients that were enrolled had stable angina (34.5%), unstable angina (34.5%), or acute myocardial infarction (30%). Temperature difference increased progressively from stable angina to acute myocardial infarction. After a median clinical follow-up period of 17.88 ± 7.16 months thermal heterogeneity was greater in patients with adverse cardiac events than in patients without events ($p<0.0001$). Moreover, temperature difference was found to be a strong predictor of adverse cardiac events during the follow-up period (OR = 2.14, $p=0.043$). However, the impact of local inflammatory activation on 1) restenosis in the era of drug-eluting stents, and 2) on the progression of non-culprit lesions remains to be determined in large prospective studies.

Impact of Statins

Intracoronary thermography has been demonstrated effective in evaluating the effect of diet and medications on atherosclerotic plaque thermal heterogeneity. The only cardiovascular medication with proved anti-inflammatory action in atherosclerotic plaques is statins. Therefore, an increased interest has been shown in preventing rather than healing plaque rupture with the administration of statins.

Statins have well-recognized anti-inflammatory effects and can reduce the number of macro-phages while increasing the collagen content and the thickness of the fibrous cap of atherosclerotic plaques (as assessed by optical coherence tomography), hence stabilizing the plaque (Libby & Aikawa, 2003). The possible stabilizing effect of statin on hot plaques has been investigated in several studies. In a study of 72 patients (37 patients receiving statins for more than 4 weeks and 35 not receiving statins) thermal heterogeneity of the culprit lesion was lower in patients under treatment, independently of the clinical syndrome (Stefanadis, *et al.*, 2002). The effect of statin on temperature was independent of the serum cholesterol level at hospital admission and patients' presenting clinical syndrome. Furthermore, statin intake showed to have a beneficial effect in patients with diabetes mellitus. In this study patients with diabetes mellitus under statins showed decreased temperature difference compared with untreated patients, suggesting that statins have a favorable effect in patients with diabetes mellitus and coronary artery disease (Toutouzas, *et al.*, 2005), (Toutouzas, 2005). The effect of statin therapy on non-culprit lesion thermal heterogeneity has been investigated in 71 patients undergoing percutaneous coronary intervention (40 patients treated with statin and 31 untreated patients). This study demonstrated that thermal heterogeneity was decreased both in patients with acute coronary syndrome and patients with stable angina receiving statins (Toutouzas, *et al.*, 2007). These findings indicate that aggressive treatment with statins may be essential for the stabilization of the vulnerable atherosclerotic plaque in patients with coronary artery disease. This is likely secondary to the proven anti-inflammatory "pleiotropic" vascular effects of statins. Intracoronary thermography remains the only method demonstrating the effect of statin treatment on *in vivo* local inflammatory status.

Systemic Markers of Inflammation

It is increasingly recognized that the mechanisms leading to an acute coronary event involve the complete coronary tree and can be regarded as a pancoronary process. In a study that recruited 20 patients (6 with unstable angina and 14 with stable angina) the investigators after choosing a cut-off temperature value ≥0.1°C, identified 10 patients without temperature heterogeneity, 4 with a single hot spot, 3 with 2 hot spots, and 3 with 3 hot spots (Webster, Stewart, & Ruygrok, 2002). Thermal heterogeneity of non-culprit lesions was investigated in a study of 40 patients with acute coronary syndrome by a multisensor thermography basket catheter (Volcano Therapeutics, Rancho Cordova, CA, USA). The temperature difference was measured, defined as the maximum temperature difference between blood and any thermal couple. This study showed increased temperature difference in non-culprit segments, still though, lower than that of culprit. Temperature difference had inverse correlation with blood flow during thermal mapping. Thus, the presence of blood flow led to a significant decrease in the recorded temperature difference between culprit and non-culprit segments (Dudek, *et al.*, 2005). However, another study including 42 patients (23 with stable angina and 19 with acute coronary syndrome) thermal heterogeneity in non-culprit intermediate lesions was found to be similar to that of culprit lesions (Toutouzas, *et al.*, 2006). In the same study patients with acute coronary syndrome had increased thermal heterogeneity in both culprit and non-culprit lesions compared to patients with stable angina supporting a pan-coronary inflammatory activation. Accordingly another study with 71 patients with acute coronary syndrome or stable angina undergoing percutaneous coronary intervention at culprit lesion, thermography of the intermediate non-culprit lesion showed increased thermal heterogeneity (Toutouzas, *et al.*, 2007). Patients with acute coronary syndrome had higher temperature differences compared to patients with stable angina in non-culprit lesions. These results provided new insights supporting the concept of diffuse destabilization of coronary atherosclerotic plaques: although a single lesion is clinically symptomatic, acute coronary syndrome was associated with diffuse thermal heterogeneity.

Several studies have demonstrated a correlation between systemic inflammation determined by elevated levels of serum biomarkers, such as C-reactive protein, and local plaque temperature. The correlation of systemic inflammatory markers with potential plaque vulnerability has been investigated in 60 patients with coronary artery disease (20 with stable angina, 20 with unstable angina, and 20 with acute myocardial infarction) and 20 sex- and age-matched controls without coronary artery disease. In this study, there was a strong correlation between C-reactive protein and serum amyloid A levels, with detected differences in temperature (Stefanadis, *et al.*, 2000). This study demonstrated that systemic inflammatory activation assessed by the levels of C-reactive protein correlates with local inflammatory activity of non-culprit intermediate lesions (Toutouzas, *et al.*, 2007). An apparently higher mean C-reactive protein level has been demonstrated in patients with higher temperature heterogeneity compared to those without elevated temperature (14.0 vs. 6.2 mg/l) (Wainstein, Costa, Ribeiro, Zago, & Rogers, 2007). Some other studies however, such as that by Webster *et al*, failed to show such a relationship, as most patients had normal CRP levels possibly as a result of a higher use of statins and anti-inflammatory medications (Webster, Stewart, & Ruygrok, 2002).

Based on these findings blood temperature differences between the coronary sinus and the right atrium were measured in patients with symptomatic coronary artery disease, thus evaluating whether diffuse coronary inflammation increases blood temperature as it flows into the coronary arterial tree and ends into the coronary sinus. Thermography was performed by a catheter possessing a steering arm that passes through the lumen of the catheter and is attached to its tip. The catheter has a thermistor probe at the center of the tip with a sensitivity of 0.05°C and a time constant of 300msec. Temperature difference between the coronary sinus and the right atrium was greater in patients with acute coronary syndrome and with stable angina compared to patients without angiographically significant coronary artery disease. Though patients with acute coronary syndrome had greater thermal heterogeneity compared to patients' stable angina, the difference did not reach statistical significance. The levels of C-reactive protein were well correlated with thermal heterogeneity (R=0.35, p<0.01) (Toutouzas, *et al.*, 2006). This study showed that systemic inflammation correlates with coronary sinus blood temperature suggesting thus that an inflammatory process is potentially the underlying mechanism for increased heat production from the myocardium. Moreover, coronary sinus blood temperature was found to be greater than right atrium blood temperature in patients with angiographically significant lesions, independently of the site of the lesion, compared to subjects without coronary artery disease. These findings further support the extensive inflammatory process within the coronary arterial tree in patients with coronary artery disease.

"Cooling Effect" of Blood Flow

Although inflammation leads to increased heat release from the atherosclerotic plaque, a discrepancy between ex-vivo and in-vivo temperature measurements has been observed (Casscells, *et al.*, 1996), (Verheye, *et al.*, 2004). This has been attributed to the 'cooling effect' of coronary flow on the measured blood temperature. Complete obstruction of blood flow has been shown to increase the degree of detected temperature heterogeneity by 60% to 76% (Stefanadis, *et al.*, 2003). However, other studies have shown that normal physiological flow conditions reduce temperature heterogeneity only by 8% to 13% compared to surface temperature measured in the absence of flow (Verheye, *et al.*, 2004). An *in vitro* model of a focal, eccentric, heat-generating lesion demonstrated that a guidewire-based system (Themocoil System) can detect changes in surface temperature.

However, temperature measurements increased linearly with source temperature and decreased with increases in flow by an exponent of -0.33 (p<0.001 for both). This study showed that flow rates and heat source properties can significantly influence the measurement and interpretation of thermographic data (Courtney, *et al.*, 2004). Accordingly, another mathematical simulation of a model of a coronary artery segment also containing a heat source predicted that measured temperature is strongly affected by blood flow, cap thickness, source geometry and maximal flow velocity. In specific, maximal temperature differences at the lumen wall decreased when the source volume increased and blood flow was acting as a coolant to the lumen wall (ten Have, Gijsen, Wentzel, Slager, & van der Steen, 2004), (ten Have, Gijsen, Wentzel, Slager, Serruys, & van der Steen, 2006), (ten Have, *et al.*, 2007). Additionally, when cap thickness increased, maximal temperatures decreased and the influence of flow increased. *In vitro* investigations in a model of 'hot' plaque showed that the sensor of the Radi-Wire could detect changes in temperature of the wall of 0.58°C as long as the distance from the wall was less than 0.5 mm and the flow less than 60mL/min. For flow values larger than 60mL/min, the pressure wire could not detect any significant increase in temperature when passed in front of the "hot spot". An inverse correlation was observed between the flow and the observed temperature changes (Cuisset, *et al.*, 2009). On the basis of these studies, to assess the possible influence of coronary blood flow, temperature measurements have been performed during complete interruption of flow (Stefanadis, Toutouzas, Vavuranakis, Tsiamis, Vaina, & Toutouzas, 2003). During vessel occlusion the observed temperature was elevated both in patients with stable angina and patients with acute coronary syndrome, suggesting that coronary flow has a 'cooling effect' on thermal heterogeneity, which may lead to underestimation of local heat production. Rzeszutko *et al.* performed intracoronary thermography in 40 patients with acute coronary syndrome using a thermography catheter containing 5 thermocouples measuring vessel wall temperature, and 1 thermocouple measuring blood temperature (accuracy 0.05°C). Temperature gradient between blood temperature and the maximum wall temperature was measured. In 40% of patients temperature gradient was found to be >0.10°C. There was a significant difference in ΔT between culprit and adjacent non-culprit segments when blood flow was interrupted during thermography. However, this difference was marginally non-significant when the flow was preserved. The most important observation from this pilot study appears to be the impact of blood flow on the thermography readings. In patients with transient blood flow interruption lower temperatures (cooling) were recorded in proximal reference segments. There was a significant inverse correlation between plaque temperature and the presence of blood flow at the beginning of the thermographic evaluation. This effect of bloodstream on vessel wall temperature has been investigated *in vitro* and *in vivo*, as well as by mathematical modeling (ten Have, Gijsen, Wentzel, Slager, & van der Steen, 2004). To eliminate these shortcomings, especially in intermediate lesions in which attachment of the thermistor cannot be ensured, other catheter designs have been introduced. Verheye *et al.* observed more pronounced temperature differences when blood flow was stopped by balloon occlusion in rabbit aorta (Verheye, *et al.*, 2004). Belardi *et al.* presented preliminary results with a basket-catheter with multiple thermistors which can also measure atheromatic plaque temperature during complete interruption of coronary blood flow (Belardi, *et al.*, 2005). All these devices need to be investigated in a large number of patients in order to draw conclusions regarding their safety and prognostic value.

Clinical Implication and Current Shortcomings of Thermography

In light of the complex pathophysiological background of coronary atherosclerosis and inflammation, intracoronary thermography has provided important information regarding the mechanisms involved. However, although coronary thermography is a safe and feasible method for the functional evaluation of atherosclerotic plaques, it has certain technical limitations. The discrepancy observed in temperature differences between ex vivo and *in vivo* measurements raise concern over the accuracy of the method. This discrepancy has been attributed to the 1) 'cooling effect' of coronary blood flow, and 2) inability of the sensors to contact the arterial vessel wall, thus underestimating plaque heat production in clinical practice. As a result, a cut-off value of temperature in order to characterize a plaque as 'inflamed' is infeasible and thus the clinical application of intracoronary thermography cannot be applicable.

Another limitation is the inability of the proposed devices to scan the coronary arteries but rather obtain spot measurements in the coronary arteries. Thus, early local inflammatory activation cannot be detected in intermediate lesions and a prospective study for investigating the prognostic role of local inflammatory activation cannot be performed.

All these shortcomings prohibit the performance of large prospective clinical trials with intravascular thermography. Improvement of technology is required targeting at ensuring accurate thermal scanning of the coronary arterial tree. In order to achieve these technological requirements the use of thermistors does not seem to fulfill the necessary criteria. Therefore, research should be focused in alternative pathways. Another important development, that would provide more comprehensive description of anatomical and functional characteristics of the atherosclerotic plaques, is the combination of intracoronary thermography with an imaging method such as

Table 1. Detection of vulnerable atherosclerotic plaque components by different imaging modalities

Method	Fibrous Cap	Lipid Pool	Inflammation	Calcium	Thrombus	VV
IVUS	+	++	-	+++	+	-
Angioscopy	+	++	-	-	+++	-
OCT	+++	+++	+	+++	+	-
MRI	+	++	+	++	+	-
IVUS+contrast	+	++	+	++	+	++

IVUS: Intravascular Ultrasound
OCT: Optical Coherence Tomography
MRI: Magnetic Resonance Imaging
VV: Vasa Vasorum

intravascular ultrasound or optical coherence tomography (OCT) in one single device. Optical coherence tomography generates real-time tomographic images from backscattered reflections of infrared light (Honda & Fitzgerald, 2008), (Yasuhiro & Fitzgerald, 2008). The greatest advantage of this method is its resolution that is significantly higher than ultrasound-based approaches. This improvement however, comes at the expense of poorer penetration through blood and tissue (1 to 3 mm). The potential feasibility of OCT for *in vivo* vulnerable plaque macrophage quantification has been demonstrated in recent studies (Tearney, *et al.*, 2006). In a clinical study, macrophage densities determined by OCT were significantly higher in unstable patients for both lipid-rich and fibrous plaques (Tearney, *et al.*, 2006). Particularly in culprit lesions, surface macrophage infiltration was more strongly associated with unstable clinical presentation than was subsurface infiltration. Moreover, sites of plaque rupture also showed a greater density than non-ruptured sites. Prospective clinical studies using this novel technique, with or without anti-inflammatory pharmacological interventions, may help prove the classic hypothesis that vulnerable plaques with increased local inflammation predict future acute coronary events. Several other invasive techniques are currently being explored to improve the intravascular assessment of vulnerable plaque morphologic and functional characteristics (Honda & Fitzgerald,

2008), (Hamdan, Assal, Fuchs, Battler, & Kornowski, 2007), (MacNeil, Lowe, Takano, Fuster, & Jang, 2003). The advantages and limitations of current technology are shown in Table 1.

The non-invasive assessment of 'hot' plaques in coronary arteries and in peripheral arteries, (e.g. carotids) however, would be ideal for the primary prevention of adverse cardiovascular events. A promising method is the microwave radiometry (RTM-01-RES system), a new method, already applied in oncology, for the non-invasive temperature measurement. Microwave radiometry detects natural electromagnetic radiation from internal tissues at microwave frequencies, and as the intensity of the radiation is proportional to the temperature of tissue, microwave radiometry can provide accurate temperature measurements. Theoretically, thermal scanning by microwave radiometry can be performed in all arterial segments in a depth of 1-7 cm from the skin. This proposal of thermal mapping in arterial segments has been already investigated in an experimental hypercholesterolemic model successfully. In specific, 24 New Zealand rabbits were randomized to either a normal (n=12) or cholesterol-rich (0.3%) diet (n=12) for 6 months (Toutouzas, *et al.*). Thereafter, temperature measurements of the abdominal aortas were performed 1) invasively with intravascular catheter-based thermography and 2) noninvasively with microwave radiometry. All animals were euthanized

Figure 4. A) Microwave radiometry detected that ΔT of the atherosclerotic carotid arteries was significantly higher compared to the ΔT of the controls (0.99±0.29 °C vs. 0.28 ±0.08°C, p<0.001) B) Fatty plaques had higher temperature differences measured my microwave radiometry (DT) compared to mixed and calcified plaques (1.180±3.11°C vs 1.00±0.19°C vs 0.75±0.25°C accordingly, p<0.01 for all comparisons).

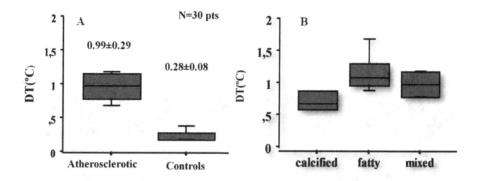

after the procedure and aortas were extracted for histological and immunohistochemical analysis. Both techniques detected that temperature differences of atherosclerotic aortic segments were significantly higher compared to temperature differences of the controls (p<0.001). In all segments, temperature differences detected by the two methods, correlated positively (p<0.001, R=0.94). Mean plaque thickness of atherosclerotic aortic segments was 357.361±159.099µm. Temperature heterogeneity of atherosclerotic segments assessed by both methods had good correlation with plaque thickness assessed by histology (p=0.006). Moreover, histological analysis showed good correlates between temperature differences and inflammatory cell density (Toutouzas, *et al*.), (Drakopoulou, *et al*.).

The method is also currently under clinical evaluation in human carotid arteries (Toutouzas, *et al*.). A recent study in 30 carotid arteries (15 with significant atherosclerosis and fifteen without documented atherosclerosis by ultrasound), showed that thermal heterogeneity detected by microwave thermography along the atherosclerotic carotid arteries was significantly higher compared to that detected in controls (0.99±0.29 °C vs 0.28 ±0.08°C, p<0.001) (Figure 3) (Tout-

ouzas, *et al*.). Moreover, among atherosclerotic carotid arteries fatty plaques had higher temperature differences compared to mixed and calcified plaques as detected by ultrasound (1.180±3.11°C vs. 1.00±0.19°C vs. 0.75±0.25°C accordingly, p<0.01 for all comparisons). Similarly, plaques with ulcerated surface had higher temperature differences compared to plaques with irregular and regular surfaces (1.33±3.21°C vs. 1.08±0.13°C vs. 0.79±0.19°C accordingly, p<0.01 for all comparisons) (Figure 4) (Toutouzas, *et al*.). Further clinical evaluation is needed to validate the clinical application of this promising method.

CONCLUSION

Inflammation plays a crucial role not only in initiation and propagation, but also in development of acute complications of atherosclerosis. Methods for detection (and treatment) of inflammatory foci in the arterial wall could help improve detection, treatment, and control of coronary artery disease. Temperature heterogeneity assessed by intracoronary thermography devices along the inner surface of a coronary artery may be a surrogate marker of impending plaque rupture and has been associated

Figure 5. Fatty atheromatic plaque with low echogenicity, in a patient with carotid artery atherosclerosis provoking 80% stenosis at the left carotid artery. Maximal thermal heterogeneity across the carotid artery (DT): 1,3°C.

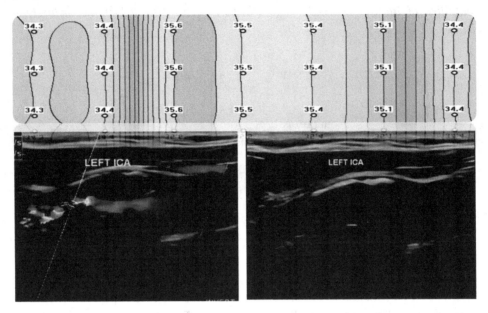

with an increased likelihood of future coronary events. Although intracoronary thermography provided important information regarding the functional characteristics of the vulnerable plaque, its clinical application has several shortcomings. Future technological achievements will hopefully lead to the detection of inflamed plaques, and thus determine the role of inflammation in plaque destabilization.

REFERENCES

Belardi, J., Albertal, M., Cura, F., Mendiz, O., Balino, P., & Padilla, L. (2005). Intravascular thermographic assessment in human coronary atherosclerotic plaques by a novel flow-occluding sensing catheter: A safety and feasibility study. *The Journal of Invasive Cardiology, 17*, 663–666.

Casscells, W., Hathorn, B., David, M., Krabach, T., Vaughn, W., & McAllister, H. (1996). Thermal detection of cellular infiltrates in living atherosclerotic plaques: Possible implications for plaque rupture and thrombosis. *Lancet, 347*, 1447–1451. doi:10.1016/S0140-6736(96)91684-0

Courtney, B., Nakamura, M., Tsugita, R., Lilly, R., Basisht, R., & Grube, E. (2004). Validation of a thermographic guidewire for endoluminal mapping of atherosclerotic disease: An *in vitro* study. *Catheterization and Cardiovascular Interventions, 62*, 221–229. doi:10.1002/ccd.10750

Cuisset, T., Beauloye, C., Melikian, N., Hamilos, M., Sarma, J., & Sarno, G. (2009). *In vitro* and *in vivo* studies on thermistor-based intracoronary temperature measurements: effect of pressure and flow. *Catheterization and Cardiovascular Interventions, 73*, 224–230. doi:10.1002/ccd.21780

Drakopoulou, M., Toutouzas, K., Karanasos, A., Synetos, A., Moldovan, C., Grassos, H., *et al.* (2010). *Association of the extent of early atheromatic lesions with thermal heterogeneity assessed non-invasively by microwave radiometry. An experimental study.* ESC2010.

Dudek, D., Rzeszutko, L., Legutko, J., Wizimirski, M., Chyrchel, M., & Witanek, B. (2005). High-risk coronary artery plaques diagnosed by intracoronary thermography. *Kardiologia Polska, 62,* 383–389.

Hamdan, A., Assal, A., Fuchs, S., Battler, A., & Kornowski, R. (2007). Imaging of vulnerable coronary artery plaques. *Catheterization and Cardiovascular Interventions, 70,* 65–74. doi:10.1002/ccd.21117

Honda, Y., & Fitzgerald, P. (2008). Frontiers in intravascular imaging technologies. *Circulation, 117,* 2024–2037. doi:10.1161/CIRCULATIONAHA.105.551804

Krams, R., Verheye, S., van Damme, L., Tempel, D., Mousavi Gourabi, B., & Boersma, E. (2005). *In vivo* temperature heterogeneity is associated with plaque regions of increased MMP-9 activity. *European Heart Journal, 26,* 2200–2205. doi:10.1093/eurheartj/ehi461

Libby, P., & Aikawa, M. (2003). Mechanisms of plaque stabilization with statins. *The American Journal of Cardiology, 91,* 4B–8B. doi:10.1016/S0002-9149(02)03267-8

MacNeil, B., Lowe, H., Takano, M., Fuster, V., & Jang, I. (2003). Intravascular modalities for detection of vulnerable plaque: current status. *Arteriosclerosis, Thrombosis, and Vascular Biology, 23,* 1333–1342. doi:10.1161/01.ATV.0000080948.08888.BF

Madjid, M., Naghavi, M., Malik, B., Litovsky, S., Willerson, J., & Casscells, W. (2002). Thermal detection of vulnerable plaque. *The American Journal of Cardiology, 90,* 36L–39L. doi:10.1016/S0002-9149(02)02962-4

Naghavi, M., John, R., Naguib, S., Siadaty, M., Grasu, R., & Kurian, K. (2002). pH Heterogeneity of human and rabbit atherosclerotic plaques; a new insight into detection of vulnerable plaque. *Atherosclerosis,* 164.

Naghavi, M., Libby, P., Falk, E., Casscells, S., Litovsky, S., & Rumberger, J. (2003). From vulnerable plaque to vulnerable patient: a call for new definitions and risk assessment strategies: Part I. *Circulation, 108,* 1664–1672. doi:10.1161/01.CIR.0000087480.94275.97

Naghavi, M., Madjid, M., Gul, K., Siadaty, M., Litovsky, S., & Willerson, J. (2003). Thermography basket catheter: *In vivo* measurement of the temperature of atherosclerotic plaques for detection of vulnerable plaques. *Catheterization and Cardiovascular Interventions, 59,* 52–59. doi:10.1002/ccd.10486

Riga, M., Toutouzas, K., Tsiamis, E., Karanasos, A., Tsioufis, C., & Stefanadi, E. (2008). Increased local inflammatory activation is associated with thin fibrous caps in culprit lesions of patients with acute myocardial infarction. New insights by optical coherence tomography. *European Heart Journal, 29,* 4825.

Rosamond, W., Flegal, K., Furie, K., Go, A., Greenlund, K., & Haase, N. (2008). Heart disease and stroke statistics--2008 update: A report from the American Heart Association Statistics Committee and Stroke Statistics Subcommittee. *Circulation, 117,* e25–e146. doi:10.1161/CIRCULATIONAHA.107.187998

Schmermund, A., Rodermann, J., & Erbel, R. (2003). Intracoronary thermography. *Herz, 28,* 505–512. doi:10.1007/s00059-003-2495-7

Stefanadis, C., Diamantopoulos, L., Dernellis, J., Economou, E., Tsiamis, E., & Toutouzas, K. (2000). Heat production of atherosclerotic plaques and inflammation assessed by the acute phase proteins in acute coronary syndromes. *Journal of Molecular and Cellular Cardiology, 32,* 43–52. doi:10.1006/jmcc.1999.1049

Stefanadis, C., Diamantopoulos, L., Vlachopoulos, C., Tsiamis, E., Dernellis, J., & Toutouzas, K. (1999). Thermal heterogeneity within human atherosclerotic coronary arteries detected *in vivo*: A new method of detection by application of a special thermography catheter. *Circulation, 99,* 1965–1971.

Stefanadis, C., Toutouzas, K., Tsiamis, E., Mitropoulos, I., Tsioufis, C., & Kallikazaros, I. (2003). Thermal heterogeneity in stable human coronary atherosclerotic plaques is underestimated *in vivo*: The "cooling effect" of blood flow. *Journal of the American College of Cardiology, 41,* 403–408. doi:10.1016/S0735-1097(02)02817-6

Stefanadis, C., Toutouzas, K., Tsiamis, E., Stratos, C., Vavuranakis, M., & Kallikazaros, I. (2001). Increased local temperature in human coronary atherosclerotic plaques: An independent predictor of clinical outcome in patients undergoing a percutaneous coronary intervention. *Journal of the American College of Cardiology, 37,* 1277–1283. doi:10.1016/S0735-1097(01)01137-8

Stefanadis, C., Toutouzas, K., Vavuranakis, M., Tsiamis, E., Tousoulis, D., & Panagiotakos, D. (2002). Statin treatment is associated with reduced thermal heterogeneity in human atherosclerotic plaques. *European Heart Journal, 23,* 1664–1669.

Stefanadis, C., Toutouzas, K., Vavuranakis, M., Tsiamis, E., Vaina, S., & Toutouzas, P. (2003). New balloon-thermography catheter for *in vivo* temperature measurements in human coronary atherosclerotic plaques: A novel approach for thermography? *Catheterization and Cardiovascular Interventions, 58,* 344–350. doi:10.1002/ccd.10449

Stone, G. (2009). *First presentation of the baseline features & plaque characteristics from the PROSPECT trial.* TCT.

Takumi, T., Lee, S., Hamasaki, S., Toyonaga, K., Kanda, D., & Kusumoto, K. (2007). Limitation of angiography to identify the culprit plaque in acute myocardial infarction with coronary total occlusion utility of coronary plaque temperature measurement to identify the culprit plaque. *Journal of the American College of Cardiology, 50,* 2197–2203. doi:10.1016/j.jacc.2007.07.079

Tearney, G., Yabushita, H., Houser, S., Aretz, H., Jang, I., & Schlendorf, K. (2006). Quantification of macrophage content in atherosclerotic plaques by optical coherence tomography. *Circulation, 107,* 113–119. doi:10.1161/01.CIR.0000044384.41037.43

ten Have, A., Draaijers, E., Gijsen, F., Wentzel, J., Slager, C., & Serruys, P. (2007). Influence of catheter design on lumen wall temperature distribution in intracoronary thermography. *Journal of Biomechanics, 40,* 281–288. doi:10.1016/j.jbiomech.2006.01.016

ten Have, A., Gijsen, F., Wentzel, J., Slager, C., Serruys, P., & van der Steen, A. (2006). A numerical study on the influence of vulnerable plaque composition on intravascular thermography measurements. *Physics in Medicine and Biology, 51,* 5875–5887. doi:10.1088/0031-9155/51/22/010

ten Have, A., Gijsen, F., Wentzel, J., Slager, C., & van der Steen, A. (2004). Temperature distribution in atherosclerotic coronary arteries: influence of plaque geometry and flow (a numerical study). *Physics in Medicine and Biology, 49,* 4447–4462. doi:10.1088/0031-9155/49/19/001

Toutouzas, K., Drakopoulou, M., Markou, V., Karabelas, I., Vaina, S., & Vavuranakis, M. (2007). Correlation of systemic inflammation with local inflammatory activity in non-culprit lesions: Beneficial effect of statins. *International Journal of Cardiology, 119,* 368–373. doi:10.1016/j.ijcard.2006.08.026

Toutouzas, K., Drakopoulou, M., Markou, V., Stougianos, P., Tsiamis, E., Tousoulis, D., *et al.* (2006). Increased coronary sinus blood temperature: Correlation with systemic inflammation. *Eur J Clin Invest.*

Toutouzas, K., Drakopoulou, M., Mitropoulos, J., Tsiamis, E., Vaina, S., & Vavuranakis, M. (2006). Elevated plaque temperature in non-culprit de novo atheromatous lesions of patients with acute coronary syndromes. *Journal of the American College of Cardiology, 47*, 301–306. doi:10.1016/j.jacc.2005.07.069

Toutouzas, K., Drakopoulou, M., Synetos, A., Stathogiannis, K., Klonaris, C., Liasis, N., *et al.* (2010). *Non-invasive detection of local inflammatory activation in atherosclerotic carotid arteries: First clinical application of microwave radiometry.* ESC2010.

Toutouzas, K., Markou, V., Drakopoulou, M., Mitropoulos, I., Tsiamis, E., & Stefanadis, C. (2005). Patients with type two diabetes mellitus: Increased local inflammatory activation in culprit atheromatous plaques. *Hellenike Kardiologike Epitheoresis. Hellenic Journal of Cardiology, 46*, 283–288.

Toutouzas, K., Markou, V., Drakopoulou, M., Mitropoulos, I., Tsiamis, E., & Vavuranakis, M. (2005). Increased heat generation from atherosclerotic plaques in patients with type 2 diabetes: An increased local inflammatory activation. *Diabetes Care, 28*, 1656–1661. doi:10.2337/diacare.28.7.1656

Toutouzas, K., Riga, M., Synetos, A., Karanasos, A., Tsiamis, E., & Tousoulis, D. (2009). Optical coherence tomography analysis of culprit lesions of patients with acute myocardial infarction in combination with intracoronary thermography: Excessive macrophage infiltration of thin fibrous caps are associated with increased local temperature. *Journal of the American College of Cardiology, 53*, 2523.

Toutouzas, K., Riga, M., Vaina, S., Patsa, C., Synetos, A., & Vavuranakis, M. (2008). In acute coronary syndromes thin fibrous cap and ruptured plaques are associated with increased local inflammatory activation: a combination of intravascular optical coherence tomography and intracoronary thermography study. *Journal of the American College of Cardiology, 51*, 1033.

Toutouzas, K., Spanos, V., & Ribichini, F. (2003). A correlation of coronary plaque temperature with inflammatory markers obtained from atherectomy specimens in humans. *The American Journal of Cardiology, 92*.

Toutouzas, K., Synetos, A., Drakopoulou, M., Moldovan, C., Siores, E., Grassos, C., *et al.* (2010). *A new non-invasive method for detection of local inflammatory activation in atheromatic plaques: Experimental evaluation of microwave thermography.* ESC2010.

Toutouzas, K., Synetos, A., Stefanadi, E., Vaina, S., Markou, V., & Vavuranakis, M. (2007). Correlation between morphologic characteristics and local temperature differences in culprit lesions of patients with symptomatic coronary artery disease. *Journal of the American College of Cardiology, 49*, 2264–2271. doi:10.1016/j.jacc.2007.03.026

Toutouzas, K., Tsiamis, E., Drakopoulou, M., Synetos, A., Karampelas, J., & Riga, M. (2009). Impact of type 2 Diabetes Mellitus on diffuse inflammatory activation of de novo atheromatous lesions: Implications for systemic inflammation. *Diabetes & Metabolism, 35*, 299–304. doi:10.1016/j.diabet.2009.01.005

Toutouzas, K., Vaina, S., Tsiamis, E., Vavuranakis, M., Mitropoulos, J., & Bosinakou, E. (2004). Detection of increased temperature of the culprit lesion after recent myocardial infarction: The favorable effect of statins. *American Heart Journal, 148*, 783–788. doi:10.1016/j.ahj.2004.05.013

Verheye, S., De Meyer, G., Krams, R., Kockx, M., Van Damme, L., & Mousavi, G. B. (2004). Intravascular thermography: Immediate functional and morphological vascular findings. *European Heart Journal, 25*, 158–165. doi:10.1016/j.ehj.2003.10.023

Verheye, S., De Meyer, G., Van Langenhove, G., Knaapen, M., & Kockx, M. (2002). *In vivo* temperature heterogeneity of atherosclerotic plaques is determined by plaque composition. *Circulation, 105*, 1596–1601. doi:10.1161/01.CIR.0000012527.94843.BF

Wainstein, M., Costa, M., Ribeiro, J., Zago, A., & Rogers, C. (2007). Vulnerable plaque detection by temperature heterogeneity measured with a guidewire system: Clinical, intravascular ultrasound and histopathologic correlates. *The Journal of Invasive Cardiology, 19*, 49–54.

Webster, M., Stewart, J., & Ruygrok, P. (2002). Intracoronary thermography with a multiple thermocouple catheter: initial human experience. *The American Journal of Cardiology, 90*, 24H.

Worthley, S., Farouque, M., Worthley, M., Baldi, M., Chew, D., & Meredith, I. (2006). The RADI PressureWire high-sensitivity thermistor and culprit lesion temperature in patients with acute coronary syndromes. *The Journal of Invasive Cardiology, 18*, 528–531.

Yasuhiro, H., & Fitzgerald, P. (2008). Frontiers in intravascular imaging technologies. *Circulation, 117*, 2024–2037. doi:10.1161/CIRCULATIONAHA.105.551804

Zarrabi, A., Gul, K., Willerson, J., Casscell, W., & Naghavi, M. (2002). Intravascular thermography: A novel approach for detection of vulnerable plaque. *Current Opinion in Cardiology, 17*, 656–662. doi:10.1097/00001573-200211000-00012

Section 4
Optical Coherence Tomography

Chapter 10
Optical Coherence Tomography:
Basic Principles of Image Acquisition

Lambros S. Athanasiou
University of Ioannina, Greece

Nico Bruining
Erasmus MC, The Netherlands

Francesco Prati
San Giovanni Hospital, Italy

Dimitris Koutsouris
National Technical University of Athens, Greece

ABSTRACT

This chapter is devoted to the description of the basic principles of data acquisition of the Optical Coherence Tomography imaging technique. The physical mechanisms of the tissue optics are detailed, while the architecture of the OCT system is provided, emphasizing on both the TD-OCT and FD-OCT. Then, after discussing about the OCT image resolution, a parametric comparison of OCT with regard to IVUS imaging technique is attempted. Finally, the limitations of the technique are described, along with the safety of its application to the clinical practice.

INSIGHTS INTO THE PRINCIPLES OF OCT IMAGING

Introduction

Optical Coherence Tomography (OCT) (Huang et al., 1991) is a new imaging modality which produces high resolution tomographic images of the internal vessel microstructure. The concept of

OCT imaging is based on measuring the echo time delay and the magnitude of backscattered light. OCT can be applied to a variety of applications with special focus on medical applications. A major advantage of OCT is the high transversal resolution. OCT is used in three fields of medical optical imaging:

- In macroscopic imaging of structures where the structures can be identified with naked eye,

DOI: 10.4018/978-1-61350-095-8.ch010

- In microscopic imaging by magnifying the image up to the limits of microscopic resolution,
- In endoscopic imaging where low and medium magnification is used.

OCT enables real time visualization of tissue making it a powerful imaging tool for medical applications. OCT could be used in the following clinical situations:

- If standard excisional biopsy is not possible such as in coronary arteries and nervous tissues or in the eye,
- If sampling errors affect standard excisional biopsy. For diagnosing many diseases including cancer, excisional biopsy after which histopathology is performed are the standard applied techniques. However, in such a sampling procedure as biopsy, if a lesion is not included in the sample then we might obtain a false-negative result. OCT is being evaluated in order to improve the accuracy of excisional biopsies to increase the number of samples that include lesions,
- And to guide interventional procedures. OCT has the ability to see beneath the tissue surface, enabling guidance and assessment of microsurgical procedures.

Basic Tissue Optics

For the correct interpretation of OCT images, a general understanding of some basic optical properties of tissue is crucial. Absorption and scattering are two basic optical properties of living tissues. The absorption coefficient $\mu_a[m^{-1}]$ is defined as the probability of absorption of a photon at an infinitesimal distance Δd when the photon propagates over the infinitesimal distance. This probability is μ_a times the distance Δd. In other words for an absorption event the mean free path is $1/\mu_a$. Similarly with the definition of the

absorption coefficient, the scattering coefficient μ_s is the probability of scattering of a photon at an infinitesimal distance Δd. This probability is μ_s times the distance Δd. When single scattered photons are detected in OCT, the relevant light from the source that is collected by the interferometer detector travels in the tissue a distance *2d*. This distance is the sum of two distances. The first distance is the distance in the tissue from the source to the point where the light is backscattered or reflected. The second distance is the distance from the point where the light is backscattered or reflected to the detector. These two distances are equal and the light is attenuated twice over that distance. Lamber-Beer's law describes the light attenuation in a non-scattering media:

$$I(d) = I_0 e^{-\mu_a d} \tag{1}$$

where $I(d)$ denotes the intensity at a distance d and I_0 denotes the light intensity incident on the tissue. Lambert–Beer's law is used to calculate the total attenuation, using the total attenuation coefficient μ_t ($\mu_t = \mu_a + \mu_s$) instead of μ_a.

The OCT System

The aim of the OCT technique is to measure the echo time delay of light using interferometric techniques (Rollins & Izatt, 1999). By using interferometric techniques the tissue backscattered light signal is correlated with the light which has traveled a reference path length that is already known. The use of interferometry techniques to determine the echo time delay of light is crucial since the speed of light is faster than the speed of sound. Using interferometry both the magnitude of backscattering light properties and the echo time delay can be measured. A frequent detection method used is the Michelson interferometer, which applies a scanning reference delay arm (Kersey, Marrone, & Davis, 1991). OCT uses interferometric techniques to perform high resolution performance of light echoes. In an OCT system, the fiber-optic coupler of the interferometer is analogous to an optical beam splitter and divides the input light into a reference arm and a measurement arm. A catheter or other image device is connected to the optical fiber in the measurement arm. The catheter scans the transverse position of the measurement beam and focuses the beam onto the tissue that is being imaged. The catheter collects the light echoes as backscattered by the tissue. The collected light echoes are returned back to the measurement arm. A retro-reflecting mirror at a calibrated distance is attached in the reference arm. The echo light of the reference arm is returned with a calibrated delay. At the fiber coupler the two echoes of light, one from the tissue and one from the reference arm are combined.

A high-speed photo-detector detects the intensity of the interference. Finally the electronic signal is processed in order to extract a measurement of echo time delay. In Figure 1 a schematic presentation of an OCT system and the above described procedure is shown.

Several detection methods are used to measure the echo time delay of light. OCT uses the interferometry to perform measurements. There are two interferometric techniques used in Intravascular OCT systems:

- The first technique applies an interferometer with a low-coherence light source and scanning reference delay is used, which is called Time - Domain (Huang, et al., 1991) (TD-OCT),
- The second technique applies a narrow-bandwidth, frequency-swept light source and a stationary reference delay interferometer is used and is called Fourier - Domain OCT (FD-OCT) (Leitgeb et al., 2004).

Time – Domain OCT (TD-OCT)

The Time - Domain OCT (TD-OCT) systems are based on a low-coherence interferometer, which is in fact a Michelson-type interferometer. The back scattered light echoes from the tissue are correlated with scattered light. The light travels a known reference path delay. We can observe interference when light from the reference arm arrives at the same time as light from the tissue (when using a low-coherence light source). By detecting the envelope of the modulated interference signal we can obtain axial information. In the Time - Domain

Figure 1. Schematic presentation of an OCT interferometer system for catheter/endoscope imaging. The OCT system is built using fiber-optics.

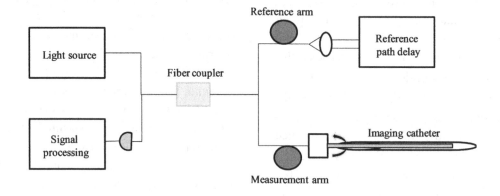

Figure 2. Schematic representation of the used interferometer (low-coherence) by the Time - Domain OCT technique

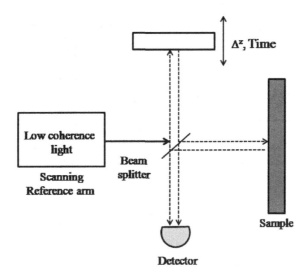

detection method, as the reference path is scanned, the echoes are measured sequentially at different depths. In Figure 2, a schematic representation of a Time - Domain (low-coherence) interferometer is presented.

A beam splitter splits the beam from a light source in two beams. The first light beam is directed to the tissue and is backscattered from the structures of tissue at different depths. From the backscattered light beam, which consists of multiple echoes, relevant information can be derived about the depth or range of the different tissue structures. A reference mirror reflects the second light beam. The position of the reference mirror in time, thus the reference beam has a variable time delay. At the beam splitter the reference beam and the measurement beam are interfered. A photodetector detects the output. In order to understand how the low-coherence interferometer works, the light beam must be considered as light pulses. If the tissue backscattered light pulse and the mirror reflected light pulse arrive synchronously within the pulse duration then the two pulses will coincide. This happens if the two distances, the distance that light travels in the

interferometer measurement arm when it is backscattered from the tissue and the distance that light travels in the interferometer reference path, are similar. A modulation in intensity is produced when the two light pulses interfere. This happens when the light pulses coincide. The modulation in intensity is measured by a photodetector. The approach in order to measure the time delays of light echoes coming from different structures of the tissue and from different depths is to scan mechanically the position of the reference mirror so that the time delay of the reference light pulse varies continuously. Concluding, the key idea of the Time - Domain interferometer (low-coherence interferometer) is to measure the time delays of optical echoes sequentially. This is done by scanning a reference path, so that different echo delays are measured at different times.

Fourier - Domain OCT (FD-OCT)

FD-OCT systems are using a narrow bandwidth light source. This light source is frequency swept in time and the reference arm in the interferometer that is used is stable. A schematic presentation

Figure 3. Schematic representation of the used interferometer by the Fourier - Domain OCT technique

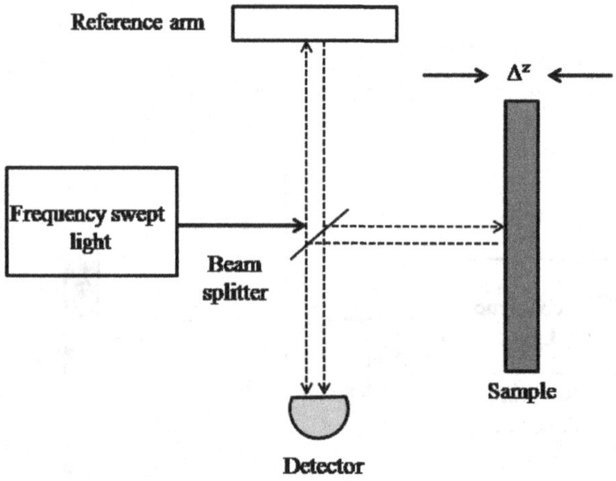

of the interferometer that is used in the Fourier - Domain technique is presented in Figure 3.

The backscattered tissue light echoes are interfered with scattered light. This light travels an already known reference path delay. The two light beams: the one coming from the tissue and the other traveling the reference path have different frequencies. This is due to the fact that the light coming from the tissue is delayed in time when compared to the light traveling the reference path. The interference varies according to the differences in frequency. By applying the Fourier transform in the signal of the detector, axial scan information is obtained. All the echoes of light are measured at once when using the Fourier - Domain detection instead of sequentially as in Time - Domain detection. Thus, the imaging speed of the Fourier - Domain detection is higher than the imaging speed of the Time - Domain detection.

This is the most important difference between the Fourier - Domain detection and the Time - Domain detection.

The basic similarities and differences between TD-OCT and FD-OCT are summarized in Table 1.

ACQUISITION AND DISPLAY TECHNIQUES

Intravascular OCT Image Acquisition

OCT technology is based on fiber optics. By combining OCT with many optical diagnostic instruments it is possible to image the retina (Wojtkowski, Leitgeb, Kowalczyk, Bajraszewski, & Fercher, 2002). By combining OCT with small-diameter endoscopes and catheters, intra-luminal imaging can be performed. Intravascular OCT is

Table 1. Key similarities and differences between TD-OCT and FD-OCT

		TD-OCT	FD-OCT
Similarities		An interferometer is used in both techniques	
	Source	Low Coherence light	A narrow bandwidth light
Differences	Speed	The light echoes are measured sequentially	All light echoes are measures at once
		TD-OCT$_{speed}$< FD-OCT$_{speed}$	TD-OCT$_{speed}$< FD-OCT$_{speed}$

a recently applied imaging technique to visualize the vessel's lumen and outer wall. A specialized catheter-endoscope can be used in order to produce cross sectional images of the vessel in a fashion similar to that of intravascular ultrasound. A disadvantage of OCT is that it is unable to "look" through blood due to the red blood cells as they are causing a high optical scatter. Therefore, blood must be cleared from the blood vessels before OCT imaging can be performed. This can be achieved by both occlusive and non-occlusive techniques (Tanigawa, Barlis, & Di Mario, 2007).

In the occlusive technique, during imaging acquisition, blood flow of the coronary artery is stopped by inflating a proximal occlusion balloon. Afterwards a crystalloid solution is flushed through the end-hole of the balloon catheter. The vessel occlusion time varies according to the patient symptoms and severity of ECG changes and the infusion stops automatically after 35 seconds, in order to avoid hemodynamic instability or arrhythmias (Regar, Prati, & Serruys, 2006; Tanigawa, et al., 2007). When using the occlusive technique, multiple pullbacks could be performed to achieve a complete lesion assessment. However, the occlusive technique has the following limitations:

1. The image clarity could be affected if the lumen is inadequately cleared. Inadequate clearing of the lumen is mostly caused by mismatch between the size of the vessel and the occlusive balloon's,
2. Long diseased lesions can only be imaged by multiple sequential pullback's (Regar, et al., 2006; Tanigawa, et al., 2007),
3. Ostial and very proximal lesions are not suitable for imaging.

In the non-occlusive technique an OCT probe (e.g. a Light Lab Image Wire) replaces the standard intracoronary guide-wire. Hereafter, a viscous iso-osmolar solution is infused, under high-pressure using an automated pump (mostly a Medrad),

through the guiding catheter to clear the vessel from blood. A high-speed pullback could then be performed at speeds varying between 20- to 40 mm/s, allowing imaging in seconds large parts of the coronary vessel. Even for long pullbacks it is possible to use this method to remove the blood from the coronary vessel during the acquisition as has been published recently (Rogowska, Patel, Fujimoto, & Brezinski, 2004). This non-occlusive technique has been shown to be an easy and safe alternative approach.

The first *in vivo* intravascular OCT imaging studies were performed in porcine (Prati et al., 2007; Prati et al., 2008). Since then many human *in vivo* intravascular OCT studies have been performed comparing OCT to the standard intravascular imaging method, e.g. IVUS (Tearney et al., 2000). The first commercially available OCT imaging system was produced by LightLab technology (Lightlab technology, St. Jude Medical, Inc. One St. Jude Medical Drive St. Paul, MN 55117-9983, USA) and applies a tiny laser imaging catheter that can be placed into coronary vessels. The LightLab OCT system uses the Fourier - Domain OCT (FD-OCT) imaging method and uses a much faster imaging engine. This engine is able to obtain a scan of up to 50 mm of an artery in approximately 3 seconds. This FD-OCT system has also additional performance advantages (Bouma et al., 2003; Jang et al., 2002) compared to conventional TD-OCT. These advantages include a higher sampling line density per frame, a wider scan range and a faster frame rate. The imaging catheter of the LightLab OCT system is called the "LightLab DragonFly Optical Coherence Tomography Imaging Probe", and is presented in Figure 4. In Figure 5, a LightLab OCT imaging console is presented. Figure 6 presents the result of an imaged coronary vessel as obtained by the LightLab OCT system (FD-OCT system).

In OCT images, the lumen can be clearly detected, due to the clearance of the blood from the lumen (Figure 7 (a)). Contrary to the detection of the lumen border, the detection of the media

Figure 4. An OCT imaging catheter. The catheter is called the LightLab DragonFly Optical Coherence Tomography Imaging Probe.

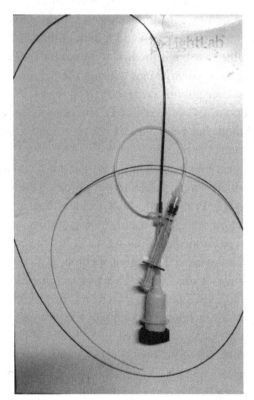

Figure 5. A light lab imaging console

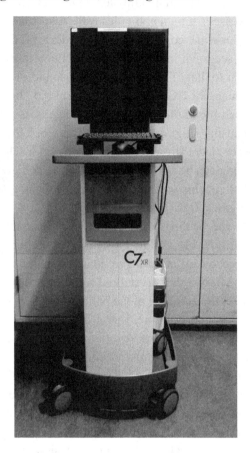

adventitia-border is not always possible as it is not always visualized, and thus also not distinguishable, due to the limited penetration depth of light in tissues (Figure 7 (b)).

OCT Image Resolution

The high resolutions of OCT images are playing an important role in its clinical use. Different mechanisms determine the resolution of an OCT image in the axial and in the traverse directions. The focused spot size of the optical beam determines the traverse resolution. The resolution of the measurement for the echo time delay determines the resolution of the image in the axial direction. In fact, the light source used for the measurement determines this axial resolution. If a low-coherence light source is used to measure the echo time-delay, the coherence length of the source determines the

Figure 6. An OCT image from a coronary artery. The image is acquired using an FD-OCT system (Light Lab).

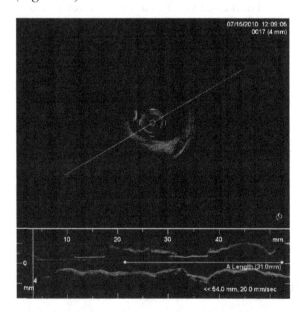

Figure 7. (a) An OCT image from a coronary artery. (b) The lumen border marked with red and the media-adventitia border which can be easily distinguished. The images are acquired using an FD-OCT system (Light Lab).

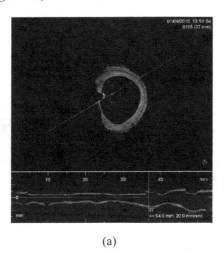

(a)

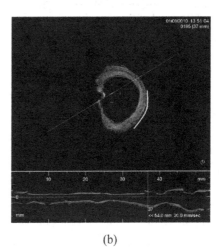

(b)

axial resolution. If a frequency light is used then the axial resolution is determined by the tuning range of the light. The axial resolution for standard OCT systems is 10-15 μm. An OCT image of the human retina with high resolution provides better differentiation of intra-retinal layers. Thus, more detailed features of the photoreceptor layer can be extracted which enables the diagnosis of an early disease (Takarada et al., 2010). For an intravascular OCT image (e.g. of a coronary artery) improvements for increasing transverse pixel density and improvements for increasing the speed of imaging (FD-OCT) are very important.

In an OCT image the number of axial scans determines the number of pixels in the transverse direction. The image acquisition time increases proportionately to the number of transverse pixels. By increasing the transverse pixel density the image quality can be improved. High-definition images are produced by high axial scan density. In these images the improvement of visualization is obvious. FD-OCT systems use Fourier - Domain detection methods that enable higher axial scan densities providing high quality OCT images by reducing the examination time.

INTRAVASCULAR OCT IMAGING

OCT vs. IVUS

OCT is an imaging modality similar to IVUS having as main difference that OCT uses light and IVUS sound. A major advantage of OCT over IVUS is its much higher resolution, but that comes at the cost of a reduced tissue penetration depth (Ko et al., 2005). OCT's resolution is about 15 μm and that of IVUS's about 100μm (Jang, et al., 2002; Jang, Tearney, & Bouma, 2001). In contrast, due to the specific optical properties of calcium, OCT is able to penetrate calcified areas within coronary plaques. This is not possible with IVUS as thick layers of calcium will reflect the acoustic signal visualizing calcium mostly as a bright rim accompanied with a so-called acoustic shadowed region behind it.

In the IVUS imaging technique the backscattered sound signals are digitized. This signal corresponds to the pressure variation in the scattered wave and is called radio frequency signal (RF). This RF signal contains the amplitude and the phase. A grayscale IVUS image consists of the amplitude data. In OCT the separation of the phase and the amplitude is performed by the Hilbert transform (Virmani, Burke, Kolodgie, & Farb, 2002) before its digitization.

In order to identify a type of tissue, the spectrum of the detected signal, in both OCT and IVUS can be analyzed. Each tissue absorbs light for specific wavelengths and for specific frequencies within OCT and IVUS imaging modalities, respectively. Thus each tissue type is attached with the spectral content of the detected signal. IVUS is able to use this technique called Virtual Histology (VH) (Zhao, Chen, Ding, Ren, & Nelson, 2002) in order to identify different tissue formations in an IVUS image. VH is a commercial technique and available for clinical applications. VH identifies 5 different tissue types (4 plaque types and the Media) and is trained and tested (Konig & Klauss, 2007) on histological data. Similar approaches based on OCT are still under investigation) (Nair, Margolis, Kuban, & Vince, 2007)).

The practical difference between OCT and IVUS is the catheter used. In IVUS an ultrasound transducer is both source and detector and is located at the tip of the catheter. Both the transmitted and recorded signals are traveling electrically to the console. In OCT, the detector and the source are distinct and an interferometer is used for detection. Due to their size, the detector and interferometer are outside the patient. A rotational optical fiber is integrated in the catheter and transmits the light to the imaged location scanning the vessel wall.

A commonly used type of IVUS catheter is the so-called phased array. This catheter does not need to be rotated which makes it advantageous to others as the sensitivity to non - uniform rotations defects is much smaller. For an OCT catheter (Figure 8) the previously described concept cannot be applied.

The OCT image wire system has an advantage over IVUS in the visualization of the lumen border. The clear, and sharp, visualization of the lumen border in the OCT images is caused by: 1) The high-resolution of the OCT images and 2)

Figure 8. An OCT catheter of 0.018-inch (ImageWire™, LightLab Imaging, Westford, MA)

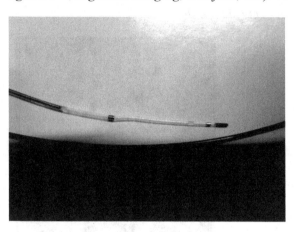

the clearing of the blood from the vessel, which is not performed during an IVUS examination. Both imaging techniques have limited visibility of the outer vessel border (which for I IVUS is mostly the external elastic membrane (EEM)). In OCT, the main cause of poor visibility is the insufficient penetration depth, especially in areas with large plaques, while in IVUS it is mostly caused due to the presence of calcium which will result in shadowed areas behind it preventing to be able to visualize the EEM.

To summarize, the main differences of the two techniques are:

- OCT has higher resolution than IVUS,
- IVUS has better tissue penetration depth than OCT,
- OCT has a more complicated image formation process than IVUS due to the interferometric detection.

Tissue Appearance in OCT Images

In OCT images non-diseased vessels appear as a three-layer structure (Jang, et al., 2002; Yamaguchi et al., 2008). The media can be visualized easily by the resolution of OCT since the thickness of the media ranges from 125 - 350 μm with a mean of 200µm (Fitzgerald et al., 1992). In an OCT image, calcium appears as a low back-scattering heterogeneous region fully bordered as depicted in Figure 9 (a). Fibrous tissue (Kawasaki et al., 2006; Kume et al., 2005) appears as high back-scattering homogeneous areas (Figure 9 (b)). Lipid pools appear as more heterogeneous back-scattering than fibrous plaques (Figure 9 (c)). In an OCT image there is high contrast between the appearance of a lipid pool and fibrous tissue. In contrary to calcific regions, lipid pools appear diffusely bordered (Yabushita et al., 2002). The appearance of mixed plaques is heterogeneous back-scattering regions similar to lipid pools and fibrous tissue (Figure 9 (d)).

Thrombi appear as masses that extrudes into the lumen of the vessel (Yabushita, et al., 2002).

There are three different types of thrombi: red, white and mixed thrombi. Red thrombi appear in OCT images as high-backscattering protrusions with signal free shadowing while the appearance of white thrombi is characterized by a signal rich and low backscattering projection that protrudes into the lumen. The two different types of thrombi are depicted in Figure 10.

Table 2 summarizes the appearance of the above described atherosclerotic plaque features in OCT images.

Limitations of OCT

OCT has some physical limitations and is still under development. The major limitation of OCT is its limited tissue penetration depth (1-3 mm),

Figure 9. (a)Calcium appearance (highlighted with red) in an OCT image, (b) Fibrous tissue appearance (highlighted with yellow) in an OCT image, (c) Lipid pool appearance (highlighted with white) in OCT images, (d) Mixed plaque appearance (highlighted with green) in OCT images. The images are acquired using an FD-OCT system (Light Lab).

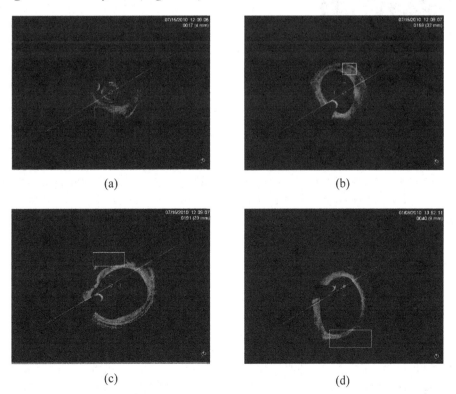

(a)

(b)

(c)

(d)

Figure 10. (a) Example of white thrombus in an OCT image, (b) Example of red thrombus in an OCT image. The images are acquired using an FD-OCT system (Light Lab).

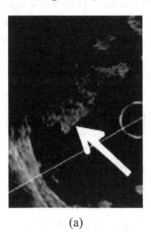

(a)

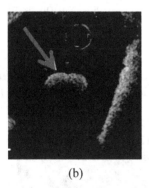

(b)

Table 2. OCT appearance in OCT images for various plaque types.

Plaque type	OCT appearance
Calcium	Bordered edges Low reflectivity Low attenuation
Fibrous tissue	Homogeneous High reflectivity Low attenuation
Lipid pool	Diffuse edges High reflectivity High attenuation
Mixed plaque	Medium reflectivity Diffuse edges
Red thrombus	Medium reflectivity High attenuation
White thrombus	Medium reflectivity Low attenuation

caused by the extensive scattering of the light by the tissue. A method to overcome this limitation is to use a fine needle and to perform imaging at the tip of the needle by inserting it into the targeted tissue (Kume et al., 2006). However, this approach cannot be applied in blood vessels. Some other limitations of OCT are:

- A non-radiopaque body,
- A wire tip that is too long (15 mm),
- A radio lucent lens,
- Possibly on-uniform rotational distortion.

In addition, the imaging wire could rotate itself when it is being manipulated (e.g. during the pullback imaging procedure). Another limitation is the necessary clearing of the blood from the artery before imaging becomes possible with OCT. Finally, implanted permanent metallic stents are causing shadowed areas within the OCT images as can be appreciated in Figure 11.

Safety of Intracoronary OCT

Due to the size and anatomical position of the coronary arteries it is extremely difficult to have access using non-invasive techniques. Thus, an intracoronary approach is needed. Intracoronary OCT has very important restrains, regarding mostly the safety issues of the OCT imaging device (Li, Chudoba, Ko, Pitris, & Fujimoto, 2000).

In an OCT intravascular system the applied energies are very low, in the range from 5.0 - 8.0 mW for the output power. These energies are not causing structural or functional damage to the imaged tissue (Bouma, et al., 2003). Consequently all safety issues in an intravascular OCT examination depend on the design of the catheter and on the ischemia caused by the necessary obstruction of blood flow from the catheter.

The first attempt in human application of OCT was in 2002 (Hausmann et al., 1995). There were

Figure 11. An OCT image from a stented segment of a coronary artery. The image is acquired using an FD-OCT system (Light Lab).

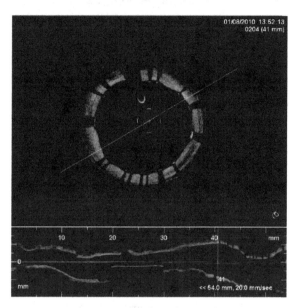

no complications in all patients who tolerated very well the procedure and the safety of the OCT examination can be considered as excellent. The study concluded that imaging a human coronary artery using OCT imaging technique is a safe and reliable technique. In studies where a comparison between OCT and IVUS was made, the safety of the intracoronary OCT imaging was evaluated for a large number of patients (Jang, et al., 2002). Intracoronary OCT imaging is becoming a commonly used invasive imaging method and so far no complications in patients were reported (Jang, et al., 2002; Yamaguchi, et al., 2008). In addition, the non-occlusive technique that is now used in order to remove the blood from the vessel and the FD-OCT system enhances the safety of intracoronary OCT imaging (Jang, et al., 2002; Kawase et al., 2005; Yamaguchi, et al., 2008). Thus we can state that intracoronary OCT is a safe imaging technique and it is as safe as IVUS.

REFERENCES

Bouma, B. E., Tearney, G. J., Yabushita, H., Shishkov, M., Kauffman, C. R., & Gauthier, D. D. (2003). Evaluation of intracoronary stenting by intravascular optical coherence tomography. *Heart (British Cardiac Society)*, *89*(3), 317–320. doi:10.1136/heart.89.3.317

Fitzgerald, P. J., St Goar, F. G., Connolly, A. J., Pinto, F. J., Billingham, M. E., & Popp, R. L. (1992). Intravascular ultrasound imaging of coronary arteries. Is three layers the norm? *Circulation*, *86*(1), 154–158.

Hausmann, D., Erbel, R., Alibellichemarin, M. J., Boksch, W., Caracciolo, E., & Cohn, J. M. (1995). The safety of intracoronary ultrasound - A multicenter survey of 2207 examinations. *Circulation*, *91*(3), 623–630.

Huang, D., Swanson, E. A., Lin, C. P., Schuman, J. S., Stinson, W. G., & Chang, W. (1991). Optical coherence tomography. *Science*, *254*(5035), 1178–1181. doi:10.1126/science.1957169

Jang, I. K., Bouma, B. E., Kang, D. H., Park, S. J., Park, S. W., & Seung, K. B. (2002). Visualization of coronary atherosclerotic plaques in patients using optical coherence tomography: Comparison with intravascular ultrasound. *Journal of the American College of Cardiology*, *39*(4), 604–609. doi:10.1016/S0735-1097(01)01799-5

Jang, I. K., Tearney, G., & Bouma, B. (2001). Visualization of tissue prolapse between coronary stent struts by optical coherence tomography - Comparison with intravascular ultrasound. *Circulation*, *104*(22), 2754–2754. doi:10.1161/hc4701.098069

Kawasaki, M., Bouma, B. E., Bressner, J., Houser, S. L., Nadkarni, S. K., & MacNeill, B. D. (2006). Diagnostic accuracy of optical coherence tomography and integrated backscatter intravascular ultrasound images for tissue characterization of human coronary plaques. *Journal of the American College of Cardiology, 48*(1), 81–88. doi:10.1016/j.jacc.2006.02.062

Kawase, Y., Hoshino, K., Yoneyama, R., McGregor, J., Hajjar, R. J., & Jang, I. K. (2005). In vivo volumetric analysis of coronary stent using optical coherence tomography with a novel balloon occlusion-flushing catheter: A comparison with intravascular ultrasound. *Ultrasound in Medicine & Biology, 31*(10), 1343–1349. doi:10.1016/j.ultrasmedbio.2005.05.010

Kersey, A. D., Marrone, M. J., & Davis, M. A. (1991). Polarization-insensitive fiber optic Michelson interferometer. *Electronics Letters, 27*(6), 518–520. doi:10.1049/el:19910325

Ko, T. H., Fujimoto, J. G., Schuman, J. S., Paunescu, L. A., Kowalevicz, A. M., Hartl, I., et al. (2005). Comparison of ultrahigh- and standard-resolution optical coherence tomography for imaging macular pathology. *Ophthalmology, 112*(11), 1922 e1921-1915.

Konig, A., & Klauss, V. (2007). Virtual histology. *Heart (British Cardiac Society), 93*(8), 977–982. doi:10.1136/hrt.2007.116384

Kume, T., Akasaka, T., Kawamoto, T., Ogasawara, Y., Watanabe, N., & Toyota, E. (2006). Assessment of coronary arterial thrombus by optical coherence tomography. *The American Journal of Cardiology, 97*(12), 1713–1717. doi:10.1016/j.amjcard.2006.01.031

Kume, T., Akasaka, T., Kawamoto, T., Watanabe, N., Toyota, E., & Neishi, Y. (2005). Assessment of coronary intima--media thickness by optical coherence tomography: Comparison with intravascular ultrasound. *Circulation Journal, 69*(8), 903–907. doi:10.1253/circj.69.903

Leitgeb, R., Drexler, W., Unterhuber, A., Hermann, B., Bajraszewski, T., & Le, T. (2004). Ultrahigh resolution Fourier domain optical coherence tomography. *Optics Express, 12*(10), 2156–2165. doi:10.1364/OPEX.12.002156

Li, X. D., Chudoba, C., Ko, T., Pitris, C., & Fujimoto, J. G. (2000). Imaging needle for optical coherence tomography. *Optics Letters, 25*(20), 1520–1522. doi:10.1364/OL.25.001520

Nair, A., Margolis, M. P., Kuban, B. D., & Vince, D. G. (2007). Automated coronary plaque characterisation with intravascular ultrasound backscatter: Ex vivo validation. *EuroIntervention, 3*(1), 113–120.

Prati, F., Cera, M., Ramazzotti, V., Imola, F., Giudice, R., & Albertucci, M. (2007). Safety and feasibility of a new non-occlusive technique for facilitated intracoronary optical coherence tomography (OCT) acquisition in various clinical and anatomical scenarios. *EuroIntervention, 3*(3), 365–370. doi:10.4244/EIJV3I3A66

Prati, F., Cera, M., Ramazzotti, V., Imola, F., Giudice, R., & Giudice, M. (2008). From bench to bed side: A novel technique to acquire OCT images. *Ciculation, 72*, 839–843. doi:10.1253/circj.72.839

Regar, E., Prati, F., & Serruys, P. W. (2006). *Intracoronary OCT application: Methodological considerations.* Abingdon, UK: Taylor & Francis.

Rogowska, J., Patel, N. A., Fujimoto, J. G., & Brezinski, M. E. (2004). Optical coherence tomographic elastography technique for measuring deformation and strain of atherosclerotic tissues. *Heart (British Cardiac Society), 90*(5), 556–562. doi:10.1136/hrt.2003.016956

Rollins, A. M., & Izatt, J. A. (1999). Optimal interferometer designs for optical coherence tomography. *Optics Letters, 24*(21), 1484–1486. doi:10.1364/OL.24.001484

Takarada, S., Imanishi, T., Liu, Y., Ikejima, H., Tsujioka, H., & Kuroi, A. (2010). Advantage of next-generation frequency-domain optical coherence tomography compared with conventional time-domain system in the assessment of coronary lesion. *Catheterization and Cardiovascular Interventions, 75*(2), 202–206. doi:10.1002/ccd.22273

Tanigawa, J., Barlis, P., & Di Mario, C. (2007). Intravascular optical coherence tomography: Optimisation of image acquisition and quantitative assessment of stent strut apposition. *EuroIntervention, 3*(1), 128–136.

Tearney, G. J., Jang, I. K., Kang, D. H., Aretz, H. T., Houser, S. L., & Brady, T. J. (2000). Porcine coronary imaging in vivo by optical coherence tomography. *Acta Cardiologica, 55*(4), 233–237. doi:10.2143/AC.55.4.2005745

Virmani, R., Burke, A. P., Kolodgie, F. D., & Farb, A. (2002). Vulnerable plaque: The pathology of unstable coronary lesions. *Journal of Interventional Cardiology, 15*(6), 439–446. doi:10.1111/j.1540-8183.2002.tb01087.x

Wojtkowski, M., Leitgeb, R., Kowalczyk, A., Bajraszewski, T., & Fercher, A. F. (2002). In vivo human retinal imaging by Fourier domain optical coherence tomography. *Journal of Biomedical Optics, 7*(3), 457–463. doi:10.1117/1.1482379

Yabushita, H., Bouma, B. E., Houser, S. L., Aretz, H. T., Jang, I. K., & Schlendorf, K. H. (2002). Characterization of human atherosclerosis by optical coherence tomography. *Circulation, 106*(13), 1640–1645. doi:10.1161/01.CIR.0000029927.92825.F6

Yamaguchi, T., Terashima, M., Akasaka, T., Hayashi, T., Mizuno, K., & Muramatsu, T. (2008). Safety and feasibility of an intravascular optical coherence tomography image wire system in the clinical setting. *The American Journal of Cardiology, 101*(5), 562–567. doi:10.1016/j.amjcard.2007.09.116

Zhao, Y. H., Chen, Z. P., Ding, Z. H., Ren, H. W., & Nelson, J. S. (2002). Real-time phase-resolved functional optical coherence tomography by use of optical Hilbert transformation. *Optics Letters, 27*(2), 98–100. doi:10.1364/OL.27.000098

KEY TERMS AND DEFINITIONS

Beer – Lambert Law: Relates the absorption of light to the properties of the material through which the light is traveling.

Fourier - Domain OCT: Interferometric technique used in intravascular OCT systems with the imaging speed than Time - domain OCT.

Intravascular OCT: The combination of OCT with a specialized catheter-endoscope to produce cross sectional images of the vessel.

Michelson Interferometer: Is the most common configuration for optical interferometry. It was invented by Albert Abraham Michelson.

OCT: Optical Coherence Tomography (OCT) is a new imaging modality which produces high resolution tomographic images of the internal vessel microstructure.

Time - Domain OCT: Interferometric technique used in intravascular OCT systems.

Tissue Appearance: The appearance of the various tissue components over an OCT image.

Chapter 11
Optical Coherence Tomography Image Interpretation and Image Processing Methodologies

Simon D. Thackray
Castle Hill Hospital, UK

Christos V. Bourantas
Castle Hill Hospital, UK

Poay Huan Loh
Castle Hill Hospital, UK

Vasilios D. Tsakanikas
University of Ioannina, Greece

Dimitrios I. Fotiadis
University of Ioannina, Greece

ABSTRACT

Optical coherence tomography (OCT) is a light-based invasive imaging method allowing accurate evaluation of coronary luminal morphology and reliable characterization of plaque. Its high resolution (10-20μm) offers the unique possibility of identifying clinically important coronary plaque microstructures such as macrophages, the presence and type of thrombus, stent expansion and endothelization and provides accurate assessment of the fibrous cap thickness in high risk plaques. These attributes placed OCT in a unique position as useful tool in research and clinical practice. As a new image modality, many interventional cardiologists are not familiar with its interpretation. In addition, there are only few developed methodologies able to process the OCT data and give comprehensive vessel representation and reliable measurements. Thus, this chapter focuses on the interpretation of OCT images and discusses the available image processing methodologies.

DOI: 10.4018/978-1-61350-095-8.ch011

INTRODUCTION

Optical coherence tomography (OCT) is an invasive catheter based imaging modality that provides high resolution cross-sectional images of coronary artery. In contrast to intravascular ultrasound (IVUS) OCT is based on the analysis of reflected light instead of acoustic waves and this allows visualization of intra-coronary features with a by far higher axial resolution (10-20μm vs. 100-150μm). Thus, OCT allows accurate evaluation of stent deployment and endothelization as well as identification of vessel wall trauma and thrombus with higher sensitivity and specificity than the other available invasive imaging modalities (Kubo *et al.* 2007, Guagliumi and Sirbu 2008). In addition, OCT provides reliable characterization of plaque's composition and is considered as the gold standard for assessing plaque's pathology (Kawasaki *et al.* 2006, Kume *et al.* 2006).

Although OCT has unique features its applicability remains limited. This has been attributed to the fact that it is a relatively new imaging modality and that most of the interventional cardiologists are Not familiar with the interpretation of OCT. Another significant limitation is the time required for processing and identification of the regions of interest in the large number of the obtained images. Thus, over the last years there has been an increased interest in standardizing the interpretation of OCT and developing new methodologies for quantitative analysis of the acquired sequence. The aim of this chapter is to provide useful guidance about the interpretation of OCT and present the available image processing methodologies.

Background: Normal Coronary Anatomy

In contrast to IVUS which can visualize only the intima-medial thickness, OCT imaging with its high resolution, allows complete imaging of the vessel wall. More specifically the internal elastic lamina, though it has thickness ≈ 3μm, is shown as

Figure 1. OCT image showing a coronary segment with mild intima-medial thickening. The bright zone corresponds to the intima-media while the dark layer surrounding the intima-media corresponds to the media. It is apparent that the high resolution of OCT allows accurate measurements of vessel wall structure.

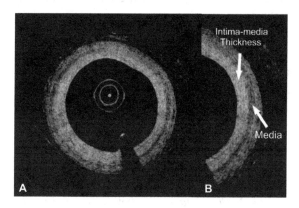

an echo lucent layer proximal to the lumen while the tunica media is illustrated as a medium dark layer structure. This can be attributed to the fact that the internal elastic lamina generates a signal-rich band (around 20 mm) probably caused by the different tissue composition of the internal elastic lamina the tunica media and intima (Prati *et al.* 2010). The media corresponds to the low signal area outer of the internal elastic lamina while the signal rich layer which surrounds the media corresponds to the external elastic lamina (Figure 1).

The feasibility of OCT to detect the vessel wall structures in the coronaries has been assessed by Kume *et al.* (2005) using histological data as the gold standard. The results confirmed the superiority of OCT compared to IVUS in measuring the intima-medial thickness (r=0.95, p<0.001, mean difference=–0.01±0.07 mm for vs. r=0.88, p<0.001, mean difference=–0.03±0.10 mm for IVUS) and showed that OCT in contrast to IVUS provides also accurate assessment of intima thickness.

MAIN FOCUS

Identification of Coronary Pathology

Plaque Characterization

Several studies have examined the accuracy of OCT in identifying plaque composition using histology as the gold standard (Jang *et al.* 2002, Yabushita *et al.* 2002, Kawasaki *et al.* 2006). OCT provided reliable categorization of the type of the atherosclerotic plaque and constitutes the gold standard for *in vivo* plaque characterization. More specifically the following components can be detected within an area of atheroma.

Calcified Plaques

The calcified plaques are well-outlined regions with a heterogeneous morphology and reduced signal density. OCT appears to have high sensitivity and specificity in detecting calcified plaques (>95%) (Yabushita *et al.* 2002, Kawasaki *et al.* 2006) and in contrast to IVUS where there is a shadowing artifact behind the calcium deposits, it allows visualization of the plaque behind the calcium and thus more accurate assessment of plaque burden in heavily calcified regions (Figure 2).

Fibrous Plaques

The fibrous plaques appear as homogenous high signal density regions (Figure 3A).

Figure 2. OCT image (A) showing a calcified lesion (arrow) with thrombus formation (*). In contrast to IVUS (B) in OCT allows evaluation of calcific component and the extent of the plaque behind the calcium deposit.

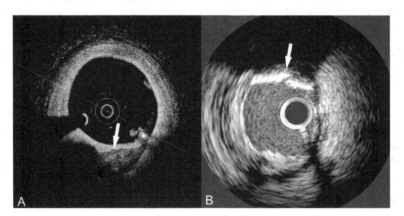

Figure 3. Example of a fibrotic (arrow in panel A) and a lipid rich plaque (arrow in panel B) revealed by OCT images

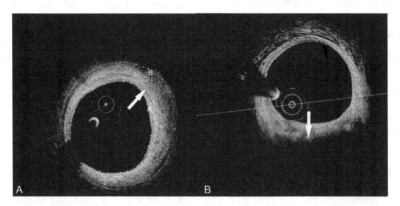

Figure 4. OCT image showing the presence of red thrombus (arrow in panel A) in a patient hospitalized because of an acute coronary syndrome and white thrombus in a patient with in-stent restenosis (arrow in panel B).

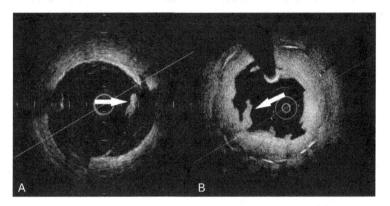

Lipid Pools

The necrotic lipid pools are diffusely bordered regions with low signal density with overlying signal rich bands, which correspond to fibrous caps (Figure 3B). A significant limitation of OCT is its low penetration in these plaques which often does not allow measurement of their thickness (Yabushita *et al.* 2002).

Identification of Culprit Lesions

Thrombus

OCT imaging allows not only reliable identification of thrombus but also classification of its constitution (Kume *et al.* 2006). In OCT thrombus appear as a mass which is discontinuous from the vessel wall and protrudes into the lumen. Red thrombi consisting mainly of red cells are characterized as high backscattering protrusions with signal free shadowing while the white thrombi which consist of platelets and white cells appear as signal-rich low-backscattering masses (Figure 4).

Plaque Dissection

In images dissected plaque is seen as a flap between the lumen and the cavity of the plaque (Figure 5A).

Plaque Erosion

Is characterized by the loss of the endothelial covering with laceration of the superficial intima without evidence of fibrous cap rupture (Figure 5B).

Figure 5. OCT imaging revealing a ruptured plaque with a rim of dissection (arrow) located at 11-2 o clock (panel A). Panel B shows plaque rupture at the site of its shoulders (arrow).

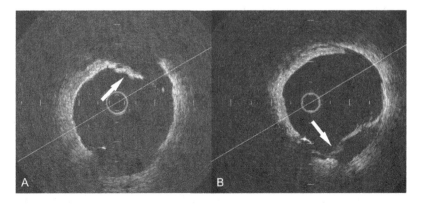

The ability of OCT in identifying a culprit lesion has been examined by Kubo *et al.* (2007) who compared OCT, angioscopy and IVUS. The results confirmed the superiority of OCT as it being more sensitive than IVUS and angioscopy in identifying plaque erosion and dissection and as reliable as angioscopy (but superior to IVUS) in revealing the presence of a thrombus.

Assessment of Plaque Vulnerability

OCT allows identification of microstructures that are unseen by other image modalities and are associated with increased plaque vulnerability. More specifically the following plaque components can be identified.

Macrophages

Infiltration of a thin cap fibroatheroma by macrophages has been associated with increased risk for acute coronary events. It has been speculated that macrophages produce metaloproteinases which digest the extra-cellular matrix leading to the thinning of the fibrous cap and thus increase the risk for plaque disruption (Davies *et al.* 1993). Tearney *et al.* (2003) used histological findings as gold standard to assess the ability of OCT in detecting the presence of macrophages in lipid pools and found that in plaques with high macrophage content the OCT images showed a heterogeneous fibrous cap with punctate, highly reflective regions. In this study further processing of the raw OCT signal allows reliable quantification of macrophage content. However, the ability of OCT to assess macrophages' infiltration has not been evaluated yet in large scale trials and thus further validation of this methodology is required before its broad implementation in research.

Fibrous Cap Thickness

Reduced thickness (<65μm) of the fibrous cap in vulnerable plaques is associated with an increased risk for plaque rupture (Naghavi *et al.* 2003,

Virmani *et al.* 2006). OCT allows accurate measurement of cap thickness and thus can provide more accurate assessment of plaque vulnerability (Kubo *et al.* 2007). However, the prognostic role of cap thickness in high risk patients is not definite and needs to be investigated in large scale multicentre studies.

Micro-calcification

Superficial calcified micro-deposits within or very close to the fibrous cap are often seen in vulnerable plaque. OCT allows identification of these microstructures that are depicted as small superficial low back-scattered heterogeneous regions.

Although not confirmed by histological studies it has been suggested that OCT can also reveal plaque hemorrhage and identify angiogenesis (Prati, *et al.* 2010). Comparing to other invasive imaging modalities OCT appears to be the best modality for identifying plaque characteristics associated with increased vulnerability (Table 1). The only limitation is that OCT has is poor penetration which does not allow evaluation of the severity of a lesion and detection of positive remodeling. Thus, potentially hybrid invasive imaging such as combination of OCT and radiofrequency analysis of the IVUS signal (IVUS-RF) may provide more thorough assessment of plaque characteristics (Sawada *et al.* 2008).

OCT and Coronary Stenting

In comparison to IVUS, OCT imaging provides detailed evaluation of stent expansion and accurate assessment of strut coverage. According to Guagliumi and Sirbu 2008 OCT allows classification of strut apposition into five categories: (a) entirely embedded struts into the vessel wall; (b) embedded sub-intimally struts without disruption of luminal border; (c) totally embedded struts with disruption of lumen; (d) partially embedded with extension of strut into lumen and (e) complete strut malapposition (blood exists between strut and lu-

Table 1. Histological features of vulnerable plaque (Naghavi et al. 2003) – ability of invasive imaging modalities in identifying vulnerable plaque characteristics.

Criteria for defining Vulnerable plaque	Intravascular imaging modalities						
Major Criteria	OCT	IVUS – IVUS-RF	Palpography	Angioscopy	Thermography	NIRS*	IV-MRI*
Active inflammation	++	-	++	-	+++	-	-
Thin fibrous cap	+++	+	+	+	-	-	+
Lipid core	+++	++	+	-	-	++	++
Disrupted plaques	+++	+	-	++	-	-	-
Stenosis > 90%	+	+++	-	-	-	-	++
Minor Criteria							
Superficial calcified nodule	++	-	-	-	-	-	-
Yellow colour on angioscopy plaque	-	-	-	+++	-	-	-
Intraplaque hemorrhage	+	-	-	-	-	-	-
Endothelial dysfunction	-	-	-	-	-	-	-
Positive remodelling	+	+++	-	-	-	-	++
Angiogenesis	+/-	+/-	-	-	-	-	-

IVUS, intracoronary ultrasound; RF, radiofrequency analysis; OCT, optical coherence tomography; NIRS, near infrared spectroscopy; IV-MRI, intravascular magnetic resonance imaging. The ability of each imaging modality in identifying vulnerable plaque characteristics is graded as: unable (-), low capability (+), moderate capability (++) and high capability (+++). The evaluation of the methods that have not been used in clinical practice (indicated with *) was based on the *in vitro* and animal studies.

minal wall). This information is useful especially in the case of drug eluting stent where delayed strut endothelialization is a common phenomenon and has been associated with in-stent thrombosis (Ishigami *et al.* 2009).

OCT appears also a reliable modality in detecting and measuring neointimal hyperplasia and was found to be superior to IVUS in cases of limited neointimal thickness (Guagliumi and Sirbu 2008). Another advantage of OCT comparing to IVUS is its high sensitivity in detecting thrombus and

Figure 6. OCT images showing stented segments of coronary artery: A) well apposed but uncovered stent struts; B) sent struts entirely embedded into the vessel wall and C) neointimal hyperplasia 6 months after bare metal stent implantation.

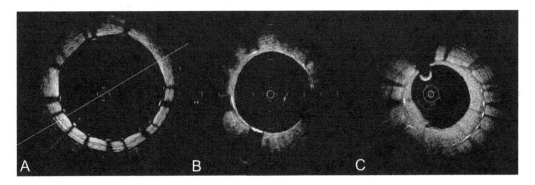

vessel wall trauma after stent implantation (Garg *et al.* 2008) and identify incomplete stent apposition or malapposition but on the other hand it is unable to assess the effect of vascular late stent malapposition remodeling to late stent malapposition due to its limited vessel penetration (Bouma *et al.* 2003).

Measurements in OCT Imaging

In contrast to IVUS which allows complete vessel visualization OCT imaging with its poor penetration quite often fails to demonstrate the outer vessel wall. Thus, in most cases only the luminal derived measurements can be obtained which are performed after image calibration in a similar manner to IVUS (Mintz *et al.* 2001).

1. **Luminal Cross-Sectional Area:** The area defined by the luminal border.
2. **Minimum Luminal Diameter:** The shorter diameter of the luminal area.
3. **Maximum Luminal Diameter:** The maximum diameter of the luminal area.
4. **Luminal Eccentricity:** The ratio maximum versus minimum luminal diameter.
5. **Stenosis:** A lesion that compromises the lumen area by at least 50% compared with a predefined reference segment.
6. **Luminal Area Stenosis:** The ratio (reference luminal cross-sectional area – minimum luminal cross section area) / reference luminal cross-sectional area.
7. **Stent Cross-Sectional Area:** The area defined by the stent border.
8. **Minimum Stent Diameter:** The shorter diameter of the stent.
9. **Maximum Stent Diameter:** The maximum diameter of the stent.
10. **Stent Symmetry:** The ratio maximum to minimum stent diameter.
11. **In-Stent Restenosis Area:** The deference between stent and luminal cross-sectional area.

12. **Plaque Area:** In case of small calibre segments where the internal elastic lamina is visible then plaque area can be defined as external elastic lamina area minus luminal cross sectional area.

Image Processing Methodologies

The ability of OCT to depict coronary anatomy and to allow more reliable identification of the type of plaque has rendered it a useful tool in clinical practice and research. However, the attenuation of light by the blood has limited its application since both approaches, suggested to overcome this problem (proximal balloon occlusion and brief saline purge though the guide catheter), have significant drawbacks. The former may cause ischemia or vessel wall injury and is not recommended whilst the latter only allows a short period of imaging time and thus depiction of short coronary segments. These limitations have been addressed by the introduction of a second generation OCT technology called optical frequency domain imaging (OFDI) which enables the acquisition of much higher number of OCT images in short time interval and thus visualization of longer segments (Yun *et al.* 2003). This has lead to interest in the development of fast and accurate semi-automated algorithms enhancing clinical applicability of OCT by allowing quick and accurate identification of regions of interest, comprehensive visualization of the studied artery and precise volumetric measurements. In this section we discuss the available image processing methodologies and introduce a locally developed segmentation algorithm for automated luminal and stent border detection and a fusion methodology for three dimensional (3-D) reconstruction of coronary arteries using OCT and angiographic data.

Comprehensive 3-D Visualisation of OCT

To visualize the vessel morphology and to quantify plaque composition in OFDI Tearney *et al.* (2008) suggested the integration of OCT sequence into a 3-D object. This process incorporates pre-processing of the initial data to include removal of the frames where the luminal silhouette is not well visible and the correction of rotational artefact. Then, in each frame the arterial wall, lipid pools, calcium, macrophages and stent borders are manually detected. After segmentation, arterial data are imported into a 3-D volume rendering program and displayed in colour for comprehensive visualization (Figure 7). This is similar to the approach suggested by Roelandt *et al.* (1994) for IVUS reconstruction and may allow complete visualization of the arterial wall and volumetric measurements. A disadvantage is that this technique is time consuming as it is performed manually and gives no data regarding arterial geometry and the location of plaque onto the artery. To overcome the former limitation, automated quantitative analysis of OCT images has been proposed whilst the latter two can be addressed with the reliable combination of the 3-D arterial geometry (obtained from angiographic images) with the luminal and vessel wall data obtained from OCT.

Quantitative Analysis of OCT

The first semi-automated quantitative OCT analysis was performed by Tanimoto *et al.* (2008) using a software named CURAD, initially developed for the processing of IVUS images. Two observers utilized this system to analyse 772 OCT frames obtained from *ex-vivo* arteries, 1807 frames from native coronary segments and 2331 frames from stented segments. The time needed to identify the luminal borders was significantly reduced (~40min for a segment with length 15mm) whilst the Bland and Altman analysis showed a low

Figure 7. Panel A: right anterior oblique angiographic view after stent deployment, showing stent site (s) and 4.2-cm OFDI pullback segment (ps). Panel B shows a maximum intensity projection while panel (C) a cutaway view of the 3-D volume-rendered OFDI data set. In these views scattered calcium deposits and a large lipid pool at the distal segment (red arrowhead) can been seen. The red colour corresponds to the artery wall, green to macrophages, yellow to lipid pool, blue to stent, white to calcium and grey to the guide wire. (From Tearney et al. 2008).

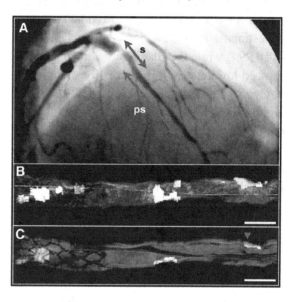

interobserver variability for the measured areas in all cases (relative difference 0.3±0.5% for ex-vivo segments, 0.6±0.5% for native segments, 1.6±0.1% for luminal area in stented segments and 0.2±0.7% for the sent area). These results demonstrated for the first time that the use of semi-automated segmentation methods for OCT border detection is feasible and provides reliable and faster identification of the regions of interest.

Sihan *et al.* (2009) presented a year later the first fully automated segmentation method of OCT images. This method used a Gaussian filter to remove noise and a Canny filter for edge detection. From the detected edges the luminal border was identified and further processed. The post-processing included noise removal, border smoothing and closure of the gaps created by side branches or guide wire artefact. Finally, poor quality images were detected and their luminal borders were represented in the final sequence by the correct border identified in the adjacent images. This method was validated in 4167 frames using the CURAD software as a gold standard. The time needed for the segmentation of each frame was 2 to 5 seconds. Only in 3% of the analysed frames the algorithm failed to identify the luminal borders and manual correction became necessary. A high correlation coefficient was noted between the estimations of the new method and CURAD (R=0.999) while the Bland and Altman analysis showed low relative differences for the luminal borders (0.4±1.8%). These results indicate that the proposed method is reliable and able to provide rapid measurements.

New Automated Border Detection Algorithm

The proposed approach for the fully automated processing of an OCT sequence is based on the active contour theory which has already been proven to be effective in the segmentation of images acquired by other medical imaging modalities, such as IVUS (Plissiti *et al.* 2004) or magnetic resonance angiography (Mansard *et al.* 2004). This segmentation methodology uses a sequential rationale, where the border detected in the previous frame (*n*) is used for the identification of the luminal border in the next frame (*n+1*). The algorithm comprises of three steps.

Preprocessing

The pre-processing procedure reformats the initial data and includes conversion of the OCT file in a sequence of OCT frames in which a 3 x 3 median filter is applied to increase the signal to noise ratio without compromising the quality of image's edges.

Calculation of the Luminal Border in the 1st Frame

To initialize the sequential algorithm, the identification of the luminal border in the 1st frame is necessary. To achieve this, the 1st frame is transformed from Cartesian to Polar coordinates and a knowledge based algorithm is implemented to remove the catheter artifact. A Gaussian low pass filter is applied and then the Canny method is used to detect the luminal border. In our approach for each angle the edge of the minimum radius is considered to correspond to the luminal border. The outcome of these steps may contain gaps, and is interpolated using a cubic function before initializing an active contour which is then deformed to approximate the lumen.

Sequential Border Detection Algorithm

After the calculation of the luminal border in the 1st frame, a sequential segmentation methodology is implemented. This procedure uses the border of the frame *n* as an initial approximation for the luminal border in the frame *n+1*. Following this rationale, the algorithm segments the entire sequence through to the last frame.

The segmentation of an OCT sequence is a challenging process. In many cases the presence of artifact does not allow reliable border detection. To facilitate this process, and avoid false detections and possible incorrect measurement, the proposed approach automatically detects the frames that do not contain adequate information. For this, a quality criterion has been established, which compares the luminal borders of the previous and following frame. Based on a knowledge based approach (sampling over 20 OCT examinations), a threshold for the luminal areas on succeeding frames has been established. When the criterion is not meet, the detected border is omitted and the sequential algorithm is applied to the next frame. If the segmentation of the next frame is successful, the algorithm continues to the following frame. However, if the algorithm fails to detect the luminal border in more than ten consecutive frames, the sequential algorithm stops on the frame after the first failure and the step II of the segmentation process is applied to re-identify the luminal border.

The described approach has been developed in MATLAB and allows quantitative assessment of luminal dimensions (maximum luminal diameter, minimum luminal diameter, luminal eccentricity, luminal area and luminal area stenosis etc). Though it has not been fully validated our preliminary results appears to be promising (Figure 8) while the average processing time on a standard workstation is only 1.5sec per frame.

Figure 8. Lumen border as has been detected by the newly developed segmentation algorithm

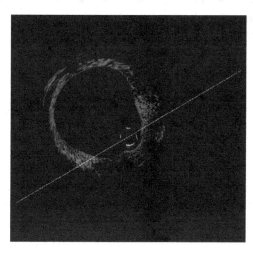

FUTURE TRENDS: FUSION OF OCT WITH ANGIOGRAPHIC DATA

The 3-D visualization approach presented by Tearney, *et al.* (2008) allows comprehensive representation of vessel wall morphology and plaque distribution but gives no data regarding vessel geometry and the location of the plaque into the artery. Similar drawbacks have been observed during the 3-D visualization of IVUS and have been addressed with the fusion of IVUS with coronary angiographic data (Wahle *et al.* 1999, Slager *et al.* 2000, Bourantas *et al.* 2005). These data fusion methodologies involve the extraction of the catheter path from the angiographic images, detection of the regions of interest in the IVUS images, placement of the detected borders onto the extracted 3-D path and finally the estimation of their absolute orientation. Recently, we have implemented the abovementioned steps to fuse

Figure 9. Biplane projections (A: left anterior oblique and D: right anterior oblique view) of a right coronary artery. The 3-D reconstructed segment is depicted in the figures B and E. As it is shown in figures C and F the reconstructed coronary segment matches well with the luminal silhouette.

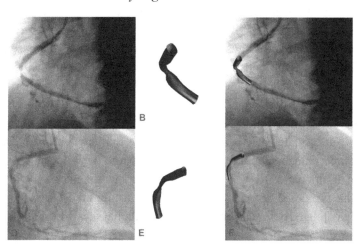

OCT and angiographic data, though our experience has shown, the whole methodology appears to be more challenging (Figure 9).

More specifically, to extract the catheter path from the angiographic images a 2nd guide wire has to be advanced in the vessel distally to the OCT wire before beginning the pull-back and after the end of the procedure. The wire is pulled-back while OCT imaging is performed. The position of the OCT probe corresponds to the tip of the guide wire when this is not visible in the OCT images. After identifying the position of the OCT probe, biplane angiography is performed to visualize simultaneously the luminal silhouette and the OCT wire. Then, pull-back of the OCT catheter is performed under brief saline purge. During this process the ECG should be recorded and the vessel should be visible in all the OCT images. Both ECG and OCT data are transferred in a vision mixer to have synchronized recordings.

The catheter path is extracted using the algorithm described by Bourantas *et al.* (2008), while the end-diastolic OCT images (peak of R wave on ECG) are selected and the luminal borders are manually detected. In the frames that the lumen is not well visualized the borders identified in the previous and next frame are utilized to estimate the intermediate border using the interpolation approach described by Goshtasby *et al.* (1992). The final borders are placed perpendicular onto the catheter path and then their orientation is estimated using the sequential triangulation algorithm and the methodology presented by Slager *et al.* (2000). The outcome of the abovementioned stages is a set of point cloud which is used to construct a non-uniform rational B-Spline (NURBS) surface that represents the morphology of the lumen. As it is shown in Figure 9 our initial results appear encouraging as there is a good match between the projections of the 3-D object onto the angiographic images and the luminal silhouette. However, it is clearly important the presented approach be fully and quantitatively validated before its broad implementation in research.

Recently, Tu *et al.* (2011) proposed the co-registration of quantitative computed angiography (QCA) and IVUS/OCT images. Initially, the QCA data were used to reconstruct the segment of interest in 3-D space and then anatomical landmarks seen in both 3-D QCA and IVUS/OCT images were detected. These landmarks were used to identify correspondence between the two imaging modalities and register the IVUS/OCT images onto the reconstructed (by the QCA data) segment. The proposed approach may allow fast fusion of the QCA and OCT data but also has significant limitations including the lack of precise orientation of the IVUS/OCT images onto the 3-D QCA model and the fact that it doesn't take into consideration the cardiac motion which may often influence the axial position of the IVUS/OCT images. Finally, the proposed validation was performed only *in vitro* and did not allow detailed quantification of the registration errors.

In the past the 3-D objects created by the combination of IVUS and angiography had provided useful information and helped explain the regional localization of atherosclerosis. Nowadays it is apparent that low or oscillating shear stress promotes atherosclerosis in native segments (Stone *et al.* 2007), in-stent restenosis in bare metal stents (Papafaklis *et al.* 2009) and contributes to the development of vulnerable plaque (Chatzizisis *et al.* 2008). However, the intrinsic limitation of IVUS does not allow these models to be used to study the role of flow heamodynamic in plaque destabilization and rupture. Slager *et al.* (2005) speculated that an increased axial tensile stress may be involved in plaque rupture but there are insufficient data to support this hypothesis. We believe that the 3-D objects obtained by fusing OCT (which is the gold standard modality for plaque characterisation and assessment of vessel wall pathology) and angiographic images, will provide us the necessary information and allow us to further investigate the association between endothelial shear stress and plaque constitution, as well as to study the role of flow heamodynamics in acute coronary syndromes.

CONCLUSION

OCT imaging allows reliable assessment of luminal dimensions and identification of plaque characteristics associated with increased vulnerability. In addition it permits visualization of microstructures (e.g. thrombus, macrophages, micro-calcification etc) which cannot be imaged using IVUS and constitutes the gold standard for the characterization of plaque morphology. A standardized interpretation of OCT images and the new developments in OCT image processing may provide fast, reliable and reproducible segmentation of the OCT images and thus enhance its clinical and research applicability. Finally, the fusion of angiographic and OCT data allow geometrically correct luminal representation and can be used to study *in vivo* the role of local heamodynamics in plaque development, destabilization and rupture.

REFERENCES

Bouma, B. E., Tearney, G. J., Yabushita, H., Shishkov, M., Kauffman, C. R., & DeJoseph Gauthier, D. (2003). Evaluation of intracoronary stenting by intravascular optical coherence tomography. *Heart (British Cardiac Society)*, *89*(3), 317–320. doi:10.1136/heart.89.3.317

Bourantas, C. V., Kalatzis, F. G., Papafaklis, M. I., Fotiadis, D. I., Tweddel, A. C., & Kourtis, I. C. (2008). ANGIOCARE: An automated system for fast three-dimensional coronary reconstruction by integrating angiographic and intracoronary ultrasound data. *Catheterization and Cardiovascular Interventions*, *72*(2), 166–175. doi:10.1002/ccd.21527

Bourantas, C. V., Kourtis, I. C., Plissiti, M. E., Fotiadis, D. I., Katsouras, C. S., & Papafaklis, M. I. (2005). A method for 3D reconstruction of coronary arteries using biplane angiography and intravascular ultrasound images. *Computerized Medical Imaging and Graphics*, *29*(8), 597–606. doi:10.1016/j.compmedimag.2005.07.001

Chatzizisis, Y. S., Jonas, M., Coskun, A. U., Beigel, R., Stone, B. V., & Maynard, C. (2008). Prediction of the localization of high-risk coronary atherosclerotic plaques on the basis of low endothelial shear stress: An intravascular ultrasound and histopathology natural history study. *Circulation*, *117*(8), 993–1002. doi:10.1161/CIRCULATIONAHA.107.695254

Cilingiroglu, M., Oh, J. H., Sugunan, B., Kemp, N. J., Kim, J., & Lee, S. (2006). Detection of vulnerable plaque in a murine model of atherosclerosis with optical coherence tomography. *Catheterization and Cardiovascular Interventions*, *67*(6), 915–923. doi:10.1002/ccd.20717

Davies, M. J., Richardson, P. D., Woolf, N., Katz, D. R., & Mann, J. (1993). Risk of thrombosis in human atherosclerotic plaques: Role of extracellular lipid, macrophage, and smooth muscle cell content. *British Heart Journal*, *69*(5), 377–381. doi:10.1136/hrt.69.5.377

Garg, S., Bourantas, C., & Thackray, S. (2008). Suspected coronary artery dissection post-stenting, confirmed by optical coherence tomography. *Heart (British Cardiac Society)*, *94*(3), 335. doi:10.1136/hrt.2006.108878

Goshtasby, A., Turner, D. A., & Ackerman, L. V. (1992). Matching of tomographic slices for interpolation. *IEEE Transactions on Medical Imaging*, *11*(4), 507–516. doi:10.1109/42.192686

Guagliumi, G., & Sirbu, V. (2008). Optical coherence tomography: High resolution intravascular imaging to evaluate vascular healing after coronary stenting. *Catheterization and Cardiovascular Interventions*, *72*(2), 237–247. doi:10.1002/ccd.21606

Ishigami, K., Uemura, S., Morikawa, Y., Soeda, T., Okayama, S., & Nishida, T. (2009). Long-term follow-up of neointimal coverage of sirolimus-eluting stents-evaluation with optical coherence tomography. *Circulation Journal*, *73*(12), 2300–2307. doi:10.1253/circj.CJ-08-1116

Jang, I. K., Bouma, B. E., Kang, D. H., Park, S. J., Park, S. W., & Seung, K. B. (2002). Visualization of coronary atherosclerotic plaques in patients using optical coherence tomography: Comparison with intravascular ultrasound. *Journal of the American College of Cardiology*, *39*(4), 604–609. doi:10.1016/S0735-1097(01)01799-5

Kawasaki, M., Bouma, B. E., Bressner, J., Houser, S. L., Nadkarni, S. K., & MacNeill, B. D. (2006). Diagnostic accuracy of optical coherence tomography and integrated backscatter intravascular ultrasound images for tissue characterization of human coronary plaques. *Journal of the American College of Cardiology*, *48*(1), 81–88. doi:10.1016/j.jacc.2006.02.062

Kubo, T., Imanishi, T., Takarada, S., Kuroi, A., Ueno, S., & Yamano, T. (2007). Assessment of culprit lesion morphology in acute myocardial infarction: Ability of optical coherence tomography compared with intravascular ultrasound and coronary angioscopy. *Journal of the American College of Cardiology*, *50*(10), 933–939. doi:10.1016/j.jacc.2007.04.082

Kume, T., Akasaka, T., Kawamoto, T., Ogasawara, Y., Watanabe, N., & Toyota, E. (2006). Assessment of coronary arterial thrombus by optical coherence tomography. *The American Journal of Cardiology*, *97*(12), 1713–1717. doi:10.1016/j.amjcard.2006.01.031

Kume, T., Akasaka, T., Kawamoto, T., Watanabe, N., Toyota, E., & Neishi, Y. (2005). Assessment of coronary intima--media thickness by optical coherence tomography: Comparison with intravascular ultrasound. *Circulation Journal*, *69*(8), 903–907. doi:10.1253/circj.69.903

Kume, T., Akasaka, T., Kawamoto, T., Watanabe, N., Toyota, E., & Neishi, Y. (2006). Assessment of coronary arterial plaque by optical coherence tomography. *The American Journal of Cardiology*, *97*(8), 1172–1175. doi:10.1016/j.amjcard.2005.11.035

Mansard, C. D., Canet Soulas, E. P., Anwander, A., Chaabane, L., Neyran, B., & Serfaty, J. M. (2004). Quantification of multicontrast vascular MR images with NLSnake, an active contour model: In vitro validation and in vivo evaluation. *Magnetic Resonance in Medicine*, *51*(2), 370–379. doi:10.1002/mrm.10722

Mintz, G. S., Nissen, S. E., Anderson, W. D., Bailey, S. R., Erbel, R., & Fitzgerald, P. J. (2001). American College of Cardiology clinical expert consensus document on standards for acquisition, measurement and reporting of intravascular ultrasound studies (IVUS). A report of the American College of Cardiology Task Force on Clinical Expert Consensus Documents. *Journal of the American College of Cardiology*, *37*(5), 1478–1492. doi:10.1016/S0735-1097(01)01175-5

Naghavi, M., Libby, P., Falk, E., Casscells, S. W., Litovsky, S., & Rumberger, J. (2003). From vulnerable plaque to vulnerable patient: a call for new definitions and risk assessment strategies: Part I. *Circulation*, *108*(14), 1664–1672. doi:10.1161/01.CIR.0000087480.94275.97

Papafaklis, M. I., Bourantas, C. V., Theodorakis, P. E., Katsouras, C. S., Fotiadis, D. I., & Michalis, L. K. (2009). Relationship of shear stress with in-stent restenosis: Bare metal stenting and the effect of brachytherapy. *International Journal of Cardiology*, *134*(1), 25–32. doi:10.1016/j.ijcard.2008.02.006

Plissiti, M. E., Fotiadis, D. I., Michalis, L. K., & Bozios, G. E. (2004). An automated method for lumen and media-adventitia border detection in a sequence of IVUS frames. *IEEE Transactions on Information Technology in Biomedicine, 8*(2), 131–141. doi:10.1109/TITB.2004.828889

Prati, F., Regar, E., Mintz, G. S., Arbustini, E., Di Mario, C., & Jang, I. K. (2010). Expert review document on methodology, terminology, and clinical applications of optical coherence tomography: Physical principles, methodology of image acquisition, and clinical application for assessment of coronary arteries and atherosclerosis. *European Heart Journal, 31*(4), 401–415. doi:10.1093/eurheartj/ehp433

Roelandt, J. R., di Mario, C., Pandian, N. G., Wenguang, L., Keane, D., & Slager, C. J. (1994). Three-dimensional reconstruction of intracoronary ultrasound images. Rationale, approaches, problems, and directions. *Circulation, 90*(2), 1044–1055.

Sawada, T., Shite, J., Garcia-Garcia, H. M., Shinke, T., Watanabe, S., & Otake, H. (2008). Feasibility of combined use of intravascular ultrasound radiofrequency data analysis and optical coherence tomography for detecting thin-cap fibroatheroma. *European Heart Journal, 29*(9), 1136–1146. doi:10.1093/eurheartj/ehn132

Sihan, K., Botha, C., Post, F., de Winter, S., Gonzalo, N., & Regar, E. (2009). Fully automatic three-dimensional quantitative analysis of intracoronary optical coherence tomography: Method and validation. *Catheterization and Cardiovascular Interventions, 74*(7), 1058–1065. doi:10.1002/ccd.22125

Slager, C. J., Wentzel, J. J., Gijsen, F. J., Thury, A., van der Wal, A. C., & Schaar, J. A. (2005). The role of shear stress in the destabilization of vulnerable plaques and related therapeutic implications. *Nature Clinical Practice. Cardiovascular Medicine, 2*(9), 456–464. doi:10.1038/ncpcardio0298

Slager, C. J., Wentzel, J. J., Schuurbiers, J. C., Oomen, J. A., Kloet, J., & Krams, R. (2000). True 3-dimensional reconstruction of coronary arteries in patients by fusion of angiography and IVUS (ANGUS) and its quantitative validation. *Circulation, 102*(5), 511–516.

Stone, P. H., Coskun, A. U., Kinlay, S., Popma, J. J., Sonka, M., & Wahle, A. (2007). Regions of low endothelial shear stress are the sites where coronary plaque progresses and vascular remodelling occurs in humans: an in vivo serial study. *European Heart Journal, 28*(6), 705–710. doi:10.1093/eurheartj/ehl575

Tanimoto, S., Rodriguez-Granillo, G., Barlis, P., de Winter, S., Bruining, N., & Hamers, R. (2008). A novel approach for quantitative analysis of intracoronary optical coherence tomography: High inter-observer agreement with computer-assisted contour detection. *Catheterization and Cardiovascular Interventions, 72*(2), 228–235. doi:10.1002/ccd.21482

Tearney, G. J., Waxman, S., Shishkov, M., Vakoc, B. J., Suter, M. J., & Freilich, M. I. (2008). Three-dimensional coronary artery microscopy by intracoronary optical frequency domain imaging. *JACC: Cardiovascular Imaging, 1*(6), 752–761. doi:10.1016/j.jcmg.2008.06.007

Tearney, G. J., Yabushita, H., Houser, S. L., Aretz, H. T., Jang, I. K., & Schlendorf, K. H. (2003). Quantification of macrophage content in atherosclerotic plaques by optical coherence tomography. *Circulation, 107*(1), 113–119. doi:10.1161/01.CIR.0000044384.41037.43

Tu, S., Holm, N. R., Koning, G., Huang, Z., & Reiber, J. H. C. (2011). Fusion of 3D QCA and IVUS/OCT. *The International Journal of Cardiovascular Imaging, 25.*

Virmani, R., Burke, A. P., Farb, A., & Kolodgie, F. D. (2006). Pathology of the vulnerable plaque. *Journal of the American College of Cardiology, 47*(8Suppl), C13–C18. doi:10.1016/j.jacc.2005.10.065

Wahle, A., Prause, P. M., DeJong, S. C., & Sonka, M. (1999). Geometrically correct 3-D reconstruction of intravascular ultrasound images by fusion with biplane angiography--Methods and validation. *IEEE Transactions on Medical Imaging, 18*(8), 686–699. doi:10.1109/42.796282

Yabushita, H., Bouma, B. E., Houser, S. L., Aretz, H. T., Jang, I. K., & Schlendorf, K. H. (2002). Characterization of human atherosclerosis by optical coherence tomography. *Circulation, 106*(13), 1640–1645. doi:10.1161/01.CIR.0000029927.92825.F6

Yun, S., Tearney, G., de Boer, J., Iftimia, N., & Bouma, B. (2003). High-speed optical frequency-domain imaging. *Optics Express, 11*(22), 2953–2963. doi:10.1364/OE.11.002953

KEY TERMS AND DEFINITIONS

Angioscopy: Is an intravascular modality that involves advancing a catheter with illumination fibres on its tip into the coronary artery and allows detection of luminal pathology (e.g. presence of thrombus, plaque rupture and dissection) and provides information regarding the composition of the superficial plaque.

Atherosclerosis: The word atherosclerosis is a composite word coming from the Greek words athere which means gruel and skleros which means hard. This term is used to describe the build up of a waxy plaque on the inside of the arterial wall.

Intravascular Magnetic Resonance Imaging (IV-MRI): Is an invasive imaging modality which uses intravascular receiver coils to increase the signal to noise ratio and obtain high resolution magnetic resonance images of the vessel wall morphology.

Intravascular Ultrasound (IVUS): Is an invasive catheter based imaging modality that requires the insertion of a catheter with a transducer on its tip that transmits and receives ultrasound signal generating real – time, high resolution, cross – sectional images of coronary arteries.

Near Infrared Spectroscopy (NIRS): Is a catheter based invasive image modality. It relies on the principle that different organic molecules absorb and scatter the near infrared light to different degrees and at various wavelengths and it appears to provide accurate detection of the lipid-rich plaques.

Non-Uniform Rational B-Spline (NURBS): Is a mathematical model used in computer graphics for generating and representing curves and surfaces that allows precise definition and manipulation of their morphology.

Palpography: Is an invasive technique that utilizes intravascular ultrasound imaging to assess the local strain of the vessel wall and atheroma and has been implemented to detect high risk plaques.

Radiofrequency Analysis of the IVUS Signal (IVUS-RF): Includes the analysis of the IVUS backscatter signal for more accurate characterization of the type of the plaque. Several methodologies have been proposed for this purpose including the integrated backscatter analysis the wavelet analysis and the autoregressive modeling of the radiofrequency data. These methodologies appear to be useful in the detection of the vulnerable plaques and in the study of the atherosclerotic evolution.

Thermography: Allows detection of the heat derived by the vessel wall and has been implemented for the identification of the vulnerable plaques as these have increased temperature due to the local inflammation.

Vulnerable Plaque: Is the atherosclerotic plaque which is prone to thrombosis or has high probability of undergoing rapid progression and causing coronary events.

Chapter 12
OCT in the Clinical Practice and Data from Clinical Studies

Francesco Prati
San Giovanni Hospital, Italy & CLI Foundation, Italy

Alessandro Di Giorgio
Ferrarotto Hospital, Italy, & ETNA Foundation, Italy

Vito Ramazzotti
San Giovanni Hospital, Italy

Maria Teresa Mallus
San Giovanni Hospital, Italy

ABSTRACT

This chapter provides a detailed description of the role of the OCT technique in the clinical practice. A review section on data from clinical studies is provided, underlining the extent usage of OCT during the last years. Finally, the capability of OCT to assess ambiguous lesions and deferral of interventions is discussed just before describing the role of the technique during the post procedural assessment.

INTRODUCTION

The introduction of stents in clinical practice was initially burdened by an unacceptably high incidence of sub-acute thrombosis. Later on the use of intravascular ultrasound (IVUS) opened the way to the understanding the reasons for stent failure. IVUS clarified that despite optimal angiographic results many first generation stents were still having a marked under-expansion with irregular eccentric lumen and incomplete apposition of the

stent struts to the vessel wall. These findings led to a new strategy for stent deployment based on high-pressure balloon dilatation inside the stent, to be done with angiographic guidance (Goldberg, Colombo, Nakamura, Almagor, Maiello, & Tobis, 1994), (Serruys & Di Mario, 1995), (Colombo, *et al.*, 1995), (Spanos, Stankovic, Tobis, & Colombo, 2003). In other words, IVUS taught us how to implant a stent but then it failed to become the technique to be used for routine guidance.

The last two decades were characterized by the growth of new technical solutions to improve percutaneous coronary intervention. Stents are

DOI: 10.4018/978-1-61350-095-8.ch012

nowadays capable of eluting drugs or exerting an anti-thrombotic action due to specific coverage. Other new concepts are being investigated; for instance bioabsorbable stents capable of eluting drugs may have a role in the next future.

Since the clinical introduction of IVUS, new imaging modalities came out, with optical coherence tomography (OCT) being the most promising to improve results of interventional cardiology.

OCT is an optical analogue of IVUS, based on infra-red light emission. In comparison with IVUS, OCT has improved resolution (10 mm) and contrast and a limited penetration that does not exceed 1.3 mm, offering therefore a high resolution superficial picture of coronary arteries. This feature of OCT allows the visualization of specific components of the atherosclerotic plaques and details the architecture of stented segments, providing information similar to histology (Tanigawa, Barlis, & Di Mario, 2007), (Jang, *et al.*, 2005), (Prati, *et al.*, 2010), (Guagliumi & Sirbu, 2008).

METHODOLOGICAL ISSUES

Technical Details and Image Acquisition

The main obstacle to the adoption of TD-OCT imaging in clinical practice is that OCT cannot image through a blood field, and therefore requires clearing or flushing of blood from the lumen (Prati, *et al.*, 2010). Time domain (TD) was the first OCT technology to be used in Europe and Japan. TD-OCT was complex and time consuming, requiring a soft occlusion balloon and saline injection in the coronary artery. This modality of acquisition was limiting the OCT widespread application in the clinical arena, focusing its role to the research settings.

Vessel imaging by TD-OCT is now much simpler due to the introduction from our group of a non occlusive modality of image acquisition (Prati, *et al.*, 2008), (Prati, Cera, Ramazzotti,

Imola, Giuduce, & Albertucci, 2007). This technique, that simply requires the administration of contrast through the guiding catheter, has been recently applied for the novel frequency domain (FD) catheters. We will discuss in detail only the FD acquisition as it is replacing the TD technique.

The LightLab Dragonfly™ FD-OCT catheter, is so far the only in the market. The Dragonfly™ catheter has a distal diameter of 2.7 Fr and is compatible with 6 Fr guiding catheters. It has a larger crossing profile as compared to the first generation of the ImageWire, and this may limit the use in very stenotic segments. On the other hand, the higher profile of the catheter precludes extremes wire eccentricity, resulting in fewer artifacts and out of focus images.

The OCT probe is first advanced over a regular guide wire, distal to the region of interest. Identification of the pull-back starting point is a simple task as a dedicated marker identifies the exact position of the OCT lens, located 10 mm proximal to the marker itself. The infusion rate of contrast is usually set to 3-4 ml/sec for the left coronary artery and 2-3 ml/sec for the right coronary, but can be modified based on the vessel run-off and size. When the OCT catheter is positioned and blood clearance is visually obtained distally by mean of the contrast injection, the acquisition of a rapid OCT image sequence with fast pull-back can be automatically or manually started. Contrast is injected through the guiding catheter, with the acquisition speed set between 5 and 25 mm/sec. Most expert users advocate the use of automated contrast injection to optimize image quality.

With an acquisition speed of 20 mm/sec, it is possible to obtain 200 cross-sectional image frames over 4-5 cm length of artery in 3.5 sec with a total infused volume of 14 ml contrast. This allows the quick evaluation of the treated artery. The FD-OCT pull-back speed is too fast to interpret the run during the acquisition but the recorded images, that are digitally stored, can be reviewed in a slow playback loop (Tearney, *et al.*, 2008), (Imola, *et al.*, 2010).

Safety and Efficacy of OCT

OCT acquisition with time domain technology, both occlusive and non-occlusive, proved to be safe and efficient. A few procedural complications, including ventricular tachycardia, ventricular fibrillation or acute vessel occlusion were reported by preliminary studies. In the largest registry on the safety of the use of time domain OCT, including 468 patients, ventricular fibrillation occurred in 1.1% of patients, air embolism in 0.6% and vessel dissection in 0.2% (Barlis, *et al.*, 2009).

Preliminary data on the safety for the use of FD-OCT technology are even more promising. The marked increase of pull-back speed and the consequent reduction in the required contrast volume abolish ECG changes or arrhythmias that were observed with the time domain technology (Imola, *et al.*, 2010), (Takarada, *et al.*, 2010).

FD-OCT is highly effective and provides clear images in longer segments compared to TD-OCT (Prati, *et al.*, 2010), (Imola, *et al.*, in press). As compared to IVUS, OCT provides excellent differentiation between the lumen and the arterial wall, facilitating the determination of lumen areas and volumes and the depiction of stent struts with high accuracy (Bezerra, Costa, Guagliumi, Rollins, & Simon, 2009), (Capodanno, *et al.*, 2009).

Assessment of target lesions by IVUS is frequently a demanding issue. In spite of the miniaturization of ultrasound catheters, IVUS probes tend to occlude the lumen in tight lesions during the time required to acquire pull-back images at a relatively low 1 mm/sec pull-back speed and consequently the symptoms and signs of myocardial ischaemia may develop. Moreover, blood stagnation can complicate image interpretation. As FD-OCT probes have a slightly thinner profile than IVUS probes and pull-back imaging can be done at very high speeds (normally 20 mm/sec), a significant fraction of severely diseased target lesions can be imaged without causing luminal obstruction, with symptomatic ischemia being less likely. If the probe causes luminal obstruc-

tion however, blood cannot be cleared and OCT imaging becomes impossible beyond or at the level of the most severe stenosis. Therefore in sub-occlusive lesions it can be more convenient to perform OCT after a gentle pre-dilatation. As accurate acquisition of OCT images has a key role, it is of utmost importance to optimize guiding catheter engagement.

For both TD-OCT and FD-OCT techniques, accurate calibration is mandatory in order to take full advantage of the high spatial accuracy of the technology. The size of the OCT image is calibrated by adjusting the z-offset, the zero-point setting of the system. In FD-OCT systems, the calibration procedure can be done in a fully automated modality

ASSESSMENT OF AMBIGUOUS LESIONS AND DEFERRAL OF INTERVENTIONS

OCT provides very accurate luminal measurements of lesion severity in case of ambiguity, due to an excellent delineation of the lumen-wall interface. Sub-optimal angiographic visualization may happen in presence of intermediate lesions of uncertain severity, very short lesions, pre- or post-aneurysmal lesions, ostial or left main stenoses, disease at branching sites, sites with focal spasm, or angiographically hazy lesions (Prati, *et al.*, 2010). In a relevant number of cases with these angiographic characteristics, OCT use can change the operator intention-to-treat, avoiding unnecessary, uncertain, interventional procedures in some cases. OCT, compared to IVUS, offers more accurate information on the superficial composition of the plaque. This feature further improves the accuracy of the definition of the culprit lesion in uncertain cases and seems particularly worthwhile in presence of thrombus or calcifications that create ambiguous images with haziness at angiography. In a recent Expert Review Document On Methodology, Terminology And

Clinical Applications of OCT, the assessment of intermediate lesion and the identification of culprit plaques of acute coronary syndromes were considered two important clinical applications of OCT (7). OCT can visualize abrupt plaque ulceration or rupture, which can be visualized as ruptured fibrous cup that connects the lumen with the lipid pool and thrombus. The thrombus is poorly studied by IVUS, being a well-known Achille's heel of the technique (Prati, *et al.*, 2010).

Like IVUS, OCT can quantify lesion severity more accurately than quantitative coronary angiography, by measuring MLA, with 3.5 mm^2 or 4 mm^2 being considered the significant cut-off threshold for a clinically significant flow-limiting stenosis in appropriately sized (>3 mm) vessels. For left main coronary stenosis a higher 6-7 mm^2 cut-off value should be applied (Barlis, *et al.*, 2009). However, as luminal measurements by OCT are slightly smaller than corresponding IVUS ones, further validation studies of comparison between OCT and fractional flow reserve may be needed to corroborate this issue. The only technical draw-back of the technique is that plaques located

at the very ostium of the left or right coronaries cannot be accurately addressed by OCT; in fact, at the current stage of technology, neither of the two OCT acquisition techniques (occlusive or non occlusive) appears to be suitable for aorto-ostial assessment (Prati, *et al.*, 2010).

Data from our center showed that OCT can be used to resolve ambiguous angiographic anatomy in stable and unstable clinical scenarios, including identification of culprit complicated plaques in the setting of acute coronary syndromes and assessment of lesion severity in stable patients (Imola, *et al.*, 2010). Pre-intervention FD-OCT was performed to evaluate ambiguous/intermediate lesions at basal angiography in 40 patients; eight patients had an acute coronary syndrome and haziness at angiography, whilst the remaining 32 had intermediate narrowing and a stable syndrome. Of the 40 patients with ambiguous lesions 24 were treated with PCI, whilst in the remaining 16 the coronary interventions were deferred.

OCT findings among the 16 patients undergoing PCI were a minimal lumen area less than 3.5 mm^2 in 11 and presence of thrombus with signs

Figure 1. Left panel shows an angiographic image of an ambiguous lesion with haziness. IVUS (right panels) was able to identify calcific components of the plaque but it did not show the features of ruptured plaque that was revealed by OCT (central panel).

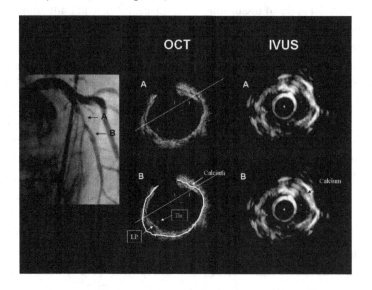

Figure 2. Left panel: Angiogram of a patient with anterior STEMI shows a severe narrowing of left anterior descending complicated by thrombus formation. Right panel: OCT shows the fibrous cap rupture.

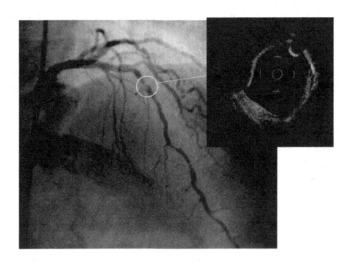

of plaque ulceration indicative of unstable plaque in the remaining 5. All patients in which coronary intervention was deferred based on OCT findings did not experience coronary events and were symptoms free.

An additional group of 22 cases with haziness at angiography underwent both IVUS and OCT. OCT confirmed the presence of complicated plaques (61% of cases), that were under-diagnosed by IVUS (48% of cases) (unpublished data).

POST PROCEDURAL ASSESSMENT

A burning question to be addressed is whether OCT will have in the future a role for guidance of routine stenting interventions. Routine IVUS guidance of elective bare stenting procedures is not supported by the results of previous studies. In fact, meta-analysis on the ability of IVUS to reduce restenosis after stenting have given conflicting results, with the most important published randomized trial being completely negative (Mintz, Nissen, & Anderson, 2001), (Gerber & Colombo, 2008).

However data on IVUS use for optimization of drug eluting stents (DES) deployment were more encouraging. Roy *et al.* (Roy, *et al.*, 2008) recently compared 884 IVUS-guided intracoronary DES implantations with the outcomes of a propensity-score matched population having angiographic guidance alone. The rate of definite stent thrombosis at 12 months, that was the primary end-point of the study was significantly lower in the IVUS guided group and there was a trend was seen in favor of the IVUS group in target lesion revascularization.

OCT offers a superb visualization of stent surface and depicts the spatial interactions between stent struts and vessel wall; it is reasonable to think of this technique as superior for guidance of interventions requiring novel devices including DES.

Stent under-expansion is a well-known cause of restenosis also for DES. In a sub-study of the SIRIUS trial, the post-intervention minimal stent area (MSA) that best separated "adequate" from "inadequate" patency was 5.0 mm², with a 90% positive predictive value for this cut-off point (Mintz & Weissman, 2006). In line with this finding a second study performed in 670 native coronary artery lesions treated with Cypher stents, the IVUS cut-offs that best predicted angiographic restenosis were an MSA of 5.5 mm² and a stent length of 40 mm (Sonoda, *et al.*, 2004). Therefore, at least for the Cypher MSA values between 5.0 and 5.5 mm² is the threshold that should identify stent that are prone to restenosis.

Interestingly, IVUS data showed that first generation stent rarely achieve the nominal area, with 66±17% of predicted MSA being the average value (Mintz & Weissman, 2006).

These findings support the concept that an imaging modality capable of measuring cross-sectional stent area can further decrease DES failure. Obviously OCT, with its high resolution can accomplish this task very well and, as an added information can identify even the smallest degree of strut malapposition, which can be misdiagnosed by IVUS. Malapposition is potentially a cause of late restenosis, due to the fact that the non adhering struts to the vessel wall cannot appropriately elute the drug. However, this finding was found to have a limited role in the process of restenosis, as shown by IVUS data.

Undoubtedly OCT could become the most useful technique to guide DES positioning if post-deployment findings will be critical in preventing thrombosis.

Apart from the risk of late thrombosis, which is now an issue for DES, the vast majority of thromboses occur in the acute and sub-acute phase, affecting both bare and DES (Wijns, 2009), (Cook & Windecker, 2009).

A final look after DES interventions with OCT should be done to address under-expansion that is rather common in presence of calcified vessels and sometimes difficult to document by angiography. Under-expansion is simply diagnosed by measuring the stent minimal lumen area, which is a well known parameter related to stent thrombosis, and adopting the most used IVUS criterion for optimal stent expansion, that is the comparison between minimal stent lumen areas with reference ones (de Jaegere, *et al.*, 1998).

The ability of OCT to directly identify malapposition, uneven stent strut distribution or intra-stent small thrombotic formations with its high resolution, make the technique a very attractive approach to prevent thrombosis. Malapposition still has an uncertain clinical significance but it is intuitive that a complete apposition of equi-spaced stent struts is an important requisite to reduce thrombogenicity (Takebayashi, *et al.*, 2004), (Otake, *et al.*, 2009). Malapposition can be misdiagnosed by IVUS and is easily visualized by OCT. Malapposition can contribute to stent thrombosis with different mechanism. It may favor thrombus formation by reducing blood flow and allowing fibrin and platelet deposition. Also, persistence of acute and late-acquired malapposition is associated with less neointimal hyperplasia and reduced re-endothelialisation, which promote platelet adhesion, and subsequent thrombotic stent occlusion.

Despite this rationale IVUS data failed to show a link between malapposition and risk of major cardiac event (Alfonso, *et al.*, 2007), (Hoffmann, *et al.*, 2008). A possible cause for this failure may be associated with the fact that IVUS studies detected a surprisingly small number of malapposed stents (less than 7.2%) using the IVUS derived criterion of at least 1 malapposed strut. The proportion of malapposed struts, addressed by OCT is much higher, even after optimal high pressure post-dilatation. In particular, malapposition is particularly evident in regions of stent overlap (Tanigawa, Barlis, Dimopoulos, & Di Mario, 2008) after deployment of DES or long stents and in type C lesions (Tanigawa, Barlis, Dimopoulos, & Di Mario, 2008), (Tanigawa, Barlis, Dimopoulos, Dalby, Moore, & Di Mario, 2009), (Kyono, *et al.*, 2010), (Kubo, *et al.*, 2008).

OCT is capable of detecting very small thrombotic depositions on stent struts, a common finding in patients with acute coronary syndromes after stenting of the culprit lesions (Prati, *et al.*, 2010). Although the clinical significance of this finding is still unknown, it is reasonable to hypothesize that the presence of thrombus after stenting elevates the risk for acute and sub-acute stent thrombosis. This may also influence the decision to use adjuvant pharmacological therapies including glycoprotein IIb/IIIa receptor antagonists at time of stenting. Di Giorgio et al studied 19 patients with ACS treated with stenting. Despite the achievement of an optimal angiographic result OCT showed some thrombus prolapsed in all. The mean intra-stent thrombus was in 4.5±3.1% whilst the percentage of thrombus area in the cross section with most severe narrowing was 19.4% ± 8.1%. Thrombus burden was significantly reduced after additional prolonged inflation with the above mentioned mean values being reduced to 3.9±2.1 and 13.9±7.1 respectively (submitted data).

Other factors such as incomplete coverage of stents struts at follow-up, uneven stent strut distribution and symmetry index may play a role in the genesis of stent thrombosis (Gonzalo, *et al.*, 2009). All of them are easily addressed by OCT and the last two factors can be assessed at the post-intervention study, possibly providing

Figure 3. After stenting of a culprit lesion OCT revealed thrombus prolapse encroaching the lumen

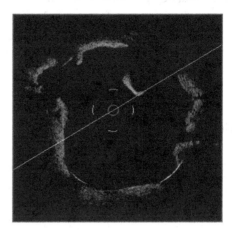

operators with adjunctive information on the propensity of stent toward acute-sub-acute and possibly late thrombosis.

Initial data on the application of OCT criteria for stent positioning were provided by Imola et al (Imola, *et al.*, 2010). Post-intervention FD-OCT

Figure 4. Lower panel: Angiography shows a good result after of LMCA-LAD stenting.

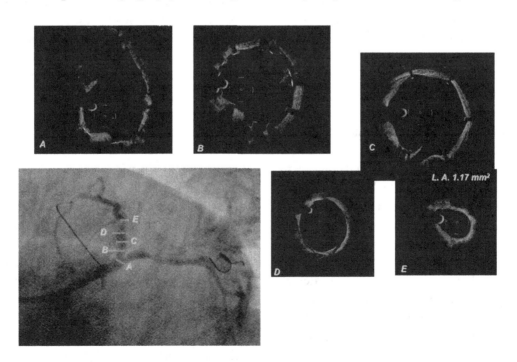

was performed in 74 patients to verify the adequacy of stent deployment and absence of vessel injury at reference sites. In total 113 deployed stents were imaged with OCT. Thirty-eight (33.6%) were chromium-cobaltium stents, whilst 75 (66.4%) were DES.

OCT findings led to additional interventions in 24 out of 74 patients (32%): 15 had further balloon inflations, 9 had additional stent deployment whilst 2 had both treatments.

The additional balloon inflations were done to: correct a significant malapposition (1 case), to treat a significant tissue prolapse (4 cases), to treat under-expansion (3 cases) and for the presence of multiple criteria (7 cases). In all 9 cases who received an additional stent, OCT showed a significant dissection at stent edges. Lastly, in two cases both further balloon expansion and stent deployment were performed due to presence of dissection and underexpansion in one case and dissection and malapposition in the second one.

Clinical follow up was obtained in 88 patients with a mean duration of 4.6±3.2 months. The minimal duration of follow-up was 1 month. There were no death, acute myocardial infarctions and cases of certain, probable or possible stent thrombosis. Three patients had a new occurrence of chest pain and two of them underwent revascularization, due to occurrence of restenosis, CABG was done in one case and re-PTCA in the other.

The main limitation of OCT resides in the inability to measure plaque burden whose thickness exceeds 1.3-1.5 mm. This may have some clinical implications as the most accreditated criterion to identify reference segments by IVUS is a plaque burden less than 40%. This definition derives from the IVUS finding that a plaque burden greater than 40% at stent margin represents a risk factor for late restenosis and thrombosis (Okabe, *et al.*, 2007). This draw-back requires new strategies to be applied to OCT guided intervention with attention to be paid to the luminal assessment of treated arteries, according to the concept that optimal lumen enlargement should have a key role

to improve outcome after intervention (Mintz & Weissman, 2006), (Park, *et al.*, 2009).

This concept is further corroborated by the recent finding that the physiologic assessment of lesion severity by means of fractional flow reserve can impact on patient clinical outcome (Tonino, De Bruyne, & Pijls, 2009). Reduction in lumen areas, presence of flaps due to plaque rupture capable of reducing flow, or thrombotic formations encroaching on the lumen, are probably the only morphological findings that can affect coronary flow, while plaque burden per se and vessel remodelling should not interfere with coronary rheology.

The use of OCT for guidance of interventional procedures must be done according to a new philosophy, that requires utmost attention at the luminal findings provided by OCT. OCT is capable of identifying the plaque-lumen contour at a very high resolution and its use should be restricted to the assessment of luminal areas, based on the concept that only luminal reduction and not the increase in plaque dimension can cause flow impairment. Obviously the same concept can be applied to post-intervention, and in particular to post-stenting assessment; presence of or reduction of lumen areas in the stented segments or at stent margins due to flow limiting dissection, lesion prolapse or large plaque burden, can affect the clinical outcome.

The inability of OCT to quantify the plaque burden does not allow an accurate selection of stent size and diameter. In an OCT guided approach these information may be obtained by angiography, or alternatively will be based on OCT luminal assessment. An OCT fast final look will have a critical role in the procedure guidance. Future studies will clarify whether this major limitation of OCT will be offset by the extraordinary definition of the stent surface, provided by the technique.

Most of the IVUS guided criteria for stent expansion used at the time of BMS, including the OPTICUS (Mudra, *et al.*, 2001) and AVID criteria (Gerber & Colombo, 2008), and the cut-off IVUS thresholds predictive of late stent failure in the DES era are based on a comparison with the lumen area in the reference segments and are easily obtained with OCT.

OCT has also an easier application for treatment of late in-stent restenosis because the strong reflective power of the stent struts allow their detection though thick layers of hyperplasia, allowing optimal sizing of high pressure balloons to correct under-expansion and of cutting balloons to deeply score up to the level of the previously implanted stent the intimal hyperplasia, when restenosis is mainly due to excessive proliferation.

After all blood flows on the endothelial surface, thus we will soon know if "high definition surfing" of the endothelium or of the stent immediately after deployment, is of critical importance or just a good exercise.

REFERENCES

Alfonso, F., Suárez, A., Pérez-Vizcayno, M., Moreno, R., Escaned, J., & Bañuelos, C. (2007). Intravascular ultrasound findings during episodes of drug-eluting stent thrombosis. *Journal of the American College of Cardiology, 50,* 2095–2097. doi:10.1016/j.jacc.2007.08.015

Barlis, P., Gonzalo, N., Di Mario, C., Prati, F., Buellesfeld, L., & Rieber, J. (2009). A multicentre evaluation of the safety intracoronary optical coherence tomography. *EuroInterv, 5,* 90–95. doi:10.4244/EIJV5I1A14

Bezerra, H., Costa, M., Guagliumi, G., Rollins, A., & Simon, D. (2009). Intracoronary optical coherence tomography: a comprehensive review clinical and research applications. *J Am Coll Cardiol Intv, 2,* 1035–1046.

Capodanno, D., Prati, F., Pawlowsky, T., Cera, M., La Manna, A., & Albertucci, M. (2009). Comparison of optical coherence tomography and intravascular ultrasound for the assessment of in-stent tissue coverage after stent implantation. *EuroInterv, 5,* 538–543. doi:10.4244/EIJV5I5A88

Colombo, A., Hall, P., Nakamura, S., Almagor, Y., Maiello, L., & Martini, G. (1995). Intracoronary stenting without anticoagulation accomplished with intravascular ultrasound guidance. *Circulation, 91,* 1676–1688.

Cook, S., & Windecker, S. (2009). Early stent thrombosis: Past, present, and future. *Circulation, 119,* 657–659. doi:10.1161/CIRCULATIONAHA.108.842757

de Jaegere, P., Mudra, H., Figulla, H., Almagor, Y., Doucet, S., & Penn, I. (1998). Intravascular ultrasound-guided optimized stent deployment. Immediate and 6 months clinical and angiographic results from the Multicenter Ultrasound Stenting in Coronaries Study (MUSIC Study). *European Heart Journal, 19,* 1214–1223. doi:10.1053/euhj.1998.1012

Gerber, R., & Colombo, A. (2008). Does IVUS guidance of coronary interventions affect outcome? A prime example of the failure of randomized clinical trials. *Catheterization and Cardiovascular Interventions, 71,* 646–654. doi:10.1002/ccd.21489

Goldberg, S., Colombo, A., Nakamura, S., Almagor, Y., Maiello, L., & Tobis, J. (1994). Benefit of intracoronary ultrasound in the deployment of Palmaz– Schatz stents. *Journal of the American College of Cardiology, 24,* 996–1003. doi:10.1016/0735-1097(94)90861-3

Gonzalo, N., Barlis, P., Serruys, P., Garcia-Garcia, H., Onuma, Y., & Ligthart, J. (2009). Incomplete stent apposition and delayed tissue coverage are more frequent in drug-eluting stents implanted during primary percutaneous coronary intervention for ST-segment elevation myocardial infarction than in drug-eluting stents implanted for stable/un. *J Am Coll Cardiol Intv, 2,* 445–452.

Guagliumi, G., & Sirbu, V. (2008). Optical coherence tomography: High resolution intravascular imaging to evaluate vascular healing after coronary stenting. *Cath & Cardiovasc Int, 72,* 237–247. doi:10.1002/ccd.21606

Hoffmann, R., Morice, M., Moses, J., Fitzgerald, P., Mauri, L., & Breithardt, G. (2008). Impact of late incomplete stent apposition after sirolimus-eluting stent implantation on 4-year clinical events: Intravascular ultrasound analysis from the multicentre, randomised, RAVEL, E-SIRIUS and SIRIUS trials. *Heart (British Cardiac Society)*, *94*, 322–328. doi:10.1136/hrt.2007.120154

Imola, F., Mallus, M., Ramazzotti, V., Manzoli, A., Pappalardo, A., & Di Giorgio, A. (2010). Safety and feasibility of frequency domain optical co-herence tomography to guide decision making in percutaneous coronary intervention. *EuroInterv*, *6*, 575–581. doi:10.4244/EIJV6I5A97

Jang, I., Tearney, G., MacNeill, B., Takano, M., Moselewski, F., & Iftima, N. (2005). In vivo characterization of coronary atherosclerotic plaque by use of Optical Coherence Tomography. *Circulation*, *111*, 1551–1555. doi:10.1161/01.CIR.0000159354.43778.69

Kubo, T., Imanishi, T., Kitabata, H., Kuroi, A., Ueno, S., & Yamano, T. (2008). Comparison of vascular response after sirolimus-eluting stent implantation between patients with unstable and stable angina pectoris: a serial optical tomography study. *J Am Coll Cardiol Img*, *1*, 475–484.

Kyono, H., Guagliumi, G., Sirbu, V., Rosenthal, N., Tahara, S., & Musumeci, G. (2010). Optical coherence tomography strut level analysis of drug eluting stents in human coronary bifurcations. *EuroInterv*, *6*, 69–77. doi:10.4244/EIJV6I1A11

Mintz, G., Nissen, S., & Anderson, W. (2001). ACC clinical expert consensus document on standards for the acquisition, measurement and reporting of intravascular ultrasound studies: A report of the American College of Cardiology Task Force on Clinical Expert Consensus Documents (Committee to Develop. *Journal of the American College of Cardiology*, *37*, 1478–1492. doi:10.1016/S0735-1097(01)01175-5

Mintz, G., & Weissman, N. (2006). Intravascular ultrasound in the drug-eluting stent era. *Journal of the American College of Cardiology*, *48*, 421–429. doi:10.1016/j.jacc.2006.04.068

Mudra, H., Di Mario, C., de Jaegere, P., Figulla, H., Macaya, C., & Zahn, R. (2001). Randomized comparison of coronary stent implantation under ultrasound or angiographic guidance to reduce stent restenosis (OPTICUS study). *Circulation*, *104*, 1343–1349. doi:10.1161/hc3701.096064

Okabe, T., Mintz, G., Ashesh, N., Roy, P., Hong, Y., & Smith, K. (2007). Intravascular ultrasound parameters associated with stent thrombosis after drug-eluting stent deployment. *J Am Coll Cardiol Intv*, *100*, 615–620.

Otake, H., Shite, J., Ako, J., Shinke, T., Tanino, Y., & Ogasawara, D. (2009). Local determinants of thrombus formation following sirolimus-eluting stent implantation assessed by Optical Coherence Tomography. *J Am Coll Cardiol Intv*, *2*, 459–466.

Park, S., Kim, Y., Park, D., Lee, S., Kim, W., & Suh, J. (2009). Impact of intravascular ultrasound guidance on long-term mortality in stenting for unprotected left main coronary artery stenosis. *Circ Cardiovasc Interv*, *3*, 167–177. doi:10.1161/CIRCINTERVENTIONS.108.799494

Prati, F., Cera, M., Ramazzotti, V., Imola, F., Giudice, R., & Albertucci, M. (2007). Safety and feasibility of a new non-occlusive technique for facilitated intracoronary optical coherence tomography (OCT) acquisition in various clinical and anatomical scenarios. *EuroInterv*, *3*, 365–370. doi:10.4244/EIJV3I3A66

Prati, F., Cera, M., Ramazzotti, V., Imola, F., Giudice, R., & Giudice, M. (2008). From bench to bedside: A novel technique to acquire OCT images. *Circulation Journal*, *72*, 839–843. doi:10.1253/circj.72.839

Prati, F., Regar, E., Mintz, G., Arbustini, A., Di Mario, C., & Jang, I. (2010). Expert review document on methodology and clinical applications of OCT. Physical principles, methodology of image acquisition and clinical application for assessment of coronary arteries and atherosclerosis. *European Heart Journal, 31*, 401–415. doi:10.1093/eurheartj/ehp433

Roy, P., Steinberg, D., Sushinsky, S., Okabe, T., Pinto, S. T., & Kaneshige, K. (2008). The potential clinical utility of intravascular ultrasound guidance in patients undergoing percutaneous coronary intervention with drug-eluting stents. *European Heart Journal, 29*, 1851–1857. doi:10.1093/eurheartj/ehn249

Serruys, W., & Di Mario, C. (1995). Who was thrombogenic: The stent or the doctor? *Circulation, 91*, 1891–1893.

Sonoda, S., Morino, Y., Ako, J., Terashima, M., Hassan, A., & Bonneau, H. (2004). Impact of final stent dimensions on long-term results following sirolimus-eluting stent implantation: Serial intravascular ultrasound analysis from the SIRIUS trial. *Journal of the American College of Cardiology, 43*, 1959–1963. doi:10.1016/j.jacc.2004.01.044

Spanos, V., Stankovic, G., Tobis, A., & Colombo, A. (2003). The challenge of in-stent restenosis: Insights from intravascular ultrasound. *European Heart Journal, 24*, 138–150. doi:10.1016/S0195-668X(02)00418-9

Takarada, S., Imanishi, T., Liu, Y., Ikejima, H., Tsujioka, H., & Kuroi, A. (2010). Advantage of next-generation frequency-domain optical coherence tomography compared with conventional time-domain system in the assessment of coronary lesion. *Catheterization and Cardiovascular Interventions, 75*, 202–206. doi:10.1002/ccd.22273

Takebayashi, H., Mintz, G., Carlier, S., Kobayashi, Y., Fujii, K., & Yasuda, T. (2004). Non-uniform strut distribution correlates with more neointimal hyperplasia after sirolimus-eluting stent implantation. *Circulation, 110*, 3430–3434. doi:10.1161/01.CIR.0000148371.53174.05

Tanigawa, J., Barlis, P., & Di Mario, C. (2007). Intravascular optical coherence tomography: Optimisation of image acquisition and quantitative assessment of stent strut apposition. *EuroInterv, 3*, 128–136.

Tanigawa, J., Barlis, P., Dimopoulos, K., Dalby, M., Moore, P., & Di Mario, C. (2009). The influence of strut thickness and cell design on immediate apposition of drug-eluting stents assessed by optical coherence tomography. *International Journal of Cardiology, 134*, 180–188. doi:10.1016/j.ijcard.2008.05.069

Tanigawa, J., Barlis, P., Dimopoulos, K., & Di Mario, C. (2008). Optical coherence tomography to assess malapposition in overlapping drug-eluting stents. *EuroInterv, 3*, 580–583. doi:10.4244/EIJV3I5A104

Tearney, G., Waxman, S., Shishkov, M., Vakoc, B., Suter, M., & Freilich, M. (2008). Three-dimensional coronary artery microscopy by intracoronary Optical Frequency Domain Imaging. *J Am Coll Cardiol Img, 1*, 752–761.

Tonino, P., De Bruyne, B., & Pijls, N. (2009). Fractional flow reserve versus angiography for guiding percutaneous coronary intervention for the FAME study investigators. *The New England Journal of Medicine, 360*, 213–224. doi:10.1056/NEJMoa0807611

Wijns, W. (2009). Late stent thrombosis after drug-eluting stent: Seeing is understanding. *Circulation, 120*, 364–365. doi:10.1161/CIRCULATIONAHA.109.882001

Chapter 13
Research Utility of Optical Coherence Tomography (OCT)

Konstantinos Toutouzas
Athens Medical School, Greece

Antonios Karanasos
Athens Medical School, Greece

Christodoulos Stefanadis
Athens Medical School, Greece

ABSTRACT

Within this chapter, the research utility of OCT is detailed. Issues like the potential of OCT for plaque characterization are covered. Additionally, a comparative evaluation of OCT with other invasive imaging techniques, as far as plaque components identification is concerned, is attempted. Finally, the role of OCT for the evaluation of plaque progression is discussed as well as its part in the future research arena.

INTRODUCTION

Despite progress in pharmacological and interventional treatment, acute coronary syndromes (ACS) remain one of the leading causes of mortality and morbidity. In the era of optical medical therapy and advanced revascularization strategies, mortality after ACS can be as high as 13% (Savonitto, Ardissino, & Granger, 1999), (Volmink, Newton, Hicks, Sleight, Fowler, & Neil, 1998). The majority of ACS are attributed to acute thrombosis associated with certain pathologies (plaque rupture, plaque erosion, calcified nodules) (Virmani, Burke,

DOI: 10.4018/978-1-61350-095-8.ch013

Farb, & Kolodgie, 2006). Furthermore, it has been shown recently that certain morphological features are associated with the risk of developing a new ACS in a non-culprit lesion after coronary intervention for ACS. Thus, in vivo imaging of plaque morphology has been a subject of intense research investigation.

Optical coherence tomography (OCT) has recently emerged as a high-resolution ($\approx 15\mu m$) intracoronary imaging modality with the ability to differentiate between various plaque morphologies and provide quantitative measurements of vessel dimensions and plaque components. Two major limitations, however, associated with OCT are 1) the need to temporarily displace blood flow during acquisition and 2) the limited penetration of OCT (1.5-2.0 mm), which makes the evaluation of the deeper structures of the plaque difficult. The first limitation is diminished by the introduction of the non-occlusive image acquisition method and more recently of the second-generation optical Fourier-domain imaging (OFDI) systems, which have improved the safety and efficacy of image acquisition (Takarada, Imanishi, & Liu, 2010). As far as the second limitation is concerned, the increased resolution balances the limited penetration, given that most features of plaque vulnerability are located superficially in the plaque. Consequently, OCT is a method that can provide useful insights into atheromatosis and constitutes a valuable research tool (Prati, Regar, & Mintz, 2010). Therefore, in this chapter we are going to analyze the potential of OCT for plaque characterization compared to histology or other imaging methods, recapitalize the insights gained from OCT studies, review the ability of OCT for research in stent technology and discuss the future perspectives of OCT for atheromatosis research.

POTENTIAL OF OCT FOR PLAQUE CHARACTERIZATION

A recent pathologic classification of coronary lesions (Virmani, Kolodgie, Burke, Farb, & Schwartz, 2000) distinguishes between non-atherosclerotic intimal lesions and progressive atherosclerotic lesions. The first category consists of intimal thickening and intimal xanthomas, while the latter consists of pathological intimal thickening, fibrous cap atheroma with thin or thick cap, and fibrocalcific plaque. The morphologies of the second category are prone to acute thrombosis amenable to one of three pathological mechanisms: plaque rupture, plaque erosion and calcified nodule. OCT has the potential of imaging all of the aforementioned morphologies and is also capable of imaging thrombosis and distinguishing between fibrin-rich and platelet-rich thrombus.

Studies performed in *ex vivo* specimens from human cadavers or animal studies have demonstrated that OCT is capable of imaging non-atherosclerotic intimal lesions and of performing precise measurements of the intimal and medial thickness. By the high-resolution of OCT it is possible to overcome the limitations of intravascular ultrasound (IVUS), which cannot clearly distinguish between the intimal and the medial layer of the coronary arterial wall, and thus assess intimal thickening or accumulation of lipid in the intima (Jang, Bouma, & Kang, 2002). Therefore, OCT has a much greater sensitivity and specificity for the detection of normal artery wall than IVUS (91/88 versus 55/79) (Rieber, Meissner, & Babaryka, 2006). A comparative study between OCT and integrated backscatter IVUS (IB-IVUS) has shown that despite both methods have excellent specificity for the detection of intimal hyperplasia (100% versus 99%), OCT is a much more sensitive method (86% versus 67%) (Kawasaki, Bouma, & Bressner, 2006). Experiments in specimens from rabbit carotid arteries have shown that OCT has high sensitivity and specificity (80% and 95% respectively) in detecting Stary III lesions, which correspond to intimal xanthomas (Zimarino, Prati, & Stabile, 2007). Furthermore, by OCT it is feasible to perform exact measurements of intimal thickness with excellent agreement with the histology (mean difference 0.01±0.04 mm, r=0.98), and the measurements of intimal-medial thickness are more accurate than the corresponding measurements performed by IVUS (Kume, Akasaka, & Kawamoto, 2005).

Additionally, OCT has excellent potential for atherosclerotic lesion characterization as it yields good diagnostic accuracy for fibrous plaques, lipid-rich plaques (fibroatheromas), and fiblocalcific plaques (Prati, Regar, & Mintz, 2010), (Yabushita, Bouma, & Houser, 2002) (Figure 1). Various studies that have examined the potential of OCT for plaque characterization on coronary specimens from human cadavers using histology as the golden standard are listed in Table 1 (Rieber,

Figure 1. Optical coherence tomography images demonstrating (A) fibrous plaque, (B) eccentric lipid-rich plaque with thin fibrous cap, and (C) fibrocalcific plaque.

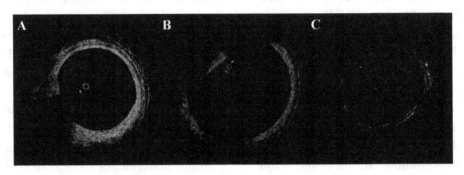

Table 1. Sensitivity and specificity of optical coherence tomography for detection of fibrous, lipid-rich and fibrocalcific plaque

	Fibrous plaque		Lipid-rich plaque		Fibrocalcific plaque	
	Sensitivity	Specificity	Sensitivity	Specificity	Sensitivity	Specificity
(Yabushita, Bouma, & Houser, 2002)	71-79	97-98	90-94	90-92	95-96	97
(Manfrini, Mont, & Leone, 2006)	83	82	45	83	68	76
(Kawasaki, Bouma, & Bressner, 2006)	98	94	95	98	100	100
(Rieber, Meissner, & Babaryka, 2006)	64	88	77	94	67	97
(Kume, Okura, & Kawamoto, 2008)	N/A	N/A	77	75	N/A	N/A

Meissner, & Babaryka, 2006), (Kawasaki, Bouma, & Bressner, 2006), (Yabushita, Bouma, & Houser, 2002), (Kume, Okura, & Kawamoto, Relationship between coronary remodeling and plaque characterization in patients without clinical evidence of coronary artery disease, 2008), (Manfrini, Mont, & Leone, 2006). All studies suggest that OCT has very good sensitivity and specificity for the detection of fibrous and fibrocalcific plaques, but there is controversy concerning the ability of OCT to identify lipid-rich plaques. This contradiction among the trials can be attributed to the low penetration of the OCT signal that can lead to poor visualization of a deeply located lipid-pool and

to the fact that the necrotic core composition is inconsistent with varying quantities of calcium, necrotic debris and lipids (Manfrini, Mont, & Leone, 2006). Despite this discrepancy among the trials about the ability of OCT to identify lipid-rich plaques, it is worth noting that OCT study has high reproducibility in the assessment of plaque morphology, as in the majority of the trials both the inter-observer and intra-observer variability of OCT assessment were low.

Apart from plaque characterization, OCT is capable of performing quantitative measurements of plaque components. OCT can perform precise measurements of cap thickness on the area above a lipid pool, having excellent correlation with the histologic measurements (Cilingiroglu, Oh, & Sugunan, 2006), (Kume, Akasaka, & Kawamoto, 2006). As a result, OCT has been shown to have good diagnostic accuracy for the detection of thin-cap atheromas (Kume, Okura, & Kawamoto, 2008), (Kume, Okura, & Yamada, 2009). Furthermore, by OCT, semi-quantitative measurements of lipid content can be performed, by measuring the quadrants of the lipid content in the cross-sectional image. Another feature that has been proposed as suggestive of plaque instability is the infiltration of the fibrous cap. It has been suggested that measurement of signal intensity values by OCT can enable the recognition of fibrous cap areas that are rich in macrophages, however the algorithm used is operator-dependent as it requires a proper selection of a region to be analyzed (Tearney, Yabushita, & Houser, 2003). Finally, identification of microcalcifications inside lipid pools –a feature suggested as a characteristic of plaque instability- is feasible by OCT, however further validation is required (Cilingiroglu, Oh, & Sugunan, 2006).

One of the major advantages of OCT is that it allows the identification of the complicated plaques that are typically characterized by the presence of thrombus. In cadaver studies, OCT had 100% sensitivity and specificity for the detection of thrombus (Manfrini, Mont, & Leone, 2006). Furthermore OCT is able to distinguish between red and white thrombus (Kume, Akasaka, & Kawamoto, 2006). An in vivo study in ACS has shown that OCT is the best imaging method for the detection of thrombus and plaque rupture, while there has been speculation that OCT is also able to detect plaque erosion (Kubo, Imanishi, & Takarada, 2007). It should be noted, however, that the presence of large thrombus burden, especially red thrombus, could lead to underestimation of the incidence of plaque rupture (Prati, Regar, & Mintz, 2010). Finally, with the increased resolution of OCT, it is possible to identify rare causes of ACS, such as calcified nodules (Figure 2).

Figure 2. Second generation optical coherence tomography image demonstrating a calcified nodule at 6 o'clock

COMPARATIVE EVALUATION WITH OTHER INVASIVE IMAGING METHODS AND COMBINED ASSESSMENT OF PLAQUE CHARACTERISTICS

The increased resolution of OCT allows for more detailed characterization of superficial morphological features of the plaque; however it comes at a cost of limited penetration that makes the assessment of deeper structures difficult. Taking that into account, it is worth reviewing the comparison of OCT with other invasive imaging methods used for plaque characterization. The first studies of comparative evaluation of OCT for plaque characterization were performed with IVUS, considered at the time the "golden standard" for plaque imaging. A pilot study comparing OCT and IVUS in an in-vivo population pointed out two major advantages of OCT: a) precise measurement of the thickness of the fibrous cap, and b) assessment of structures located behind superficial macrocalcification (Jang, Bouma, & Kang, 2002). Furthermore, OCT could identify the internal and the external elastic laminae in the majority of the cases, and detected more cases of intimal hyperplasia and lipid-rich plaques than IVUS (Jang, Bouma, & Kang, 2002). In post-mortem studies OCT has been shown to have superior sensitivity and specificity than IVUS for the detection of all plaque types and especially for the detection of lipid-rich plaque (Rieber, Meissner, & Babaryka, 2006), (Kawasaki, Bouma, & Bressner, 2006), (Kume, Okura, & Kawamoto, 2008). Further in vivo studies have also shown that OCT has greater potential than IVUS for characterizing stable and complicated plaques (Kubo, Imanishi, & Takarada, 2007), (Gonzalo, Serruys, Barlis, Ligthart, Garcia-Garcia, & Regar, 2010), (Low, Kawase, Chan, Tearney, Bouma, & Jang, 2009). All these advantages, however, are partially offset by OCT inability to accurately identify vessel remodeling and measure plaque size, two important features of plaque vulnerability (Jang, Bouma, & Kang, 2002).

Other imaging methods have also been compared to OCT for plaque characterization. Angioscopy, the use of which is restricted to some research centers in Japan, has been shown to be less effective than OCT for characterization of the ruptured plaque in vivo (Kubo, Imanishi, & Takarada, 2007). An in vivo comparison of OCT and angioscopy has shown that the plaque color observed in angioscopy is strongly associated with the thickness of the fibrous cap and not the size of the lipid core (Takano, Jang, & Inami, 2008). Tissue characterization by intravascular ultrasound using radiofrequency data analysis [IVUS radiofrequency data (IVUS-RFD) and IB-IVUS is widely used for plaque characterization. In an in vivo study comparing the potential of OCT and VH-IVUS for plaque characterization, despite an excellent agreement for the detection of calcified plaques, minor discrepancies were present, due to the differences of the imaging methods in resolution and penetration depth, and to the lack of common nomenclature and variation (Gonzalo, Serruys, Barlis, Ligthart, Garcia-Garcia, & Regar,

2010). Studies comparing OCT with IVUS-RFD and IB-IVUS respectively, using histology as the "golden standard" have shown that all methods have similar sensitivity and specificity for the detection of various plaque types, with each method being biased by its own inherent limitations (Kawasaki, Bouma, & Bressner, 2006), (Goderie, van Soest, & Garcia-Garcia, 2010). Interestingly, the combined used of OCT and IVUS-RFD has resulted in slightly better plaque classification (Goderie, van Soest, & Garcia-Garcia, 2010).

The combined use of OCT and IVUS-RFD for plaque characterization has been used in several clinical settings as it combines the excellent resolution of OCT with the increased depth of imaging of IVUS-RFD (Sawada, Shite, & Garcia-Garcia, 2008). In a feasibility study, the combination of OCT and IVUS-RFD resulted in a more accurate characterization of TCFA, by combining the measurement of the fibrous cap thickness by OCT with the amount of the necrotic core by IVUS-RFD (Sawada, Shite, & Garcia-Garcia, 2008). Thin-cap fibroatheromas, as detected by this combination of imaging methods, were associated with lower adiponectin levels in men with stable angina (Sawada, Shite, & Shinke, Low plasma adiponectin levels are associated with presence of thin-cap fibroatheroma in men with stable coronary artery disease, 2009). The combination of OCT and IVUS-RFD was also used by another group for the characterization of plaques located near bifurcations, demonstrating that plaques in the proximal rim of bifurcations had thinner fibrous cap and greater percentage of lipid core (Gonzalo, Garcia-Garcia, & Regar, 2009).

However, the combined use of the two techniques, improves only the morphological characterization of the vulnerable plaque. An ideal combination of methods would allow the simultaneous study of morphological and functional characteristics of the plaque. Our group has demonstrated, by combined used of IVUS and thermography, that plaques with expansive remodeling and ruptured plaques are associated with increased local inflammatory activation, as demonstrated by increased temperature difference (Toutouzas, Synetos, & Stefanadi, 2007). Results from our laboratory also suggest that morphological features derived by OCT, such as thin fibrous cap and increased macrophage concentration in the fibrous cap, are also associated with increased plaque temperature (Toutouzas, Riga, & Drakopoulou, 2009). Furthermore, the development of algorithms capable of detecting plaque deformation (Rogowska, Patel, Fujimoto, & Brezinski, 2004), (van Soest, Mastik, de Jong, & van der Steen, 2007) or calculating shear stress using OCT, would provide an excellent combination of morphological and functional imaging with the use of a single catheter.

INSIGHTS INTO PLAQUE MORPHOLOGY AND PATHOPHYSIOLOGY

Clinical Presentation and Plaque Morphology

There is a large number of studies performed that takes advantage of the potential of OCT for detection of critical elements of plaque vulnerability in order to provide useful insights into the pathophysiology of atheromatosis. Pathological examination of coronary plaques harvested from patients with acute coronary syndromes has revealed that the majority of ruptured plaques are large plaques with expansive remodelling, neovascularization, reduced calcification, great lipid core and thin fibrous cap with macrophage infiltration (Virmani, Burke, Farb, & Kolodgie, 2006). In vivo OCT studies have confirmed that culprit plaques of patients with ACS have greater lipid content, lower fibrous cap thickness, greater macrophage concentration, reduced calcification and increased incidence of plaque rupture and TCFA (Fujii, Masutani, & Okumura, 2008), (Jang, Tearney, & MacNeill, In vivo characterization of

coronary atherosclerotic plaque by use of optical coherence tomography, 2005), (MacNeill, Jang, & Bouma, 2004). Patients with acute myocardial infarction were also associated with greater incidence of thrombus and TCFA in the non-culprit lesion (Fujii, Masutani, & Okumura, 2008), (Kubo, Imanishi, & Kashiwagi, 2010). Coronary artery morphology seems also to be implicated in the pathogenesis of spastic angina. In a study enrolling patients without angiographically evident coronary heart disease, patients suffering from spastic angina, as confirmed by acetylcholine provocation test, had no evidence of calcific or lipid deposits and greater intimal area than patients with normal coronary arteries without evidence of coronary spasm (Morikawa, Uemura, & Ishigami, 2009).

Moreover, morphological differences are not restricted to patients with or without ACS, but are also present between different presentations of acute coronary syndromes. In a study by our group focusing on the morphological differences of ruptured plaques in non-ST-elevation and in ST-elevation myocardial infarction, we have demonstrated that differences in the clinical presentation are due to discrepancies in the morphology of the ruptured plaque (Toutouzas, Karanasos & Tsiamis, 2011). Specifically, ruptured plaques in patients with ST-elevation myocardial infarction have greater cap disruption than ruptured plaques in non-ST-elevation myocardial infarction. Tanaka *et al.* have studied the differences in ruptured plaque morphology in exertion-onset ACS and in rest-onset ACS and have found that plaque rupture in exertion-onset ACS is associated with greater fibrous cap thickness and greater incidence of thrombus and is more often located at the shoulder of the plaque (Tanaka, Imanishi, & Kitabata, 2008). Fascinatingly, in both studies ruptured cap thickness was greater than 65μm in a number of cases, bringing into question the threshold for characterizing a thin cap (Tanaka, Imanishi, & Kitabata, 2008), (Toutouzas, Karanasos & Tsiamis, 2011).

Plaque Morphology and Clinical Characteristics

Another field of research in plaque morphology by OCT is whether specific populations have distinct morphological characteristics. It was found that gender is not a factor affecting plaque morphology, as no significant differences in culprit plaque morphology were found between men and women with coronary heart disease (Chia, Christopher, Takano, Tearney, Bouma, & Jang, 2007). Diabetes as well, does not seem to be associated with plaque morphology, considering that plaque characteristics were similar among diabetics and non-diabetics (Chia, Raffel, Takano, Tearney, Bouma, & Jang, 2008). On the other hand, statin therapy seems to be associated with plaque characteristics. Patients under statin therapy have reduced incidence of plaque rupture compared to statin-naïve patients and there is a strong trend towards increased cap thickness in this population (Chia, Raffel, Takano, Tearney, Bouma, & Jang, 2008). Furthermore, in a prospective study with three-month follow-up OCT examination, statin therapy increased the thickness of the fibrous cap in the culprit lesion of patients with stable angina, an effect noticed in plaques with thin fibrous cap, but not in plaques with thick fibrous cap (Takarada, Imanishi, & Kubo, 2009).

Localization of Plaques with High-Risk Morphology

OCT has also contributed to the knowledge about the location of vulnerable plaques. It is known that the majority of coronary syndromes are attributed to plaques located near the coronary ostium (Wang, Normand, Mauri, & Kuntz, 2004). In a post-mortem study with the use of histology and OCT, 70% of the 30 TCFAs found in 108 major epicardial arteries were located in the first 30 mm, whereas further along the vessels the frequency was significantly lower (Kume, Okura, & Yamada, 2009). An in vivo three-vessel OCT study in patients with stable angina and acute coronary syndromes showed that 76% of the TCFAs in the left anterior descending artery (LAD) were located between 0 and 30 mm from the LAD ostium, while in the other arteries TCFAs were evenly distributed throughout the entire coronary length (Fujii, Kawasaki, & Masutani, 2010). In the same study, the clustering of the TCFAs was similar in culprit segments as compared with nonculprit segments (Fujii, Kawasaki, & Masutani, 2010). Moreover, examination by OCT of the culprit lesion in patients with ACS has shown that culprit lesion TCFAs are located in the proximal segment of the LAD, while the distribution is even at the right coronary artery (RCA) (Tanaka, Imanishi, & Kitabata, 2008). These studies come into agreement with results from our group showing that culprit lesions of patients with ACS located more proximally have thinner fibrous cap and increased incidence of plaque rupture (Karanasos, Toutouzas, & Riga, 2010).

Plaque Characteristics and Outcome of Thrombolysis

Thus, it is established that pharmacologic agents can affect plaque morphology. However, it is possible that plaque morphology is associated with the outcome of various therapies. We have shown recently in a multicentre study that plaques with high-risk characteristics are associated with impaired flow following thrombolytic administration (Toutouzas, Tsiamis, & Karanasos, 2010). The thickness of the fibrous cap, plaque rupture and lipid-rich plaque were associated with low TIMI flow grade after thrombolysis, indicating that vulnerable plaque morphology can affect the outcome of thrombolysis.

Plaque Morphology and Markers of Systemic Inflammation

OCT has also been used as a tool for assessing the relation between plaque morphology and markers of systemic inflammation. Raffel *et al.* have examined the association between morphological characteristics of the culprit lesion, such as the thickness of the fibrous cap and the infiltration of the cap by macrophages, and a systemic marker of inflammation, as is the white blood cell count (Raffel, Tearney, Gauthier, Halpern, Bouma, & Jang, 2007). Culprit plaques with evidence of "vulnerability" –thin fibrous cap and high concentration of macrophages in the cap- were associated with evidence of systemic inflammation, as assessed by the white blood cell count. Additionally, high-sensitivity C-reactive protein (hs-CRP), a controversial marker of vascular inflammation has been linked with high-risk morphological characteristics. In a number of studies, coronary heart disease patients with TCFA had higher levels of hs-CRP than patients without TCFA (Tanaka, Imanishi, & Kitabata, 2008), (Kashiwagi, Tanaka, & Kitabata, 2009), (Li, Fu, & Shi, 2010). Hs-CRP has also been proposed as an independent predictor of the presence of multiple TCFAs in the coronary tree (Fujii, Masutani, & Okumura, 2008).

Furthermore, in a study assessing the association of various inflammatory biomarkers with the morphological characteristics of the culprit lesion in patients with coronary artery disease, a hs-CRP cut-off of 1.66 mg/L was the only significant independent predictor of TCFA, with a sensitivity of 96% and specificity of 90% in the ROC curve analysis (Li, Fu, & Shi, 2010). In the same study, plasma levels of hs-CRP as well as other inflammatory markers (interleukin-18, tumor necrosis factor α, and white blood cell count) had a significant inverse linear correlation with fibrous cap thickness (natural logarithm of fibrous cap thickness) and had also a trend toward higher levels with increasing plaque lipid content (the highest number of quadrants with lipid pools displaying lipid-rich plaque appearance). No association existed however for any inflammatory marker with the incidence of thrombus and calcium, and only levels of hs-CRP and white blood cell count

were significantly associated with the incidence of plaque rupture.

Conversely, in a study with multi-vessel examination by combined used of OCT and IVUS-RFD in men with stable coronary disease, TCFA was not associated with plasma levels of hs-CRP nor interleukin 6(Sawada, Shite, & Shinke, 2009). However, the incidence of TCFA was independently associated with the plasma concentration of adiponectin (Sawada, Shite, & Shinke, 2009). In particular, patients with TCFA had lower levels of adiponectin than patients without TCFA, and moreover the levels of adiponectin in patients with multi-vessel TCFA were significantly lower than in patients with single-vessel TCFA. Additionally, plaque rupture by OCT in patients with unstable angina was found by another group to be associated with increased plasma levels of fractalkine, a chemokine, and increased populations of inflammatory cells expressing its receptor CX3CR1 (Ikejima, Imanishi, & Tsujioka, 2010). All the aforementioned observations collectively underscore the association of systemic inflammation with high-risk plaque morphology, as assessed by OCT, but warrant further investigation as they have been made in small samples and have not been evaluated prospectively.

EVALUATION OF PLAQUE PROGRESSION

One major future goal of invasive plaque imaging would be the identification of plaques that are in high risk of causing an acute coronary syndrome in the future. We know today that plaques with great stenosis are not necessarily the plaques that are more prone to disrupt and initiate thrombosis. As mentioned above, post-mortem studies have pointed out specific morphological characteristics associated with plaque rupture and thrombosis. These characteristics include eccentric remodeling, large plaque size with a great necrotic core, thin fibrous cap, infiltration of the cap by inflammatory cells, reduced or spotty calcification and increased neovascularization. However, at the moment there is no definite proof that plaques with such morphology identified in vivo will rupture and cause acute coronary syndromes. Angiographic studies have shown that complex angiographic morphology, which has been associated with plaque rupture and thin fibrous cap in the OCT assessment (Karanasos, Toutouzas, & Riga, 2010), is associated with non-culprit lesion progression (Tsiamis, Toutouzas, & Synetos, 2010), (Goldstein, Demetriou, Grines, Pica, Shoukfeh, & O'Neill, 2000), (The PROSPECT authors, 2009). Yet, there is a need for prospective invasive imaging studies that will look into the natural history of atheromatosis and provide evidence concerning which plaques are more probable to cause an acute coronary syndrome in the future.

The PROSPECT trial was the first large trial using invasive imaging with IVUS-RFD that tried to investigate the natural history of non-culprit plaques in patients with acute coronary syndromes (The PROSPECT authors, 2009). The first results showed that non-culprit lesions have almost the same probability to cause an event with the culprit lesions. The independent predictors for a non-culprit lesion event were quantitative factors such as the degree of stenosis and the plaque size, but also the presence of TCFA as identified by IVUS–RFD, providing the first evidence that plaque morphology is associated with clinical outcome. Despite the positive messages from the PROSPECT trial, it should be kept in mind that this study was performed by IVUS-RFD, a method lacking the ability to identify crucial elements of the plaque vulnerability such as the thin fibrous cap. OCT on the other hand, has a very good potential for plaque characterization (Toutouzas, Karanasos, & Stefanadis, 2010), as it can measure fibrous cap thickness and detect lipid-rich plaques, cap infiltration by macrophages and plaques with reduced or spotty calcification near the lumen (Prati, Regar, & Mintz, 2010). Furthermore, the greater potential for identification of plaque rup-

ture and thrombus could answer more questions about the natural history of the ruptured plaque and the role of thrombus in plaque progression. Consequently, the implementation of a prospective study using OCT or combined used of IVUS-RFD and OCT for the assessment of plaque morphology would probably lead to more comprehensive insights into the natural history of atheromatosis.

Apart from natural history studies, OCT can also help in identifying high-risk plaques in studies of prophylactic stenting. The ongoing SECRITT-1 trial (Ramcharitar, Gonzalo, & van Geuns, 2009) has randomized patients with non-flow-limiting plaques with vulnerable morphology by combined use of IVUS-RFD and OCT (thin fibrous cap by OCT and large plaque burden and percentage of necrotic core by IVUS-RFD) to medical therapy or stenting with a dedicated stent tailored to shield vulnerable plaques. The development of new stents dedicated to the treatment of vulnerable plaques by targeting neovascularization (Synetos, Toutouzas, & Drakopoulou, 2010), (Stefanadis, Toutouzas, Stefanadi, Lazaris, Patsouris, & Kipshidze, 2007), (Stefanadis, Toutouzas, Tsiamis, Vavuranakis, Stefanadi, & Kipshidze, 2008) warrants evaluation of the plaque before the intervention and at the follow-up in order to assess the effect of the intervention.

OCT FOR RESEARCH IN STENT TECHNOLOGY

The use of OCT is not restricted to research on the field of plaque morphology, but it also expands to investigation of the vessel response to stenting and plaque modification by the intervention. In particular, OCT can provide useful insights into stent thrombosis, endothelialization of the stents, the mechanisms of restenosis and the follow-up of bioabsorbable stents. IVUS has been used traditionally to assess the effects of stenting on the vessel wall. However, due to the limited resolution of IVUS, features such features as edge dissections, tissue prolapse and residual thrombus were not imaged, so their clinical relevance was unknown. It has been demonstrated that OCT has an ability to detect stent edge dissection (Toutouzas, Vaina, Riga, & Stefanadis, 2009), tissue protrusion, and stent malapposition, at a level that is two to three times better than that of IVUS (Suzuki, Ikeno, & Koizumi, 2008), (Kubo, Imanishi, & Kitabata, 2008). Furthermore, by OCT it is possible to fully assess the type and the extent of the dissection and visualize any concurring tissue prolapse (Gonzalo, Serruys, & Okamura, 2009). (Kubo, Imanishi, & Kitabata, 2008) have demonstrated that differences in the clinical syndrome and plaque morphology are associated with different vessel response post-intervention and at the follow-up. Figure 3 demonstrates an example of a case with plaque rupture pre-stenting and tissue protrusion post-stenting. Additionally, OCT is the best method for assessing the extent and type of the malapposition post-implantation (Radu, Jorgensen, Kelbaek, Helqvist, Skovgaard, & Saunamaki, 2010), and provide insights into the association of malapposition with stent type, plaque morphology and stent overlapping (Kim, Kim, & Kim, 2010), (Tanigawa, Barlis, Dimopoulos, Dalby, Moore, & Di Mario, 2009), (Tanigawa, Barlis, Dimopoulos, & Di Mario, 2008), (Tanigawa, Barlis, & Di Mario, 2008).

Moreover, by OCT we can assess the vessel response to stenting at the follow-up. Incomplete stent coverage and incomplete apposition have been associated with late thrombosis in pathologic studies (Joner, Finn, & Farb, 2006). (Prati, Zimarino, & Stabile, 2008) have shown in an animal model the ability of OCT to visualize stent coverage as well as the association between histological and OCT measurements of neointimal thickness. Consequently, OCT has been used in numerous follow-up studies in order to assess the extent of stent coverage and neointimal thickness, as well as the differences of vessel healing patterns between various types of stents (Fan, Kim, & Lee), (Kim, Jang, & Fan, 2009), (Kim, Kim, & Kim, 2010), (Motreff, Souteyrand, & Levesque, 2009), (Chen, Ma, & Luo, 2008), (Guagliumi, Musumeci, & Sirbu, 2010). It must be noted however that OCT lacks the required resolution to distinguish between true endothelialization and fibrin deposition. Various researchers have also attempted to classify neointimal tissue in a qualitative manner, without having however proven an association between the OCT appearance of neointimal tissue and histological features or clinical events (Suzuki, Kozuma, & Maeno, 2010), (Nagai, Ishibashi-Ueda, & Fujii, 2010), (Takano, Yamamoto, & Inami, 2009), (Habara, Terashima, & Suzuki, 2009), (Gonzalo, Serruys, & Okamura, Optical coherence tomography patterns of stent restenosis, 2009). Finally, OCT examination of stents at follow-up is being used

Figure 3. Optical coherence tomography images of a plaque before (A,B) and after (C) intervention. Figures A and B show a thin cap fibroatheroma and plaque rupture with cavity formation, respectively. Figure C shows tissue protrusion after stenting located at 5 o'clock.

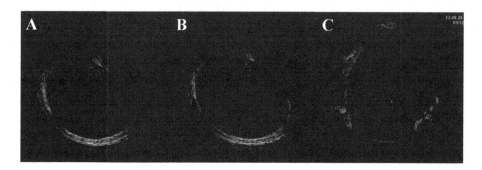

for assessment of incomplete stent apposition, a feature associated with the clinical syndrome (Gonzalo, Barlis, & Serruys, 2009). Follow-up studies (Ozaki, Okumura, & Ismail, 2010) can reveal whether a malapposition was present from the time of stent implantation or it was indeed late stent malapposition (Rathore, Terashima, & Suzuki, 2009), (Bouki, Chatzopoulos, Katsafados, Elaiopoulos, Psychari, & Apostolou, 2009). Finally, stent follow-up study by OCT can also be used in the case of biodegradable stents, and demonstrate the rate of degradation as well as vessel morphology following the degradation (Serruys, Ormiston, & Onuma, 2009), (Ormiston, Serruys, & Regar, 2008), (Pinto, Pakala, Lovec, Tio, & Waksman, 2007), (Pinto, Pakala, & Waksman, 2008).

FUTURE RESEARCH DIRECTIONS

Various technologies are being currently developed and promise to increase the diagnostic potential of OCT. OFDI systems that are already available, have improved the safety and efficacy of image acquisition and have reduced the duration of the examination (Takarada, Imanishi, & Liu, 2010). In addition, edge and strut detection systems with automated quantification of vessel and stent dimensions are being evaluated (Sihan, Botha, & Post, 2009), (Gurmeric, Isguder, Carlier, & Unal, 2009), (Tanimoto, Rodriguez-Granillo, & Barlis, 2008). Tissue characterization algorithms based on the intensity and the attenuation of the OCT signal have been developed to facilitate the efforts for plaque characterization (van Soest, Goderie, & Regar, 2010), (Xu, Schmitt, Carlier, & Virmani, 2008).

Meanwhile, (Tearney, Waxman, & Shishkov, 2008) have made possible the three-dimensional reconstruction of OFDI images by specific software. Finally, several technology improvements such as polarization-sensitive OCT (Oh, Yun, & Vakoc, 2008), (Nadkarni, Bouma, de Boer, & Tearney, 2009), (Kuo, Chou, & Chou, 2007), ultra-high resolution OCT (Wang, Fleming, & Rollins, 2007) and contrast-enhanced OCT (Luo, Marks, Ralston, & Boppart, 2006) promise to improve the visualization of plaque components, while others such as Doppler OCT or OCT elastography (Rogowska, Patel, Fujimoto, & Brezinski, 2004), (van Soest, Mastik, de Jong, & van der Steen, 2007) try to incorporate functional assessment to the morphological study.

CONCLUSION

Optical coherence tomography (OCT) is a new high-resolution method with significant research potential. OCT has very good sensitivity and specificity for coronary plaque characterization, while it can image critical components of plaque vulnerability, such as fibrous cap thickness and infiltration of cap by macrophages, at a cost of limited penetration. Numerous OCT studies have been performed, providing useful insights into the association of plaque morphology with systemic inflammation, clinical presentation and clinical characteristics, as well as into the location of high-risk plaques and their natural history. Furthermore, OCT has expanded our knowledge regarding the vessel response to stenting and can be used for more detailed stent evaluation. Finally, future developments promise further enhancement of the diagnostic potential of OCT for plaque characterization.

REFERENCES

Bouki, K., Chatzopoulos, D., Katsafados, M., Elaiopoulos, D., Psychari, S., & Apostolou, T. (2009). Late acquired stent malapposition detected by optical coherence tomography examination. *International Journal of Cardiology, 137*, e77–e78. doi:10.1016/j.ijcard.2009.04.039

Chen, B., Ma, F., & Luo, W. (2008). Neointimal coverage of bare-metal and sirolimus-eluting stents evaluated with optical coherence tomography. *Heart (British Cardiac Society), 94,* 566–570. doi:10.1136/hrt.2007.118679

Chia, S., Christopher, R. O., Takano, M., Tearney, G., Bouma, B., & Jang, I. (2007). In-vivo comparison of coronary plaque characteristics using optical coherence tomography in women vs. men with acute coronary syndrome. *Coronary Artery Disease, 18,* 423–427. doi:10.1097/MCA.0b013e3282583be8

Chia, S., Raffel, O., Takano, M., Tearney, G., Bouma, B., & Jang, I. (2008). Association of statin therapy with reduced coronary plaque rupture: An optical coherence tomography study. *Coronary Artery Disease, 19,* 237–242. doi:10.1097/MCA.0b013e32830042a8

Chia, S., Raffel, O., Takano, M., Tearney, G., Bouma, B., & Jang, I. (2008). Comparison of coronary plaque characteristics between diabetic and non-diabetic subjects: An in vivo optical coherence tomography study. *Diabetes Research and Clinical Practice, 81,* 155–160. doi:10.1016/j.diabres.2008.03.014

Cilingiroglu, M., Oh, J., & Sugunan, B. (2006). Detection of vulnerable plaque in a murine model of atherosclerosis with optical coherence tomography. *Catheterization and Cardiovascular Interventions, 67,* 915–923. doi:10.1002/ccd.20717

Fan, C., Kim, J., & Lee, J. (2010). Different vascular healing patterns with various drug-eluting stents in primary percutaneous coronary intervention for ST-segment elevation myocardial infarction: Optical coherence tomographic findings. *The American Journal of Cardiology, 105,* 972–976. doi:10.1016/j.amjcard.2009.11.018

Fujii, K., Kawasaki, D., & Masutani, M. (2010). OCT assessment of thin-cap fibroatheroma distribution in native coronary arteries. *JACC: Cardiovascular Imaging, 3,* 168–175. doi:10.1016/j.jcmg.2009.11.004

Fujii, K., Masutani, M., & Okumura, T. (2008). Frequency and predictor of coronary thin-cap fibroatheroma in patients with acute myocardial infarction and stable angina pectoris a 3-vessel optical coherence tomography study. *Journal of the American College of Cardiology, 52,* 787–788. doi:10.1016/j.jacc.2008.05.030

Goderie, T., van Soest, G., & Garcia-Garcia, H. (2010). Combined optical coherence tomography and intravascular ultrasound radio frequency data analysis for plaque characterization. Classification accuracy of human coronary plaques in vitro. *The International Journal of Cardiovascular Imaging, 26*(8). doi:10.1007/s10554-010-9631-2

Goldstein, J., Demetriou, D., Grines, C., Pica, M., Shoukfeh, M., & O'Neill, W. (2000). Multiple complex coronary plaques in patients with acute myocardial infarction. *The New England Journal of Medicine, 343,* 915–922. doi:10.1056/NEJM200009283431303

Gonzalo, N., Barlis, P., & Serruys, P. (2009). Incomplete stent apposition and delayed tissue coverage are more frequent in drug-eluting stents implanted during primary percutaneous coronary intervention for ST-segment elevation myocardial infarction than in drug-eluting stents implanted for stable/un. *JACC: Cardiovascular Interventions, 2,* 445–452. doi:10.1016/j.jcin.2009.01.012

Gonzalo, N., Garcia-Garcia, H., & Regar, E. (2009). In vivo assessment of high-risk coronary plaques at bifurcations with combined intravascular ultrasound and optical coherence tomography. *JACC: Cardiovascular Imaging, 2,* 473–482. doi:10.1016/j.jcmg.2008.11.016

Gonzalo, N., Serruys, P., Barlis, P., Ligthart, J., Garcia-Garcia, H., & Regar, E. (2010). Multi-modality intra-coronary plaque characterization: A pilot study. *International Journal of Cardiology*, *138*, 32–39. doi:10.1016/j.ijcard.2008.08.030

Gonzalo, N., Serruys, P., & Okamura, T. (2009). Optical coherence tomography assessment of the acute effects of stent implantation on the vessel wall: A systematic quantitative approach. *Heart (British Cardiac Society)*, *95*, 1913–1919. doi:10.1136/hrt.2009.172072

Gonzalo, N., Serruys, P., & Okamura, T. (2009). Optical coherence tomography patterns of stent restenosis. *American Heart Journal*, *158*, 284–293. doi:10.1016/j.ahj.2009.06.004

Guagliumi, G., Musumeci, G., & Sirbu, V. (2010). Optical coherence tomography assessment of in vivo vascular response after implantation of overlapping bare-metal and drug-eluting stents. *JACC: Cardiovascular Interventions*, *3*, 531–539. doi:10.1016/j.jcin.2010.02.008

Gurmeric, S., Isguder, G., Carlier, S., & Unal, G. (2009). A new 3-D automated computational method to evaluate in-stent neointimal hyperplasia in in-vivo intravascular optical coherence tomography pullbacks. *Med Image Comput Comput Assist Interv*, *12*, 776–785.

Habara, M., Terashima, M., & Suzuki, T. (2009). Detection of atherosclerotic progression with rupture of degenerated in-stent intima five years after bare-metal stent implantation using optical coherence tomography. *The Journal of Invasive Cardiology*, *21*, 552–553.

Ikejima, H., Imanishi, T., & Tsujioka, H. (2010). Upregulation of fractalkine and its receptor, CX3CR1, is associated with coronary plaque rupture in patients with unstable angina pectoris. *Circulation Journal*, *74*, 337–345. doi:10.1253/circj.CJ-09-0484

Jang, I., Bouma, B., & Kang, D. (2002). Visualization of coronary atherosclerotic plaques in patients using optical coherence tomography: Comparison with intravascular ultrasound. *Journal of the American College of Cardiology*, *39*, 604–609. doi:10.1016/S0735-1097(01)01799-5

Jang, I., Tearney, G., & MacNeill, B. (2005). In vivo characterization of coronary atherosclerotic plaque by use of optical coherence tomography. *Circulation*, *111*, 1551–1555. doi:10.1161/01.CIR.0000159354.43778.69

Joner, M., Finn, A., & Farb, A. (2006). Pathology of drug-eluting stents in humans: Delayed healing and late thrombotic risk. *Journal of the American College of Cardiology*, *48*, 193–202. doi:10.1016/j.jacc.2006.03.042

Karanasos, A., Toutouzas, K., & Riga, M. (2010). Complex angiographic morphology is associated with ruptured plaques and thinner fibrous cap by optical coherence tomography. *ECS2010*. (abstract)

Karanasos, A., Toutouzas, K., & Riga, M. (2010). Culprit lesions in proximal segments of coronary arteries are associated with thin fibrous cap and plaque rupture as assessed by optical coherence tomography. *ESC2010*. (abstract)

Kashiwagi, M., Tanaka, A., & Kitabata, H. (2009). Relationship between coronary arterial remodeling, fibrous cap thickness and high-sensitivity C-reactive protein levels in patients with acute coronary syndrome. *Circulation Journal*, *73*, 1291–1295. doi:10.1253/circj.CJ-08-0968

Kawasaki, M., Bouma, B., & Bressner, J. (2006). Diagnostic accuracy of optical coherence tomography and integrated backscatter intravascular ultrasound images for tissue characterization of human coronary plaques. *Journal of the American College of Cardiology*, *48*, 81–88. doi:10.1016/j.jacc.2006.02.062

Kim, J., Jang, I., & Fan, C. (2009). Evaluation in 3 months duration of neointimal coverage after zotarolimus-eluting stent implantation by optical coherence tomography: The ENDEAVOR OCT trial. *JACC: Cardiovascular Interventions, 2,* 1240–1247. doi:10.1016/j.jcin.2009.10.006

Kim, J., Kim, J., & Kim, T. (2010). Comparison of neointimal coverage of sirolimus-eluting stents and paclitaxel-eluting stents using optical coherence tomography at 9 months after implantation. *Circulation Journal, 74,* 320–326. doi:10.1253/circj.CJ-09-0546

Kim, U., Kim, J., & Kim, J. (2010). The initial extent of malapposition in ST-elevation myocardial infarction treated with drug-eluting stent: The usefulness of optical coherence tomography. *Yonsei Medical Journal, 51,* 332–338. doi:10.3349/ymj.2010.51.3.332

Kubo, T., Imanishi, T., & Kashiwagi, M. e. (2010). Multiple coronary lesion instability in patients with acute myocardial infarction as determined by optical coherence tomography. *The American Journal of Cardiology, 105,* 318–322. doi:10.1016/j.amjcard.2009.09.032

Kubo, T., Imanishi, T., & Kitabata, H. (2008). Comparison of vascular response after sirolimus-eluting stent implantation between patients with unstable and stable angina pectoris: a serial optical coherence tomography study. *JACC: Cardiovascular Imaging, 1,* 475–484. doi:10.1016/j.jcmg.2008.03.012

Kubo, T., Imanishi, T., & Takarada, S. (2007). Assessment of culprit lesion morphology in acute myocardial infarction: ability of optical coherence tomography compared with intravascular ultrasound and coronary angioscopy. *Journal of the American College of Cardiology, 50,* 933–939. doi:10.1016/j.jacc.2007.04.082

Kume, T., Akasaka, T., & Kawamoto, T. (2005). Assessment of coronary intima--media thickness by optical coherence tomography: Comparison with intravascular ultrasound. *Circulation Journal, 69,* 903–907. doi:10.1253/circj.69.903

Kume, T., Akasaka, T., & Kawamoto, T. (2006). Assessment of coronary arterial thrombus by optical coherence tomography. *The American Journal of Cardiology, 97,* 1713–1717. doi:10.1016/j.amjcard.2006.01.031

Kume, T., Akasaka, T., & Kawamoto, T. (2006). Measurement of the thickness of the fibrous cap by optical coherence tomography. *Am Heart J, 152,* 755 e1-4.

Kume, T., Okura, H., & Kawamoto, T. (2008). Relationship between coronary remodeling and plaque characterization in patients without clinical evidence of coronary artery disease. *Atherosclerosis, 197,* 799–805. doi:10.1016/j.atherosclerosis.2007.07.028

Kume, T., Okura, H., & Yamada, R. (2009). Frequency and spatial distribution of thin-cap fibroatheroma assessed by 3-vessel intravascular ultrasound and optical coherence tomography: An ex vivo validation and an initial in vivo feasibility study. *Circulation Journal, 73,* 1086–1091. doi:10.1253/circj.CJ-08-0733

Kuo, W., Chou, N., & Chou, C. (2007). Polarization-sensitive optical coherence tomography for imaging human atherosclerosis. *Applied Optics, 46,* 2520–2527. doi:10.1364/AO.46.002520

Li, Q., Fu, Q., & Shi, S. (2010). Relationship between plasma inflammatory markers and plaque fibrous cap thickness determined by intravascular optical coherence tomography. *Heart (British Cardiac Society), 96*(3), 196–201. doi:10.1136/hrt.2009.175455

Low, A., Kawase, Y., Chan, Y., Tearney, G., Bouma, B., & Jang, I. (2009). In vivo characterisation of coronary plaques with conventional grey-scale intravascular ultrasound: Correlation with optical coherence tomography. *EuroIntervention, 4,* 626–632. doi:10.4244/EIJV4I5A105

Luo, W., Marks, D., Ralston, T., & Boppart, S. (2006). Three-dimensional optical coherence tomography of the embryonic murine cardiovascular system. *Journal of Biomedical Optics, 11,* 021014. doi:10.1117/1.2193465

MacNeill, B., Jang, I., & Bouma, B. (2004). Focal and multi-focal plaque macrophage distributions in patients with acute and stable presentations of coronary artery disease. *Journal of the American College of Cardiology, 44,* 972–979. doi:10.1016/j.jacc.2004.05.066

Manfrini, O., Mont, E., & Leone, O. (2006). Sources of error and interpretation of plaque morphology by optical coherence tomography. *The American Journal of Cardiology, 98,* 156–159. doi:10.1016/j.amjcard.2006.01.097

Morikawa, Y., Uemura, S., & Ishigami, K. (2011). Morphological features of coronary arteries in patients with coronary spastic angina: Assessment with intracoronary optical coherence tomography. *International Journal of Cardiology, 46*(3).

Motreff, P., Souteyrand, G., & Levesque, S. (2009). Comparative analysis of neointimal coverage with paclitaxel and zotarolimus drug-eluting stents: Using optical coherence tomography 6 months after implantation. *Arch Cardiovasc Dis, 102,* 617–624. doi:10.1016/j.acvd.2009.05.010

Nadkarni, S., Bouma, B., de Boer, J., & Tearney, G. (2009). Evaluation of collagen in atherosclerotic plaques: the use of two coherent laser-based imaging methods. *Lasers in Medical Science, 24,* 439–445. doi:10.1007/s10103-007-0535-x

Nagai, H., Ishibashi-Ueda, H., & Fujii, K. (2010). Histology of highly echolucent regions in optical coherence tomography images from two patients with sirolimus-eluting stent restenosis. *Catheterization and Cardiovascular Interventions, 75,* 961–963.

Oh, W., Yun, S., & Vakoc, B. e. (2008). High-speed polarization sensitive optical frequency domain imaging with frequency multiplexing. *Optics Express, 16,* 1096–1103. doi:10.1364/OE.16.001096

Ormiston, J., Serruys, P., & Regar, E. (2008). A bioabsorbable everolimus-eluting coronary stent system for patients with single de-novo coronary artery lesions (ABSORB): A prospective open-label trial. *Lancet, 371,* 899–907. doi:10.1016/S0140-6736(08)60415-8

Ozaki, Y., Okumura, M., & Ismail, T. (2010). The fate of incomplete stent apposition with drug-eluting stents: an optical coherence tomography-based natural history study. *European Heart Journal, 31,* 1470–1476. doi:10.1093/eurheartj/ehq066

Pinto, S. T., Pakala, R., Lovec, R., Tio, F., & Waksman, R. (2007). Optical coherence tomographic imaging of a bioabsorbable magnesium stent lost in a porcine coronary artery. *Cardiovascular Revascularization Medicine; Including Molecular Interventions, 8,* 293–294. doi:10.1016/j.carrev.2007.09.002

Pinto, S. T., Pakala, R., & Waksman, R. (2008). Serial imaging and histology illustrating the degradation of a bioabsorbable magnesium stent in a porcine coronary artery. *European Heart Journal, 29,* 314. doi:10.1093/eurheartj/ehm365

Prati, F., Regar, E., & Mintz, G. (2010). Expert review document on methodology, terminology, and clinical applications of optical coherence tomography: Physical principles, methodology of image acquisition, and clinical application for assessment of coronary arteries and atherosclerosis. *European Heart Journal, 31,* 401–415. doi:10.1093/eurheartj/ehp433

Prati, F., Zimarino, M., & Stabile, E. (2008). Does optical coherence tomography identify arterial healing after stenting? An in vivo comparison with histology, in a rabbit carotid model. *Heart (British Cardiac Society), 94*, 217–221. doi:10.1136/hrt.2006.112482

Radu, M., Jorgensen, E., Kelbaek, H., Helqvist, S., Skovgaard, L., & Saunamaki, K. (2010). Strut apposition after coronary stent implantation visualised with optical coherence tomography. *EuroIntervention, 6*, 86–93. doi:10.4244/EIJV6I1A13

Raffel, O., Tearney, G., Gauthier, D., Halpern, E., Bouma, B., & Jang, I. (2007). Relationship between a systemic inflammatory marker, plaque inflammation, and plaque characteristics determined by intravascular optical coherence tomography. *Arteriosclerosis, Thrombosis, and Vascular Biology, 27*, 1820–1827. doi:10.1161/ATVBAHA.107.145987

Ramcharitar, S., Gonzalo, N., & van Geuns, R. (2009). First case of stenting of a vulnerable plaque in the SECRITT I trial-the dawn of a new era? *Nat Rev Cardiol, 6*, 374–378. doi:10.1038/nrcardio.2009.34

Rathore, S., Terashima, M., & Suzuki, T. (2009). Late-acquired stent malapposition after sirolimus-eluting stent implantation following acute coronary syndrome: Angiographic, IVUS, OCT and coronary angioscopic observation. *The Journal of Invasive Cardiology, 21*, 666–667.

Rieber, J., Meissner, O., & Babaryka, G. (2006). Diagnostic accuracy of optical coherence tomography and intravascular ultrasound for the detection and characterization of atherosclerotic plaque composition in ex-vivo coronary specimens: A comparison with histology. *Coronary Artery Disease, 17*, 425–430. doi:10.1097/00019501-200608000-00005

Rogowska, J., Patel, N., Fujimoto, J., & Brezinski, M. (2004). Optical coherence tomographic elastography technique for measuring deformation and strain of atherosclerotic tissues. *Heart (British Cardiac Society), 90*, 556–562. doi:10.1136/hrt.2003.016956

Savonitto, S., Ardissino, D., & Granger, C. (1999). Prognostic value of the admission electrocardiogram in acute coronary syndromes. *Journal of the American Medical Association, 281*, 707–713. doi:10.1001/jama.281.8.707

Sawada, T., Shite, J., & Garcia-Garcia, H. (2008). Feasibility of combined use of intravascular ultrasound radiofrequency data analysis and optical coherence tomography for detecting thin-cap fibroatheroma. *European Heart Journal, 29*, 1136–1146. doi:10.1093/eurheartj/ehn132

Sawada, T., Shite, J., & Shinke, T. (2009). Low plasma adiponectin levels are associated with presence of thin-cap fibroatheroma in men with stable coronary artery disease. *International Journal of Cardiology, 142*(3).

Serruys, P., Ormiston, J., & Onuma, Y. (2009). A bioabsorbable everolimus-eluting coronary stent system (ABSORB): 2-year outcomes and results from multiple imaging methods. *Lancet, 373*, 897–910. doi:10.1016/S0140-6736(09)60325-1

Sihan, K., Botha, C., & Post, F. (2009). Fully automatic three-dimensional quantitative analysis of intracoronary optical coherence tomography: Method and validation. *Catheterization and Cardiovascular Interventions, 74*, 1058–1065. doi:10.1002/ccd.22125

Stefanadis, C., Toutouzas, K., Stefanadi, E., Lazaris, A., Patsouris, E., & Kipshidze, N. (2007). Inhibition of plaque neovascularization and intimal hyperplasia by specific targeting vascular endothelial growth factor with bevacizumab-eluting stent: An experimental study. *Atherosclerosis, 195*, 269–276. doi:10.1016/j.atherosclerosis.2006.12.034

Stefanadis, C., Toutouzas, K., Tsiamis, E., Vavuranakis, M., Stefanadi, E., & Kipshidze, N. (2008). First-in-man study with bevacizumab-eluting stent: A new approach for the inhibition of atheromatic plaque neovascularisation. *EuroIntervention*, *3*, 460–464. doi:10.4244/EIJV3I4A82

Suzuki, N., Kozuma, K., & Maeno, Y. e. (2010). Quantitative coronary optical coherence tomography image analysis for the signal attenuation observed in-stent restenotic tissue. *International Journal of Cardiology*, *145*(2). doi:10.1016/j.ijcard.2010.04.020

Suzuki, Y., Ikeno, F., & Koizumi, T. (2008). In vivo comparison between optical coherence tomography and intravascular ultrasound for detecting small degrees of in-stent neointima after stent implantation. *JACC: Cardiovascular Interventions*, *1*, 168–173. doi:10.1016/j.jcin.2007.12.007

Synetos, A., Toutouzas, K., & Drakopoulou, M. (2010). *Biodegradable bevacizumab eluting stent effectively inhibits revascularization and intimal hyperplasia: An experimental study. ESC2010.* (abstract)

Takano, M., Jang, I., & Inami, S. (2008). In vivo comparison of optical coherence tomography and angioscopy for the evaluation of coronary plaque characteristics. *The American Journal of Cardiology*, *101*, 471–476. doi:10.1016/j.amjcard.2007.09.106

Takano, M., Yamamoto, M., & Inami, S. (2009). Appearance of lipid-laden intima and neovascularization after implantation of bare-metal stents extended late-phase observation by intracoronary optical coherence tomography. *Journal of the American College of Cardiology*, *55*, 26–32. doi:10.1016/j.jacc.2009.08.032

Takarada, S., Imanishi, T., & Kubo, T. (2009). Effect of statin therapy on coronary fibrous-cap thickness in patients with acute coronary syndrome: assessment by optical coherence tomography study. *Atherosclerosis*, *202*, 491–497. doi:10.1016/j.atherosclerosis.2008.05.014

Takarada, S., Imanishi, T., & Liu, Y. (2010). Advantage of next-generation frequency-domain optical coherence tomography compared with conventional time-domain system in the assessment of coronary lesion. *Catheterization and Cardiovascular Interventions*, *75*, 202–206. doi:10.1002/ccd.22273

Tanaka, A., Imanishi, T., & Kitabata, H. (2008). Distribution and frequency of thin-capped fibroatheromas and ruptured plaques in the entire culprit coronary artery in patients with acute coronary syndrome as determined by optical coherence tomography. *The American Journal of Cardiology*, *112*, 975–979. doi:10.1016/j.amjcard.2008.05.062

Tanaka, A., Imanishi, T., & Kitabata, H. (2008). Morphology of exertion-triggered plaque rupture in patients with acute coronary syndrome: An optical coherence tomography study. *Circulation*, *118*, 2368–2373. doi:10.1161/CIRCULATIONAHA.108.782540

Tanigawa, J., Barlis, P., & Di Mario, C. (2008). Heavily calcified coronary lesions preclude strut apposition despite high pressure balloon dilatation and rotational atherectomy: In-vivo demonstration with optical coherence tomography. *Circulation Journal*, *72*, 157–160. doi:10.1253/circj.72.157

Tanigawa, J., Barlis, P., Dimopoulos, K., Dalby, M., Moore, P., & Di Mario, C. (2009). The influence of strut thickness and cell design on immediate apposition of drug-eluting stents assessed by optical coherence tomography. *International Journal of Cardiology*, *134*, 180–188. doi:10.1016/j.ijcard.2008.05.069

Tanigawa, J., Barlis, P., Dimopoulos, K., & Di Mario, C. (2008). Optical coherence tomography to assess malapposition in overlapping drug-eluting stents. *EuroIntervention, 3*, 580–583. doi:10.4244/EIJV3I5A104

Tanimoto, S., Rodriguez-Granillo, G., & Barlis, P. (2008). A novel approach for quantitative analysis of intracoronary optical coherence tomography: High inter-observer agreement with computer-assisted contour detection. *Catheterization and Cardiovascular Interventions, 72*, 228–235. doi:10.1002/ccd.21482

Tearney, G., Waxman, S., & Shishkov, M. (2008). Three-dimensional coronary artery microscopy by intracoronary optical frequency domain imaging. *JACC: Cardiovascular Imaging, 1*, 752–761. doi:10.1016/j.jcmg.2008.06.007

Tearney, G., Yabushita, H., & Houser, S. (2003). Quantification of macrophage content in atherosclerotic plaques by optical coherence tomography. *Circulation, 107*, 113–119. doi:10.1161/01.CIR.0000044384.41037.43

The_PROSPECT_authors. (2009). *The multicenter, prospective, international providing regional observations to study predictors of events in the coronary tree (PROSPECT) trial.* (ClinicalTrials.gov identifier NCT00180466). TCT. (abstract)

Toutouzas, K., Karanasos, A., & Stefanadis, C. (2010). Multiple plaque morphologies assessed by optical coherence tomography in a patient with acute coronary syndrome. *Heart (British Cardiac Society), 96*, 1335–1336. doi:10.1136/hrt.2010.194928

Toutouzas, K., Karanasos, A., & Tsiamis, E. (2011). New insights by optical coherence tomography into the differences and similarities of culprit ruptured plaque morphology in non-ST-elevation myocardial infarction and ST-elevation myocardial infarction. *American Heart Journal, 161*, 1162–1169. doi:10.1016/j.ahj.2011.03.005

Toutouzas, K., Riga, M., & Drakopoulou, M. (2009). *Combination of optical coherence tomography and intracoronary thermography for the morphological and functional assessment of the culprit lesion in patients with acute coronary syndromes.* ESC2010. (abstract)

Toutouzas, K., Synetos, A., & Stefanadi, E. (2007). Correlation between morphologic characteristics and local temperature differences in culprit lesions of patients with symptomatic coronary artery disease. *Journal of the American College of Cardiology, 49*, 2264–2271. doi:10.1016/j.jacc.2007.03.026

Toutouzas, K., Tsiamis, E., & Karanasos, A. e. (2010). Morphological characteristics of culprit atheromatic plaque are associated with coronary flow after thrombolytic therapy: New implications of optical coherence tomography from a multicenter study. *JACC: Cardiovascular Interventions, 3*, 507–514. doi:10.1016/j.jcin.2010.02.010

Toutouzas, K., Vaina, S., Riga, M., & Stefanadis, C. (2009). Evaluation of dissection after coronary stent implantation by intravascular optical coherence tomography. *Clinical Cardiology, 32*, E47–E48. doi:10.1002/clc.20173

Tsiamis, E., Toutouzas, K., & Synetos, A. (2010). Prognostic clinical and angiographic characteristics for the development of a new significant lesion in remote segments after successful percutaneous coronary intervention. *International Journal of Cardiology, 143*, 29–34. doi:10.1016/j.ijcard.2009.01.026

van Soest, G., Goderie, T., & Regar, E. (2010). Atherosclerotic tissue characterization in vivo by optical coherence tomography attenuation imaging. *Journal of Biomedical Optics, 15*, 011105. doi:10.1117/1.3280271

van Soest, G., Mastik, F., de Jong, N., & van der Steen, A. (2007). Robust intravascular optical coherence elastography by line correlations. *Physics in Medicine and Biology, 52*, 2445–2458. doi:10.1088/0031-9155/52/9/008

Virmani, R., Burke, A., Farb, A., & Kolodgie, F. (2006). Pathology of the vulnerable plaque. *Journal of the American College of Cardiology*, *47*, C13–C18. doi:10.1016/j.jacc.2005.10.065

Virmani, R., Kolodgie, F., Burke, A., Farb, A., & Schwartz, S. (2000). Lessons from sudden coronary death: A comprehensive morphological classification scheme for atherosclerotic lesions. *Arteriosclerosis, Thrombosis, and Vascular Biology*, *20*, 1262–1275. doi:10.1161/01.ATV.20.5.1262

Volmink, J., Newton, J., Hicks, N., Sleight, P., Fowler, G., & Neil, H. (1998). Coronary event and case fatality rates in an English population: Results of the Oxford myocardial infarction incidence study. The Oxford Myocardial Infarction Incidence Study Group. *Heart (British Cardiac Society)*, *80*, 40–44.

Wang, H., Fleming, C., & Rollins, A. (2007). Ultrahigh-resolution optical coherence tomography at 1.15 mum using photonic crystal fiber with no zero-dispersion wavelengths. *Optics Express*, *15*, 3085–3092. doi:10.1364/OE.15.003085

Wang, J., Normand, S., Mauri, L., & Kuntz, R. (2004). Coronary artery spatial distribution of acute myocardial infarction occlusions. *Circulation*, *110*, 278–284. doi:10.1161/01.CIR.0000135468.67850.F4

Xu, C., Schmitt, J., Carlier, S., & Virmani, R. (2008). Characterization of atherosclerosis plaques by measuring both backscattering and attenuation coefficients in optical coherence tomography. *Journal of Biomedical Optics*, *13*, 034003. doi:10.1117/1.2927464

Yabushita, H., Bouma, B., & Houser, S. (2002). Characterization of human atherosclerosis by optical coherence tomography. *Circulation*, *106*, 1640–1645. doi:10.1161/01.CIR.0000029927.92825.F6

Zimarino, M., Prati, F., & Stabile, E. (2007). Optical coherence tomography accurately identifies intermediate atherosclerotic lesions--An in vivo evaluation in the rabbit carotid artery. *Atherosclerosis*, *139*, 94–101. doi:10.1016/j.atherosclerosis.2006.08.047

Section 5
Intracoronary Near-Infrared Spectroscopy

Chapter 14
Intravascular Imaging of Lipid Core Plaque by Near-Infrared Spectroscopy

Emmanouil S. Brilakis
Dallas VA Medical Center, USA

Stephen T. Sum
InfraReDx, Inc., USA

Sean P. Madden
InfraReDx, Inc., USA

James E. Muller
InfraReDx, Inc., USA

ABSTRACT

Intracoronary near-infrared spectroscopy (NIRS) is a novel catheter-based technique that allows determination of the chemical composition of the coronary artery wall. This is accomplished by measuring the proportion of near-infrared light diffusely reflected by the arterial wall after scattering and absorption have occurred. Histology and clinical studies have validated that NIRS can detect with high accuracy the presence of coronary lipid core plaques, which form the substrate for most acute coronary syndromes and complicate stenting procedures. Coronary NIRS is currently being evaluated as a tool to: (Clarke, Figg, & Maguire, 2006) optimize the outcomes of percutaneous coronary interventions (PCI), (Ross, 1999) identify coronary lesions at risk for causing events and optimize the medical management of such patients, and (Kagan, Livsic, Sternby, & Vihert, 1968) allow evaluation of novel anti-atherosclerotic treatments.

DOI: 10.4018/978-1-61350-095-8.ch014

INTRODUCTION

Coronary plaques with a lipid-rich, necrotic core are believed to be the cause of most acute coronary syndromes (Clarke, Figg, & Maguire, 2006), (Ross, 1999). In such events, a thrombus is frequently found over a rupture site in the thin fibrous cap of the plaque (Kagan, Livsic, Sternby, & Vihert, 1968). The effective detection of lipid core plaques (LCP) in coronary arteries has presented a long-standing challenge for vascular diagnostic methods.

For the past 50 years, coronary angiography has been the principal technique utilized to evaluate the extent and severity of coronary artery disease (Goldstein, 2009), (Giroud, Li, Urban, & Rutishauer, 1992). The angiogram provides an overall image of the blood circulation through the coronary tree and highlights areas of stenosis and irregular luminal surfaces that may be indicative of atherosclerotic plaque. A significant limitation of angiography, however, is that the angiogram does not provide information about the vessel wall. Thus, angiography cannot adequately characterize the structure of arterial plaque or its composition.

Given the limitations of angiography, a number of intravascular imaging methods have been developed to improve the assessment of coronary artery disease. In general, these methods utilize either sound or light to generate intra-coronary images. The former include intravascular ultrasound (IVUS), IVUS virtual histology (VH), integrated backscatter (IB), elastography, and palpography (Gonzalo, Garcia-Garcia, & Ligthart, 2008), (Nair, Kuban, Tuzcu, Schoenhagen, Nissen, & Vince, 2002), (Okubo, Kawasaki, & Ishihara, 2008), (de Korte, van der Steen, Cespedes, & Pasterkamp, 1998), (Doyley, Mastik, & de Korte, 2001). The latter category includes angioscopy, optical coherence tomography (OCT) and optical frequency domain imaging (OFDI), Raman spectroscopy, and near-infrared spectroscopy (NIRS) (Ishibashi, Aziz, Abela, & Waxman, 2006), (Patel, Stamper, & Brezinski, 2005), (Yun, Tearney, &

Vakoc, 2006), (Bezerra, Costa, Guagliumi, Rollins, & Simon, 2009), (Brennan, Nazemi, Motz, & Ramcharitar, 2008), (van de Pol, Romer, Puppels, & van der Laarse, 2002). While offering a number of advantages over angiography for plaque characterization, each modality possesses its own limitations (Schaar, Mastik, & Regar, 2007), (Jan, Patrick, & Luc, 2008), (Escolar, Weigold, Fuisz, & Weissman, 2006), (Honda & Fitzgerald, 2008). Table 1 summarizes the strengths and weaknesses of the different intra-coronary imaging methods (modified from Maehara *et al.* (Maehara, Mintz, & Weissman, 2009)).

NIRS in cardiovascular imaging analyzes the amount of light reflected in a range of wavelengths to determine the chemical composition of tissue, including lipids such as cholesterol and cholesteryl esters. This chapter explains the basic principles of NIRS technology, summarizes the various studies performed to support the use of NIRS for detection of LCP, and discusses the potential research and clinical utility of NIRS.

PRINCIPLES OF DIFFUSE REFLECTANCE NEAR-INFRARED SPECTROSCOPY

Physical Principles

Spectroscopy is the measurement of the wavelength-dependent interaction of electromagnetic radiation with matter. In diffuse reflectance NIRS, a detector measures as a function of wavelength the proportion of light diffusely reflected by a sample irradiated with near-infrared light. The diffusely reflected light results from scattering (the deflection of light in random directions from structures in the sample), and absorption (the absorption of light by molecular bonds and the transformation of the energy to mainly molecular vibrations).

Scattering and absorption are both wavelength-dependent phenomena characteristic of the material with which the light is interacting. Quantum

Table 1. Strengths and weaknesses of intravascular imaging methods for coronary plaque characterization and PCI

	Angiography	IVUS (40 MHz)	IVUS-VH (20 MHz)	Angioscopy	OCT/ OFDI	Raman Spectroscopy	Near-Infrared Spectroscopy	NIRS-IVUS (40 MHz)
Axial resolution, µm	NA	100	200	10-50	10	NA	NA	100
Necrotic core	-	±	+	+	+	++	++	++
Calcium	-	++	++	-	++	-	-	++
Thin cap	-	±	+	+	++	-	*	*
Thrombus	±	±	-	++	+	-	*	*
Inflammation	-	-	-	-	±	-	-	-
Expansive remodeling	-	++	++	-	-	-	-	++
Measurement through blood	++	++	++	-	-	-	+	++
Stent tissue coverage	-	+	+	++	++	-	-	+
PCI (stent expansion and complications)	+	++	±	±	++	-	-	++

++, excellent; +, good; ±, possible; -, impossible; *, potential under investigation.
PCI, percutaneous coronary intervention. OCT, optical coherence tomography; OFDI, Optical Frequency Domain Imaging
Modified from Maehara et al. (Maehara, Mintz, & Weissman, 2009)

theory dictates that only light of specific wavelengths can be absorbed by a chemical bond and these wavelengths differ for different bonds. The wavelengths of light in NIRS are approximately in the 800-2500 nm range (Figure 1), mainly involving vibrations of carbon-hydrogen, oxygen-hydrogen, and nitrogen- hydrogen bonds. The term "near" in near-infrared refers to its closeness to the visible region of the electromagnetic spectrum (mid- and far-infrared regions occur at wavelengths greater than 2500 nm).

Deviations from ideality of quantum vibrational spectroscopy theory arise in the near-infrared region where so-called forbidden transitions

Figure 1. Electromagnetic spectrum and the energy-matter phenomena associated with its different regions. The near-infrared region is adjacent to the visible region at approximately 800-2500 nm.

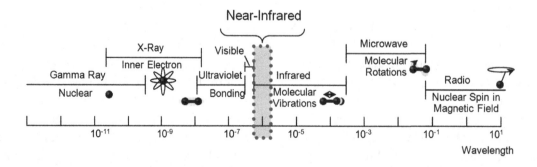

Figure 2. Example near-infrared spectra of pure substances. Each substance has a characteristic spectral shape determined by its chemical structure.

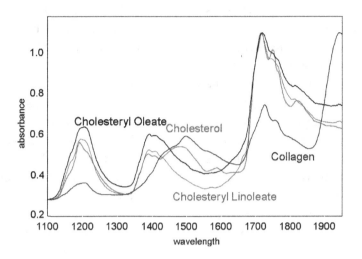

between vibrational energy levels occur as overtones and combinations of the fundamental mid-infrared bands. The NIRS bands tend be rather broad and featureless compared to those in the mid-infrared and thus lack the "fingerprinting" of the mid-infrared region. However, near-infrared is far more practicable for imaging in a broad array of applications due to the lower molar absorptivity of water and other constituents, allowing NIRS to penetrate materials to analytically useful depths.

Chemical Analysis

Since scattering and absorption vary as a function of wavelength for different materials, spectroscopic signatures can potentially be exploited for material identification (Figure 2). For mixed substances, as in most materials of interest, the spectrum is a composite of spectral contributions from the multiple constituents. This mixture spectrum can be viewed as the weighted sum of the individual component spectra, where the weights correspond to the proportions of the components in the mixture (Figure 3).

Figure 3. Mixture spectrum illustration. The spectrum of a mixed sample consists of the combined spectral contributions from the individual components of the mixture. The mixture spectrum is the weighted sum of the spectra of the pure components (ignoring component interactions). The weights are determined by the relative proportions of the individual components.

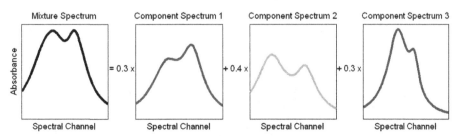

In practice, the broad-featured NIRS spectra of mixtures are difficult to interpret visually and typically require multivariate methods of analysis to extract information. The extraction of such information is achieved with a mathematical model built from a calibration set of samples whose chemical and physical properties span the expected range of future samples to be analyzed. Reference values for the target analytes in these samples are obtained by an independent method (e.g. histology in the case of tissue). Models constructed from these calibration samples relate the NIRS signals with the reference values, allowing the estimation of samples of unknown analyte levels on the basis of their NIRS measurements. The methodology employed in this process is derived from "Chemometrics," the discipline concerned with the application of mathematical and statistical techniques to chemical data analysis (Lavine & Workman, 2008).

NIRS can provide direct, rapid and accurate measurements with little or no sample preparation. As a result, NIRS has been widely adopted in a variety of areas including agriculture, food, petroleum, astronomy, pharmaceuticals, and medicine (Williams & Norris, 2001), (Ciurczak & Drennen, 2002). In agriculture, NIRS is commonly used for the analysis of grain to qualitatively and quantitatively determine components such as protein, starch, cellulose, moisture, and oil. In pharmaceuticals, powdered formulations are analyzed for active ingredients, impurities, moisture, and particle size. One of many examples of medical applications of NIRS is the measurement of hemoglobin and oxyhemoglobin to determine oxygen saturation (Mendelson, 1992).

NIRS is well-suited to form the basis of a system for analysis of coronary tissue for several reasons:

- *Near-infrared light can be delivered and collected using fiber optics.* Fiber optics contained in a cardiac catheter allows for access to the coronary artery. By coupling the catheter with a pullback and rotation device, the entire artery can be scanned.

- *NIRS measurements can be carried out through blood.* The ability of near-infrared light to penetrate blood eliminates the need to contact the tissue or clear the field of view via saline flush or vessel occlusion.

- *NIRS light can be generated with an ultra-fast laser.* The rapid generation and acquisition of spectral signal (~5 ms) reduces the effect of cardiac motion and allows an arterial segment of interest to be scanned quickly.

- *NIRS can determine chemical composition at millimeter depths.* The ability of NIRS to identify the chemical composition of substances allows for the detection of compositional features (e.g. lipid) characteristic of plaque.

INTRAVASCULAR IMAGING USING NEAR-INFRARED SPECTROSCOPY

Pre-Clinical Studies

Initial studies to assess the ability of NIRS to detect atherosclerosis were performed using an off-the-shelf commercial system. Aortic specimens were examined by several groups with such a system. Using a prototype fiber optic probe, Lodder and Cassis (Lodder, Cassis, & Ciurczak, 1990), (Cassis & Lodder, 1993) demonstrated that NIRS could detect the accumulation of low-density lipoprotein cholesterol (LDL) in the aorta of hypercholesterolemic rabbits. Jaross and coworkers demonstrated that the NIRS determination of cholesterol content of human aortic samples agreed strongly with that of high-pressure liquid chromatography (Jaross, Neumeister, Lattke, & Schuh, 1999). This same group later also measured the cholesterol and collagen content of human aortic specimens by NIRS (Neumeister, Scheibe, Lattke, & Jaross, 2002). Moreno *et al.* (Moreno, Lodder, Purushothaman, Charash, O'Connor, & Muller, 2002) also studied atherosclerosis in human aorta, validating an algorithm for the determination of lipid pool, thin cap, and inflammatory infiltrate with a sensitivity/specificity of 90%/93%, 77%/93%, and 84%/91%, respectively. They (Moreno, Ryan, & Hopkins, 2001) also measured the aorta of rabbits with diet-induced atherosclerosis to show that NIRS could identify lipid-rich plaques *in vivo* through blood. Lilledahl *et al.* (Lilledahl, Haugen, Barkost, & Svaasand, 2006) investigated the detection of vulnerable plaque in human aortic specimens based on lipid content using reflection spectroscopy in the visible and near-infrared regions.

Human carotid and coronary arteries were also studied for the ability of NIRS to detect atherosclerosis in tissue. Dempsey *et al.* (Dempsey, Davis, Buice, & Lodder, 1996) developed a NIRS algorithm to determine lipoprotein composition in carotid endarterectomy specimens using gel electrophoresis as a reference method. Wang *et al.* (Wang, Geng, & Guo, 2002) reported that direct measurement of lipid-protein ratios in carotid samples correlated with NIRS spectroscopic findings and suggested that these ratios could be used to characterize advanced lesion types with superficial necrotic cores. Moreno *et al.* (Moreno, Ryan, & Hopkins, 2001) measured the NIRS spectra of fixed human coronary artery samples and validated an algorithm against histology for determination of lipid area. The sensitivity and specificity for the detection of lipid-rich coronary plaques were 83% and 94%, respectively.

While initial studies proved the feasibility of using NIRS to detect plaque in tissue, all had one or more significant practical limitations. These limitations included the absence of blood, a fixed probe-to-target distance, and the use of fixed or frozen tissue. Marshik *et al.* (Marshik, Tan, & Tang, 2002) showed that a NIRS system could accurately detect lipid-rich plaques in fresh human aorta samples through blood at depths of up to 3 mm with a sensitivity of 88% and a specificity of 79%. Such a system could also classify these plaques based on cap thickness. The performance

of a similar system with improved laser scanning speed was later evaluated against histology with good results for the detection of thin cap fibroatheroma (TCFA) and disrupted plaques (Marshik, Tan, & Tang, 2003).

Research efforts were subsequently turned to the development of a catheter-based instrument. Such a system was required to access the coronary arteries *in vivo* and rapidly perform thousands of measurements through circulating blood (Waxman, Ishibashi, & Caplan, 2007), (Caplan, Waxman, Nesto, & Muller, 2006). In an early feasibility study, a human coronary autopsy specimen was affixed to the surface of a beating pig heart in a human-to-porcine xenograft model (Waxman, Tang, & Marshik, 2004), (Waxman, Khabbaz, & Connolly, 2008). The prototype 3.2 F NIRS catheter was able to correctly identify a spectrally distinct target attached to the surface of the graft in the presence of flowing blood and cardiac motion.

The early catheter-based system was later improved with the addition of an automated pullback and rotation device (PBR), allowing the system to circumferentially scan the length of a vessel. In an early assessment of the system, measurements were taken in the coronary arteries of familial hypercholesterolemic pigs with complex atherosclerotic lesions. Measurements taken *in vivo* and *ex vivo* demonstrated good correlation between absorbance images on repeat pullbacks with multiple catheters (unpublished data, InfraReDx).

Calibration and Validation Studies

The foregoing prototype system was then employed in a large *ex vivo* study with human coronary autopsy specimens to develop an algorithm for the detection of LCP (Gardner, Tan, & Hull, 2008). NIRS spectra and histological data were collected in human autopsy hearts to build a calibration model capable of recognizing the NIRS spectral shapes associated with LCP.

Figure 4. NIRS autopsy study apparatus for calibration and validation of LCP detection system. A. Human coronary segment with epicardial backing tissue mounted in custom perfusion fixture. Rods enable accurate cutting of 2-mm thick cross-sections and registration of NIRS signals with histology. B. Autopsy study experimental setup with artery in perfusion fixture and equipment for control of human blood pressure, temperature and pulsatile flow.

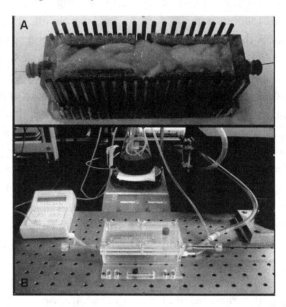

Coronary arteries from human autopsy specimens were mounted in a tissue fixture and connected to a blood circulation system with physiologic pressure, temperature and flow (Figure 4). NIRS spectra of the arterial segment were collected at a rate of approximately 40 Hertz with a PBR-driven catheter at 0.5 millimeters/second, resulting in nearly 4,000 measurements per 50 millimeters of pullback. Each spectral measurement interrogated a volume defined by 1 to 2 mm^2 of luminal surface, and approximately 1 mm of tissue depth.

Following scanning, the arterial segments were cut into 2-mm thick cross-sectional blocks and analyzed by histology. The resulting set of NIRS spectra and corresponding histology data were used to construct and validate an LCP detection algorithm. A total of 84 hearts and 216 segments were used in the calibration and validation. The prospective validation was double-blinded with respect to collection of the validation data and development of the algorithm.

In order to develop and evaluate the LCP detection algorithm, a definition of LCP of interest was needed. For this purpose, LCP was defined as a fibroatheroma containing a necrotic core at least 200 microns thick with a circumferential span of at least 60 degrees on cross-section. The primary endpoint of the algorithm validation was the accuracy of detecting such LCP. A secondary endpoint was the accuracy of detecting LCP with the additional constraint of a cap thickness of less than 450 microns. Additional secondary and exploratory endpoints included accuracy of a lipid core burden index (LCBI), segment level agreement rate, and image repeatability.

Each spectral measurement was assigned a probability of LCP by the detection algorithm and displayed in a false color map known as a chemogram (Figure 5A) with colors ranging from red (low probability of LCP) to yellow (high prob-

Figure 5. NIRS pullback and selected histologic findings from human coronary artery segment

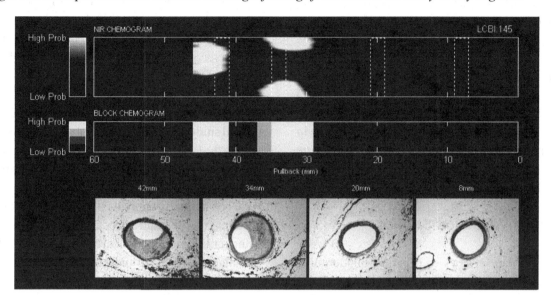

ability of LCP). From the chemogram, a summary metric of the probability that an LCP was present in a 2-mm interval of the pullback was computed and displayed in a supplementary false color map called a block chemogram (Figure 5B). Blocks corresponded to one of four discrete bins, each represented by a distinct color (red, orange, tan, and yellow, in increasing order of LCP probability).

An additional metric, the lipid core burden index (LCBI), was devised to quantify the amount of LCP in a scanned artery segment. The LCBI was defined as the proportion of yellow pixels in the chemogram on a 0-1000 scale. Figure 6 illustrates the computation of the LCBI.

The 2-mm block chemogram values were compared to histology (presence or absence of

Figure 6. Illustration of the lipid core burden index (LCBI). The LCBI (top right) shows the proportion of lipid in a scanned artery on a 0 to 1,000 scale. The LCBI is calculated as the fraction of valid pixels in the Chemogram that are yellow, multiplied by a factor of 1000. Yellow pixels are those whose values (probability of LCP) exceed a specified threshold, as indicated by the horizontal plane in the bottom panel.

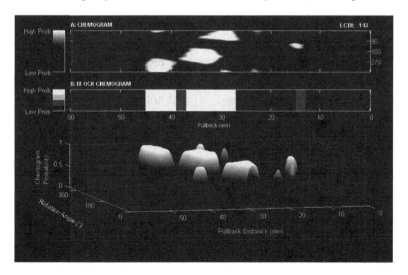

structures meeting the LCP definition) in each 2-mm block in a receiver operating characteristic (ROC) curve analysis of diagnostic accuracy. Prospective validation of the system for detection of LCP in nearly 2000 individual blocks from 51 hearts yielded an area under the ROC curve (AUC) of 0.80 for average lumen diameters of up to 3.0 mm. The detection of any-sized fibroatheroma in an artery segment using the LCBI as a measure of lipid burden resulted in an AUC of 0.86 (Gardner, Tan, & Hull, 2008).

Clinical Validation Studies

The coronary arteries of 6 patients undergoing PCI for stable angina were scanned with an early prototype (2002, Lahey Clinic, Burlington, MA) in a first use of NIRS in patients. The study demonstrated that spectra could be safely collected in patients and that these spectra carried information from the artery wall. Significant motion artifacts, however, were observed due to slow signal acquisition time (2.5 s). An improved prototype NIRS system coupled with a PBR and a faster scanning laser (5 ms acquisition time) was later employed in a feasibility study of 10 patients (2006, Lahey Clinic, Burlington, MA). Spectra were safely collected in all patients and the ability to discriminate between signals measured in a vessel and those from blood alone was demonstrated with no measurable artifacts from motion.

In a subsequent pivotal study, the similarity of NIRS signals collected in the coronary arteries of patients to those obtained in autopsy specimens was assessed. While the autopsy study in which the LCP detection algorithm was developed and validated was designed to approximate *in vivo* conditions (physiologic blood pressure, pulsatile flow rate, and temperature) (Gardner, Tan, & Hull, 2008), the experimental apparatus could not adequately simulate other potentially relevant factors of the *in vivo* environment (e.g. respiratory and cardiac motion). Thus, the SPECTroscopic Assessment of Coronary Lipid (SPECTACL)

study was conducted to determine if the spectra recorded in patients (in whom tissue is not available for validation), were equivalent to the spectra recorded in autopsy specimens (in which histology was available for validation). Spectral similarity was prospectively analyzed using common multivariate outlier metrics. This multicenter pivotal study enrolled 106 patients from 6 clinical sites in the USA and Canada. SPECTACL showed prospectively in a blinded subset of 59 cases that the spectral features of coronary arteries in patients were substantially equivalent to those of autopsy specimens. This equivalence was demonstrated using multivariate statistical metrics based on the Mahalanobis distance and spectral F-ratio. Demonstration of spectral similarity between NIRS measurements collected *in vivo* and *ex vivo* showed the applicability of the autopsy- tissue-based LCP detection algorithm to patients (Waxman, Dixon, & L'Allier, 2009).

NIRS System

A clinical NIRS system (InfraReDx, Inc., Burlington, MA) consists of a console, a pullback and rotation device (PBR), and an intravascular catheter. The console comprises a near-infrared scanning laser, computer, power system, and two monitors (for operator and physician). The PBR contains the electronic, optical and mechanical components for delivering and detecting light, as well as translating and rotating the imaging core of the catheter. The 3.2-F rapid exchange catheter has a sealed imaging window (no priming required) with two optical fibers inside a drive cable comprising the core. The delivery and collection fibers in the core are terminated by mirrors embedded in an optical tip for directing incident light through blood onto the artery wall and receiving the diffusely reflected light (Figure 7). The imaging core rotates at 240 rpm with automated pullback at a linear rate of 0.5 mm/s, interrogating tissue in a helical pattern as the laser scans across multiple wavelengths in

Figure 7. Drawing of NIRS catheter optical tip showing optical fibers and mirrors of delivery and collection channels

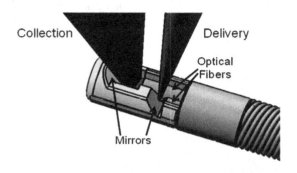

the near-infrared region of the electromagnetic spectrum. The resulting spectra are processed and interpreted by the LCP detection algorithm to generate a longitudinal image (chemogram) of the scanned artery segment displaying regions of high and low probability of LCP (Figure 5).

The principal strength of the NIRS system is its ability to determine the chemical composition of the artery wall through blood, rendering the system particularly well-suited for the detection of lipid core plaque. The main limitation of the system is its inability to provide structural measurements such as lumen and vessel size, plaque thickness, and stent size. A new system that combines NIRS and IVUS was recently developed that enables simultaneous, co-registered acquisition of compositional and structural information (Garg, Serruys, & van der Ent, 2010).

RESEARCH AND CLINICAL UTILITY OF NEAR-INFRARED SPECTROSCOPY

Based on the results of the autopsy validation (Gardner, Tan, & Hull, 2008) and the demonstration of similarity between clinical and autopsy spectra (Waxman, Dixon, & L'Allier, 2009), coronary NIRS was approved by the US Food and Drug Administration (FDA) for clinical use

in the United States in April 2008 (U.S. Food and Drug Administration. Press Annoucements) for the detection of lipid core containing plaques of interest (LCP) and the assessment of lipid core burden in coronary arteries. The new combination NIRS-IVUS system was approved by the FDA in June 2010. By January 2011, the systems had been used in over 1600 patients in 25 hospitals.

Coronary NIRS has multiple potential uses, all of which are currently under investigation (Maini, 2008), (Goldstein, Grines, & Fischell, 2009), (Maini, Brilakis, & Kim, 2010), (Garcia, Wood, Cipher, Banerjee, & Brilakis, 2010), (Schultz, Serruys, & van der Ent, 2010), (Muller, Tawakol, Kathiresan, & Narula, 2006), (Sum, Madden, Hendricks, Chartier, & Muller, 2009). NIRS can be used to (Clarke, Figg, & Maguire, 2006) optimize the outcomes of percutaneous coronary interventions (PCI), (Ross, 1999) identify coronary lesions at risk for causing events and optimize the medical management of such patients and (Kagan, Livsic, Sternby, & Vihert, 1968) allow evaluation of novel anti-atherosclerotic treatments.

Optimization of PCI Outcomes

Coronary NIRS could be used to optimize PCI outcomes by (a) helping determine the optimum stent length for adequate lesion coverage; (b) helping determine the optimum stent type; (c) allowing prediction of the risk of peri-procedural complications, such as no-reflow and peri-procedural acute myocardial infarction.

When drug-eluting stents (DES) are currently used for PCI, the operators usually attempt to cover from a proximal to a distal normal reference segment. However, occasionally these angiographically "normal" sites may contain a large amount of LCP that does not compromise the lumen due to positive remodeling. Disruption or incomplete coverage of such plaques could lead to stent thrombosis (Farb, Burke, Kolodgie, & Virmani, 2003). Use of coronary NIRS could aid selection

Figure 8. Coronary angiography demonstrating an eccentric lesion in the mid left anterior descending artery with TIMI 3 flow, and circumferential LCP and ulcerated appearance by IVUS (panel A). After stenting (panel B) no-reflow occurred and plaque prolapse through the stent struts was observed by intravascular ultrasonography. After intracoronary vasodilator administration coronary flow improved but the cardiac biomarkers subsequently increased consistent with a post-procedural acute myocardial infarction.

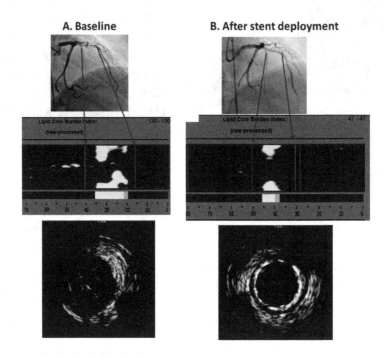

of the appropriate stent length for complete lesion and adjacent LCP coverage.

Stent implantation in lesions with large LCP may be associated with plaque prolapse through the stent struts (Figure 8) (Kawai, Hisamatsu, & Matsubara, 2009). DES implantation can lead to incomplete healing and increased risk for stent thrombosis (Farb, Burke, Kolodgie, & Virmani, 2003). Pre-stenting coronary NIRS could detect such plaques. Bare metal stents might be preferred for treating such lesions, especially in large diameter vessels with low in-stent restenosis risk.

Post-PCI acute myocardial infarction has complex pathophysiology, but distal embolization appears to play a significant role (Kawai, Hisamatsu, & Matsubara, 2009). An increasing number of reports demonstrate that NIRS-detected LCPs may be more likely to embolize and cause

acute myocardial infarction (Goldstein, Grines, & Fischell, Coronary Embolization Following Balloon Dilation of Lipid-Core Plaques, 2009), (Maini, Brilakis, & Kim, 2010), (Schultz, Serruys, & van der Ent, 2010), (Saeed, Banerjee, & Brilakis, 2010), (Raghunathan, Abdel Karim, & DaSilva, 2011). The decrease in LCP after stenting, observed in several studies, further supports distal plaque embolization as the cause for no reflow and myocardial infarction (Goldstein, Grines, & Fischell, 2009), (Garcia, Wood, Cipher, Banerjee, & Brilakis, 2010), (Raghunathan, Abdel Karim, & DaSilva, 2011). Preliminary analyses from the COLOR registry have demonstrated that LCPs with the following 3 characteristics (a. $\geq$ 300° angular extent of chemogram yellow for any 2 mm vertical chemogram slice; b. $\geq$ 4mm longitudinal extent of yellow blocks in block che-

Figure 9. Incidence of post-procedural acute myocardial infarction among 28 patients with pre-stenting NIRS imaging of their coronary artery lesion, demonstrating that myocardial infarction occurred in patients with large circumferential LCPs located in the proximal or mid coronary artery segments (48).

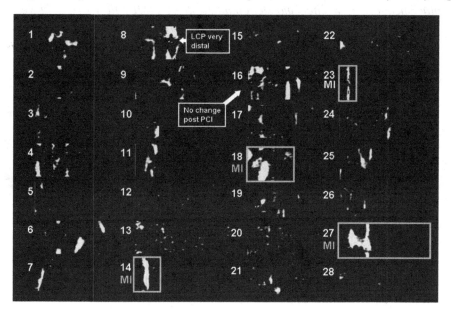

mogram; and c. proximal or mid location in the scanned artery) are more likely to cause post-PCI acute myocardial infarction (Figure 9). Occasionally no reflow during PCI can have serious consequences (Figure 8), including death. Plaque prolapse through the stent struts has been associated with increased risk for post-procedural myocardial infarction (Kim, Mintz, & Ohlmann, 2006) and may be more likely to occur in plaques with large lipid cores (Figure 9).

NIRS-enabled pre-PCI identification of coronary plaques at risk for developing no-reflow could allow for appropriate prevention and treatments strategies. Pretreatment of a lesion with vasodilators might minimize distal plugging of the microvasculature by debris liberated post PCI (Kawai, Hisamatsu, & Matsubara, 2009), but would not prevent embolization per se. Embolic protection devices, both distal and proximal, could capture liberated debris before distal embolization occurs. Use of embolic protection devices is currently approved only in saphenous vein grafts (Figure 10) (Banerjee & Brilakis, 2009), but not

in native coronary arteries, as several studies (such as the Enhanced Myocardial Efficacy and Removal by Aspiration of Liberalized Debris - EMERALD trial (Stone, Webb, & Cox, 2005), the Drug Elution and Distal Protection in ST-Elevation Myocardial Infarction – DEDICATION trial (Kelbaek, Terkelsen, & Helqvist, 2008), and the UpFlow MI trial (Guetta, Mosseri, & Shechter, 2007)) did not find benefit of the routine use of distal protection during primary PCI. However, use of embolic protection devices may be beneficial when used in high-risk lesions and coronary NIRS may help identify such lesions in patients with either stable angina or acute coronary syndromes. The angiographic lesion appearance alone may be insufficient to estimate the risk of distal embolization: as shown in Figures 11 and 12, although both lesions appear to be eccentric and ulcerated and a filter was used in both lesions, debris was retrieved only from the lesion with a large LCP by coronary NIRS (Figure 11). Ostial saphenous vein graft lesions are known to have low risk for distal embolization (Hong, Mehran,

Figure 10. No reflow in a patient undergoing intervention of a lesion in the proximal portion of a saphenous vein graft to the right coronary artery (panel A). After balloon angioplasty TIMI 0 flow occurred (panel B) and the patient developed chest pain and ST- segment elevation. After debris aspiration, filter retrieval and placement of a new filter and stent implantation, TIMI 3 flow was achieved.

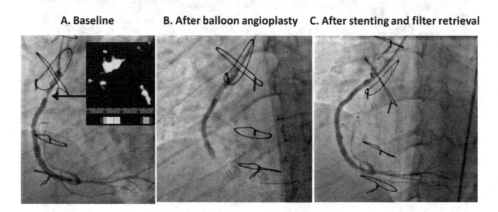

Figure 11. Near-infrared spectroscopy of the right coronary artery in a patient with unstable angina and diffuse mid right coronary artery disease (Panel A). Stenting was performed using a Spider (ev3, Plymouth, Minnesota) filter resulting in an excellent angiographic result and retrieval of a large amount of yellow debris.

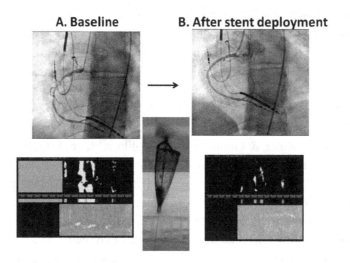

& Dangas, 1999), (Sdringola, Assali, & Ghani, 2001), (Badhey, Lichtenwalter, & de Lemos, 2010) and may have fewer LCPs compared to saphenous vein graft body lesions (Figure 13). The ability of NIRS to identify lesions at high risk of peri-procedural rupture and distal embolization and the mitigation of this risk with an embolic protection device is being tested in a prospective, randomized trial named CANARY (Coronary As-

sessment by Near-infrared of Atherosclerotic Rupture-prone Yellow, NCT01268319).

Identification of High-Risk Coronary Lesions and Optimization of Medical Management

Coronary NIRS may identify high-risk non-obstructive coronary lesions and optimize the

Figure 12. Stenting of an eccentric mid right coronary artery lesion in patient with non-ST elevation acute myocardial infarction. Baseline near-infrared spectroscopy did not demonstrate any significant lipid core plaque. Stenting was performed using a Spider embolic protection device without complications. No debris was retrieved in the filter.

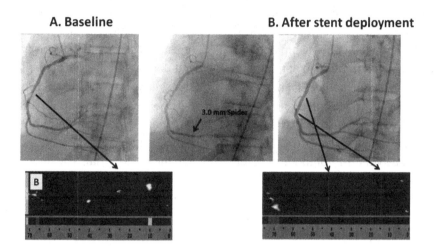

Figure 13. Near infrared spectroscopy of an ostial (panel A) and a body (panel B) saphenous vein graft lesion demonstrating significant differences in the amount of LCP (significant in the body and minimal in the ostial lesions).

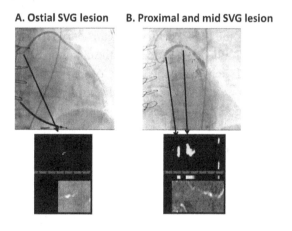

management of such patients (Muller, Tawakol, Kathiresan, & Narula, 2006). Although stenting of non-obstructive coronary lesions is currently not indicated, a provocative pilot study of prophylactic drug-eluting stent implantation in intermediate saphenous vein graft lesions showed improved outcomes in the stenting group (Rodes-Cabau, Bertrand, & Larose, 2009). In a pilot study of native coronary arteries, the SECRITT I (Santorini Criteria for Investigating and Treating Thin Capped Fibroatheroma) trial, patients with intermediate (40-50% diameter stenosis), non-culprit lesions with a fractional flow reserve (FFR) > 0.75 and VH-IVUS-derived high-risk plaque were randomized 1:1 to treatment with a self-expanding stent or medication (Ramcharitar, Gonzalo, & van Geuns, 2009). If intermediate native coronary artery lesions with large LCPs are shown to carry significant risk for subsequent events, then the detection and treatment of such lesions could prevent the occurrence of events.

Local shear stress conditions have been linked to the formation of high-risk, rupture-prone plaques. Wentzel *et al.* combined NIRS, IVUS, and multi-slice computed tomography (MSCT) measurements to study the relationship between shear stress and LCP distribution in coronary arteries (Wentzel, van der Giessen, & Garg, 2010).

Even in the absence of obstructive coronary lesions, patients with extensive LCPs might benefit from intensive plaque modification treatments, such an intensive anti-thrombotic regimen, aggressive low-density lipoprotein cholesterol lowering, high-density lipoprotein infusion, low-density lipoprotein apheresis, or with medications such as niacin, fibrates or in the future with novel compounds that are currently under clinical trial evaluation (Sacks, Rudel, & Conner, 2009).

Evaluation of Novel Anti-Atherosclerotic Treatments

Coronary NIRS could also become a powerful tool for the evaluation of new anti-atherosclerotic treatments. Currently the effect of such treatments on coronary plaque is based on intravascular ultrasonography imaging of a target coronary segment looking at longitudinal changes in percent atheroma volume before and after treatment (Bose, von Birgelen, & Erbel, 2007). Determination of the lipid core burden in the target coronary segment by NIRS could allow a more specific evaluation of the artery wall components that may be at higher risk for causing subsequent events and are more likely to change in response to treatments. In order to distinguish treatment-induced change from other sources of variability, it is essential to characterize the reproducibility of a measurement technique used in a baseline/follow-up scenario. Excellent reproducibility of the NIRS findings during repeat pullbacks has been demonstrated (Spearman's rho 0.927, intra-class correlation coefficient 0.925 in a 36 vessel analysis) (Garcia, Wood, Cipher, Banerjee, & Brilakis, 2010). Ongoing studies are further examining the reproducibility of NIRS measurements, and are evaluating other sources of variation such as multiple placements of the catheter, different catheters and different wires (Figure 14). The recent availability of the combined NIRS-IVUS catheter will allow for simultaneous, co-registered assessment of coronary plaque volume and composition, offering enhanced capacity to assess novel anti-atherosclerotic strategies (Garg, Serruys, & van der Ent, 2010).

Several studies are currently utilizing coronary NIRS as an endpoint, such as the AtheroREMO and the IBIS-3 trial. The ongoing COLOR (Chemometric Observations of Lipid Core Containing Plaques of Interest in Native Coronary Arteries, NCT00831116) registry is currently enrolling patients (target enrollment is 1,000 patients) at 19 sites and will provide valuable insights on the clinical utility and implications of coronary NIRS.

CONCLUSION

Coronary NIRS is a powerful new technology for the assessment of coronary lipid core plaques. Coronary NIRS has been extensively validated in clinical and histologic studies and can have significant impact on optimizing the outcomes of percutaneous coronary interventions, identifying high-risk coronary lesions and assessing novel anti-atherosclerotic treatments.

REFERENCES

Badhey, N., Lichtenwalter, C., & de Lemos, J. (2010). Contemporary use of embolic protection devices in saphenous vein graft interventions: Insights from the stenting of saphenous vein grafts trial. *Catheterization and Cardiovascular Interventions, 76,* 263–269. doi:10.1002/ccd.22438

Banerjee, S., & Brilakis, E. (2009). Embolic protection during saphenous vein graft interventions. *The Journal of Invasive Cardiology, 21,* 415–417.

Figure 14. Evaluation of the in-vivo reproducibility of intracoronary near-infrared spectroscopy using two different spectroscopy catheters and different wires

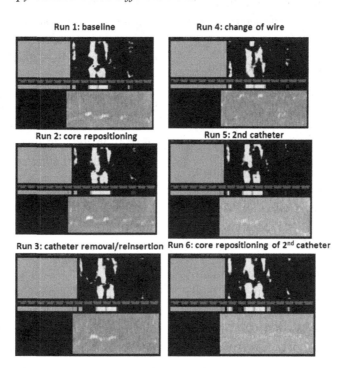

Bezerra, H., Costa, M., Guagliumi, G., Rollins, A., & Simon, D. (2009). Intracoronary optical coherence tomography: A comprehensive review clinical and research applications. *JACC: Cardiovascular Interventions, 2*, 1035–1046. doi:10.1016/j.jcin.2009.06.019

Bose, D., von Birgelen, C., & Erbel, R. (2007). Intravascular ultrasound for the evaluation of therapies targeting coronary atherosclerosis. *Journal of the American College of Cardiology, 49*, 925–932. doi:10.1016/j.jacc.2006.08.067

Brennan, J., Nazemi, J., Motz, J., & Ramcharitar, S. (2008). The vPredict optical catheter system: Intravascular raman spectroscopy. *EuroIntervention, 3*, 635–638. doi:10.4244/EIJV3I5A113

Caplan, J., Waxman, S., Nesto, R., & Muller, J. (2006). Near infrared spectroscopy for the detection of vulnerable coronary artery plaques. *Journal of the American College of Cardiology, 47*, C92–C96. doi:10.1016/j.jacc.2005.12.045

Cassis, L., & Lodder, R. (1993). Near-IR imaging of atheromas in living arterial tissue. *Analytical Chemistry, 65*, 1247–1256. doi:10.1021/ac00057a023

Ciurczak, E., & Drennen, J. (2002). *Pharmaceutical and medical applications of near-infrared spectroscopy*. CRC Press.

Clarke, M., Figg, N., & Maguire, J. (2006). Apoptosis of vascular smooth muscle cells induces features of plaque vulnerability in atherosclerosis. *Nature Medicine, 12*, 1075–1080. doi:10.1038/nm1459

de Korte, C., van der Steen, A., Cespedes, E., & Pasterkamp, G. (1998). Intravascular ultrasound elastography in human arteries: Initial experience in vitro. *Ultrasound in Medicine & Biology, 24*, 401–408. doi:10.1016/S0301-5629(97)00280-9

Dempsey, R., Davis, D., Buice, R., & Lodder, R. (1996). Biological and medical applications of near-infrared spectrometry. *Applied Spectroscopy*, 5018A–5034A.

Doyley, M., Mastik, F., & de Korte, C. (2001). Advancing intravascular ultrasonic palpation toward clinical applications. *Ultrasound in Medicine & Biology*, *27*, 1471–1480. doi:10.1016/S0301-5629(01)00457-4

Escolar, E., Weigold, G., Fuisz, A., & Weissman, N. (2006). New imaging techniques for diagnosing coronary artery disease. *Canadian Medical Association Journal*, *174*, 487–495. doi:10.1503/cmaj.050925

Farb, A., Burke, A., Kolodgie, F., & Virmani, R. (2003). Pathological mechanisms of fatal late coronary stent thrombosis in humans. *Circulation*, *108*, 1701–1706. doi:10.1161/01.CIR.0000091115.05480.B0

Garcia, B., Wood, F., Cipher, D., Banerjee, S., & Brilakis, E. (2010). Reproducibility of near-infrared spectroscopy for the detection of lipid core coronary plaques and observed changes after coronary stent implantation. *Catheterization and Cardiovascular Interventions*, *76*, 359–365. doi:10.1002/ccd.22500

Gardner, C., Tan, H., & Hull, E. e. (2008). Detection of lipid core coronary plaques in autopsy specimens with a novel catheter-based near-infrared spectroscopy system. *JACC: Cardiovascular Imaging*, *1*, 638–648. doi:10.1016/j.jcmg.2008.06.001

Garg, S., Serruys, P., & van der Ent, M. (2010). First use in patients of a combined near infrared spectroscopy and intra-vascular ultrasound catheter to identify composition and structure of coronary plaque. *EuroIntervention*, *5*, 755–756. doi:10.4244/EIJV5I6A126

Giroud, D., Li, J., Urban, P. B. M., & Rutishauer, W. (1992). Relation of the site of acute myocardial infarction to the most severe coronary arterial stenosis at prior angiography. *The American Journal of Cardiology*, *69*, 729–732. doi:10.1016/0002-9149(92)90495-K

Goldstein, J. (2009). CT angiography: Imaging anatomy to deduce coronary physiology. *Catheterization and Cardiovascular Interventions*, *73*, 503–505. doi:10.1002/ccd.22005

Goldstein, J., Grines, C., & Fischell, T. (2009). Coronary embolization following balloon dilation of lipid-core plaques. *JACC: Cardiovascular Imaging*, *2*, 1420–1424. doi:10.1016/j.jcmg.2009.10.003

Gonzalo, N., Garcia-Garcia, H., & Ligthart, J. (2008). Coronary plaque composition as assessed by greyscale intravascular ultrasound and radiofrequency spectral data analysis. *The International Journal of Cardiovascular Imaging*, *24*, 811–818. doi:10.1007/s10554-008-9324-2

Guetta, V., Mosseri, M., & Shechter, M. e. (2007). Safety and efficacy of the FilterWire EZ in acute ST-segment elevation myocardial infarction. *The American Journal of Cardiology*, *99*, 911–915. doi:10.1016/j.amjcard.2006.11.037

Honda, Y., & Fitzgerald, P. (2008). Frontiers in intravascular imaging technologies. *Circulation*, *117*, 2024–2037. doi:10.1161/CIRCULATIONAHA.105.551804

Hong, M., Mehran, R., & Dangas, G. (1999). Creatine kinase-MB enzyme elevation following successful saphenous vein graft intervention is associated with late mortality. *Circulation*, *100*, 2400–2405.

Ishibashi, F., Aziz, K., Abela, G., & Waxman, S. (2006). Update on coronary angioscopy: Review of a 20-year experience and potential application for detection of vulnerable plaque. *Journal of Interventional Cardiology*, *19*, 17–25. doi:10.1111/j.1540-8183.2006.00099.x

Jan, G., Patrick, S., & Luc, M. (2008). Identifying the vulnerable plaque: A review of invasive and non-invasive imaging modalities. *Artery Research, 2*(1), 21–34. doi:10.1016/j.artres.2007.11.002

Jaross, W., Neumeister, V., Lattke, P., & Schuh, D. (1999). Determination of cholesterol in atherosclerotic plaques using near infrared diffuse reflection spectroscopy. *Atherosclerosis, 147*, 327–337. doi:10.1016/S0021-9150(99)00203-8

Kagan, A., Livsic, A., Sternby, N., & Vihert, A. (1968). Coronary-artery thrombosis and the acute attack of coronary heart-disease. *Lancet, 2*, 1199–1200. doi:10.1016/S0140-6736(68)91688-7

Kawai, Y., Hisamatsu, K., & Matsubara, H. (2009). Intravenous administration of nicorandil immediately before percutaneous coronary intervention can prevent slow coronary flow phenomenon. *European Heart Journal, 30*, 765–772. doi:10.1093/eurheartj/ehp077

Kelbaek, H., Terkelsen, C., & Helqvist, S. (2008). Randomized comparison of distal protection versus conventional treatment in primary percutaneous coronary intervention: The drug elution and distal protection in ST-elevation myocardial infarction (DEDICATION) trial. *Journal of the American College of Cardiology, 51*, 899–905.

Kim, S.-W., Mintz, G., & Ohlmann, P. e. (2006). Frequency and severity of plaque prolapse within cypher and taxus stents as determined by sequential intravascular ultrasound analysis. *The American Journal of Cardiology, 98*, 1206–1211. doi:10.1016/j.amjcard.2006.06.014

Lavine, B., & Workman, J. (2008). Chemometrics. *Analytical Chemistry, 80*, 4519–4531. doi:10.1021/ac800728t

Lilledahl, M., Haugen, O., Barkost, M., & Svaasand, L. (2006). Reflection spectroscopy of atherosclerotic plaque. *Journal of Biomedical Optics, 11*, 021005. doi:10.1117/1.2186332

Lodder, R., Cassis, L., & Ciurczak, E. (1990). Arterial analysis with a novel near-IR fiber-optic probe. *Spectroscopy, 5*, 12–17.

Maehara, A., Mintz, G., & Weissman, N. (2009). Advances in intravascular imaging. *Circulation: Cardiovascular Interventions, 2*, 482–490. doi:10.1161/CIRCINTERVENTIONS.109.868398

Maini, B. (2008). Clinical coronary chemograms and lipid core containing coronary plaques. *JACC Imaging, 1*, 689–690. doi:10.1016/j.jcmg.2008.07.010

Maini, B., Brilakis, E., & Kim, M. (2010). Association of large lipid core plaque detected by near infrared spectroscopy with post percutaneous coronary intervention myocardial infarction. *Journal of the American College of Cardiology, 55*, A179.E1672.

Marshik, B., Tan, H., & Tang, J. (2002). Discrimination of lipid-rich plaques in human aorta specimens with NIR spectroscopy through whole blood. *The American Journal of Cardiology, 90*(Suppl 6A), 129H.

Marshik, B., Tan, H., & Tang, J. (2003). Detection of thin-capped fibroatheromas in human aorta tissue with near infrared spectroscopy through blood. *Journal of the American College of Cardiology, 41*(Suppl 1).

Mendelson, Y. (1992). Pulse oximetry: Theory and applications for noninvasive monitoring. *Clinical Chemistry, 38*, 1601–1607.

Moreno, P., Lodder, R., Purushothaman, K., Charash, W., O'Connor, W., & Muller, J. (2002). Detection of lipid pool, thin fibrous cap, and inflammatory cells in human aortic atherosclerotic plaques by near-infrared spectroscopy. *Circulation, 105*, 923–927. doi:10.1161/hc0802.104291

Moreno, P., Ryan, S., & Hopkins, D. (2001). Identification of lipid-rich aortic atherosclerotic plaques in living rabbits with a near infrared spectroscopy catheter. *Journal of the American College of Cardiology, Suppl A: 3A*(37).

Muller, J., Tawakol, A., Kathiresan, S., & Narula, J. (2006). New opportunities for identification and reduction of coronary risk: Treatment of vulnerable patients, arteries, and plaques. *Journal of the American College of Cardiology, C*(47), 2–6. doi:10.1016/j.jacc.2005.12.044

Nair, A., Kuban, B., Tuzcu, E., Schoenhagen, P., Nissen, S., & Vince, D. (2002). Coronary plaque classification with intravascular ultrasound radiofrequency data analysis. *Circulation, 106*, 2200–2206. doi:10.1161/01.CIR.0000035654.18341.5E

Neumeister, V., Scheibe, M., Lattke, P., & Jaross, W. (2002). Determination of the cholesterol-collagen ratio of arterial atherosclerotic plaques using near infrared spectroscopy as a possible measure of plaque stability. *Atherosclerosis, 165*, 251–257. doi:10.1016/S0021-9150(02)00279-4

Okubo, M., Kawasaki, M., & Ishihara, Y. (2008). Development of integrated backscatter intravascular ultrasound for tissue characterization of coronary plaques. *Ultrasound in Medicine & Biology, 34*, 655–663. doi:10.1016/j.ultrasmedbio.2007.09.015

Patel, N., Stamper, D., & Brezinski, M. (2005). Review of the ability of optical coherence tomography to characterize plaque, including a comparison with intravascular ultrasound. *Cardiovascular and Interventional Radiology, 28*, 1–9. doi:10.1007/s00270-003-0021-1

Raghunathan, D., Abdel Karim, A., & DaSilva, M. (2011). (in press). Association between the presence and extent of coronary lipid core plaques detected by near-infrared spectroscopy with post percutaneous coronary intervention myocardial infarction. *The American Journal of Cardiology*. doi:10.1016/j.amjcard.2011.01.044

Ramcharitar, S., Gonzalo, N., & van Geuns, R. e. (2009). First case of stenting of a vulnerable plaque in the SECRITT I trial-the dawn of a new era? *Nature Reviews Cardiology, 6*, 374–378. doi:10.1038/nrcardio.2009.34

Rodes-Cabau, J., Bertrand, O., & Larose, E. e. (2009). Comparison of plaque sealing with paclitaxel-eluting stents versus medical therapy for the treatment of moderate nonsignificant saphenous vein graft lesions. The moderate vein graft lesion stenting with the taxus stent and intravascular ultrasound (VELETI). *Circulationm, 120*, 1978–1986. doi:10.1161/CIRCULATIONAHA.109.874057

Ross, R. (1999). Atherosclerosis--An inflammatory disease. *The New England Journal of Medicine, 340*, 115–126. doi:10.1056/NEJM199901143400207

Sacks, F., Rudel, L., & Conner, A. (2009). Selective delipidation of plasma HDL enhances reverse cholesterol transport in vivo. *Journal of Lipid Research, 50*, 894–907. doi:10.1194/jlr.M800622-JLR200

Saeed, B., Banerjee, S., & Brilakis, E. (2010). Slow flow after stenting of a coronary lesion with a large lipid core plaque detected by near-infrared spectroscopy. *EuroIntervention, 6*, 545. doi:10.4244/EIJ30V6I4A90

Schaar, J., Mastik, F., & Regar, E. (2007). Current diagnostic modalities for vulnerable plaque detection. *Current Pharmaceutical Design, 13*, 995–1001. doi:10.2174/138161207780487511

Schultz, C., Serruys, P., & van der Ent, M. (2010). Prospective identification of a large lipid core coronary plaque with a novel near-infrared spectroscopy and intravascular ultrasound (NIR-IVUS) catheter: Infarction following stenting possibly due to distal embolization of plaque contents. *Journal of the American College of Cardiology, 314*, 314. doi:10.1016/j.jacc.2009.10.090

Sdringola, S., Assali, A., & Ghani, M. (2001). Risk assessment of slow or no-reflow phenomenon in aortocoronary vein graft percutaneous intervention. *Catheterization and Cardiovascular Interventions, 54*, 318–324. doi:10.1002/ccd.1290

Stone, G., Webb, J., & Cox, D. (2005). Distal microcirculatory protection during percutaneous coronary intervention in acute ST-segment elevation myocardial infarction: A randomized controlled trial. *Journal of the American Medical Association, 293*, 1063–1072. doi:10.1001/jama.293.9.1063

Sum, S., Madden, S., Hendricks, M., Chartier, S., & Muller, J. (2009). Near-infrared spectroscopy for the detection of lipid core coronary plaques. *Current Cardiovascular Imaging Reports, 2*, 307–315. doi:10.1007/s12410-009-0036-3

U.S. Food and Drug Administration. (n.d.). *Press annoucements.* Retrieved from http://www.fda.gov/ NewsEvents/Newsroom/ PressAnnouncements/2008/ ucm116888.html 2008

van de Pol, S., Romer, T., Puppels, G., & van der Laarse, A. (2002). Imaging of atherosclerosis. Raman spectroscopy of atherosclerosis. *Journal of Cardiovascular Risk, 9*, 255–261. doi:10.1097/00043798-200210000-00005

Wang, J., Geng, Y., & Guo, B. (2002). Near-infrared spectroscopic characterization of human advanced atherosclerotic plaques. *Journal of the American College of Cardiology, 39*, 1305–1313. doi:10.1016/S0735-1097(02)01767-9

Waxman, S., Dixon, S., & L'Allier, P. (2009). In vivo validation of a catheter-based near-infrared spectroscopy system for detection of lipid core coronary plaques: Initial results of the SPECTACL study. *JACC: Cardiovascular Imaging, 2*, 858–868. doi:10.1016/j.jcmg.2009.05.001

Waxman, S., Ishibashi, F., & Caplan, J. (2007). Rationale and use of near-infrared spectroscopy for detection of lipid-rich and vulnerable plaques. *Journal of Nuclear Cardiology, 14*, 719–728. doi:10.1016/j.nuclcard.2007.08.001

Waxman, S., Khabbaz, K., & Connolly, R. e. (2008). Intravascular imaging of atherosclerotic human coronaries in a porcine model: A feasibility study. *The International Journal of Cardiovascular Imaging, 24*, 37–44. doi:10.1007/s10554-007-9227-7

Waxman, S., Tang, J., & Marshik, B. (2004). In vivo detection of a coronary artificial target with a near infrared spectroscopy catheter. *American Journal of Cardiology. Suppl, 6A*(94), 141E.

Wentzel, J., van der Giessen, A., & Garg, S. e. (2010). In vivo 3D distribution of lipid-core plaque in human coronary artery as assessed by fusion of near infrared spectroscopy-intravascular ultrasound and multislice computed tomography scan. *Circulation: Cardiovascular Imaging, e*(3), 6-7.

Williams, P., & Norris, K. (2001). *Near-infrared technology in the agriculture and food industries.* American Association of Cereal Chemists.

Yun, S., Tearney, G., & Vakoc, B. (2006). Comprehensive volumetric optical microscopy in vivo. *Nature Medicine, 12*, 1429–1433. doi:10.1038/nm1450

Section 6
Intracardiac Echocardiography

Chapter 15
Intracardiac Echocardiography:
Procedural Steps and Clinical Application

Rajesh K Nair
Rigshospitalet, Denmark

Poay Huan Loh
Rigshospitalet, Denmark

Lars Sondergaard
Rigshospitalet, Denmark

ABSTRACT

Intracardiac echocardiography (ICE) represents one of the major recent advancements in cardiovascular imaging that has directly widened the scope of structural heart disease intervention. It has replaced trans-esophageal echocardiography in many of the structural heart disease interventional procedures and hence, precluded the need for general anaesthetic and its associated clinical and logistic issues. Although ICE has been available for more than two decades, it is still not widely used, and many interventional cardiologists remain unfamiliar to this technology. It is the aim of this chapter to provide a comprehensive overview of the commercially available devices with specific reference to the AcuNav™ catheter (Biosense Webster, California, USA), the procedural steps, and clinical applications of this imaging technique.

INTRODUCTION

Over the last decade, advancements in imaging modalities have widened the scope of structural heart disease intervention. What was once performed predominantly for diagnostic work up for congenital heart disease is now done with a therapeutic purpose. This way non-coronary inter-vention is rapidly evolving to a sub-speciality of its own. Many of the percutaneous approaches require interventional cardiologists to understand various imaging modalities other than conventional fluoroscopy. Echocardiography gains particular importance as it gives intra-operative structural and functional assessment of cardiac structures in real time. One major advance that has revolutionalized structural heart disease intervention is intracardiac echocardiography (ICE). In this

DOI: 10.4018/978-1-61350-095-8.ch015

chapter, the clinical use of the ICE with specific reference to AcuNav™ ICE catheter (Siemens, Mountain View, CA) will be discussed in detail.

BACKGROUND

Intra-cardiac echocardiography (ICE) refers to ultrasonographic imaging from within the cardiac chambers and the major blood vessels. ICE was first introduced in the early 1980s to visualize vascular lumen using mechanical higher frequency transducers (20–40 MHz). (Pandian, 1989) (Foster & Picard, 2001) With time advancements in catheter technology have made ICE catheters smaller, more maneuverable and thus more user friendly. The invasive cardiologist is often able to use simultaneous ICE and fluoroscopy guidance during the manipulation of devices or catheters inside confined cardiac chambers. Dependence on fluoroscopy and consequent exposure to X-rays for patients and laboratory personnel is thereby reduced.

The 3 commercially available ICE catheters at present are the AcuNav™ catheter (Biosense Webster, California, USA), the ViewFlex™ catheter (EP Medsystems, New Jersey, USA) and the Ultra ICE™ catheter (EP technologies, Boston Scientific, Boston, USA). The Ultra ICE™ catheter is a 8F sheath based catheter that houses a 9MHz beveled, single-element mechanical transducer which rotates at 1800 rpm. The distal 1 cm long sono-lucent sheath shields the mechanical transducer from direct contact with the endocardium. Providing a depth of field of approximately 5cm, the catheter acquires crossectional images perpendicular to its long axis, ideal for 3 dimensional reconstruction. This catheter is used primarily for electrophysiological studies. The other 2 available catheter systems (AcuNav™ and ViewFlex™) have multiple electronically directed piezoelectric crystals with lower frequency ranges. They provide improved depth of imaging, deeper sonar penetration and better visualization of cardiac anatomy. (Packer et al., 2002)

MAIN FOCUS OF THE CHAPTER

Parts of the Equipment and Procedure

The AcuNav™ catheter incorporates 64-element vector phased-array transducer (5.5-10MHz) with full spectral, colour and tissue Doppler capabilities. (Bartel, Caspari, Mueller, & Erbel, 2002) The transducer scans in a longitudinal plane with respect to the catheter providing a 90° sector image. The AcuNav™ catheter is for single use and can be attached to a standard ultrasound machines using adaptors. The catheter is available at 10F and 8F sizes, which are introduced via 11F and 9F sheaths respectively. The depth of ultra sound tissue penetration is up to 12cm for the 10F catheter and 16cm for the 8F catheter. This allows effective visualization of left sided heart structures from the right heart chambers. As there are no guide wires, the catheters should be carefully manipulated under fluoroscopy using 2 proximal rings. (Figure 1) Bi-plane fluoroscopy complements maneuvering of ICE catheter through tortuous iliac vessels or in complex cardiac anatomy with the radio-opaque transducer at the catheter tip as guide. Once inside the vascular system, the distal catheter tip may be articulated to 4 directions (anterior, posterior, left and right) using 2 proximal rings for optimal imaging. (Figure 1) The handle also has a 'locking knob' allowing the tip of the catheter to be 'locked' in order to maintain a desired plane and to provide 'hands-free' imaging. With experience, the catheter can be advanced with tip deflectability without fluoroscopy within the RA, through the tricuspid valve or even through a patent foramen ovale into LA. Different imaging planes are described below for optimal imaging of various cardiac structures with ICE.

"Home View": Tricuspid Valve

The 'home view' may be regarded as a good starting point for systematic ICE examination for the novice as this needs very little in way of catheter

Figure 1. AcuNav™ ICE catheter - note the three control rings at the handle, the most proximal one the 'locking knob' which locks the tip direction, the middle ring controls the left / right direction and the distal ring controls the anterior / posterior movement of the tip.

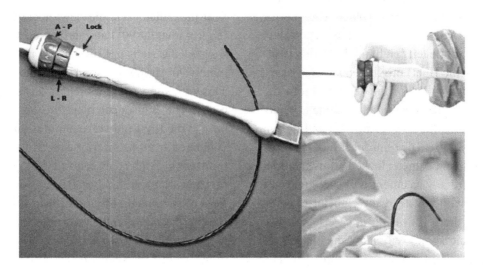

manipulation and is easily reproducible. The tip of the ICE catheter is placed in the mid right atrium (RA) with all the directional control rings set to neutral. Under fluoroscopy, radio-opaque transducer at the ICE catheter tip usually faces the 7th intervertebral disk of the thoracic spine. (Figure 2) Subtle anterior and leftward movement of the control rings may be required to align the imaging palette at the catheter tip to orient towards the tricuspid valve. The 'home view' position shows the right atrium (RA), tricuspid valve (TV),

right ventricle (RV) and right ventricular outflow tract (RVOT) clearly. Occasionally the long axis view of the pulmonary valve and the short axis view of the aortic valve may also appear in this imaging plane.

Atrial Septal View: Inter Atrial Septum (IAS)

From the home view, the catheter tip is slightly advanced further towards the superior vena cava

Figure 2. Home view showing RA, RV and RVOT. The shaded area represents structures seen in this view. ICE catheter (arrow) in the mid-right atrium with the transducer facing the tricuspid valve. The tricuspid valve and right ventricle in- and out-flow are seen.

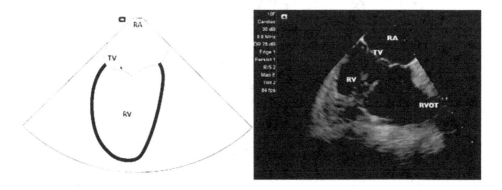

(SVC). The entire catheter is then rotated clockwise (approximately 160°) and the tip deflected posteriorly (using the directional ring) bringing the inter atrial septum (IAS) in plane. The anterior aspect of the IAS is seen towards the aortic valve. Figure 3 (a) Subtle left / right tip deflection (usually towards the right) might become necessary for further evaluation of the septum. From the septal view, further cranial advancement of the catheter towards the SVC brings RA and IAS in view with the SVC. The transducer faces the IAS and SVC. With the catheter locked in this position, gentle forward advancement will show more of SVC while withdrawal of the catheter towards the IVC (to the level of 8th intervertebral disc of the thoracic spine) will show the entire IAS in the superior / inferior plane. Figure 3 (b) The inferior rim in particular is often challenging to be visualized using trans-oesophageal echocardiography (TOE).

Short Axis View: IAS, Aortic Valve, LVOT

With the catheter in home view, clockwise rotation (approximately 90°) and deflection towards the right of the right-left directional ring (approximately 90°) brings the short axis of aorta in plane. This view shows the IAS in its anterior - posterior plane. The transducer plane in this position is near to the tricuspid valve annulus and the aorta is imaged from its inferior aspect. In contrast to the trans-oesophageal echo (TOE), RA is seen towards the near field and LA towards the far field of the image. Figure 4 (a) In this position, the tip of the ICE catheter is adjacent to the TV annulus, inferior to the aorta. On fluoroscopy, the radio-opaque transducer pane should be between the 6th and 7th intervertebral discs of the thoracic spine, oriented anterior-superior plane (facing cranially) Figure 5 (a). Quite like in TOE, further interrogation or off axis views of cardiac structures

Figure 3. (a) Short axis view, showing the anterior (towards the aortic valve) and the posterior rim of the inter atrial septum (IAS). (b) Long axis view (catheter tip at the junction of SVC and RA), showing the superior and inferior rim of the IAS. Note the transeptal puncture needle. (c) IAS with atrial septal closure device in situ. (d) X Ray AP view showing the ICE catheter position for optimal view of IAS. Note a PFO closure device in situ.

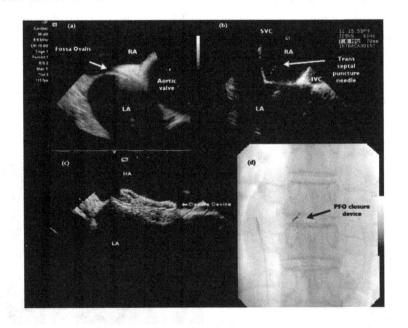

Figure 4. (a) Short axis view of the aortic valve (AV), showing non (NCC), right (RCC) and left (LCC) coronary cusps. (b) Long axis view of the aortic valve. (c) Corevalve aortic prosthesis in situ (d) Short axis view of the aortic valve in relation to the long axis view of the pulmonary valve (PV) and right ventricular outflow tract (RVOT).

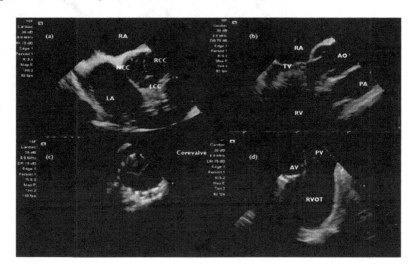

Figure 5. (a) X-Ray AP view of ICE catheter position (black arrow head) for short axis view of the aortic valve (AV). Note the atrial septal position with PFO closure device in situ (black star). (b) X-Ray AP view of the ICE catheter position (black arrow head) for long axis view of the aortic valve. Note pigtail catheter (white arrow head) marking the aortic valve, Amplatzer stiff guide wire at LV apex (white arrow) and a pacing lead at the RV apex (black arrow).

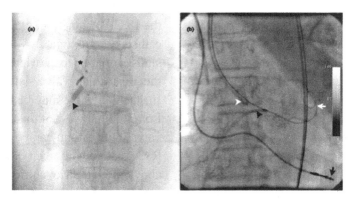

are obtained by subtle catheter tip manipulation from the standard views.

Septal, short axis and long axis views are useful to examine the entire IAS anatomy and its morphological variants. IAS runs obliquely from the anterior aspect of the heart, extending posteriorly and to the right. When seen from the right atrium, the fibro-membranous fossa ovalis is clearly visualized as a central crater, surrounded by a muscular rim. An ostium primum ASD is seen as a defect along the anteroinferior rim of the IAS and a secundum ASD is seen as a clear defect within the fossa ovalis. Micro bubble contrast study to ascertain functional characteristics

Figure 6. (a), (b) Left atrium with colour flow Doppler along the ostia of left inferior and superior pulmonary veins. (c) Right inferior and superior pulmonary veins.

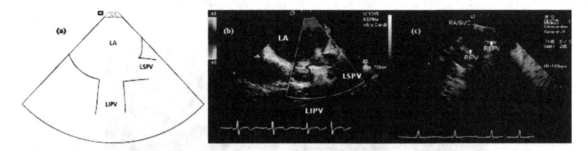

of an ASD is best performed in these views. Other abnormalities such as an aneurysmal IAS or lipomatous hypertrophy of the IAS may be also be seen. (Zanchetta et al., 2003) Combination of short axis and long axis views are used to measure the anterior - posterior and inferior - superior diameters of an ASD respectively. Doppler colour flow beside an inflated sizing balloon across the ASD and appropriate position for atrial septal puncture may be visualized in these views. Abnormalities of the aortic valve and the origin of the right and left coronary ostia may also be assessed.

Pulmonary Veins

Depending on the transducer position, pulmonary veins (PV) may be seen in the septal, short or long axis views. Anatomic configuration of PV drainage into the left atrium may have considerable variation, including the presence of a common ostium. (Scharf et al., 2003) From the atrial septal view, further clockwise rotation and mild caudal withdrawal of the catheter to mid to low RA shows the left atrial appendage (LAA) and the drainage of left superior and inferior pulmonary veins into the postero-lateral aspect of the LA. Left atrial appendage thrombus is imaged clearly during invasive procedures in this view. The right superior and inferior pulmonary veins are visualized by advancing the probe cranially into the SVC (from home view) and rotating clockwise

the catheter 180° Minor anterior flexion of the catheter tip may be required such that the transducer aligns to the lateral wall of the RA/SVC. PV inflow can be assessed in these views using pulsed wave Doppler (Figure 6).

IVC-RA Junction: Coronary Sinus (CS)

With the directional rings in neutral position, the catheter is withdrawn caudally into to inferior vena cava (IVC) - RA junction (level of 8th intervertebral disc of the thoracic spine). From the IVC-RA junction, clockwise rotation of the catheter (approximately 140°) shows the coronary sinus in relation to the tricuspid valve, its annulus, the Eustachian valve, lateral wall of RA. The Eustachian valve may be mistaken for an ASD. Longitudinal view of the CS with the Thebesian valve at its ostium can be seen draining into the RA. Anatomically the CS is situated posteriorly above the left atrioventricular junction, opening into the right atrium between the inferior vena cava and the tricuspid valve.

This view is frequently used by cardiac electrophysiologists as anatomical landmarks for ablation procedures and coronary sinus catheterisation. The 'extra-septal' nature of an inferior sinus venosus ASD is easily visualized as overriding of the IVC and infero-posterior bi-atrial connection on this view. Largely intact inferior-posterior rim of the fossa ovalis is seen continuous along the septal,

Figure 7. (a) Short axis view of coronary sinus (CS) in relation to the right (RA) and left (LA) atria (b) ICE image showing CS with catheter in situ and mitral valve (MV) and left ventricle (LV) (c) Long axis view of coronary sinus with catheter in situ.

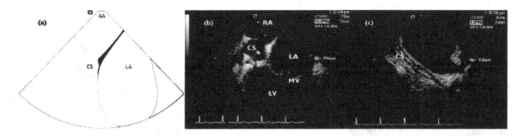

short axis and long axis views as described earlier. Pericardial effusion outside the lateral wall of RA, persistent redundant ridge of Eustachian valve or an unusually prominent Chiari's net- work can also be seen in this view.

Four Chamber View

Four chamber view is obtained from the mid RA. With the catheter in neutral position, the tip is slightly anteflexed (using anterior - posterior deflection ring), rotated clockwise and gently advanced to abut the IAS. On fluoroscopy, the transducer plane should face the LV apex. In this view, the entire LA, LV, mitral valve (MV) and part of RA and RV comes into plane. Minor left

and right adjustments will show the membranous inter ventricular septum (IVS) and left atrial appendage (LAA). This view is used for VSD closure, (Cao, Zabal, Koenig, Sandhu, & Hijazi, 2005) interrogate the LAA for thrombus, and MV intervention (optimal balloon positioning during mitral valvotomy). (Applebaum et al., 1998)

Imaging from the RV

With the catheter controls in neutral, the tip is advanced gently to the roof of the RA. From this position, the ICE catheter is ante-flexed (using the anterior - posterior directional ring) to see RV, TV and its sub-valvular apparatus. The catheter tip under ICE guidance is gently advanced through

Figure 8. (a) 4 chamber view of the heart, ICE catheter positioned within right atrium, showing inter-ventricular septum (IVS), right ventricle (RV) and the left ventricle (LV). (b) Modified 4 chamber view showing mitral valve (MV) and left atrium (LA). Note Amplatzer stiff wire positioned inside the LV (white arrow).

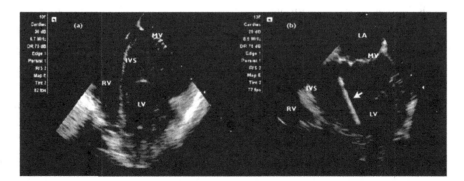

Figure 9. Long-axis view of the left ventricle (LV) obtained from within the right ventricular outflow tract. Note the mitral valve (MV), inter ventricular septum (IVS) and small loculated posterior pericardial effusion (PE). (b) X-Ray AP view showing ICE catheter position for LV long axis. Note ICE catheter position (black arrow heads) in relation to the aortic valve marked by a pigtail catheter (white arrow head), pace maker lead at the RV apex (black arrows) and the tip of Amplatzer stiff guide wire at the LV apex (white arrow) (c) Short axis view of the mitral valve showing the anterior (AMVL) and posterior (PMVL) mitral valve leaflets.

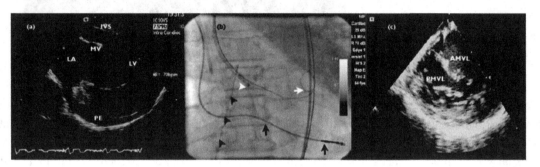

the tricuspid orifice into the RV. As the tip passes near the septal commissure towards the base of the RVOT, the anterior flexion is reduced and the tip straightened. This maneuver allows the catheter tip to advance towards the low lateral base of the RVOT and gives good images of the mitral valve and LV. Clockwise rotation of the catheter at this position is often necessary to shift from off-axis images to true long axis views of LV. Equivalent parasternal long axis views which are seen during TTE can be obtained this way. Paradoxical motion artifacts may occur on tissue Doppler when the catheter tip floats inside the RV chamber. Hence for an accurate assessment of LV wall motion, the catheter tip is allowed to touch the RV walls by minor adjustments of the directional rings. Adjusting the transducer plane to face the MV from within the RV gives short axis views of the MV. To get optimal images of the MV, the catheter tip is maintained close to the IVS. This view is particularly useful in patients with atrial enlargement where images of the MV alongside the IAS are suboptimal.

With the catheter tip positioned along the RVOT, the catheter is manipulated gently, guided by echo images and fluoroscopy to visualize the pulmonary valve (PV). The ultrasound probe is aimed towards the RVOT and under fluoroscopy, the radio-opaque transducer plane at the distal catheter tip usually faces upwards. The relation of the PV to the main pulmonary truck and its branches are also clearly seen in this position.

Clinical Applications of ICE

Innovative ways of replacing conventional ultrasound techniques (trans-thoracic or trans-oesophageal) by ICE offer numerous advantages during an percutaneous non-coronary cardiac interventions.

ICE is usually performed under local anesthetic and eliminates risks associated with TOE like oesophageal tear, need for general anesthesia or heavy sedation. Patients are able to communicate to the operator of any discomfort during the procedure. In comparison to TTE or TOE, there is little interference to cardio respiratory cycles and virtually no acoustic barriers between the transducer and cardiac structures. High resolution ICE images coupled with Doppler analysis reliably differentiates specific pathology like constrictive pericarditis from restrictive cardiomyopathy, better than standard TOE or TTE approaches. Intraluminal or intracardiac thrombi, can be visualised directly and if need be disrupted endoluminally using an ICE catheter. During cardiac interventions, ICE images appear to provide comparable or better images to other imaging modalities (Chi et al., 2001) (Bartel, Müller, Caspari, & Erbel, 2002) (Liu et al., 2004) (Bartel et al., 2005) (Koenig & Cao, 2005) Unlike TTE or TEE, ICE has relatively larger field of view and better acoustic contrast between soft tissue structures. RV, IAS (particularly the long axis views, detecting inferior or superior sinus venosus ASD), pulmonary veins (partial anomalous pulmonary venous system), tricuspid, pulmonary and aortic valves and their associated morphological variants (strands or pathological vegetation) are better appreciated using ICE. The newer generation of phase array ICE catheters, provide high resolution images in familiar anatomical sector formats as in conventional TOE. The catheter can be locked in a desired imaging plane, providing continuous real time anatomical and functional guidance for the operator. The interventional cardiologist can often perform ICE safely during a procedure. (Johnson, Seward, & Packer, 2002) Cost burden and X-ray exposure to additional operators assigned for imaging are reduced. This often offsets the cost implications of a single use ICE catheter. (Alboliras & Hijazi, 2004) Evidence of post-procedure or intra-procedure complications like interference of a closure or occlusion devices with valve function or residual paraprosthetic leaks may be quickly identified using ICE. Furthermore, real time imaging using ICE alerts the operator to potentially dangerous complications like thrombus formation on catheters, ablation electrodes, endocardial lesion sites, LAA or cardiac tamponade.

Trans-septal Puncture (TSP)

Successful access of the left atrium from the right side of the heart is a crucial step in performing procedures like mitral valvuloplasty, left sided electrophysiological studies, closure of mitral paravalvular leak or occlusion of left atrial appendage. Experienced operators perform routine transeptal puncture under fluoroscopy alone. Tactile response from the TSP apparatus falling into the fossa ovalis and radiographic clues from catheters placed over the aortic root, coronary sinus or His bundle electrode catheters are used to perform TSP. Even with the aid of bi-plane fluoroscopy, due to anatomic variability, there is an inherent risk in perforating the LA free wall or even the aorta with the Brockenbrough needle, which is used for TSP. Incidence of cardiac perforation under fluoroscopy guidance ranges from 1.0% to 4.3%. (Hahn et al., 2009) Whilst TOE images are adequate for visualizing IAS, images from ICE catheters can be just as informative, safe and effective. (Hijazi et al., 2001) (Chi et al., 2001) (Szili-Torok et al., 2001) (Daoud, Kalbfletsch & Hummel, 1999) (Koenig & Cao, 2005) The near field images obtained using ICE is thought to be better than TOE images, proving its utility for TSP. (Herrmann et al., 2005) (Epstein, Smith, & Ten Hoff, 2007) ICE guidance allows direct visualization of anatomical structures adjacent to the septum that could cause potential complications. ICE helps in distorted anatomy both in procedures related to electrophysiology (Shalganov, Paprika, Borbás, Temesvári, & Szili-Török, 2005) and mitral valve intervention. (Cafri, de la Guardia, Barasch, Brink, & Smalling, 2000) Furthermore, overall laboratory time, procedure time and fluoroscopy time were reduced when operators relied on imaging using ICE compared to TOE for percutaneous ASD/PFO closure. (Boccalandro, Baptista, Muench, Carter, & Smalling, 2004) (Bartel et al., 2003) Depending on atrial anatomy the site of trans-septal puncture may also be relevant to the overall outcome of certain procedures. Ultrasound guidance is particularly useful in the presence of complex cardiac anatomy or when double TSP is warranted. ICE does offer excellent images of the atrial septum in multiple planes, allowing accurate localization of a site for TSP, optimal for specific cardiac procedure. (Bazaz & Schwartzman, 2003) Figure 3(b).

Transcatheter ASD/PFO Closure

ICE is most commonly used for atrial septal interventions. Patent foramen ovale (PFO) in the presence of an aneursymal atrial septum is an indication for device closure in order to prevent paradoxical embolism in patients with a history of cryptogenic stroke. (Mareedu, Shah, Mesa, & McCauley, 2007) (Knebel et al., 2004) Guide catheters, guide wires, sizing balloons and various closure devices are clearly visualized across the IAS with ICE. Combination of different views described above are utilized for the choice of a particular closure device, its optimal deployment, residual shunts and anatomical relation of the device to adjacent structures. Figure 3 ICE is considered a better clinical tool than TOE with similar cost implications. (Chi et al., 2001) (Hijazi et al., 2001) (Alboliras & Hijazi, 2004)

Ventricular Septal Defect (VSD) Closure

Surgery remains the gold standard treatment for VSD. However in selected patients, percutaneous closure is a safe option. Echocardiographic guidance is crucial in identifying the precise location of VSD and optimal placement of a closure device. ICE provides excellent image windows to evaluate interventricular septum (IVS). (Cao et al., 2005) Figure 8

Mitral Valve Intervention

Percutaneous balloon valvuloplasty offers a safe and effective therapeutic option to mitral stenosis in selected patients. (Feldman, 2000) Although many operators perform the procedure using fluoroscopy alone, in patients with mitral stenosis and distorted atrial anatomy real time echocardiographic guidance improves safety

during the procedure. ICE helps in optimal TSP, placement of balloon across the mitral valve, anatomical and functional evaluation of the valve prior to and immediately after mitral valvotomy. (Hung, Fu, Yeh, Wu, & Wong, 1996) (Salem et al., 2002) (Green, Hansgen, & Carroll, 2004) Figure 8,9 LAA may also be visualized for presence of thrombus using ICE.

Percutaneous mitral valve repair using Mitraclip is an evolving therapy for patients with functional and degenerative mitral valve insufficiency. Although placement of Mitraclip is currently performed using 2D or 3D TOE under general anaesthesia, successful repair of the mitral valve has been reported in swine model using ICE. (Liddicoat et al., 2003) (Naqvi, Zarbatany, Molloy, Logan, & Buchbinder, 2006) As operators gain familiarity with the Mitraclip catheters, there is the potential of performing complex procedures like percutaneous mitral valve repair using ICE.

Pulmonary Valve Implant

Percutaneous pulmonary valve implantation using the Melody (Medtronic) or Edwards Sapien THV (Transcatheter Heart Valve, Edwards Lifesciences, Irvine, California) is usually performed by fluoroscopy alone. However in an occasional patient with challenging anatomy, excellent images of the pulmonary valve can be obtained using an ICE catheter positioned along the RVOT. Figure 4(d) Using ICE catheters the relation of the pulmonary valve to the main pulmonary trunk and its branches are clearly seen, while ICE can be used to assess the degree of functional stenosis or residual regurgitation after a pulmonary valve intervention.

Transcatheter Aortic Valve Implant (TAVI)

Interventional cardiologists rely heavily on fluoroscopic markers (using catheters placed in the right coronary sinus or calcification along aortic annulus) for positioning trans-catheter aortic valve implants (TAVI). In patients with excessive LV hypertrophy, concomitant mitral valve disease, native bicuspid aortic valve or prosthetic mitral valve, ultrasound guidance is crucial. Many centers perform intra procedural TOE for direct visualization aortic annulus. However as the TOE probe is placed at the level of upper or mid oesophagus, it hinders simultaneous fluoroscopic guidance. Experienced centers have started performing TAVI (trans-femoral and subclavian artery approaches) under local anaesthesia and sedation using ICE. ICE shows excellent views of the aortic valve (both short axis and long axis), aortic root, coronary ostia and LVOT. Figure 4(c), 10

Cardiac Biopsy

Obtaining myocardial tissue during cardiac biopsy safely is often challenging when patients have complex cardiac anatomy. ICE provides excellent images for targeted biopsy of intra cardiac tumours, post transplant screening. (Segar, Bourdillon, Elsner, Kesler, & Feigenbaum, 1995)

Electrophysiological Procedures

The close relation of many accessory pathways to the natural atrioventricular conduction system, coronary ostia or cardiac valves means that direct visualization of the arrhythmic substrate improves safety in ablation procedures. Direct contact between the ablation catheter and endo-cardial tissue plays an important role in successful electrophysiological ablation. ICE provides accurate, real time, site specific guidance during complex electrophysiological ablation (Chugh, Chan, Johnson, & Packer, 1999) (Callans et al., 1999) (Anderson & Ho, 2006) (Daccarett et al., 2007) Meticulous observation of pulmonary vein ostia by planimetry (Mangrum, Mounsey, Kok, DiMarco, & Haines, 2002) and Doppler (Ren, Marchlinski, Callan, & Sado, 2002) helps to prevent pulmonary vein stenosis, a recognized

complication of PV ablation. (Saad et al., 2003) During complex EP studies, use of ICE helps to reduce fluoroscopy time. (Kalman, Olgin, Karch, & Lesh, 1997) (Lesh, Kalman, & Karch, 1998)

LIMITATIONS

The learning curve performing procedures with ICE guidance is often more superior than with fluoroscopy alone. (Epstein, Smith, & TenHoff, 1998) This may be particularly relevant for operators who are conventionally not used to 'echocardiographic imaging' of the heart. Distorted cardiac anatomy due to chamber dilatation or complex congenital heart disease might prove suboptimal in orienting cardiac structures in standard ICE views as described above. In comparison with TOE, detailed images of mitral valve, LAA, 4 chamber views may be more difficult to obtain with ICE, especially when the transducer tip is in the RA. Monoplane ICE catheters are less versatile and demand careful tip articulation and rotation for comprehensive evaluation of intra cardiac structures or devices. Most of the ICE catheters lack forward facing transducers. Hence, fluoroscopy is still necessary for safe negotiation of the catheter through blood vessels.

Conventional 5 chamber view seen in TOE (obtained upper oesophagus level at 0 degree) showing the relation of LVOT, aortic valve and the anterior mitral valve leaflet is virtually impossible to be obtained using ICE. This is a drawback of using ICE during deployment of Corevalve (where a bioprosthetic tissue valve is stitched on a stent skirt ideally positioned in LVOT), especially in patients with significant LV hypertrophy (Figure 10).

FUTURE RESEARCH DIRECTIONS

Incorporation of omniplane transducers with 3D capability (Ding, Rao, Nagueh, & Khoury,

Figure 10. Limitations of ICE, TOE images (a) Long axis view of aortic valve stenosis in relation to the mitral valve (MV) (b) Long axis view of Corevalve in situ, deployed percutaneously, in relation with MV. (c) Residual moderate paraprosthetic incompetence from Corevalve.

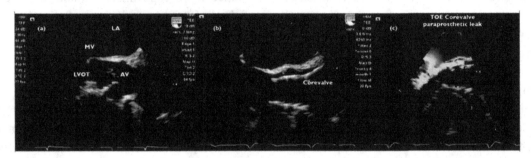

2005) will decrease learning curve and perhaps extend the use of ICE for more complex invasive procedures like percutaneous mitral valve repair. Advancements in catheter techniques may also decrease the size of catheters (Lee, Idriss, Wolf, & Smith, 2004) allowing retrograde transarterial access for visualization of the left heart via the aortic valve or PDA closure.

CONCLUSION

Over the last decade, ICE has emerged as a promising tool in interventional cardiology. Real time structural, functional and haemodynamic information and early identification of complications has widened the scope of percutaneous intervention for structural heart disease and electrophysiology.

REFERENCES

Alboliras, E. T., & Hijazi, Z. M. (2004). Comparison of costs of intracardiac echocardiography and transesophageal echocardiography in monitoring percutaneous device closure of atrial septal defect in children and adults. *The American Journal of Cardiology*, *94*(5), 690–692. doi:10.1016/j.amjcard.2004.05.048

Anderson, R. H., & Ho, S. Y. (2006). Anatomy of the atrioventricular junctions with regard to ventricular preexcitation. *Pacing and Clinical Electrophysiology*, *20*(8), 2072–2076. doi:10.1111/j.1540-8159.1997.tb03631.x

Applebaum, R. M., Kasliwal, R. R., Kanojia, A., Seth, A., Bhandari, S., & Trehan, N. (1998). Utility of three-dimensional echocardiography during balloon mitral valvuloplasty. *Journal of the American College of Cardiology*, *32*(5), 1405–1409. doi:10.1016/S0735-1097(98)00386-6

Bartel, T., Caspari, G., Mueller, S., & Erbel, R. (2002). Intracardiac echocardiography-technology and clinical role. *Journal of Clinical and Basic Cardiology*, *5*(2), 133–138.

Bartel, T., Konorza, T., Arjumand, J., Ebradlidze, T., Eggebrecht, H., & Caspari, G. (2003). Intracardiac echocardiography is superior to conventional monitoring for guiding device closure of interatrial communications. *Circulation*, *107*(6), 795–797. doi:10.1161/01.CIR.0000057547.00909.1C

Bartel, T., Konorza, T., Neudorf, U., Ebralize, T., Eggebrecht, H., Gutersohn, A., & Erbel, R. (2005). Intracardiac echocardiography: An ideal guiding tool for device closure of interatrial communications. *European Journal of Echocardiography*, *6*(2), 92–96. doi:10.1016/j.euje.2004.07.007

Bartel, T., Müller, S., Caspari, G., & Erbel, R. (2002). Intracardiac and intraluminal echocardiography: Indications and standard approaches. *Ultrasound in Medicine & Biology*, *28*(8), 997–1003. doi:10.1016/S0301-5629(02)00551-3

Bazaz, R., & Schwartzman, D. (2003). Site-Selective atrial septal puncture. *Journal of Cardiovascular Electrophysiology*, *14*(2), 196–199. doi:10.1046/j.1540-8167.2003.02377.x

Boccalandro, F., Baptista, E., Muench, A., Carter, C., & Smalling, R. W. (2004). Comparison of intracardiac echocardiography versus transesophageal echocardiography guidance for percutaneous transcatheter closure of atrial septal defect. *The American Journal of Cardiology*, *93*(4), 437–440. doi:10.1016/j.amjcard.2003.10.037

Cafri, C., de la Guardia, B., Barasch, E., Brink, J., & Smalling, R. W. (2000). Transseptal puncture guided by intracardiac echocardiography during percutaneous transvenous mitral commissurotomy in patients with distorted anatomy of the fossa ovalis. *Catheterization and Cardiovascular Interventions*, *50*(4), 463–467. doi:10.1002/1522-726X(200008)50:4<463::AID-CCD21>3.0.CO;2-E

Callans, D. J., Ren, J. F., Schwartzman, D., Gottlieb, C. D., Chaudhry, F. A., & Marchlinski, F. E. (1999). Narrowing of the superior vena cava-right atrium junction during radiofrequency catheter ablation for inappropriate sinus tachycardia: Analysis with intracardiac echocardiography. *Journal of the American College of Cardiology*, *33*(6), 1667–1670. doi:10.1016/S0735-1097(99)00047-9

Cao, Q. L., Zabal, C., Koenig, P., Sandhu, S., & Hijazi, Z. M. (2005). Initial clinical experience with intracardiac echocardiography in guiding transcatheter closure of perimembranous ventricular septal defects: Feasibility and comparison with transesophageal echocardiography. *Catheterization and Cardiovascular Interventions*, *66*(2), 258–267. doi:10.1002/ccd.20463

Chugh, S. S., Chan, R. C., Johnson, S. B., & Packer, D. L. (1999). Catheter tip orientation affects radiofrequency ablation lesion size in the canine left ventricle. *Pacing and Clinical Electrophysiology*, *22*(3), 413–420. doi:10.1111/j.1540-8159.1999.tb00469.x

Daccarett, M., Segerson, N. M., Günther, J., Nölker, G., Gutleben, K., Brachmann, J., & Marrouche, N. F. (2007). Blinded correlation study of three-dimensional electro-anatomical image integration and phased array intra-cardiac echocardiography for left atrial mapping. *Europace*, *9*(10), 923–926. doi:10.1093/europace/eum192

Daoud, E. G., Kalbfletsch, S. J., & Hummel, J. D. (1999). Intracardiac echocardiography to guide transseptal left heart catheterization for radiofrequency catheter ablation. *Journal of Cardiovascular Electrophysiology*, *10*(3), 358–363. doi:10.1111/j.1540-8167.1999.tb00683.x

Ding, C., Rao, L., Nagueh, S. F., & Khoury, D. S. (2005). Dynamic three-dimensional visualization of the left ventricle by intracardiac echocardiography. *Ultrasound in Medicine & Biology*, *31*(1), 15–21. doi:10.1016/j.ultrasmedbio.2004.09.016

Epstein, L. M., Smith, T., & Ten Hoff, H. (2007). Nonfluoroscopic transseptal catheterization. *Journal of Cardiovascular Electrophysiology*, *9*(6), 625–630. doi:10.1111/j.1540-8167.1998.tb00945.x

Epstein, L. M., Smith, T., & TenHoff, H. (1998). Nonfluoroscopic transseptal catheterization: Safety and efficacy of intracardiac echocardiographic guidance. *Journal of Cardiovascular Electrophysiology*, *9*(6), 625–630. doi:10.1111/j.1540-8167.1998.tb00945.x

Feldman, T. (2000). Rheumatic mitral stenosis. *Current Treatment Options in Cardiovascular Medicine*, *2*(2), 93–103. doi:10.1007/s11936-000-0002-5

Foster, G. P., & Picard, M. H. (2001). Intracardiac echocardiography: Current uses and future directions. *Echocardiography-Jnl Cardiovascular Ultrasound & Allied Techniques, 18*(1), 43–48.

Green, N. E., Hansgen, A. R., & Carroll, J. D. (2004). Initial clinical experience with intracardiac echocardiography in guiding balloon mitral valvuloplasty: Technique, safety, utility, and limitations. *Catheterization and Cardiovascular Interventions, 63*(3), 385–394. doi:10.1002/ccd.20177

Hahn, K., Gal, R., Sarnoski, J., Kubota, J., Schmidt, D. H., & Bajwa, T. K. (2009). Transesophageal echocardiographically guided atrial transseptal catheterization in patients with normal-sized atria: Incidence of complications. *Clinical Cardiology, 18*(4), 217–220. doi:10.1002/clc.4960180408

Herrmann, H. C., Silvestry, F. E., Glaser, R., See, V., Kasner, S., & Bradbury, D. (2005). Percutaneous patent foramen ovale and atrial septal defect closure in adults: Results and device comparison in 100 consecutive implants at a single center. *Catheterization and Cardiovascular Interventions, 64*(2), 197–203. doi:10.1002/ccd.20260

Hijazi, Z. M., Wang, Z., Cao, Q. L., Koenig, P., Waight, D., & Lang, R. (2001). Transcatheter closure of atrial septal defects and patent foramen ovale under intracardiac echocardiographic guidance: Feasibility and comparison with transesophageal echocardiography. *Catheterization and Cardiovascular Interventions, 52*(2), 194–199. doi:10.1002/1522-726X(200102)52:2<194::AID-CCD1046>3.0.CO;2-4

Hung, J. S., Fu, M., Yeh, K. H., Wu, C. J., & Wong, P. (1996). Usefulness of intracardiac echocardiography in complex transseptal catheterization during percutaneous transvenous mitral commissurotomy. In *Mayo Clinic Proceedings*.

Jan, S. L., Hwang, B., Lee, P. C., Fu, Y. C., Chiu, P. S., & Chi, C. S. (2001). Intracardiac ultrasound assessment of atrial septal defect: Comparison with transthoracic echocardiographic, angiocardiographic, and balloon-sizing measurements. *Cardiovascular and Interventional Radiology, 24*(24). doi:10.1007/s002700000397

Johnson, S. B., Seward, J. B., & Packer, D. L. (2002). Phased-array intracardiac echocardiography for guiding transseptal catheter placement: Utility and learning curve. *Pacing and Clinical Electrophysiology, 25*(4 Pt 1), 402–407. doi:10.1046/j.1460-9592.2002.00402.x

Kalman, J. M., Olgin, J. E., Karch, M. R., & Lesh, M. D. (1997). Use of intracardiac echocardiography in interventional electrophysiology. *Pacing and Clinical Electrophysiology, 20*(9), 2248–2262. doi:10.1111/j.1540-8159.1997.tb04244.x

Knebel, F., Gliech, V., Walde, T., Panda, A., Sanad, W., & Eddicks, S. (2004). Percutaneous closure of interatrial communications in adults - prospective embolism prevention study with two- and three-dimensional echocardiography. *Cardiovascular Ultrasound, 2*, 5. doi:10.1186/1476-7120-2-5

Koenig, P., & Cao, Q. L. (2005). Echocardiographic guidance of transcatheter closure of atrial septal defects intracardiac echocardiography better than transesophageal echocardiography? *Pediatric Cardiology, 26*(2), 135–139. doi:10.1007/s00246-004-0952-6

Lee, W., Idriss, S. F., Wolf, P. D., & Smith, S. W. (2004). A miniaturized catheter 2-D array for real-time, 3-D intracardiac echocardiography. *IEEE Transactions on Ultrasonics, Ferroelectrics, and Frequency Control, 51*(10), 1334–1346. doi:10.1109/TUFFC.2004.1350962

Lesh, M. D., Kalman, J. M., & Karch, M. R. (1998). Use of intracardiac echocardiography during electrophysiologic evaluation and therapy of atrial arrhythmias. *Journal of Cardiovascular Electrophysiology*, *9*(8Suppl), S40–S47.

Liddicoat, J. R., Mac Neill, B. D., Gillinov, A. M., Cohn, W. E., Chin, C. H., & Prado, A. D. (2003). Percutaneous mitral valve repair: A feasibility study in an ovine model of acute ischemic mitral regurgitation. *Catheterization and Cardiovascular Interventions*, *60*(3), 410–416. doi:10.1002/ccd.10662

Liu, Z., McCormick, D., Dairywala, I., Surabhi, S., Goldberg, S., Turi, Z., & Vannan, M. A. (2004). Catheter-based intracardiac echocardiography in the interventional cardiac laboratory. *Catheterization and Cardiovascular Interventions*, *63*(1), 63–71. doi:10.1002/ccd.20106

Mangrum, J. M., Mounsey, J. P., Kok, L. C., DiMarco, J. P., & Haines, D. E. (2002). Intracardiac echocardiography-guided, anatomically based radiofrequency ablation of focal atrial fibrillation originating from pulmonary veins. *Journal of the American College of Cardiology*, *39*(12), 1964–1972. doi:10.1016/S0735-1097(02)01893-4

Mareedu, R. K., Shah, M. S., Mesa, J. E., & McCauley, C. S. (2007). Percutaneous closure of patent foramen ovale: A case series and literature review. *Clinical Medicine & Research*, *5*(4), 218. doi:10.3121/cmr.2007.764

Naqvi, T. Z., Zarbatany, D., Molloy, M. D., Logan, J., & Buchbinder, M. (2006). Intracardiac echocardiography for percutaneous mitral valve repair in a swine model. *Journal of the American Society of Echocardiography*, *19*(2), 147–153. doi:10.1016/j.echo.2005.09.008

Packer, D. L., Stevens, C. L., Curley, M. G., Bruce, C. J., Miller, F. A., & Khandheria, B. K. (2002). Intracardiac phased-array imaging: Methods and initial clinical experience with high resolution, under blood visualization: Initial experience with intracardiac phased-array ultrasound. *Journal of the American College of Cardiology*, *39*(3), 509–516. doi:10.1016/S0735-1097(01)01764-8

Pandian, N. G. (1989). Intravascular and intracardiac ultrasound imaging. An old concept, now on the road to reality. *Circulation*, *80*(4), 1091. doi:10.1161/01.CIR.80.4.1091

Ren, J. F., Marchlinski, F. E., Callan, D. J., & Zado, E. S. (2002). Intracardiac doppler echocardiographic quantification of pulmonary vein flow velocity: An effective technique for monitoring pulmonary vein ostia narrowing during focal atrial fibrillation ablation. *Journal of Cardiovascular Electrophysiology*, *13*(11), 1076–1081. doi:10.1046/j.1540-8167.2002.01076.x

Saad, E. B., Marrouche, N. F., Saad, C. P., Ha, E., Bash, D., & White, R. D. (2003). Pulmonary vein stenosis after catheter ablation of atrial fibrillation: Emergence of a new clinical syndrome. *Annals of Internal Medicine*, *138*, 634–638.

Salem, M. I., Makaryus, A. N., Kort, S., Chung, E., Marchant, D., Ong, L., & Mangion, J. (2002). Intracardiac echocardiography using the acunav ultrasound catheter during percutaneous balloon mitral valvuloplasty. *Journal of the American Society of Echocardiography*, *15*(12), 1533–1537. doi:10.1067/mje.2002.126771

Scharf, C., Sneider, M., Case, I., Chugh, A., Lai, S. W. K., & Pelosi, F. Jr (2003). Anatomy of the pulmonary veins in patients with atrial fibrillation and effects of segmental ostial ablation analyzed by computed tomography. *Journal of Cardiovascular Electrophysiology*, *14*(2), 150–155. doi:10.1046/j.1540-8167.2003.02444.x

Segar, D. S., Bourdillon, P. D. V., Elsner, G., Kesler, K., & Feigenbaum, H. (1995). Intracardiac echocardiography-guided biopsy of intracardiac masses. *Journal of the American Society of Echocardiography, 8*(6), 927–929. doi:10.1016/S0894-7317(05)80018-5

Shalganov, T. N., Paprika, D., Borbás, S., Temesvári, A., & Szili-Török, T. (2005). Preventing complicated transseptal puncture with intracardiac echocardiography: Case report. *Cardiovascular Ultrasound, 3*, 5. doi:10.1186/1476-7120-3-5

Szili-Torok, T., Kimman, G. P., Theuns, D., Res, J., Roelandt, J., & Jordaens, L. J. (2001). Transseptal left heart catheterisation guided by intracardiac echocardiography. *Heart (British Cardiac Society), 86*(5), e11. doi:10.1136/heart.86.5.e11

Zanchetta, M., Rigatelli, G., Pedon, L., Zennaro, M., Maiolino, A., & Onorato, P. (2003). Role of intracardiac echocardiography in atrial septal abnormalities. *Journal of Interventional Cardiology, 16*(1), 63–77. doi:10.1046/j.1540-8183.2003.08004.x

Section 7
Fusion Methodologies

Chapter 16
Analysis of the Existing Data Fusion Methodologies for 3D Coronary Imaging

Panagiotis Siogkas
University of Ioannina, Greece

Dimitrios I. Fotiadis
University of Ioannina, Greece

Christos V. Bourantas
Castle Hill Hospital, UK

Ann C. Tweddel
Castle Hill Hospital, UK

Scot Garg
Royal Blackburn Hospital, UK

Lampros K. Michalis
University of Ioannina, Greece

Dimitris Koutsouris
National Technical University of Athens, Greece

ABSTRACT

New developments in the treatment of coronary artery disease have increased the demand for a more detailed, accurate, and comprehensive evaluation of coronary artery functional anatomy. Though there are a multitude of modalities available for the study of coronary anatomy, each has significant limitations, and thus, do not permit a complete functional assessment of coronary anatomy. To overcome these drawbacks, fusion of different imaging modalities has been proposed. The aim of this chapter is to describe the most prevalent and emerging of these fused imaging modalities and present their current and potential applications, highlighting their impact in the clinical and research arena.

DOI: 10.4018/978-1-61350-095-8.ch016

INTRODUCTION

Accurate evaluation of coronary artery geometry and morphology is crucial for both the assessment of the extent and severity of coronary artery disease, as well as the progression of atherosclerosis. Conventional contrast coronary angiography currently constitutes the method of choice for visualizing coronary anatomy and estimating the severity of a luminal stenosis. However, it provides little information regarding the composition of the plaque, its vulnerability and the overall atherosclerotic burden. Additional data may be sought from other invasive imaging techniques (e.g. intravascular ultrasound (IVUS), optical coherence tomography (OCT), near infrared spectroscopy (NIRS) or angioscopy), and the interventional cardiologist must then mentally integrate this information with the angiographic findings so as to appreciate details of coronary morphology. In clinical practice this process is sufficient in most cases, however in research, precise vessel reconstruction and comprehensive representation is necessary in order to examine plaque morphology and assess its distribution and evolution. To address these issues several methods have been developed which are able to integrate information provided by invasive and non-invasive imaging modalities.

In this chapter we identify some of the published data on fusion methodologies for 3D coronary imaging and discuss their clinical and research applications. We are focused on the approaches applied in intra-vascular imaging and present the most important data on fusion methodologies currently in use implemented in non-invasive cardiac imaging, aiming to highlight the potential clinical and research value of hybrid imaging.

BACKGROUND

Technology in medical imaging has made substantial progress. Miniaturization of medical devices and advances in signal processing has allowed the development of numerous invasive imaging modalities which address the limitations of coronary angiography and provide detailed intravascular coronary imaging. The first methodology available for research and clinical purposes was IVUS and subsequently other modalities ensued including angioscopy, thermography, OCT and most recently NIRS.

However, although these new imaging techniques provide a plethora of data which add substantially to our understanding of the mechanisms involved in the progression of atherosclerosis, none of them allows complete representation of vessel morphology and geometry. For example IVUS does not describe arterial geometry and has limited capability in identifying the type of plaque, while its moderate resolution restricts its ability to detect plaque features associated with increased vulnerability. Some of these limitations are addressed by OCT (e.g. detailed visualization of luminal morphology, accurate characterization of the type of plaque and identification of microstructures [macrophages, microcalcifications, fibrous cap thickness] seen in high risk plaques) which has a higher resolution but again does define vessel's geometry. In addition, its poor penetration often does not allow imaging of the whole vessel wall (Kubo et al., 2007), (Kawasaki et al., 2006). Angioscopy is restricted to the luminal surface and cannot provide data regarding the vessel wall morphology and plaque burden while the other two available imaging techniques (NIRS and thermography) may be useful for the detection of the high risk plaques as the first allows identification of the lipid pools and the second determination of the plaque heating but are unable to portray vessel's geometry, anatomy and histology (Takumi et al., 2007), (Moreno et al., 2002).

Taking the best from each modality and integrating the information seems the obvious solution. This can be achieved either through the development of micro-devices that allow simultaneous multi-coronary imaging (e.g. combination of IVUS and NIRS) or through the development of efficient methodologies that permit offline integration of the information provided by the different imaging techniques (e.g. coronary angiography and IVUS, IVUS and computed tomography [CT] etc). A major European project currently in progress called ARTreat implements the fusion of the aforementioned image modalities. Although simultaneous imaging is superior, as it does not require additional processing time and overcomes the problem of accurate co-registration, it is off-line co-registration that is currently the most frequently used approach in hybrid imaging.

MAIN FOCUS

IVUS Based Hybrid Imaging

Combination of IVUS and NIRS Data

Conventional gray scale IVUS appears to have limited capability in identifying lipid pools. To overcome this drawback radiofrequency analysis of the backscatter IVUS signal (IVUS-RF) has been suggested, which allowed identification of the lipid plaques with higher sensitivity (84% vs. 67%) and specificity (97% vs. 95%) than grayscale IVUS (Kawasaki et al., 2006). However, although IVUS-RF is more reliable it cannot be regarded as the gold standard for the identification of the lipid rich plaques. A new technology recently available is the Apollo catheter (InfraRedx, Burlington, MA), which has both a NIRS light source and an IVUS source on its tip allowing thus simultaneous NIRS and IVUS imaging. The catheter has already be used *in vivo* (Figure 1) (Garg, Serruys, van der Ent, Schultz, & van Soest, 2010) and in one case report it appeared that it may be useful in the prediction of distal embolisation after stent implantation (Schultz et al., 2010). However, although its feasibility has been confirmed and the first results appear promising, further studies are necessary in order to define the clinical and research utility of this hybrid imaging technique.

Figure 1. Left anterior oblique view of the right coronary artery showing the Apollo catheter (A). The NIRS source is located more proximally while the IVUS transducer is at the distal end of the catheter's tip (B, C). The combined IVUS and chemical information from a pullback is showed on the panels D, E and F.

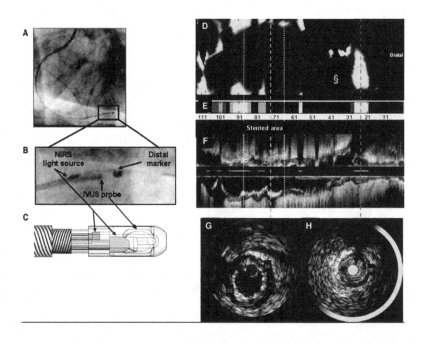

Combination of IVUS and Coronary Angiography

The limitations of coronary angiography (lack of information regarding luminal morphology and the composition of plaque) and IVUS (unable to provide information regarding coronary geometry and locate plaque within the artery) can be addressed with fusion of these two imaging techniques. The first fusion technique was proposed by Klein et al. and though it had significant methodological limitations it opened new horizons in coronary representation. Since then several reconstruction approaches have been proposed (Lengyel et al., 1995, Evans et al., 1996, Shekhar et al., 1999) however most have made substantial approximations in coronary reconstruction (Lengyel et al., 1995, Evans et al., 1996) or were not clinically applicable as they required multiple angiographic images and thus increased screening time and radiation dose (Subramanian, et al., 2000, Shekhar et al., 1999).

The first clinically applicable method was proposed by Wahle (Wahle, Prause, DeJong, & Sonka, 1998). This method used the position of the guidewire in the lumen to approximate the trajectory of the IVUS catheter and required only two sets of orthogonal angiographic images to extract the IVUS catheter path. The first set was used to define the distal end of the pull-back and the other the proximal end. The IVUS catheter path was then automatically extracted in each projection and two dimensional (2D) curves were defined. In these curves corresponding points were identified which were used to extract 3D points that defined the 3D path of the IVUS catheter. In a next step the borders detected in the IVUS frames were placed perpendicularly onto the extracted path and their relative orientation was estimated using the sequential triangulation algorithm which is a modification of the Frennet-Serret formula. Finally, an efficient methodology which compared the projections of the path and final model onto the angiographic images and their silhouette in these was implemented to define their absolute orientation. The only drawback of this approach was the approximations made during the catheter path extraction. More specifically often the "normal" lines drawn from corresponding points did not intersect in 3D space. In this case the 3D point was approximated in the middle of the distance between these lines. This approximation may result in a distorted 3D path and an erroneous estimation of the relative axial twist of the IVUS images.

Slager et al. (2000) proposed an approach which followed similar steps to reconstruct the coronaries but implemented a different catheter path extraction methodology. In brief, they used a 3D circular segment, to define the 3D trajectory of the IVUS path, which was stepwise adapted in 3D until its computed biplane projections optimally matched with the silhouette of the IVUS catheter in both angiographic images. However, the *in vivo* validation of this approach showed a considerable error between the projection of the 3D path and the guidewire which could be up to 1.6mm provided a considerable source of error.

More recently, Bourantas et al. (2005) proposed an advanced methodology to extract the catheter path. They used a cubic B-spline to approximate the catheter paths in the each biplane projection. Both B-splines were extruded parallel to their plane forming two surfaces and their intersection was assumed that corresponded to the trajectory of the IVUS catheter. The proposed approach was validated *in vivo* and *in vitro* and the results showed that this technique was able to overcome common problems such as the presence of foreshortening during the reconstruction of S – shaped arteries and the reconstruction of small segments where the catheter trajectory is not well visualised.

The above mentioned reconstruction methodologies provide complete coronary representation and give reliable information about the plaque volume and its distribution. The obtained 3D objects permit comprehensive visualization of coronary geometry and plaque and have been extensively used in research and especially in the study of the association between local heamodynamics and the progression of atherosclerosis. Thus, today it is known that low and oscillatory shear stresses increase the risk for in-stent restenosis and atherosclerosis progression in native coronary segments and coronary bifurcations while recently, it was shown that low shear stresses not only act as an atherogenic factor but also promote the development of vulnerable plaque. (Papafaklis et al., 2007, Stone et al., 2007, Chatzizisis et al., 2008, Papafaklis et al., 2009).

To enhance the research applicability of these methodologies integration of the developed algorithms into commercially available systems is required. Today there are two systems available (Wahle et al., 2004, Bourantas et al., 2008). Both of them operate in a user-friendly environment, are easy to use, and incorporate a visualization module which provides comprehensive visualization of the final object. In addition, ANGIOCARE system, introduced by Bourantas et al., (2008) allows rapid coronary reconstruction almost in real time and provides accurate quantification of the extent of atherosclerosis which can be useful for treatment planning at the time of intervention in the catheterization laboratory (Figure 2).

Combination of IVUS and CT

The previously described methodologies provide geometrically correct models of the coronaries and allow accurate assessment of both plaque burden and distribution. However, they cannot include coronary bifurcations or portray the anatomy and morphology of side branches. The two approaches developed specifically for this purpose are tedious

Figure 2. 3D reconstruction of a coronary artery and blood flow simulation. (A) Extraction of the IVUS trajectory from biplane angiography; (B) IVUS segmentation; (C) placement of the detected borders onto the catheter path and determination of their absolute orientation; (D) virtual endoscopy of the reconstructed vessel; (E) blood flow simulation into the final object and quantitative assessment of the local heamodynamics (From Bourantas et al., 2011).

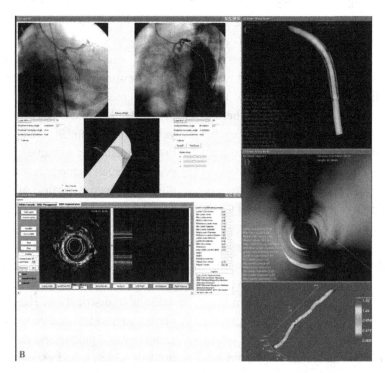

and time consuming and thus their implementation in all side branches is not feasible (Papafaklis et al., 2007), (Gijsen et al., 2007). To overcome these drawbacks van der Giessen et al. (2010) proposed the fusion of IVUS to coronary CT.

Using this approach the centerline of the lumen is defined from the CT images and then 0.2mm cross-sectional images are generated perpendicular to the centerline. Anatomical landmarks (e.g. the origin of side branches) are identified on both IVUS and CT cross-sections and used to identify corresponding images. The end-diastolic IVUS frames showing these landmarks are placed perpendicularly onto the luminal centerline over the corresponding CT cross-sections and then their absolute orientation is estimated. The remaining IVUS frames are placed between the frames with the identified landmarks using linear interpolation (Figure 3). In these models blood flow can be simulated and local shear stresses can be computed.

Van der Giessen's method was validated using 35 arteries from 23 patients. 3D reconstruction was feasible in 31 cases (89%) while in 4 arteries there were insufficient anatomical landmarks. It appeared that variations in the identification of the correspondence between CT and IVUS cross-sections as well as in the exact orientation of the IVUS landmarks did not affect the shear stress pattern and the relation between the shear stresses and the plaque thickness. Having confirmed the reproducibility of the blood flow measurements the authors concluded that the models provided by this method can be used to study the impact of blood flow on the progress of atherosclerosis.

A significant limitation of the proposed reconstruction methodology is its inability to reconstruct segments without side-branches, as the identification of at least two landmarks is necessary in order to identify correspondence between CT and IVUS and to determine the orientation of the IVUS frames onto the luminal centerline. This approach appears also to be laborious and time consuming as human interaction is necessary in most of the reconstruction steps. Finally, although the authors

Figure 3. Integration of IVUS and CT angiography. (a) The centerline of the lumen is defined in the CT angiography and then CT cross-sectional images are generated perpendicular to this centerline. (b) In these images anatomical landmarks seen also in IVUS images are identified. (c, d) The absolute orientation of the IVUS images is defined and then these are placed perpendicular onto the luminal centerline. (From Van der Giessen et al., 2010. Reproduced with permission of The International Journal of Cardiovascular Imaging).

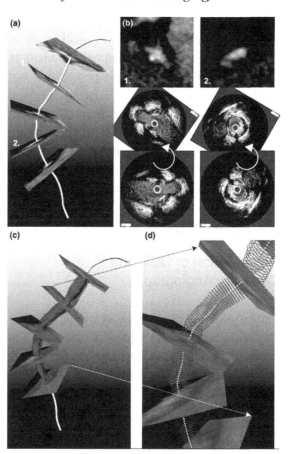

tested the reproducibility of the blood flow measurements, they did not examine the accuracy of the reconstruction methodology.

Though this method has considerable drawbacks it also has potential for important research applications. In contrast to the other reconstruction techniques, it permits full representation of the coronary anatomy and geometry including side branches and thus provides models which allow the study of the complex blood flow patterns noted in coronary bifurcations (Nazemi, Kleinstreuer, Archie, & Sorrell, 1989). In addition, the credible registration of the IVUS frames onto the CT images offers the potentiality for direct comparison of the CT and IVUS frames and thus this technique can be implemented to evaluate the ability of CT in characterizing the type of the plaque. It can be used in cases where the reconstruction from IVUS and coronary angiography is not feasible, e.g. when simultaneous X-ray visualization of the IVUS catheter and the luminal silhouette is not possible or when biplane angiography is not available.

An interesting recent case report (Wentzel et al., 2010) fused CT, IVUS and NIRS to create 3D models that can be implemented to study the impact of shear stresses on the natural history and destabilization of lipid-rich plaques.

OCT Based Hybrid Imaging

Combination of OCT and Coronary Angiography

The fusion of IVUS and X-ray or CT angiography may allow accurate assessment of plaque burden and its distribution and investigation of the role of blood flow on plaque development, but has the indigenous drawbacks of IVUS imaging; mainly poor axial resolution and moderate accuracy in identifying the type of the plaque. As a result does not allow reliable identification of vulnerable plaques or culprit lesions and thus, these models cannot be used to study the role of blood flow on vulnerable plaque formation and plaque destabilization.

To overcome this limitation fusion of OCT imaging and coronary angiography has been proposed. Two approaches have been developed both of which are described in chapter eleven. The first shown in Figure 4 is similar to the technique

applied to reconstruct the coronaries from IVUS and angiographic data (Bourantas, et al., 2005). Another technique described by Tu et al. (2011) integrates quantitative coronary angiography (QCA) and OCT data. According to this approach the information provided by QCA is initially used to reconstruct the segment of interest in 3D and then anatomical landmarks seen in both 3D QCA and OCT images are detected. These landmarks are used to identify corresponding images between the two imaging modalities and orientate the OCT images onto the reconstructed (by the QCA) segment. Limitations of this methodology include the lack of precise orientation of OCT onto the 3D QCA model and the fact that it is time consuming and requires multiple manual interactions.

It has been reported that shear and tensile stresses may contribute to plaque destabilization and rupture; however there are not sufficient data to confirm these hypotheses (Slager et al., 2005). This is mainly due to the inability to identify *in vivo* the exact location and geometry of the culprit lesions and especially the site of plaque rupture. It is possible that the integration of OCT and coronary angiography may address this problem and provide the substrate to study *in vivo* models of the impact of blood flow heamodynamics in acute coronary syndromes.

Other Hybrid Imaging Techniques

Further to the already described techniques, which at least partially employ data from invasive imaging modalities other to coronary angiography a number of methodologies have been developed for the integration of different non-invasive imaging modalities with or without coronary angiography data. Some of these have provided promising results and either have already or are going to be adopted in clinical practice. In this section we describe the most prevalent of these methodologies and discuss their clinical and research value with a final aim to highlight the perspective and potential value of hybrid imaging.

Figure 4. Fusion of OCT and angiographic data: (A) Extraction of the OCT catheter from two angiographic images; (B) detection of the luminal borders onto the OCT frames; (C) placement of the OCT borders onto the catheter path. Two steps are then followed to identify the orientation of the OCT frames. Firstly the relative axial twist of the OCT frames is determined using the sequential triangulation method and then the absolute orientation of the 1st frame is estimated by rotating this frame at an arbitrary angle and comparing the projections of the 3D model with the luminal silhouette of the vessel in the angiographic images (B). The angle at which a good matching is obtained corresponds to the correct absolute orientation (E, F).

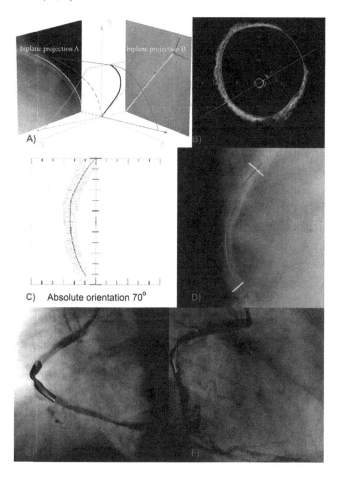

The first integration methodology with potential clinical value was proposed by Walimbe et al. (Walimbe et al., 2003) who suggested fusion of 3D echocardiography and scintigraphic data. The models obtained are likely to allow more accurate detection of coronary artery disease than the gated scintigraphic data alone, since 3D ultrasound has a higher sensitivity in detecting regional wall motion abnormalities. Though this hypothesis has been confirmed in a small feasibility study further validation is needed before its broad application in clinical practice (Walimbe, Jaber, Garcia, & Shekhar, 2009).

A year later Nishimura et al. (Nishimura et al., 2004) proposed the fusion of the anatomical data provided by coronary angiography with the functional data given by scintigraphy. Initially, they re-orientated of the single-photon emission computed tomographic (SPECT) cross sections and then they used these to reconstruct the left

Figure 5. Superimposition of the reconstructed using SPECT data (at stress A and rest B) left ventricle onto the coronary angiography. The lesion seen in the left anterior descending artery (arrow) results in a reversible antero-apical ischaemia as shown in the reconstructed left ventricle (Nishimura, et al., 2004. Reproduced with permission of Journal of Nuclear Medicine).

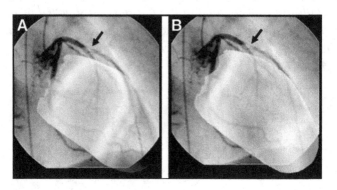

ventricle which was finally superimposed onto the angiographic images (Figure 5). This simplistic approach allowed evaluation of the extent of myocardial ischemia caused by a coronary lesion but could be performed only in specific angiographic views and provided only vely limited evaluation regarding the status of the right coronary artery.

To overcome these drawbacks Faber et al. (2004) suggested the fusion of the coronary tree reconstructed from the angiographic data with the left ventricle reconstructed from the scintigraphic images. The proposed automated methodology used anatomical landmarks to identify corresponding areas between the two models. To validate

their approach, they computed the overlap between the physiologic area assessed by SPECT and the anatomical area at risk determined using the coronary artery anatomy. The measured overlap was >80% indicating that the developed methodology was relatively accurate. Though there is as yet no clinical evidence, it is likely that the additional information provided by the co-registration of the anatomical (given by the coronary angiography) and the functional data (provided by SPECT or positron emission tomography (PET)) can change patient management and optimize treatment (Figure 6).

Figure 6. Fusion of the angiographic and the scintigraphic data (obtained after stress) in a patient with typical angina symptoms. Coronary angiography showed a moderate lesion in the middle of the left anterior descending artery while scintigraphy a reversible defect in the antero-anteroseptal wall which covered 10% of the left ventricle. Though this may suggest anterior ischemia caused by the lesion in the left anterior descending artery the fusion of the two imaging modalities demonstrated that the reversible defect is likely to be due to a lesion located in a septal branch.

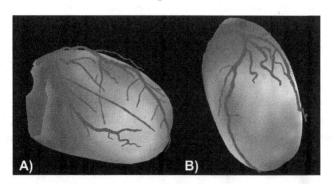

The most dramatic impact on clinical practice was occurred with the fusion of the angiographic data provided by CT and the perfusion data obtained by PET or SPECT. First, Rispler et al. (2007) using the methodology suggested by Faber et al. (2004) integrated data from these two imaging modalities and found that the hybrid models have higher specificity (95% vs. 63%) and positive predictive value (31% vs. 77%) for the detection of obstructive coronary artery disease than CT angiography. Gaemperli Schepis, Kalff, et al. (2007) presented the first workstation developed by General Electric that allowed fast semi-automated co-registration of CT angiography and scintigraphy. Extensive validation showed that these models permitted a more reliable diagnosis of obstructive coronary artery disease compared to scintigraphy, CT angiography or even to side-by-side interpretation of scintigraphy and CT angiography (Santana et al., 2009; Gaemperli, Schepis, Valenta, et al., 2007). It seems that these hybrid models provide additional information to coronary angiography and can be used to identify the culprit lesion in patients with stable angina and multi vessel disease and to classify the haemodynamic significance of moderate lesions (Figure 7). More excitingly, the unification of PET and CT imaging can be applied in the detection of the vulnerable plaques as it allows anatomic identification of nuclear tracers attracted by inflamed plaques (Wykrzykowska et al., 2009).

Recently, Stolzmann et al. (2010) proposed the co-registration of CT angiography and the perfusion given by Gadolinium magnetic resonance imaging. Though the utility of these has not been tested in a clinical setting yet, it is likely from the extent of scar to thrive robust information regarding the myocardial viability and the association between coronary lesions and viable/non viable myocardium and thus to predict functional recovery in heart failure patients after coronary revascularization (Kim et al., 2000).

CONCLUSION

Though there is a multitude of invasive and non-invasive imaging modalities available to portray coronary morphology and anatomy none of them provide complete and comprehensive information regarding vessel functional anatomy. To overcome the indigenous limitations of the existing imaging modalities integration of different imaging techniques has been proposed. This can be achieved either by the development of devices that allow simultaneous coronary imaging or through the de-

Figure 7. Perfusion polar maps at stress and rest showing a partial reversible anterior perfusion defect (A, arrow). 3D volume rendering CT angiography showing a lesion in the mid left anterior descending and in the first diagonal. Fusion of the SPECT/CT data revealed that the culprit lesion is the one located in the first diagonal. (Gaemperli et al., 2007. Reproduced with permission of Journal of Nuclear Medicine).

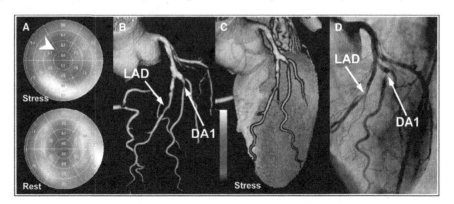

velopment of efficient methodologies that permit offline integration of the information provided by different imaging techniques. Advancements in technology and image processing have provided a variety of hybrid imaging models that give a more thorough and detailed assessment of coronary artery pathology. These models may prove themselves useful in clinical decision making and definitely will help in the research of progression/regression of atherosclerosis and of myocardial viability.

REFERENCES

Bourantas, C. V., Garg, S., Naka, K. K., Thury, A., Hoye, A., & Michalis, L. K. (2011). Focus on the research utility of intravascular ultrasound - Comparison with other invasive modalities. *Cardiovascular Ultrasound*, 9.

Bourantas, C. V., Kalatzis, F. G., Papafaklis, M. I., Fotiadis, D. I., Tweddel, A. C., & Katsouras, C. S. (2008). ANGIOCARE: An automated system for fast three dimensional coronary reconstruction using angiographic and intracoronary ultrasound data. *Catheterization and Cardiovascular Interventions*, 72(2), 166–175. doi:10.1002/ccd.21527

Bourantas, C. V., Kourtis, I. C., Plissiti, M. E., Fotiadis, D. I., Katsouras, C. S., & Papafaklis, M. I. (2005). A method for 3D reconstruction of coronary arteries using biplane angiography and intravascular ultrasound images. *Computerized Medical Imaging and Graphics*, 29(8), 597–606. doi:10.1016/j.compmedimag.2005.07.001

Chatzizisis, Y. S., Jonas, M., Coskun, A. U., Beigel, R., Stone, B. V., & Maynard, C. (2008). Prediction of the localization of high-risk coronary atherosclerotic plaques on the basis of low endothelial shear stress: An intravascular ultrasound and histopathology natural history study. *Circulation*, 117(8), 993–1002. doi:10.1161/CIRCULATIONAHA.107.695254

Evans, J. L., Ng, K. H., Wiet, S. G., Vonesh, M. J., Burns, W. B., & Radvany, M. G. (1996). Accurate three-dimensional reconstruction of intravascular ultrasound data: Spatially correct three-dimensional reconstructions. *Circulation*, 93, 567–576.

Faber, T. L., Santana, C. A., Garcia, E. V., Candell-Riera, J., Folks, R. D., & Peifer, J. W. (2004). Three-dimensional fusion of coronary arteries with myocardial perfusion distributions: Clinical validation. *Journal of Nuclear Medicine*, 45(5), 745–753.

Gaemperli, O., Husmann, L., Schepis, T., Koepfli, P., Valenta, I., & Jenni, W. (2009). Coronary CT angiography and myocardial perfusion imaging to detect flow-limiting stenoses: A potential gatekeeper for coronary revascularization? *European Heart Journal*, 30(23), 2921–2929. doi:10.1093/eurheartj/ehp304

Gaemperli, O., Schepis, T., Kalff, V., Namdar, M., Valenta, I., & Stefani, L. (2007). Validation of a new cardiac image fusion software for three-dimensional integration of myocardial perfusion SPECT and stand-alone 64-slice CT angiography. *European Journal of Nuclear Medicine and Molecular Imaging*, 34(7), 1097–1106. doi:10.1007/s00259-006-0342-9

Gaemperli, O., Schepis, T., Valenta, I., Husmann, L., Scheffel, H., & Duerst, V. (2007). Cardiac image fusion from stand-alone SPECT and CT: Clinical experience. *Journal of Nuclear Medicine*, 48(5), 696–703. doi:10.2967/jnumed.106.037606

Garcia-Garcia, H. M., Costa, M. A., & Serruys, P. W. (2010). Imaging of coronary atherosclerosis: Intravascular ultrasound. *European Heart Journal*, 31(20), 2456–2469C. doi:10.1093/eurheartj/ehq280

Garg, S., Serruys, P. W., van der Ent, M., Schultz, C., & van Soest, G. (2010). First use in patients of a combined near infrared spectroscopy and intravascular ultrasound catheter to identify composition and structure of coronary plaque. *EuroIntervention*, *5*(6), 755–756. doi:10.4244/EIJV5I6A126

Gijsen, F. J., Wentzel, J. J., Thury, A., Lamers, B., Schuurbiers, J. C., & Serruys, P. W. (2007). A new imaging technique to study 3-D plaque and shear stress distribution in human coronary artery bifurcations in vivo. *Journal of Biomechanics*, *40*(11), 2349–2357. doi:10.1016/j.jbiomech.2006.12.007

Kawasaki, M., Bouma, B. E., Bressner, J., Houser, S. L., Nadkarni, S. K., & MacNeill, B. D. (2006). Diagnostic accuracy of optical coherence tomography and integrated backscatter intravascular ultrasound images for tissue characterization of human coronary plaques. *Journal of the American College of Cardiology*, *48*(1), 81–88. doi:10.1016/j.jacc.2006.02.062

Kim, R. J., Wu, E., Rafael, A., Chen, E. L., Parker, M. A., & Simonetti, O. (2000). The use of contrast-enhanced magnetic resonance imaging to identify reversible myocardial dysfunction. *The New England Journal of Medicine*, *343*(20), 1445–1453. doi:10.1056/NEJM200011163432003

Kubo, T., Imanishi, T., Takarada, S., Kuroi, A., Ueno, S., & Yamano, T. (2007). Assessment of culprit lesion morphology in acute myocardial infarction: Ability of optical coherence tomography compared with intravascular ultrasound and coronary angioscopy. *Journal of the American College of Cardiology*, *50*(10), 933–939. doi:10.1016/j.jacc.2007.04.082

Lengyel, J., Greenberg, D. P., & Pop, R. (1995). Time–dependent three-dimensional intravascular ultrasound. In R. Cook (Ed.), *The SIGGRAPH 95 Conference on Comp Graphics*, (pp. 457-64).

Moreno, P. R., Lodder, R. A., Purushothaman, K. R., Charash, W. E., O'Connor, W. N., & Muller, J. E. (2002). Detection of lipid pool, thin fibrous cap, and inflammatory cells in human aortic atherosclerotic plaques by near-infrared spectroscopy. *Circulation*, *105*(8), 923–927. doi:10.1161/hc0802.104291

Nazemi, M., Kleinstreuer, C., Archie, J. P., & Sorrell, F. Y. (1989). Fluid-flow and plaque-formation in an aortic bifurcation. *Journal of Biomechanical Engineering-Transactions of the ASME*, *111*(4), 316–324. doi:10.1115/1.3168385

Nishimura, Y., Fukuchi, K., Katafuchi, T., Sagou, M., Oka, H., & Ishida, Y. (2004). Superimposed display of coronary artery on gated myocardial perfusion scintigraphy. *Journal of Nuclear Medicine*, *45*(9), 1444–1449.

Papafaklis, M. I., Bourantas, C. V., Theodorakis, P. E., Katsouras, C. S., Fotiadis, D. I., & Michalis, L. K. (2007). Association of endothelial shear stress with plaque thickness in a real three-dimensional left main coronary artery bifurcation model. *International Journal of Cardiology*, *115*(2), 276–278. doi:10.1016/j.ijcard.2006.04.030

Papafaklis, M. I., Bourantas, C. V., Theodorakis, P. E., Katsouras, C. S., Fotiadis, D. I., & Michalis, L. K. (2009). Relationship of shear stress with in-stent restenosis: Bare metal stenting and the effect of brachytherapy. *International Journal of Cardiology*, *134*(1), 25–32. doi:10.1016/j.ijcard.2008.02.006

Rispler, S., Keidar, Z., Ghersin, E., Roguin, A., Soil, A., & Dragu, R. (2007). Integrated single-photon emission computed tomography and computed tomography coronary angiography for the assessment of hemodynamically significant coronary artery lesions. *Journal of the American College of Cardiology*, *49*(10), 1059–1067. doi:10.1016/j.jacc.2006.10.069

Santana, C. A., Garcia, E. V., Faber, T. L., Sirineni, G. K. R., Esteves, F. P., & Sanyal, R. (2009). Diagnostic performance of fusion of myocardial perfusion imaging (MPI) and computed tomography coronary angiography. *Journal of Nuclear Cardiology, 16*(2), 201–211. doi:10.1007/s12350-008-9019-z

Schultz, C. J., Serruys, P. W., van der Ent, M., Ligthart, J., Mastik, F., & Garg, S. (2010). First-in-man clinical use of combined near-infrared spectroscopy and intravascular ultrasound: A potential key to predict distal embolization and no-reflow? *Journal of the American College of Cardiology, 56*(4), 314–314. doi:10.1016/j.jacc.2009.10.090

Shekhar, R., Cothern, R. M., Vince, D. G., Chandra, S., Thomas, J. D., & Cornhill, J. F. (1999). Three – dimensional segmentation of luminal and adventitial borders in serial intravascular ultrasound images. *Computerized Medical Imaging and Graphics, 23*, 299–309. doi:10.1016/S0895-6111(99)00029-4

Slager, C. J., Wentzel, J. J., Gijsen, F. J., Thury, A., van der Wal, A. C., & Schaar, J. A. (2005). The role of shear stress in the destabilization of vulnerable plaques and related therapeutic implications. *Nature Clinical Practice. Cardiovascular Medicine, 2*(9), 456–464. doi:10.1038/ncpcardio0298

Slager, C. J., Wentzel, J. J., Schuurbiers, J. C., Oomen, J. A., Kloet, J., & Krams, R. (2000). True 3-dimensional reconstruction of coronary arteries in patients by fusion of angiography and IVUS (ANGUS) and its quantitative validation. *Circulation, 102*(5), 511–516.

Stolzmann, P., Alkadhi, H., Scheffel, H., Hennemuth, A., Kuehnel, C., & Baumueller, S. (2010). Image fusion of coronary CT angiography and cardiac perfusion MRI: A pilot study. *European Radiology, 20*(5), 1174–1179. doi:10.1007/s00330-010-1746-2

Stone, P. H., Coskun, A. U., Kinlay, S., Popma, J. J., Sonka, M., & Wahle, A. (2007). Regions of low endothelial shear stress are the sites where coronary plaque progresses and vascular remodelling occurs in humans: An in vivo serial study. *European Heart Journal, 28*(6), 705–710. doi:10.1093/eurheartj/ehl575

Subramanian, K. R., Thubrikar, M. J., Fowler, B., Mostafavi, M. T., & Funk, M. W. (2000). Accurate 3D reconstruction of complex blood vessel geometries from intravascular ultrasound images: In vitro study. *Journal of Medical Engineering & Technology, 24*(4), 131–140. doi:10.1080/03091900050163391

Takumi, T., Lee, S., Hamasaki, S., Toyonaga, K., Kanda, D., & Kusumoto, K. (2007). Limitation of angiography to identify the culprit plaque in acute myocardial infarction with coronary total occlusion utility of coronary plaque temperature measurement to identify the culprit plaque. *Journal of the American College of Cardiology, 50*(23), 2197–2203. doi:10.1016/j.jacc.2007.07.079

Tu, S., Holm, N. R., Koning, G., Huang, Z., & Reiber, J. H. C. (2011). Fusion of 3D QCA and IVUS/OCT. *The International Journal of Cardiovascular Imaging, 25*.

van der Giessen, A. G., Schaap, M., Gijsen, F. J., Groen, H. C., van Walsum, T., & Mollet, N. R. (2010). 3D fusion of intravascular ultrasound and coronary computed tomography for in-vivo wall shear stress analysis: A feasibility study. *The International Journal of Cardiovascular Imaging, 26*(7), 781–796. doi:10.1007/s10554-009-9546-y

Wahle, A., Olszewski, M. E., & Sonka, M. (2004). Interactive virtual endoscopy in coronary arteries based on multimodality fusion. *IEEE Transactions on Medical Imaging, 23*(11), 1391–1403. doi:10.1109/TMI.2004.837109

Wahle, A., Prause, G. P. M., DeJong, S. C., & Sonka, M. (1998). 3-D fusion of biplane angiography and intravascular ultrasound for accurate visualization and volumetry. *Medical Image Computing and Computer-Assisted Intervention - Miccai'98, 1496*, (pp. 146-155).

Walimbe, V., Jaber, W. A., Garcia, M. J., & Shekhar, R. (2009). Multimodality cardiac stress testing: Combining real-time 3-dimensional echocardiography and myocardial perfusion SPECT. *Journal of Nuclear Medicine, 50*(2), 226–230. doi:10.2967/jnumed.108.053025

Walimbe, V., Zagrodsky, V., Raja, S., Jaber, W. A., DiFilippo, F. P., & Garcia, M. J. (2003). Mutual information-based multimodality registration of cardiac ultrasound and SPECT images: A preliminary investigation. *The International Journal of Cardiovascular Imaging, 19*(6), 483–494. doi:10.1023/B:CAIM.0000004325.48512.5a

Weichert, F., Muller, H., Quast, U., Kraushaar, A., Spilles, P., & Heintz, M. (2003). Virtual 3D IVUS vessel model for intravascular brachytherapy planning, I. 3D segmentation, reconstruction, and visualization of coronary artery architecture and orientation. *Medical Physics, 30*(9), 2530–2536. doi:10.1118/1.1603964

Wentzel, J. J., van der Giessen, A. G., Garg, S., Schultz, C., Mastik, F., & Gijsen, F. J. H. (2010). In vivo 3D distribution of lipid-core plaque in human coronary artery as assessed by fusion of near infrared spectroscopy-Intravascular ultrasound and multislice computed tomography scan. *Circulation-Cardiovascular Imaging, 3*(6), E6–E7. doi:10.1161/CIRCIMAGING.110.958850

Wykrzykowska, J., Lehman, S., Williams, G., Parker, J. A., Palmer, M. R., & Varkey, S. (2009). Imaging of inflamed and vulnerable plaque in coronary arteries with F-18-FDG PET/CT in patients with suppression of myocardial uptake using a low-carbohydrate, high-fat preparation. *Journal of Nuclear Medicine, 50*(4), 563–568. doi:10.2967/jnumed.108.055616

KEY TERMS AND DEFINITIONS

3D Reconstruction: Is the process of capturing the three dimensional shape and appearance of a real object.

B-splines: Parametrical curves which are described by the following formula.

Frennet – Serret Formula: A mathematical formula developed by Jean Frédéric Frenet and Joseph Alfred Serret to calculate the curvature and torsion of a 3-D curve.

Hybrid Imaging: It constitutes the current state of the art in cardiac imaging and is based on the fusion of data provided by different imaging modalities. This integration results in models which allow simultaneous visualization of all the information provided by the combined imaging techniques and thus a more complete representation of the cardiac structure.

Shear Stress: Any fluid moving along the vessel wall will incur in a parallel to the surface of the vessel stress which is called shear stress. The shear stresses in the arterial wall have recently attracted attention as it appears that they may affect the atherosclerotic process.

Viable Myocardium: Is defined as the ischaemic myocardium which has impaired systolic function (due to stunning or hibernation) that improves after revascularization.

Vulnerable Plaque: Atherosclerotic plaque which is prone to thrombosis, rupture or it has high probability of undergoing rapid progression and causing coronary events.

Section 8
Current Status of Vascular Imaging

Chapter 17

Current Status of Intravascular Imaging with IVUS and OCT:
The Clinical Implications of Intravascular Imaging

Angela Hoye
Castle Hill Hospital, UK

ABSTRACT

When undertaking coronary intervention, the use of intravascular imaging is an important adjunct to gain additional information regarding the procedure and help to optimise the results. Intra-vascular ultrasound (IVUS) is a familiar modality that is particularly useful at assessing the vessel both prior to and following intervention with stent implantation. Optical coherence tomography (OCT) has been introduced more recently and provides highly detailed images enabling assessment of features such as tissue coverage of individual stent struts. However, OCT has only limited tissue penetration as compared with IVUS. The following chapter aims to provide an overview as to the strengths and weaknesses of both imaging techniques, which should be seen as complementary, and discusses the implications of these modalities in current clinical practice.

INTRODUCTION

As far back as 1991, Davidson and colleagues described the potential use of intravascular ultrasound (IVUS) to examine the coronary vessels and evaluate what was happening during coronary intervention. Using a mechanically rotated 4.8Fr IVUS catheter, in 65 patients, they found that they were better able to identify plaque and

the occurrence of dissection than with standard cineangiography. Since that time, interventional cardiologists have used intravascular imaging both as a research and clinical tool to better understand the pathophysiology of coronary disease and the response to coronary intervention / treatments. The technology of IVUS has developed greatly with modern rapid-exchange catheters that are far more trackable. Multiple (64) elements are mounted on the tip of a catheter and the elements are excited one by one or pair-wise, resulting in an

DOI: 10.4018/978-1-61350-095-8.ch017

electronically rotating beam. The IVUS catheters operate on frequencies between 20MHz (phased array catheters) and 40MHz (mechanical catheters), resulting in a resolution of approximately 80 microns axially and 200-250 microns laterally. Adjunctive use of IVUS has been shown to improve outcomes following stent implantation (Fitzgerald et al., 2000; Oemrawsingh et al., 2003), and may also facilitate the ability to perform optimal percutaneous coronary intervention (PCI) with a reduced volume of contrast.

Optical coherence tomography (OCT) is a catheter-based imaging technique analogous to IVUS but using near infra-red light emission. This generates detailed images which have a much higher resolution (10µm) than those obtained with IVUS. The downside however is a more limited depth of tissue penetration (see Table 1). Until recently, OCT had been viewed predominantly as merely a research tool; however the technology has developed such that real-time images can now be made extremely rapidly without the need for prolonged occlusion of the vessel (OCT cannot image through blood). Using frequency domain OCT catheters with an acquisition speed of 20mm/sec, it is possible to obtain 200 cross-sectional images over a 4-5cm length of vessel in just 3.5

seconds, and the information obtained is proving to have a potentially much broader application in everyday clinical practice. The following chapter aims to compare the modalities of IVUS and OCT, and summarise the potential application of both imaging techniques in specific situations encountered in contemporary clinical practice.

It is important to appreciate the strengths and weaknesses for each of these imaging techniques to determine which may be the most appropriate modality for a particular situation. The key to understanding which modality is to be preferred is the appreciation of the differences in resolution and penetration. OCT is undoubtedly superior to IVUS in the detail of the images that are generated but has less tissue penetration. OCT is therefore better able to identify detailed information about what is going on close to the lumen eg plaque rupture, neointimal coverage of stent struts etc, but is not particularly good at imaging the diameter of the vessel as a whole, particularly when evaluating relatively large (>5mm) vessels, and should not be used to assess positive remodelling. The detail of the luminal image means that it is far easier with OCT to clearly define the endoluminal border to facilitate accurate assessment of minimal lumen area with a high degree

Table 1. Comparison of the features of intravascular ultrasound (IVUS) versus optical coherence tomography (OCT)

	IVUS	**FD-OCT***
Size of catheter	3.2-3.5Fr	2.7Fr
Guiding catheter compatibility	6Fr (≥0.64")**	6Fr (≥0.64")
Max frame rate	30fps	100-200fps
Max pullback speed	1 mm/sec	20-40 mm/sec
Wave length	35-80 um	1.3 um
Axial resolution	150 um	10-15 um
Lateral resolution	250 um	40-90 um
Tissue penetration	7mm	2-3.5mm
Scan diameter	15mm	Approx 10mm

* C7 Dragonfly catheter (St Jude Medical)

** 20MHz Eagle eye from Volcano Corp is compatible with 5Fr (0.056")

Table 2. Rate of major adverse cardiac events at >1 year follow-up in 300 patients (357 intermediate lesions), with respect to the minimum lumen area (MLA) as determined by IVUS

IVUS MLA (mm²)	N	Adverse event rate (%)
2.0-2.9	17	31
3.0-3.9	36	22
4.0-4.9	55	7
≥5.0	193	4

IVUS: intravascular ultrasound; MLA: minimum lumen area

Reproduced from Abizaid AS et al. Long-term follow-up after percutaneous transluminal coronary angioplasty was not performed based on intravascular ultrasound findings: importance of lumen dimensions. Circulation. 1999 Jul 20;100(3):256-61.

of reproducibility (Gonzalo et al., 2009). IVUS has the advantage of a much greater tissue penetration and scan diameter. In addition, it is more widely available and the majority of interventionists are familiar with and better trained in interpreting the images.

Satoko and colleagues (in press) compared the results of imaging with IVUS and OCT in phantom models. Both modalities were able to measure vessel diameter accurately, though the less detailed imaging obtained from IVUS imaging was associated with observations with a broader range of observations (wider standard deviation); in addition IVUS imaging results tended to underestimate length.

Assessment of Coronary Disease

Lesions of Moderate Severity

IN clinical practice for patients with stable disease, PCI is only indicated when a lesion is flow-limiting. Quantitative coronary angiography is neither particularly sensitive nor specific at determining lesion significance, however when combined with IVUS evaluation, studies have demonstrated a good degree of correlation with fractional flow reserve (FFR). A minimum lumen area (MLA) <3.0-4.0mm² and % diameter stenosis (%DS) >60-70% has a good correlation with an FFR <0.75 (Takagi et al., 1999; Briguori et al., 2001). Abizaid and colleagues (1999) evaluated

300 patients, (357 lesions of moderate severity), and demonstrated that those with a MLA >4.0 mm² had a low major adverse cardiac event (MACE) rate at >1 year follow-up of 4.4%, driven by target lesion revascularization in 2.8% (Table 2). For large vessels therefore, revascularization is recommended for an MLA of <4.0mm². It is however important to appreciate that for smaller diameter vessels (eg ≤2.5mm), in terms of correlation with an FFR <0.75, the cut-off for intervention will be a smaller MLA. An example of a moderate lesion affecting the ostium of the left anterior descending artery is depicted in Figure 1.

Left Main Stem Disease

In clinical practice, one of the most critical lesions that requires optimal evaluation is that of the left main stem (LMS). In 1978, Conley et al showed that with medical therapy, a significant (≥50%) LMS lesion on diagnostic coronary angiography has a 3-year rate of survival of 50%. Importantly, angiography tends to underestimate LMS stenosis severity compared with findings on autopsy (Isner et al., 1981). Abizaid and colleagues (1999) evaluated the 1-year outcome of 122 patients with moderate LMS disease treated (initially) with medical therapy alone. At follow-up the overall event rate (death, myocardial infarction, or LMS revascularization) was 14%, with minimum lumen diameter (MLD) on IVUS being the most important quantitative predictor of cardiac events. For

Figure 1. IVUS examination of an intermediate lesion affecting the ostium of the left anterior descending artery (LAD)

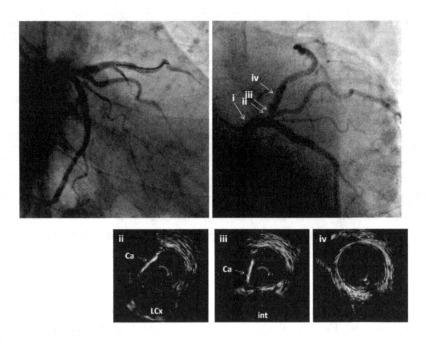

the 18 patients with an event, the MLD and MLA were 2.30 ± 0.69mm and 6.8 ± 4.4mm^2 respectively, as compared with MLD and MLA of 2.94 ± 0.81mm and 10.0 ± 5.3mm^2 in the remainder (p=0.01). Similar findings were seen in another study of 107 patients with moderate LMS disease (Ricciardi et al., 2003); multivariate predictors of late cardiac events were diabetes (hazard ratio 2.69, P=.014) and minimum lumen area by IVUS (hazard ratio 0.59, P=.015).

Jasti and colleagues (2004) compared IVUS parameters with FFR, a significant FFR (<0.75) correlated to a MLD by IVUS of 2.8mm with a sensitivity and specificity of 93% and 98% respectively; and a MLA of 5.9mm^2 with a sensitivity and specificity of 93% and 95% respectively. Therefore most clinicians take these IVUS measurements (a MLD <2.8mm or MLA <6mm^2) to suggest a physiologically important LMS stenosis. In some patients, imaging of the LMS with IVUS evaluation has potential advantages over OCT which may provide only limited imaging due to the large size of the LMS.

IVUS guidance is very useful during LMS PCI to help plan the technique of stenting, choose an appropriate stent size, and to evaluate the results after stent implantation. An IVUS pullback made from both the left anterior descending artery (LAD) and left circumflex artery (LCx) will allow the operator to fully appreciate the distribution of plaque and to evaluate the most suitable strategy for stenting (Figure 2). Data from registries suggest that, where possible, use of a single stent within the LMS is associated with a lower rate of MACE compared with a "routine" 2-stent strategy. However, the presence of significant plaque within the ostia of both the LAD and LCx at baseline may direct the operator to undertake PCI with a 2-stent strategy from the outset. Most importantly, IVUS will then allow the operator to choose the best size of stent(s) to use, and ensure a good final result. Obtaining an optimal result is of particular importance when treating the LMS as it subtends

Figure 2. The use of intra-vascular imaging (IVUS) to guide treatment of the left main stem (LMS)

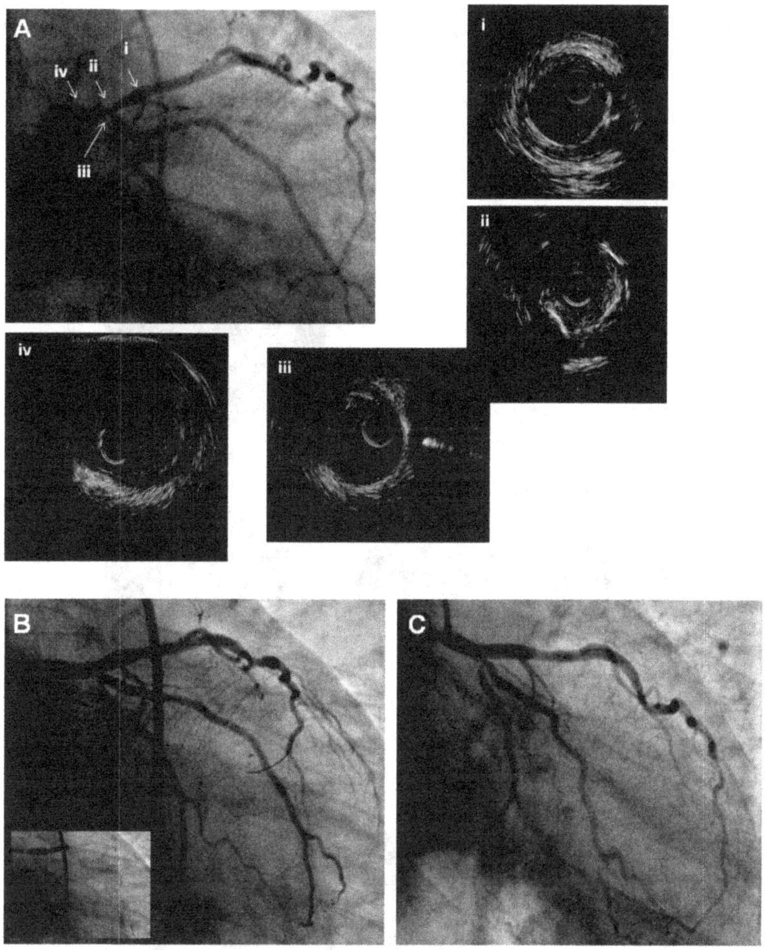

a large mass of myocardium and the occurrence of a serious event such as stent thrombosis thereby carries an extremely high mortality risk.

Ostial Lesions

It may sometimes be very difficult to differentiate between true ostial disease and an apparent stenosis caused by "spasm" related to positioning of the coronary catheter. Such spasm may not always respond well to intra-coronary nitrates yet the presence / absence of such a lesion may form the basis of treatment (Figure 3). Intra-vascular imaging is very helpful in this situation to determine the presence and burden of plaque; when the left

main stem is being evaluated, this may be better performed with IVUS in preference to OCT which may not always be able to image a particularly large vessel in its entirety.

Calcification

Heavy calcification of a coronary vessel will reduce the image quality for both IVUS and OCT as it will not allow penetration of either ultrasound or infra-red waves and therefore does not allow for imaging behind the calcium. The presence of significant calcification will potentially impact on the result of PCI with sub-optimal stent expansion leading to an increased risk of stent thrombosis

Figure 3. A) Angiographic image (left anterior oblique view) of the right coronary artery (RCA) of a 58 year old man with a history of exertional chest pain. There was no evidence of significant disease in the left coronary artery. Cannulation of the RCA was associated with pressure damping, however it was unclear as to whether this was due to the presence of plaque or related to severe vessel spasm. Intravascular ultrasound imaging was extremely helpful in identifying a very short but severe atheromatous lesion right at the ostium (ii). B) the lesion was successfully treated with a 3.0x15mm Multilink Vision stent (Abbott Vascular). IVUS performed following stent implantation demonstrated a good stent result and complete coverage of the lesion – this necessitated a few struts to jut into the aorta (Ao).

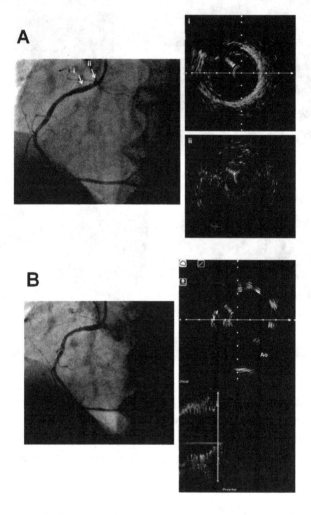

and restenosis, and aggressive pre-dilatation may be required to avoid this. Intravascular imaging is far superior compared with coronary angiography in identifying the presence of calcium and, most importantly, determining the site – within the plaque as opposed to simply epicardial. Particularly when a confluent ring of calcification is evident by IVUS or OCT, plaque modification such as with a rotablator is indicated and should preferably be performed prior to balloon dilatation. Both modalities (IVUS and OCT) have a high sensitivity to identify areas of calcification and although tissue penetration is generally better

Table 3. Assessment of culprit lesion morphology in acute myocardial infarction: ability of optical coherence tomography compared with intravascular ultrasound and coronary angioscopy

	OCT (n=30)	Coronary angioscopy (n=30)	IVUS (n=30)	p value
Fibrous cap disruption	73%*†	47%	40%	0.021
Fibrous cap erosion	23%*†	3%	0%	0.003
thrombus	100%†	100%‡	33%	<0.001

* p<0.05 OCT versus angioscopy

† p<0.01 OCT versus IVUS

‡ p<0.01 angioscopy versus IVUS

Reproduced from Kubo et al. (2007). Assessment of culprit lesion morphology in acute myocardial infarction: ability of optical coherence tomography compared with intravascular ultrasound and coronary angioscopy. J Am Coll Cardiol. Sep 4;50(10):933-9

with IVUS, OCT may demonstrate better tissue penetration in some calcified plaques.

Acute Coronary Syndromes (Vulnerable Plaque)

Vulnerable plaque is characterised by certain features such as a thin cap (<65μm) and lipid-rich pool, the most well-established parameter being the presence of a thin fibrous cap. OCT is best placed to image these characteristics - even VH-IVUS has been shown to be unreliable at determining necrotic core in porcine arteries (Thim et al., 2010). OCT imaging provides such detailed information that it enables actual measurement of the cap diameter and is therefore well-placed to identify plaque atheroma with high-risk characteristics; something which is not possible with IVUS. Indeed, the resolution of IVUS is insufficient for this purpose (in the range of 150μm). Accurate measurement of the fibrous cap thickness has been validated by Kume and colleagues (2006) in 35 lipid-rich plaques from human cadavers. OCT was compared with the corresponding histology and demonstrated good degree of correlation (r=0.90, p<0.001).

Recently, investigators have realised the potential applicability of this in clinical practice in patients who present with an acute coronary syndrome (ACS). Most notably, it may be extremely difficult to identify the site of the culprit lesion in patients with ACS, particularly those with multivessel or "non-flow-limiting" disease. As compared with IVUS (and angioscopy) in one study of 30 patients with AMI (Kubo et al., 2007), OCT was far superior at identifying fibrous cap disruption, fibrous cap erosion, and thrombus (see Table 3). Only OCT could estimate the fibrous cap thickness, which was 49 ± 21 microns; the incidence of thin cap fibroatheroma (TCFA) was 83% in this population by OCT. An example of the potential clinical utility of OCT in this situation is depicted in Figure 4.

In acute myocardial infarction associated with a heavy burden of intra-coronary thrombus, OCT evaluation is able to identify the precise site of plaque rupture. Thrombus that develops secondary to plaque rupture will often propagate longitudinally along the vessel. When undertaking PCI, the thrombus is often extracted, and stent implantation is then performed usually at the site of what appears to be the most important area of disease by angiography. However, investigators have shown that by OCT imaging, the actual site of plaque rupture may in fact sometimes be more proximal and is then "missed" by the operator. This has significant implications in that the unstable plaque is not stabilised by stent implantation, and may lead to a risk of recurrent acute coronary syndrome. An example of a site of plaque rupture as seen on OCT is depicted in Figure 5.

Figure 4. OCT images of a patient with a previous history of stent implantation, admitted with a troponin positive acute coronary syndrome. The stent, seen in the distal vessel (D) has healed well. However, there is plaque rupture evident in the proximal vessel. A: an intimal flap is seen at 5 o'clock, and a thin cap fibroatheroma is evident at 1 o'clock, there is a large lipid pool from 1 to 5 o'clock (A). B: the actual point of plaque rupture is seen at 5 o'clock. C: red thrombus is seen overlying the burst cap which was measured to be 70 microns in thickness.

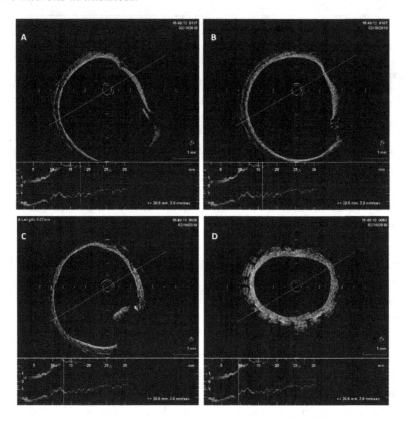

Guide to Therapy

Complex PCI

In current clinical practice IVUS is well placed to accurately determine vessel size (diameter) and allow optimal choice of stent size. IVUS is used most commonly when performing PCI in complex lesions in order to try to reduce the risk of adverse events, particularly restenosis. An example of a complex case where IVUS was critical is depicted in Figure 6. There is data from Roy et al., (2008) to suggest that IVUS-guidance in routine practice may reduce the rate of stent thrombosis and re-stenosis when treating patients with drug-eluting stents. The outcomes of a cohort of 884 patients treated with IVUS-guided PCI were compared to those of a propensity-matched group treated without IVUS. At 30 days and 12-months, the rate of definite stent thrombosis was lower in those with IVUS (0.5% versus 1.4%, p=0.046), and (0.7% versus 2.0%, p=0.014) respectively. There was also a trend in favour of the IVUS treated group in the reduction of target vessel revascularization (5.1% versus 7.2%, p=0.07). Particularly when small or very long lengths of stent are implanted it is vital to ensure that they are well-expanded and intravascular imaging is indicated to ensure

Figure 5. Optical coherence tomography (OCT) images from a patient with acute non-ST segment eleva-tion myocardial infarction. The presence of intra-coronary thrombus can be clearly seen (red arrows). In addition, OCT was able to detect a thin-cap fibroatheroma just proximal to the thrombus. The detail obtained by OCT imaging enabled measurement of the cap thickness which was 63 μm in diameter (A) in this example. In view of these features, the operator chose to treat the lesion with a longer length of stent to ensure that this (high risk) plaque was also covered.

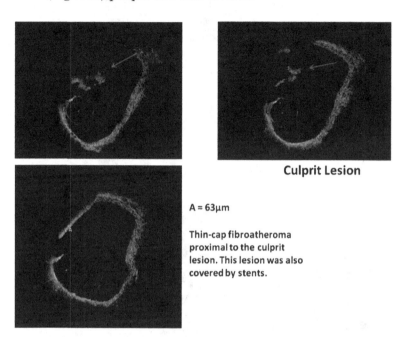

Culprit Lesion

A = 63μm

Thin-cap fibroatheroma
proximal to the culprit
lesion. This lesion was also
covered by stents.

that there are no problems that could predispose the patient to future problems. These include the presence of a gap between stents, malapposition, and edge dissection, all of which can be seen with both IVUS and OCT.

Interventional cardiologists are familiar with IVUS and the IVUS-indications to perform additional therapy eg post-dilatation when the stent is under-expanded, additional stent implantation if there is a gap or edge dissection. One of the current issues with OCT imaging to evaluate the results after stenting is that it is extremely sensitive at detecting problems such as minute dissections, tissue prolapse through the stent struts, intra-stent dissections, single strut malapposition etc. These abnormalities may be so minuscule that they may not be evident at all on IVUS, and it currently remains unclear as to the clinical importance of these findings and whether any

additional intervention is indicated. Some operators favour the use of additional balloon post-dilatation when tissue prolapse is seen on OCT, however there is no data as to whether this impacts on long-term results. In 2009, Rosenthal presented data to demonstrate that OCT is superior to IVUS in detecting strut malapposition. Indeed, OCT demonstrates a relatively high rate of strut malapposition particularly in regions of stent overlap and in severely calcified lesions (Tan-igawa et al 2008). Once again however, the clinical significance of this and potential need for additional intervention is still unknown. Therefore, at the present time, IVUS can be seen as a useful and established tool to guide the results of stent implantation; the implications of some of the detailed imaging obtained from OCT imaging are still to be defined.

Figure 6. The use of IVUS to optimise therapy in complex disease. A 68 year old man was admitted with a troponin positive acute coronary syndrome and underwent coronary angiography which demonstrated a significant lesion in the distal left main stem that divided into 4 separate branches.

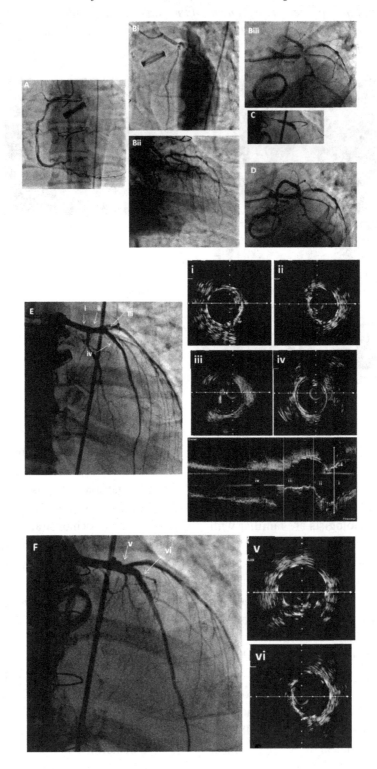

Left Main Stem and Bifurcation Lesions

Even for experienced operators, the use of adjunctive IVUS has been shown to be beneficial when performing PCI of the left main stem and bifurcation lesions (Furukawa et al., 2005; Park et al., 2009). In the MAIN-COMPARE registry published by Park and colleagues in 2009, the benefits of IVUS-guidance were shown in patients treated with drug-eluting stent implantation for left main stem disease (as compared with a propensity-matched group without IVUS-guidance). At 3-years, the mortality of the IVUS group was significantly lower (4.7% versus 16.0%, log-rank p=0.048). When treating bifurcation lesions, angiography has been shown to underestimate the significance of disease at the ostium of side branch. However, this has a significant impact on the occurrence of complications relating to side branch occlusion; Furukawa et al (2005) showed that intra-coronary imaging is able to accurately identify the presence of plaque and may therefore impact on the type of bifurcation stenting strategy undertaken (see Figure 2). Following stent implantation in the main vessel, OCT in particular can identify the presence of stent struts / malapposition covering the side branch ostium. The treatment of bifurcation lesions is still associated with a relatively increased rate of stent failure and OCT may provide insights into the mechanisms of this. However, the data thus far is only preliminary and further work is needed before OCT can be introduced more routinely into clinical practice in this situation.

Chronic Total Occlusions

Chronic total occlusions (CTO) are a particular group where adjunctive IVUS has a role in facilitating successful recanalization. The point of occlusion is not always easily identifiable, and lesions without a tapered stump have a significantly lower rate of successful recanalization. When the anatomy allows (presence of a side branch at the point of occlusion in the main vessel), IVUS evaluation (typically with the 20MHz phased array catheter from Volcano) can be performed in the side branch to accurately pinpoint the site of occlusion and facilitate correct positioning of a guidewire (Park et al., 2009). After guidewire penetration of the occlusion cap, IVUS can then be used to ensure that the wire appears to be in the true lumen of the vessel. Another use of IVUS during CTO PCI occurs when the guidewire has been passed into the sub-intima. This space is dilated to enable the IVUS catheter to pass and Rathore and colleagues have demonstrated that the imaging may then be used to facilitate successful puncture of the guidewire back into the true lumen of the vessel.

Stent Failure: Thrombosis and Restenosis

Though the risk of stent thrombosis is low, its occurrence may be catastrophic leading to death or significant myocardial infarction in the majority of cases. In the 1990's, adjunctive IVUS imaging was shown to reduce stent thrombosis rates by evaluating the presence of stent under-expansion, thereby guiding the need for balloon post-dilatation to optimise the results (Colombo et al., 1995; Moussa et al., 1997). An example of stent thrombosis due to under-expansion is seen in Figure 7. Subsequent studies have identified several features which are associated with the risk of stent thrombosis and can be seen on both IVUS and OCT. Early stent thrombosis is associated with mechanical causes such as stent under-expansion, malapposition, stent fracture etc. However late stent thrombosis may be related to delayed endothelialisation of (drug-eluting) stents, something which is only possible to assess accurately with OCT. OCT is able to clearly image the surface of stent struts (it cannot measure the strut thickness) and therefore identify the presence and thickness of neointima and evidence of malapposed stent struts (Figure 8). Absence of healing may indicate the need for prolonged duration of dual anti-platelet therapy.

Figure 7. The use of intra-vascular imaging (IVUS) to understand the mechanism of stent thrombosis

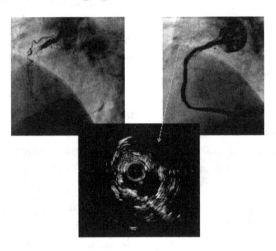

Figure 8. OCT image of a patient with a non-ST elevation acute myocardial infarction with ECG changes in the territory of previous stent implantation. Coronary angiography demonstrated no significant abnormalities with a widely patent stent. However OCT was able to clearly identify that there was an underlying problem, the image demonstrates 2 malapposed stent struts with adherent thrombus (at 4 and 5 o`clock). Other struts seen in the frame are well apposed with clear neointimal formation and no thrombus.

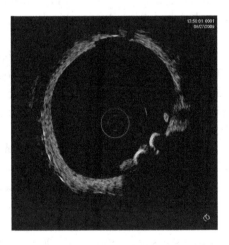

Another mechanism of stent thrombosis is the patients` resistance to anti-platelet therapy and it is therefore vital to perform intravascular imaging in this situation to understand the most appropri-

ate treatment strategy. Does the stent require additional balloon dilatation? In the absence of a problem with expansion of the stent itself, does the patient need testing for resistance to anti-platelet therapy / clopidogrel? The results of stent implantation cannot be assessed adequately enough with coronary angiography and intravascular imaging is strongly indicated in this situation. It is important to appreciate that OCT provides such detailed images that even very small thrombi may be visualised (Otake et al., 2009). However, these may not necessarily be associated with thrombotic clinical events and the clinical significance of such findings is not yet understood.

Restenosis is another cause of morbidity after stent implantation, occurring due to over proliferation of neointima. The occurrence of restenosis has been reduced since the introduction and widespread adoption of drug-eluting stents. However it does still occur particularly when complex lesions are treated. Once again, it is important to understand the mechanism behind the occurrence of restenosis. Factors associated with it include stent under-expansion, stent fracture, presence of a gap between stents, and incomplete lesions coverage. All of these may be visible with both modalities – IVUS and OCT though the latter will provide more detailed information. In particular, stent fracture is identified by a lack of circumferential struts and may be difficult to visualise particularly in stents with an open-cell design. OCT has the potential advantage over IVUS in that the detailed images are obtained with a fast pullback rate and are therefore less susceptible to movement. With future developments in technology, this will facilitate the possibility of on-line 3D-reconstruction of the stent morphology thereby enabling a clearer understanding of the geometry.

Cost-Effectiveness

There is no doubt that the adjunctive use of intravascular imaging is superior to coronary angiography in providing more detailed information about the coronary vessel and/or result after intervention. However, in most countries, the additional cost involved is the main factor that limits its' use to only selected situations. The use of IVUS does however reduce the subsequent clinical event rate and therefore reduce the cost implications that these have. In 2003, Mueller and colleagues published a study of 269 patients (356 lesions) who were randomised to the use of IVUS or angiography-guided provisional stenting, the 2-year rate of MACE was significantly lower in the IVUS group (80% versus 69%, p<0.04). The slight increase in procedural costs related to the IVUS were offset by the slightly higher costs related to re-hospitalizations. In a separate study of 108 men (Gaster et al., 2003), the use of IVUS was shown to increase procedural costs due to the catheter expense as well as a higher usage of balloons etc. At a median follow-up of 2.5 years, the IVUS-guided group were significantly more likely to be free from MACE (78% versus 59%, p=0.04), and had a significantly lower cumulative cost (€163,672 versus €313,706, p=0.01). However, both these studies were conducted some years ago (in the era of bare metal stents) and PCI practice has since changed. The introduction of drug-eluting stents has led to an increase in complex PCI and there is a need for the cost-effectiveness of IVUS to be re-evaluated.

The major drawback of OCT, in terms of its' introduction to routine clinical practice, is that it is more expensive than IVUS, and in most clinical situations its' role has yet to be defined. There is, as yet, a lack of data to demonstrate how OCT may reduce adverse events and therefore cost-effectiveness information is not available.

FUTURE RESEARCH DIRECTIONS

Future studies are needed to better define the role of OCT in routine clinical practice, and understand the implications of changes such as minute dissections and tissue prolapse. Future developments for both modalities will hopefully incorporate real-time 3D-reconstruction to better visualise the vessel / implanted stent(s). In addition, forward-looking IVUS and OCT are both under evaluation and may be of particular help in improving the success rates of PCI of chronic total occlusions through facilitating correct guidewire passage (Rogers, J 2009; Munce et al 2007).

CONCLUSION

Both IVUS and OCT provide additional detailed information over and above what is possible with angiography alone and are extremely useful in helping to guide therapy. The role of IVUS in clinical practice is better understood and defined. IVUS is able to evaluate the significance of "moderate" disease better than angiography-alone, and has an important role when undertaking complex PCI such as in the left main stem, or treating long lesions / diffuse disease to ensure an optimal strategy and result. Both IVUS and OCT provide information regarding the mechanism of stent failure, though the exquisitely detailed images obtained from OCT can provide additional information such as the extent of stent endothelialisation. Compared with IVUS, OCT imaging is particularly beneficial when trying to identify the culprit site of plaque rupture in patients with an acute coronary syndrome, though OCT is limited by its reduced penetration capability. Each imaging modality therefore has strengths and weaknesses and the two should be seen as complementary techniques in optimising coronary intervention.

REFERENCES

Abizaid, A. S., Mintz, G. S., Abizaid, A., Mehran, R., Lansky, A. J., & Pichard, A. D. (1999). One-year follow-up after intravascular ultrasound assessment of moderate left main coronary artery disease in patients with ambiguous angiograms. *Journal of the American College of Cardiology, 34*(3), 707–715. doi:10.1016/S0735-1097(99)00261-2

Abizaid, A. S., Mintz, G. S., Mehran, R., Abizaid, A., Lansky, A. J., & Pichard, A. D. (1999). Long-term follow-up after percutaneous transluminal coronary angioplasty was not performed based on intravascular ultrasound findings: Importance of lumen dimensions. *Circulation, 100*(3), 256–261.

Briguori, C., Anzuini, A., Airoldi, F., Gimelli, G., Nishida, T., & Adamian, M. (2001). Intravascular ultrasound criteria for the assessment of the functional significance of intermediate coronary artery stenoses and comparison with fractional flow reserve. *The American Journal of Cardiology, 87*(2), 136–141. doi:10.1016/S0002-9149(00)01304-7

Colombo, A., Hall, P., Nakamura, S., Almagor, Y., Maiello, L., & Martini, G. (1995). Intracoronary stenting without anticoagulation accomplished with intravascular ultrasound guidance. *Circulation, 91*(6), 1676–1688.

Conley, M. J., Ely, R. L., Kisslo, J., Lee, K. L., McNeer, J. F., & Rosati, R. A. (1978). The prognostic spectrum of left main stenosis. *Circulation, 57*(5), 947–952.

Davidson, C. J., Sheikh, K. H., Kisslo, K. B., Phillips, H. R., Peter, R. H., & Behar, V. S. (1991). Intracoronary ultrasound evaluation of interventional technologies. *The American Journal of Cardiology, 68*(13), 1305–1309. doi:10.1016/0002-9149(91)90236-E

Fitzgerald, P. J., Oshima, A., Hayase, M., Metz, J. A., Bailey, S. R., & Baim, D. S. (2000). Final results of the can routine ultrasound influence stent expansion (CRUISE) study. *Circulation, 102*(5), 523–530.

Furukawa, E., Hibi, K., Kosuge, M., Nakatogawa, T., Toda, N., & Takamura, T. (2005). Intravascular ultrasound predictors of side branch occlusion in bifurcation lesions after percutaneous coronary intervention. *Circulation Journal, 69*(3), 325–330. doi:10.1253/circj.69.325

Gaster, A. L., Slothuus Skjoldborg, U., Larsen, J., Korsholm, L., von Birgelen, C., & Jensen, S. (2003). Continued improvement of clinical outcome and cost effectiveness following intravascular ultrasound guided PCI: Insights from a prospective, randomised study. *Heart (British Cardiac Society), 89*(9), 1043–1049. doi:10.1136/heart.89.9.1043

Gonzalo, N., Garcia-Garcia, H. M., & Serruys, P. W. (2009). Reproducibility of quantitative optical coherence tomography for stent analysis. *EuroIntervention, 5*(2), 224–232. doi:10.4244/EIJV5I2A35

Isner, J. M., Kishel, J., & Kent, K. M. (1981). Accuracy of angiographic determination of left main coronary arterial narrowing. Angiographic-histologic correlative analysis in 28 patients. *Circulation, 63*(5), 1056–1064. doi:10.1161/01.CIR.63.5.1056

Jasti, V., Ivan, E., Yalamanchili, V., Wongpraparut, N., & Leesar, M. A. (2004). Correlations between fractional flow reserve and intravascular ultrasound in patients with an ambiguous left main coronary artery stenosis. *Circulation, 110*(18), 2831–2836. doi:10.1161/01.CIR.0000146338.62813.E7

Kubo, T., Imanishi, T., & Takarada, S. (2007). Assessment of culprit lesion morphology in acute myocardial infarction: Ability of optical coherence tomography compared with intravascular ultrasound and coronary angioscopy. *Journal of the American College of Cardiology, 50*(10), 933–939. doi:10.1016/j.jacc.2007.04.082

Kume, T., Akasaka, T., & Kawamoto, T. (2006). Measurement of the thickness of the fibrous cap by optical coherence tomography. *Am Heart J, 152*(4), 755.e1-4.

Moussa, I., Di Mario, C., & Reimers, B. (1997). Subacute stent thrombosis in the era of intravascular ultrasound-guided coronary stenting without anticoagulation: Frequency, predictors and clinical outcome. *Journal of the American College of Cardiology, 29*(1), 6–12. doi:10.1016/S0735-1097(96)00452-4

Mueller, C., Hodgson, J. M., & Schindler, C. (2003). Cost-effectiveness of intracoronary ultrasound for percutaneous coronary interventions. *The American Journal of Cardiology, 91*(2), 143–147. doi:10.1016/S0002-9149(02)03099-0

Munce, N. R., Yang, V. X., & Standish, B. A. (2007). Ex vivo imaging of chronic total occlusions using forward-looking optical coherence tomography. *Lasers in Surgery and Medicine, 39*(1), 28–35. doi:10.1002/lsm.20449

Oemrawsingh, P. V., Mintz, G. S., & Schalij, M. J. (2003). Intravascular ultrasound guidance improves angiographic and clinical outcome of stent implantation for long coronary artery stenoses: Final results of a randomized comparison with angiographic guidance (TULIP Study). *Circulation, 107*(1), 62–67. doi:10.1161/01.CIR.0000043240.87526.3F

Otake, H., Shite, J., & Ako, J. (2009). Local determinants of thrombus formation following sirolimus-eluting stent implantation assessed by optical coherence tomography. *JACC: Cardiovascular Interventions, 2*(5), 459–466. doi:10.1016/j.jcin.2009.03.003

Park, S. J., Kim, Y. H., & Park, D. W. (2009). Impact of intravascular ultrasound guidance on long-term mortality in stenting for unprotected left main coronary artery stenosis. *Circ Cardiovasc Interv, 2*(3), 167–177. doi:10.1161/CIRCINTERVENTIONS.108.799494

Park, Y., Park, H. S., & Jang, G. L. (2009). Intravascular ultrasound guided recanalization of stumpless chronic total occlusion. *International Journal of Cardiology, 148*(2).

Rathore, S., Katoh, O., & Tuschikane, E. (2010). A novel modification of the retrograde approach for the recanalization of chronic total occlusion of the coronary arteries intravascular ultrasound-guided reverse controlled antegrade and retrograde tracking. *JACC: Cardiovascular Interventions, 3*(2), 155–164. doi:10.1016/j.jcin.2009.10.030

Ricciardi, M. J., Meyers, S., & Choi, K. (2003). Angiographically silent left main disease detected by intravascular ultrasound: a marker for future adverse cardiac events. *American Heart Journal, 146*(3), 507–512. doi:10.1016/S0002-8703(03)00239-4

Rogers J. (2009 June/July). Forward-looking IVUS in chronic total occlusions. A new approach to an old problem. *Cardiac Interventions Today,* (pp. 21-24).

Rosenthal, N., Guagliumi, G., Sirbu, V., & Zocai, G. B. (2009). *Comparing intravascular ultrasound and optical coherence tomography for the evaluation of stent segment malapposition.* Paper presented at the Transcatheter Therapeutics meeting (TCT), San Francisco.

Roy, P., Steinberg, D. H., Sushinsky, S. J., Okabe, T., Pinto Slottow, T. L., & Kaneshige, K. (2008). The potential clinical utility of intravascular ultrasound guidance in patients undergoing percutaneous coronary intervention with drug-eluting stents. *European Heart Journal, 29*(15), 1851–1857. doi:10.1093/eurheartj/ehn249

Satoko, T., Bezerra, H. G., & Hiroyuki, S. (in press). Ex vivo comparison of the accuracy of measurements by OCT and IVUS. *EuroIntervention*.

Takagi, A., Tsurumi, Y., & Ishii, Y. (1999). Clinical potential of intravascular ultrasound for physiological assessment of coronary stenosis: Relationship between quantitative ultrasound tomography and pressure-derived fractional flow reserve. *Circulation, 100*(3), 250–255.

Tanigawa, J., Barlis, P., Dimopoulos, K., & Di Mario, C. (2008). Optical coherence tomography to assess malapposition in overlapping drug-eluting stents. *EuroIntervention, 3*(5), 580–583. doi:10.4244/EIJV3I5A104

Thim, T., Hagensen, M. K., & Wallace-Bradley, D. (2010). Unreliable assessment of necrotic core by virtual histology intravascular ultrasound in porcine coronary artery disease. *Circ Cardiovasc Imaging, 3*(4), 384–391. doi:10.1161/CIRCIMAGING.109.919357

ADDITIONAL READING

Bourantas, C. V., Naka, K. k., Garg, S., Thackray, S., Papadopoulos, D., & Alamgir, F. M. (2010). Clinical indications for intravascular ultrasound imaging. *Echocardiography (Mount Kisco, N.Y.), 27*(10), 1280–1290. doi:10.1111/j.1540-8175.2010.01259.x

Di Mario, C., Heyndrickx, G. R., Prati, F., & Pijls, N. H. J. (2009). Invasive imaging and haemodynamics. Chapter 8 of European Society of Cardiology Textbook of Cardiovascular Medicine. 2nd edition. Oxford press

Gonzalo N., Escaned J,. Alfonso F., Jiménez-Quevedo P., Zakhem B., Bañuelos C., Hernández-Antolin R., Macaya C. (2010). Is refined OCT guidance of stent implantation needed? *Eurointervention* Suppl G:G145-53

Herrero-Garibi, J., Cruz-González, I., Parejo-Diaz, P., & Jang, I. K. (2010). Optical coherence tomography: its value in intravascular diagnosis today. *Revista Espanola de Cardiologia, 63*(8), 951–962. doi:10.1016/S1885-5857(10)70189-4

Tuzcu, E. M., Bayturan, O., & Kapadia, S. (2010). Coronary intravascular ultrasound: a closer view. *Heart (British Cardiac Society), 96*, 1318–1324. doi:10.1136/hrt.2009.178434

KEY TERMS AND DEFINITIONS

Adjunctive Device: The use of an additional tool to facilitate an optimal result.

Coronary Intravascular Imaging: A method whereby detailed pictures of the vessel wall and lumen are made usually by inserting a catheter into the coronary artery.

Intravascular Ultrasound: Imaging performed from within the vessel using reflected ultrasound waves to obtain images.

Optical Coherence Tomography: Imaging performed from within the vessel using reflected near infra-red light waves to obtain detailed images.

Restenosis: Re-narrowing of the vessel lumen following previous angioplasty. When referring to stent restenosis this relates to over-proliferation of neointima.

Stent Endothelialization: The formation of neointima on the luminal surface of the stent struts.

Stent Thrombosis: Formation of a blood clot within a stent.

Chapter 18
Current Clinical Status of Vascular Non-Invasive Imaging Methodologies

Thanjavur Bragadeesh
University of Hull, UK

Ann C. Tweddel
University of Hull, UK

ABSTRACT

Rupture of high risk atherosclerotic plaque is responsible for acute vascular events such as myocardial infarction and sudden cardiac death. Several non-invasive vascular imaging methods have been developed to identify and characterise atherosclerotic plaques at risk of rupture. In this chapter we will discuss the background, rationale, and current state of non-invasive vascular imaging.

INTRODUCTION

Many risk factors and physiological responses contribute to the development of atherosclerotic plaques, a disease process that primarily affects large and medium sized arteries. Fatty streaks appear within the vascular intima early in adolescence and evolve over many decades into atherosclerotic plaques with the deposition of lipids, necrotic debris, migration of smooth muscle and inflammatory cells (Ross & Glomset, 1976a, 1976b; Stary, 1992, 2000). A fibrous cap produced by smooth muscle cells maintain the

stability of the plaque and separates the thrombogenic core of the plaque from the blood stream. In the early stages of development the plaques do not obstruct the vessel lumen due to outward expansion of the vessel wall (positive remodeling) (Glagov, Weisenberg, Zarins, Stankunavicius, & Kolettis, 1987).

The stability of the fibrous cap and the entire plaque is regulated by the lymphocytes and macrophages cells within the plaque(Daugherty & Rateri, 2002). Lymphocytes and macrophages when activated secrete interferon, matrix degrading proteases and other cytokines that inhibit smooth muscle cells, reduce collagen production and effect thinning of the fibrous cap (Davies,

DOI: 10.4018/978-1-61350-095-8.ch018

1996; Libby, Ridker, & Maseri, 2002; Packard & Libby, 2008; Virmani, Burke, Farb, & Kolodgie, 2006). Eventual erosion and/or rupture of the fibrous cap expose the necrotic core to the blood stream leading to thrombus formation and abrupt closure of the vessel lumen. Several postmortem studies have confirmed the presence of plaque erosion (Farb *et al.*, 1996) and rupture (Burke *et al.*, 1997)in patients who presented with acute vascular events. Other characteristic features such as increased neovascularisation and macrophage accumulation especially in the shoulder region of the plaque have also been noted in ruptured plaques(Moreno *et al.*, 2004; Muller, Abela, Nesto, & Tofler, 1994). Plaque components and hallmarks of a rupture prone plaque are summarized in Table 1.

Assessment of coronary atherosclerosis by coronary angiography is limited since atherosclerotic plaques do not affect the arterial lumen until late in the disease process(Kim *et al.*, 2002; Topol & Nissen, 1995). Furthermore, non-critical coronary stenoses are more often the culprit lesion in patients presenting with acute coronary syndrome (Hackett, Davies, & Maseri, 1988). Majority of patients who present with an acute coronary syndrome do not have prior symptoms of myocardial ischaemia. It is therefore essential to measure plaque burden and function before symptoms develop(Fayad & Fuster, 2001). Intravascular ultrasound, optical coherence tomography, thermography, intravascular magnetic resonance imaging and other intravascular imaging techniques were developed to assess the structure and function of atherosclerotic plaques early in their development when they are still confined to the arterial wall. However the techniques are invasive and can be utilised only in selected patients.

Non-invasive vascular imaging modalities include magnetic resonance imaging (MRI), cardiovascular computed tomography angiography (CCTA), and nuclear imaging techniques. Until recently the primary role of non-invasive imaging has been to identify myocardial ischaemia in symptomatic patients and act as a gatekeeper for coronary revascularization. In this chapter we discuss in detail the various non-invasive methods used to image atherosclerosis.

NON-INVASIVE VASCULAR IMAGING

Non-invasive vascular imaging can provide information about the size and distribution of plaques, the total atherosclerotic burden and in addition, can characterize plaque morphology, composition,

Table1. Plaque components and factors that predispose to plaque rupture

Plaque components	Atheromatous core – lipid, necrotic debris
	Extracellular matrix
	Calcium
	Fibrous cap
Features of high risk plaque	Thin cap fibroatheroma
	Large lipid/necrotic core
	Active inflammation – plaque infiltration with macrophages and lymphocytes
	Outward positive remodeling
	Increased plaque microneovascularisation
	Plaque ulceration / Plaque fissure
	Spotty calcification
	Platelet aggregation and thrombus formation

and thrombus formation. Non-invasive imaging has therefore the potential to identify plaques at high risk of rupture (vulnerable plaques) and influence patient management.

Cardiovascular Computed Tomography (CT)

There are two methods of imaging the coronary arteries with CT; Electron beam CT (EBCT) and multislice CT (MSCT). In EBCT, images are acquired by moving the x-ray beam in an arc around the patient while with MSCT, the x-ray source (gantry) and the patient are moved during image acquisition. EBCT has a superior temporal resolution (50 to 100ms) but poorer spatial resolution (1.5 mm) when compared to MSCT. MSCT has a temporal resolution of 83 to 200 ms and spatial resolution of 0.5 mm.

Calcium score is a highly reproducible method of quantifying coronary artery calcification (Agatston *et al.*, 1994). Coronary calcification does not represent critically narrowed coronary segments nor signifies plaques at risk of rupture but is an indirect measure of total plaque burden (Agatston *et al.*, 1994). Since the amount of calcium in the coronary arteries is directly proportional to the extent of atherosclerosis, a high coronary calcium score is an excellent marker of adverse vascular events (Budoff & Malpeso, ; Detrano, Doherty, Davies, & Stary, 2000) such as acute myocardial infarction and cardiovascular death. In many epidemiological studies EBCT was the method used to quantify coronary calcium and is therefore considered to be the gold standard. However in current routine clinical practice mechanical multislice computed tomography (MSCT) is utilized to calculate calcium score(Becker *et al.*, 2001).

Briefly, non-contrast enhanced ECG gated axial images are acquired, which are then post processed in a dedicated workstation (Figure 1 A.). Based on x-ray attenuation (HU) the calcified segments are given a density factor between 1 and 4; density factor is 1 when the x-ray at-

tenuation is between 130 to 199 HU, 2 for values between 200 to 299 HU, 3 for 300 to 399 HU and 4 for attenuation values of >400 HU. Agatston's calcium score, the most validated method to measure coronary calcium, is given by sum of the product of the calcified lesion area times the density factor (Σ (calcified lesion area x density factor)) and is dimensionless. The disadvantage of Agatston's score is the interscan variability

Figure 1. A) Calcified plaques of the left coronary artery with non-contrast enhanced MSCT. B) and C) Severe stenosis of right coronary artery with MSCT with corresponding view during cardiac catheterization. MSCT – multislice computed tomography.

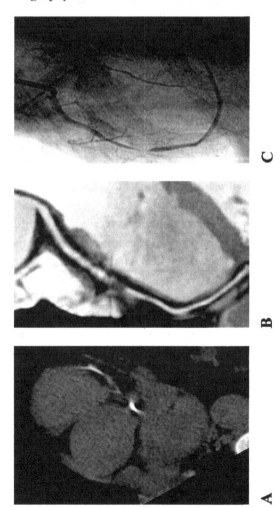

of 15% (Achenbach *et al.*, 2001). Hence other methods of quantifying coronary calcium such as volume score and calcium mass determination were developed. Irrespective of the method used coronary calcium score has its limitations. A high calcium score may not provide additional predictive value in patients who are considered to be high-risk on the basis of conventional risk factors (O'Rourke *et al.*, 2000). Conversely, a low or zero calcium score do not exclude the presence of non-calcified atherosclerotic plaques. In the study by Hwang *et al.*, 12% of asymptomatic and 7% of symptomatic patients with a calcium score of zero demonstrated non-calcified plaques (Hwang, Kim, Chung, Ryu, & Park). Similarly, in a study by Marwan *et al.* significant coronary stenosis was present in patients with no coronary calcium (Marwan, Ropers, Pflederer, Daniel, & Achenbach). In study, Gottlieb *et al* found that the overall sensitivity for CS = 0 to predict the absence of >or=50% stenosis was 45%, with a negative predictive value of 68% (Gottlieb *et al.*). The main advantage of calcium score is that it can provide an estimate of atherosclerotic burden quickly without the need for contrast administration using a relatively low radiation dose.

Contrast enhanced cardiovascular computed tomographic angiography (CCTA) with MSCT can demonstrate and characterize non-calcified plaques in coronary arteries in-vivo. Several studies have shown that CCTA has very high sensitivity and negative predictive values in identifying patients with significant coronary disease(Budoff *et al.*, 2008; Miller *et al.*, 2008) (Figures 1 B. and Figures 1 C.). In addition CCTA can reveal early non-obstructive coronary disease at a time when invasive coronary angiography and stress myocardial perfusion studies are normal(Carrigan *et al.*, 2009). CCTA can also provide information about plaque numbers, location within the coronary arterial tree, distribution, plaque area, extent of calcification and remodeling (Figure 2). Hence, CCTA provides incremental prognostic value over and above conventional tests (Min *et al.*, 2007).

Figure 2. Top panel shows the long axis view of the proximal left main coronary artery and the bottom panel corresponds to the short axis view. Yellow arrow is an eccentric non-calcified plaque that has expanded outward – positive remodeling. There is calcification in the inferior part of the vessel – yellow arrow. The arterial lumen (L) is patent.

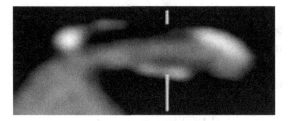

More recently a number of investigators have tried to identify high-risk vulnerable plaques with CCTA (Kashiwagi *et al.*, 2009; Kitagawa *et al.*, 2009). Pflederer *et al.* compared CCTA findings of 55 unstable angina patients with age matched controls who were diagnosed to have stable angina (Pflederer *et al.*). Culprit lesions were found to have lower signal densities (85.6 ± 45.1HU v 143.8 ± 104.1 HU), spotty calcification, higher positive remodeling indices (1.6 ± 0.4 v 0.97 ± 0.17), contrast rim and larger plaques volumes (192.8 ± 114.9 mm v 103.8 ± 51.8 mm) when compared to stable plaques. Similar studies that compared CCTA with intravascular imaging such as intravascular ultrasound (Pundziute *et al.*, 2008) and OCT (Kashiwagi *et al.*, 2009) showed that contrast rim and mixed plaque were features of thin cap fibroatheroma. Motoyama *et al* prospectively studied the relation of low attenuation plaques (LAP), plaques with low signal density, and positive remodeling (PR) to outcomes over 2years (Motoyama *et al.*, 2009). ACS developed in 10 (22.2%) with both LAP and PR compared with 1 (3.7%) of the 27 patients with plaques displaying either feature (1-feature positive plaques). In only 4 (0.5%) of the 820 patients with neither PR nor LAP (2-feature negative plaques) did ACS develop. None of the 167 patients with normal angiograms had acute coronary events (p < 0.001).

Targeted imaging with nanoparticles and spectral CT is now possible with metal based contrast agents such as gold. In a recent preclinical study Cordmore *et al* used a gold high-density lipoprotein contrast agent (Au-HDL), for characterization of macrophage burden in atherosclerotic plaques in the aorta of Apolipoprotein E knockout and wild type control mice(Cormode *et al.*, 2010). Similarly Hyafil *et al* used iodinated nanoparticles dispersed with surfactant to image macrophages in atherosclerotic plaques of rabbits(Hyafil *et al.*, 2007).

In summary CCTA is a relatively quick imaging technique that can quantify plaque burden and composition (Table 2). The major disadvantage is the poor positive predictive value (<50%) to identify critical coronary stenosis and hence provides little incremental value in patients with a high pretest probability of coronary disease.

MRI

Identification and characterisation of vascular plaques with magnetic resonance imaging can be achieved by one of three methods. In the first method, differences in tissue response to a radiofrequency pulse in the presence of a magnetic field is utilised to produce tissue contrast. T1, T2 and proton density weighted spin echo images have been used to characterise plaque composition in ex-vivo (Toussaint, Southern, Fuster, & Kantor, 1995) (Serfaty *et al.*, 2001) (Shinnar *et al.*, 1999) and in-vivo (Cai *et al.*, 2002; Skinner *et al.*, 1995; Toussaint, LaMuraglia, Southern, Fuster, & Kantor, 1996) (Mitsumori *et al.*, ; Yuan *et al.*) experiments. Atheromatous core appear dark compared to the fibrous cap and media in T2 weighted images (Toussaint *et al.*, 1996). Similarly plaque calcification appears dark in T1 weighted images due to their low water content (Toussaint *et al.*, 1995). Though the lipid core can be differentiated from the media of the arterial wall some investigators found an overlap of signal intensities between the two(Coombs, Rapp, Ursell, Reilly, & Saloner, 2001). Mulitcontrast MRI imaging improves the accuracy of plaque characterisation (Shinnar *et al.*, 1999). Differentiation of intact from thin and ruptured fibrous caps with a 3-dimensional (3D)

Table 2. Assessment of atherosclerosis with CT

Method	Finding	Remarks
Non-contrast enhanced CT	Calcium score	Measure of total atherosclerotic burden
Contrast enhanced CT angiography	Positive remodeling	Features of high risk plaque
	Low attenuation plaque	
	Spotty calcification	
	Contrast rim enhancement	
	Luminal stenosis severity	
	Plaque volume	
Targeted contrast agent	Uptake by macrophages within plaques	Animal studies using spectral CT

multiple overlapping thin slab MR angiography has been validated in human carotid artery plaques by Hatsukami *et al.*(Hatsukami, Ross, Polissar, & Yuan, 2000). The presence of a dark band between the bright arterial lumen and grey plaque core corresponds to a thick fibrous cap. Absence of the dark band signify a thin fibrous cap and the presence of a bright signal adjacent to the plaque core represents a mural thrombus

Both fresh and old plaque haemorrhages are identifiable by multicontrast MRI with a relatively high sensitivity (90%). Recent intraplaque haemorrhages appear hyperintense on pre-contrast T1-weighted MRI and time-of-flight vascular MRI while older haemorrhagic areas appear hypointense in multicontrast MRI (Chu *et al.*, 2004). High resolution MRI of carotid arteries in patients with acute cerebrovascular events has revealed thin fibrous caps (Yuan *et al.*, 2002), plaque haemorrhages and large lipid cores (Saam *et al.*, 2006).

In the second method, gadolinium based MR contrast agents that alter spin-lattice interaction of adjacent protons are used to characterise plaque and identify thrombus. Gadolinium enhancement improves accuracy of discriminating lipid core from surrounding vessel wall. Furthermore an increase in signal intensity of 80% and above after contrast enhancement in T1 weighted images was observed in plaques with elevated levels of neovascularisation (Yuan *et al.*, 2002); a factor known to cause plaque instability. Kerwin *et al.*(Kerwin *et al.*, 2003)found a significant correlation (correlation coefficient of 0.8) between the extent of plaque neovascularisation as measured by dynamic gadolinium enhanced MRI and by histology. Thick fibrous cap and ulceration of the fibrous cap are also more easily identified with gadolinium enhanced MRI.

In the third method, molecular imaging of macrophages, inflammation and thrombus is achieved with targeted contrast enhanced MRI such as paramagnetic iron oxide. The sensitivity of MR to iron oxide based contrast agents is also far superior to that of gadolinium based contrast agents (Ren-

Figure 3. MRI of carotid plaque in a 3T scanner. Lipid-rich plaque which has a necrotic core (solid arrow). A thin fibrous cap can be seen in the bottom-left of the image (dashed arrow). Image courtesy of Dr.Scott Murray (Lindsay, Murray, & Choudhury 2010).

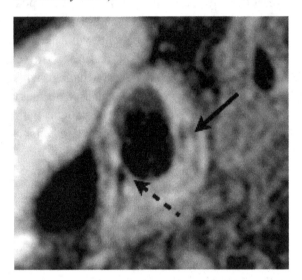

shaw, Owen, McLaughlin, Frey, & Leigh, 1986). Iron oxide based contrast agents are taken up by macrophages and any signal produced signify accumulated macrophages. Macrophages within aortic plaques of hyperlipidemic rabbits have been imaged with T2* weighted MRI (Ruehm, Corot, Vogt, Kolb, & Debatin, 2001) and in patients with symptomatic carotid arterial plaques (Kooi *et al.*, 2003). Contrast agents targeted against activated fibrin within thrombus(Botnar *et al.*, 2004; Yu *et al.*, 2000), activated platelets(von zur Muhlen *et al.*, 2008) and albumin(Cornily *et al.*, 2008) are also available for experimental use and should eventually be available for clinical use.

Plaque assessment with MRI is summarised in Table 3. Most vascular MRI studies in humans have been on carotid and aortic atheromatous plaques. Replicating the above experiments to image the coronary vascular bed is difficult because coronary arteries are smaller and more tortuous compared to the aorta and carotid arteries. Furthermore cardiac and respiratory motions

Table 3. Assessment of atherosclerosis with MRI

Method	Finding
T1, T2, PD weighted MRI and Time-of-flight MRI without exogenous contrast agent.	Vessel wall thickness
	Plaque size / lipid core
	Plaque calcification
	Thin fibrous cap
	Ruptured fibrous cap
	Plaque haemorrhage
Gadolinium contrast enhanced MRI	Plaque neovascularisation
	Plaque size
	Plaque thrombus
Targeted contrast agents	Macrophages within plaques
	Activated platelets
	Activated fibrin in thrombus

have to be taken into account during coronary imaging. Recent advances in coil design, and pulse sequences have enabled coronary MR imaging with submillimeter spatial resolution(Botnar *et al.*, 2001; Botnar *et al.*, 2000). Large scale outcome studies on the clinical utility of coronary MRI and further refinements in hardware and pulse sequences are necessary before coronary vascular MR can be used in routine clinical practice.

Nuclear Imaging

Nuclear imaging of vascular plaques is based on single photon emission tomography (SPECT) or positron emission tomography (PET). Both SPECT and PET vascular imaging employ radionuclide tracers bound to active molecules that are targeted to specific tissue types or cell surface receptors. The target of the active molecules can be plaque components such as the lipid core, inflammatory cells or thrombus.

Radionuclide tracer is injected intravenously and allowed to accumulate over time at the site of interest. Radioactivity from the accumulated tracer is then measured and amplified to create an image. Gamma ray emitting radioisotopes such as Technitium-99, Iodine-125 and Indium-111 are used as tracers in SPECT imaging. On the other hand isotopes that emit high energy (511 KeV) gamma rays (positron emitters) such as Fluorine-18, Rubidium-82 and 13N-Ammonia are used to generate PET images. Signal-to-noise ratio and spatial resolution is superior with PET (5mm) compared to SPECT (10mm).

Several animal and human studies have used nuclear tracers to characterise vascular plaques. Early studies of SPECT vascular imaging utilised ^{99m}Tc labelled low density lipoproteins in animals and humans(Lees & Lees, 1991). Though accumulation of ^{99m}Tc-LDL within atherosclerotic plaques was detectable, the signal was weak and compounded further by the presence of residual radioactivity within the blood pool.

Foam cells are formed by the binding to and internalization of oxidised LDL by macrophages(Gerrity, 1981). Lectin-like ox-LDL receptor 1 (LOX-1) on the endothelial cells that also binds to oxidized LDL seems to play an important role in plaque progression and instability(Kume *et al.*, 1998). Ishino *et al* successfully demonstrated imaging of high risk plaque with ^{99m}Tc labeled anti-LOX-1 antibody in hyperlipidaemic rabbits (Ishino *et al.*, 2008).

Figure 4. PET-CT of coronary artery. Hot spot shown in RCA (top arrow in panel D). Reprinted with permission from Rudd et al.(Rudd et al.)

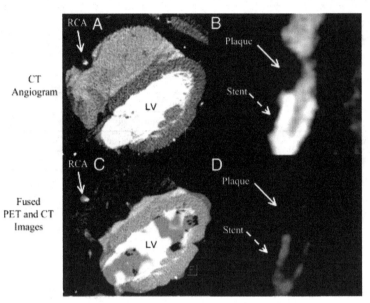

Several other studies have focused on the identification and quantification of inflammation within atherosclerotic plaques since inflammation is central to the transition of stable to unstable plaques. Radiolabelled monocyte chemotactic peptide 1 (MCP-1) (Hartung, Petrov, Cheng, & Narula, 2004), interleukins (Leung, 2004), monocytes (Kircher *et al.*, 2008; Swirski *et al.*, 2006) and macrophages (Nahrendorf *et al.*, 2008)have all been used in targeted imaging of plaque inflammation. ^{18}F-Flurodeoxyglucose (FDG), a PET tracer is taken up almost exclusively by activated macrophages within atheromatous plaques due to increased metabolic rate. Hence PET imaging with FDG tracer provides additional information about the metabolic activity of plaques. "Hotspots", regions with high signal in PET images, correspond to high risk atheromatous plaques(Rogers *et al.*, ; Tahara *et al.*, 2007; Tawakol *et al.*, 2005). Furthermore nuclear imaging has been used to track the effect of anti-inflammatory therapeutic interventions (Fujimoto *et al.*, 2008). Tahara *et al.* demonstrated that anti-inflammatory therapy

with statins cause a reduction in the magnitude of signal within the plaques (Tahara *et al.*, 2006).

Apart from inflammation other biological processes within atheromatous plaque that predispose to acute ischaemic events like apoptosis of macrophages, expansive remodelling of the vessel lumen and thrombus formation have also been imaged. Annexin A5, a naturally occurring protein actively binds phosphatidylserine molecules expressed on the cell membrane of apoptotic cells. [99m]Tc labelled annexinA5 has been used to image apoptosis within atherosclerotic plaques of animal models (Laufer, Winkens, Corsten *et al.*, 2009; Laufer, Winkens, Narula, & Hofstra, 2009).

Positive remodelling of arterial wall to accommodate the expanding plaque reduces the risk of ischaemia but increases the risk of plaque rupture (Varnava, Mills, & Davies, 2002). Positive remodelling is mediated via the degradation of extracellular matrix by a family of proteases called matrix metalloproteinases (MMPs). Radiolabelled monoclonal antibody and broad spectrum MMP inhibitors are used as tracers to image biological

Table 4. Assessment of atherosclerosis with nuclear imaging

Biological process	Target
Plaque composition	Foam cells
	Lipids
	Lipoproteins
Inflammation	Macrophages
	Lymphocytes
	Neutrophils
	Cytokine receptor expression
Metabolic activity	FDG uptake by macrophages
Thrombus	Fibrin
	Platelets
Apoptosis	Phosphatidylserine expression in cell membrane
Positive remodeling	Expression of metalloproteinase
Plaque neovascularisation	$\alpha_v\beta_3$ integrins on cell membranes

markers of positive remodeling within vascular plaques (Kuge *et al.*, ; Tekabe *et al.*).

Though the data with nuclear vascular imaging, summarized in Table 4, is promising there are several disadvantages with nuclear imaging of vascular plaques. Firstly, most studies have been on carotid and aortic plaques with little data on the feasibility of imaging coronary plaques. Imaging of coronary arterial plaques is challenging due to the relatively smaller size of coronary arteries, the need for cardiac gating and the presence of background signal from both the myocardium and blood pool. Secondly, the radiolabelled molecular probes have been used mostly in animal studies and their value in humans is yet to be tested.

Limitations

Differences between the non-invasive imaging techniques are tabulated in Table 5. There are several limitations with non-invasive vascular imaging. Firstly, The spatial resolution is limited to 0.5 mm with CT, which has the best spatial resolution of all non-invasive imaging modalities, compared to 0.2mm that can be achieved with invasive angiography and few microns in the case

of optical coherence tomography. Secondly, apart from calcium scoring and CT coronary angiography there is little data on the clinical utility of non-invasive vascular imaging in human coronary disease. Assessment of coronary disease with CT is indicated in asymptomatic individuals with high risk of vascular disease (high Framingham score). However there is little outcome data on MRI and nuclear imaging methods based on which patients can be selected for scanning. Thirdly, non-invasive imaging provides a snapshot about the state of atherosclerosis at a given point in time while atherosclerosis is a dynamic process that evolves over time. Perhaps there is a group of patients who will need periodic scanning at regular intervals. Lastly, there is no prospective data on the appropriate management strategy in patients with a positive result on non-invasive imaging, i.e., a high calcium score or a high risk plaque on CT angiography.

CONCLUSION

Non-invasive imaging has come a long way in the last three decades. Continued improvements

Table 5. Comparison of noninvasive vascular imaging techniques

	CT	MRI	Nuclear imaging
Spatial resolution	Submillimeter spatial resolution.	Spatial resolution much better than nuclear imaging. Usually around 1 mm.	Spatial resolution between 5 mm with PET and 10 mm with SPECT.
Sensitivity to contrast agent	Least sensitive to contrast agents.	Can detect contrast agents at micromolar concentrations.	Most sensitive to detect contrast agents. Can detect tracers at nanomolar concentrations
Targeted imaging	Very few animal studies with spectral CT	Contrast agents based on iron oxides are available for targeted imaging. Most studies are on animal models.	Wide variety of targeted tracers available. Metabolic imaging possible with FDG-PET.
Disadvantages	Interpretation of image is difficult in the presence of heavy calcification. Positive predictive value of <50% to identify severe coronary stenosis	Overlap of signal intensities between plaque and normal vessel wall.	Interference from radioactivity in blood pool and myocardium
Vessels visualised	Aorta Carotid Peripheral Coronary *Coronary artery imaging available for clinical use. Data from multicentre studies available.*	Aorta Carotid Peripheral *Very few studies on coronary artery imaging.*	Aorta Carotid Peripheral *Very limited data on the feasibility of coronary artery imaging*

in hardware, software and molecular biology will allow the development of newer techniques to assess atherosclerosis that are more sensitive and specific than current methods. These are exciting times, as the future for non-invasive vascular imaging is bright.

REFERENCES

Achenbach, S., Ropers, D., Mohlenkamp, S., Schmermund, A., Muschiol, G., Groth, J., *et al.* (2001). Variability of repeated coronary artery calcium measurements by electron beam tomography. *Am J Cardiol, 87*(2), 210-213, A218.

Agatston, A. S., Janowitz, W. R., Kaplan, G., Gasso, J., Hildner, F., & Viamonte, M. Jr. (1994). Ultrafast computed tomography-detected coronary calcium reflects the angiographic extent of coronary arterial atherosclerosis. *The American Journal of Cardiology, 74*(12), 1272–1274. doi:10.1016/0002-9149(94)90563-0

Becker, C. R., Kleffel, T., Crispin, A., Knez, A., Young, J., & Schoepf, U. J. (2001). Coronary artery calcium measurement: agreement of multirow detector and electron beam CT. *AJR. American Journal of Roentgenology, 176*(5), 1295–1298.

Botnar, R. M., Buecker, A., Wiethoff, A. J., Parsons, E. C. Jr, Katoh, M., & Katsimaglis, G. (2004). In vivo magnetic resonance imaging of coronary thrombosis using a fibrin-binding molecular magnetic resonance contrast agent. *Circulation, 110*(11), 1463–1466. doi:10.1161/01.CIR.0000134960.31304.87

Botnar, R. M., Kim, W. Y., Bornert, P., Stuber, M., Spuentrup, E., & Manning, W. J. (2001). 3D coronary vessel wall imaging utilizing a local inversion technique with spiral image acquisition. *Magnetic Resonance in Medicine, 46*(5), 848–854. doi:10.1002/mrm.1268

Botnar, R. M., Stuber, M., Kissinger, K. V., Kim, W. Y., Spuentrup, E., & Manning, W. J. (2000). Noninvasive coronary vessel wall and plaque imaging with magnetic resonance imaging. *Circulation, 102*(21), 2582–2587.

Budoff, M. J., Dowe, D., Jollis, J. G., Gitter, M., Sutherland, J., & Halamert, E. (2008). Diagnostic performance of 64-multidetector row coronary computed tomographic angiography for evaluation of coronary artery stenosis in individuals without known coronary artery disease: results from the prospective multicenter ACCURACY (assessment by coronary computed tomographic angiography of individuals undergoing invasive coronary angiography) trial. *Journal of the American College of Cardiology, 52*(21), 1724–1732. doi:10.1016/j.jacc.2008.07.031

Budoff, M. J., & Malpeso, J. M. (2011). Is coronary artery calcium the key to assessment of cardiovascular risk in asymptomatic adults? *Journal of Cardiovascular Computed Tomography, 5*(1). doi:10.1016/j.jcct.2010.11.004

Burke, A. P., Farb, A., Malcom, G. T., Liang, Y. H., Smialek, J., & Virmani, R. (1997). Coronary risk factors and plaque morphology in men with coronary disease who died suddenly. *The New England Journal of Medicine, 336*(18), 1276–1282. doi:10.1056/NEJM199705013361802

Cai, J. M., Hatsukami, T. S., Ferguson, M. S., Small, R., Polissar, N. L., & Yuan, C. (2002). Classification of human carotid atherosclerotic lesions with in vivo multicontrast magnetic resonance imaging. *Circulation, 106*(11), 1368–1373. doi:10.1161/01.CIR.0000028591.44554.F9

Carrigan, T. P., Nair, D., Schoenhagen, P., Curtin, R. J., Popovic, Z. B., & Halliburton, S. (2009). Prognostic utility of 64-slice computed tomography in patients with suspected but no documented coronary artery disease. *European Heart Journal, 30*(3), 362–371. doi:10.1093/eurheartj/ehn605

Chu, B., Kampschulte, A., Ferguson, M. S., Kerwin, W. S., Yarnykh, V. L., & O'Brien, K. D. (2004). Hemorrhage in the atherosclerotic carotid plaque: a high-resolution MRI study. *Stroke, 35*(5), 1079–1084. doi:10.1161/01. STR.0000125856.25309.86

Coombs, B. D., Rapp, J. H., Ursell, P. C., Reilly, L. M., & Saloner, D. (2001). Structure of plaque at carotid bifurcation: high-resolution MRI with histological correlation. *Stroke, 32*(11), 2516–2521. doi:10.1161/hs1101.098663

Cormode, D. P., Roessl, E., Thran, A., Skajaa, T., Gordon, R. E., & Schlomka, J. P. (2010). Atherosclerotic plaque composition: analysis with multicolor CT and targeted gold nanoparticles. *Radiology, 256*(3), 774–782. doi:10.1148/radiol.10092473

Cornily, J. C., Hyafil, F., Calcagno, C., Briley-Saebo, K. C., Tunstead, J., & Aguinaldo, J. G. (2008). Evaluation of neovessels in atherosclerotic plaques of rabbits using an albumin-binding intravascular contrast agent and MRI. *Journal of Magnetic Resonance Imaging, 27*(6), 1406–1411. doi:10.1002/jmri.21369

Daugherty, A., & Rateri, D. L. (2002). T lymphocytes in atherosclerosis: the yin-yang of Th1 and Th2 influence on lesion formation. *Circulation Research, 90*(10), 1039–1040. doi:10.1161/01. RES.0000021397.28936.F9

Davies, M. J. (1996). Stability and instability: Two faces of coronary atherosclerosis. The Paul Dudley White Lecture 1995. *Circulation, 94*(8), 2013–2020.

Detrano, R. C., Doherty, T. M., Davies, M. J., & Stary, H. C. (2000). Predicting coronary events with coronary calcium: Pathophysiologic and clinical problems. *Current Problems in Cardiology, 25*(6), 374–402. doi:10.1067/mcd.2000.104848

Farb, A., Burke, A. P., Tang, A. L., Liang, T. Y., Mannan, P., & Smialek, J. (1996). Coronary plaque erosion without rupture into a lipid core. A frequent cause of coronary thrombosis in sudden coronary death. *Circulation, 93*(7), 1354–1363.

Fayad, Z. A., & Fuster, V. (2001). Clinical imaging of the high-risk or vulnerable atherosclerotic plaque. *Circulation Research, 89*(4), 305–316. doi:10.1161/hh1601.095596

Fujimoto, S., Hartung, D., Ohshima, S., Edwards, D. S., Zhou, J., & Yalamanchili, P. (2008). Molecular imaging of matrix metalloproteinase in atherosclerotic lesions: Resolution with dietary modification and statin therapy. *Journal of the American College of Cardiology, 52*(23), 1847–1857. doi:10.1016/j.jacc.2008.08.048

Gerrity, R. G. (1981). The role of the monocyte in atherogenesis: I. Transition of blood-borne monocytes into foam cells in fatty lesions. *American Journal of Pathology, 103*(2), 181–190.

Glagov, S., Weisenberg, E., Zarins, C. K., Stankunavicius, R., & Kolettis, G. J. (1987). Compensatory enlargement of human atherosclerotic coronary arteries. *The New England Journal of Medicine, 316*(22), 1371–1375. doi:10.1056/NEJM198705283162204

Gottlieb, I., Miller, J. M., Arbab-Zadeh, A., Dewey, M., Clouse, M. E., & Sara, L.. The absence of coronary calcification does not exclude obstructive coronary artery disease or the need for revascularization in patients referred for conventional coronary angiography. *Journal of the American College of Cardiology, 55*(7), 627–634. doi:10.1016/j.jacc.2009.07.072

Hackett, D., Davies, G., & Maseri, A. (1988). Preexisting coronary stenoses in patients with first myocardial infarction are not necessarily severe. *European Heart Journal, 9*(12), 1317–1323.

Hartung, D., Petrov, A., Cheng, K. T., & Narula, J. (2004). *99mTc-Monocyte chemoattractant protein-1.*

Hatsukami, T. S., Ross, R., Polissar, N. L., & Yuan, C. (2000). Visualization of fibrous cap thickness and rupture in human atherosclerotic carotid plaque in vivo with high-resolution magnetic resonance imaging. *Circulation, 102*(9), 959–964.

Hwang, Y., Kim, Y., Chung, I. M., Ryu, J., & Park, H. Coronary heart disease risk assessment and characterization of coronary artery disease using coronary CT angiography: Comparison of asymptomatic and symptomatic groups. *Clinical Radiology, 65*(8), 601–608. doi:10.1016/j.crad.2010.04.009

Hyafil, F., Cornily, J. C., Feig, J. E., Gordon, R., Vucic, E., & Amirbekian, V. (2007). Noninvasive detection of macrophages using a nanoparticulate contrast agent for computed tomography. *Nature Medicine, 13*(5), 636–641. doi:10.1038/nm1571

Ishino, S., Mukai, T., Kuge, Y., Kume, N., Ogawa, M., & Takai, N. (2008). Targeting of lectinlike oxidized low-density lipoprotein receptor 1 (LOX-1) with 99mTc-labeled anti-LOX-1 antibody: Potential agent for imaging of vulnerable plaque. *Journal of Nuclear Medicine, 49*(10), 1677–1685. doi:10.2967/jnumed.107.049536

Kashiwagi, M., Tanaka, A., Kitabata, H., Tsujioka, H., Kataiwa, H., & Komukai, K. (2009). Feasibility of noninvasive assessment of thin-cap fibroatheroma by multidetector computed tomography. *JACC: Cardiovascular Imaging, 2*(12), 1412–1419. doi:10.1016/j.jcmg.2009.09.012

Kerwin, W., Hooker, A., Spilker, M., Vicini, P., Ferguson, M., & Hatsukami, T. (2003). Quantitative magnetic resonance imaging analysis of neovasculature volume in carotid atherosclerotic plaque. *Circulation, 107*(6), 851–856. doi:10.1161/01.CIR.0000048145.52309.31

Kim, W. Y., Stuber, M., Bornert, P., Kissinger, K. V., Manning, W. J., & Botnar, R. M. (2002). Three-dimensional black-blood cardiac magnetic resonance coronary vessel wall imaging detects positive arterial remodeling in patients with nonsignificant coronary artery disease. *Circulation, 106*(3), 296–299. doi:10.1161/01. CIR.0000025629.85631.1E

Kircher, M. F., Grimm, J., Swirski, F. K., Libby, P., Gerszten, R. E., & Allport, J. R. (2008). Noninvasive in vivo imaging of monocyte trafficking to atherosclerotic lesions. *Circulation, 117*(3), 388–395. doi:10.1161/CIRCULATIONAHA.107.719765

Kitagawa, T., Yamamoto, H., Horiguchi, J., Ohhashi, N., Tadehara, F., & Shokawa, T. (2009). Characterization of noncalcified coronary plaques and identification of culprit lesions in patients with acute coronary syndrome by 64-slice computed tomography. *JACC: Cardiovascular Imaging, 2*(2), 153–160. doi:10.1016/j.jcmg.2008.09.015

Kooi, M. E., Cappendijk, V. C., Cleutjens, K. B., Kessels, A. G., Kitslaar, P. J., & Borgers, M. (2003). Accumulation of ultrasmall superparamagnetic particles of iron oxide in human atherosclerotic plaques can be detected by in vivo magnetic resonance imaging. *Circulation, 107*(19), 2453–2458. doi:10.1161/01.CIR.0000068315.98705.CC

Kuge, Y., Takai, N., Ogawa, Y., Temma, T., Zhao, Y., & Nishigori, K.. Imaging with radiolabelled anti-membrane type 1 matrix metalloproteinase (MT1-MMP) antibody: Potentials for characterizing atherosclerotic plaques. *European Journal of Nuclear Medicine and Molecular Imaging, 37*(11), 2093–2104. doi:10.1007/s00259-010-1521-2

Kume, N., Murase, T., Moriwaki, H., Aoyama, T., Sawamura, T., & Masaki, T. (1998). Inducible expression of lectin-like oxidized LDL receptor-1 in vascular endothelial cells. *Circulation Research, 83*(3), 322–327.

Laufer, E. M., Winkens, H. M., Corsten, M. F., Reutelingsperger, C. P., Narula, J., & Hofstra, L. (2009). PET and SPECT imaging of apoptosis in vulnerable atherosclerotic plaques with radiolabeled Annexin A5. *The Quarterly Journal of Nuclear Medicine and Molecular Imaging, 53*(1), 26–34.

Laufer, E. M., Winkens, M. H., Narula, J., & Hofstra, L. (2009). Molecular imaging of macrophage cell death for the assessment of plaque vulnerability. *Arteriosclerosis, Thrombosis, and Vascular Biology, 29*(7), 1031–1038. doi:10.1161/ATVBAHA.108.165522

Lees, A. M., & Lees, R. S. (1991). 99mTechnetium-labeled low density lipoprotein: receptor recognition and intracellular sequestration of radiolabel. *Journal of Lipid Research, 32*(1), 1–8.

Leung, K. (2004). *99mTc-Interleukin-2.*

Libby, P., Ridker, P. M., & Maseri, A. (2002). Inflammation and atherosclerosis. *Circulation, 105*(9), 1135–1143. doi:10.1161/hc0902.104353

Lindsay, A. C., Murray, S. W., & Choudhury, R. P. (2010). Contemporary coronary imaging from patient to plaque: Part 4 magnetic resonance imaging. *Br J Cardiol, 17*(6), 290–292.

Marwan, M., Ropers, D., Pflederer, T., Daniel, W. G., & Achenbach, S. (2009). Clinical characteristics of patients with obstructive coronary lesions in the absence of coronary calcification: An evaluation by coronary CT angiography. *Heart (British Cardiac Society), 95*(13), 1056–1060. doi:10.1136/hrt.2008.153353

Miller, J. M., Rochitte, C. E., Dewey, M., Arbab-Zadeh, A., Niinuma, H., & Gottlieb, I. (2008). Diagnostic performance of coronary angiography by 64-row CT. *The New England Journal of Medicine, 359*(22), 2324–2336. doi:10.1056/NEJMoa0806576

Min, J. K., Shaw, L. J., Devereux, R. B., Okin, P. M., Weinsaft, J. W., & Russo, D. J. (2007). Prognostic value of multidetector coronary computed tomographic angiography for prediction of all-cause mortality. *Journal of the American College of Cardiology, 50*(12), 1161–1170. doi:10.1016/j.jacc.2007.03.067

Mitsumori, L. M., Hatsukami, T. S., Ferguson, M. S., Kerwin, W. S., Cai, J., & Yuan, C. (2003). In vivo accuracy of multisequence MR imaging for identifying unstable fibrous caps in advanced human carotid plaques. *Journal of Magnetic Resonance Imaging, 17*(4), 410–420. doi:10.1002/jmri.10264

Moreno, P. R., Purushothaman, K. R., Fuster, V., Echeverri, D., Truszczynska, H., & Sharma, S. K. (2004). Plaque neovascularization is increased in ruptured atherosclerotic lesions of human aorta: Implications for plaque vulnerability. *Circulation, 110*(14), 2032–2038. doi:10.1161/01.CIR.0000143233.87854.23

Motoyama, S., Sarai, M., Harigaya, H., Anno, H., Inoue, K., & Hara, T. (2009). Computed tomographic angiography characteristics of atherosclerotic plaques subsequently resulting in acute coronary syndrome. *Journal of the American College of Cardiology, 54*(1), 49–57. doi:10.1016/j.jacc.2009.02.068

Muller, J. E., Abela, G. S., Nesto, R. W., & Tofler, G. H. (1994). Triggers, acute risk factors and vulnerable plaques: The lexicon of a new frontier. *Journal of the American College of Cardiology, 23*(3), 809–813. doi:10.1016/0735-1097(94)90772-2

Nahrendorf, M., Zhang, H., Hembrador, S., Panizzi, P., Sosnovik, D. E., & Aikawa, E. (2008). Nanoparticle PET-CT imaging of macrophages in inflammatory atherosclerosis. *Circulation, 117*(3), 379–387. doi:10.1161/CIRCULATIONAHA.107.741181

O'Rourke, R. A., Brundage, B. H., Froelicher, V. F., Greenland, P., Grundy, S. M., & Hachamovitch, R. (2000). American College of Cardiology/American Heart Association expert consensus document on electron-beam computed tomography for the diagnosis and prognosis of coronary artery disease. *Journal of the American College of Cardiology, 36*(1), 326–340. doi:10.1016/S0735-1097(00)00831-7

Packard, R. R. S., & Libby, P. (2008). Inflammation in atherosclerosis: From vascular biology to biomarker discovery and risk prediction. *Clinical Chemistry, 54*(1), 24–38. doi:10.1373/clinchem.2007.097360

Pflederer, T., Marwan, M., Schepis, T., Ropers, D., Seltmann, M., & Muschiol, G. Characterization of culprit lesions in acute coronary syndromes using coronary dual-source CT angiography. *Atherosclerosis, 211*(2), 437–444. doi:10.1016/j.atherosclerosis.2010.02.001

Pundziute, G., Schuijf, J. D., Jukema, J. W., Decramer, I., Sarno, G., & Vanhoenacker, P. K. (2008). Head-to-head comparison of coronary plaque evaluation between multislice computed tomography and intravascular ultrasound radiofrequency data analysis. *JACC: Cardiovascular Interventions, 1*(2), 176–182. doi:10.1016/j.jcin.2008.01.007

Renshaw, P. F., Owen, C. S., McLaughlin, A. C., Frey, T. G., & Leigh, J. S. Jr. (1986). Ferromagnetic contrast agents: a new approach. *Magnetic Resonance in Medicine, 3*(2), 217–225. doi:10.1002/mrm.1910030205

Rogers, I. S., Nasir, K., Figueroa, A. L., Cury, R. C., Hoffmann, U., & Vermylen, D. A. Feasibility of FDG imaging of the coronary arteries: comparison between acute coronary syndrome and stable angina. *JACC: Cardiovascular Imaging, 3*(4), 388–397. doi:10.1016/j.jcmg.2010.01.004

Ross, R., & Glomset, J. A. (1976a). The pathogenesis of atherosclerosis (first of two parts). *The New England Journal of Medicine, 295*(7), 369–377. doi:10.1056/NEJM197608122950707

Ross, R., & Glomset, J. A. (1976b). The pathogenesis of atherosclerosis (second of two parts). *The New England Journal of Medicine, 295*(8), 420–425. doi:10.1056/NEJM197608192950805

Rudd, J. H., Narula, J., Strauss, H. W., Virmani, R., Machac, J., & Klimas, M. Imaging atherosclerotic plaque inflammation by fluorodeoxyglucose with positron emission tomography: Ready for prime time? *Journal of the American College of Cardiology, 55*(23), 2527–2535. doi:10.1016/j.jacc.2009.12.061

Ruehm, S. G., Corot, C., Vogt, P., Kolb, S., & Debatin, J. F. (2001). Magnetic resonance imaging of atherosclerotic plaque with ultrasmall superparamagnetic particles of iron oxide in hyperlipidemic rabbits. *Circulation, 103*(3), 415–422.

Saam, T., Cai, J., Ma, L., Cai, Y. Q., Ferguson, M. S., & Polissar, N. L. (2006). Comparison of symptomatic and asymptomatic atherosclerotic carotid plaque features with in vivo MR imaging. *Radiology, 240*(2), 464–472. doi:10.1148/radiol.2402050390

Serfaty, J. M., Chaabane, L., Tabib, A., Chevallier, J. M., Briguet, A., & Douek, P. C. (2001). Atherosclerotic plaques: classification and characterization with T2-weighted high-spatial-resolution MR imaging-- An in vitro study. *Radiology, 219*(2), 403–410.

Shinnar, M., Fallon, J. T., Wehrli, S., Levin, M., Dalmacy, D., & Fayad, Z. A. (1999). The diagnostic accuracy of ex vivo MRI for human atherosclerotic plaque characterization. *Arteriosclerosis, Thrombosis, and Vascular Biology, 19*(11), 2756–2761. doi:10.1161/01.ATV.19.11.2756

Skinner, M. P., Yuan, C., Mitsumori, L., Hayes, C. E., Raines, E. W., & Nelson, J. A. (1995). Serial magnetic resonance imaging of experimental atherosclerosis detects lesion fine structure, progression and complications in vivo. *Nature Medicine, 1*(1), 69–73. doi:10.1038/nm0195-69

Stary, H. C. (1992). Composition and classification of human atherosclerotic lesions. *Virchows Archiv. A, Pathological Anatomy and Histopathology, 421*(4), 277–290. doi:10.1007/BF01660974

Stary, H. C. (2000). Lipid and macrophage accumulations in arteries of children and the development of atherosclerosis. *The American Journal of Clinical Nutrition, 72*(5Suppl), 1297S–1306S.

Swirski, F. K., Pittet, M. J., Kircher, M. F., Aikawa, E., Jaffer, F. A., & Libby, P. (2006). Monocyte accumulation in mouse atherogenesis is progressive and proportional to extent of disease. *Proceedings of the National Academy of Sciences of the United States of America, 103*(27), 10340–10345. doi:10.1073/pnas.0604260103

Tahara, N., Kai, H., Ishibashi, M., Nakaura, H., Kaida, H., & Baba, K. (2006). Simvastatin attenuates plaque inflammation: Evaluation by fluorodeoxyglucose positron emission tomography. *Journal of the American College of Cardiology, 48*(9), 1825–1831. doi:10.1016/j.jacc.2006.03.069

Tahara, N., Kai, H., Nakaura, H., Mizoguchi, M., Ishibashi, M., & Kaida, H. (2007). The prevalence of inflammation in carotid atherosclerosis: analysis with fluorodeoxyglucose-positron emission tomography. *European Heart Journal, 28*(18), 2243–2248. doi:10.1093/eurheartj/ehm245

Tawakol, A., Migrino, R. Q., Hoffmann, U., Abbara, S., Houser, S., & Gewirtz, H. (2005). Noninvasive in vivo measurement of vascular inflammation with F-18 fluorodeoxyglucose positron emission tomography. *Journal of Nuclear Cardiology, 12*(3), 294–301. doi:10.1016/j.nuclcard.2005.03.002

Tekabe, Y., Li, Q., Luma, J., Weisenberger, D., Sedlar, M., & Harja, E.Noninvasive monitoring the biology of atherosclerotic plaque development with radiolabeled annexin V and matrix metalloproteinase inhibitor in spontaneous atherosclerotic mice. *Journal of Nuclear Cardiology, 17*(6), 1073–1081. doi:10.1007/s12350-010-9276-5

Topol, E. J., & Nissen, S. E. (1995). Our preoccupation with coronary luminology. The dissociation between clinical and angiographic findings in ischemic heart disease. *Circulation, 92*(8), 2333–2342.

Toussaint, J. F., LaMuraglia, G. M., Southern, J. F., Fuster, V., & Kantor, H. L. (1996). Magnetic resonance images lipid, fibrous, calcified, hemorrhagic, and thrombotic components of human atherosclerosis in vivo. *Circulation, 94*(5), 932–938.

Toussaint, J. F., Southern, J. F., Fuster, V., & Kantor, H. L. (1995). T2-weighted contrast for NMR characterization of human atherosclerosis. *Arteriosclerosis, Thrombosis, and Vascular Biology, 15*(10), 1533–1542.

Varnava, A. M., Mills, P. G., & Davies, M. J. (2002). Relationship between coronary artery remodeling and plaque vulnerability. *Circulation, 105*(8), 939–943. doi:10.1161/hc0802.104327

Virmani, R., Burke, A. P., Farb, A., & Kolodgie, F. D. (2006). Pathology of the vulnerable plaque. *Journal of the American College of Cardiology, 47*(8Suppl), C13–C18. doi:10.1016/j.jacc.2005.10.065

von zur Muhlen, C., von Elverfeldt, D., Moeller, J. A., Choudhury, R. P., Paul, D., & Hagemeyer, C. E. (2008). Magnetic resonance imaging contrast agent targeted toward activated platelets allows in vivo detection of thrombosis and monitoring of thrombolysis. *Circulation, 118*(3), 258–267. doi:10.1161/CIRCULATIONAHA.107.753657

Yu, X., Song, S. K., Chen, J., Scott, M. J., Fuhrhop, R. J., & Hall, C. S. (2000). High-resolution MRI characterization of human thrombus using a novel fibrin-targeted paramagnetic nanoparticle contrast agent. *Magnetic Resonance in Medicine, 44*(6), 867–872. doi:10.1002/1522-2594(200012)44:6<867::AID-MRM7>3.0.CO;2-P

Yuan, C., Kerwin, W. S., Ferguson, M. S., Polissar, N., Zhang, S., & Cai, J. (2002). Contrast-enhanced high resolution MRI for atherosclerotic carotid artery tissue characterization. *Journal of Magnetic Resonance Imaging, 15*(1), 62–67. doi:10.1002/jmri.10030

Yuan, C., Mitsumori, L. M., Ferguson, M. S., Polissar, N. L., Echelard, D., & Ortiz, G. (2001). In vivo accuracy of multispectral magnetic resonance imaging for identifying lipid-rich necrotic cores and intraplaque hemorrhage in advanced human carotid plaques. *Circulation, 104*(17), 2051–2056. doi:10.1161/hc4201.097839

Section 9
Intravascular Imaging and Haemodynamics

Chapter 19
Intravascular Imaging and Haemodynamics:
The Role of Shear Stress in Atherosclerosis and In-Stent Restenosis

Michail I. Papafaklis
Harvard Medical School, USA & University of Ioannina, Greece

Lampros K. Michalis
University of Ioannina, Greece

ABSTRACT

Shear stress on the endothelial surface has been implicated in atherosclerosis localization, plaque vulnerability, and remodeling behavior of the arterial wall, as well as in-stent restenosis following percutaneous coronary interventions. The purposes of this chapter are to introduce haemodynamic shear stress, briefly explain the methodology for measuring and imaging shear stress in vivo, present the role of shear stress in the atherosclerotic disease process, and cite the evidence highlighting the effects of stent implantation on local blood flow patterns and linking shear stress at the stent surface to neointimal hyperplasia following coronary artery stenting.

INTRODUCTION

Atherosclerotic cardiovascular disease is characterized by chronic inflammation and fibroproliferation of large- and medium-sized arteries, and remains the leading cause of mortality and morbidity in western societies. Despite the systemic nature of risk factors (i.e., dyslipidaemia, diabetes mellitus, hypertension, cigarette smoking, social stress) associated with atherosclerosis, the disease manifestations are focal and eccentric, and evolve in an independent manner. Atherosclerosis is a site-specific disease, which affects primarily the carotid bifurcation, the coronary arteries, the infrarenal aorta and the arteries of the lower limbs having a propensity to involve branch points, bifurcations and highly curved arteries (Asakura & Karino, 1990; Ku et al., 1985). Regional haemodynamic

DOI: 10.4018/978-1-61350-095-8.ch019

factors that create a unique environment are critical determinants of the behavior of atherosclerosis at focal sites throughout the vasculature in susceptible individuals. Flow-derived shear stress, in particular, exerts its pathobiological effects on the arterial endothelium that are associated with increased atherosclerosis susceptibility and development, and plaque vulnerability (Chatzizisis, Coskun, Jonas, Edelman, Feldman et al., 2007; Davies, 2009).

The advancement of percutaneous coronary interventions during the last three decades has provided efficient non-surgical management of obstructive atherosclerotic lesions. Coronary stenting using bare metal stents or, more recently, drug-eluting stents, has currently dominated as an interventional strategy for restoring arterial blood flow in diseased arteries. However, stenting constitutes an invasive procedure involving the implantation of a foreign metal body, which affects the regional arterial geometry, and consequently, alters the local haemodynamic environment. Stent architecture influences the detailed characteristics of post-stent implantation blood flow patterns (Balossino et al., 2008), which are recognized as major determinants of the vascular response, neointima distribution and deposition of the eluted drugs.

BACKGROUND

Haemodynamic Forces and Intravascular Flow Patterns

Mechanical (haemodynamic) forces are important modulators of vascular endothelial cells lining the luminal surface of blood vessels. Flowing blood exerts a physical force on the arterial wall generating haemodynamic stress (i.e., force per unit area measured in N/m^2 or Pascal [Pa]) which has two components (vectors): (i) the normal (i.e., perpendicular to the wall) stress due to blood pressure, which results in cyclic stretch (tensile stress) of the vessel wall, and (ii) shear stress (SS), which is the tangential stress derived from the friction of blood on the vessel wall due to the fluid's viscous nature (Figure 1). The flow of viscous fluids, such as blood, is characterized by the fundamental observation and assumption in fluid mechanics, according to which the fluid layer in contact with the wall has zero velocity relative to the wall boundary (i.e., no-slip condition) (Munson et al., 2002). As a result, the velocity of adjacent layers of fluid increases from zero at the wall to a maximum value at some distance from the wall establishing a velocity gradient (shear rate = du/dy). Fluids for which SS is linearly related to the

Figure 1. Components (P: blood pressure and SS: shear stress) of haemodynamic stress exerted by the flowing blood on the endothelial surface and arterial wall. Blood pressure results in circumferential stretch (tensile stress) of the arterial wall. Flow velocity (u) increases from zero at the wall to a maximum value near the center of the artery establishing a velocity gradient. Modified from (Gijsen, 1998).

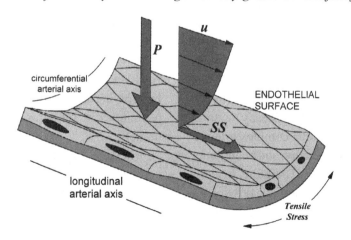

shear rate are designated as Newtonian fluids and in this case, SS is proportional to the product of the blood viscosity (μ) and shear rate at the wall. Blood does not exhibit a constant viscosity at all flow rates (i.e., viscosity depends on the shear rate) and behaves as a non-Newtonian fluid–characterized by a non-linear relationship of SS to shear rate–especially in the microcirculatory system. The non-Newtonian behavior is most evident at very low shear rates when the red blood cells aggregate forming larger particles (rouleaux). However, in most arteries, blood behaves in a Newtonian fashion, and the viscosity can be taken as a constant.

The nature of blood flow through an artery is dependent on the velocity of flow and the complex geometric characteristics (e.g., curvature and branching) or the presence of any stenoses. Based on the type of internal structure of the flow field, blood flow is classified as laminar or turbulent. In laminar, or streamline flow, blood particles flow in parallel layers, whereas in turbulent flow blood particles acquire irregular and random trajectories which vary continuously over time. The Reynolds number (Re) is a critical parameter in fluid dynamics, which defines whether flow conditions lead to laminar or turbulent flow for a given geometry. In arteries (flow in a tube), flows with low Re values (< 2,000) are considered to be laminar, whereas higher Re values lead to turbulent flow. Depending on the specific geometric irregularities, such as a post-stenotic sudden expansion of the cross-

sectional area of the vessel, and the Re values in an artery, blood flow may remain laminar but develop instabilities and become disturbed characterized by flow separation and recirculation zones with flow reversal and stagnation.

Arterial blood flow is also characterized by its pulsatile (i.e., time varying or unsteady) nature which, in combination with the complex arterial anatomy, determines the direction and magnitude of blood flow velocity and SS. Therefore, in arterial regions with undisturbed laminar flow (e.g.,

in relatively straight arterial segments), SS is pulsatile and unidirectional with positive values in the physiologic range (>1.5 Pa) over the cardiac cycle (Malek et al., 1999). In contrast, regions with disturbed flow (e.g., arterial bifurcations) are characterized by low and/or oscillatory SS; low SS is pulsatile and unidirectional but has a low time-average magnitude (<1 Pa), while oscillatory SS is bidirectional (i.e., time-dependent reversal of the direction of the SS vector) due to both forward and reverse flow resulting in time-average SS values close to zero.

In Vivo Shear Stress Assessment in Coronary Arteries

The investigation of the role of SS in atherosclerosis and in-stent restenosis in animals and humans requires *in vivo* assessment of the local SS distribution on the endothelial surface. Direct measurement of the local velocity gradient and thus, SS in coronary arteries is very difficult due to their small size and complex time-dependent three-dimensional (3D) geometry. Therefore, *in vivo* SS assessment in coronary arteries necessitates the mathematical analysis of the flow field. An approximate solution can be derived from the Hagen-Poiseuille equation (SS=$32\mu Q/\pi d^3$, μ: viscosity, Q: flow, d: luminal diameter), which is valid in idealized cases of steady (time unvarying), fully-developed laminar flow of a Newtonian fluid through a straight tube of constant circular cross-section. However, a more detailed approach compared to the simplistic Poiseuille flow involves the use of the differential equations of continuity and momentum (Navier-Stokes equation). The solution of these equations for complex flow fields like those in coronary arteries is feasible by applying computational fluid dynamics (CFD) techniques in 3D coronary artery reconstructed models.

The first step for *in vivo* SS assessment in coronary arteries is the realistic (patient-specific) 3D coronary artery reconstruction, which can be obtained by using stand-alone biplane or rotational angiography (Xie et al., 2010). However, this approach does not allow the 3D reconstruction of the outer vessel wall, and thus, the assessment of plaque distribution and its association with the local haemodynamics. To overcome this limitation, fusion of biplane angiographic and intravascular ultrasound (IVUS) data (Bourantas et al., 2005; Giannoglou et al., 2006; Slager et al., 2000; Stone, Coskun, Yeghiazarians et al., 2003; Wahle et al., 1999) has been proposed. According to the latter methodologies, the IVUS catheter is advanced in the coronary artery under fluoroscopic control distally from the coronary segment of interest (e.g., distal to a branch locator), and following intracoronary administration of nitroglycerin angiographic images from two different views are obtained during diluted contrast agent injection. IVUS is performed using a motorized pullback (typically at a speed of 0.5 mm/sec) and the ECG is recorded in both the angiographic and IVUS sequence. The biplane angiographic images (typically at end-diastole) are used to reconstruct the catheter path in 3D space. The arterial lumen and outer vessel wall are reconstructed by placing digitized and segmented end-diastolic frames (contours) onto the reconstructed 3D catheter path. The incorporation of IVUS data in the 3D reconstruction methodology is technically demanding, but increases the accuracy of the 3D models, is highly reproducible (Coskun et al., 2003) and also has the advantage of providing comprehensive 3D visualization of the lumen and outer vessel wall (media-adventitia border) (Figure 2). However, this methodology does not provide 3D coronary artery models including branches and bifurcations (i.e., regions which are considered to be highly susceptible to atherosclerosis). The 3D reconstruction of coronary artery bifurcations including both the mother and the two daughter vessels necessitates the fusion of the 3D data sets of these vessels increasing the technical difficulty. Two approaches have been presented for this purpose: (i) data of biplane angiography (lumen only)

Figure 2. Three-dimensional reconstructed surfaces of the lumen (red) and outer vessel wall (light blue) of a right coronary artery.

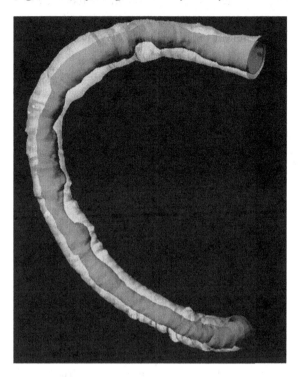

for the side branch may be fused with combined angiographic-IVUS data (lumen and outer vessel wall) for the mother vessel (Gijsen et al., 2007), and (ii) the IVUS pullback may be performed in both arteries of the bifurcation (e.g., left anterior descending and circumflex arteries) and the mother vessel (e.g., left main stem) providing two separate 3D models (lumen and outer vessel wall) for each mother-daughter vessel, which are then fused for reconstructing a unified mother-daughter vessels model (Papafaklis, 2008; Papafaklis, Bourantas et al., 2007). Furthermore, latest advancements in medical imaging have also enabled the use of computed tomography angiography for non-invasive imaging and 3D reconstruction of the coronary arterial tree (Rybicki et al., 2009; van der Giessen et al., 2009).

Shear stress computation in 3D reconstructed arteries is accomplished by using CFD modeling, according to which the complex geometry of the

3D reconstructed arterial lumen model is separated into a large number of smaller finite elements (typically tetrahedrons or hexahedron), creating a grid on which the equations describing the phenomenon are discretized. By assuming the velocity field within those elements, it is possible to solve the differential equations of fluid motion at the nodes connecting these elements, provided that the boundary conditions on the flow inlet (e.g., patient-specific flow), flow outlet, and arterial walls (application of the no-slip condition), as well as the material properties of the fluid (i.e., blood density and viscosity) are defined. Patient-specific flow rate may be determined by measuring the time required for injected contrast medium to fill a known arterial volume and patient-specific blood viscosity is estimated from the measured hematocrit. Computational fluid dynamics iterative calculations finally provide invaluable knowledge of the detailed flow characteristics (e.g., velocity profile) and spatio-temporal variations that SS may exhibit in coronary arteries (Figure 3). Three-dimensional reconstruction of coronary arteries coupled with CFD techniques can be used to track changes in lumen, plaque or neointima thickness and SS in periods as short as 6-9 months in humans or experimental animals (Koskinas, Feldman et al., 2010; Stone et al., 2007), and therefore, investigate *in vivo* the role of SS in both atherosclerosis in native arteries and neointimal hyperplasia in stents.

THE ROLE OF ENDOTHELIAL SHEAR STRESS IN THE ATHEROSCLEROTIC DISEASE PROCESS

Localized Plaque Growth and Shear Stress

In the 1960s, the previously acquired knowledge on the localized distribution of atherosclerotic

Figure 3. A) Color-coded streamlines demonstrating the flow pattern in the lumen of a patient's right coronary artery (RCA). B) Detailed view of the flow pattern showing a region of disturbed flow and recirculation (arrow) just distal to a luminal obstruction. C) Color-coded velocity vectors indicating the flow velocity profile in various cross-sections along the axial direction of the artery. D) Detailed view of the mid-RCA demonstrating skewing of the velocity profile towards the outer wall of this curved arterial segment. E) Color-coded map of the shear stress distribution on the arterial wall (endothelial surface); different views are provided.

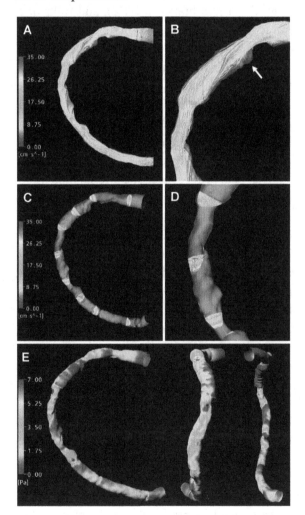

lesions in the vasculature led to the appreciation that fluid mechanics are implicated in the pathology of the disease. At that time, two opposing theories were proposed; one advocated high and the other low SS (Caro, 2009). Excessively high SS (approximately >38 Pa) was demonstrated to cause direct endothelial injury and denudation (Fry, 1968), while acutely increased SS, but below that causing damage, augmented the permeability of the endothelial surface and the transendothelial transport of protein (Fry, 1969). However, the above-mentioned high SS value is supernatural since the maximum SS in any artery of the cardiovascular system is known to be less than 10-15 Pa (Malek et al., 1999; Papaioannou et al., 2006). The low shear hypothesis of atherogenesis, proposed by Caro and colleagues (1969; 1971), postulated that the diffusional flux of lipids between the blood and the arterial wall is governed by convective and diffusive processes within the blood with local SS affecting local supply and removal rates. Atherosclerotic lesion localization at branching sites of cadaver human arteries was also investigated in parallel with theoretical models of steady flow SS patterns at a bifurcation and supported the preferential development of atherosclerosis in arterial regions experiencing low SS (i.e., the outer walls of bifurcations). Therefore, low shear regions were considered to be zones of inhibited lipid efflux resulting in fat accumulation within the arterial wall.

The initial observations by Caro, et al. were confirmed by later studies in cadaver specimens and casts of vessels demonstrating that plaque thickness in the arterial wall of abdominal aortas, carotids and coronary arteries is negatively correlated to SS magnitude (Friedman et al., 1981; Ku et al., 1985). Further support of the role of low SS in plaque development was also derived by *in vivo* animal experiments and investigations in humans using sophisticated blood flow simulations in 3D arterial models derived from angiographic and IVUS imaging of coronary arteries or magnetic resonance imaging of large vessels (Feldman et

al., 2002; Long et al., 2000). It has now been well documented that regions of moderate to high SS are spared of intimal thickening, while focal lesions develop only in areas of low and/or recirculating flow. Arterial regions of naturally occurring low or oscillatory SS, such as the inner surfaces of curvatures and the outer walls of bifurcations, are the regions primarily involved in plaque accumulation and progression (Figure 4). Spatial gradients of SS in geometrically irregular regions, as well as temporal SS gradients, have also been implicated in atherogenesis.

Recent molecular biology and histological investigations have demonstrated that different levels of SS lead to a selective up- or down-regulation of atherogenic or atheroprotective genes providing a mechanistic link among the local hemodynamic milieu, endothelial gene expression and vascular pathobiology. Low SS, in particular, exerts a multifactorial influence on the arterial wall, which involves the conversion of biomechanical stimuli to biochemical responses by endothelial cells leading to the activation of inflammatory pathways (e.g., nuclear factor kappa B) and muting of atheroprotective transcriptional factors (e.g., Krüppel-like factor-2) (Hahn & Schwartz, 2009). The result of this process is (i) the increased expression of adhesion molecules (e.g., ICAM-1, VCAM-1) (Gimbrone et al., 2000) and chemokines (e.g., MCP-1, fraktalkine) (Cheng et al., 2007), which mediate the recruitment of inflammatory cells in the intima, and (ii) the decrease of atheroprotective molecules, such as nitric oxide and prostacyclin (Davies, 2009). Conversely, normal or high SS exerts protective functions on the endothelial layer by increasing nitric oxide synthase (Nadaud et al., 1996) and reducing endothelial cell death and proliferation (Cho et al., 1997).

Figure 4. Localization of atherosclerotic plaques (yellow) in regions of low shear stress (blue) in the outer walls of arterial bifurcations (e.g., carotids) and the inner walls of curved arteries (e.g., coronary arteries). Regions with high shear stress (red) are relatively resistant to developing atherosclerosis.

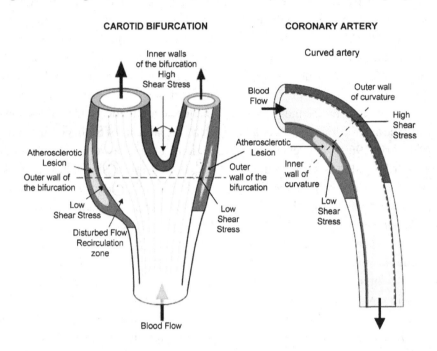

Effects of Shear Stress on Arterial Remodeling and Plaque Vulnerability

The arterial wall is capable of undergoing major reshaping, the so-called arterial remodeling, during both physiological and disease processes. If the flow rate is altered from its physiologic state for a long period, the vessel caliber responds by changing in such a way as to recover the physiologic range of shear (Kamiya & Togawa, 1980; Zarins et al., 1987). In normal arteries high SS elicits an expansive remodeling response, whereas low SS a constrictive one. Furthermore, Glagov et al. (1987) first observed in human coronary arteries the ability of the vessel wall to adapt and accommodate a growing plaque by an increase of the internal elastic lamina area. According to the observations in normal arteries, the response of the plaque-free wall to the rise in SS (when the plaque protrudes into the lumen) has been suggested as a mechanism explaining the compensa-

tory remodeling process (Slager, Wentzel, Gijsen, Schuurbiers et al., 2005; Wentzel et al., 2003), which preserves normal lumen dimensions until the lesion area encompasses 30-40% of the internal elastic lamina area. However, recent *in vivo* studies have provided evidence supporting the role of low SS in the remodeling of atherosclerotic arteries, a process regulated by the balance between extracellular matrix production and enzymatic breakdown. Animal experiments demonstrated that low SS induces matrix degradation, and thus expansive remodeling, by up-regulating the expression and activity of collagenases (e.g., MMP-1, 13) and elastases (e.g., MMP-2, 9, 12 and cathepsins K, S) relative to their inhibitors (Chatzizisis et al., 2011; Koskinas, Sukhova et al., 2010). Therefore, local SS influences key mediators in the arterial wall and can potentially determine the extent of vessel expansion. An environment of extremely low SS may lead to excessive wall inflammation, severe fragmentation of the internal elastic lamina and destruction of plaque matrix resulting in overcompensation. A disproportionate vessel expansion to plaque growth is accompanied by lumen increase, which further decreases SS, and establishes a vicious cycle between persistently very low SS and excessive expansive remodeling.

Rupture-prone plaques leading to acute coronary syndromes are typically characterized by a thin (<65 μm) inflamed fibrous cap overlying a large necrotic core and are more often located within expansively remodeled arterial regions, compared with lesions with a stable phenotype (Virmani et al., 2006). Low SS has been suggested to exert a key role in the conversion of stable lesions to high-risk plaques (Cheng et al., 2006; Koskinas et al., 2009). *In vivo* experimental studies demonstrated that the intensity of inflammatory cell infiltration is related in a dose-dependent manner to the magnitude of the preceding SS, which leads to cap thinning and the development of highly inflamed fibroatheromas (Chatzizisis et al., 2008). Further, the low SS–induced recruitment of proinflammatory cytokines contributes to augmented in-plaque oxidative stress and apoptotic death of macrophages and smooth muscle cells, which constitute a major source of necrotic debris in the expanding necrotic core. Although regions with physiologic SS are relatively resistant to lesion development, localized high SS, as that occurring at the throat of stenotic plaques, has also been implicated in endothelial detachment, platelet adhesion and induction of thrombotic occlusion without rupture (Slager, Wentzel, Gijsen, Thury et al., 2005).

SHEAR STRESS AT THE STENTED ENDOTHELIAL SURFACE AND IN-STENT NEOINTIMAL HYPERPLASIA

Neointimal hyperplasia is the major contributing pathophysiologic mechanism of in-stent restenosis and is influenced by clinical characteristics, such as diabetes (Abizaid et al., 1998), and pro-

cedural and lesion-related parameters, such as residual stenosis, number of stents, stent length and plaque burden (Hibi et al., 2002; Kasaoka et al., 1998). However, recent studies have shown that the altered geometry and associated blood flow disturbances established after stenting can also influence restenosis; stent design, material and configuration dictate intravascular flow features, thereby influencing neointimal hyperplasia (Kastrati et al., 2001; Rogers & Edelman, 1995). Neointima formation causing in-stent restenosis is often observed at specific locations in the stented segment (Thury et al., 2002) and SS–except for its role in atherosclerosis–has also being implicated in the pathobiology of in-stent restenosis and stent thrombosis (Papafaklis & Michalis, 2005; Wentzel et al., 2008).

The pathophysiology of in-stent restenosis involves accumulation of new tissue within the arterial wall, and neointima formation is caused by a cascade mechanism initiated by platelet aggregation due to vascular injury and followed by macrophage intimal infiltration. Growth factors (e.g. platelet-derived growth factor, vascular endothelial growth factor) released during vessel injury influence intracellular positive and negative regulators of cell cycle events, which ultimately control smooth muscle cell migration and proliferation in the intima (Carter et al., 1994). Smooth muscle cells migration to the intima is also characterized by their phenotypic switch from a contractile phenotype to a synthetic one, which leads to increased extracellular matrix production. SS has been demonstrated *in vitro* to act either through the endothelium or directly, as in cases of a damaged endothelial layer after stenting, and modulate smooth muscle cell gene expression, proliferation and phenotypic modulation (Chiu et al., 2004; Hastings et al., 2007).

Effect of Stent Implantation and Architecture on Local Flow Dynamics

Arterial geometry is critical in determining local flow dynamics and SS distribution. Animal studies and simulations in 3D theoretical vessels reflecting the *in vivo* environment have shown that stent implantation alters coronary artery haemodynamics due to the immediate effects of the metal scaffolding on vascular resistance and local arterial geometry. Assessment of flow dynamics indices in the left anterior descending coronary artery of anesthetized dogs demonstrated that stent implantation produces a modest increase in coronary blood flow related to a reduction in coronary vascular resistance and leads to increases in regional oscillatory SS. The same study provided significant evidence that stent deployment attenuates the alterations in fluid dynamics (i.e., reductions in coronary vascular resistance and increases in Reynolds number [Re] and SS indices) during maximal vasodilation (LaDisa et al., 2002). Stent deployment has also been shown *in vivo* to cause prominent increments in curvature (increase by 121% at the entrance and by 100% at the exit of the stent) near the stent edges resulting in local SS maxima and minima (Wentzel et al., 2000). The inherent curvature of coronary arteries along their course on the epicardial surface cannot be fully preserved after stenting; the stent-induced axial arterial straightening leads to skewing of the velocity profile at the inlet and outlet of the stented region, and causes large alterations in spatial SS distributions. Therefore, implantation of a stent that conforms to the native vessel curvature causes

Figure 5. Time-dependent alterations in spatial wall shear stress throughout the cardiac cycle in computational vessels implanted with 12 mm stents that conform to (flexible, left) or cause straightening of (inflexible, right) an idealized and curved coronary artery. Adapted from (LaDisa et al., 2006).

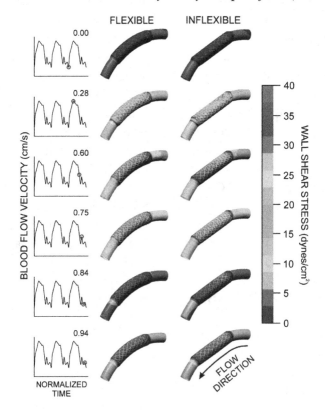

minimal changes in SS distribution and may be beneficial from a haemodynamic perspective (LaDisa et al., 2006).

Detailed knowledge on the alterations in SS caused by stent implantation has been provided by simplified representations of normal coronary arteries modeled as cylindrical tubes, but also including the individual stent struts. LaDisa, et al. (2003) showed that a slotted-tube stent design has a profound influence on near-wall velocity and wall SS patterns compared to a non-stented vessel in a 3D computational fluid dynamics model of an epicardial coronary artery using *in vivo* canine data as boundary conditions. Minimum wall SS is decreased by approximately 80% within the stent and at the outlet of the stent in stented compared to non-stented vessels, and regions of low SS are localized around stent struts and are associated with stagnation flow and boundary layer separation immediately upstream and downstream of the struts. A recent study comparing four different types of bare metal stents demonstrated that the zones with low SS values are found near the stent struts at the diastolic peak of the cardiac cycle, while the highest SS values are localized over the stent struts, which are the regions most exposed to the blood flow (Balossino et al., 2008).

Stent design characteristics, such as strut number, thickness and angle, exert a significant influence on local flow dynamics. Increasing the number of struts from four to eight has been shown to produce a 2.75–fold increase in exposure to low SS (LaDisa et al., 2004). Steady-state simulations demonstrated that a reduction in strut thickness from 0.096 to 0.056 mm is associated with a decrease in regions subjected to low SS by approximately 87% (LaDisa et al., 2004). However, thinner struts (0.05 vs. 0.15 mm) have been reported to cause an increase in the overall percentage area with low SS values in the deceleration phase of the cardiac cycle according to investigations employing pulsatile flow and more realistic arterial geometries, which incorporate

the deformed shape of the inner surface of the arterial wall (Balossino et al., 2008). Of note, larger stent struts have been associated with less endothelial coverage, underscoring the importance of stent characteristics on both flow dynamics and the response of the arterial wall (Charonko et al., 2009). Furthermore, the stent strut profile has a significant impact on the wall SS both on the struts and in between struts. Streamlined profiles (e.g., elliptical and tear-drop) exhibit better haemodynamic performance compared to the standard square and circular profiles since the former have smaller recirculation zones and a lower percentage of inter-strut area where the SS level is decreased (Jimenez & Davies, 2009; Mejia et al., 2009). Strut connectors also constitute an essential component of the stent design as their presence increases stent flexibility, which in turn improves stent deployment. Areas exposed to low SS and reverse flow are proportional to the connector length in the cross-flow direction, and the lengths of flow recirculation depend on the overall strut-connector-strut configuration (Pant et al., 2010).

Stent-related procedural parameters, namely stent-to-artery ratio, over-expansion and overlapping stents, vary among percutaneous coronary interventions and can affect SS distribution. An increase in the deployment ratio (1.1:1 vs. 1.2:1) has been demonstrated to increase the exposure to low SS by 12–fold (LaDisa et al., 2004). Over-expanding the stent with a second balloon affects the alignment of the stent geometry, and leads to higher SS at the inlet and lower values in mid-stent regions, while overlapping stents show disturbed flow and a SS deficit region downstream of the overlapped region. Therefore, the use of overlapping stents in place of a single longer stent appears to disrupt the flow within the stented region (Charonko et al., 2010). The post-procedural cross-sectional vascular shape of the stented segment also determines the local flow field. Although stent implantation with or without balloon post-dilatation is expected to result in a circular cross-section, implanted stents, especially those with a small number of stent struts in the circumference, may not have a circular profile. Polygonal computational vessels due to circumferential straightening are subjected to greater areas of low SS and elevated spatial SS gradients than those with circular geometry and may predispose to subsequent neointimal hyperplasia (LaDisa, Olson, Guler et al., 2005). Further, stent foreshortening, which is defined as the difference between the original and actual stent length after stent deployment, influences the angle created between axially aligned stent struts and the principal direction of blood flow, thereby increasing the intra-strut area of the luminal surface exposed to low SS and elevated spatial SS gradients (LaDisa, Olson, Hettrick et al., 2005).

Overall, stent implantation as well as the various stent design characteristics have a major impact on local arterial geometry and flow features causing alterations in SS distribution and thus, may contribute to restenosis risk.

The Role of Shear Stress in Neointimal Hyperplasia Following Bare Metal Stenting

Implantation of bare metal stents is beneficial in blocking vascular contraction and providing good long-term clinical results, but in-stent restenosis occurs frequently reducing the procedure's efficacy (Kimura et al., 2002). Recent *in vivo* investigations implicate SS in the restenotic process. Animal experiments have shown that neointimal hyperplasia occurs in stented arterial regions of low SS and elevated spatial SS gradients (LaDisa, Olson, Molthen et al., 2005). In the ilio-femoral bifurcation of a porcine model, stenting of the main branch led to highly eccentric restenotic lesions with a maximum at the lateral wall of the main branch; these lesions were in concert with the extent, shape and location of an area of boundary layer separation, flow stagnation and thus, decreased SS magnitude. Regions at the lateral

wall had a 3.5–fold higher neointimal thickness compared to high SS regions at the flow divider and were fibrin-rich both around the stent struts and in regions between and away the stent struts showing dense macrophage infiltration of the intima in the acute phase (Richter et al., 2004). In contrast to the adverse effect of low SS on stent patency, an artificial 2–fold increase of SS after placing a prototype flow divider in stented segments of rabbit iliac arteries has been demonstrated to result in significant lower (>50%) mean late luminal loss, reduction (>40%) in neointimal thickness and a reduced inflammation and injury score, as assessed by macrophage infiltration and internal elastic lamina disruption (Carlier et al., 2003). Evidently, in-stent SS distribution may be artificially altered; stenting devices of non-conventional shape could be tailored to increase SS and thus, reduce in-stent restenosis (Papaioannou et al., 2007).

Limited studies in a clinical setting have lately provided additional data on the role of SS in in-stent restenosis. Wentzel, et al. (2001) demonstrated a significant negative correlation (r range: –0.65 to –0.04, p<0.05) between SS and neointimal thickness in 9 out of the 14 patients studied 6 months after self-expandable Wallstent (Schneider, AG) implantation. SS and neointimal thickness were found to be geometrically interrelated such that maximal thickness was preferentially located near the inner curve of the coronary artery, where the minimal SS was also observed, whereas the minimal thickness was more frequently detected in the outer curve, which was primarily where the maximal SS was also located. Similarly, a negative correlation of in-stent neointimal thickness to baseline SS was also reported in 5 out of the 7 patients studied in a later investigation with balloon-expandable bare metal stents (Sanmartin et al., 2006). In contrast, Stone, et al. (2003) reported a limited role of SS in in-stent restenosis since neointimal hyperplasia appeared to occur to some degree in all categories of SS in the six stented coronary segments they studied. Latest patient data from our group support the role of SS in neointimal proliferation, but also indicate that SS cannot predict the exact locations of neointimal hyperplasia in all cases, since the thickening does not necessarily occur in all regions where SS is low and not all regions where SS is high are spared from neointimal hyperplasia. In-stent restenosis is a multi-factorial process and regions with low SS should thus be considered to have a higher probability for neointimal hyperplasia to occur and be more profound (Papafaklis et al., 2009). In the same study, vascular brachytherapy following bare metal stent implantation, a therapeutic modality used in the recent past for reducing in-stent restenosis, was found to diminish the inverse relationship between neointimal thickness and SS probably due to the deleterious effect of radiation on the cells which sense and are affected by SS.

Drug Deposition and Neointima Distribution in Drug-Eluting Stents: The Effect of In-Stent Haemodynamics

Localized delivery of immunosuppressive agents using drug-eluting stents (DES) inhibits the pathogenic path of restenosis occurring in the early phase of 6 months after stent implantation. Although drug-eluting stents have a potent anti-proliferative effect, neointimal hyperplasia or even in-stent restenosis may still occur especially when DES are used in complex clinical and anatomic settings (Alfonso, 2010). DES implantation has also been associated with poor endothelialization of stent struts (Jimenez-Valero et al., 2009), delayed healing (Farb et al., 2001), incomplete stent apposition and tissue regression behind the stent struts (Hong et al., 2006). The degree of drug penetration into the tissue dictates drug efficacy, but also may contribute to the side-effects of DES implantation. Drug deposition is determined by a complex interplay between strut-wall contact, amount and location of drug release, and flow profiles, which in turn depend on stent design and strut position. Simulations using coupled compu-

tational fluid dynamics and mass transfer models have revealed that direct strut contact accounts for only 38% of peak and 11% of total arterial drug, whereas non-contacting strut surfaces can contribute up to 90% of arterial drug deposition (Balakrishnan et al., 2005). Flow patterns around the stent struts determine the quantity of blood-solubilized drug, which is washed away by the free flow stream or trapped in flow stagnation zones and deposited not only under or adjacent to struts but also in distal tissue segments or in inter-strut zones (Kolachalama, Tzafriri et al., 2009). Overlapping DES dramatically affect drug distribution not only by adding to the amount of local drug and area of contact with the arterial wall, but also by influencing the degree of strut protrusion into the lumen, and consequently, flow disruption (Balakrishnan et al., 2005). In cases of bifurcational stenting, drug deposition is determined not only by stent strut configuration, but also by flow disturbances imposed by the flow divider; the presence of the side branch affects drug distribution in the stented main vessel, thereby creating zones of excessive drug deposition and areas of drug depletion, which could ultimately lead to vascular toxicity and restenosis, respectively (Kolachalama, Levine et al., 2009).

The predictive value of SS after DES implantation on neointima distribution (i.e., neointimal hyperplasia and tissue regression) at follow-up has been recently investigated in patients. An initial study by Gijsen, et al. (2003) reported that neointimal thickness 6 months following sirolimus-eluting stent (SES) implantation was inversely related to SS in 4 out of the 6 patients studied by angiography and intravascular ultrasound for 3D coronary artery reconstruction; inter-strut shallow pits were observed and attributed to tissue regression induced by high SS. Both neointimal growth and tissue regression were also demonstrated in a patient presenting with lumen enlargement and incomplete stent apposition shortly (10 weeks) after paclitaxel-eluting stent (PES) implantation; only neointimal hyperplasia thickness was found to be inversely correlated to

SS, while there was no association between tissue regression depth and SS (Papafaklis, Katsouras et al., 2007). Post-procedural stent malapposition and thrombus dissolution were potential mechanisms for the coronary dilatation in this case. In contrast to the previous reports, a study investigating the correlation between neointimal hyperplasia volume and SS in a diabetic population at 9-month follow-up after SES implantation found no association between the two variables (Suzuki et al., 2008). The limited role of SS in neointima distribution in SES is also supported by a latest study in thirty patients at 6-month follow-up after sirolimus- or paclitaxel-eluting stent implantation compared to bare metal stents. A significant negative correlation of neointimal thickness to SS was found only in PES patients, as in the bare metal stent control group, whereas sirolimus elution was demonstrated to attenuate the SS effect resulting in even more decreased neointimal hyperplasia in SES compared to PES (Papafaklis, Bourantas et al., 2010). Differences in the biologic properties between the two drugs and their association with the molecular pathways through which SS exerts its cellular effects seem to account for the differential neointimal response to SS in this study and the superior inhibition of neointimal growth by SES compared to PES as documented in large patient trials (Stefanadis & Toutouzas, 2009).

CLINICAL IMPLICATIONS AND FUTURE RESEARCH DIRECTIONS

Catheter-based approaches using angiography and intravascular imaging (primarily IVUS) allow visualization of the lumen and arterial wall providing valuable information about the wall morphology and remodeling behavior in clinical practice. Recent technological development, however, has also led to the application of sophisticated techniques for 3D coronary artery reconstruction and blood flow simulation, which enable the assessment of SS in patients. A growing

body of evidence supports the importance of SS in determining the natural history and complexity of coronary atherosclerosis (Papafaklis, Koskinas et al., 2010), and detailed knowledge of the local haemodynamic environment in coronary arteries is likely to be essential for risk-stratification and prognostication (Chatzizis, Coskun, Jonas, Edelman, Stone et al., 2007). The incorporation of SS assessment in routine patient care may be useful for characterizing early high-risk plaques and predicting the culprit lesions of subsequent adverse cardiac events.

Stent implantation and various design characteristics have a major impact on local flow dynamics since they change native arterial geometry and alter SS distribution. In the era of drug-eluting stents, theoretical simulations provide insight into the role of flow patterns in determining drug deposition and distribution in the inter-strut areas, while the first patient studies support the role of SS in in-stent restenosis. Newly acquired knowledge regarding the importance of blood flow characteristics following percutaneous coronary interventions is invaluable in guiding the construction of haemodynamically driven next-generation stenting devices and thus, improving success rates and clinical outcomes.

CONCLUSION

The role of SS in vascular pathobiology has been lately highlighted by both molecular investigations and *in vivo* studies, which demonstrated that SS distribution is critical in explaining the spatial heterogeneity of atherosclerotic lesions and their remodeling behavior, while it may also influence neointima distribution and restenosis following stent implantation. Modern imaging methodologies allow for *in vivo* serial assessment of the natural history of coronary artery disease, as well as that of the restenotic process following endovascular interventions in relation to haemodynamic factors. Incorporation of *in vivo* serial SS measurements into clinical practice could provide a more complete diagnostic approach for assessing the likelihood of a particular atherosclerotic lesion to evolve into a high-risk or stenotic plaque, and restenosis following a percutaneous coronary intervention.

REFERENCES

Abizaid, A., Kornowski, R., Mintz, G. S., Hong, M. K., Abizaid, A. S., & Mehran, R. (1998). The influence of diabetes mellitus on acute and late clinical outcomes following coronary stent implantation. *Journal of the American College of Cardiology, 32*(3), 584–589. doi:10.1016/S0735-1097(98)00286-1

Alfonso, F. (2010). Treatment of drug-eluting stent restenosis the new pilgrimage: Quo vadis? *Journal of the American College of Cardiology, 55*(24), 2717–2720. doi:10.1016/j.jacc.2010.03.026

Asakura, T., & Karino, T. (1990). Flow patterns and spatial distribution of atherosclerotic lesions in human coronary arteries. *Circulation Research, 66*(4), 1045–1066.

Balakrishnan, B., Tzafriri, A. R., Seifert, P., Groothuis, A., Rogers, C., & Edelman, E. R. (2005). Strut position, blood flow, and drug deposition: Implications for single and overlapping drug-eluting stents. *Circulation, 111*(22), 2958–2965. doi:10.1161/CIRCULATIONAHA.104.512475

Balossino, R., Gervaso, F., Migliavacca, F., & Dubini, G. (2008). Effects of different stent designs on local hemodynamics in stented arteries. *Journal of Biomechanics, 41*(5), 1053–1061. doi:10.1016/j.jbiomech.2007.12.005

Bourantas, C. V., Kourtis, I. C., Plissiti, M. E., Fotiadis, D. I., Katsouras, C. S., & Papafaklis, M. I. (2005). A method for 3D reconstruction of coronary arteries using biplane angiography and intravascular ultrasound images. *Computerized Medical Imaging and Graphics, 29*(8), 597–606. doi:10.1016/j.compmedimag.2005.07.001

Carlier, S. G., van Damme, L. C., Blommerde, C. P., Wentzel, J. J., van Langehove, G., & Verheye, S. (2003). Augmentation of wall shear stress inhibits neointimal hyperplasia after stent implantation: Inhibition through reduction of inflammation? *Circulation, 107*(21), 2741–2746. doi:10.1161/01.CIR.0000066914.95878.6D

Caro, C. G. (2009). Discovery of the role of wall shear in atherosclerosis. *Arteriosclerosis, Thrombosis, and Vascular Biology, 29*(2), 158–161. doi:10.1161/ATVBAHA.108.166736

Caro, C. G., Fitz-Gerald, J. M., & Schroter, R. C. (1969). Arterial wall shear and distribution of early atheroma in man. *Nature, 223*(5211), 1159–1160. doi:10.1038/2231159a0

Caro, C. G., Fitz-Gerald, J. M., & Schroter, R. C. (1971). Atheroma and arterial wall shear. Observation, correlation and proposal of a shear dependent mass transfer mechanism for atherogenesis. *Proceedings of the Royal Society of London. Series B. Biological Sciences, 177*(46), 109–159. doi:10.1098/rspb.1971.0019

Carter, A. J., Laird, J. R., Farb, A., Kufs, W., Wortham, D. C., & Virmani, R. (1994). Morphologic characteristics of lesion formation and time course of smooth muscle cell proliferation in a porcine proliferative restenosis model. *Journal of the American College of Cardiology, 24*(5), 1398–1405. doi:10.1016/0735-1097(94)90126-0

Charonko, J., Karri, S., Schmieg, J., Prabhu, S., & Vlachos, P. (2009). In vitro, time-resolved PIV comparison of the effect of stent design on wall shear stress. *Annals of Biomedical Engineering, 37*(7), 1310–1321. doi:10.1007/s10439-009-9697-y

Charonko, J., Karri, S., Schmieg, J., Prabhu, S., & Vlachos, P. (2010). In vitro comparison of the effect of stent configuration on wall shear stress using time-resolved particle image velocimetry. *Annals of Biomedical Engineering, 38*(3), 889–902. doi:10.1007/s10439-010-9915-7

Chatzizisis, Y. S., Baker, A. B., Sukhova, G. K., Koskinas, K. C., Papafaklis, M. I., & Beigel, R. (2011). Augmented expression and activity of extracellular matrix-degrading enzymes in regions of low endothelial shear stress colocalize with coronary atheromata with thin fibrous caps in pigs. *Circulation, 123*(6), 621–630. doi:10.1161/CIRCULATIONAHA.110.970038

Chatzizisis, Y. S., Coskun, A. U., Jonas, M., Edelman, E. R., Feldman, C. L., & Stone, P. H. (2007). Role of endothelial shear stress in the natural history of coronary atherosclerosis and vascular remodeling: Molecular, cellular, and vascular behavior. *Journal of the American College of Cardiology, 49*(25), 2379–2393. doi:10.1016/j.jacc.2007.02.059

Chatzizisis, Y. S., Coskun, A. U., Jonas, M., Edelman, E. R., Stone, P. H., & Feldman, C. L. (2007). Risk stratification of individual coronary lesions using local endothelial shear stress: A new paradigm for managing coronary artery disease. *Current Opinion in Cardiology, 22*(6), 552–564. doi:10.1097/HCO.0b013e3282f07548

Chatzizisis, Y. S., Jonas, M., Coskun, A. U., Beigel, R., Stone, B. V., & Maynard, C. (2008). Prediction of the localization of high-risk coronary atherosclerotic plaques on the basis of low endothelial shear stress: an intravascular ultrasound and histopathology natural history study. *Circulation, 117*(8), 993–1002. doi:10.1161/CIRCULATIONAHA.107.695254

Cheng, C., Tempel, D., van Haperen, R., de Boer, H. C., Segers, D., & Huisman, M. (2007). Shear stress-induced changes in atherosclerotic plaque composition are modulated by chemokines. *The Journal of Clinical Investigation, 117*(3), 616–626. doi:10.1172/JCI28180

Cheng, C., Tempel, D., van Haperen, R., van der Baan, A., Grosveld, F., & Daemen, M. J. (2006). Atherosclerotic lesion size and vulnerability are determined by patterns of fluid shear stress. *Circulation, 113*(23), 2744–2753. doi:10.1161/CIRCULATIONAHA.105.590018

Chiu, J. J., Chen, L. J., Chen, C. N., Lee, P. L., & Lee, C. I. (2004). A model for studying the effect of shear stress on interactions between vascular endothelial cells and smooth muscle cells. *Journal of Biomechanics, 37*(4), 531–539. doi:10.1016/j.jbiomech.2003.08.012

Cho, A., Mitchell, L., Koopmans, D., & Langille, B. L. (1997). Effects of changes in blood flow rate on cell death and cell proliferation in carotid arteries of immature rabbits. *Circulation Research, 81*(3), 328–337.

Coskun, A. U., Yeghiazarians, Y., Kinlay, S., Clark, M. E., Ilegbusi, O. J., & Wahle, A. (2003). Reproducibility of coronary lumen, plaque, and vessel wall reconstruction and of endothelial shear stress measurements in vivo in humans. *Catheterization and Cardiovascular Interventions, 60*(1), 67–78. doi:10.1002/ccd.10594

Davies, P. F. (2009). Hemodynamic shear stress and the endothelium in cardiovascular pathophysiology. *Nature Clinical Practice. Cardiovascular Medicine, 6*(1), 16–26. doi:10.1038/ncpcardio1397

Farb, A., Heller, P. F., Shroff, S., Cheng, L., Kolodgie, F. D., & Carter, A. J. (2001). Pathological analysis of local delivery of paclitaxel via a polymer-coated stent. *Circulation, 104*(4), 473–479. doi:10.1161/hc3001.092037

Feldman, C. L., Ilegbusi, O. J., Hu, Z., Nesto, R., Waxman, S., & Stone, P. H. (2002). Determination of in vivo velocity and endothelial shear stress patterns with phasic flow in human coronary arteries: A methodology to predict progression of coronary atherosclerosis. *American Heart Journal, 143*(6), 931–939. doi:10.1067/mhj.2002.123118

Friedman, M. H., Hutchins, G. M., Bargeron, C. B., Deters, O. J., & Mark, F. F. (1981). Correlation between intimal thickness and fluid shear in human arteries. *Atherosclerosis, 39*(3), 425–436. doi:10.1016/0021-9150(81)90027-7

Fry, D. L. (1968). Acute vascular endothelial changes associated with increased blood velocity gradients. *Circulation Research, 22*(2), 165–197.

Fry, D. L. (1969). Certain histological and chemical responses of the vascular interface to acutely induced mechanical stress in the aorta of the dog. *Circulation Research, 24*(1), 93–108.

Giannoglou, G. D., Chatzizisis, Y. S., Sianos, G., Tsikaderis, D., Matakos, A., & Koutkias, V. (2006). In-vivo validation of spatially correct three-dimensional reconstruction of human coronary arteries by integrating intravascular ultrasound and biplane angiography. *Coronary Artery Disease, 17*(6), 533–543. doi:10.1097/00019501-200609000-00007

Gijsen, F. J. (1998). *Modeling of wall shear stress in large arteries.* Doctoral Dissertation, Technische Universiteit Eindhoven, The Netherlands.

Gijsen, F. J., Oortman, R. M., Wentzel, J. J., Schuurbiers, J. C., Tanabe, K., & Degertekin, M. (2003). Usefulness of shear stress pattern in predicting neointima distribution in sirolimus-eluting stents in coronary arteries. *The American Journal of Cardiology, 92*(11), 1325–1328. doi:10.1016/j.amjcard.2003.08.017

Gijsen, F. J., Wentzel, J. J., Thury, A., Lamers, B., Schuurbiers, J. C., & Serruys, P. W. (2007). A new imaging technique to study 3-D plaque and shear stress distribution in human coronary artery bifurcations in vivo. *Journal of Biomechanics, 40*(11), 2349–2357. doi:10.1016/j.jbiomech.2006.12.007

Gimbrone, M. A. Jr, Topper, J. N., Nagel, T., Anderson, K. R., & Garcia-Cardena, G. (2000). Endothelial dysfunction, hemodynamic forces, and atherogenesis. *Annals of the New York Academy of Sciences, 902,* 230–239, discussion 239–240. doi:10.1111/j.1749-6632.2000.tb06318.x

Glagov, S., Weisenberg, E., Zarins, C. K., Stankunavicius, R., & Kolettis, G. J. (1987). Compensatory enlargement of human atherosclerotic coronary arteries. *The New England Journal of Medicine, 316*(22), 1371–1375. doi:10.1056/NEJM198705283162204

Hahn, C., & Schwartz, M. A. (2009). Mechanotransduction in vascular physiology and atherogenesis. *Nature Reviews. Molecular Cell Biology, 10*(1), 53–62. doi:10.1038/nrm2596

Hastings, N. E., Simmers, M. B., McDonald, O. G., Wamhoff, B. R., & Blackman, B. R. (2007). Atherosclerosis-prone hemodynamics differentially regulates endothelial and smooth muscle cell phenotypes and promotes pro-inflammatory priming. *American Journal of Physiology. Cell Physiology, 293*(6), C1824–C1833. doi:10.1152/ajpcell.00385.2007

Hibi, K., Suzuki, T., Honda, Y., Hayase, M., Bonneau, H. N., & Yock, P. G. (2002). Quantitative and spatial relation of baseline atherosclerotic plaque burden and subsequent in-stent neointimal proliferation as determined by intravascular ultrasound. *The American Journal of Cardiology, 90*(10), 1164–1167. doi:10.1016/S0002-9149(02)02791-1

Hong, M. K., Mintz, G. S., Lee, C. W., Park, D. W., Park, K. M., & Lee, B. K. (2006). Late stent malapposition after drug-eluting stent implantation: An intravascular ultrasound analysis with long-term follow-up. *Circulation, 113*(3), 414–419. doi:10.1161/CIRCULATIONAHA.105.563403

Jimenez, J. M., & Davies, P. F. (2009). Hemodynamically driven stent strut design. *Annals of Biomedical Engineering, 37*(8), 1483–1494. doi:10.1007/s10439-009-9719-9

Jimenez-Valero, S., Moreno, R., & Sanchez-Recalde, A. (2009). Very late drug-eluting stent thrombosis related to incomplete stent endothelialization: In-vivo demonstration by optical coherence tomography. *The Journal of Invasive Cardiology, 21*(9), 488–490.

Kamiya, A., & Togawa, T. (1980). Adaptive regulation of wall shear stress to flow change in the canine carotid artery. *The American Journal of Physiology*, *239*(1), H14–H21.

Kasaoka, S., Tobis, J. M., Akiyama, T., Reimers, B., Di Mario, C., & Wong, N. D. (1998). Angiographic and intravascular ultrasound predictors of in-stent restenosis. *Journal of the American College of Cardiology*, *32*(6), 1630–1635. doi:10.1016/S0735-1097(98)00404-5

Kastrati, A., Mehilli, J., Dirschinger, J., Pache, J., Ulm, K., & Schuhlen, H. (2001). Restenosis after coronary placement of various stent types. *The American Journal of Cardiology*, *87*(1), 34–39. doi:10.1016/S0002-9149(00)01268-6

Kimura, T., Abe, K., Shizuta, S., Odashiro, K., Yoshida, Y., & Sakai, K. (2002). Long-term clinical and angiographic follow-up after coronary stent placement in native coronary arteries. *Circulation*, *105*(25), 2986–2991. doi:10.1161/01.CIR.0000019743.11941.3B

Kolachalama, V. B., Levine, E. G., & Edelman, E. R. (2009). Luminal flow amplifies stent-based drug deposition in arterial bifurcations. *PLoS ONE*, *4*(12), e8105. doi:10.1371/journal.pone.0008105

Kolachalama, V. B., Tzafriri, A. R., Arifin, D. Y., & Edelman, E. R. (2009). Luminal flow patterns dictate arterial drug deposition in stent-based delivery. *Journal of Controlled Release*, *133*(1), 24–30. doi:10.1016/j.jconrel.2008.09.075

Koskinas, K. C., Chatzizisis, Y. S., Baker, A. B., Edelman, E. R., Stone, P. H., & Feldman, C. L. (2009). The role of low endothelial shear stress in the conversion of atherosclerotic lesions from stable to unstable plaque. *Current Opinion in Cardiology*, *24*(6), 580–590. doi:10.1097/HCO.0b013e328331630b

Koskinas, K. C., Feldman, C. L., Chatzizisis, Y. S., Coskun, A. U., Jonas, M., & Maynard, C. (2010). Natural history of experimental coronary atherosclerosis and vascular remodeling in relation to endothelial shear stress: A serial, in vivo intravascular ultrasound study. *Circulation*, *121*(19), 2092–2101. doi:10.1161/CIRCULATIONAHA.109.901678

Koskinas, K. C., Sukhova, G. K., Baker, A. B., Chatzizisis, Y. S., Papafaklis, M. I., & Coskun, A. U. (2010). Coronary thin-capped atheromata exhibit increased expression of interstitial collagenases in regions of persistently low endothelial shear stress: A serial, in vivo natural history study in pigs [Abstract]. *Circulation*, *122*(Supplement), A19592.

Ku, D. N., Giddens, D. P., Zarins, C. K., & Glagov, S. (1985). Pulsatile flow and atherosclerosis in the human carotid bifurcation. Positive correlation between plaque location and low oscillating shear stress. *Arteriosclerosis (Dallas, Tex.)*, *5*(3), 293–302. doi:10.1161/01.ATV.5.3.293

LaDisa, J. F. Jr, Guler, I., Olson, L. E., Hettrick, D. A., Kersten, J. R., & Warltier, D. C. (2003). Three-dimensional computational fluid dynamics modeling of alterations in coronary wall shear stress produced by stent implantation. *Annals of Biomedical Engineering*, *31*(8), 972–980. doi:10.1114/1.1588654

LaDisa, J. F. Jr, Hettrick, D. A., Olson, L. E., Guler, I., Gross, E. R., & Kress, T. T. (2002). Stent implantation alters coronary artery hemodynamics and wall shear stress during maximal vasodilation. *Journal of Applied Physiology*, *93*(6), 1939–1946.

LaDisa, J. F. Jr, Olson, L. E., Douglas, H. A., Warltier, D. C., Kersten, J. R., & Pagel, P. S. (2006). Alterations in regional vascular geometry produced by theoretical stent implantation influence distributions of wall shear stress: Analysis of a curved coronary artery using 3D computational fluid dynamics modeling. *Biomedical Engineering Online*, *5*, 40. doi:10.1186/1475-925X-5-40

LaDisa, J. F. Jr, Olson, L. E., Guler, I., Hettrick, D. A., Audi, S. H., & Kersten, J. R. (2004). Stent design properties and deployment ratio influence indexes of wall shear stress: A three-dimensional computational fluid dynamics investigation within a normal artery. *Journal of Applied Physiology*, *97*(1), 424–430, discussion 416. doi:10.1152/japplphysiol.01329.2003

LaDisa, J. F. Jr, Olson, L. E., Guler, I., Hettrick, D. A., Kersten, J. R., & Warltier, D. C. (2005). Circumferential vascular deformation after stent implantation alters wall shear stress evaluated with time-dependent 3D computational fluid dynamics models. *Journal of Applied Physiology*, *98*(3), 947–957. doi:10.1152/japplphysiol.00872.2004

LaDisa, J. F. Jr, Olson, L. E., Hettrick, D. A., Warltier, D. C., Kersten, J. R., & Pagel, P. S. (2005). Axial stent strut angle influences wall shear stress after stent implantation: Analysis using 3D computational fluid dynamics models of stent foreshortening. *Biomedical Engineering Online*, *4*, 59. doi:10.1186/1475-925X-4-59

LaDisa, J. F. Jr, Olson, L. E., Molthen, R. C., Hettrick, D. A., Pratt, P. F., & Hardel, M. D. (2005). Alterations in wall shear stress predict sites of neointimal hyperplasia after stent implantation in rabbit iliac arteries. *American Journal of Physiology. Heart and Circulatory Physiology*, *288*(5), H2465–H2475. doi:10.1152/ajpheart.01107.2004

Long, Q., Xu, X. Y., Ariff, B., Thom, S. A., Hughes, A. D., & Stanton, A. V. (2000). Reconstruction of blood flow patterns in a human carotid bifurcation: A combined CFD and MRI study. *Journal of Magnetic Resonance Imaging*, *11*(3), 299–311. doi:10.1002/(SICI)1522-2586(200003)11:3<299::AID-JMRI9>3.0.CO;2-M

Malek, A. M., Alper, S. L., & Izumo, S. (1999). Hemodynamic shear stress and its role in atherosclerosis. *Journal of the American Medical Association*, *282*(21), 2035–2042. doi:10.1001/jama.282.21.2035

Mejia, J., Ruzzeh, B., Mongrain, R., Leask, R., & Bertrand, O. F. (2009). Evaluation of the effect of stent strut profile on shear stress distribution using statistical moments. *Biomedical Engineering Online*, *8*, 8. doi:10.1186/1475-925X-8-8

Munson, B. R., Young, D. F., & Okiishi, T. H. (2002). *Fundamentals of fluid mechanics* (4th ed.). New York, NY: John Wiley & Sons, Inc.

Nadaud, S., Philippe, M., Arnal, J. F., Michel, J. B., & Soubrier, F. (1996). Sustained increase in aortic endothelial nitric oxide synthase expression in vivo in a model of chronic high blood flow. *Circulation Research*, *79*(4), 857–863.

Pant, S., Bressloff, N. W., Forrester, A. I., & Curzen, N. (2010). The influence of strut-connectors in stented vessels: A comparison of pulsatile flow through five coronary stents. *Annals of Biomedical Engineering*, *38*(5), 1893–1907. doi:10.1007/s10439-010-9962-0

Papafaklis, M. I. (2008). *Three-dimensional coronary artery reconstruction and blood flow simulation.* Doctoral Dissertation, University of Ioannina, Greece.

Papafaklis, M. I., Bourantas, C. V., Theodorakis, P. E., Katsouras, C. S., Fotiadis, D. I., & Michalis, L. K. (2007). Association of endothelial shear stress with plaque thickness in a real three-dimensional left main coronary artery bifurcation model. *International Journal of Cardiology*, *115*(2), 276–278. doi:10.1016/j.ijcard.2006.04.030

Papafaklis, M. I., Bourantas, C. V., Theodorakis, P. E., Katsouras, C. S., Fotiadis, D. I., & Michalis, L. K. (2009). Relationship of shear stress with in-stent restenosis: Bare metal stenting and the effect of brachytherapy. *International Journal of Cardiology*, *134*(1), 25–32. doi:10.1016/j.ijcard.2008.02.006

Papafaklis, M. I., Bourantas, C. V., Theodorakis, P. E., Katsouras, C. S., Naka, K. K., & Fotiadis, D. I. (2010). The effect of shear stress on neointimal response following sirolimus- and paclitaxel-eluting stent implantation compared to bare metal stents in humans. *Journal of the American College of Cardiology: Cardiovascular Interventions*, *3*(11), 1181–1189.

Papafaklis, M. I., Katsouras, C. S., Theodorakis, P. E., Bourantas, C. V., Fotiadis, D. I., & Michalis, L. K. (2007). Coronary dilatation 10 weeks after paclitaxel-eluting stent implantation. No role of shear stress in lumen enlargement? *Heart and Vessels*, *22*(4), 268–273. doi:10.1007/s00380-006-0970-9

Papafaklis, M. I., Koskinas, K. C., Chatzizisis, Y. S., Stone, P. H., & Feldman, C. L. (2010). In-vivo assessment of the natural history of coronary atherosclerosis: Vascular remodeling and endothelial shear stress determine the complexity of atherosclerotic disease progression. *Current Opinion in Cardiology*, *25*(6), 627–638. doi:10.1097/HCO.0b013e32833f0236

Papafaklis, M. I., & Michalis, L. K. (2005). The effect of shear stress on the onset and progression of atheromatous disease and on restenosis following transluminal therapies. *Hellenike Kardiologike Epitheoresis. Hellenic Journal of Cardiology*, *46*(3), 183–187.

Papaioannou, T. G., Christofidis, C., Mathioulakis, D. S., & Stefanadis, C. I. (2007). A novel design of a noncylindric stent with beneficial effects on flow characteristics: An experimental and numerical flow study in an axisymmetric arterial model with sequential mild stenoses. *Artificial Organs*, *31*(8), 627–638. doi:10.1111/j.1525-1594.2007.00431.x

Papaioannou, T. G., Karatzis, E. N., Vavuranakis, M., Lekakis, J. P., & Stefanadis, C. (2006). Assessment of vascular wall shear stress and implications for atherosclerotic disease. *International Journal of Cardiology*, *113*(1), 12–18. doi:10.1016/j.ijcard.2006.03.035

Richter, Y., Groothuis, A., Seifert, P., & Edelman, E. R. (2004). Dynamic flow alterations dictate leukocyte adhesion and response to endovascular interventions. *The Journal of Clinical Investigation*, *113*(11), 1607–1614.

Rogers, C., & Edelman, E. R. (1995). Endovascular stent design dictates experimental restenosis and thrombosis. *Circulation*, *91*(12), 2995–3001.

Rybicki, F. J., Melchionna, S., Mitsouras, D., Coskun, A. U., Whitmore, A. G., & Steigner, M. (2009). Prediction of coronary artery plaque progression and potential rupture from 320-detector row prospectively ECG-gated single heart beat CT angiography: Lattice Boltzmann evaluation of endothelial shear stress. *The International Journal of Cardiovascular Imaging*, *25*, 289–299. doi:10.1007/s10554-008-9418-x

Sanmartin, M., Goicolea, J., Garcia, C., Garcia, J., Crespo, A., & Rodriguez, J. (2006). Influence of shear stress on in-stent restenosis: In vivo study using 3D reconstruction and computational fluid dynamics. *Revista Espanola de Cardiologia*, *59*(1), 20–27.

Slager, C. J., Wentzel, J. J., Gijsen, F. J., Schuurbiers, J. C., van der Wal, A. C., & van der Steen, A. F. (2005). The role of shear stress in the generation of rupture-prone vulnerable plaques. *Nature Clinical Practice. Cardiovascular Medicine*, *2*(8), 401–407. doi:10.1038/ncpcardio0274

Slager, C. J., Wentzel, J. J., Gijsen, F. J., Thury, A., van der Wal, A. C., & Schaar, J. A. (2005). The role of shear stress in the destabilization of vulnerable plaques and related therapeutic implications. *Nature Clinical Practice. Cardiovascular Medicine*, *2*(9), 456–464. doi:10.1038/ncpcardio0298

Slager, C. J., Wentzel, J. J., Schuurbiers, J. C., Oomen, J. A., Kloet, J., & Krams, R. (2000). True 3-dimensional reconstruction of coronary arteries in patients by fusion of angiography and IVUS (ANGUS) and its quantitative validation. *Circulation*, *102*(5), 511–516.

Stefanadis, C., & Toutouzas, K. (2009). Paclitaxel versus sirolimus: The battle is still ongoing. *Journal of the American College of Cardiology*, *53*(8), 665–666. doi:10.1016/j.jacc.2008.10.048

Stone, P. H., Coskun, A. U., Kinlay, S., Clark, M. E., Sonka, M., & Wahle, A. (2003). Effect of endothelial shear stress on the progression of coronary artery disease, vascular remodeling, and in-stent restenosis in humans: In vivo 6-month follow-up study. *Circulation*, *108*(4), 438–444. doi:10.1161/01.CIR.0000080882.35274.AD

Stone, P. H., Coskun, A. U., Kinlay, S., Popma, J. J., Sonka, M., & Wahle, A. (2007). Regions of low endothelial shear stress are the sites where coronary plaque progresses and vascular remodelling occurs in humans: An in vivo serial study. *European Heart Journal*, *28*(6), 705–710. doi:10.1093/eurheartj/ehl575

Stone, P. H., Coskun, A. U., Yeghiazarians, Y., Kinlay, S., Popma, J. J., & Kuntz, R. E. (2003). Prediction of sites of coronary atherosclerosis progression: In vivo profiling of endothelial shear stress, lumen, and outer vessel wall characteristics to predict vascular behavior. *Current Opinion in Cardiology*, *18*(6), 458–470. doi:10.1097/00001573-200311000-00007

Suzuki, N., Nanda, H., Angiolillo, D. J., Bezerra, H., Sabate, M., & Jimenez-Quevedo, P. (2008). Assessment of potential relationship between wall shear stress and arterial wall response after bare metal stent and sirolimus-eluting stent implantation in patients with diabetes mellitus. *The International Journal of Cardiovascular Imaging*, *24*(4), 357–364. doi:10.1007/s10554-007-9274-0

Thury, A., Wentzel, J. J., Vinke, R. V., Gijsen, F. J., Schuurbiers, J. C., & Krams, R. (2002). Images in cardiovascular medicine. Focal in-stent restenosis near step-up: Roles of low and oscillating shear stress? *Circulation*, *105*(23), e185–e187. doi:10.1161/01.CIR.0000018282.32332.13

van der Giessen, A. G., Wentzel, J. J., Meijboom, W. B., Mollet, N. R., van der Steen, A. F., & van de Vosse, F. N. (2009). Plaque and shear stress distribution in human coronary bifurcations: A multislice computed tomography study. *EuroIntervention*, *4*(5), 654–661. doi:10.4244/EIJV4I5A109

Virmani, R., Burke, A. P., Farb, A., & Kolodgie, F. D. (2006). Pathology of the vulnerable plaque. *Journal of the American College of Cardiology*, *47*(8Suppl), C13–C18. doi:10.1016/j.jacc.2005.10.065

Wahle, A., Prause, P. M., DeJong, S. C., & Sonka, M. (1999). Geometrically correct 3-D reconstruction of intravascular ultrasound images by fusion with biplane angiography--methods and validation. *IEEE Transactions on Medical Imaging*, *18*(8), 686–699. doi:10.1109/42.796282

Wentzel, J. J., Gijsen, F. J., Schuurbiers, J. C., van der Steen, A. F., & Serruys, P. W. (2008). The influence of shear stress on in-stent restenosis and thrombosis. *EuroIntervention*, *4*(Suppl C), C27–C32.

Wentzel, J. J., Janssen, E., Vos, J., Schuurbiers, J. C., Krams, R., & Serruys, P. W. (2003). Extension of increased atherosclerotic wall thickness into high shear stress regions is associated with loss of compensatory remodeling. *Circulation*, *108*(1), 17–23. doi:10.1161/01.CIR.0000078637.21322.D3

Wentzel, J. J., Krams, R., Schuurbiers, J. C., Oomen, J. A., Kloet, J., & van Der Giessen, W. J. (2001). Relationship between neointimal thickness and shear stress after Wallstent implantation in human coronary arteries. *Circulation*, *103*(13), 1740–1745.

Wentzel, J. J., Whelan, D. M., van der Giessen, W. J., van Beusekom, H. M., Andhyiswara, I., & Serruys, P. W. (2000). Coronary stent implantation changes 3-D vessel geometry and 3-D shear stress distribution. *Journal of Biomechanics*, *33*(10), 1287–1295. doi:10.1016/S0021-9290(00)00066-X

Xie, L., Hu, Y., Nunes, J. C., Bellanger, J. J., Bedossa, M., & Luo, L. (2010). A model-based reconstruction method for 3-D rotational coronary angiography. *Proceedings of the IEEE Engineering Medical Biology Society, 1*, 3186–3189.

Zarins, C. K., Zatina, M. A., Giddens, D. P., Ku, D. N., & Glagov, S. (1987). Shear stress regulation of artery lumen diameter in experimental atherogenesis. *Journal of Vascular Surgery, 5*(3), 413–420.

ADDITIONAL READING

Benard, N., Perrault, R., & Coisne, D. (2004). Blood flow in stented coronary artery: numerical fluid dynamics analysis. *Conference Proceedings; Annual International Conference of the IEEE Engineering in Medicine and Biology Society. IEEE Engineering in Medicine and Biology Society. Conference, 5*, 3800–3803.

Caro, C. G., Fitz-Gerald, J. M., & Schroter, R. C. (1971). Proposal of a shear dependent mass transfer mechanism for atherogenesis. *Clinical Science, 40*(2), 5P.

Chatzizisis, Y. S., & Giannoglou, G. D. (2007). Coronary hemodynamics and atherosclerotic wall stiffness: a vicious cycle. *Medical Hypotheses, 69*(2), 349–355. doi:10.1016/j.mehy.2006.11.053

Chatzizisis, Y. S., & Giannoglou, G. D. (2010). Shear stress and inflammation: are we getting closer to the prediction of vulnerable plaque? *Expert Review of Cardiovascular Therapy, 8*(10), 1351–1353. doi:10.1586/erc.10.126

Chen, M. C., Lu, P. C., Chen, J. S., & Hwang, N. H. (2005). Computational hemodynamics of an implanted coronary stent based on three-dimensional cine angiography reconstruction. *ASAIO Journal (American Society for Artificial Internal Organs), 51*(4), 313–320. doi:10.1097/01.mat.0000169117.07070.fb

Cheng, C., de Crom, R., van Haperen, R., Helderman, F., Gourabi, B. M., & van Damme, L. C. (2004). The role of shear stress in atherosclerosis: action through gene expression and inflammation? *Cell Biochemistry and Biophysics, 41*(2), 279–294. doi:10.1385/CBB:41:2:279

Cheng, C., van Haperen, R., de Waard, M., van Damme, L. C., Tempel, D., & Hanemaaijer, L. (2005). Shear stress affects the intracellular distribution of eNOS: direct demonstration by a novel in vivo technique. *Blood, 106*(12), 3691–3698. doi:10.1182/blood-2005-06-2326

Faik, I., Mongrain, R., Leask, R. L., Rodes-Cabau, J., Larose, E., & Bertrand, O. (2007). Time-dependent 3D simulations of the hemodynamics in a stented coronary artery. *Biomedical Materials (Bristol, England), 2*(1), S28–S37. doi:10.1088/1748-6041/2/1/S05

Feldman, C. L., & Stone, P. H. (2000). Intravascular hemodynamic factors responsible for progression of coronary atherosclerosis and development of vulnerable plaque. *Current Opinion in Cardiology, 15*(6), 430–440. doi:10.1097/00001573-200011000-00010

Garcia, J., Crespo, A., Goicolea, J., Sanmartin, M., & Garcia, C. (2006). Study of the evolution of the shear stress on the restenosis after coronary angioplasty. *Journal of Biomechanics, 39*(5), 799–805. doi:10.1016/j.jbiomech.2005.02.005

Krams, R., Wentzel, J. J., Oomen, J. A., Vinke, R., Schuurbiers, J. C., & de Feyter, P. J. (1997). Evaluation of endothelial shear stress and 3D geometry as factors determining the development of atherosclerosis and remodeling in human coronary arteries in vivo. Combining 3D reconstruction from angiography and IVUS (ANGUS) with computational fluid dynamics. *Arteriosclerosis, Thrombosis, and Vascular Biology, 17*(10), 2061–2065. doi:10.1161/01.ATV.17.10.2061

Mongrain, R., & Rodes-Cabau, J. (2006). Role of shear stress in atherosclerosis and restenosis after coronary stent implantation. *Revista Espanola de Cardiologia, 59*(1), 1–4.

Moore, J. A., Rutt, B. K., Karlik, S. J., Yin, K., & Ethier, C. R. (1999). Computational blood flow modeling based on in vivo measurements. *Annals of Biomedical Engineering, 27*(5), 627–640. doi:10.1114/1.221

Murphy, J. B., & Boyle, F. J. (2010). A full-range, multi-variable, CFD-based methodology to identify abnormal near-wall hemodynamics in a stented coronary artery. *Biorheology, 47*(2), 117–132.

Nakazawa, G., Yazdani, S. K., Finn, A. V., Vorpahl, M., Kolodgie, F. D., & Virmani, R. (2010). Pathological findings at bifurcation lesions: the impact of flow distribution on atherosclerosis and arterial healing after stent implantation. *Journal of the American College of Cardiology, 55*(16), 1679–1687. doi:10.1016/j.jacc.2010.01.021

Papathanasopoulou, P., Zhao, S., Kohler, U., Robertson, M. B., Long, Q., & Hoskins, P. (2003). MRI measurement of time-resolved wall shear stress vectors in a carotid bifurcation model, and comparison with CFD predictions. *Journal of Magnetic Resonance Imaging, 17*(2), 153–162. doi:10.1002/jmri.10243

Ramaswamy, S. D., Vigmostad, S. C., Wahle, A., Lai, Y. G., Olszewski, M. E., & Braddy, K. C. (2004). Fluid dynamic analysis in a human left anterior descending coronary artery with arterial motion. *Annals of Biomedical Engineering, 32*(12), 1628–1641. doi:10.1007/s10439-004-7816-3

Resnick, N., Yahav, H., Shay-Salit, A., Shushy, M., Schubert, S., & Zilberman, L. C. (2003). Fluid shear stress and the vascular endothelium: for better and for worse. *Progress in Biophysics and Molecular Biology, 81*(3), 177–199. doi:10.1016/S0079-6107(02)00052-4

Richter, Y., & Edelman, E. R. (2006). Cardiology is flow. *Circulation, 113*(23), 2679–2682. doi:10.1161/CIRCULATIONAHA.106.632687

Silver, A. E., & Vita, J. A. (2006). Shear-stress-mediated arterial remodeling in atherosclerosis: too much of a good thing? *Circulation, 113*(24), 2787–2789. doi:10.1161/CIRCULATIONAHA.106.634378

Steinman, D. A. (2002). Image-based computational fluid dynamics modeling in realistic arterial geometries. *Annals of Biomedical Engineering, 30*(4), 483–497. doi:10.1114/1.1467679

Stone, P. H., & Feldman, C. L. (2010). In Vivo Assessment of Local Intravascular Hemodynamics and Arterial Morphology to Investigate Vascular Outcomes A Growing Field Coming of Age. *Journal of the American College of Cardiology: Cardiovascular Interventions, 3*(11), 1199–1201.

Tzima, E., Irani-Tehrani, M., Kiosses, W. B., Dejana, E., Schultz, D. A., & Engelhardt, B. (2005). A mechanosensory complex that mediates the endothelial cell response to fluid shear stress. *Nature, 437*(7057), 426–431. doi:10.1038/nature03952

Wentzel, J. J., Gijsen, F. J., Schuurbiers, J. C., Krams, R., Serruys, P. W., & De Feyter, P. J. (2005). Geometry guided data averaging enables the interpretation of shear stress related plaque development in human coronary arteries. *Journal of Biomechanics, 38*(7), 1551–1555. doi:10.1016/j.jbiomech.2004.06.022

Wentzel, J. J., Gijsen, F. J., Stergiopulos, N., Serruys, P. W., Slager, C. J., & Krams, R. (2003). Shear stress, vascular remodeling and neointimal formation. *Journal of Biomechanics, 36*(5), 681–688. doi:10.1016/S0021-9290(02)00446-3

White, C. R., & Frangos, J. A. (2007). The shear stress of it all: the cell membrane and mechanochemical transduction. *Proceedings of the Royal Society of London. Series B. Biological Sciences, 362*(1484), 1459–1467.

Williams, A. R., Koo, B. K., Gundert, T. J., Fitzgerald, P. J., & Ladisa, J. F. Jr. (2010). Local hemodynamic changes caused by main branch stent implantation and subsequent virtual side branch balloon angioplasty in a representative coronary bifurcation. *Journal of Applied Physiology, 109*(2), 532–540. doi:10.1152/japplphysiol.00086.2010

KEY TERMS AND DEFINITIONS

Disturbed Laminar Blood Flow: Disturbed laminar flow is characterized by instabilities including flow separation, reversed flow or recirculation, and reattachment to forward flow.

Laminar Flow: Streamlined blood flow in which blood particles flow in parallel layers.

Pulsatile (Unsteady) Blood Flow: Blood flow with periodically changing velocity during the cardiac cycle.

Shear Rate: The spatial gradient of blood velocity (i.e., du/dy, where du is change in flow velocity unit and dy is change in unit of radial distance from the wall), which describes how fast the blood velocity increases from areas at the arterial wall, where the velocity is zero, toward areas at the center of the lumen. Physiologically, the shear rate decreases at the center of the lumen and gradually increases toward the wall.

Shear Stress: The tangential force derived by the friction of the flowing blood on the endothelial surface. It is the product of the shear rate at the wall and the blood viscosity.

Steady Blood Flow: Blood flow in which velocity does not vary with time. This type of flow does not occur *in vivo*; however, it has been largely used in blood flow simulation investigations.

Turbulent Blood Flow: Flow in which blood particles acquire irregular and random trajectories which vary continuously over time and thus, the blood velocity vector at any given point varies continuously over time.

Section 10
Future Trends in Intravascular Imaging

Chapter 20
Future Trends in Intravascular Imaging

George D. Giannoglou
AHEPA University General Hospital, Greece & Aristotle University of Thessaloniki Medical School, Greece

Yiannis S. Chatzizisis
AHEPA University General Hospital, Greece & Aristotle University of Thessaloniki Medical School, Greece

ABSTRACT

Vulnerable plaques have certain histopathologic and regional characteristics. The advent of novel invasive and non-invasive imaging modalities aim to identify the histopathologic and regional characteristics of vulnerable plaque, thereby enabling the early diagnosis and potential application of treatments strategies to avert future acute coronary events.

INTRODUCTION

Although all coronary artery lesions are exposed to the same systemic risk factors, each of these atherosclerotic lesions presents its own potential for progression and risk. A portion of atherosclerotic lesions are thin capped fibroatheromas (also called high-risk or thrombosis-prone or vulnerable plaques) prone to acute disruption, and consequent acute coronary syndrome. Histopathology studies indicate that more than 75% of vulnerable plaques obstruct the coronary lumen by less than 50% prior to rupture, and do not limit coronary flow nor

produce angina (Kolodgie, *et al.*, 2004), (Virmani, Burke, Farb, & Kolodgie, 2006). These lesions are currently neither identified nor treated before plaque rupture. Plaque rupture with superimposed thrombosis is the predominant cause of acute coronary syndromes and sudden coronary death.

Vulnerable plaques have certain histopathologic and regional characteristics which are summarized in Table 1. The histopathologic characteristics include a thin, intensely inflamed fibrous cap measuring $< 65\,\mu m$, separating a large necrotic core from fluid-phase risk factors. The fibrous cap contains less collagen and reduced content of vascular smooth muscle cells. A dense network of neovessels may also develop in the plaque.

DOI: 10.4018/978-1-61350-095-8.ch020

Table 1. Characteristics of vulnerable plaques as potential targets of novel imaging modalities

Histopathologic characteristics	Regional characteristics
Large necrotic core	Low endothelial shear stress
Severe inflammation	Severe internal elastic lamina degradation
Extracellular matrix remodelling	Expansive vascular remodelling
Thin fibrous cap	
Reduced vascular smooth muscle cells	
Neovascularization	

The vulnerable plaques develop in regions characterized by low endothelial shear stress (ESS), severe internal elastic lamina fragmentation and expansive vascular wall remodelling.

Advent of novel invasive and non-invasive imaging modalities aim to identify the abovementioned histopathologic and regional characteristics of vulnerable plaque, thereby enabling the early diagnosis and potential application of treatments strategies to avert future acute coronary events.

Histopathologic Characteristics of Plaque Vulnerability

Expansion of Necrotic Core

Necrotic core expansion due to an ongoing oxidized LDL-C accumulation in the intima is a key factor of lesion destabilization. (Virmani, Burke, Farb, & Kolodgie, 2006), (Koskinas, Chatzizisis, Baker, Edelman, Stone, & Feldman, 2009) In the setting of intense inflammation of the plaque, the apoptotic process is not properly coupled with phagocytic clearance (efferocytosis), such that accumulating necrotic debris contributes to the expansion of the necrotic core (Seimon & Tabas, 2009) Neovascularization is also a key factor in necrotic core expansion through fragmentation of the neovessels and release of the cholesterol-rich erythrocytes in the plaque (Giannoglou, *et al.*, 2009).

Inflammation and Matrix Degradation

The extent of inflammatory cell infiltration and extracellular matrix degradation in the plaque and fibrous cap is another major factor that promotes plaque vulnerability. The extracellular matrix of vascular wall and fibrous cap is composed of a complex mixture of collagen and elastin fibers within a ground substance of proteoglycans. The extracellular matrix confers tensile strength in the fibrous cap and determines the mechanical properties and stability of atherosclerotic arteries. Interstitial collagenases, mostly matrix metalloproteinases (MMPs)-1, -8 and -13, initiate the catabolic cascade of collagen. In addition to collagen catabolism, plaques also contain potent elastases (MMP-2, -9, cathepsins K, L, S, neutrophil elastase) which break down elastin fibers in the plaque and may have important roles in adverse outward arterial remodelling and plaque destabilization. Recent evidence suggests that the enzymatic regulation of matrix glycosaminoglycans plays an important role in plaque vulnerability (Baker, *et al.*, 2010) Proteoglycans are implicated in the subendothelial lipid deposition and retention. Heparanase, an enzymatic regulator of heparan sulfate, shifts the extracellular matrix composition favouring the predominance of lipoprotein-retaining proteoglycans, and acts synergistically with MMPs in the degradation of the extracellular matrix.

Reduced Vascular Smooth Muscle Cell Content

In addition to intensive extracellular matrix degradation, reduced vascular smooth muscle cell content and attenuated extracellular matrix synthesis constitute another important feature of plaque vulnerability. IFN-γ, a pro-inflammatory cytokine derived by activated T-lymphocytes, is a potent inhibitor of collagen synthesis by vascular smooth muscle cells, which in combination with vascular smooth muscle cell apoptosis represents a further mechanism of plaque destabilization (Xu, Wang, Buttice, Sengupta, & Smith, 2003), (Tousoulis, Antoniades, Koumallos, & Stefanadis, 2006).

Neovascularization

Another key factor that critically determines plaque vulnerability is neovascularization (angiogenesis). Dense neovessels been developed within the atherosclerotic plaque from the existing adventitial vasa vasorum supply the lesion with erythrocyte membrane-derived cholesterol, inflammatory cells, reactive oxygen species and matrix proteases from the "back door", thereby reinforcing the inflamed status of the plaque and promoting plaque progression (Giannoglou, *et al.*, 2009), (Langheinrich, *et al.*, 2006).

Regional Characteristics of Plaque Vulnerability

Low ESS

Recent evidence suggests that low ESS affects multiple cellular and extracellular components implicated in plaque vulnerability. (Koskinas, Chatzizisis, Baker, Edelman, Stone, & Feldman, 2009), (Chatzizisis, *et al.*, 2008), (Koskinas, *et al.*, 2010), (Papafaklis, Koskinas, Chatzizisis, Stone, & Feldman, 2010), (Chatzizisis, Coskun, Jonas, Edelman, Feldman, & Stone, 2007) In the set-ting of local low ESS, inflammatory cell-derived mediators induce inflammation and secretion of extracellular matrix degrading proteases and potentiate vascular smooth muscle cell necrosis and apoptosis reducing thus their matrix synthetic capacity (Chatzizisis, *et al.*, 2008), (Chatzizisis, *et al.*, 2011), (Cheng, *et al.*, 2006), (Gambillara, Montorzi, Haziza-Pigeon, Stergiopulos, & Silacci, 2005), (Platt, Ankeny, Shi, Weiss, Vega, & Taylor, 2007), (Qi, *et al.*, 2008). The predominance of inflammation, cell death and extracellular matrix degradation over extracellular matrix synthesis and fibroproliferation, largely determines the evolution of rupture-prone vulnerable plaques.

Severe Internal Elastic Lamina Fragmentation

The regional disruption of the internal elastic lamina constitutes the key event that drives the formation of vulnerable plaques. Histopathology studies have shown that in the setting of very low levels of local ESS, and subsequently intense accumulation of inflammatory cells within the intima, the part of the internal elastic lamina beneath the plaque undergoes local degradation by the foam cells-derived proteases (e.g. MMP-2, -9 and cathepsins K, L, S) (Chatzizisis, *et al.*, 2008), (Chatzizisis, *et al.*, 2011). These internal elastic lamina breaks constitute the gateway for vascular smooth muscle cells, which are originally located into the media, to enter the intima and promote plaque progression. At the same time the inflammatory cells extend into the media where they elaborate matrix-degrading proteases and promote expansive remodelling of the vascular wall (Chatzizisis, Coskun, Jonas, Edelman, Stone, & Feldman, 2007), (Bentzon, Weile, Sondergaard, Hindkjaer, Kassem, & Falk, 2006).

Expansive Vascular Remodelling

The arterial wall dynamically responds to plaque formation. The nature of the wall's remodelling, regulated by systemic, genetic, and local hemodynamic factors, can range from constrictive to compensatory expansive to excessive expansive (Koskinas, Chatzizisis, Baker, Edelman, Stone, & Feldman, 2009), (Koskinas, *et al.*, 2010), (Papafaklis, Koskinas, Chatzizisis, Stone, & Feldman, 2010). Expansively remodelled coronary plaques are associated with increased inflammation and unstable clinical presentation (Virmani, Burke, Farb, & Kolodgie, 2006). A dynamic interplay between the local ESS and the vascular remodelling is a critical determinant of the natural history of an individual lesion (Chatzizisis, Coskun, Jonas, Edelman, Feldman, & Stone, 2007). Studies have recently shown that regions culminating in high-risk excessive expansive remodelling had been exposed to very low ESS throughout their natural history (Chatzizisis, *et al.*, 2008), (Koskinas, *et al.*, 2010). Excessive expansive remodelling contributes to further lowering of the low ESS milieu, thus reinforcing the intense pro-inflammatory stimulus and matrix degradation, ultimately promoting the evolution of an early atheroma to a vulnerable plaque.

CONCLUSION

Targeting all these histopathologic and regional characteristics with novel imaging modalities, invasive, non-invasive or even combination of them, is anticipated to create a new perspective in the era of vulnerable plaque diagnosis, thereby enabling the development of novel therapeutic strategies.

REFERENCES

Baker, A., Chatzizisis, Y., Beigel, R., Jonas, M., Stone, B., & Coskun, A. (2010). Regulation of heparanase in coronary artery disease. *Atherosclerosis, 213*(2). doi:10.1016/j.atherosclerosis.2010.09.003

Bentzon, J., Weile, C., Sondergaard, C., Hindkjaer, J., Kassem, M., & Falk, E. (2006). Smooth muscle cells in atherosclerosis originate from the local vessel wall and not circulating progenitor cells in ApoE knockout mice. *Arteriosclerosis, Thrombosis, and Vascular Biology, 26*, 2696–2702. doi:10.1161/01.ATV.0000247243.48542.9d

Chatzizisis, Y., Coskun, A., Jonas, M., Edelman, E., Feldman, C., & Stone, P. (2007). Role of endothelial shear stress in the natural history of coronary atherosclerosis and vascular remodeling: Molecular, cellular, and vascular behavior. *Journal of the American College of Cardiology, 49*, 2379–2393. doi:10.1016/j.jacc.2007.02.059

Chatzizisis, Y., Coskun, A., Jonas, M., Edelman, E., Stone, P., & Feldman, C. (2007). Risk stratification of individual coronary lesions using local endothelial shear stress: A new paradigm for managing coronary artery disease. *Current Opinion in Cardiology, 22*, 552–564. doi:10.1097/HCO.0b013e3282f07548

Chatzizisis, Y., Jonas, M., Coskun, A., Beigel, R., Stone, B., & Maynard, C. (2008). Prediction of the localization of high-risk coronary atherosclerotic plaques on the basis of low endothelial shear stress: An intravascular ultrasound and histopathology natural history study. *Circulation, 117*, 993–1002. doi:10.1161/CIRCULATIONAHA.107.695254

Chatzizisis, Y. S., Baker, A., Sukhova, G. K., Koskinas, K., Papafaklis, M., & Beigel, R. (2011). Augmented expression and activity of extracellular matrix–degrading enzymes in regions of low endothelial shear stress co-localize with coronary atheromata with thin fibrous caps in pigs. *Circulation, 123*, 621–630. doi:10.1161/CIRCULATIONAHA.110.970038

Cheng, C., Tempel, D., van Haperen, R., van der Baan, A., Grosveld, F., & Daemen, M. (2006). Atherosclerotic lesion size and vulnerability are determined by patterns of fluid shear stress. *Circulation, 113*, 2744–2753. doi:10.1161/CIRCULATIONAHA.105.590018

Gambillara, V., Montorzi, G., Haziza-Pigeon, C., Stergiopulos, N., & Silacci, P. (2005). Arterial wall response to ex vivo exposure to oscillatory shear stress. *Journal of Vascular Research, 42,* 535–544. doi:10.1159/000088343

Giannoglou, G., Koskinas, K., Tziakas, D., Ziakas, A., Antoniadis, A., & Tentes, I. (2009). Total cholesterol content of erythrocyte membranes and coronary atherosclerosis: An intravascular ultrasound pilot study. *Angiology, 60,* 676–682. doi:10.1177/0003319709337307

Kolodgie, F., Virmani, R., Burke, A., Farb, A., Weber, D., & Kutys, R. (2004). Pathologic assessment of the vulnerable human coronary plaque. *Heart (British Cardiac Society), 90,* 1385–1391. doi:10.1136/hrt.2004.041798

Koskinas, K., Chatzizisis, Y., Baker, A., Edelman, E., Stone, P., & Feldman, C. (2009). The role of low endothelial shear stress in the conversion of atherosclerotic lesions from stable to unstable plaque. *Current Opinion in Cardiology, 24,* 580–590. doi:10.1097/HCO.0b013e328331630b

Koskinas, K., Feldman, C., Chatzizisis, Y., Coskun, A., Jonas, M., & Maynard, C. (2010). Natural history of experimental coronary atherosclerosis and vascular remodeling in relation to endothelial shear stress: A serial, in vivo intravascular ultrasound study. *Circulation, 121,* 2092–2101. doi:10.1161/CIRCULATIONAHA.109.901678

Langheinrich, A., Michniewicz, A., Sedding, D., Walker, G., Beighley, P., & Rau, W. (2006). Correlation of vasa vasorum neovascularization and plaque progression in aortas of apolipoprotein E(-/-)/low-density lipoprotein(-/-) double knockout mice. *Arteriosclerosis, Thrombosis, and Vascular Biology, 26,* 347–352. doi:10.1161/01.ATV.0000196565.38679.6d

Papafaklis, M., Koskinas, K., Chatzizisis, Y., Stone, P., & Feldman, C. (2010). In-vivo assessment of the natural history of coronary atherosclerosis: Vascular remodeling and endothelial shear stress determine the complexity of atherosclerotic disease progression. *Current Opinion in Cardiology, 25*(6). doi:10.1097/HCO.0b013e32833f0236

Platt, M., Ankeny, R., Shi, G., Weiss, D., Vega, J., & Taylor, W. J. (2007). Expression of cathepsin K is regulated by shear stress in cultured endothelial cells and is increased in endothelium in human atherosclerosis. *American Journal of Physiology. Heart and Circulatory Physiology, 292,* H1479–H1486. doi:10.1152/ajpheart.00954.2006

Qi, Y., Qu, M., Long, D., Liu, B., Yao, Q., & Chien, S. (2008). Rho-GDP dissociation inhibitor alpha downregulated by low shear stress promotes vascular smooth muscle cell migration and apoptosis: A proteomic analysis. *Cardiovascular Research, 80,* 114–122. doi:10.1093/cvr/cvn158

Seimon, T., & Tabas, I. (2009). Mechanisms and consequences of macrophage apoptosis in atherosclerosis. *Journal of Lipid Research, 50*(Suppl), S382–S387. doi:10.1194/jlr.R800032-JLR200

Tousoulis, D., Antoniades, C., Koumallos, N., & Stefanadis, C. (2006). Pro-inflammatory cytokines in acute coronary syndromes: From bench to bedside. *Cytokine & Growth Factor Reviews, 17,* 225–233. doi:10.1016/j.cytogfr.2006.04.003

Virmani, R., Burke, A., Farb, A., & Kolodgie, F. (2006). Pathology of the vulnerable plaque. *Journal of the American College of Cardiology, 47,* C13–C18. doi:10.1016/j.jacc.2005.10.065

Xu, Y., Wang, L., Buttice, G., Sengupta, P., & Smith, B. (2003). Interferon gamma repression of collagen (COL1A2) transcription is mediated by the RFX5 complex. *The Journal of Biological Chemistry, 278,* 49134–49144. doi:10.1074/jbc.M309003200

Chapter 21
Future Trends in 3D Intravascular Ultrasound (IVUS) Reconstruction

George D. Giannoglou
AHEPA University General Hospital, Greece & Aristotle University of Thessaloniki Medical School, Greece

Antonios P. Antoniadis
AHEPA University General Hospital, Greece & Aristotle University of Thessaloniki Medical School, Greece

ABSTRACT

Recent advances in geometrically correct 3D IVUS reconstruction enable the depiction of the true coronary anatomy by combining IVUS data with biplane angiographic images. Further development of the existing 3D IVUS reconstruction software, in conjunction with advancing hardware capabilities, is expected to allow the implementation of real-time 3D IVUS reconstruction within the catheterization laboratories.

CURRENT IVUS IMAGING DEFICIENCIES

While IVUS allows accurate *in vivo* visualization of the vascular lumen and wall, (Mintz, *et al.*, 2001), (Tobis, *et al.*, 1991), (Yock, Linker, & Angelsen, 1989), (Nissen, *et al.*, 1990), (Liebson & Klein, 1992) it has certain inherent technical limitations. Being a tomographic technique, IVUS produces single plane two-dimensional images,

which are cross-sectional to the longitudinal catheter axis. Thus, it provides no direct spatial vascular information and does not clearly depict anatomical relationships (Roelandt, *et al.*, 1994). In an attempt to overcome these deficiencies, the concept of three-dimensional (3D) IVUS reconstruction has emerged as the method of choice for imaging the real coronary anatomy and it is anticipated to extend the diagnostic as well as the interventional potential in the cardiac catheterization laboratory (Rosenfield, *et al.*, 1991), (Klingensmith, *et al.*, 2003).

DOI: 10.4018/978-1-61350-095-8.ch021

Linear Versus Geometrically Correct Reconstruction

Traditionally, 3D IVUS reconstruction has been performed in a linear manner by stacking adjacent IVUS frames (von Birgelen, *et al.*, 1997). However, this approach does not take into account the vessel curvature and the axial movements of the IVUS catheter during the pullback, thus the reconstructed model is of limited precision. On the other hand, geometrically correct 3D IVUS reconstruction combines IVUS data with biplane angiographic images (views of the same vessel taken in perpendicular planes) and therefore allows depiction of the spatial trajectory of the IVUS pullback trail (Bourantas, *et al.*, 2005). The latter serves as a "backbone" on which the two-dimensional IVUS tomographic images are aligned and orientated (Coskun, *et al.*, 2003), (Cothren, Shekhar, Tuzcu, Nissen, Cornhill, & Vince, 2000), (Giannoglou, *et al.*, 2006), (Chatzizisis, *et al.*, 2008). The final outcome is a realistic representation of the 3D coronary anatomy which can be used for further analyses (Bourantas, *et al.*, 2008).

PROCESSING STEPS FOR GEOMETRICALLY CORRECT 3D IVUS RECONSTRUCTION

The methodology for the geometrically correct 3D IVUS reconstruction can be divided in the following discrete steps:

Angiographic Images Acquisition and Formation of the 3D Catheter Path

From each of the two perpendicular angiographic projections taken at the initiation of the IVUS procedure, i.e. right anterior oblique (RAO) 30° and left anterior oblique (LAO) 60° a single frame is selected corresponding to the appropriate phase of the cardiac cycle, as determined by simultaneously

recorded electrocardiogram (ECG). Generally, frames corresponding to the peak of the R-wave refer to the end-diastolic phase, while frames recorded at the end of the T-wave refer to the end-systolic phase. These images are manually processed for the detection of the IVUS catheter and vessel borders. On the basis of the course of the IVUS catheter in each angiographic projection, the 3D trajectory of the pullback is then reconstructed (Giannoglou, *et al.*, 2006).

IVUS Images Acquisition and Segmentation

When processing IVUS images it is generally desirable to examine those taken from the same phase of cardiac cycle in order to minimize the effects of cardiac movement on vascular shape and dimensions. As in the case of angiographic images, the selection is done on the basis of simultaneously recorded ECG (ECG-gated IVUS) and can be performed either manually or automatically utilizing pre-filtering, interframe difference and adaptive thresholding techniques. The selected IVUS images are further processed to detect the lumen and media-adventitia borders in each frame. This can be done manually, but as it is time consuming specific algorithms have been developed for semi- or completely automatic detection. In the semi-automatic detection, the user draws an approximation of the boundary and by employing deformable contours techniques this initial estimation is adapted to best match the actual boundary. The contour is further refined by applying low-pass filtering to produce a smooth curve. In the fully automatic detection method IVUS images are transformed in polar coordinates and truncated in order to remove the catheter. After application of specific low-pass filtering, the lumen and media-adventitia boundaries are initialized using texture and luminance features (Giannoglou, *et al.*, 2007), (Papadogiorgaki, Mezaris, Chatzizisis, Giannoglou, & Kompatsiaris, 2008), (Papadogiorgaki, Mezaris, Chatzizisis, Giannoglou, & Kompatsiaris, Texture Analysis and Radial Basis Function Approximation for IVUS Image Segmentation, 2007). In both techniques, image calibration is performed prior to contours detection, in order to convert pixel values to metric variables. This is done by manually defining a calibration parameter of known value within the IVUS image, e.g. the diameter of the IVUS catheter.

Placement and Orientation of IVUS Contours in the Catheter Path

IVUS contours are placed on a plane perpendicular to the catheter path. The correct position of each pair of contours is calculated by the known unique frame number, the catheter pullback speed and the frequency of the frame acquisition. Subsequently, the relative rotation of each contour with respect to the 3D path is estimated. This is performed with the application of the Frenet-Serret formulas to calculate the twisting of the IVUS catheter within the coronary lumen during pullback, which in turn determines the correct orientation of the contours (Wahle, Prause, DeJong, & Sonka, 1999). Then, the absolute rotation of the contours as whole around the catheter path is determined. This is done by using successive rotations and back-projections to the angiography planes where each projection is compared to the initially detected vessel borders. The angle that presents the smallest cumulative error for both projections is the absolute rotation angle of the contours. The resulting vessel model is generated by applying a mesh grid along the inner and outer contours to produce the lumen and media-adventitia surfaces respectively. The outcome of this process is an accurate 3D reconstruction of the examined vessel.

APPLICATIONS OF 3D IVUS CORONARY RECONSTRUCTION

3D coronary reconstruction opens exciting, clinical as well as research, opportunities. Firstly, the generation of a computational grid on the 3D reconstructed models and the simulation of blood flow using computational fluid dynamics software allows subsequent calculation of any hemodynamic factor of interest. Secondly, 3D reconstruction in systole and diastole permits calculation of coronary stiffness and remodeling. These parameters affect significantly the progression of atherosclerosis and therefore play a crucial role in the natural history of atherosclerotic plaques. In clinical grounds, the above methodology may yield fast and accurate morphometric and volumetric plaque analysis. Such information might facilitate individualized clinical decision-making and improve the quality of stent-positioning. Finally, it might contribute towards an effective follow-up and evaluation of the outcome of coronary interventions e.g. by examining stent placement or by identifying areas of in-stent restenosis.

FUTURE PERSPECTIVES

While 3D IVUS reconstruction has been well studied and experimentally validated, (Chatzizisis, *et al.*, 2006) it has not yet been adopted in everyday clinical practice. This may be due to the lack of widely accepted dedicated software to integrate and carry out all the aforementioned processing steps. Several potential software solutions have been announced, but the lack of consensus as to their use and efficacy, as well as the not-insignificant cost of commercial products, may act as hampering factors. Also, despite continuous progress on the data processing part, the whole procedure described above is still lengthy and can only be used for offline analysis. Further development of the existing software, in conjunction with advancing hardware processing capabilities, is expected to allow the implementation of real-time 3D IVUS reconstruction within the catheterization laboratories. Such a valuable everyday clinical tool would be welcomed by the interventional cardiologists. However, before this happens, the clinical benefit of this modality over conventional IVUS should be demonstrated in randomized clinical trials.

REFERENCES

Bourantas, C., Kalatzis, F., Papafaklis, M., Fotiadis, D., Tweddel, A., & Kourtis, I. (2008). ANGIOCARE: An automated system for fast three-dimensional coronary reconstruction by integrating angiographic and intracoronary ultrasound data. *Catheterization and Cardiovascular Interventions, 72*, 166–175. doi:10.1002/ccd.21527

Bourantas, C., Kourtis, I., Plissiti, M., Fotiadis, D., Katsouras, C., Papafaklis, M., & Michalis, L. (2005). A method for 3D reconstruction of coronary arteries using biplane angiography and intravascular ultrasound images. *Computerized Medical Imaging and Graphics, 29*, 597–606. doi:10.1016/j.compmedimag.2005.07.001

Chatzizisis, Y., Giannoglou, G., Matakos, A., Basdekidou, C., Sianos, G., & Panagiotou, A. (2006). In-vivo accuracy of geometrically correct three-dimensional reconstruction of human coronary arteries: Is it influenced by certain parameters? *Coronary Artery Disease, 17*, 545–551. doi:10.1097/00019501-200609000-00008

Chatzizisis, Y., Giannoglou, G., Sianos, G., Ziakas, A., Tsikaderis, D., & Dardas, P. (2008). In vivo comparative study of linear versus geometrically correct three-dimensional reconstruction of coronary arteries. *The American Journal of Cardiology, 101*, 263–267. doi:10.1016/j.amjcard.2007.07.070

Coskun, A., Yeghiazarians, Y., Kinlay, S., Clark, M., Ilegbusi, O., & Wahle, A. (2003). Reproducibility of coronary lumen, plaque, and vessel wall reconstruction and of endothelial shear stress measurements in vivo in humans. *Catheterization and Cardiovascular Interventions, 60*, 67–78. doi:10.1002/ccd.10594

Cothren, R., Shekhar, R., Tuzcu, E., Nissen, S., Cornhill, J., & Vince, D. (2000). Three-dimensional reconstruction of the coronary artery wall by image fusion of intravascular ultrasound and bi-plane angiography. *International Journal of Cardiac Imaging, 16*, 69–85. doi:10.1023/A:1006304419505

Giannoglou, G., Chatzizisis, Y., Koutkias, V., Kompatsiaris, I., Papadogiorgaki, M., & Mezaris, V. (2007). A novel active contour model for fully automated segmentation of intravascular ultrasound images: In vivo validation in human coronary arteries. *Computers in Biology and Medicine, 37*, 1292–1302. doi:10.1016/j.compbiomed.2006.12.003

Giannoglou, G., Chatzizisis, Y., Sianos, G., Tsikaderis, D., Matakos, A., & Koutkias, V.,…. Louridas, G. (2006). In-vivo validation of spatially correct three-dimensional reconstruction of human coronary arteries by integrating intravascular ultrasound and biplane angiography. *Coronary Artery Disease, 17*, 533–543. doi:10.1097/00019501-200609000-00007

Klingensmith, J., Schoenhagen, P., Tajaddini, A., Halliburton, S., Tuzcu, E., Nissen, S., & Vince, D. (2003). Automated three-dimensional assessment of coronary artery anatomy with intravascular ultrasound scanning. *American Heart Journal, 145*, 795–805. doi:10.1016/S0002-8703(03)00089-9

Liebson, P., & Klein, L. (1992). Intravascular ultrasound in coronary atherosclerosis: A new approach to clinical assessment. *American Heart Journal, 123*, 1643–1660. doi:10.1016/0002-8703(92)90819-H

Mintz, G., Nissen, S., Anderson, W., Bailey, S., Erbel, R., & Fitzgerald, P. (2001). Expert consensus document on standards for acquisition, measurement and reporting of intravascular ultrasound studies (IVUS). A report of the American College of Cardiology Task Force on Clinical Expert Consensus Documents. *Journal of the American College of Cardiology, 37*, 1478–1492. doi:10.1016/S0735-1097(01)01175-5

Nissen, S., Grines, C., Gurley, J., Sublett, K., Haynie, D., & Diaz, C. (1990). Application of a new phased-array ultrasound imaging catheter in the assessment of vascular dimensions. In vivo comparison to cineangiography. *Circulation, 81,* 660–666. doi:10.1161/01.CIR.81.2.660

Papadogiorgaki, M., Mezaris, V., Chatzizisis, Y., Giannoglou, G., & Kompatsiaris, I. (2007). Texture analysis and radial basis function approximation for IVUS image segmentation. *The Open Biomedical Engineering Journal, 1,* 53–59.

Papadogiorgaki, M., Mezaris, V., Chatzizisis, Y., Giannoglou, G., & Kompatsiaris, I. (2008). Image analysis techniques for automated IVUS contour detection. *Ultrasound in Medicine & Biology, 34,* 1482–1498. doi:10.1016/j.ultrasmedbio.2008.01.022

Roelandt, J., di Mario, C., Pandian, N., Wenguang, L., Keane, D., & Slager, C. (1994). Three-dimensional reconstruction of intracoronary ultrasound images. Rationale, approaches, problems, and directions. *Circulation, 90,* 1044–1055.

Rosenfield, K., Losordo, D., Ramaswamy, K., Pastore, J., Langevin, R., & Razvi, S. (1991). Three-dimensional reconstruction of human coronary and peripheral arteries from images recorded during two-dimensional intravascular ultrasound examination. *Circulation, 84,* 1938–1956.

Tobis, J., Mallery, J., Mahon, D., Lehmann, K., Zalesky, P., & Griffith, J. (1991). Intravascular ultrasound imaging of human coronary arteries in vivo. Analysis of tissue characterizations with comparison to in vitro histological specimens. *Circulation, 83,* 913–926.

von Birgelen, C., de Vrey, E., Mintz, G., Nicosia, A., Bruining, N., & Li, W.,.... de Feyter, P. (1997). ECG-gated three-dimensional intravascular ultrasound: Feasibility and reproducibility of the automated analysis of coronary lumen and atherosclerotic plaque dimensions in humans. *Circulation, 96,* 2944–2952.

Wahle, A., Prause, P., DeJong, S., & Sonka, M. (1999). Geometrically correct 3-D reconstruction of intravascular ultrasound images by fusion with biplane angiography-Methods and validation. *IEEE Transactions on Medical Imaging, 18,* 686–699. doi:10.1109/42.796282

Yock, P., Linker, D., & Angelsen, B. (1989). Two-dimensional intravascular ultrasound: Technical development and initial clinical experience. *Journal of the American Society of Echocardiography, 2,* 296–304.

Chapter 22
Future Trends in Coronary CT Angiography

George D. Giannoglou
AHEPA University General Hospital, Greece & Aristotle University Medical School, Greece

Sotirios A. Katranas
AHEPA University General Hospital, Greece & Aristotle University Medical School, Greece

ABSTRACT

Coronary computed tomography angiography (CCTA) is surrounded by the safety non-invasive methods offer and the advantages of high speed that multislice CT is associated with. While calcium score and recognition of anomalous coronary arteries are acceptable applications, CCTA reveals new fields of research on coronary artery disease, including lumen, bypass grafts, and stents patency, as well as endothelial shear stress and coronary stiffness measurements.

INTRODUCTION

Conventional coronary angiography is currently the gold standard for assessing coronary artery patency. Both spatial and temporal resolutions are excellent and permits treatment with percutaneous coronary intervention at the same session (Roberts, Bax, & Davies, 2008). The procedure usually takes about 30 minutes and demands the use of radiation and radiopaque contrast media. (Scanlon, 1999) Conventional coronary angiography, however, fails to visualize the artery wall and so is incapable

to reveal an outward remodeling, as it creates a 2D coronary "lumenogram" (Naghavi, 2003). More precise depiction of coronary arteries is achieved combining intravascular ultrasound (IVUS) and conventional coronary angiography. (Papadogiorgaki *et al.*, 2008), (Giannoglou *et al.*, 2007). Both conventional coronary angiography and IVUS are invasive methods and their application has the risk of major complications for the patient i.e. arrhythmia, stroke, coronary artery dissection and access site bleeding (1.8%, mortality rate 0.1%) (Hoffmann, 2005) which can raise in the case of a patient being in an unstable condition. Thus, the need for non-invasive methods for 3D coronary

DOI: 10.4018/978-1-61350-095-8.ch022

imaging have emerged, and modalities such as multislice computed tomography (MSCT), electron beam computed tomography and magnetic resonance imaging are now clinically available (Escolar, 2006).

MSCT is the basis for coronary computed tomography angiography (CCTA). MSCT is a spiral CT, where an increased number of detector rows (channels) allow multiple channels of data to be acquired simultaneously. At the beginning, the number of channels was 4 and subsequently has increased to 16-, 64-, 128- and lately to 256- and 320-channels. Multiple heart beats are being scanned during MSCT performing, while heart is synchronized with simultaneous ECG recording and data acquisition during all cardiac phases allows the use of data from certain parts of each consecutive cardiac cycle. Last generation MSCTs tend to be dual band and dual energy. Dual source means they contain 2 X-ray sources and 2 sets of detectors offset 90° from each other in the CT gantry increasing this way temporal resolution, while dual energy refers to the area of interest being scanned using x rays generated at different voltages, improving thus tissue differentiation and spatial resolution. Post-processing of axial images is performed on an independent workstation where retrospective reconstruction of the coronary arteries takes place. Reconstruction is achieved using special software, where maximum intensity projection [MIP] and three-dimensional multiplanar (MPR) reformats are mainly used (Roberts, Bax, & Davies, 2008), (Mark *et al.*), (Hassan, Nazir, & Alkadhi, 2010).

CCTA surmounts the complications that may arise from undergoing conventional coronary angiography. It is a high speed method (about 5 sec), takes place during a single breath and there is no need for hospitalization. CCTA offers the possibility to distinguish the arterial wall and indicate an outward remodeling. In addition fewer amounts of contrast media are needed. The mean radiation dose for 64-channel CT compared to conventional coronary angiography is 15 mSv (range 12-18

mSv) vs. 7mSv (range 2-16mSv). However, with tube current modulation the mean radiation dose for 64-channel CT is 9 mSv (range 8-18mSv) and with prospectively triggered CCTA is 3 mSv (range 2-4mSv) (Mark *et al.*). Prospective ECG-gating that is applied on latest MSCTs decreases radiation dose further compared to retrospective ECG-gating being present in most MSCTs studies: in phases of maximal cardiac movement there is tube-current modulation and less beam emission (Wijesekera, Duncan, & Padley). The entry of 320-MSCT has diminished more the radiation dose needed (4.2 vs. 8.5 mSv; $p<0.05$), as well as the volume of contrast media (80 vs. 111 ml; $p<0.001$) (Dewey *et al.*, 2009).

There are some restrictions of CCTA. Cardiac rhythm must be normal (i.e. unable to be applied on patients with atrial fibrillation) and heart rate should be less than 75 beats per minute. Thus, tiredness and caffeine should be avoided prior to the examination, while a beta blocker may be administrated when needed in order the desired heart rate and rhythm to be achieved. Whether the body mass index is increased, it is likely that the vessels will not to be very well depicted. People unable to hold their breath for 10 seconds are excluded from the examination, because of the artifacts caused by respiratory motion. Although the volume of contrast media used in CCTA is less than conventional coronary angiography, contrast media -induced nephropathy and allergic reactions are safety issues.

CURRENT APPLICATIONS

Calcium score is a major current application of CCTA. It refers on the measurement of the calcium burden on the coronary arteries' wall. Calcium score has been found to be a risk factor, independent of the traditional ones. There is a direct proportional relationship between the extent of coronary artery disease and calcium score and it provides additional prognostic information to the widely used traditional risk factors. It is very useful for intermediate-risk patients where the clinical decision making is difficult, while it seems to offer less additional prognostic value to these patients who have been considered low-risk according to clinical criteria (Loewinger & Budoff, 2007), (Prat-Gonzalez, Sanz, & Garcia, 2008).

Despite being rare, coronary artery anomalies are an important cause of premature cardiac morbidity and mortality. Coronary artery anomalies are difficult to detect using conventional coronary angiography; it is hard to visualize them in spite of using multiple projections and even if they are visualized it is difficult to evaluate their course accurately. CCTA allows defining the orifice origin and proximal path of anomalous coronary arteries and recognizes intramyocardial location of an epicardial artery (myocardial bridging) (Kim *et al.*, 2006).

FUTURE TRENDS

CCTA's most promising clinical application is to diagnose coronary artery disease. CCTA provides information not only for the lumen patency, but also for the presence of a non-obstructive plaque. CCTA can visualize a plaque characterized by an outward remodeling and reveals its relationship to the lumen. The analysis of ten studies performed using a 64-MSCT reveals sensitivity was 98% with a specificity of 90%, positive predictive value 93% and negative predictive value 95% per patient (Ramkumar *et al.*, 2009). At this point, CCTA is mainly used to exclude the presence of significant obstructive coronary artery disease in symptomatic patients with low to intermediate probability of coronary artery disease (Wijesekera, Duncan, & Padley). Extending indications of CCTA to high risk patients remains a challenging issue.

Another potential application of CCTA is the evaluation of cardiac transplant patients. The usual practice is these patients to be evaluated using conventional coronary angiography; when coronary artery disease is not detected the possibility of transplant survival is high. However, the transplant vasculopathy is diffuse and concentric and conventional coronary angiography quite often does not detect it. More studies have to be conducted in order to ensure CCTA's role in this field (Mark *et al.*).

It has been proposed for MSCT –during the CCTA procedure– to be used as a possible triple rule-out diagnostic modality for obstructive coronary disease, pulmonary embolism and acute aortic syndromes. In the emergency room, patients without ST-elevation acute myocardial infarction and when enzymes are still negative could perform CCTA in order to exclude or to confirm a coronary stenosis. The MSCT examination could be used at the same time to detect a clinically significant pulmonary embolus quicker and easier than ventilation-perfusion scans and pulmonary angiography. At the same time, aortic dissection, intramural aortic hematoma and rupture of an aortic thoracic aneurysm could be excluded as it happens with any contrast enhanced CT (Loewinger & Budoff, 2007). However, it is still challenging to compromise the optimal scan parameters for each component of the exam in order to achieve the best depiction of all vessels, as their diameter and anatomic distribution differs (Mark *et al.*).

Another highly interesting and challenging area is stent patency evaluation. Non-occlusive in-stent restenosis by neointimal hyperplasia remains a crucial topic after stent implantation. Stent's dimensions and type play a key role till now; stents with small lumen diameter (<3mm) and artifacts arising from high-density metallic material used for their construction make the assessment rather difficult. Although the spatial resolution has improved, there is still space to achieve better depiction. Currently the main role of CCTA on stent evaluation is limited to lumen's total occlusion (Wijesekera, Duncan, & Padley), (Prat-Gonzalez, Sanz, & Garcia, 2008).

During the evolution of CCTA, MSCT emerged to be a very useful tool for the evaluation of the patency and location of bypass grafts. This meant to be the first indication of MSCT for clinical use and now is the primary tool to evaluate a patient who is suspected to suffer from graft pathology (Ramkumar *et al.*, 2009), (Jankharia & Raut). Venus bypass grafts can be easily evaluated, because their caliber is larger and they are less mobile compared to native coronary arteries. Evaluation of internal mammary artery grafts is more difficult because of their smaller caliber and the artifacts arousing from the metallic clips on the sternum. Also, it may be difficult to evaluate the distal anastomotic site and the presence of atherosclerotic lesions in the native coronary arteries both distal to anastomotic site and the ungrafted vessels. So, there is still space for further development. Further and in conjuction with the clinical role of MSCT in coronary artery bypass grafting, MSCT is very useful in order to plan the graft's position relatively to the sternum prior to the operation (Mark *et al.*), (Wijesekera, Duncan, & Padley).

CCTA can also be utilized in order non-coronary cardiovascular diseases to be recognized. Such diseases include cardiac masses, pericardial diseases, congenital valve disease and complex congenital heart disease. Although there are not enough studies on this area, CCTA can be a useful tool when conventional modalities are incapable to definitely diagnose the above mentioned diseases (Chow *et al.*, 2009). Findings in other systems may also be detected with CCTA i.e. pulmonary nodules, liver cysts, hiatal hernia, thoracic aortic aneurysm and mediastinal lymph nodes altering thus the overall management of the particular patient (Mark *et al.*). Both cardiac and non-cardiac findings may be a possible cause of a patient's symptoms during diagnostic approach with CCTA when coronary artery disease is suspected..

RESEARCH DEVELOPMENTS

The expansion of the use of CCTA has opened new research fields. Endothelial shear stress (ESS) is the tangential force derived by the friction of the flowing blood on the endothelial cells (Chatzizisis & Giannoglou, 2007) and possibly is a major factor affecting the atherogenic process (Chatzizisis Y *et al.*, 2007). Till now the calculation of ESS was mainly depended on three-dimensional artery reconstruction by fusing intravascular ultrasound (IVUS) and coronary angiography data (Giannoglou *et al.*, 2007). However, both coronary angiography and IVUS are invasive procedures and embrace specific patient's risks. Also the positioning of the catheter into a coronary artery during the intravascular procedure can cause blood flow turbulences and thus alteration of the real ESS prices. The use of CCTA – beyond the non-invasive aspect and its benefits – surmounts this obstacle and provides more equitable measurements (Figure 1).

CCTA also seems to offer the possibility to study coronary stiffness in a direct way. Coronary stiffness is an emerging independent risk factor for cardiovascular diseases (Laurent, P, & Lacolley, 2005) and reflects the rigidity of the arterial wall (Cohn, DA, & Grandits, 2005). Many indices have been used for the estimation and quantification of arterial stiffness, (Yu *et al.*, 2008), (Claridge *et al.*, 2008) but all of them confront with problems in evaluation and interpretation, as they depend on indirect ways of estimating the true arterial stiffness (O'Rourke *et al.*, 2002). Direct measurement of coronary stiffness would require the measurement of arterial volumes throughout the cardiac cycle and calculation of the pressure-volume slope. 3D-coronary reconstruction during both diastole and systole depended on CCTA with the implementation of computational fluid dynamics analysis for the pressure estimation is a novel research approach which allows in-vivo non-invasive quantification of coronary stiffness (Ramaswamy *et al.*, 2004).

Figure 1: Endothelial shear stress (ESS, in Pascal) in right coronary artery, calculated using computational fluid dynamics. The three-dimensional artery reconstruction of right coronary artery was achieved using CCTA.

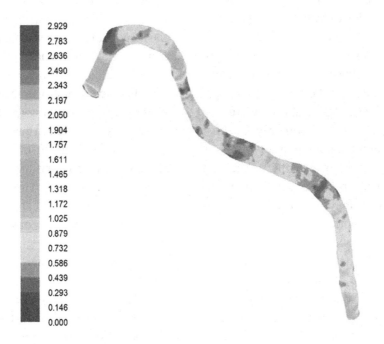

Another future role of CCTA is the detection of vulnerable atheromatic plaques. Vulnerable plaques do not cause flow restriction and may lead to acute coronary syndrome. Their identification will provide the possibility of more accurate risk stratification in a selected population and possibly intervention in high-risk patients either with pharmaceutical treatment or interventional procedures. Vulnerable plaques are usually minimally stenotic lesions associated with expansive vascular remodeling, and characterized by a thin fibrous cap and a large necrotic lipid core, while low ESS has been found to be an independent factor of their development. Plaques having these characteristics can be evaluated with research protocols applied on CCTA leading thus to their identification.

Another methodology for vulnerable plaque detection is to characterize plaque morphology and segregate plaque components by means of Hounsfield units (HU). Separation can be based upon different HU attenuation for each component. Thus lipid-rich core, mixed and calcified plaques

can be distinguished. This constitutes an important step for the risk stratification of patients with coronary artery disease. It is important to evolve a technology that could detect atheromatic lesions in an early stage and to characterize their composition in order to know their future behavior. However, there is not yet clear equivalence between HU and tissues, while artifacts created by calcium may alter the HU measurements (Mark *et al.*), (Loewinger & Budoff, 2007), (Gerber *et al.*, 2002).

Finally a possible future use of the CCTA could be the follow-up of the atheroma burden during treatment. The quantification of the atherosclerotic coronary plaques and the follow-up of their changes overtime may allow for the assessment of the effects of prescribed drugs on plaques' evolution. The mean HU change may also provide further information regarding the treatment's effect on the plaque. Current limitations include the non-accurate definition of the adventitial border, and restrictions due to spatial resolution (Mark *et al.*).

REFERENCES

Chatzizisis, Y., Coskun, A., Jonas, M., Edelman, E., Feldman, C., & Stone, P. (2007). Role of endothelial shear stress in the natural history of coronary atherosclerosis and vascular remodeling: Molecular, cellular, and vascular behavior. *Journal of the American College of Cardiology*, *49*(25), 2379–2393. doi:10.1016/j.jacc.2007.02.059

Chatzizisis, Y., & Giannoglou, G. (2007). Coronary hemodynamics and atherosclerotic wall stiffness: A vicious cycle. *Medical Hypotheses*, *69*(2), 349–355. doi:10.1016/j.mehy.2006.11.053

Chow, B., Larose, E., Bilodeau, S., Ellins, M., Galiwango, P., & Kass, M. (2009). The what, when, where, w.ho and how of cardiac computed tomography in 2009: Guidelines for the clinician. *The Canadian Journal of Cardiology*, *25*(3), 135. doi:10.1016/S0828-282X(09)70039-X

Claridge, M., Bate, G., Dineley, J., Hoskins, P., Marshall, T., & Adam, D. (2008). A reproducibility study of a TDI-based method to calculate indices of arterial stiffness. *Ultrasound in Medicine & Biology*, *34*(2), 215–220. doi:10.1016/j.ultrasmedbio.2007.08.010

Cohn, J., Duprez, D., & Grandits, G. (2005). Arterial elasticity as part of a comprehensive assessment of cardiovascular risk and drug treatment. *Hypertension*, *46*(1), 217–220. doi:10.1161/01.HYP.0000165686.50890.c3

Dewey, M., Zimmermann, E., Deissenrieder, F., Laule, M., Dübel, H., & Schlattmann, P. (2009). Noninvasive coronary angiography by 320-row computed tomography with lower radiation exposure and maintained diagnostic accuracy: Comparison of results with cardiac catheterization in a head-to-head pilot investigation. *Circulation*, *120*(10), 867–875. doi:10.1161/CIRCULATIONAHA.109.859280

Escolar, E., Weigold, G., Fuisz, A., & Weissman, N. (2006). New imaging techniques for diagnosis coronary artery disease. *Canadian Medical Association Journal*, *174*(4), 487–495. doi:10.1503/cmaj.050925

Gerber, T., Kuzo, R., Karstaedt, N., Lane, G., Morin, R., & Sheedy, P. (2002). Current results and new developments of coronary angiography with use of contrast-enhanced computed tomography of the heart. *Mayo Clinic Proceedings*, *77*(1), 55–71. doi:10.4065/77.1.55

Giannoglou, G., Chatzizisis, Y., Koutkias, V., Kompatsiaris, I., Papadogiorgaki, M., & Mezaris, V. (2007). A novel active contour model for fully automated segmentation of intravascular ultrasound images: In vivo validation in human coronary arteries. *Computers in Biology and Medicine*, *37*(9), 1292–1302. doi:10.1016/j.compbiomed.2006.12.003

Hassan, A., Nazir, S., & Alkadhi, H. (2010). Technical challenges of coronary CT angiography: Today and tomorrow. *European Journal of Radiology*, *79*(2).

Hoffmann, M., Shi, H., Schmitz, B., Schmid, F., Lieberknecht, M., & Schulze, R. (2005). Noninvasive coronary angiography with multislice computed tomography. *Journal of the American Medical Association*, *293*(20), 2471–2478. doi:10.1001/jama.293.20.2471

Jankharia, B., & Raut, A. (2010). Cardiac imaging: Current and emerging applications. *Postgraduate Medical Journal*, *56*(2), 125–130. doi:10.4103/0022-3859.65289

Kim, S., Seo, J., Do, K., Heo, J., Lee, J., & Song, J. (2006). Coronary artery anomalies: Classification and ECG-gated multi-detector row CT findings with angiographic correlation. *Radiographics*, *26*(2), 317–333, discussion 333–334. doi:10.1148/rg.262055068

Laurent, S., Boutouyrie, P., & Lacolley, P. (2005). Structural and genetic bases of arterial stiffness. *Hypertension, 45*(6), 1050–1055. doi:10.1161/01. HYP.0000164580.39991.3d

Loewinger, L., & Budoff, M. (2007). New advances in cardiac computed tomography. *Current Opinion in Cardiology, 25*(2), 408–412. doi:10.1097/HCO.0b013e3282170ac4

Mark, D., Berman, D., Budoff, M., Carr, J., Gerber, T., & Hecht, H. (2010). ACCF/ACR/AHA/ NASCI/SAIP/SCAI/SCCT 2010 expert consensus document on coronary computed tomographic angiography: A report of the American College of Cardiology Foundation Task Force on Expert Consensus Documents. *Journal of the American College of Cardiology, 55*(23), 2663–2699. doi:10.1016/j.jacc.2009.11.013

Naghavi, M., Libby, P., Falk, E., Casscells, S., Litovsky, S., & Rumberger, J. (2003). From vulnerable plaque to vulnerable patient: A call for new definitions and risk assessment strategies: Part I. *Circulation, 108*(14), 1664–1672. doi:10.1161/01. CIR.0000087480.94275.97

O'Rourke, M., Staessen, J., Vlachopoulos, C., Duprez, D., & Plante, G. (2002). Clinical applications of arterial stiffness: Definitions and reference values. *American Journal of Hypertension, 15*(5), 426–444. doi:10.1016/S0895-7061(01)02319-6

Papadogiorgaki, M., Mezaris, V., Chatzizisis, Y., Giannoglou, G., & Kompatsiaris, I. (2008). Image analysis techniques for automated IVUS contour detection. *Ultrasound in Medicine & Biology, 34*(9), 1482–1498. doi:10.1016/j.ultrasmedbio.2008.01.022

Prat-Gonzalez, S., Sanz, J., & Garcia, M. (2008). Cardiac CT: Indications and limitations. *Journal of Nuclear Medicine Technology, 36*(1), 18–24. doi:10.2967/jnmt.107.042424

Ramaswamy, S., Vigmostad, S., Wahle, A., Lai, Y., Olszewski, M., & Braddy, K. (2004). Fluid dynamic analysis in a human left anterior descending coronary artery with arterial motion. *Annals of Biomedical Engineering, 32*(12), 1628–1641. doi:10.1007/s10439-004-7816-3

Ramkumar, P., Mitsouras, D., Feldman, C., Stone, P., & Rybicki, F. (2009). New advances in cardiac computed tomography. *Current Opinion in Cardiology, 24*(6), 596–603. doi:10.1097/ HCO.0b013e3283319b84

Roberts, W., Bax, J., & Davies, L. (2008). Cardiac CT and CT coronary angiography: Technology and application. *Heart (British Cardiac Society), 94*(6), 781–792. doi:10.1136/hrt.2007.116392

Scanlon, P., Faxon, D., Audet, A., Carabello, B., Dehmer, G., & Eagle, K. (1999). ACC/AHA guidelines for coronary angiography: Executive summary and recommendations. A report of the American College of Cardiology/American Heart Association Task Force on Practice Guidelines (Committee on Coronary Angiography) developed in collaboration. *Circulation, 99*(17), 2345–2357.

Wijesekera, N., Duncan, M., & Padley, S. (2010). X-ray computed tomography of the heart. *British Medical Bulletin, 93*, 49–67. doi:10.1093/bmb/ ldp043

Yu, W., Chuang, S., Lin, Y., & Chen, C. (2008). Brachial-ankle vs carotid-femoral pulse wave velocity as a determinant of cardiovascular structure and function. *Journal of Human Hypertension, 22*(1), 24–31. doi:10.1038/sj.jhh.1002259

Chapter 23
Coronary Plaque Vulnerability:
Molecular and Cellular Mechanisms and Novel Imaging Modalities

George D. Giannoglou
AHEPA University General Hospital, Greece & Aristotle University Medical School, Greece

Konstantinos C. Koskinas
AHEPA University General Hospital, Greece & Aristotle University Medical School, Greece

ABSTRACT

Beyond structural information obtained by traditional imaging modalities, molecular imaging can now visualize inflammation and proteolytic activity in the atheroma in-vivo. In addition, visualization of plaque neovascularization, and measurement of the plaque's mechanical properties may enhance the identification of rupture-prone lesions. While limited mainly at the pre-clinical level, these novel imaging methods show promise for clinical translation.

ROLE OF MATRIX-DEGRADING PROTEASES IN PLAQUE DESTABILIZATION AND RUPTURE

The thrombotic complications of coronary atherosclerotic disease result mostly from physical disruption of a subpopulation of high-risk lesions (Virmani, Kolodgie, Burke, Farb, & Schwartz, 2000). Local inflammation and proteolytic activity within the plaque influence critically the stability of the atheroma and modulate the plaque's propensity to rupture and cause an acute coronary event (Libby, 2008).

The status of the extracellular matrix in the atherosclerotic intima is regulated by the fine balance between macromolecule synthesis and enzymatic catabolism. Extracellular matrix macromolecules, especially fibrillar interstitial collagens, confer tensile strength upon the plaque's fibrous cap and determine the mechanical properties and stability of atherosclerotic arteries, as shown by experiments in genetically altered mice that

DOI: 10.4018/978-1-61350-095-8.ch023

express collagenase-resistant collagen (Deguchi, *et al.*, 2005). Interstitial collagenases, mostly collagenolytic matrix metalloproteinases (MMPs) MMP-1, MMP-13 and MMP-8, attack the intact triple helical collagen molecule and thereby initiate the catabolic cascade of collagen (Sukhova, *et al.*, 1999), (Deguchi, Aikawa, & Libby, 2005). These active collagenases are expressed in human atherosclerotic plaques, but not in normal arteries, and promote plaque vulnerability through the degradation of the major plaque-stabilizing protein, i.e. collagen. Gelatinases MMP-2 and MMP-9 are implicated in later steps of collagen catabolism after the collagenases make the initial attack. In addition to collagen catabolism, plaques also contain potent elastases (MMP-9, cathepsins S and K, neutrophil elastase) which break down elastin fibers (Dollery & Libby, 2006) and may have important roles in adverse outward arterial remodeling and plaque destabilization (Sukhova, Shi, Simon, Chapman, & Libby, 1998), (Lutgens, *et al.*, 2006).

MOLECULAR IMAGING OF PLAQUE INFLAMMATION AND PROTEASE ACTIVITY

In the light of the well-recognized contribution of inflammation and proteolytic activity to plaque destabilization, novel imaging modalities visualizing molecular targets are increasingly appreciated for their potential to assess *in vivo* biological processes beyond the structural information that is obtained from traditional imaging modalities. While the feasibility and validation of these techniques have been tested at the pre-clinical level, the rapidly emerging strategy of optical and multimodality molecular imaging of inflammation and protease activity has shown promise for clinical translation. These techniques could provide a powerful tool to enhance our understanding of the pathophysiologic processes governing the progression

towards high-risk plaque, enable the identification of rupture-prone plaques at earlier stages of their evolution, enable monitoring of novel therapeutic interventions, and allow for individualized therapeutic strategies. Near-infrared fluorescence (NIRF) is a particularly promising technique for the *in vivo* visualization of protease activity. Detection of the NIR fluorochromes can be performed either non-invasively by fluorescence molecular tomography (FMT), or invasively, using intravascular NIRF catheters.

Non-invasive Imaging of Protease Activity by Near-Infrared Fluorescence (NIRF)

Protease presence in the plaques can be visualized *in vivo* with radiolabeled small molecule inhibitors or MRI-detectable agents (Amirbekian, *et al.*, 2009). However, because protease molecules may represent inactive zymogen precursors that lack proteolytic capacity, protease activity *per se* can be visualized by potease-activatable fluorescent probes. The principle of NIRF molecular imaging of protease activity consists of biocompatible agents that emit fluorescent signal after proteolytic cleavage of a peptide sequence specific to their target enzyme. These agents are injected and delivered to the protease-rich plaque environment and cleaved by proteases, including cathepsins -K, -L, -S, and -B, generating fluorochromes that are detectable by NIRF imaging technologies (Chen, *et al.*, 2002). More recently, experimental studies have used the first-generation protease activatable agent and incorporated peptide substrates that are specifically cleaved by selective enzymes, including MMP-2, MMP-9 (Chen, Tung, Allport, Chen, Weissleder, & Huang, 2005), cathepsin-K, (Jaffer, *et al.*, 2007) -S (Galande, Hilderbrand, Weissleder, & Tung, 2006) and -D, thereby allowing the enzyme-specific assessment of protease activity in the atherosclerotic plaque *in vivo*.

Figure 1. In vivo fluorescence molecular tomography-computed tomography imaging (FMT CT)

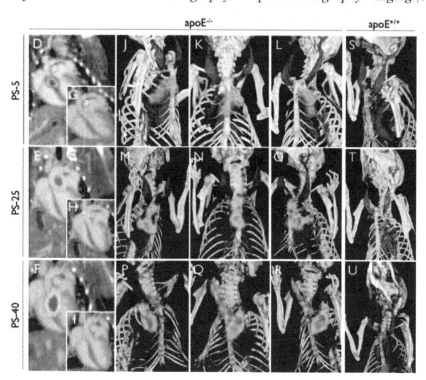

Fluorescence molecular tomography (FMT) is emerging as a quantitative modality for non-invasive detection and quantification of inflammatory protease activity (Ntziachristos, Tung, Bremer, & Weissleder, 2002). Detection of NIR fluorochromes by FMT has been applied for the visualization of cysteine protease activity in atheromata of apoE-/- mice (Chen, *et al.*, 2002); importantly, the *in vivo* signal was validated by ex vivo NIRF and fluorescence reflectance imaging, co-localized with cathepsin-B by immunostaining, affirming thus the specificity of the obtained signal. Fluorescent molecular tomography has also been applied and validated experimentally to visualize matrix metalloproteinase-mediated gelatinolytic activity *in vivo*, demonstrating the feasibility and specificity of the *in vivo* imaging of gelatinolysis (Deguchi J., *et al.*, 2006). Advantages of FMT include absence of radiation, high sensitivity, cost-effectiveness, short procedural duration, signal amplification, low background,

and the potential for concomitant imaging with multiple biomarkers (Sinusas, *et al.*, 2008).

From a clinical perspective point of view, the physical properties of NIR photons and in particular the penetration up to 10cm in tissue depth, might allow the application of non-invasive FMT for the detection of NIRF signal in human carotid plaques.

Recently, hybrid *in vivo* FMT – CT imaging of protease activity was employed in mouse atherosclerotic plaques. The combined FMT – CT approach provided the advantage of highly sensitive probes and additional anatomic information (Figure 1) (Nahrendorf, Waterman, Thurber, Groves, Rajopadhye, & Panizzi, 2009).

Intravascular NIRF Visualization of Protease Activity

To overcome the limited depth of tissue penetration of fluorescence, intravascular visualization of protease activity has been performed in animal models (Jaffer, *et al.*, 2008). An OCT wire that is already utilized in clinical practice was recently applied for the *in vivo* NIRF imaging of cysteine protease activity in the iliac arteries of rabbits. The *in vivo* signal was confirmed by *ex vivo* immunostaining for cathepsin B, validating the feasibility and specificity of visualizing protease activity *in vivo* in coronary-sized arteries, by the use of clinically available wires. With the development of intravascular fluorescence imaging platforms, these results show promise for the clinical NIRF visualization of inflamed plaques with catheter-based detectors (Zhu, Jaffer, Ntziachristos, & Weissleder, 2005).

NIRF intravital fluorescence microscopy (IVFM) has also been applied experimentally for the detection of plaque cathepsin K activity in murine carotid plaques; the carotid plaques were surgically exposed and underwent intravital fluorescence microscopy (IVFM) using a laser scanning microscope. The intravital fluorescence microscopy in surgically exposed carotid arteries might be of limited clinical extrapolation; however, coronary plaques in humans could potentially be visualized by means of clinically available confocal fluorescence microendoscopes using the same methodology (Hsiung, *et al.*, 2008).

Multimodal Molecular Imaging

Multimodality molecular imaging with probes that are detectable by optical, nuclear, and MRI techniques has allowed concomitant visualization of plaques with complementary imaging modalities. Multimodality magnetic nanoparticles have been applied for MRI-based imaging of macrophages in human carotid plaques (Tang, *et al.*, 2006). More recently, *in vivo* imaging of plaque macrophages was performed using dual-modality nanoparticles detectable by MRI and intravital microscopy (Pande, Kohler, Aikawa, Weissleder, & Jaffer, 2006), and even trimodality nanoparticles

detectable by positron emission tomography, MRI and NIRF (Nahrendorf, *et al.*, 2008). Using multiple molecular readouts enables combination of noninvasive and invasive approaches for molecular imaging and substantially improves spatial resolution. The use of integrated PET/MRI scanners may enable clinical noninvasive detection of carotid plaque macrophages coupled by additional anatomic and molecular assessment (Judenhofer, *et al.*, 2008). Furthermore, invasive catheter-based NIRF macrophage detection could be performed using trimodality nanoparticles in human coronary lesions (Jaffer, *et al.*, 2008).

In addition, novel multimodal probes raise the intriguing possibility of "theranostic", i.e. concomitant therapeutic and diagnostic, strategies that could combine compound targeting and imaging-based *in vivo* assessment of biochemical efficacy in atherosclerotic plaques.

IN VIVO ASSESSMENT OF PLAQUE NEOVASCULARIZATION

Plaque neovascularization is recognized as a feature of plaque vulnerability (Moreno, Purushothaman, Sirol, Levy, & Fuster, 2006). Ruptured coronary plaques in patients who died suddenly exhibit more frequently intraplaque hemorrhage (Virmani, Kolodgie, Burke, Farb, & Schwartz, 2000), presumably through thin-walled, immature microvessels with incomplete endothelial junctions (Sluimer, Kolodgie, & Bijnens, 2009). Accordingly, microvessel density in human aortic plaques is increased in lesions with inflammation, intraplaque hemorrhage, and characteristics of vulnerability (Moreno, *et al.*, 2004).

Local ischemia and oxidation in the plaque environment are major stimuli for the production of angiogenic factors, promoting local neovascularization. Neovessels nourish the growing plaque with lipids, inflammatory cells and cytokines, but may also contribute to plaque progression through intraplaque hemorrhage. Cholesterol-rich erythrocytes that are extravasated at sites of intraplaque hemorrhage could play a role in the expansion of the lipid core (Giannoglou, *et al.*, 2009), as suggested by the localization of erythrocyte membranes in the lipid core of atherosclerotic plaques (Kolodgie, *et al.*, 2003). In addition, total cholesterol levels (Tziakas, *et al.*, 2007) and intelleukin-8 levels (Tziakas, *et al.*, 2008) in the membrane of circulating red blood cells are increased in patients with acute coronary syndrome compared with patients with chronic stable angina, indicating that erythrocyte membranes released within the lipid core may also contribute to plaque instability.

Micro-computed tomography (CT) scanning from human autopsy hearts was recently used for the *ex vivo* assessment of vasa vasorum density, showing an association between plaque neovascularization and plaque complexity and progression (Gössl, *et al.*, 2010). MRI-based assessment of plaque neovessels has also been tested experimentally. Gadofluorine-M-enhanced MRI has been used for in vivo detection of atherosclerotic plaque inflammation and neovascularization in rabbits (Sirol, *et al.*, 2009); the plaque accumulation of gadofluorine-M correlated with increased neovessel density.

Molecular imaging of plaque neovascularization has been performed at the pre-clinical level. *Ex vivo* visualization of murine plaque neovascularization has been described by the use of a NIRF sensor targeted to the extra-domain B of fibronectin (Matter, *et al.*, 2004). In addition, the efficacy of ezetimibe in attenuating plaque neovascularization has been tested in a murine model of atehrosclerosis using the same principle of ex vivo fluorescence imaging (Graf, *et al.*, 2008). The clinical applicability of these techniques remains to be determined.

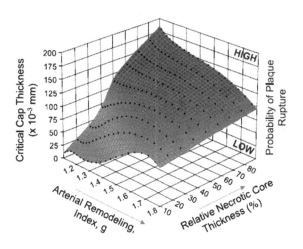

Figure 2. Three-dimensional plot highlighting the influences of remodeling index and relative necrotic core thickness on critical cap thickness

IN VIVO MEASUREMENT OF BIOMECHANICAL PLAQUE FEATURES FOR THE ASSESSMENT OF PLAQUE INSTABILITY

While IVUS is used routinely to investigate the amount of lumen stenosis in borderline lesions and to assist in stent deployment, IVUS-based methodologies have also been applied for the evaluation of plaque composition and the identification of high-risk coronary lesions. Although the thickness of the fibrous cap is a recognized feature determining the plaque's likelihood of rupture, not all thin-capped fibroatheromata have the same risk of rupture, suggesting that other morphological plaque characteristics may also be involved (Virmani, Kolodgie, Burke, Farb, & Schwartz, 2000). Recent sophisticated computational models measured cap stress value, a surrogate marker of the likelihood of cap rupture, in atherosclerotic vessel models that resembled the glagovian arterial remodeling process (Ohayon, Finet, & al., 2008). IVUS-based data from non-ruptured human coronary plaques were used to test the biomechanical interaction among anatomical features of coronary plaques, and their impact on cap stress. Necrotic core thickness, rather than core area, appeared as an emerging determinant of plaque stability, which was a multifactorial consequence of cap thickness, necrotic core thickness, and the local arterial remodeling index (Figure 2). The quantification of the mechanical stress that is imposed on the fibrous cap, based on IVUS-derived plaque measurements, may facilitate the estimation of the risk of rupture in eccentric, core-containing coronary plaques.

REFERENCES

Amirbekian, V., Aguinaldo, J., Amirbekian, S., Hyafil, F., Vucic, E., & Sirol, M. (2009). Atherosclerosis and matrix metalloproteinases: Experimental molecular MR imaging in vivo. *Radiology*, *251*, 429–438. doi:10.1148/radiol.2511080539

Chen, J., Tung, C., Allport, J., Chen, S., Weissleder, R., & Huang, P. (2005). Near-infrared fluorescent imaging of matrix metalloproteinase activity after myocardial infarction. *Circulation*, *111*, 1800–1805. doi:10.1161/01.CIR.0000160936.91849.9F

Chen, J., Tung, C., Mahmood, U., Ntziachristos, V., Gyurko, R., & Fishman, M. (2002). In vivo imaging of proteolytic activity in atherosclerosis. *Circulation*, *105*, 2766–2771. doi:10.1161/01.CIR.0000017860.20619.23

Deguchi, J., Aikawa, E., & Libby, P. (2005). Matrix metalloproteinase-13/collagenase-3 deletion promotes collagen accumulation and organization in mouse atherosclerotic plaques. *Circulation*, *112*, 2708–2715. doi:10.1161/CIRCULATIONAHA.105.562041

Deguchi, J., Aikawa, E., Libby, P., Vachon, J., Inada, M., & Krane, S. (2005). Matrix metalloproteinase-13/collagenase-3 deletion promotes collagen accumulation and organization in mouse atherosclerotic plaques. *Circulation*, *112*, 2708–2715. doi:10.1161/CIRCULATIONAHA.105.562041

Deguchi, J., Aikawa, M., Tung, C., Aikawa, E., Kim, D., & Ntziachristos, V. (2006). Inflammation in atherosclerosis: Visualizing matrix metalloproteinase action in macrophages in vivo. *Circulation*, *114*, 55–62. doi:10.1161/CIRCULATIONAHA.106.619056

Dollery, C., & Libby, P. (2006). Atherosclerosis and proteinase activation. *Cardiovascular Research*, *69*, 625–635. doi:10.1016/j.cardiores.2005.11.003

Galande, A., Hilderbrand, S., Weissleder, R., & Tung, C. (2006). Enzyme-targeted fluorescent imaging probes on a multiple antigenic peptide core. *Journal of Medicinal Chemistry*, *49*, 4715–4720. doi:10.1021/jm051001a

Giannoglou, G., Koskinas, K., Tziakas, D., Ziakas, A., Tentes, I., & Antoniadis, A. (2009). Total cholesterol content of erythrocyte membranes and coronary atherosclerosis: An intravascular ultrasound pilot study. *Angiology*, *60*, 676–682. doi:10.1177/0003319709337307

Gössl, M., Versari, D., Hildebrandt, H., Bajanowski, T., Sangiorgi, G., & Erbel, R. (2010). Segmental heterogeneity of vasa vasorum neovascularization in human coronary atherosclerosis. *JACC: Cardiovascular Imaging*, *3*(1), 32–40. doi:10.1016/j.jcmg.2009.10.009

Graf, K., Dietrich, T., Tachezy, M., Scholle, F., Licha, K., & Stawowy, P. (2008). Monitoring therapeutical intervention with ezetimibe using targeted near-infrared fluorescence imaging in experimental atherosclerosis. *Molecular Imaging*, *7*, 68–76.

Hsiung, P., Hardy, J., Friedland, S., Soetikno, R., Du, C., & Wu, A. (2008). Detection of colonic dysplasia in vivo using a targeted heptapeptide and confocal microendoscopy. *Nature Medicine*, *14*, 454–458. doi:10.1038/nm1692

Jaffer, F., Kim, D., Quinti, L., Tung, C., Aikawa, E., & Pande, A. (2007). Optical visualization of cathepsin K activity in atherosclerosis with a novel, protease-activatable fluorescence sensor. *Circulation, 115*, 2292–2298. doi:10.1161/CIRCULATIONAHA.106.660340

Jaffer, F., Vinegoni, C., John, M., Aikawa, E., Gold, H., & Finn, A. (2008). Real-time catheter molecular sensing of inflammation in proteolytically active atherosclerosis. *Circulation, 118*, 1802–1809. doi:10.1161/CIRCULATIONAHA.108.785881

Judenhofer, M., Wehrl, H., Newport, D., Catana, C., Siegel, S., & Becker, M. (2008). Simultaneous PET-MRI: A new approach for functional and morphological imaging. *Nature Medicine, 14*, 459–465. doi:10.1038/nm1700

Kolodgie, F., Gold, H., Burke, A., Fowler, D., Kruth, H., & Weber, D. (2003). Intraplaque hemorrhage and progression of coronary atheroma. *The New England Journal of Medicine, 349*, 2316–2325. doi:10.1056/NEJMoa035655

Libby, P. (2008). The molecular mechanisms of the thrombotic complications of atherosclerosis. *Journal of Internal Medicine, 263*, 517–527. doi:10.1111/j.1365-2796.2008.01965.x

Lutgens, E., Lutgens, S., Faber, B., Heeneman, S., Gijbels, M., & de Winther, M. (2006). Disruption of the cathepsin K gene reduces atherosclerosis progression and induces plaque fibrosis but accelerates macrophage foam cell formation. *Circulation, 113*, 98–107. doi:10.1161/CIRCULATIONAHA.105.561449

Matter, C., Schuler, P., Alessi, P., Meier, P., Ricci, R., & Zhang, D. (2004). Molecular imaging of atherosclerotic plaques using a human antibody against the extra-domain B of fibronectin. *Circulation Research, 95*, 1225–1233. doi:10.1161/01.RES.0000150373.15149.ff

Moreno, P., Purushothaman, K., Fuster, V., Echeverri, D., Truszczynska, H., & Sharma, S. (2004). Plaque neovascularization is increased in ruptured atherosclerotic lesions of human aorta: Implications for plaque vulnerability. *Circulation, 110*, 2032–2038. doi:10.1161/01.CIR.0000143233.87854.23

Moreno, P., Purushothaman, K., Sirol, M., Levy, A., & Fuster, V. (2006). Neovascularization in human atherosclerosis. *Circulation, 113*, 2245–2252. doi:10.1161/CIRCULATIONAHA.105.578955

Nahrendorf, M., Waterman, P., Thurber, G., Groves, K., Rajopadhye, M., & Panizzi, P. (2009). Hybrid in vivo FMT-CT imaging of protease activity in atherosclerosis with customized nanosensors. *Arteriosclerosis, Thrombosis, and Vascular Biology, 29*, 1444–1451. doi:10.1161/ATVBAHA.109.193086

Nahrendorf, M., Zhang, H., Hembrador, S., Panizzi, P., Sosnovik, D., & Aikawa, E. (2008). Nanoparticle PET-CT imaging of macrophages in inflammatory atherosclerosis. *Circulation, 117*, 379–387. doi:10.1161/CIRCULATIONAHA.107.741181

Ntziachristos, V., Tung, C., Bremer, C., & Weissleder, R. (2002). Fluorescence molecular tomography resolves protease activity in vivo. *Nature Medicine, 8*, 757–760. doi:10.1038/nm729

Ohayon, J., & Finet, G., & al., G. A. (2008). Necrotic core thickness and positive arterial remodeling index: Emergent biomechanical factors for evaluating the risk of plaque rupture. *American Journal of Physiology. Heart and Circulatory Physiology, 295*, H717–H727. doi:10.1152/ajpheart.00005.2008

Pande, A., Kohler, R., Aikawa, E., Weissleder, R., & Jaffer, F. (2006). Detection of macrophage activity in atherosclerosis in vivo using multichannel, highresolution laser scanning fluorescence microscopy. *Journal of Biomedical Optics, 11*, 021009. doi:10.1117/1.2186337

Sinusas, A., Bengel, F., Nahrendorf, M., Epstein, F., Wu, J., & Villanueva, F. (2008). Multimodality cardiovascular molecular imaging: Part I. *Circulation: Cardiovascular Imaging*, *1*, 244–256. doi:10.1161/CIRCIMAGING.108.824359

Sirol, M., Moreno, P., Purushothaman, K., Vucic, E., Amirbekian, V., & Weinmann, H. (2009). Increased neovascularization in advanced lipid-rich atherosclerotic lesions detected by gadofluorine-M-enhanced MRI: Implications for plaque vulnerability. *Circulation: Cardiovascular Imaging*, *2*(5), 391–396. doi:10.1161/CIRCIM-AGING.108.801712

Sluimer, J., Kolodgie, F., & Bijnens, A. (2009). Thin-walled microvessels in human coronary atherosclerotic plaques show incomplete endothelial junctions relevance of compromised structural integrity for intraplaque microvascular leakage. *Journal of the American College of Cardiology*, *53*, 1517–1527. doi:10.1016/j.jacc.2008.12.056

Sukhova, G., Schoenbeck, U., Rabkin, E., Schoen, F., Poole, A., & Billinghurst, R. (1999). Evidence of increased collagenolysis by interstitial collagenases-1 and -3 in vulnerable human atheromatous plaques. *Circulation*, *99*, 2503–2509.

Sukhova, G., Shi, G., Simon, D., Chapman, H., & Libby, P. (1998). Expression of the elastolytic cathepsins S and K in human atheroma and regulation of their production in smooth muscle cells. *The Journal of Clinical Investigation*, *102*, 576–583. doi:10.1172/JCI181

Tang, T., Howarth, S., Miller, S., Trivedi, R., & Graves, M., U-King-Im, J., *et al.* (2006). Assessment of inflammatory burden contralateral to the symptomatic carotid stenosis using high-resolution ultrasmall, superparamagnetic iron oxide-enhanced MRI. *Stroke*, *37*, 2266–2270. doi:10.1161/01.STR.0000236063.47539.99

Tziakas, D., Chalikias, G., Tentes, I., Stakos, D., Chatzikyriakou, S., & Mitrousi, K. (2008). Interleukin-8 is increased in the membrane of circulating erythrocytes in patients with acute coronary syndrome. *European Heart Journal*, *29*, 2713–2722. doi:10.1093/eurheartj/ehn382

Tziakas, D., Kaski, J., Chalikias, G., Romero, C., Fredericks, S., & Tentes, I. (2007). Total cholesterol content of erythrocyte membranes is increased in patients with acute coronary syndrome. *Journal of the American College of Cardiology*, *49*, 2081–2089. doi:10.1016/j.jacc.2006.08.069

Virmani, R., Kolodgie, F., Burke, A., Farb, A., & Schwartz, S. (2000). Lessons from sudden coronary death: A comprehensive morphological classification scheme for atherosclerotic lesions. *Arteriosclerosis, Thrombosis, and Vascular Biology*, *20*, 1262–1275. doi:10.1161/01.ATV.20.5.1262

Zhu, B., Jaffer, F., Ntziachristos, V., & Weissleder, R. (2005). Development of a near infrared fluorescence catheter: Operating characterisitics and feasibility for atherosclerotic plaque detection. *Journal of Physics. D, Applied Physics*, *38*, 2701–2707. doi:10.1088/0022-3727/38/15/024

Compilation of References

Abizaid, A. S., Mintz, G. S., Abizaid, A., Mehran, R., Lansky, A. J., & Pichard, A. D. (1999a). One-year follow-up after intravascular ultrasound assessment of moderate left main coronary artery disease in patients with ambiguous angiograms. *Journal of the American College of Cardiology*, *34*(3), 707–715. doi:10.1016/S0735-1097(99)00261-2

Abizaid, A. S., Mintz, G. S., Mehran, R., Abizaid, A., Lansky, A. J., & Pichard, A. D. (1999b). Long-term follow-up after percutaneous transluminal coronary angioplasty was not performed based on intravascular ultrasound findings: importance of lumen dimensions. *Circulation*, *100*(3), 256–261.

Abizaid, A., Costa, M. A., Blanchard, D., Albertal, M., Eltchaninoff, H., & Guagliumi, G. (2004). Sirolimus-eluting stents inhibit neointimal hyperplasia in diabetic patients. Insights from the RAVEL Trial. *European Heart Journal*, *25*(2), 107–112. doi:10.1016/j.ehj.2003.11.002

Abizaid, A. S., Mintz, G. S., Mehran, R., Abizaid, A., Lansky, A. J., & Pichard, A. D. (1999). Long-term follow-up after percutaneous transluminal coronary angioplasty was not performed based on intravascular ultrasound findings: Importance of lumen dimensions. *Circulation*, *100*(3), 256–261.

Abizaid, A., Kornowski, R., Mintz, G. S., Hong, M. K., Abizaid, A. S., & Mehran, R. (1998). The influence of diabetes mellitus on acute and late clinical outcomes following coronary stent implantation. *Journal of the American College of Cardiology*, *32*(3), 584–589. doi:10.1016/S0735-1097(98)00286-1

Achenbach, S., Ropers, D., Mohlenkamp, S., Schmermund, A., Muschiol, G., Groth, J., *et al.* (2001). Variability of repeated coronary artery calcium measurements by electron beam tomography. *Am J Cardiol*, *87*(2), 210-213, A218.

Adelman, A., Cohen, E., Kimball, B., Bonan, R., Ricci, D., & Webb, J. (1993). A comparison of directional atherectomy with balloon angioplasty for lesions of the left anterior descending coronary artery. *The New England Journal of Medicine*, *329*, 228–233. doi:10.1056/NEJM199307223290402

Agatston, A. S., Janowitz, W. R., Kaplan, G., Gasso, J., Hildner, F., & Viamonte, M. Jr. (1994). Ultrafast computed tomography-detected coronary calcium reflects the angiographic extent of coronary arterial atherosclerosis. *The American Journal of Cardiology*, *74*(12), 1272–1274. doi:10.1016/0002-9149(94)90563-0

Alboliras, E. T., & Hijazi, Z. M. (2004). Comparison of costs of intracardiac echocardiography and transesophageal echocardiography in monitoring percutaneous device closure of atrial septal defect in children and adults. *The American Journal of Cardiology*, *94*(5), 690–692. .doi:10.1016/j.amjcard.2004.05.048

Alfonso, F. (2006). Pathophysiology of stent thrombosis: platelet activation, mechanical factors, or both? *Journal of the American College of Cardiology*, *47*(5), 1086–1087, author reply 1087. doi:10.1016/j.jacc.2005.12.008

Alfonso, F. (2008). The "vulnerable" stent: Why so dreadful? *Journal of the American College of Cardiology*, *51*(25), 2403–2406. doi:10.1016/j.jacc.2008.03.029

Alfonso, F., Perez-Vizcayno, M. J., Hernandez, R., Bethencourt, A., Marti, V., & Lopez-Minguez, J. R. (2006). A randomized comparison of sirolimus-eluting stent with balloon angioplasty in patients with in-stent restenosis: Results of the Restenosis Intrastent: Balloon Angioplasty Versus Elective Sirolimus-Eluting Stenting (RIBS-II) trial. *Journal of the American College of Cardiology*, *47*(11), 2152–2160. doi:10.1016/j.jacc.2005.10.078

Alfonso, F., Suarez, A., Angiolillo, D. J., Sabate, M., Escaned, J., & Moreno, R. (2004). Findings of intravascular ultrasound during acute stent thrombosis. *Heart (British Cardiac Society)*, *90*(12), 1455–1459. doi:10.1136/hrt.2003.026047

Alfonso, F., Suarez, A., Perez-Vizcayno, M. J., Moreno, R., Escaned, J., & Banuelos, C. (2007). Intravascular ultrasound findings during episodes of drug-eluting stent thrombosis. *Journal of the American College of Cardiology*, *50*(21), 2095–2097. doi:10.1016/j.jacc.2007.08.015

Alfonso, F., Suárez, A., Pérez-Vizcayno, M., Moreno, R., Escaned, J., & Bañuelos, C. (2007). Intravascular ultrasound findings during episodes of drug-eluting stent thrombosis. *Journal of the American College of Cardiology*, *50*, 2095–2097. doi:10.1016/j.jacc.2007.08.015

Alfonso, F. (2010). Treatment of drug-eluting stent restenosis the new pilgrimage: Quo vadis? *Journal of the American College of Cardiology*, *55*(24), 2717–2720. doi:10.1016/j.jacc.2010.03.026

Amano, T., Matsubara, T., Uetani, T., Kato, M., Kato, B., & Yoshida, T. (2011). Lipid-rich plaques predict non-target-lesion ischemic events in patients undergoing percutaneous coronary intervention: Insights from integrated backscatter intravascular ultrasound & ndash. *Circulation Journal*, *75*(1), 157–166. doi:10.1253/circj.CJ-10-0612

Ambrose, J. A. (2008). In search of the "vulnerable plaque": Can it be localized and will focal regional therapy ever be an option for cardiac prevention? *Journal of the American College of Cardiology*, *51*(16), 1539–1542. doi:10.1016/j.jacc.2007.12.041

Ambrose, J. A., Winters, S. L., Arora, R. R., Eng, A., Riccio, A., & Gorlin, R. (1986). Angiographic evolution of coronary artery morphology in unstable angina. *Journal of the American College of Cardiology*, *7*(3), 472–478. doi:10.1016/S0735-1097(86)80455-7

Amirbekian, V., Aguinaldo, J., Amirbekian, S., Hyafil, F., Vucic, E., & Sirol, M. (2009). Atherosclerosis and matrix metalloproteinases: Experimental molecular MR imaging in vivo. *Radiology*, *251*, 429–438. doi:10.1148/radiol.2511080539

Anderson, R. H., & Ho, S. Y. (2006). Anatomy of the atrioventricular junctions with regard to ventricular pre-excitation. *Pacing and Clinical Electrophysiology*, *20*(8), 2072–2076. doi:10.1111/j.1540-8159.1997.tb03631.x

Aoki, J., Mintz, G. S., Weissman, N. J., Mann, J. T., Cannon, L., & Greenberg, J. (2008). Chronic arterial responses to overlapping paclitaxel-eluting stents: Insights from serial intravascular ultrasound analyses in the TAXUS-V and -VI trials. *JACC: Cardiovascular Interventions*, *1*(2), 161–167. doi:10.1016/j.jcin.2007.12.005

Applebaum, R. M., Kasliwal, R. R., Kanojia, A., Seth, A., Bhandari, S., & Trehan, N. (1998). Utility of three-dimensional echocardiography during balloon mitral valvuloplasty. *Journal of the American College of Cardiology*, *32*(5), 1405–1409. doi:10.1016/S0735-1097(98)00386-6

Arampatzis, C. A., Ligthart, J. M., Schaar, J. A., Nieman, K., Serruys, P. W., & de Feyter, P. J. (2003). Images in cardiovascular medicine. Detection of a vulnerable coronary plaque: A treatment dilemma. *Circulation*, *108*(5), e34–e35. doi:10.1161/01.CIR.0000075303.04340.EF

Asakura, T., & Karino, T. (1990). Flow patterns and spatial distribution of atherosclerotic lesions in human coronary arteries. *Circulation Research*, *66*(4), 1045–1066.

Ashley, S., Brooks, S., Kester, R., & Rees, M. (1990). Thermal characteristics of sapphire contact probe delivery systems for laser angioplasty. *Lasers in Surgery and Medicine*, 10.

Ashley, S., Brooks, S., Wright, H., Gehani, A., & Rees, M. (1991). Acute effects of a copper vapour laser on atheroma. *Lasers in Medical Science*, *6*(1), 23–27. doi:10.1007/BF02042642

Badhey, N., Lichtenwalter, C., & de Lemos, J. (2010). Contemporary use of embolic protection devices in saphenous vein graft interventions: Insights from the stenting of saphenous vein grafts trial. *Catheterization and Cardiovascular Interventions*, *76*, 263–269. doi:10.1002/ccd.22438

Baker, A., Chatzizisis, Y., Beigel, R., Jonas, M., Stone, B., & Coskun, A. (2010). Regulation of heparanase in coronary artery disease. *Atherosclerosis*, *213*(2). doi:10.1016/j.atherosclerosis.2010.09.003

Balakrishnan, B., Tzafriri, A. R., Seifert, P., Groothuis, A., Rogers, C., & Edelman, E. R. (2005). Strut position, blood flow, and drug deposition: Implications for single and overlapping drug-eluting stents. *Circulation*, *111*(22), 2958–2965. doi:10.1161/CIRCULATIONAHA.104.512475

Baldewsing, R. A., Danilouchkine, M. G., Mastik, F., Schaar, J. A., Serruys, P. W., & van der Steen, A. F. (2008). An inverse method for imaging the local elasticity of atherosclerotic coronary plaques. *IEEE Transactions on Information Technology in Biomedicine, 12*(3), 277–289. doi:10.1109/TITB.2007.907980

Baldewsing, R. A., de Korte, C. L., Schaar, J. A., Mastik, F., & van der Steen, A. F. (2004). A finite element model for performing intravascular ultrasound elastography of human atherosclerotic coronary arteries. *Ultrasound in Medicine & Biology, 30*(6), 803–813. doi:10.1016/j.ultrasmedbio.2004.04.005

Balossino, R., Gervaso, F., Migliavacca, F., & Dubini, G. (2008). Effects of different stent designs on local hemodynamics in stented arteries. *Journal of Biomechanics, 41*(5), 1053–1061. doi:10.1016/j.jbiomech.2007.12.005

Banerjee, S., & Brilakis, E. (2009). Embolic protection during saphenous vein graft interventions. *The Journal of Invasive Cardiology, 21*, 415–417.

Barlis, P., Gonzalo, N., Di Mario, C., Prati, F., Buellesfeld, L., & Rieber, J. (2009). A multicentre evaluation of the safety intracoronary optical coherence tomography. *EuroInterv, 5*, 90–95. doi:10.4244/EIJV5I1A14

Bartel, T., Caspari, G., Mueller, S., & Erbel, R. (2002). Intracardiac echocardiography-technology and clinical role. *Journal of Clinical and Basic Cardiology, 5*(2), 133–138.

Bartel, T., Konorza, T., Arjumand, J., Ebradlidze, T., Eggebrecht, H., & Caspari, G. (2003). Intracardiac echocardiography is superior to conventional monitoring for guiding device closure of interatrial communications. *Circulation, 107*(6), 795–797. doi:10.1161/01.CIR.0000057547.00909.1C

Bartel, T., Konorza, T., Neudorf, U., Ebralize, T., Eggebrecht, H., Gutersohn, A., & Erbel, R. (2005). Intracardiac echocardiography: An ideal guiding tool for device closure of interatrial communications. *European Journal of Echocardiography, 6*(2), 92–96. doi:10.1016/j.euje.2004.07.007

Bartel, T., Müller, S., Caspari, G., & Erbel, R. (2002). Intracardiac and intraluminal echocardiography: Indications and standard approaches. *Ultrasound in Medicine & Biology, 28*(8), 997–1003. doi:10.1016/S0301-5629(02)00551-3

Bazaz, R., & Schwartzman, D. (2003). Site-Selective atrial septal puncture. *Journal of Cardiovascular Electrophysiology, 14*(2), 196–199. doi:10.1046/j.1540-8167.2003.02377.x

Becker, C. R., Kleffel, T., Crispin, A., Knez, A., Young, J., & Schoepf, U. J. (2001). Coronary artery calcium measurement: agreement of multirow detector and electron beam CT. *AJR. American Journal of Roentgenology, 176*(5), 1295–1298.

Belardi, J., Albertal, M., Cura, F., Mendiz, O., Balino, P., & Padilla, L. (2005). Intravascular thermographic assessment in human coronary atherosclerotic plaques by a novel flow-occluding sensing catheter: A safety and feasibility study. *The Journal of Invasive Cardiology, 17*, 663–666.

Bentzon, J., Weile, C., Sondergaard, C., Hindkjaer, J., Kassem, M., & Falk, E. (2006). Smooth muscle cells in atherosclerosis originate from the local vessel wall and not circulating progenitor cells in ApoE knockout mice. *Arteriosclerosis, Thrombosis, and Vascular Biology, 26*, 2696–2702. doi:10.1161/01.ATV.0000247243.48542.9d

Berry, C., L'Allier, P. L., Gregoire, J., Lesperance, J., Levesque, S., & Ibrahim, R. (2007). Comparison of intravascular ultrasound and quantitative coronary angiography for the assessment of coronary artery disease progression. *Circulation, 115*(14), 1851–1857. doi:10.1161/CIRCULATIONAHA.106.655654

Bezerra, H., Costa, M., Guagliumi, G., Rollins, A., & Simon, D. (2009). Intracoronary optical coherence tomography: a comprehensive review clinical and research applications. *J Am Coll Cardiol Intv, 2*, 1035–1046.

Bhatti, S., Hakeem, A., & Cilingiroglu, M. (2010). Lp-PLA(2) as a marker of cardiovascular diseases. *Current Atherosclerosis Reports, 12*(2), 140–144. doi:10.1007/s11883-010-0095-6

Blasini, R., Neumann, F. J., Schmitt, C., Bökenkamp, J., & Schömig, A. (1997). Comparison of angiography and intravascular ultrasound for the assessment of lumen size after coronary stent placement: Impact of dilation pressures. *Catheterization and Cardiovascular Diagnosis, 42*(2), 113–119. doi:10.1002/(SICI)1097-0304(199710)42:2<113::AID-CCD2>3.0.CO;2-G

Boccalandro, F., Baptista, E., Muench, A., Carter, C., & Smalling, R. W. (2004). Comparison of intracardiac echocardiography versus transesophageal echocardiography guidance for percutaneous transcatheter closure of atrial septal defect. *The American Journal of Cardiology*, *93*(4), 437–440. .doi:10.1016/j.amjcard.2003.10.037

Bonello, L., De Labriolle, A., Lemesle, G., Roy, P., Steinberg, D. H., & Pichard, A. D. (2009). Intravascular ultrasound-guided percutaneous coronary interventions in contemporary practice. *Arch Cardiovasc Dis*, *102*(2), 143–151. doi:10.1016/j.acvd.2008.11.002

Bose, D., von Birgelen, C., & Erbel, R. (2007). Intravascular ultrasound for the evaluation of therapies targeting coronary atherosclerosis. *Journal of the American College of Cardiology*, *49*, 925–932. doi:10.1016/j.jacc.2006.08.067

Boston Scientific. (2009). News release: Boston Scientific announces release of next-generation iLab® system software. Retrieved from http://bostonscientific.mediaroom.com/index.php?s=43&item=864

Botnar, R. M., Buecker, A., Wiethoff, A. J., Parsons, E. C. Jr, Katoh, M., & Katsimaglis, G. (2004). In vivo magnetic resonance imaging of coronary thrombosis using a fibrin-binding molecular magnetic resonance contrast agent. *Circulation*, *110*(11), 1463–1466. doi:10.1161/01.CIR.0000134960.31304.87

Botnar, R. M., Kim, W. Y., Bornert, P., Stuber, M., Spuentrup, E., & Manning, W. J. (2001). 3D coronary vessel wall imaging utilizing a local inversion technique with spiral image acquisition. *Magnetic Resonance in Medicine*, *46*(5), 848–854. doi:10.1002/mrm.1268

Botnar, R. M., Stuber, M., Kissinger, K. V., Kim, W. Y., Spuentrup, E., & Manning, W. J. (2000). Noninvasive coronary vessel wall and plaque imaging with magnetic resonance imaging. *Circulation*, *102*(21), 2582–2587.

Bouki, K., Chatzopoulos, D., Katsafados, M., Elaiopoulos, D., Psychari, S., & Apostolou, T. (2009). Late acquired stent malapposition detected by optical coherence tomography examination. *International Journal of Cardiology*, *137*, e77–e78. doi:10.1016/j.ijcard.2009.04.039

Bouma, C., Niessen, W., Zuiderveld, K., Gussenhoven, E., & Viergever, M. (1997). Automated lumen definition from 30 MHz intravascular ultrasound images. *Medical Image Analysis*, *1*(4), 363–377. doi:10.1016/S1361-8415(97)85007-4

Bouma, B. E., Tearney, G. J., Yabushita, H., Shishkov, M., Kauffman, C. R., & Gauthier, D. D. (2003). Evaluation of intracoronary stenting by intravascular optical coherence tomography. *Heart (British Cardiac Society)*, *89*(3), 317–320. doi:10.1136/heart.89.3.317

Bouma, B. E., Tearney, G. J., Yabushita, H., Shishkov, M., Kauffman, C. R., & DeJoseph Gauthier, D. (2003). Evaluation of intracoronary stenting by intravascular optical coherence tomography. *Heart (British Cardiac Society)*, *89*(3), 317–320. doi:10.1136/heart.89.3.317

Bourantas, C. V., Garg, S., Naka, K. K., Thury, A., Hoye, A., & Michalis, L. K. (2011). Focus on the research utility of intravascular ultrasound - Comparison with other invasive modalities. *Cardiovascular Ultrasound*, *9*(1), 2. doi:10.1186/1476-7120-9-2

Bourantas, C. V., Naka, K. K., Garg, S., Thackray, S., Papadopoulos, D., & Alamgir, F. M. (2010). Clinical indications for intravascular ultrasound imaging. *Echocardiography (Mount Kisco, N.Y.)*, *27*(10), 1282–1290. doi:10.1111/j.1540-8175.2010.01259.x

Bourantas, C. V., Kalatzis, F. G., Papafaklis, M. I., Fotiadis, D. I., Tweddel, A. C., & Kourtis, I. C. (2008). Angiocare: An automated system for fast three-dimensional coronary reconstruction by integrating angiographic and intracoronary ultrasound data. *Catheterization and Cardiovascular Interventions*, *72*(2), 166–175. doi:10.1002/ccd.21527

Bourantas, C. V., Kourtis, I. C., Plissiti, M. E., Fotiadis, D. I., Katsouras, C. S., Papafaklis, M. I., & Michalis, L. K. (2005). A method for 3D reconstruction of coronary arteries using biplane angiography and intravascular ultrasound images. *Computerized Medical Imaging and Graphics*, *29*(8), 597–606. doi:10.1016/j.compmedimag.2005.07.001

Bourantas, C. V., Kalatzis, F. G., Papafaklis, M. I., Fotiadis, D. I., Tweddel, A. C., & Katsouras, C. S. (2008). ANGIOCARE: An automated system for fast three dimensional coronary reconstruction using angiographic and intracoronary ultrasound data. *Catheterization and Cardiovascular Interventions*, *72*(2), 166–175. doi:10.1002/ccd.21527

Bourantas, C. V., Tweddel, A. C., Papafaklis, M. I., Karvelis, P. S., Fotiadis, D. I., & Katsouras, C. S. (2009). Comparison of quantitative coronary angiography with intracoronary ultrasound. Can quantitative coronary angiography accurately estimate the severity of a luminal stenosis? *Angiology*, *60*(2), 169–179.

Bourantas, C. V., Kalatzis, F. G., Papafaklis, M. I., Fotiadis, D. I., Tweddel, A. C., & Kourtis, I. C. (2008). ANGIO-CARE: An automated system for fast three-dimensional coronary reconstruction by integrating angiographic and intracoronary ultrasound data. *Catheterization and Cardiovascular Interventions*, *72*(2), 166–175. doi:10.1002/ccd.21527

Bourantas, C. V., Kourtis, I. C., Plissiti, M. E., Fotiadis, D. I., Katsouras, C. S., & Papafaklis, M. I. (2005). A method for 3D reconstruction of coronary arteries using biplane angiography and intravascular ultrasound images. *Computerized Medical Imaging and Graphics*, *29*(8), 597–606. doi:10.1016/j.compmedimag.2005.07.001

Bourantas, C. V., Garg, S., Naka, K. K., Thury, A., Hoye, A., & Michalis, L. K. (2011). Focus on the research utility of intravascular ultrasound - Comparison with other invasive modalities. *Cardiovascular Ultrasound*, *9*.

Brennan, J., Nazemi, J., Motz, J., & Ramcharitar, S. (2008). The vPredict optical catheter system: Intravascular raman spectroscopy. *EuroIntervention*, *3*, 635–638. doi:10.4244/EIJV3I5A113

Briguori, C., Anzuini, A., Airoldi, F., Gimelli, G., Nishida, T., & Adamian, M. (2001). Intravascular ultrasound criteria for the assessment of the functional significance of intermediate coronary artery stenoses and comparison with fractional flow reserve. *The American Journal of Cardiology*, *87*(2), 136–141. doi:10.1016/S0002-9149(00)01304-7

Brown, B. G., & Zhao, X. Q. (2007). Is intravascular ultrasound the gold standard surrogate for clinically relevant atherosclerosis progression? *Journal of the American College of Cardiology*, *49*(9), 933–938. doi:10.1016/j.jacc.2006.12.014

Brugaletta, S., Garcia-Garcia, H. M., Garg, S., Gomez-Lara, J., Diletti, R., & Onuma, Y. (2010). Temporal changes of coronary artery plaque located behind the struts of the everolimus eluting bioresorbable vascular scaffold. *The International Journal of Cardiovascular Imaging*, *27*(6).

Brugaletta, S., Ribamar Costa Jr, J., & Garcia-Garcia, H. M. (2011). (in press). Assessment of drug-eluting stents and bioresorbable stents by grayscale IVUS and IVUS-based imaging modalities. *The International Journal of Cardiovascular Imaging*. doi:10.1007/s10554-010-9788-8

Bruining, N., Verheye, S., Knaapen, M., Somers, P., Roelandt, J. R., & Regar, E. (2007). Three-dimensional and quantitative analysis of atherosclerotic plaque composition by automated differential echogenicity. *Catheterization and Cardiovascular Interventions*, *70*(7), 968–978. doi:10.1002/ccd.21310

Brunenberg, E., Pujol, O., Romeny, B., & Radeva, P. (2006). Automatic IVUS Segmentation of atherosclerotic plaque with Stop & Go Snake. *Proceedings of Medical Image Computing and Computer-Assisted Intervention: MICCAI*, *9*, 9–16.

Brusseau, E., de Korte, C. L., Mastik, F., Schaar, J., & van der Steen, A. F. W. (2004). Fully automatic luminal contour segmentation in intracoronary ultrasound imaging – A statistical approach. *IEEE Transactions on Medical Imaging*, *23*(5), 554–566. doi:10.1109/TMI.2004.825602

Budoff, M. J., Dowe, D., Jollis, J. G., Gitter, M., Sutherland, J., & Halamert, E. (2008). Diagnostic performance of 64-multidetector row coronary computed tomographic angiography for evaluation of coronary artery stenosis in individuals without known coronary artery disease: results from the prospective multicenter ACCURACY (assessment by coronary computed tomographic angiography of individuals undergoing invasive coronary angiography) trial. *Journal of the American College of Cardiology*, *52*(21), 1724–1732. doi:10.1016/j.jacc.2008.07.031

Budoff, M. J., & Malpeso, J. M. (2011). Is coronary artery calcium the key to assessment of cardiovascular risk in asymptomatic adults? *Journal of Cardiovascular Computed Tomography*, *5*(1). doi:10.1016/j.jcct.2010.11.004

Burke, A. P., Farb, A., Malcom, G. T., Liang, Y. H., Smialek, J., & Virmani, R. (1997). Coronary risk factors and plaque morphology in men with coronary disease who died suddenly. *The New England Journal of Medicine*, *336*(18), 1276–1282. doi:10.1056/NEJM199705013361802

Burke, A. P., Joner, M., & Virmani, R. (2006). IVUS-VH: A predictor of plaque morphology? *European Heart Journal*, *27*(16), 1889–1890. doi:10.1093/eurheartj/ehl126

Burke, A. P., Farb, A., Malcom, G. T., Liang, Y. H., Smialek, J., & Virmani, R. (1997). Coronary risk factors and plaque morphology in men with coronary disease who died suddenly. *The New England Journal of Medicine, 336*(18), 1276–1282. doi:10.1056/NEJM199705013361802

Butterworth, R. (1951). A new operating cardioscope. *The Journal of Thoracic and Cardiovascular Surgery, 22*, 319–322.

Caballero, K. L., Barajas, J., Pujol, O., Rodriguez, O., & Radeva, P. (2007). Using reconstructed IVUS images for coronary plaque classification. *Proceedings of Engineering in Medicine and Biology Society in 29th Annual International Conference of the IEEE,* (pp. 2167–2170).

Cafri, C., de la Guardia, B., Barasch, E., Brink, J., & Smalling, R. W. (2000). Transseptal puncture guided by intracardiac echocardiography during percutaneous transvenous mitral commissurotomy in patients with distorted anatomy of the fossa ovalis. *Catheterization and Cardiovascular Interventions, 50*(4), 463–467. doi:10.1002/1522-726X(200008)50:4<463::AID-CCD21>3.0.CO;2-E

Cai, J. M., Hatsukami, T. S., Ferguson, M. S., Small, R., Polissar, N. L., & Yuan, C. (2002). Classification of human carotid atherosclerotic lesions with in vivo multicontrast magnetic resonance imaging. *Circulation, 106*(11), 1368–1373. doi:10.1161/01.CIR.0000028591.44554.F9

Callans, D. J., Ren, J. F., Schwartzman, D., Gottlieb, C. D., Chaudhry, F. A., & Marchlinski, F. E. (1999). Narrowing of the superior vena cava-right atrium junction during radiofrequency catheter ablation for inappropriate sinus tachycardia: Analysis with intracardiac echocardiography. *Journal of the American College of Cardiology, 33*(6), 1667–1670. doi:10.1016/S0735-1097(99)00047-9

Cannon, C. P., Braunwald, E., McCabe, C. H., Rader, D. J., Rouleau, J. L., & Belder, R. (2004). Intensive versus moderate lipid lowering with statins after acute coronary syndromes. *The New England Journal of Medicine, 350*(15), 1495–1504. doi:10.1056/NEJMoa040583

Cao, Q. L., Zabal, C., Koenig, P., Sandhu, S., & Hijazi, Z. M. (2005). Initial clinical experience with intracardiac echocardiography in guiding transcatheter closure of perimembranous ventricular septal defects: Feasibility and comparison with transesophageal echocardiography. *Catheterization and Cardiovascular Interventions, 66*(2), 258–267. .doi:10.1002/ccd.20463

Caplan, J., Waxman, S., Nesto, R., & Muller, J. (2006). Near infrared spectroscopy for the detection of vulnerable coronary artery plaques. *Journal of the American College of Cardiology, 47*, C92–C96. doi:10.1016/j.jacc.2005.12.045

Capodanno, D., Prati, F., Pawlowsky, T., Cera, M., La Manna, A., & Albertucci, M. (2009). Comparison of optical coherence tomography and intravascular ultrasound for the assessment of in-stent tissue coverage after stent implantation. *EuroInterv, 5*, 538–543. doi:10.4244/EIJV5I5A88

Cardinal, M., Meunier, J., Soulez, G., Maurice, R., Therasse, E., & Cloutier, G. (2006). Intravascular ultrasound image segmentation: A three-dimensional fast-marching method based on gray level distributions. *IEEE Transactions on Medical Imaging, 25*, 590–601. doi:10.1109/TMI.2006.872142

Carlier, S., Kakadiaris, I., Dib, N., Vavuranakis, M., O'Malley, S., & Gul, K. (2005). Vasa vasorum imaging: A new window to the clinical detection of vulnerable atherosclerotic plaques. *Current Atherosclerosis Reports, 7*(4).

Carlier, S. G., Mintz, G. S., & Stone, G. W. (2006). Imaging of atherosclerotic plaque using radiofrequency ultrasound signal processing. *Journal of Nuclear Cardiology, 13*(6), 831–840. doi:10.1016/j.nuclcard.2006.10.013

Carlier, S. G., van Damme, L. C., Blommerde, C. P., Wentzel, J. J., van Langehove, G., & Verheye, S. (2003). Augmentation of wall shear stress inhibits neointimal hyperplasia after stent implantation: Inhibition through reduction of inflammation? *Circulation, 107*(21), 2741–2746. doi:10.1161/01.CIR.0000066914.95878.6D

Caro, C. G. (2009). Discovery of the role of wall shear in atherosclerosis. *Arteriosclerosis, Thrombosis, and Vascular Biology, 29*(2), 158–161. doi:10.1161/ATVBAHA.108.166736

Caro, C. G., Fitz-Gerald, J. M., & Schroter, R. C. (1969). Arterial wall shear and distribution of early atheroma in man. *Nature, 223*(5211), 1159–1160. doi:10.1038/2231159a0

Caro, C. G., Fitz-Gerald, J. M., & Schroter, R. C. (1971). Atheroma and arterial wall shear. Observation, correlation and proposal of a shear dependent mass transfer mechanism for atherogenesis. *Proceedings of the Royal Society of London. Series B. Biological Sciences, 177*(46), 109–159. doi:10.1098/rspb.1971.0019

Carrigan, T. P., Nair, D., Schoenhagen, P., Curtin, R. J., Popovic, Z. B., & Halliburton, S. (2009). Prognostic utility of 64-slice computed tomography in patients with suspected but no documented coronary artery disease. *European Heart Journal, 30*(3), 362–371. doi:10.1093/eurheartj/ehn605

Carter, A. J., Laird, J. R., Farb, A., Kufs, W., Wortham, D. C., & Virmani, R. (1994). Morphologic characteristics of lesion formation and time course of smooth muscle cell proliferation in a porcine proliferative restenosis model. *Journal of the American College of Cardiology, 24*(5), 1398–1405. doi:10.1016/0735-1097(94)90126-0

Casscells, W., Hathorn, B., David, M., Krabach, T., Vaughn, W., & McAllister, H. (1996). Thermal detection of cellular infiltrates in living atherosclerotic plaques: Possible implications for plaque rupture and thrombosis. *Lancet, 347*, 1447–1451. doi:10.1016/S0140-6736(96)91684-0

Casscells, W., Hathorn, B., David, M., Krabach, T., Vaughn, W., & McAllister, H. (1996). Thermal detection of cellular infiltrates in living atherosclerotic plaques: Possible implications for plaque rupture and thrombosis. *Lancet, 347*, 1447–1451. doi:10.1016/S0140-6736(96)91684-0

Cassis, L., & Lodder, R. (1993). Near-IR imaging of atheromas in living arterial tissue. *Analytical Chemistry, 65*, 1247–1256. doi:10.1021/ac00057a023

Cespedes, I., Huang, Y., Ophir, J., & Spratt, S. (1995). Methods for estimation of subsample time delays of digitized echo signals. *Ultrasonic Imaging, 17*(2), 142–171. doi:10.1006/uimg.1995.1007

Cespedes, I., Ophir, J., Ponnekanti, H., & Maklad, N. (1993). Elastography: Elasticity imaging using ultrasound with application to muscle and breast in vivo. *Ultrasonic Imaging, 15*(2), 73–88. doi:10.1006/uimg.1993.1007

Chalana, V., & Kim, Y. (1997). A methodology for evaluation of boundary detection algorithms on medical images. *IEEE Transactions on Medical Imaging, 16*(5), 642–652. doi:10.1109/42.640755

Charonko, J., Karri, S., Schmieg, J., Prabhu, S., & Vlachos, P. (2009). In vitro, time-resolved PIV comparison of the effect of stent design on wall shear stress. *Annals of Biomedical Engineering, 37*(7), 1310–1321. doi:10.1007/s10439-009-9697-y

Charonko, J., Karri, S., Schmieg, J., Prabhu, S., & Vlachos, P. (2010). In vitro comparison of the effect of stent configuration on wall shear stress using time-resolved particle image velocimetry. *Annals of Biomedical Engineering, 38*(3), 889–902. doi:10.1007/s10439-010-9915-7

Chatzizisis, Y. S., Jonas, M., Coskun, A. U., Beigel, R., Stone, B. V., & Maynard, C. (2008). Prediction of the localization of high-risk coronary atherosclerotic plaques on the basis of low endothelial shear stress: An intravascular ultrasound and histopathology natural history study. *Circulation, 117*(8), 993–1002. doi:10.1161/CIRCULATIONAHA.107.695254

Chatzizisis, Y. S., Jonas, M., Coskun, A. U., Beigel, R., Stone, B. V., & Maynard, C. (2008). Prediction of the localization of high-risk coronary atherosclerotic plaques on the basis of low endothelial shear stress: An intravascular ultrasound and histopathology natural history study. *Circulation, 117*(8), 993–1002. doi:10.1161/CIRCULATIONAHA.107.695254

Chatzizisis, Y. S., Baker, A. B., Sukhova, G. K., Koskinas, K. C., Papafaklis, M. I., & Beigel, R. (2011). Augmented expression and activity of extracellular matrix-degrading enzymes in regions of low endothelial shear stress colocalize with coronary atheromata with thin fibrous caps in pigs. *Circulation, 123*(6), 621–630. doi:10.1161/CIRCULATIONAHA.110.970038

Chatzizisis, Y. S., Coskun, A. U., Jonas, M., Edelman, E. R., Feldman, C. L., & Stone, P. H. (2007). Role of endothelial shear stress in the natural history of coronary atherosclerosis and vascular remodeling: Molecular, cellular, and vascular behavior. *Journal of the American College of Cardiology, 49*(25), 2379–2393. doi:10.1016/j.jacc.2007.02.059

Chatzizisis, Y. S., Coskun, A. U., Jonas, M., Edelman, E. R., Stone, P. H., & Feldman, C. L. (2007). Risk stratification of individual coronary lesions using local endothelial shear stress: A new paradigm for managing coronary artery disease. *Current Opinion in Cardiology, 22*(6), 552–564. doi:10.1097/HCO.0b013e3282f07548

Chatzizisis, Y. S., Jonas, M., Coskun, A. U., Beigel, R., Stone, B. V., & Maynard, C. (2008). Prediction of the localization of high-risk coronary atherosclerotic plaques on the basis of low endothelial shear stress: an intravascular ultrasound and histopathology natural history study. *Circulation*, *117*(8), 993–1002. doi:10.1161/CIRCULATIONAHA.107.695254

Chatzizisis, Y., Coskun, A., Jonas, M., Edelman, E., Feldman, C., & Stone, P. (2007). Role of endothelial shear stress in the natural history of coronary atherosclerosis and vascular remodeling: Molecular, cellular, and vascular behavior. *Journal of the American College of Cardiology*, *49*, 2379–2393. doi:10.1016/j.jacc.2007.02.059

Chatzizisis, Y. S., Baker, A., Sukhova, G. K., Koskinas, K., Papafaklis, M., & Beigel, R. (2011). Augmented expression and activity of extracellular matrix–degrading enzymes in regions of low endothelial shear stress co-localize with coronary atheromata with thin fibrous caps in pigs. *Circulation*, *123*, 621–630. doi:10.1161/CIRCULATIONAHA.110.970038

Chatzizisis, Y., Giannoglou, G., Matakos, A., Basdekidou, C., Sianos, G., & Panagiotou, A. (2006). In-vivo accuracy of geometrically correct three-dimensional reconstruction of human coronary arteries: Is it influenced by certain parameters? *Coronary Artery Disease*, *17*, 545–551. doi:10.1097/00019501-200609000-00008

Chatzizisis, Y., Giannoglou, G., Sianos, G., Ziakas, A., Tsikaderis, D., & Dardas, P. (2008). In vivo comparative study of linear versus geometrically correct three-dimensional reconstruction of coronary arteries. *The American Journal of Cardiology*, *101*, 263–267. doi:10.1016/j.amjcard.2007.07.070

Chatzizisis, Y., & Giannoglou, G. (2007). Coronary hemodynamics and atherosclerotic wall stiffness: A vicious cycle. *Medical Hypotheses*, *69*(2), 349–355. doi:10.1016/j.mehy.2006.11.053

Chen, B., Ma, F., & Luo, W. (2008). Neointimal coverage of bare-metal and sirolimus-eluting stents evaluated with optical coherence tomography. *Heart (British Cardiac Society)*, *94*, 566–570. doi:10.1136/hrt.2007.118679

Chen, J., Tung, C., Allport, J., Chen, S., Weissleder, R., & Huang, P. (2005). Near-infrared fluorescent imaging of matrix metalloproteinase activity after myocardial infarction. *Circulation*, *111*, 1800–1805. doi:10.1161/01.CIR.0000160936.91849.9F

Chen, J., Tung, C., Mahmood, U., Ntziachristos, V., Gyurko, R., & Fishman, M. (2002). In vivo imaging of proteolytic activity in atherosclerosis. *Circulation*, *105*, 2766–2771. doi:10.1161/01.CIR.0000017860.20619.23

Cheng, G. C., Loree, H. M., Kamm, R. D., Fishbein, M. C., & Lee, R. T. (1993). Distribution of circumferential stress in ruptured and stable atherosclerotic lesions. A structural analysis with histopathological correlation. *Circulation*, *87*(4), 1179–1187.

Cheng, C., Tempel, D., van Haperen, R., de Boer, H. C., Segers, D., & Huisman, M. (2007). Shear stress-induced changes in atherosclerotic plaque composition are modulated by chemokines. *The Journal of Clinical Investigation*, *117*(3), 616–626. doi:10.1172/JCI28180

Cheng, C., Tempel, D., van Haperen, R., van der Baan, A., Grosveld, F., & Daemen, M. J. (2006). Atherosclerotic lesion size and vulnerability are determined by patterns of fluid shear stress. *Circulation*, *113*(23), 2744–2753. doi:10.1161/CIRCULATIONAHA.105.590018

Cheng, C., Tempel, D., van Haperen, R., van der Baan, A., Grosveld, F., & Daemen, M. (2006). Atherosclerotic lesion size and vulnerability are determined by patterns of fluid shear stress. *Circulation*, *113*, 2744–2753. doi:10.1161/CIRCULATIONAHA.105.590018

Cheruvu, P. K., Finn, A. V., Gardner, C., Caplan, J., Goldstein, J., & Stone, G. W. (2007). Frequency and distribution of thin-cap fibroatheroma and ruptured plaques in human coronary arteries: A pathologic study. *Journal of the American College of Cardiology*, *50*(10), 940–949. doi:10.1016/j.jacc.2007.04.086

Chevalier, B., Silber, S., Park, S. J., Garcia, E., Schuler, G., & Suryapranata, H. (2009). Randomized comparison of the Nobori Biolimus A9-eluting coronary stent with the Taxus Liberte paclitaxel-eluting coronary stent in patients with stenosis in native coronary arteries: The NOBORI 1 trial--Phase 2. *Circ Cardiovasc Interv*, *2*(3), 188–195. doi:10.1161/CIRCINTERVENTIONS.108.823443

Chia, S., Christopher, R. O., Takano, M., Tearney, G., Bouma, B., & Jang, I. (2007). In-vivo comparison of coronary plaque characteristics using optical coherence tomography in women vs. men with acute coronary syndrome. *Coronary Artery Disease, 18*, 423–427. doi:10.1097/MCA.0b013e3282583be8

Chia, S., Raffel, O., Takano, M., Tearney, G., Bouma, B., & Jang, I. (2008). Association of statin therapy with reduced coronary plaque rupture: An optical coherence tomography study. *Coronary Artery Disease, 19*, 237–242. doi:10.1097/MCA.0b013e32830042a8

Chia, S., Raffel, O., Takano, M., Tearney, G., Bouma, B., & Jang, I. (2008). Comparison of coronary plaque characteristics between diabetic and non-diabetic subjects: An in vivo optical coherence tomography study. *Diabetes Research and Clinical Practice, 81*, 155–160. doi:10.1016/j.diabres.2008.03.014

Chiu, J. J., Chen, L. J., Chen, C. N., Lee, P. L., & Lee, C. I. (2004). A model for studying the effect of shear stress on interactions between vascular endothelial cells and smooth muscle cells. *Journal of Biomechanics, 37*(4), 531–539. doi:10.1016/j.jbiomech.2003.08.012

Cho, A., Mitchell, L., Koopmans, D., & Langille, B. L. (1997). Effects of changes in blood flow rate on cell death and cell proliferation in carotid arteries of immature rabbits. *Circulation Research, 81*(3), 328–337.

Chow, B., Larose, E., Bilodeau, S., Ellins, M., Galiwango, P., & Kass, M. (2009). The what, when, where, w.ho and how of cardiac computed tomography in 2009: Guidelines for the clinician. *The Canadian Journal of Cardiology, 25*(3), 135. doi:10.1016/S0828-282X(09)70039-X

Chu, B., Kampschulte, A., Ferguson, M. S., Kerwin, W. S., Yarnykh, V. L., & O'Brien, K. D. (2004). Hemorrhage in the atherosclerotic carotid plaque: a high-resolution MRI study. *Stroke, 35*(5), 1079–1084. doi:10.1161/01.STR.0000125856.25309.86

Chugh, S. S., Chan, R. C., Johnson, S. B., & Packer, D. L. (1999). Catheter tip orientation affects radiofrequency ablation lesion size in the canine left ventricle. *Pacing and Clinical Electrophysiology, 22*(3), 413–420. doi:10.1111/j.1540-8159.1999.tb00469.x

Chung, I. M., Gold, H. K., Schwartz, S. M., Ikari, Y., Reidy, M. A., & Wight, T. N. (2002). Enhanced extracellular matrix accumulation in restenosis of coronary arteries after stent deployment. *Journal of the American College of Cardiology, 40*(12), 2072–2081. doi:10.1016/S0735-1097(02)02598-6

Cilingiroglu, M., Oh, J. H., Sugunan, B., Kemp, N. J., Kim, J., & Lee, S. (2006). Detection of vulnerable plaque in a murine model of atherosclerosis with optical coherence tomography. *Catheterization and Cardiovascular Interventions, 67*(6), 915–923. doi:10.1002/ccd.20717

Cilingiroglu, M., Oh, J., & Sugunan, B. (2006). Detection of vulnerable plaque in a murine model of atherosclerosis with optical coherence tomography. *Catheterization and Cardiovascular Interventions, 67*, 915–923. doi:10.1002/ccd.20717

Ciurczak, E., & Drennen, J. (2002). *Pharmaceutical and medical applications of near-infrared spectroscopy.* CRC Press.

Claridge, M., Bate, G., Dineley, J., Hoskins, P., Marshall, T., & Adam, D. (2008). A reproducibility study of a TDI-based method to calculate indices of arterial stiffness. *Ultrasound in Medicine & Biology, 34*(2), 215–220. doi:10.1016/j.ultrasmedbio.2007.08.010

Clarke, M., Figg, N., & Maguire, J. (2006). Apoptosis of vascular smooth muscle cells induces features of plaque vulnerability in atherosclerosis. *Nature Medicine, 12*, 1075–1080. doi:10.1038/nm1459

ClinicalTrials.gov. (2006). *PROSPECT: An imaging study in patients with unstable atherosclerotic lesions.* Retrieved from http://www.clinicaltrials.gov/ct/gui/show/NCT00180466;jsessionid=732C53C19413A1117791F0BE7FE99369?order=9

ClinicalTrials.gov. (2009). Assessment of dual antiplatelet therapy with drug eluting stents (ADAPT-DES). Retrieved from http://clinicaltrials.gov/ct2/show/NCT00638794

Cohn, J., Duprez, D., & Grandits, G. (2005). Arterial elasticity as part of a comprehensive assessment of cardiovascular risk and drug treatment. *Hypertension, 46*(1), 217–220. doi:10.1161/01.HYP.0000165686.50890.c3

Colombo, A., De Gregorio, J., Moussa, I., Kobayashi, Y., Karvouni, E., & Di Mario, C. (2001). Intravascular ultrasound-guided percutaneous transluminal coronary angioplasty with provisional spot stenting for treatment of long coronary lesions. *Journal of the American College of Cardiology*, *38*(5), 1427–1433. doi:10.1016/S0735-1097(01)01557-1

Colombo, A., Hall, P., Nakamura, S., Almagor, Y., Maiello, L., & Martini, G. (1995). Intracoronary stenting without anticoagulation accomplished with intravascular ultrasound guidance. *Circulation*, *91*, 1676–1688.

Colombo, A., Drzewiecki, J., Banning, A., Grube, E., Hauptmann, K., & Silber, S. (2003). Randomized study to assess the effectiveness of slow- and moderate-release polymer-based paclitaxel-eluting stents for coronary artery lesions. *Circulation*, *108*(7), 788–794. doi:10.1161/01.CIR.0000086926.62288.A6

Conley, M. J., Ely, R. L., Kisslo, J., Lee, K. L., McNeer, J. F., & Rosati, R. A. (1978). The prognostic spectrum of left main stenosis. *Circulation*, *57*(5), 947–952.

Cook, S., Wenaweser, P., Togni, M., Billinger, M., Morger, C., & Seiler, C. (2007). Incomplete stent apposition and very late stent thrombosis after drug-eluting stent implantation. *Circulation*, *115*(18), 2426–2434. doi:10.1161/CIRCULATIONAHA.106.658237

Cook, S., Ladich, E., Nakazawa, G., Eshtehardi, P., Neidhart, M., & Vogel, R. (2009). Correlation of intravascular ultrasound findings with histopathological analysis of thrombus aspirates in patients with very late drug-eluting stent thrombosis. *Circulation*, *120*(5), 391–399. doi:10.1161/CIRCULATIONAHA.109.854398

Cook, S., & Windecker, S. (2009). Early stent thrombosis: Past, present, and future. *Circulation*, *119*, 657–659. doi:10.1161/CIRCULATIONAHA.108.842757

Coombs, B. D., Rapp, J. H., Ursell, P. C., Reilly, L. M., & Saloner, D. (2001). Structure of plaque at carotid bifurcation: high-resolution MRI with histological correlation. *Stroke*, *32*(11), 2516–2521. doi:10.1161/hs1101.098663

Cormode, D. P., Roessl, E., Thran, A., Skajaa, T., Gordon, R. E., & Schlomka, J. P. (2010). Atherosclerotic plaque composition: analysis with multicolor CT and targeted gold nanoparticles. *Radiology*, *256*(3), 774–782. doi:10.1148/radiol.10092473

Cornily, J. C., Hyafil, F., Calcagno, C., Briley-Saebo, K. C., Tunstead, J., & Aguinaldo, J. G. (2008). Evaluation of neovessels in atherosclerotic plaques of rabbits using an albumin-binding intravascular contrast agent and MRI. *Journal of Magnetic Resonance Imaging*, *27*(6), 1406–1411. doi:10.1002/jmri.21369

Corti, R., Hutter, R., Badimon, J., & Fuster, V. (2004). Evolving concepts in the triad of atherosclerosis, inflammation and thrombosis. *Journal of Thrombosis and Thrombolysis*, *17*, 35–44. doi:10.1023/B:THRO.0000036027.39353.70

Cortis, B., Hussein, H., Khandekar, C., Principe, J., & Tkaczuk, R. (1984). Angioscopy in vivo. *Catheterization and Cardiovascular Diagnosis*, *10*(5), 493–500. doi:10.1002/ccd.1810100513

Coskun, A. U., Yeghiazarians, Y., Kinlay, S., Clark, M. E., Ilegbusi, O. J., & Wahle, A. (2003). Reproducibility of coronary lumen, plaque, and vessel wall reconstruction and of endothelial shear stress measurements in vivo in humans. *Catheterization and Cardiovascular Interventions*, *60*(1), 67–78. doi:10.1002/ccd.10594

Costa, J. R. Jr, Abizaid, A., Costa, R., Feres, F., Tanajura, L. F., & Maldonado, G. (2009). 1-year results of the hydroxyapatite polymer-free sirolimus-eluting stent for the treatment of single de novo coronary lesions: The VESTASYNC I trial. *JACC: Cardiovascular Interventions*, *2*(5), 422–427. doi:10.1016/j.jcin.2009.02.009

Costa, J. R. Jr, Abizaid, A., Feres, F., Costa, R., Seixas, A. C., & Maia, F. (2008). EXCELLA First-in-Man (FIM) study: Safety and efficacy of novolimus-eluting stent in de novo coronary lesions. *EuroIntervention*, *4*(1), 53–58. doi:10.4244/EIJV4I1A10

Cothren, R., Shekhar, R., Tuzcu, E., Nissen, S., Cornhill, J., & Vince, D. (2000). Three-dimensional reconstruction of the coronary artery wall by image fusion of intravascular ultrasound and bi-plane angiography. *International Journal of Cardiac Imaging*, *16*, 69–85. doi:10.1023/A:1006304419505

Courtney, B., Nakamura, M., Tsugita, R., Lilly, R., Basisht, R., & Grube, E. (2004). Validation of a thermographic guidewire for endoluminal mapping of atherosclerotic disease: An in vitro study. *Catheterization and Cardiovascular Interventions*, *62*, 221–229. doi:10.1002/ccd.10750

•

Cuisset, T., Beauloye, C., Melikian, N., Hamilos, M., Sarma, J., & Sarno, G. (2009). In vitro and in vivo studies on thermistor-based intracoronary temperature measurements: Effect of pressure and flow. *Catheterization and Cardiovascular Interventions, 73*, 224–230. doi:10.1002/ccd.21780

Cunningham, K. S., & Gotlieb, A. I. (2005). The role of shear stress in the pathogenesis of atherosclerosis. *Laboratory Investigation, 85*(1), 9–23.

Cutler, E., Levine, S., & Beck, C. (1924). The surgical treatment of mitral stenosis. *Experimental and Clinical Studies Arch Surg, 9*, 689–821.

Daccarett, M., Segerson, N. M., Günther, J., Nölker, G., Gutleben, K., Brachmann, J., & Marrouche, N. F. (2007). Blinded correlation study of three-dimensional electro-anatomical image integration and phased array intra-cardiac echocardiography for left atrial mapping. *Europace, 9*(10), 923–926. .doi:10.1093/europace/eum192

Daoud, E. G., Kalbfletsch, S. J., & Hummel, J. D. (1999). Intracardiac echocardiography to guide transseptal left heart catheterization for radiofrequency catheter ablation. *Journal of Cardiovascular Electrophysiology, 10*(3), 358–363. .doi:10.1111/j.1540-8167.1999.tb00683.x

Daugherty, A., & Rateri, D. L. (2002). T lymphocytes in atherosclerosis: the yin-yang of Th1 and Th2 influence on lesion formation. *Circulation Research, 90*(10), 1039–1040. doi:10.1161/01.RES.0000021397.28936.F9

Davidson, C. J., Sheikh, K. H., Kisslo, K. B., Phillips, H. R., Peter, R. H., & Behar, V. S. (1991). Intracoronary ultrasound evaluation of interventional technologies. *The American Journal of Cardiology, 68*(13), 1305–1309. doi:10.1016/0002-9149(91)90236-E

Davies, M. J., Richardson, P. D., Woolf, N., Katz, D. R., & Mann, J. (1993). Risk of thrombosis in human atherosclerotic plaques: Role of extracellular lipid, macrophage, and smooth muscle cell content. *British Heart Journal, 69*(5), 377–381. doi:10.1136/hrt.69.5.377

Davies, M. J. (1996). Stability and instability: Two faces of coronary atherosclerosis. The Paul Dudley White Lecture 1995. *Circulation, 94*(8), 2013–2020.

Davies, P. F. (2009). Hemodynamic shear stress and the endothelium in cardiovascular pathophysiology. *Nature Clinical Practice. Cardiovascular Medicine, 6*(1), 16–26. doi:10.1038/ncpcardio1397

De Franco, A. C., Nissen, S. E., Tuzcu, E. M., & Whitlow, P. L. (1996). Incremental value of intravascular ultrasound during rotational coronary atherectomy. *Catheterization and Cardiovascular Diagnosis*, (Suppl), 23–33.

de Jaegere, P., Mudra, H., Figulla, H., Almagor, Y., Doucet, S., & Penn, I. (1998). Intravascular ultrasound-guided optimized stent deployment. Immediate and 6 months clinical and angiographic results from the Multicenter Ultrasound Stenting in Coronaries Study (MUSIC Study). *European Heart Journal, 19*, 1214–1223. doi:10.1053/euhj.1998.1012

de Korte, C. L., Pasterkamp, G., van der Steen, A. F., Woutman, H. A., & Bom, N. (2000). Characterization of plaque components with intravascular ultrasound elastography in human femoral and coronary arteries in vitro. *Circulation, 102*(6), 617–623.

de Korte, C. L., Sierevogel, M. J., Mastik, F., Strijder, C., Schaar, J. A., & Velema, E. (2002). Identification of atherosclerotic plaque components with intravascular ultrasound elastography in vivo: A Yucatan pig study. *Circulation, 105*(14), 1627–1630. doi:10.1161/01.CIR.0000014988.66572.2E

de Korte, C., van der Steen, A., Cespedes, E., & Pasterkamp, G. (1998). Intravascular ultrasound elastography in human arteries: Initial experience in vitro. *Ultrasound in Medicine & Biology, 24*, 401–408. doi:10.1016/S0301-5629(97)00280-9

de Winter, S., Heller, I., Hamers, R., de Feyter, P., Serruys, P., & Roelandt, J. (2003). Computer assisted three-dimensional plaque characterization in ultracoronary ultrasound studies. *Computers in Cardiology, 30*, 73–76.

Dee, P., & Crosby, I. (1977). Fibreoptic studies of the aortic valve in dogs. *British Heart Journal, 39*, 459–461. doi:10.1136/hrt.39.4.459

Deguchi, J., Aikawa, E., Libby, P., Vachon, J., Inada, M., & Krane, S. (2005). Matrix metalloproteinase-13/collagenase-3 deletion promotes collagen accumulation and organization in mouse atherosclerotic plaques. *Circulation, 112*, 2708–2715. doi:10.1161/CIRCULATIONAHA.105.562041

Deguchi, J., Aikawa, M., Tung, C., Aikawa, E., Kim, D., & Ntziachristos, V. (2006). Inflammation in atherosclerosis: Visualizing matrix metalloproteinase action in macrophages in vivo. *Circulation*, *114*, 55–62. doi:10.1161/CIRCULATIONAHA.106.619056

DeMaria, A. N., Narula, J., Mahmud, E., & Tsimikas, S. (2006). Imaging vulnerable plaque by ultrasound. *Journal of the American College of Cardiology*, *47*(8Suppl), C32–C39. doi:10.1016/j.jacc.2005.11.047

Dempsey, R., Davis, D., Buice, R., & Lodder, R. (1996). Biological and medical applications of near-infrared spectrometry. *Applied Spectroscopy*, 5018A–5034A.

Detrano, R. C., Doherty, T. M., Davies, M. J., & Stary, H. C. (2000). Predicting coronary events with coronary calcium: Pathophysiologic and clinical problems. *Current Problems in Cardiology*, *25*(6), 374–402. doi:10.1067/mcd.2000.104848

Dewey, M., Zimmermann, E., Deissenrieder, F., Laule, M., Dübel, H., & Schlattmann, P. (2009). Noninvasive coronary angiography by 320-row computed tomography with lower radiation exposure and maintained diagnostic accuracy: Comparison of results with cardiac catheterization in a head-to-head pilot investigation. *Circulation*, *120*(10), 867–875. doi:10.1161/CIRCULATIONAHA.109.859280

Dhawale, P., Rasheed, Q., Griffin, N., Wilson, D., & Hodgson, J. (1993). Intracoronary ultrasound plaque volume quantification . In *Proc Comput Cardiol* (pp. 121–124). Los Alamitos, CA: IEEE Computer Society Press.

Di Mario, C., Gorge, G., Peters, R., & Kearney, P., F., P., Hausmann, D., et al. (1998). Clinical application and image interpretation in intracoronary ultrasound. *European Heart Journal*, *19*, 207–229. doi:10.1053/euhj.1996.0433

Di Mario, C., Gorge, G., Peters, R., Kearney, P., Pinto, F., & Hausmann, D. (1998). Clinical application and image interpretation in intracoronary ultrasound. Study Group on Intracoronary Imaging of the Working Group of Coronary Circulation and of the Subgroup on Intravascular Ultrasound of the Working Group of Echocardiography of the European Society of Cardiology. *European Heart Journal*, *19*(2), 207–229. doi:10.1053/euhj.1996.0433

Diethrich, E. B., Pauliina Margolis, M., Reid, D. B., Burke, A., Ramaiah, V., & Rodriguez-Lopez, J. A. (2007). Virtual histology intravascular ultrasound assessment of carotid artery disease: the Carotid Artery Plaque Virtual Histology Evaluation (CAPITAL) study. *Journal of Endovascular Therapy*, *14*(5), 676–686. doi:10.1583/1545-1550(2007)14[676:VHIUAO]2.0.CO;2

Ding, C., Rao, L., Nagueh, S. F., & Khoury, D. S. (2005). Dynamic three-dimensional visualization of the left ventricle by intracardiac echocardiography. *Ultrasound in Medicine & Biology*, *31*(1), 15–21. doi:10.1016/j.ultrasmedbio.2004.09.016

Doi, H., Maehara, A., Mintz, G. S., Yu, A., Wang, H., & Mandinov, L. (2009). Impact of post-intervention minimal stent area on 9-month follow-up patency of paclitaxel-eluting stents an integrated intravascular ultrasound analysis from the TAXUS IV, V, and VI and TAXUS ATLAS workhorse, long lesion, and direct stent trials. *JACC: Cardiovascular Interventions*, *2*(12), 1269–1275. doi:10.1016/j.jcin.2009.10.005

Dollery, C., & Libby, P. (2006). Atherosclerosis and proteinase activation. *Cardiovascular Research*, *69*, 625–635. doi:10.1016/j.cardiores.2005.11.003

Doyley, M. M., Mastik, F., de Korte, C. L., Carlier, S. G., Cespedes, E. I., & Serruys, P. W. (2001). Advancing intravascular ultrasonic palpation toward clinical applications. *Ultrasound in Medicine & Biology*, *27*(11), 1471–1480. doi:10.1016/S0301-5629(01)00457-4

Doyley, M., Mastik, F., & de Korte, C. (2001). Advancing intravascular ultrasonic palpation toward clinical applications. *Ultrasound in Medicine & Biology*, *27*, 1471–1480. doi:10.1016/S0301-5629(01)00457-4

Drakopoulou, M., Toutouzas, K., Karanasos, A., Synetos, A., Moldovan, C., Grassos, H., *et al.* (2010). *Association of the extent of early athetomatic lesions with thermal heterogeneity assessed non-invasively by microwave radiometry. An experimental study.* ESC2010.

Dudek, D., Rzeszutko, L., Legutko, J., Wizimirski, M., Chyrchel, M., & Witanek, B. (2005). High-risk coronary artery plaques diagnosed by intracoronary thermography. *Kardiologia Polska*, *62*, 383–389.

Ehara, S., Kobayashi, Y., Yoshiyama, M., Shimada, K., Shimada, Y., & Fukuda, D. (2004). Spotty calcification typifies the culprit plaque in patients with acute myocardial infarction: An intravascular ultrasound study. *Circulation*, *110*(22), 3424–3429. doi:10.1161/01.CIR.0000148131.41425.E9

Epstein, L. M., Smith, T., & TenHoff, H. (1998). Nonfluoroscopic transseptal catheterization: Safety and efficacy of intracardiac echocardiographic guidance. *Journal of Cardiovascular Electrophysiology*, *9*(6), 625–630. doi:10.1111/j.1540-8167.1998.tb00945.x

Escolar, E., Mintz, G. S., Popma, J., Michalek, A., Kim, S. W., & Mandinov, L. (2007). Meta-analysis of angiographic versus intravascular ultrasound parameters of drug-eluting stent efficacy (from TAXUS IV, V, and VI). *The American Journal of Cardiology*, *100*(4), 621–626. doi:10.1016/j.amjcard.2007.03.076

Escolar, E., Weigold, G., Fuisz, A., & Weissman, N. (2006). New imaging techniques for diagnosing coronary artery disease. *Canadian Medical Association Journal*, *174*, 487–495. doi:10.1503/cmaj.050925

Evans, J. L., Ng, K. H., Wiet, S. G., Vonesh, M. J., Burns, W. B., & Radvany, M. G. (1996). Accurate three-dimensional reconstruction of intravascular ultrasound data: Spatially correct three-dimensional reconstructions. *Circulation*, *93*, 567–576.

Faber, T. L., Santana, C. A., Garcia, E. V., Candell-Riera, J., Folks, R. D., & Peifer, J. W. (2004). Three-dimensional fusion of coronary arteries with myocardial perfusion distributions: Clinical validation. *Journal of Nuclear Medicine*, *45*(5), 745–753.

Falk, E., Shah, P. K., & Fuster, V. (1995). Coronary plaque disruption. *Circulation*, *92*(3), 657–671.

Fan, C., Kim, J., & Lee, J. (2010). Different vascular healing patterns with various drug-eluting stents in primary percutaneous coronary intervention for ST-segment elevation myocardial infarction: Optical coherence tomographic findings. *The American Journal of Cardiology*, *105*, 972–976. doi:10.1016/j.amjcard.2009.11.018

Farb, A., Burke, A., Kolodgie, F., & Virmani, R. (2003). Pathological mechanisms of fatal late coronary stent thrombosis in humans. *Circulation*, *108*, 1701–1706. doi:10.1161/01.CIR.0000091115.05480.B0

Farb, A., Burke, A. P., Tang, A. L., Liang, T. Y., Mannan, P., & Smialek, J. (1996). Coronary plaque erosion without rupture into a lipid core. A frequent cause of coronary thrombosis in sudden coronary death. *Circulation*, *93*(7), 1354–1363.

Farb, A., Heller, P. F., Shroff, S., Cheng, L., Kolodgie, F. D., & Carter, A. J. (2001). Pathological analysis of local delivery of paclitaxel via a polymer-coated stent. *Circulation*, *104*(4), 473–479. doi:10.1161/hc3001.092037

Fayad, Z. A., & Fuster, V. (2001). Clinical imaging of the high-risk or vulnerable atherosclerotic plaque. *Circulation Research*, *89*(4), 305–316. doi:10.1161/hh1601.095596

Feldman, T. (2000). Rheumatic mitral stenosis. *Current Treatment Options in Cardiovascular Medicine*, *2*(2), 93–103. doi:10.1007/s11936-000-0002-5

Feldman, C. L., Ilegbusi, O. J., Hu, Z., Nesto, R., Waxman, S., & Stone, P. H. (2002). Determination of in vivo velocity and endothelial shear stress patterns with phasic flow in human coronary arteries: A methodology to predict progression of coronary atherosclerosis. *American Heart Journal*, *143*(6), 931–939. doi:10.1067/mhj.2002.123118

Feres, F., Andrade, P. B., Costa, R. A., de Ribamar Costa, J. Jr, Abizaid, A., & Staico, R. (2009). Angiographic and intravascular ultrasound findings following implantation of the Endeavor zotarolimus-eluting stents in patients from the real-world clinical practice. *EuroIntervention*, *5*(3), 355–362. doi:10.4244/V5I3A56

Feres, F., Munoz, J. S., Abizaid, A., Albertal, M., Mintz, G. S., & Staico, R. (2005). Comparison between sirolimus-eluting stents and intracoronary catheter-based beta radiation for the treatment of in-stent restenosis. *The American Journal of Cardiology*, *96*(12), 1656–1662. doi:10.1016/j.amjcard.2005.07.081

Filho, E. S., Saijo, Y., Tanaka, A., & Yoshizawa, M. (2008). Detection and quantification of calcifications in intravascular ultrasound images by automatic thresholding. *Ultrasound in Medicine & Biology*, *34*(1), 160–165. doi:10.1016/j.ultrasmedbio.2007.06.025

Filho, S., Saijo, Y., Tanaka, A., Yambe, T., Li, S., & Yoshizawa, M. (2007). Automated calcification detection and quantification in intravascular ultrasound images by adaptive thresholding. *Proceedings of World Congress on Medical Physics and Biomedical Engineering*, *14*, 1421–1425. doi:10.1007/978-3-540-36841-0_348

Finet, G., Maurincomme, E., Reiber, J., Savalle, L., Magnin, I., & Beaune, J. (1998). Evaluation of an automatic intraluminal edge detection technique for intravascular ultrasound images. *Circulation Journal, 62*(2), 115–121. doi:10.1253/jcj.62.115

Finn, A. V., Chandrashekhar, Y., & Narula, J. (2010). Seeking alternatives to hard end points: Is imaging the best approach? *Circulation, 121*(10), 1165–1168. doi:10.1161/CIR.0b013e3181d83b4f

Finn, A. V., Nakano, M., Narula, J., Kolodgie, F. D., & Virmani, R. (2010). Concept of vulnerable/unstable plaque. *Arteriosclerosis, Thrombosis, and Vascular Biology, 30*(7), 1282–1292. doi:10.1161/ATVBAHA.108.179739

Finn, A. V., Nakazawa, G., Joner, M., Kolodgie, F. D., Mont, E. K., & Gold, H. K. (2007). Vascular responses to drug eluting stents: importance of delayed healing. *Arteriosclerosis, Thrombosis, and Vascular Biology, 27*(7), 1500–1510. doi:10.1161/ATVBAHA.107.144220

Fischell, T., & Drexler, H. (1996, Jun). Pullback atherectomy (PAC) for the treatment of complex bifurcation coronary artery disease. *Catheterization and Cardiovascular Diagnosis, 38*(2), 218–2. doi:10.1002/(SICI)1097-0304(199606)38:2<218::AID-CCD23>3.0.CO;2-D

Fitzgerald, P. J., St Goar, F. G., Connolly, A. J., Pinto, F. J., Billingham, M. E., & Popp, R. L. (1992). Intravascular ultrasound imaging of coronary arteries. Is three layers the norm? *Circulation, 86*(1), 154–158.

Fitzgerald, P. J., Oshima, A., Hayase, M., Metz, J. A., Bailey, S. R., & Baim, D. S. (2000). Final results of the can routine ultrasound influence stent expansion (CRUISE) study. *Circulation, 102*(5), 523–530.

Foster, G. P., & Picard, M. H. (2001). Intracardiac echocardiography: Current uses and future directions. *Echocardiography-Jnl Cardiovascular Ultrasound & Allied Techniques, 18*(1), 43–48.

Friedman, M. H., Hutchins, G. M., Bargeron, C. B., Deters, O. J., & Mark, F. F. (1981). Correlation between intimal thickness and fluid shear in human arteries. *Atherosclerosis, 39*(3), 425–436. doi:10.1016/0021-9150(81)90027-7

Fry, D. L. (1968). Acute vascular endothelial changes associated with increased blood velocity gradients. *Circulation Research, 22*(2), 165–197.

Fry, D. L. (1969). Certain histological and chemical responses of the vascular interface to acutely induced mechanical stress in the aorta of the dog. *Circulation Research, 24*(1), 93–108.

Fujii, K., Carlier, S. G., Mintz, G. S., Yang, Y. M., Moussa, I., & Weisz, G. (2005). Stent underexpansion and residual reference segment stenosis are related to stent thrombosis after sirolimus-eluting stent implantation: An intravascular ultrasound study. *Journal of the American College of Cardiology, 45*(7), 995–998. doi:10.1016/j.jacc.2004.12.066

Fujii, K., Mintz, G. S., Kobayashi, Y., Carlier, S. G., Takebayashi, H., & Yasuda, T. (2004). Contribution of stent underexpansion to recurrence after sirolimus-eluting stent implantation for in-stent restenosis. *Circulation, 109*(9), 1085–1088. doi:10.1161/01.CIR.0000121327.67756.19

Fujii, K., Kawasaki, D., & Masutani, M. (2010). OCT assessment of thin-cap fibroatheroma distribution in native coronary arteries. *JACC: Cardiovascular Imaging, 3*, 168–175. doi:10.1016/j.jcmg.2009.11.004

Fujii, K., Masutani, M., & Okumura, T. (2008). Frequency and predictor of coronary thin-cap fibroatheroma in patients with acute myocardial infarction and stable angina pectoris a 3-vessel optical coherence tomography study. *Journal of the American College of Cardiology, 52*, 787–788. doi:10.1016/j.jacc.2008.05.030

Fujimoto, H., Tao, S., Dohi, T., Ito, S., Masuda, J., & Haruo, M. (2008). Primary and mid-term outcome of sirolimus-eluting stent implantation with angiographic guidance alone. *Journal of Cardiology, 51*(1), 18–24. doi:10.1016/j.jjcc.2007.09.002

Fujimoto, S., Hartung, D., Ohshima, S., Edwards, D. S., Zhou, J., & Yalamanchili, P. (2008). Molecular imaging of matrix metalloproteinase in atherosclerotic lesions: Resolution with dietary modification and statin therapy. *Journal of the American College of Cardiology, 52*(23), 1847–1857. doi:10.1016/j.jacc.2008.08.048

Funada, R., Oikawa, Y., Yajima, J., Kirigaya, H., Nagashima, K., & Ogasawara, K. (2009). The potential of RF backscattered IVUS data and multidetector-row computed tomography images for tissue characterization of human coronary atherosclerotic plaques. *The International Journal of Cardiovascular Imaging, 25*(5), 471–478. doi:10.1007/s10554-009-9446-1

Furukawa, E., Hibi, K., Kosuge, M., Nakatogawa, T., Toda, N., & Takamura, T. (2005). Intravascular ultrasound predictors of side branch occlusion in bifurcation lesions after percutaneous coronary intervention. *Circulation Journal, 69*(3), 325–330. doi:10.1253/circj.69.325

Gaemperli, O., Husmann, L., Schepis, T., Koepfli, P., Valenta, I., & Jenni, W. (2009). Coronary CT angiography and myocardial perfusion imaging to detect flow-limiting stenoses: A potential gatekeeper for coronary revascularization? *European Heart Journal, 30*(23), 2921–2929. doi:10.1093/eurheartj/ehp304

Gaemperli, O., Schepis, T., Kalff, V., Namdar, M., Valenta, I., & Stefani, L. (2007). Validation of a new cardiac image fusion software for three-dimensional integration of myocardial perfusion SPECT and stand-alone 64-slice CT angiography. *European Journal of Nuclear Medicine and Molecular Imaging, 34*(7), 1097–1106. doi:10.1007/s00259-006-0342-9

Gaemperli, O., Schepis, T., Valenta, I., Husmann, L., Scheffel, H., & Duerst, V. (2007). Cardiac image fusion from stand-alone SPECT and CT: Clinical experience. *Journal of Nuclear Medicine, 48*(5), 696–703. doi:10.2967/jnumed.106.037606

Galande, A., Hilderbrand, S., Weissleder, R., & Tung, C. (2006). Enzyme-targeted fluorescent imaging probes on a multiple antigenic peptide core. *Journal of Medicinal Chemistry, 49*, 4715–4720. doi:10.1021/jm051001a

Gambillara, V., Montorzi, G., Haziza-Pigeon, C., Stergiopulos, N., & Silacci, P. (2005). Arterial wall response to ex vivo exposure to oscillatory shear stress. *Journal of Vascular Research, 42*, 535–544. doi:10.1159/000088343

Gamble, W., & Ennis, R. (1967). Experimental intracardiac visualisation. *The New England Journal of Medicine, 276*, 1397–1403. doi:10.1056/NEJM196706222762502

Garcia, B., Wood, F., Cipher, D., Banerjee, S., & Brilakis, E. (2010). Reproducibility of near-infrared spectroscopy for the detection of lipid core coronary plaques and observed changes after coronary stent implantation. *Catheterization and Cardiovascular Interventions, 76*, 359–365. doi:10.1002/ccd.22500

Garcia-Garcia, H. M., Costa, M. A., & Serruys, P. W. (2010). Imaging of coronary atherosclerosis: Intravascular ultrasound. *European Heart Journal, 31*(20), 2456–2469. doi:10.1093/eurheartj/ehq280

Garcia-Garcia, H. M., Goedhart, D., Schuurbiers, J. C., Kukreja, N., Tanimoto, S., & Daemen, J. (2006). Virtual histology and remodelling index allow in vivo identification of allegedly high-risk coronary plaques in patients with acute coronary syndromes: A three vessel intravascular ultrasound radiofrequency data analysis. *EuroIntervention, 2*(3), 338–344.

Garcia-Garcia, H. M., Mintz, G. S., Lerman, A., Goedhart, D., Schuurbiers, J. C., & Kukreja, N. (2009). Tissue characterisation using intravascular radiofrequency data analysis: Recommendations for aquisition, analysis, interpretation and reporting. *EuroIntervention, 5*, 177–189. doi:10.4244/EIJV5I2A29

Garcia-Garcia, H. M., Goedhart, D., Schuurbiers, J. C., Kukreja, N., Tanimoto, S., & Daemen, J. (2006). Virtual histology and remodelling index allow in vivo identification of allegedly high-risk coronary plaques in patients with acute coronary syndromes: a three vessel intravascular ultrasound radiofrequency data analysis. *EuroIntervention, 2*(3), 338–344.

Garcia-Garcia, H. M., Gonzalo, N., Kukreja, N., & Alfonso, F. (2008). Greyscale intravascular ultrasound and IVUS-radiofrequency tissue characterisation to improve understanding of the mechanisms of coronary stent thrombosis in drug-eluting stents. *EuroIntervention, 4*(Suppl C), C33–C38.

Garcia-Garcia, H. M., Gonzalo, N., Pawar, R., Kukreja, N., Dudek, D., & Thuesen, L. (2009). Assessment of the absorption process following bioabsorbable everolimus-eluting stent implantation: Temporal changes in strain values and tissue composition using intravascular ultrasound radiofrequency data analysis. A substudy of the ABSORB clinical trial. *EuroIntervention, 4*(4), 443–448. doi:10.4244/EIJV4I4A77

Garcia-Garcia, H. M., Costa, M. A., & Serruys, P. W. (2010). Imaging of coronary atherosclerosis: Intravascular ultrasound. *European Heart Journal, 31*(20), 2456–2469C. doi:10.1093/eurheartj/ehq280

Gardner, C. M., Tan, H., Hull, E. L., Lisauskas, J. B., Sum, S. T., & Meese, T. M. (2008). Detection of lipid core coronary plaques in autopsy specimens with a novel catheter-based near-infrared spectroscopy system. *JACC: Cardiovascular Imaging, 1*(5), 638–648. doi:10.1016/j.jcmg.2008.06.001

Gardner, C., Tan, H., & Hull, E. e. (2008). Detection of lipid core coronary plaques in autopsy specimens with a novel catheter-based near-infrared spectroscopy system. *JACC: Cardiovascular Imaging, 1*, 638–648. doi:10.1016/j.jcmg.2008.06.001

Garg, S., Serruys, P. W., van der Ent, M., Schultz, C., Mastik, F., & van Soest, G. (2010). First use in patients of a combined near infra-red spectroscopy and intra-vascular ultrasound catheter to identify composition and structure of coronary plaque. *EuroIntervention, 5*(6), 755–756. doi:10.4244/EIJV5I6A126

Garg, S., Bourantas, C., & Thackray, S. (2008). Suspected coronary artery dissection post-stenting, confirmed by optical coherence tomography. *Heart (British Cardiac Society), 94*(3), 335. doi:10.1136/hrt.2006.108878

Gaster, A. L., Slothuus Skjoldborg, U., Larsen, J., Korsholm, L., von Birgelen, C., & Jensen, S. (2003). Continued improvement of clinical outcome and cost effectiveness following intravascular ultrasound guided PCI: Insights from a prospective, randomised study. *Heart (British Cardiac Society), 89*(9), 1043–1049. doi:10.1136/heart.89.9.1043

Gehan, I. A., Ashley, S., Brooks, S., Kester, R., Ball, S., & Rees, M. (1988). Percutaneous angioscopy and sapphire tip lasing of intimal flaps following angioplasty. *Heart and Vessels, 4*(1), 52.

Gehani, A., Davies, A., Stoodley, K., Ashley, S., Brooks, S., & Rees, M. (1991). Does the Kensey catheter keep a coaxial position inside the arterial lumen? An in vitro angioscopic study. *Cardiovascular and Interventional Radiology, 14*, 222–229. doi:10.1007/BF02578463

Gerber, R., & Colombo, A. (2008). Does IVUS guidance of coronary interventions affect outcome? A prime example of the failure of randomized clinical trials. *Catheterization and Cardiovascular Interventions, 71*, 646–654. doi:10.1002/ccd.21489

Gerber, T., Kuzo, R., Karstaedt, N., Lane, G., Morin, R., & Sheedy, P. (2002). Current results and new developments of coronary angiography with use of contrast-enhanced computed tomography of the heart. *Mayo Clinic Proceedings, 77*(1), 55–71. doi:10.4065/77.1.55

Gerrity, R. G. (1981). The role of the monocyte in atherogenesis: I. Transition of blood-borne monocytes into foam cells in fatty lesions. *American Journal of Pathology, 103*(2), 181–190.

Gerstein, H. C., Ratner, R. E., Cannon, C. P., Serruys, P. W., Garcia-Garcia, H. M., & van Es, G. A. (2010). Effect of rosiglitazone on progression of coronary atherosclerosis in patients with type 2 diabetes mellitus and coronary artery disease: The assessment on the prevention of progression by rosiglitazone on atherosclerosis in diabetes patients with cardiovascular history trial. *Circulation, 121*(10), 1176–1187. doi:10.1161/CIRCULATIONAHA.109.881003

Giannoglou, G., Chatzizisis, Y., Koutkias, V., Kompatsiaris, I., Papadogiorgaki, M., & Mezaris, V. (2007). A novel active contour model for fully automated segmentation of intravascular ultrasound images: in vivo validation in human coronary arteries. *Computers in Biology and Medicine, 37*(9), 1292–1302. doi:10.1016/j.compbiomed.2006.12.003

Giannoglou, G., Chatzizisis, Y., Sianos, G., Tsikaderis, D., Matakos, A., & Koutkias, V. (2006). Integration of multi–modality imaging for accurate 3D reconstruction of human coronary arteries in vivo. *Nuclear Instruments and Methods in Physics Research, 569*, 310–313. doi:10.1016/j.nima.2006.08.057

Giannoglou, G. D., Chatzizisis, Y. S., Sianos, G., Tsikaderis, D., Matakos, A., & Koutkias, V. (2006). In-vivo validation of spatially correct three-dimensional reconstruction of human coronary arteries by integrating intravascular ultrasound and biplane angiography. *Coronary Artery Disease, 17*(6), 533–543. doi:10.1097/00019501-200609000-00007

Giannoglou, G., Koskinas, K., Tziakas, D., Ziakas, A., Antoniadis, A., & Tentes, I. (2009). Total cholesterol content of erythrocyte membranes and coronary atherosclerosis: An intravascular ultrasound pilot study. *Angiology, 60*, 676–682. doi:10.1177/0003319709337307

Giannoglou, G., Chatzizisis, Y., Koutkias, V., Kompatsiaris, I., Papadogiorgaki, M., & Mezaris, V. (2007). A novel active contour model for fully automated segmentation of intravascular ultrasound images: In vivo validation in human coronary arteries. *Computers in Biology and Medicine*, *37*, 1292–1302. doi:10.1016/j.compbiomed.2006.12.003

Giannoglou, G., Chatzizisis, Y., Sianos, G., Tsikaderis, D., Matakos, A., & Koutkias, V.,.... Louridas, G. (2006). In-vivo validation of spatially correct three-dimensional reconstruction of human coronary arteries by integrating intravascular ultrasound and biplane angiography. *Coronary Artery Disease*, *17*, 533–543. doi:10.1097/00019501-200609000-00007

Gijsen, F. J., Wentzel, J. J., Thury, A., Mastik, F., Schaar, J. A., & Schuurbiers, J. C. (2008). Strain distribution over plaques in human coronary arteries relates to shear stress. *American Journal of Physiology. Heart and Circulatory Physiology*, *295*(4), H1608–H1614. doi:10.1152/ajpheart.01081.2007

Gijsen, F. J., Wentzel, J. J., Thury, A., Lamers, B., Schuurbiers, J. C., & Serruys, P. W. (2007). A new imaging technique to study 3-D plaque and shear stress distribution in human coronary artery bifurcations in vivo. *Journal of Biomechanics*, *40*(11), 2349–2357. doi:10.1016/j.jbiomech.2006.12.007

Gijsen, F. J., Oortman, R. M., Wentzel, J. J., Schuurbiers, J. C., Tanabe, K., & Degertekin, M. (2003). Usefulness of shear stress pattern in predicting neointima distribution in sirolimus-eluting stents in coronary arteries. *The American Journal of Cardiology*, *92*(11), 1325–1328. doi:10.1016/j.amjcard.2003.08.017

Gijsen, F. J. (1998). *Modeling of wall shear stress in large arteries.* Doctoral Dissertation, Technische Universiteit Eindhoven, The Netherlands.

Gil, R. J., Pawłowski, T., Dudek, D., Horszczaruk, G., Zmudka, K., & Lesiak, M. (2007). Investigators of direct stenting vs optimal angioplasty trial (DIPOL): Comparison of angiographically guided direct stenting technique with direct stenting and optimal balloon angioplasty guided with intravascular ultrasound. The multicenter, randomized trial results. *American Heart Journal*, *154*(4), 669–675. doi:10.1016/j.ahj.2007.06.017

Gimbrone, M. A. Jr, Topper, J. N., Nagel, T., Anderson, K. R., & Garcia-Cardena, G. (2000). Endothelial dysfunction, hemodynamic forces, and atherogenesis. *Annals of the New York Academy of Sciences*, *902*, 230–239, discussion 239–240. doi:10.1111/j.1749-6632.2000.tb06318.x

Giroud, D., Li, J., Urban, P. B. M., & Rutishauer, W. (1992). Relation of the site of acute myocardial infarction to the most severe coronary arterial stenosis at prior angiography. *The American Journal of Cardiology*, *69*, 729–732. doi:10.1016/0002-9149(92)90495-K

Glagov, S., Weisenberg, E., Zarins, C. K., Stankunavicius, R., & Kolettis, G. J. (1987). Compensatory enlargement of human atherosclerotic coronary arteries. *The New England Journal of Medicine*, *316*(22), 1371–1375. doi:10.1056/NEJM198705283162204

Glaser, R., Selzer, F., Faxon, D. P., Laskey, W. K., Cohen, H. A., & Slater, J. (2005). Clinical progression of incidental, asymptomatic lesions discovered during culprit vessel coronary intervention. *Circulation*, *111*(2), 143–149. doi:10.1161/01.CIR.0000150335.01285.12

Godbout, B., de Guise, J., Soulez, G., & Cloutier, G. (2005). 3D elastic registration of vessel structures from IVUS data on biplane angiography. *Academic Radiology*, *12*(1), 10–16. doi:10.1016/j.acra.2004.10.058

Goderie, T., van Soest, G., & Garcia-Garcia, H. (2010). Combined optical coherence tomography and intravascular ultrasound radio frequency data analysis for plaque characterization. Classification accuracy of human coronary plaques in vitro. *The International Journal of Cardiovascular Imaging*, *26*(8). doi:10.1007/s10554-010-9631-2

Goldberg, S., Colombo, A., Nakamura, S., Almagor, Y., Maiello, L., & Tobis, J. (1994). Benefit of intracoronary ultrasound in the deployment of Palmaz– Schatz stents. *Journal of the American College of Cardiology*, *24*, 996–1003. doi:10.1016/0735-1097(94)90861-3

Goldstein, J. A., Demetriou, D., Grines, C. L., Pica, M., Shoukfeh, M., & O'Neill, W. W. (2000). Multiple complex coronary plaques in patients with acute myocardial infarction. *The New England Journal of Medicine*, *343*(13), 915–922. doi:10.1056/NEJM200009283431303

Goldstein, J. (2009). CT angiography: Imaging anatomy to deduce coronary physiology. *Catheterization and Cardiovascular Interventions, 73*, 503–505. doi:10.1002/ccd.22005

Goldstein, J., Grines, C., & Fischell, T. (2009). Coronary embolization following balloon dilation of lipid-core plaques. *JACC: Cardiovascular Imaging, 2*, 1420–1424. doi:10.1016/j.jcmg.2009.10.003

Gonzalo, N., Garcia-Garcia, H. M., Ligthart, J., Rodriguez-Granillo, G., Meliga, E., & Onuma, Y. (2008). Coronary plaque composition as assessed by greyscale intravascular ultrasound and radiofrequency spectral data analysis. *The International Journal of Cardiovascular Imaging, 24*(8), 811–818. doi:10.1007/s10554-008-9324-2

Gonzalo, N., Garcia-Garcia, H. M., Regar, E., Barlis, P., Wentzel, J., & Onuma, Y. (2009). In vivo assessment of high-risk coronary plaques at bifurcations with combined intravascular ultrasound and optical coherence tomography. *JACC: Cardiovascular Imaging, 2*(4), 473–482. doi:10.1016/j.jcmg.2008.11.016

Gonzalo, N., Serruys, P. W., Barlis, P., Ligthart, J., Garcia-Garcia, H. M., & Regar, E. (2010). Multi-modality intra-coronary plaque characterization: A pilot study. *International Journal of Cardiology, 138*(1), 32–39. doi:10.1016/j.ijcard.2008.08.030

Gonzalo, N., Barlis, P., Serruys, P., Garcia-Garcia, H., Onuma, Y., & Ligthart, J. (2009). Incomplete stent apposition and delayed tissue coverage are more frequent in drug-eluting stents implanted during primary percutaneous coronary intervention for ST-segment elevation myocardial infarction than in drug-eluting stents implanted for stable/un. *J Am Coll Cardiol Intv, 2*, 445–452.

Gonzalo, N., Garcia-Garcia, H., & Regar, E. (2009). In vivo assessment of high-risk coronary plaques at bifurcations with combined intravascular ultrasound and optical coherence tomography. *JACC: Cardiovascular Imaging, 2*, 473–482. doi:10.1016/j.jcmg.2008.11.016

Gonzalo, N., Serruys, P., Barlis, P., Ligthart, J., Garcia-Garcia, H., & Regar, E. (2010). Multi-modality intra-coronary plaque characterization: A pilot study. *International Journal of Cardiology, 138*, 32–39. doi:10.1016/j.ijcard.2008.08.030

Gonzalo, N., Serruys, P., & Okamura, T. (2009). Optical coherence tomography assessment of the acute effects of stent implantation on the vessel wall: A systematic quantitative approach. *Heart (British Cardiac Society), 95*, 1913–1919. doi:10.1136/hrt.2009.172072

Gonzalo, N., Serruys, P., & Okamura, T. (2009). Optical coherence tomography patterns of stent restenosis. *American Heart Journal, 158*, 284–293. doi:10.1016/j.ahj.2009.06.004

Gonzalo, N., Garcia-Garcia, H., & Ligthart, J. (2008). Coronary plaque composition as assessed by greyscale intravascular ultrasound and radiofrequency spectral data analysis. *The International Journal of Cardiovascular Imaging, 24*, 811–818. doi:10.1007/s10554-008-9324-2

Gonzalo, N., Garcia-Garcia, H. M., & Serruys, P. W. (2009). Reproducibility of quantitative optical coherence tomography for stent analysis. *EuroIntervention, 5*(2), 224–232. doi:10.4244/EIJV5I2A35

Goshtasby, A., Turner, D. A., & Ackermann, L. V. (1992). Matching of tomographic slices for interpolation. *IEEE Transactions on Medical Imaging, 11*, 507–516. doi:10.1109/42.192686

Gössl, M., Versari, D., Hildebrandt, H., Bajanowski, T., Sangiorgi, G., & Erbel, R. (2010). Segmental heterogeneity of vasa vasorum neovascularization in human coronary atherosclerosis. *JACC: Cardiovascular Imaging, 3*(1), 32–40. doi:10.1016/j.jcmg.2009.10.009

Gottlieb, I., Miller, J. M., Arbab-Zadeh, A., Dewey, M., Clouse, M. E., & Sara, L.. The absence of coronary calcification does not exclude obstructive coronary artery disease or the need for revascularization in patients referred for conventional coronary angiography. *Journal of the American College of Cardiology, 55*(7), 627–634. doi:10.1016/j.jacc.2009.07.072

Graf, K., Dietrich, T., Tachezy, M., Scholle, F., Licha, K., & Stawowy, P. (2008). Monitoring therapeutical intervention with ezetimibe using targeted near-infrared fluorescence imaging in experimental atherosclerosis. *Molecular Imaging, 7*, 68–76.

Granada, J. F., Wallace-Bradley, D., Win, H. K., Alviar, C. L., Builes, A., & Lev, E. I. (2007). In vivo plaque characterization using intravascular ultrasound-virtual histology in a porcine model of complex coronary lesions. *Arteriosclerosis, Thrombosis, and Vascular Biology*, *27*(2), 387–393. doi:10.1161/01.ATV.0000253907.51681.0e

Green, N. E., Hansgen, A. R., & Carroll, J. D. (2004). Initial clinical experience with intracardiac echocardiography in guiding balloon mitral valvuloplasty: Technique, safety, utility, and limitations. *Catheterization and Cardiovascular Interventions*, *63*(3), 385–394. .doi:10.1002/ccd.20177

Guagliumi, G., & Sirbu, V. (2008). Optical coherence tomography: High resolution intravascular imaging to evaluate vascular healing after coronary stenting. *Catheterization and Cardiovascular Interventions*, *72*(2), 237–247. doi:10.1002/ccd.21606

Guagliumi, G., & Sirbu, V. (2008). Optical coherence tomography: High resolution intravascular imaging to evaluate vascular healing after coronary stenting. *Cath & Cardiovasc Int*, *72*, 237–247. doi:10.1002/ccd.21606

Guedes, A., Keller, P. F., L'Allier, P. L., Lesperance, J., Gregoire, J., & Tardif, J. C. (2005). Long-term safety of intravascular ultrasound in nontransplant, nonintervened, atherosclerotic coronary arteries. *Journal of the American College of Cardiology*, *45*(4), 559–564. doi:10.1016/j.jacc.2004.10.063

Guetta, V., Mosseri, M., & Shechter, M. e. (2007). Safety and efficacy of the FilterWire EZ in acute ST-segment elevation myocardial infarction. *The American Journal of Cardiology*, *99*, 911–915. doi:10.1016/j.amjcard.2006.11.037

Gurmeric, S., Isguder, G., Carlier, S., & Unal, G. (2009). A new 3-D automated computational method to evaluate in-stent neointimal hyperplasia in in-vivo intravascular optical coherence tomography pullbacks. *Med Image Comput Comput Assist Interv*, *12*, 776–785.

Haas, C., Ermert, H., Holt, S., Grewe, P., Machraoui, A., & Barmeyer, J. (2000). Segmentation of 3D intravascular ultrasonic images based on a random field model. *Ultrasound in Medicine & Biology*, *26*(2), 297–306. doi:10.1016/S0301-5629(99)00139-8

Habara, M., Terashima, M., & Suzuki, T. (2009). Detection of atherosclerotic progression with rupture of degenerated in-stent intima five years after bare-metal stent implantation using optical coherence tomography. *The Journal of Invasive Cardiology*, *21*, 552–553.

Hackett, D., Davies, G., & Maseri, A. (1988). Pre-existing coronary stenoses in patients with first myocardial infarction are not necessarily severe. *European Heart Journal*, *9*(12), 1317–1323.

Hagenaars, T., Gussenhoven, E. J., Van Der Linden, E., & Bom, N. (2000). Reproducibility of calcified lesion quantification: A longitudinal intravascular ultrasound study. *Ultrasound in Medicine & Biology*, *26*, 1075–1079. doi:10.1016/S0301-5629(00)00246-5

Hahn, K., Gal, R., Sarnoski, J., Kubota, J., Schmidt, D. H., & Bajwa, T. K. (2009). Transesophageal echocardiographically guided atrial transseptal catheterization in patients with normal-sized atria: Incidence of complications. *Clinical Cardiology*, *18*(4), 217–220. doi:10.1002/clc.4960180408

Hahn, C., & Schwartz, M. A. (2009). Mechanotransduction in vascular physiology and atherogenesis. *Nature Reviews. Molecular Cell Biology*, *10*(1), 53–62. doi:10.1038/nrm2596

Hamdan, A., Assali, A., Fuchs, S., Battler, A., & Kornowski, R. (2007). Imaging of vulnerable coronary artery plaques. *Catheterization and Cardiovascular Interventions*, *70*, 65–74. doi:10.1002/ccd.21117

Hammers, R., Bruining, N., Knook, M., Sabate, M., & Roelandt, J. R. T. C. (2001). A novel approach to quantitative analysis of intravascular ultrasound images. *IEEE J*, *28*, 589–592.

Hansen, A., Hehrlein, C., Hardt, S., Bekeredjian, R., Brachmann, J., & Kubler, W. (2001). Is the "candy-wrapper" effect of (32)P radioactive beta-emitting stents due to remodeling or neointimal hyperplasia? Insights from intravascular ultrasound. *Catheterization and Cardiovascular Interventions*, *54*(1), 41–48. doi:10.1002/ccd.1235

Hara, H., Tsunoda, T., Moroi, M., Kubota, T., Kunimasa, T., & Shiba, M. (2006). Ultrasound attenuation behind coronary atheroma without calcification: Mechanism revealed by autopsy. *Acute Cardiac Care*, *8*(2), 110–112. doi:10.1080/14628840600637781

Harken, D., & Glidden, E. (1932). Experiments in intracardiac surgery. *The Journal of Thoracic and Cardiovascular Surgery, 12*, 566–572.

Hartmann, M., Mattern, E. S., Huisman, J., van Houwelingen, G. K., de Man, F. H., & Stoel, M. G. (2009). Reproducibility of volumetric intravascular ultrasound radiofrequency-based analysis of coronary plaque composition in vivo. *The International Journal of Cardiovascular Imaging, 25*(1), 13–23. doi:10.1007/s10554-008-9338-9

Hartung, D., Petrov, A., Cheng, K. T., & Narula, J. (2004). *99mTc-Monocyte chemoattractant protein-1.*

Hasegawa, T., Ako, J., Koo, B. K., Miyazawa, A., Sakurai, R., & Chang, H. (2009). Analysis of left main coronary artery bifurcation lesions treated with biolimus-eluting DEVAX AXXESS plus nitinol self-expanding stent: intravascular ultrasound results of the AXXENT trial. *Catheterization and Cardiovascular Interventions, 73*(1), 34–41. doi:10.1002/ccd.21765

Hassan, A., Nazir, S., & Alkadhi, H. (2010). Technical challenges of coronary CT angiography: Today and tomorrow. *European Journal of Radiology, 79*(2).

Hastings, N. E., Simmers, M. B., McDonald, O. G., Wamhoff, B. R., & Blackman, B. R. (2007). Atherosclerosis-prone hemodynamics differentially regulates endothelial and smooth muscle cell phenotypes and promotes proinflammatory priming. *American Journal of Physiology. Cell Physiology, 293*(6), C1824–C1833. doi:10.1152/ajpcell.00385.2007

Hatsukami, T. S., Ross, R., Polissar, N. L., & Yuan, C. (2000). Visualization of fibrous cap thickness and rupture in human atherosclerotic carotid plaque in vivo with high-resolution magnetic resonance imaging. *Circulation, 102*(9), 959–964.

Hausmann, D., Erbel, R., Alibelli-Chemarin, M. J., Boksch, W., Caracciolo, E., & Cohn, J. M. (1995). The safety of intracoronary ultrasound. A multicenter survey of 2207 examinations. *Circulation, 91*(3), 623–630.

Henneke, K. H., Regar, E., König, A., Werner, F., Klauss, V., & Metz, J. (1999). Impact of target lesion calcification on coronary stent expansion after rotational atherectomy. *American Heart Journal, 137*(1), 93–99. doi:10.1016/S0002-8703(99)70463-1

Hernandez, A., Rotger, D., & Gil, D. (2008). Image-based ECG sampling of IVUS sequences. *IEEE Ultrasonics Symposium*, (pp. 1330–1333).

Herrmann, H. C., Silvestry, F. E., Glaser, R., See, V., Kasner, S., & Bradbury, D. (2005). Percutaneous patent foramen ovale and atrial septal defect closure in adults: Results and device comparison in 100 consecutive implants at a single center. *Catheterization and Cardiovascular Interventions, 64*(2), 197–203. .doi:10.1002/ccd.20260

Hibi, K., Suzuki, T., Honda, Y., Hayase, M., Bonneau, H. N., & Yock, P. G. (2002). Quantitative and spatial relation of baseline atherosclerotic plaque burden and subsequent in-stent neointimal proliferation as determined by intravascular ultrasound. *The American Journal of Cardiology, 90*(10), 1164–1167. doi:10.1016/S0002-9149(02)02791-1

Hijazi, Z. M., Wang, Z., Cao, Q. L., Koenig, P., Waight, D., & Lang, R. (2001). Transcatheter closure of atrial septal defects and patent foramen ovale under intracardiac echocardiographic guidance: Feasibility and comparison with transesophageal echocardiography. *Catheterization and Cardiovascular Interventions, 52*(2), 194–199. doi:10.1002/1522-726X(200102)52:2<194::AID-CCD1046>3.0.CO;2-4

Hiro, T., Fujii, T., Yasumoto, K., Murata, T., Murashige, A., & Matsuzaki, M. (2001). Detection of fibrous cap in atherosclerotic plaque by intravascular ultrasound by use of color mapping of angle-dependent echo-intensity variation. *Circulation, 103*(9), 1206–1211.

Hiro, T., Leung, C. Y., De Guzman, S., Caiozzo, V. J., Farvid, A. R., & Karimi, H. (1997). Are soft echoes really soft? Intravascular ultrasound assessment of mechanical properties in human atherosclerotic tissue. *American Heart Journal, 133*(1), 1–7. doi:10.1016/S0002-8703(97)70241-2

Hiro, T., Kimura, T., Morimoto, T., Miyauchi, K., Nakagawa, Y., & Yamagishi, M. (2009). Effect of intensive statin therapy on regression of coronary atherosclerosis in patients with acute coronary syndrome: a multicenter randomized trial evaluated by volumetric intravascular ultrasound using pitavastatin versus atorvastatin (JAPAN-ACS [Japan assessment of pitavastatin and atorvastatin in acute coronary syndrome] study). *Journal of the American College of Cardiology, 54*(4), 293–302. doi:10.1016/j.jacc.2009.04.033

Hoffmann, R., Mintz, G. S., Dussaillant, G. R., Popma, J. J., Pichard, A. D., & Satler, L. F. (1996). Patterns and mechanisms of in-stent restenosis. A serial intravascular ultrasound study. *Circulation, 94*(6), 1247–1254.

Hoffmann, R., Morice, M., Moses, J., Fitzgerald, P., Mauri, L., & Breithardt, G. (2008). Impact of late incomplete stent apposition after sirolimus-eluting stent implantation on 4-year clinical events: Intravascular ultrasound analysis from the multicentre, randomised, RAVEL, E-SIRIUS and SIRIUS trials. *Heart (British Cardiac Society), 94*, 322–328. doi:10.1136/hrt.2007.120154

Hoffmann, M., Shi, H., Schmitz, B., Schmid, F., Lieberknecht, M., & Schulze, R. (2005). Noninvasive coronary angiography with multislice computed tomography. *Journal of the American Medical Association, 293*(20), 2471–2478. doi:10.1001/jama.293.20.2471

Honda, Y., & Fitzgerald, P. (2008). Frontiers in intravascular imaging technologies. *Circulation, 117*, 2024–2037. doi:10.1161/CIRCULATIONAHA.105.551804

Hong, M. K., Mintz, G. S., Popma, J. J., Kent, K. M., Pichard, A. D., & Satler, L. F. (1994). Limitations of angiography for analyzing coronary atherosclerosis progression or regression. *Annals of Internal Medicine, 121*(5), 348–354.

Hong, Y. J., Mintz, G. S., Kim, S. W., Lu, L., Bui, A. B., & Pichard, A. D. (2007). Impact of remodeling on cardiac events in patients with angiographically mild left main coronary artery disease. *The Journal of Invasive Cardiology, 19*(12), 500–505.

Hong, Y. J., Jeong, M. H., Choi, Y. H., Ko, J. S., Lee, M. G., & Kang, W. Y. (2009). Impact of plaque components on no-reflow phenomenon after stent deployment in patients with acute coronary syndrome: A virtual histology-intravascular ultrasound analysis. *European Heart Journal, 32*.

Hong, Y. J., Jeong, M. H., Choi, Y. H., Ma, E. H., Ko, J. S., & Lee, M. G. (2010). Impact of baseline plaque components on plaque progression in nonintervened coronary segments in patients with angina pectoris on rosuvastatin 10 mg/day. *The American Journal of Cardiology, 106*(9), 1241–1247. doi:10.1016/j.amjcard.2010.06.046

Hong, Y. J., Jeong, M. H., Kim, S. W., Choi, Y. H., Ma, E. H., & Ko, J. S. (2010). Relation between plaque components and plaque prolapse after drug-eluting stent implantation--Virtual histology-intravascular ultrasound. *Circulation Journal, 74*(6), 1142–1151. doi:10.1253/circj.CJ-09-0781

Hong, M. K., Mintz, G. S., Lee, C. W., Kim, Y. H., Lee, S. W., & Song, J. M. (2004). Comparison of coronary plaque rupture between stable angina and acute myocardial infarction: A three-vessel intravascular ultrasound study in 235 patients. *Circulation, 110*(8), 928–933. doi:10.1161/01.CIR.0000139858.69915.2E

Hong, M. K., Mintz, G. S., Lee, C. W., Lee, J. W., Park, J. H., & Park, D. W. (2008). A three-vessel virtual histology intravascular ultrasound analysis of frequency and distribution of thin-cap fibroatheromas in patients with acute coronary syndrome or stable angina pectoris. *The American Journal of Cardiology, 101*(5), 568–572. doi:10.1016/j.amjcard.2007.09.113

Hong, M. K., Park, D. W., Lee, C. W., Lee, S. W., Kim, Y. H., & Kang, D. H. (2009). Effects of statin treatments on coronary plaques assessed by volumetric virtual histology intravascular ultrasound analysis. *JACC: Cardiovascular Interventions, 2*(7), 679–688. doi:10.1016/j.jcin.2009.03.015

Hong, M., Mehran, R., & Dangas, G. (1999). Creatine kinase-MB enzyme elevation following successful saphenous vein graft intervention is associated with late mortality. *Circulation, 100*, 2400–2405.

Hong, M. K., Mintz, G. S., Lee, C. W., Park, D. W., Park, K. M., & Lee, B. K. (2006). Late stent malapposition after drug-eluting stent implantation: An intravascular ultrasound analysis with long-term follow-up. *Circulation, 113*(3), 414–419. doi:10.1161/CIRCULATIONAHA.105.563403

Honye, J., Mahon, D. J., Jain, A., White, C. J., Ramee, S. R., & Wallis, J. B. (1992). Morphological effects of coronary balloon angioplasty in vivo assessed by intravascular ultrasound imaging. *Circulation, 85*(3), 1012–1025.

Hsiung, P., Hardy, J., Friedland, S., Soetikno, R., Du, C., & Wu, A. (2008). Detection of colonic dysplasia in vivo using a targeted heptapeptide and confocal microendoscopy. *Nature Medicine, 14*, 454–458. doi:10.1038/nm1692

Hu, F. B., Tamai, H., Kosuga, K., Kyo, E., Hata, T., & Okada, M. (2003). Intravascular ultrasound-guided directional coronary atherectomy for unprotected left main coronary stenoses with distal bifurcation involvement. *The American Journal of Cardiology*, *92*(8), 936–940. doi:10.1016/S0002-9149(03)00973-1

Huang, D., Swanson, E. A., Lin, C. P., Schuman, J. S., Stinson, W. G., & Chang, W. (1991). Optical coherence tomography. *Science*, *254*(5035), 1178–1181. doi:10.1126/science.1957169

Huisman, J., Egede, R., Rdzanek, A., Bose, D., Erbel, R., & Kochman, J. (2010). Between-centre reproducibility of volumetric intravascular ultrasound radiofrequency-based analyses in mild-to-moderate coronary atherosclerosis: An international multicentre study. *EuroIntervention*, *5*(8), 925–931. doi:10.4244/EIJV5I8A156

Hung, J. S., Fu, M., Yeh, K. H., Wu, C. J., & Wong, P. (1996). Usefulness of intracardiac echocardiography in complex transseptal catheterization during percutaneous transvenous mitral commissurotomy. In *Mayo Clinic Proceedings*.

Hwang, Y., Kim, Y., Chung, I. M., Ryu, J., & Park, H. Coronary heart disease risk assessment and characterization of coronary artery disease using coronary CT angiography: Comparison of asymptomatic and symptomatic groups. *Clinical Radiology*, *65*(8), 601–608. doi:10.1016/j.crad.2010.04.009

Hyafil, F., Cornily, J. C., Feig, J. E., Gordon, R., Vucic, E., & Amirbekian, V. (2007). Noninvasive detection of macrophages using a nanoparticulate contrast agent for computed tomography. *Nature Medicine*, *13*(5), 636–641. doi:10.1038/nm1571

Ikejima, H., Imanishi, T., & Tsujioka, H. (2010). Up-regulation of fractalkine and its receptor, CX3CR1, is associated with coronary plaque rupture in patients with unstable angina pectoris. *Circulation Journal*, *74*, 337–345. doi:10.1253/circj.CJ-09-0484

Imola, F., Mallus, M., Ramazzotti, V., Manzoli, A., Pappalardo, A., & Di Giorgio, A. (2010). Safety and feasibility of frequency domain optical coherence tomography to guide decision making in percutaneous coronary intervention. *EuroInterv*, *6*, 575–581. doi:10.4244/EIJV6I5A97

Inaba, S., Okayama, H., Funada, J. I., Hashida, H., Hiasa, G., & Sumimoto, T. (2009). Relationship between smaller calcifications and lipid-rich plaques on integrated backscatter-intravascular ultrasound. *International Journal of Cardiology*, *145*(2).

Inoue, F., Ueshima, K., Fujimoto, T., & Kihyon, A. (2010). Effect of angiotensin receptor blockade on the coronary plaque component in patients with stable angina: Virtual histology intravascular ultrasound study. *Circulation*, *122*, A13580.

Ishibashi, F., Aziz, K., Abela, G., & Waxman, S. (2006). Update on coronary angioscopy: Review of a 20-year experience and potential application for detection of vulnerable plaque. *Journal of Interventional Cardiology*, *19*, 17–25. doi:10.1111/j.1540-8183.2006.00099.x

Ishigami, K., Uemura, S., Morikawa, Y., Soeda, T., Okayama, S., & Nishida, T. (2009). Long-term follow-up of neointimal coverage of sirolimus-eluting stents-evaluation with optical coherence tomography. *Circulation Journal*, *73*(12), 2300–2307. doi:10.1253/circj.CJ-08-1116

Ishino, S., Mukai, T., Kuge, Y., Kume, N., Ogawa, M., & Takai, N. (2008). Targeting of lectinlike oxidized low-density lipoprotein receptor 1 (LOX-1) with 99mTc-labeled anti-LOX-1 antibody: Potential agent for imaging of vulnerable plaque. *Journal of Nuclear Medicine*, *49*(10), 1677–1685. doi:10.2967/jnumed.107.049536

Iskurt, A., Candemir, S., & Akgul, Y. S. (2006). Identification of luminal and medial adventitial borders in intravascular ultrasound images using level sets. *Lecture Notes in Computer Science, Lecture Notes in Artificial Intelligence, and Lecture Notes in Bioinformatics, 4263 LNCS*, (pp. 572-582).

Isner, J. M., Kishel, J., & Kent, K. M. (1981). Accuracy of angiographic determination of left main coronary arterial narrowing. Angiographic-histologic correlative analysis in 28 patients. *Circulation*, *63*(5), 1056–1064. doi:10.1161/01.CIR.63.5.1056

Isoda, K., Satomura, K., & Ohsuzu, F. (n.d.). Pathological characterization of yellow and white plaques under angioscopy. *International Journal of Angiology*, *10*(3), 183-187.

Jaffer, F., Kim, D., Quinti, L., Tung, C., Aikawa, E., & Pande, A. (2007). Optical visualization of cathepsin K activity in atherosclerosis with a novel, protease-activatable fluorescence sensor. *Circulation, 115*, 2292–2298. doi:10.1161/CIRCULATIONAHA.106.660340

Jaffer, F., Vinegoni, C., John, M., Aikawa, E., Gold, H., & Finn, A. (2008). Real-time catheter molecular sensing of inflammation in proteolytically active atherosclerosis. *Circulation, 118*, 1802–1809. doi:10.1161/CIRCULATIONAHA.108.785881

Jan, G., Patrick, S., & Luc, M. (2008). Identifying the vulnerable plaque: A review of invasive and non-invasive imaging modalities. *Artery Research, 2*(1), 21–34. doi:10.1016/j.artres.2007.11.002

Jan, S. L., Hwang, B., Lee, P. C., Fu, Y. C., Chiu, P. S., & Chi, C. S. (2001). Intracardiac ultrasound assessment of atrial septal defect: Comparison with transthoracic echocardiographic, angiocardiographic, and balloon-sizing measurements. *Cardiovascular and Interventional Radiology, 24*(24). doi:.doi:10.1007/s002700000397

Jang, I. K., Bouma, B. E., Kang, D. H., Park, S. J., Park, S. W., & Seung, K. B. (2002). Visualization of coronary atherosclerotic plaques in patients using optical coherence tomography: Comparison with intravascular ultrasound. *Journal of the American College of Cardiology, 39*(4), 604–609. doi:10.1016/S0735-1097(01)01799-5

Jang, I. K., Tearney, G., & Bouma, B. (2001). Visualization of tissue prolapse between coronary stent struts by optical coherence tomography - Comparison with intravascular ultrasound. *Circulation, 104*(22), 2754–2754. doi:10.1161/hc4701.098069

Jang, I., Tearney, G., MacNeill, B., Takano, M., Moselewski, F., & Iftima, N. (2005). In vivo characterization of coronary atherosclerotic plaque by use of Optical Coherence Tomography. *Circulation, 111*, 1551–1555. doi:10.1161/01.CIR.0000159354.43778.69

Jankharia, B., & Raut, A. (2010). Cardiac imaging: Current and emerging applications. *Postgraduate Medical Journal, 56*(2), 125–130. doi:10.4103/0022-3859.65289

Jaross, W., Neumeister, V., Lattke, P., & Schuh, D. (1999). Determination of cholesterol in atherosclerotic plaques using near infrared diffuse reflection spectroscopy. *Atherosclerosis, 147*, 327–337. doi:10.1016/S0021-9150(99)00203-8

Jasti, V., Ivan, E., Yalamanchili, V., Wongpraparut, N., & Leesar, M. A. (2004). Correlations between fractional flow reserve and intravascular ultrasound in patients with an ambiguous left main coronary artery stenosis. *Circulation, 110*(18), 2831–2836. doi:10.1161/01.CIR.0000146338.62813.E7

Jensen, L. O., Maeng, M., Mintz, G. S., Christiansen, E. H., Hansen, K. N., & Galloe, A. (2009). Serial intravascular ultrasound analysis of peri-stent remodeling and proximal and distal edge effects after sirolimus-eluting or paclitaxel-eluting stent implantation in patients with diabetes mellitus. *The American Journal of Cardiology, 103*(8), 1083–1088. doi:10.1016/j.amjcard.2008.12.035

Jensen, L. O., Thayssen, P., Mintz, G. S., Egede, R., Maeng, M., & Junker, A. (2008). Comparison of intravascular ultrasound and angiographic assessment of coronary reference segment size in patients with type 2 diabetes mellitus. *The American Journal of Cardiology, 101*(5), 590–595. doi:10.1016/j.amjcard.2007.10.020

Jensen, L. O., Maeng, M., Thayssen, P., Christiansen, E. H., Hansen, K. N., & Galloe, A. (2008). Neointimal hyperplasia after sirolimus-eluting and paclitaxel-eluting stent implantation in diabetic patients: the Randomized Diabetes and Drug-Eluting Stent (DiabeDES) Intravascular Ultrasound Trial. *European Heart Journal, 29*(22), 2733–2741. doi:10.1093/eurheartj/ehn434

Jensen, L. O., Thayssen, P., Pedersen, K. E., Stender, S., & Haghfelt, T. (2004). Regression of coronary atherosclerosis by simvastatin: a serial intravascular ultrasound study. *Circulation, 110*(3), 265–270. doi:10.1161/01.CIR.0000135215.75876.41

Jim, M., Hau, W., Ko, R., Siu, C., Ho, H., & Yiu, K. (2010). Virtual histology by intravascular ultrasound study on degenerative aortocoronary saphenous vein grafts. *Heart and Vessels, 25*(3), 175–181. doi:10.1007/s00380-009-1185-7

Jimenez, J. M., & Davies, P. F. (2009). Hemodynamically driven stent strut design. *Annals of Biomedical Engineering*, 37(8), 1483–1494. doi:10.1007/s10439-009-9719-9

Jimenez-Quevedo, P., Sabate, M., Angiolillo, D. J., Costa, M. A., Alfonso, F., & Gomez-Hospital, J. A. (2006). Vascular effects of sirolimus-eluting versus bare-metal stents in diabetic patients: three-dimensional ultrasound results of the Diabetes and Sirolimus-Eluting Stent (DIABETES) Trial. *Journal of the American College of Cardiology*, 47(11), 2172–2179.

Jimenez-Valero, S., Moreno, R., & Sanchez-Recalde, A. (2009). Very late drug-eluting stent thrombosis related to incomplete stent endothelialization: In-vivo demonstration by optical coherence tomography. *The Journal of Invasive Cardiology*, 21(9), 488–490.

Johnson, S. B., Seward, J. B., & Packer, D. L. (2002). Phased-array intracardiac echocardiography for guiding transseptal catheter placement: Utility and learning curve. *Pacing and Clinical Electrophysiology*, 25(4 Pt 1), 402–407. doi:10.1046/j.1460-9592.2002.00402.x

Joner, M., Finn, A., & Farb, A. (2006). Pathology of drug-eluting stents in humans: Delayed healing and late thrombotic risk. *Journal of the American College of Cardiology*, 48, 193–202. doi:10.1016/j.jacc.2006.03.042

Judenhofer, M., Wehrl, H., Newport, D., Catana, C., Siegel, S., & Becker, M. (2008). Simultaneous PET-MRI: A new approach for functional and morphological imaging. *Nature Medicine*, 14, 459–465. doi:10.1038/nm1700

Kaaresen, K. F., & Bolviken, E. (1999). Blind deconvolution of ultrasonic traces accounting for pulse variance. *IEEE Transactions on Ultrasonics, Ferroelectrics, and Frequency Control*, 46(3), 564–573. doi:10.1109/58.764843

Kagan, A., Livsic, A., Sternby, N., & Vihert, A. (1968). Coronary-artery thrombosis and the acute attack of coronary heart-disease. *Lancet*, 2, 1199–1200. doi:10.1016/S0140-6736(68)91688-7

Kallel, F., & Ophir, J. (1998). Limits on the contrast of strain concentrations in elastography. *Ultrasound in Medicine & Biology*, 24(8), 1215–1219. doi:10.1016/S0301-5629(98)00106-9

Kalman, J. M., Olgin, J. E., Karch, M. R., & Lesh, M. D. (1997). Use of intracardiac echocardiography in interventional electrophysiology. *Pacing and Clinical Electrophysiology*, 20(9), 2248–2262. doi:10.1111/j.1540-8159.1997.tb04244.x

Kamiya, A., & Togawa, T. (1980). Adaptive regulation of wall shear stress to flow change in the canine carotid artery. *The American Journal of Physiology*, 239(1), H14–H21.

Kaple, R. K., Maehara, A., Sano, K., Missel, E., Castellanos, C., & Tsujita, K. (2009). The axial distribution of lesion-site atherosclerotic plaque components: An in vivo volumetric intravascular ultrasound radio-frequency analysis of lumen stenosis, necrotic core and vessel remodeling. *Ultrasound in Medicine & Biology*, 35(4), 550–557. doi:10.1016/j.ultrasmedbio.2008.09.024

Karanasos, A., Toutouzas, K., & Riga, M. (2010). Complex angiographic morphology is associated with ruptured plaques and thinner fibrous cap by optical coherence tomography. *ECS2010*. (abstract)

Karanasos, A., Toutouzas, K., & Riga, M. (2010). Culprit lesions in proximal segments of coronary arteries are associated with thin fibrous cap and plaque rupture as assessed by optical coherence tomography. *ESC2010*. (abstract)

Kasaoka, S., Tobis, J. M., Akiyama, T., Reimers, B., Di Mario, C., & Wong, N. D. (1998). Angiographic and intravascular ultrasound predictors of in-stent restenosis. *Journal of the American College of Cardiology*, 32(6), 1630–1635. doi:10.1016/S0735-1097(98)00404-5

Kashiwagi, M., Tanaka, A., & Kitabata, H. (2009). Relationship between coronary arterial remodeling, fibrous cap thickness and high-sensitivity C-reactive protein levels in patients with acute coronary syndrome. *Circulation Journal*, 73, 1291–1295. doi:10.1253/circj.CJ-08-0968

Kashiwagi, M., Tanaka, A., Kitabata, H., Tsujioka, H., Kataiwa, H., & Komukai, K. (2009). Feasibility of noninvasive assessment of thin-cap fibroatheroma by multidetector computed tomography. *JACC: Cardiovascular Imaging*, 2(12), 1412–1419. doi:10.1016/j.jcmg.2009.09.012

Kass, M., & Haddad, H. (2006). Cardiac allograft vasculopathy: Pathology, prevention and treatment. *Current Opinion in Cardiology*, 21(2), 132–137. doi:10.1097/01.hco.0000203184.89158.16

Kass, M., Witkin, A., & Terzopoulos, D. (1987). Snakes: Active contour models. *International Journal of Computer Vision*, *1*, 321–331. doi:10.1007/BF00133570

Kastrati, A., Mehilli, J., Dirschinger, J., Pache, J., Ulm, K., & Schuhlen, H. (2001). Restenosis after coronary placement of various stent types. *The American Journal of Cardiology*, *87*(1), 34–39. doi:10.1016/S0002-9149(00)01268-6

Katouzian, A., Sathyanarayana, S., Baseri, B., Konofagou, E., & Carlier, S. (2008). Challenges in atherosclerotic plaque characterization with intravascular ultrasound (IVUS): From data collection to classification. *Information Technology in Biomedicine . IEEE Transactions*, *12*(3), 315–327.

Kawaguchi, R., Oshima, S., Jingu, M., Tsurugaya, H., Toyama, T., & Hoshizaki, H. (2007). Usefulness of virtual histology intravascular ultrasound to predict distal embolization for ST-segment elevation myocardial infarction. *Journal of the American College of Cardiology*, *50*(17), 1641–1646. doi:10.1016/j.jacc.2007.06.051

Kawaguchi, R., Tsurugaya, H., Hoshizaki, H., Toyama, T., Oshima, S., & Taniguchi, K. (2008). Impact of lesion calcification on clinical and angiographic outcome after sirolimus-eluting stent implantation in real-world patients. *Cardiovascular Revascularization Medicine; Including Molecular Interventions*, *9*(1), 2–8. doi:10.1016/j.carrev.2007.07.004

Kawai, Y., Hisamatsu, K., & Matsubara, H. (2009). Intravenous administration of nicorandil immediately before percutaneous coronary intervention can prevent slow coronary flow phenomenon. *European Heart Journal*, *30*, 765–772. doi:10.1093/eurheartj/ehp077

Kawamoto, T., Okura, H., Koyama, Y., Toda, I., Taguchi, H., & Tamita, K. (2007). The relationship between coronary plaque characteristics and small embolic particles during coronary stent implantation. *Journal of the American College of Cardiology*, *50*(17), 1635–1640. doi:10.1016/j.jacc.2007.05.050

Kawasaki, M., Bouma, B. E., Bressner, J., Houser, S. L., Nadkarni, S. K., & MacNeill, B. D. (2006). Diagnostic accuracy of optical coherence tomography and integrated backscatter intravascular ultrasound images for tissue characterization of human coronary plaques. *Journal of the American College of Cardiology*, *48*(1), 81–88. doi:10.1016/j.jacc.2006.02.062

Kawasaki, M., Hattori, A., Ishihara, Y., Okubo, M., Nishigaki, K., & Takemura, G. (2010). Tissue Characterization of coronary plaques and assessment of thickness of fibrous cap using integrated backscatter intravascular ultrasound. *Circulation Journal*, *74*(12). doi:10.1253/circj.CJ-10-0547

Kawasaki, M., Sano, K., Okubo, M., Yokoyama, H., Ito, Y., & Murata, I. (2005). Volumetric quantitative analysis of tissue characteristics of coronary plaques after statin therapy using three-dimensional integrated backscatter intravascular ultrasound. *Journal of the American College of Cardiology*, *45*(12), 1946–1953. doi:10.1016/j.jacc.2004.09.081

Kawasaki, M., Takatsu, H., Noda, T., Ito, Y., Kunishima, A., & Arai, M. (2001). Noninvasive quantitative tissue characterization and two-dimensional color-coded map of human atherosclerotic lesions using ultrasound integrated backscatter: Comparison between histology and integrated backscatter images. *Journal of the American College of Cardiology*, *38*(2), 486–492. doi:10.1016/S0735-1097(01)01393-6

Kawasaki, M., Takatsu, H., Noda, T., Sano, K., Ito, Y., & Hayakawa, K. (2002). In vivo quantitative tissue characterization of human coronary arterial plaques by use of integrated backscatter intravascular ultrasound and comparison with angioscopic findings. *Circulation*, *105*(21), 2487–2492. doi:10.1161/01.CIR.0000017200.47342.10

Kawasaki, M., Bouma, B. E., Bressner, J., Houser, S. L., Nadkarni, S. K., & MacNeill, B. D. (2006). Diagnostic accuracy of optical coherence tomography and integrated backscatter intravascular ultrasound images for tissue characterization of human coronary plaques. *Journal of the American College of Cardiology*, *48*(1), 81–88. doi:10.1016/j.jacc.2006.02.062

Kawasaki, M., Sano, K., Okubo, M., Yokoyama, H., Ito, Y., & Murata, I. (2005). Volumetric quantitative analysis of tissue characteristics of coronary plaques after statin therapy using three-dimensional integrated backscatter intravascular ultrasound. *Journal of the American College of Cardiology, 45*(12), 1946–1953. doi:10.1016/j.jacc.2004.09.081

Kawase, Y., Hoshino, K., Yoneyama, R., McGregor, J., Hajjar, R. J., & Jang, I. K. (2005). In vivo volumetric analysis of coronary stent using optical coherence tomography with a novel balloon occlusion-flushing catheter: A comparison with intravascular ultrasound. *Ultrasound in Medicine & Biology, 31*(10), 1343–1349. doi:10.1016/j.ultrasmedbio.2005.05.010

Kelbaek, H., Terkelsen, C., & Helqvist, S. (2008). Randomized comparison of distal protection versus conventional treatment in primary percutaneous coronary intervention: The drug elution and distal protection in ST-elevation myocardial infarction (DEDICATION) trial. *Journal of the American College of Cardiology, 51*, 899–905.

Kersey, A. D., Marrone, M. J., & Davis, M. A. (1991). Polarization-insensitive fiber optic Michelson interferometer. *Electronics Letters, 27*(6), 518–520. doi:10.1049/el:19910325

Kerwin, W., Hooker, A., Spilker, M., Vicini, P., Ferguson, M., & Hatsukami, T. (2003). Quantitative magnetic resonance imaging analysis of neovasculature volume in carotid atherosclerotic plaque. *Circulation, 107*(6), 851–856. doi:10.1161/01.CIR.0000048145.52309.31

Kim, J., Jang, I., & Fan, C. (2009). Evaluation in 3 months duration of neointimal coverage after zotarolimus-eluting stent implantation by optical coherence tomography: The ENDEAVOR OCT trial. *JACC: Cardiovascular Interventions, 2*, 1240–1247. doi:10.1016/j.jcin.2009.10.006

Kim, J., Kim, J., & Kim, T. (2010). Comparison of neointimal coverage of sirolimus-eluting stents and paclitaxel-eluting stents using optical coherence tomography at 9 months after implantation. *Circulation Journal, 74*, 320–326. doi:10.1253/circj.CJ-09-0546

Kim, U., Kim, J., & Kim, J. (2010). The initial extent of malapposition in ST-elevation myocardial infarction treated with drug-eluting stent: The usefulness of optical coherence tomography. *Yonsei Medical Journal, 51*, 332–338. doi:10.3349/ymj.2010.51.3.332

Kim, S.-W., Mintz, G., & Ohlmann, P. e. (2006). Frequency and severity of plaque prolapse within cypher and taxus stents as determined by sequential intravascular ultrasound analysis. *The American Journal of Cardiology, 98*, 1206–1211. doi:10.1016/j.amjcard.2006.06.014

Kim, R. J., Wu, E., Rafael, A., Chen, E. L., Parker, M. A., & Simonetti, O. (2000). The use of contrast-enhanced magnetic resonance imaging to identify reversible myocardial dysfunction. *The New England Journal of Medicine, 343*(20), 1445–1453. doi:10.1056/NEJM200011163432003

Kim, W. Y., Stuber, M., Bornert, P., Kissinger, K. V., Manning, W. J., & Botnar, R. M. (2002). Three-dimensional black-blood cardiac magnetic resonance coronary vessel wall imaging detects positive arterial remodeling in patients with nonsignificant coronary artery disease. *Circulation, 106*(3), 296–299. doi:10.1161/01.CIR.0000025629.85631.1E

Kim, S., Seo, J., Do, K., Heo, J., Lee, J., & Song, J. (2006). Coronary artery anomalies: Classification and ECG-gated multi-detector row CT findings with angiographic correlation. *Radiographics, 26*(2), 317–333, discussion 333–334. doi:10.1148/rg.262055068

Kimura, S., Kakuta, T., Yonetsu, T., Suzuki, A., Iesaka, Y., & Fujiwara, H. (2009). Clinical significance of echo signal attenuation on intravascular ultrasound in patients with coronary artery disease. *Circ Cardiovasc Interv, 2*(5), 444–454. doi:10.1161/CIRCINTERVENTIONS.108.821124

Kimura, B. J., Bhargava, V., & DeMaria, A. N. (1995). Value and limitations of intravascular ultrasound imaging in characterizing coronary atherosclerotic plaque. *American Heart Journal, 130*(2), 386–396. doi:10.1016/0002-8703(95)90457-3

Kimura, M., Mintz, G. S., Weissman, N. J., Dawkins, K. D., Grube, E., & Ellis, S. G. (2008). Meta-analysis of the effects of paclitaxel-eluting stents versus bare metal stents on volumetric intravascular ultrasound in patients with versus without diabetes mellitus. *The American Journal of Cardiology, 101*(9), 1263–1268. doi:10.1016/j.amjcard.2007.12.025

Kimura, T., Abe, K., Shizuta, S., Odashiro, K., Yoshida, Y., & Sakai, K. (2002). Long-term clinical and angiographic follow-up after coronary stent placement in native coronary arteries. *Circulation, 105*(25), 2986–2991. doi:10.1161/01.CIR.0000019743.11941.3B

Kircher, M. F., Grimm, J., Swirski, F. K., Libby, P., Gerszten, R. E., & Allport, J. R. (2008). Noninvasive in vivo imaging of monocyte trafficking to atherosclerotic lesions. *Circulation, 117*(3), 388–395. doi:10.1161/CIRCULATIONAHA.107.719765

Kitagawa, T., Yamamoto, H., Horiguchi, J., Ohhashi, N., Tadehara, F., & Shokawa, T. (2009). Characterization of noncalcified coronary plaques and identification of culprit lesions in patients with acute coronary syndrome by 64-slice computed tomography. *JACC: Cardiovascular Imaging, 2*(2), 153–160. doi:10.1016/j.jcmg.2008.09.015

Klingensmith, J. D., Shekhar, R., & Vince, D. G. (2000). Evaluation of three-dimensional segmentation algorithms for the identification of luminal and medial–adventitial borders in intravascular ultrasound images. *IEEE Transactions on Medical Imaging, 19*(10), 996–1011. doi:10.1109/42.887615

Klingensmith, J., Schoenhagen, P., Tajaddini, A., Halliburton, S., Tuzcu, E., Nissen, S., & Vince, D. (2003). Automated three-dimensional assessment of coronary artery anatomy with intravascular ultrasound scanning. *American Heart Journal, 145*, 795–805. doi:10.1016/S0002-8703(03)00089-9

Knebel, F., Gliech, V., Walde, T., Panda, A., Sanad, W., & Eddicks, S. (2004). Percutaneous closure of interatrial communications in adults - prospective embolism prevention study with two- and three-dimensional echocardiography. *Cardiovascular Ultrasound, 2*, 5. .doi:10.1186/1476-7120-2-5

Ko, T. H., Fujimoto, J. G., Schuman, J. S., Paunescu, L. A., Kowalevicz, A. M., Hartl, I., et al. (2005). Comparison of ultrahigh- and standard-resolution optical coherence tomography for imaging macular pathology. *Ophthalmology, 112*(11), 1922 e1921-1915.

Koenig, P., & Cao, Q. L. (2005). Echocardiographic guidance of transcatheter closure of atrial septal defects intracardiac echocardiography better than transesophageal echocardiography? *Pediatric Cardiology, 26*(2), 135–139. doi:10.1007/s00246-004-0952-6

Kolachalama, V. B., Levine, E. G., & Edelman, E. R. (2009). Luminal flow amplifies stent-based drug deposition in arterial bifurcations. *PLoS ONE, 4*(12), e8105. doi:10.1371/journal.pone.0008105

Kolachalama, V. B., Tzafriri, A. R., Arifin, D. Y., & Edelman, E. R. (2009). Luminal flow patterns dictate arterial drug deposition in stent-based delivery. *Journal of Controlled Release, 133*(1), 24–30. doi:10.1016/j.jconrel.2008.09.075

Kolodgie, F. D., Burke, A. P., Farb, A., Gold, H. K., Yuan, J., & Narula, J. (2001). The thin-cap fibroatheroma: A type of vulnerable plaque: The major precursor lesion to acute coronary syndromes. *Current Opinion in Cardiology, 16*(5), 285–292. doi:10.1097/00001573-200109000-00006

Kolodgie, F., Virmani, R., Burke, A., Farb, A., Weber, D., & Kutys, R. (2004). Pathologic assessment of the vulnerable human coronary plaque. *Heart (British Cardiac Society), 90*, 1385–1391. doi:10.1136/hrt.2004.041798

Kolodgie, F., Gold, H., Burke, A., Fowler, D., Kruth, H., & Weber, D. (2003). Intraplaque hemorrhage and progression of coronary atheroma. *The New England Journal of Medicine, 349*, 2316–2325. doi:10.1056/NEJMoa035655

Konig, A., & Klauss, V. (2007). Virtual histology. *Heart (British Cardiac Society), 93*(8), 977–982. doi:10.1136/hrt.2007.116384

Koning, G., Dijkstra, J., Von Birgelen, C., Tuinenburg, J. C., Brunette, J., & Tardif, C. (2002). Advanced contour detection for three–dimensional intracoronary ultrasound: A validation in–vitro and in vivo. *The International Journal of Cardiovascular Imaging, 18*, 235–248. doi:10.1023/A:1015551920382

Konofagou, E., & Ophir, J. (1998). A new elastographic method for estimation and imaging of lateral displacements, lateral strains, corrected axial strains and Poisson's ratios in tissues. *Ultrasound in Medicine & Biology*, *24*(8), 1183–1199. doi:10.1016/S0301-5629(98)00109-4

Kooi, M. E., Cappendijk, V. C., Cleutjens, K. B., Kessels, A. G., Kitslaar, P. J., & Borgers, M. (2003). Accumulation of ultrasmall superparamagnetic particles of iron oxide in human atherosclerotic plaques can be detected by in vivo magnetic resonance imaging. *Circulation*, *107*(19), 2453–2458. doi:10.1161/01.CIR.0000068315.98705.CC

Koskinas, K. C., Chatzizisis, Y. S., Baker, A. B., Edelman, E. R., Stone, P. H., & Feldman, C. L. (2009). The role of low endothelial shear stress in the conversion of atherosclerotic lesions from stable to unstable plaque. *Current Opinion in Cardiology*, *24*(6), 580–590. doi:10.1097/HCO.0b013e328331630b

Koskinas, K. C., Feldman, C. L., Chatzizisis, Y. S., Coskun, A. U., Jonas, M., & Maynard, C. (2010). Natural history of experimental coronary atherosclerosis and vascular remodeling in relation to endothelial shear stress: A serial, in vivo intravascular ultrasound study. *Circulation*, *121*(19), 2092–2101. doi:10.1161/CIRCULATIONAHA.109.901678

Koskinas, K. C., Sukhova, G. K., Baker, A. B., Chatzizisis, Y. S., Papafaklis, M. I., & Coskun, A. U. (2010). Coronary thin-capped atheromata exhibit increased expression of interstitial collagenases in regions of persistently low endothelial shear stress: A serial, in vivo natural history study in pigs [Abstract]. *Circulation*, *122*(Supplement), A19592.

Koskinas, K., Chatzizisis, Y., Baker, A., Edelman, E., Stone, P., & Feldman, C. (2009). The role of low endothelial shear stress in the conversion of atherosclerotic lesions from stable to unstable plaque. *Current Opinion in Cardiology*, *24*, 580–590. doi:10.1097/HCO.0b013e328331630b

Kotani, J., Mintz, G. S., Castagna, M. T., Pinnow, E., Berzingi, C. O., & Bui, A. B. (2003). Intravascular ultrasound analysis of infarct-related and non-infarct-related arteries in patients who presented with an acute myocardial infarction. *Circulation*, *107*(23), 2889–2893. doi:10.1161/01.CIR.0000072768.80031.74

Kovalski, G., Beyar, R., Shofti, R., & Azhari, H. (2000). Three-dimensional automatic quantitative analysis of intravascular ultrasound images. *Ultrasound in Medicine & Biology*, *26*(4), 527–537. doi:10.1016/S0301-5629(99)00167-2

Krams, R., Verheye, S., van Damme, L., Tempel, D., Mousavi Gourabi, B., & Boersma, E. (2005). In vivo temperature heterogeneity is associated with plaque regions of increased MMP-9 activity. *European Heart Journal*, *26*, 2200–2205. doi:10.1093/eurheartj/ehi461

Ku, D. N., Giddens, D. P., Zarins, C. K., & Glagov, S. (1985). Pulsatile flow and atherosclerosis in the human carotid bifurcation. Positive correlation between plaque location and low oscillating shear stress. *Arteriosclerosis (Dallas, Tex.)*, *5*(3), 293–302. doi:10.1161/01.ATV.5.3.293

Kubo, T., Maehara, A., Mintz, G. S., Garcia-Garcia, H. M., Serruys, P. W., & Suzuki, T. (2010). Analysis of the long-term effects of drug-eluting stents on coronary arterial wall morphology as assessed by virtual histology intravascular ultrasound. *American Heart Journal*, *159*(2), 271–277. doi:10.1016/j.ahj.2009.11.008

Kubo, T., Imanishi, T., Takarada, S., Kuroi, A., Ueno, S., & Yamano, T. (2007). Assessment of culprit lesion morphology in acute myocardial infarction: Ability of optical coherence tomography compared with intravascular ultrasound and coronary angioscopy. *Journal of the American College of Cardiology*, *50*(10), 933–939. doi:10.1016/j.jacc.2007.04.082

Kubo, T., Imanishi, T., Kitabata, H., Kuroi, A., Ueno, S., & Yamano, T. (2008). Comparison of vascular response after sirolimus-eluting stent implantation between patients with unstable and stable angina pectoris: a serial optical tomography study. *J Am Coll Cardiol Img*, *1*, 475–484.

Kubo, T., Imanishi, T., & Kashiwagi, M. e. (2010). Multiple coronary lesion instability in patients with acute myocardial infarction as determined by optical coherence tomography. *The American Journal of Cardiology*, *105*, 318–322. doi:10.1016/j.amjcard.2009.09.032

Kubo, T., Imanishi, T., & Takarada, S. (2007). Assessment of culprit lesion morphology in acute myocardial infarction: ability of optical coherence tomography compared with intravascular ultrasound and coronary angioscopy. *Journal of the American College of Cardiology, 50*, 933–939. doi:10.1016/j.jacc.2007.04.082

Kubo, T., Imanishi, T., Takarada, S., Kuroi, A., Ueno, S., & Yamano, T. (2007). Assessment of culprit lesion morphology in acute myocardial infarction: Ability of optical coherence tomography compared with intravascular ultrasound and coronary angioscopy. *Journal of the American College of Cardiology, 50*(10), 933–939. doi:10.1016/j.jacc.2007.04.082

Kuge, Y., Takai, N., Ogawa, Y., Temma, T., Zhao, Y., & Nishigori, K.. Imaging with radiolabelled anti-membrane type 1 matrix metalloproteinase (MT1-MMP) antibody: Potentials for characterizing atherosclerotic plaques. *European Journal of Nuclear Medicine and Molecular Imaging, 37*(11), 2093–2104. doi:10.1007/s00259-010-1521-2

Kume, T., Akasaka, T., Kawamoto, T., Ogasawara, Y., Watanabe, N., & Toyota, E. (2006). Assessment of coronary arterial thrombus by optical coherence tomography. *The American Journal of Cardiology, 97*(12), 1713–1717. doi:10.1016/j.amjcard.2006.01.031

Kume, T., Akasaka, T., Kawamoto, T., Watanabe, N., Toyota, E., & Neishi, Y. (2005). Assessment of coronary intima--media thickness by optical coherence tomography: Comparison with intravascular ultrasound. *Circulation Journal, 69*(8), 903–907. doi:10.1253/circj.69.903

Kume, T., Akasaka, T., & Kawamoto, T. (2006). Assessment of coronary arterial thrombus by optical coherence tomography. *The American Journal of Cardiology, 97*, 1713–1717. doi:10.1016/j.amjcard.2006.01.031

Kume, T., Okura, H., & Kawamoto, T. (2008). Relationship between coronary remodeling and plaque characterization in patients without clinical evidence of coronary artery disease. *Atherosclerosis, 197*, 799–805. doi:10.1016/j.atherosclerosis.2007.07.028

Kume, T., Okura, H., & Yamada, R. (2009). Frequency and spatial distribution of thin-cap fibroatheroma assessed by 3-vessel intravascular ultrasound and optical coherence tomography: An ex vivo validation and an initial in vivo feasibility study. *Circulation Journal, 73*, 1086–1091. doi:10.1253/circj.CJ-08-0733

Kume, N., Murase, T., Moriwaki, H., Aoyama, T., Sawamura, T., & Masaki, T. (1998). Inducible expression of lectin-like oxidized LDL receptor-1 in vascular endothelial cells. *Circulation Research, 83*(3), 322–327.

Kume, T., Akasaka, T., & Kawamoto, T. (2006). Measurement of the thickness of the fibrous cap by optical coherence tomography. *Am Heart J, 152*, 755 e1-4.

Kuo, W., Chou, N., & Chou, C. (2007). Polarization-sensitive optical coherence tomography for imaging human atherosclerosis. *Applied Optics, 46*, 2520–2527. doi:10.1364/AO.46.002520

Kyono, H., Guagliumi, G., Sirbu, V., Rosenthal, N., Tahara, S., & Musumeci, G. (2010). Optical coherence tomography strut level analysis of drug eluting stents in human coronary bifurcations. *EuroInterv, 6*, 69–77. doi:10.4244/EIJV6I1A11

LaDisa, J. F. Jr, Guler, I., Olson, L. E., Hettrick, D. A., Kersten, J. R., & Warltier, D. C. (2003). Three-dimensional computational fluid dynamics modeling of alterations in coronary wall shear stress produced by stent implantation. *Annals of Biomedical Engineering, 31*(8), 972–980. doi:10.1114/1.1588654

LaDisa, J. F. Jr, Hettrick, D. A., Olson, L. E., Guler, I., Gross, E. R., & Kress, T. T. (2002). Stent implantation alters coronary artery hemodynamics and wall shear stress during maximal vasodilation. *Journal of Applied Physiology, 93*(6), 1939–1946.

LaDisa, J. F. Jr, Olson, L. E., Douglas, H. A., Warltier, D. C., Kersten, J. R., & Pagel, P. S. (2006). Alterations in regional vascular geometry produced by theoretical stent implantation influence distributions of wall shear stress: Analysis of a curved coronary artery using 3D computational fluid dynamics modeling. *Biomedical Engineering Online, 5*, 40. doi:10.1186/1475-925X-5-40

LaDisa, J. F. Jr, Olson, L. E., Guler, I., Hettrick, D. A., Audi, S. H., & Kersten, J. R. (2004). Stent design properties and deployment ratio influence indexes of wall shear stress: A three-dimensional computational fluid dynamics investigation within a normal artery. *Journal of Applied Physiology*, *97*(1), 424–430, discussion 416. doi:10.1152/japplphysiol.01329.2003

LaDisa, J. F. Jr, Olson, L. E., Guler, I., Hettrick, D. A., Kersten, J. R., & Warltier, D. C. (2005). Circumferential vascular deformation after stent implantation alters wall shear stress evaluated with time-dependent 3D computational fluid dynamics models. *Journal of Applied Physiology*, *98*(3), 947–957. doi:10.1152/japplphysiol.00872.2004

LaDisa, J. F. Jr, Olson, L. E., Hettrick, D. A., Warltier, D. C., Kersten, J. R., & Pagel, P. S. (2005). Axial stent strut angle influences wall shear stress after stent implantation: Analysis using 3D computational fluid dynamics models of stent foreshortening. *Biomedical Engineering Online*, *4*, 59. doi:10.1186/1475-925X-4-59

LaDisa, J. F. Jr, Olson, L. E., Molthen, R. C., Hettrick, D. A., Pratt, P. F., & Hardel, M. D. (2005). Alterations in wall shear stress predict sites of neointimal hyperplasia after stent implantation in rabbit iliac arteries. *American Journal of Physiology. Heart and Circulatory Physiology*, *288*(5), H2465–H2475. doi:10.1152/ajpheart.01107.2004

Langheinrich, A., Michniewicz, A., Sedding, D., Walker, G., Beighley, P., & Rau, W. (2006). Correlation of vasa vasorum neovascularization and plaque progression in aortas of apolipoprotein E(-/-)/low-density lipoprotein(-/-) double knockout mice. *Arteriosclerosis, Thrombosis, and Vascular Biology*, *26*, 347–352. doi:10.1161/01.ATV.0000196565.38679.6d

Laufer, E. M., Winkens, H. M., Corsten, M. F., Reutelingsperger, C. P., Narula, J., & Hofstra, L. (2009). PET and SPECT imaging of apoptosis in vulnerable atherosclerotic plaques with radiolabeled Annexin A5. *The Quarterly Journal of Nuclear Medicine and Molecular Imaging*, *53*(1), 26–34.

Laufer, E. M., Winkens, M. H., Narula, J., & Hofstra, L. (2009). Molecular imaging of macrophage cell death for the assessment of plaque vulnerability. *Arteriosclerosis, Thrombosis, and Vascular Biology*, *29*(7), 1031–1038. doi:10.1161/ATVBAHA.108.165522

Laurent, S., Boutouyrie, P., & Lacolley, P. (2005). Structural and genetic bases of arterial stiffness. *Hypertension*, *45*(6), 1050–1055. doi:10.1161/01.HYP.0000164580.39991.3d

Lavine, B., & Workman, J. (2008). Chemometrics. *Analytical Chemistry*, *80*, 4519–4531. doi:10.1021/ac800728t

Le Floc'h, S., Cloutier, G., Finet, G., Tracqui, P., Pettigrew, R. I., & Ohayon, J. (2010). On the potential of a new IVUS elasticity modulus imaging approach for detecting vulnerable atherosclerotic coronary plaques: In vitro vessel phantom study. *Physics in Medicine and Biology*, *55*(19), 5701–5721. doi:10.1088/0031-9155/55/19/006

Leborgne, L., Dascotte, O., Jarry, G., Levy, F., Kamel, S., & Maizel, J. (2005). *Multi-vessel coronary plaque temperature heterogeneity in patients with acute coronary syndromes. First study with the Radi Medical System wire*. In AHA.

Lee, C. H., Tai, B. C., Soon, C. Y., Low, A. F., Poh, K. K., & Yeo, T. C. (2010). New set of intravascular ultrasound-derived anatomic criteria for defining functionally significant stenoses in small coronary arteries (results from Intravascular Ultrasound Diagnostic Evaluation of Atherosclerosis in Singapore [IDEAS] study). *The American Journal of Cardiology*, *105*(10), 1378–1384. doi:10.1016/j.amjcard.2010.01.002

Lee, R. T., & Libby, P. (1997). The unstable atheroma. *Arteriosclerosis, Thrombosis, and Vascular Biology*, *17*(10), 1859–1867. doi:10.1161/01.ATV.17.10.1859

Lee, R. T., Richardson, S. G., Loree, H. M., Grodzinsky, A. J., Gharib, S. A., & Schoen, F. J. (1992). Prediction of mechanical properties of human atherosclerotic tissue by high-frequency intravascular ultrasound imaging. An in vitro study. *Arteriosclerosis and Thrombosis*, *12*(1), 1–5. doi:10.1161/01.ATV.12.1.1

Lee, S. W., Hau, W. K., Kong, S. L., & Chan, R. W. (2010). Virtual histology findings of the effects of atorvastatin treatment on coronary plaque volume and composition (the venus study): final results. *Circulation*, *122*, a13301.

Lee, S. Y., Mintz, G. S., Kim, S. Y., Hong, Y. J., Kim, S. W., & Okabe, T. (2009). Attenuated plaque detected by intravascular ultrasound: clinical, angiographic, and morphologic features and post-percutaneous coronary intervention complications in patients with acute coronary syndromes. *JACC: Cardiovascular Interventions*, *2*(1), 65–72. doi:10.1016/j.jcin.2008.08.022

Lee, D. Y., Eigler, N., Luo, H., Nishioka, T., Tabak, S. W., & Forrester, J. S. (1995). Effect of intracoronary ultrasound imaging on clinical decision making. *American Heart Journal*, *129*(6), 1084–1093. doi:10.1016/0002-8703(95)90387-9

Lee, W., Idriss, S. F., Wolf, P. D., & Smith, S. W. (2004). A miniaturized catheter 2-D array for real-time, 3-D intracardiac echocardiography. *IEEE Transactions on Ultrasonics, Ferroelectrics, and Frequency Control*, *51*(10), 1334–1346. doi:10.1109/TUFFC.2004.1350962

Lees, A. M., & Lees, R. S. (1991). 99mTechnetium-labeled low density lipoprotein: receptor recognition and intracellular sequestration of radiolabel. *Journal of Lipid Research*, *32*(1), 1–8.

Leitgeb, R., Drexler, W., Unterhuber, A., Hermann, B., Bajraszewski, T., & Le, T. (2004). Ultrahigh resolution Fourier domain optical coherence tomography. *Optics Express*, *12*(10), 2156–2165. doi:10.1364/OPEX.12.002156

Lemos, P. A., Saia, F., Ligthart, J. M., Arampatzis, C. A., Sianos, G., & Tanabe, K. (2003). Coronary restenosis after sirolimus-eluting stent implantation: Morphological description and mechanistic analysis from a consecutive series of cases. *Circulation*, *108*(3), 257–260. doi:10.1161/01.CIR.0000083366.33686.11

Lengyel, J., Greenberg, D. P., & Pop, R. (1995). Time–dependent three-dimensional intravascular ultrasound. In R. Cook (Ed.), *The SIGGRAPH 95 Conference on Comp Graphics*, (pp. 457-64).

Lesh, M. D., Kalman, J. M., & Karch, M. R. (1998). Use of intracardiac echocardiography during electrophysiologic evaluation and therapy of atrial arrhythmias. *Journal of Cardiovascular Electrophysiology*, *9*(8Suppl), S40–S47.

Leung, K. (2004). *99mTc-Interleukin-2*.

Li, X. D., Chudoba, C., Ko, T., Pitris, C., & Fujimoto, J. G. (2000). Imaging needle for optical coherence tomography. *Optics Letters*, *25*(20), 1520–1522. doi:10.1364/OL.25.001520

Li, Q., Fu, Q., & Shi, S. (2010). Relationship between plasma inflammatory markers and plaque fibrous cap thickness determined by intravascular optical coherence tomography. *Heart (British Cardiac Society)*, *96*(3), 196–201. doi:10.1136/hrt.2009.175455

Li, W., Carrillo, R., Jian, Y., Tat-Jin, T., & Thomas, L. (2008). Multi-frequency processing for lumen enhancement with wideband intravascular ultrasound. *IEEE Ultrasonics Symposium*, 2-5 Nov. 2008, (pp. 371–374).

Libby, P. (2005). The forgotten majority: Unfinished business in cardiovascular risk reduction. *Journal of the American College of Cardiology*, *46*(7), 1225–1228. doi:10.1016/j.jacc.2005.07.006

Libby, P., & Theroux, P. (2005). Pathophysiology of coronary artery disease. *Circulation*, *111*(25), 3481–3488. doi:10.1161/CIRCULATIONAHA.105.537878

Libby, P., Ridker, P., & Maseri, A. (2002). Inflammation and atherosclerosis. *Circulation*, *105*, 1135–1143. doi:10.1161/hc0902.104353

Libby, P., & Aikawa, M. (2003). Mechanisms of plaque stabilization with statins. *The American Journal of Cardiology*, *91*, 4B–8B. doi:10.1016/S0002-9149(02)03267-8

Libby, P., Ridker, P. M., & Maseri, A. (2002). Inflammation and atherosclerosis. *Circulation*, *105*(9), 1135–1143. doi:10.1161/hc0902.104353

Libby, P. (2008). The molecular mechanisms of the thrombotic complications of atherosclerosis. *Journal of Internal Medicine*, *263*, 517–527. doi:10.1111/j.1365-2796.2008.01965.x

Liddicoat, J. R., Mac Neill, B. D., Gillinov, A. M., Cohn, W. E., Chin, C. H., & Prado, A. D. (2003). Percutaneous mitral valve repair: A feasibility study in an ovine model of acute ischemic mitral regurgitation. *Catheterization and Cardiovascular Interventions*, *60*(3), 410–416. doi:10.1002/ccd.10662

Liebson, P., & Klein, L. (1992). Intravascular ultrasound in coronary atherosclerosis: A new approach to clinical assessment. *American Heart Journal*, *123*, 1643–1660. doi:10.1016/0002-8703(92)90819-H

Lilledahl, M., Haugever, O., Barkost, M., & Svaasand, L. (2006). Reflection spectroscopy of atherosclerotic plaque. *Journal of Biomedical Optics, 11*, 021005. doi:10.1117/1.2186332

Lin, C. P., Honye, J., & Saito, S. (2010). New modality for evaluating plaque characteristics of the culprit lesion in a patient with acute coronary syndrome and no reflow phenomenon. *International Heart Journal, 51*(3), 207–210. doi:10.1536/ihj.51.207

Lindsay, A. C., Murray, S. W., & Choudhury, R. P. (2010). Contemporary coronary imaging from patient to plaque: Part 4 magnetic resonance imaging. *Br J Cardiol, 17*(6), 290–292.

Little, W. C., Constantinescu, M., Applegate, R. J., Kutcher, M. A., Burrows, M. T., & Kahl, F. R. (1988). Can coronary angiography predict the site of a subsequent myocardial infarction in patients with mild-to-moderate coronary artery disease? *Circulation, 78*(5 Pt 1), 1157–1166. doi:10.1161/01.CIR.78.5.1157

Liu, Z., McCormick, D., Dairywala, I., Surabhi, S., Goldberg, S., Turi, Z., & Vannan, M. A. (2004). Catheter-based intracardiac echocardiography in the interventional cardiac laboratory. *Catheterization and Cardiovascular Interventions, 63*(1), 63–71. doi:10.1002/ccd.20106

Lizzi, F. L., Greenebaum, M., Feleppa, E. J., Elbaum, M., & Coleman, D. J. (1983). Theoretical framework for spectrum analysis in ultrasonic tissue characterization. *The Journal of the Acoustical Society of America, 73*(4), 1366–1373. doi:10.1121/1.389241

Lobregt, S., & Viergever, M. A. (1995). Discrete dynamic control model. *IEEE Transactions on Medical Imaging, 14*, 12–24. doi:10.1109/42.370398

Lodder, R., Cassis, L., & Ciurczak, E. (1990). Arterial analysis with a novel near-IR fiber-optic probe. *Spectroscopy, 5*, 12–17.

Loewinger, L., & Budoff, M. (2007). New advances in cardiac computed tomography. *Current Opinion in Cardiology, 25*(2), 408–412. doi:10.1097/HCO.0b013e3282170ac4

Long, Q., Xu, X. Y., Ariff, B., Thom, S. A., Hughes, A. D., & Stanton, A. V. (2000). Reconstruction of blood flow patterns in a human carotid bifurcation: A combined CFD and MRI study. *Journal of Magnetic Resonance Imaging, 11*(3), 299–311. doi:10.1002/(SICI)1522-2586(200003)11:3<299::AID-JMRI9>3.0.CO;2-M

Loree, H. M., Tobias, B. J., Gibson, L. J., Kamm, R. D., Small, D. M., & Lee, R. T. (1994). Mechanical properties of model atherosclerotic lesion lipid pools. *Arteriosclerosis and Thrombosis, 14*(2), 230–234. doi:10.1161/01.ATV.14.2.230

Lotan, C., Almagor, Y., Kuiper, K., Suttorp, M. J., & Wijns, W. (2006). Sirolimus-eluting stent in chronic total occlusion: the SICTO study. *Journal of Interventional Cardiology, 19*(4), 307–312. doi:10.1111/j.1540-8183.2006.00151.x

Low, A., Kawase, Y., Chan, Y., Tearney, G., Bouma, B., & Jang, I. (2009). In vivo characterisation of coronary plaques with conventional grey-scale intravascular ultrasound: Correlation with optical coherence tomography. *EuroIntervention, 4*, 626–632. doi:10.4244/EIJV4I5A105

Luo, W., Marks, D., Ralston, T., & Boppart, S. (2006). Three-dimensional optical coherence tomography of the embryonic murine cardiovascular system. *Journal of Biomedical Optics, 11*, 021014. doi:10.1117/1.2193465

Luscher, T. F., Pieper, M., Tendera, M., Vrolix, M., Rutsch, W., & van den Branden, F. (2009). A randomized placebo-controlled study on the effect of nifedipine on coronary endothelial function and plaque formation in patients with coronary artery disease: the ENCORE II study. *European Heart Journal, 30*(13), 1590–1597. doi:10.1093/eurheartj/ehp151

Lutgens, E., Lutgens, S., Faber, B., Heeneman, S., Gijbels, M., & de Winther, M. (2006). Disruption of the cathepsin K gene reduces atherosclerosis progression and induces plaque fibrosis but accelerates macrophage foam cell formation. *Circulation, 113*, 98–107. doi:10.1161/CIRCULATIONAHA.105.561449

MacNeil, B., Lowe, H., Takano, M., Fuster, V., & Jang, I. (2003). Intravascular modalities for detection of vulnerable plaque: current status. *Arteriosclerosis, Thrombosis, and Vascular Biology, 23*, 1333–1342. doi:10.1161/01.ATV.0000080948.08888.BF

MacNeill, B., Jang, I., & Bouma, B. (2004). Focal and multi-focal plaque macrophage distributions in patients with acute and stable presentations of coronary artery disease. *Journal of the American College of Cardiology*, *44*, 972–979. doi:10.1016/j.jacc.2004.05.066

Madjid, M., Willerson, J., & Casscells, S. (2006). Intracoronary thermography for detection of high-risk vulnerable plaques. *Journal of the American College of Cardiology*, *47*, C80–C85. doi:10.1016/j.jacc.2005.11.050

Madjid, M., Naghavi, M., Malik, B., Litovsky, S., Willerson, J., & Casscells, W. (2002). Thermal detection of vulnerable plaque. *The American Journal of Cardiology*, *90*, 36L–39L. doi:10.1016/S0002-9149(02)02962-4

Maehara, A., Mintz, G. S., Bui, A. B., Walter, O. R., Castagna, M. T., & Canos, D. (2002). Morphologic and angiographic features of coronary plaque rupture detected by intravascular ultrasound. *Journal of the American College of Cardiology*, *40*(5), 904–910. doi:10.1016/S0735-1097(02)02047-8

Maehara, A., Mintz, G., & Weissman, N. (2009). Advances in intravascular imaging. *Circulation: Cardiovascular Interventions*, *2*, 482–490. doi:10.1161/CIRCINTERVENTIONS.109.868398

Maini, B. (2008). Clinical coronary chemograms and lipid core containing coronary plaques. *JACC Imaging*, *1*, 689–690. doi:10.1016/j.jcmg.2008.07.010

Maini, B., Brilakis, E., & Kim, M. (2010). Association of large lipid core plaque detected by near infrared spectroscopy with post percutaneous coronary intervention myocardial infarction. *Journal of the American College of Cardiology*, *55*, A179.E1672.

Malek, A. M., Alper, S. L., & Izumo, S. (1999). Hemodynamic shear stress and its role in atherosclerosis. *Journal of the American Medical Association*, *282*(21), 2035–2042. doi:10.1001/jama.282.21.2035

Maluenda, G., Pichard, A. D., & Waksman, R. (2010). Is there still a role for intravascular ultrasound in the current practice era? *EuroIntervention, 6 Suppl G*, G139-144.

Manfrini, O., Mont, E., & Leone, O. (2006). Sources of error and interpretation of plaque morphology by optical coherence tomography. *The American Journal of Cardiology*, *98*, 156–159. doi:10.1016/j.amjcard.2006.01.097

Mangrum, J. M., Mounsey, J. P., Kok, L. C., DiMarco, J. P., & Haines, D. E. (2002). Intracardiac echocardiography-guided, anatomically based radiofrequency ablation of focal atrial fibrillation originating from pulmonary veins. *Journal of the American College of Cardiology*, *39*(12), 1964–1972. doi:10.1016/S0735-1097(02)01893-4

Mansard, C. D., Canet Soulas, E. P., Anwander, A., Chaabane, L., Neyran, B., & Serfaty, J. M. (2004). Quantification of multicontrast vascular MR images with NLSnake, an active contour model: In vitro validation and in vivo evaluation. *Magnetic Resonance in Medicine*, *51*(2), 370–379. doi:10.1002/mrm.10722

Mareedu, R. K., Shah, M. S., Mesa, J. E., & McCauley, C. S. (2007). Percutaneous closure of patent foramen ovale: A case series and literature review. *Clinical Medicine & Research*, *5*(4), 218. doi:10.3121/cmr.2007.764

Mark, D., Berman, D., Budoff, M., Carr, J., Gerber, T., & Hecht, H. (2010). ACCF/ACR/AHA/NASCI/SAIP/SCAI/SCCT 2010 expert consensus document on coronary computed tomographic angiography: A report of the American College of Cardiology Foundation Task Force on Expert Consensus Documents. *Journal of the American College of Cardiology*, *55*(23), 2663–2699. doi:10.1016/j.jacc.2009.11.013

Marshik, B., Tan, H., & Tang, J. (2002). Discrimination of lipid-rich plaques in human aorta specimens with NIR spectroscopy through whole blood. *The American Journal of Cardiology*, *90*(Suppl 6A), 129H.

Marshik, B., Tan, H., & Tang, J. (2003). Detection of thin-capped fibroatheromas in human aorta tissue with near infrared spectroscopy through blood. *Journal of the American College of Cardiology*, *41*(Suppl 1).

Marwan, M., Ropers, D., Pflederer, T., Daniel, W. G., & Achenbach, S. (2009). Clinical characteristics of patients with obstructive coronary lesions in the absence of coronary calcification: An evaluation by coronary CT angiography. *Heart (British Cardiac Society)*, *95*(13), 1056–1060. doi:10.1136/hrt.2008.153353

Masamichi, T., Kyoichi, M., Kentaro, O., Shinya, Y., Takayoshi, O., & Shunta, S. (2001). Mechanical and structural characteristics of vulnerable plaques: Analysis by coronary angioscopy and intravascular ultrasound. *Journal of the American College of Cardiology*, *38*, 99–104. doi:10.1016/S0735-1097(01)01315-8

Matsumoto, M. S., Lemos, P. A., Yoneyama, T., & Furuie, S. S. (2009). Cardiac phase detection in intravascular ultrasound images, progress in biomedical optics and imaging. *Proceedings of the Society for Photo-Instrumentation Engineers, 6920,* 69200D.

Matter, C. M., Stuber, M., & Nahrendorf, M. (2009). Imaging of the unstable plaque: How far have we got? *European Heart Journal, 30*(21), 2566–2574. doi:10.1093/eurheartj/ehp419

Matter, C., Schuler, P., Alessi, P., Meier, P., Ricci, R., & Zhang, D. (2004). Molecular imaging of atherosclerotic plaques using a human antibody against the extra-domain B of fibronectin. *Circulation Research, 95,* 1225–1233. doi:10.1161/01.RES.0000150373.15149.ff

McPherson, J. A., Maehara, A., Mintz, G. S., Serruys, P. W., & Stone, P. H. (2010). Are vulnerable plaques widely disseminated or focal? A baseline 3-vessel IVUS analysis from the PROSPECT trial. *Journal of the American College of Cardiology, 55*(10A), A178. doi:10.1016/S0735-1097(10)61670-1

Mehta, S. K., McCrary, J. R., Frutkin, A. D., Dolla, W. J., & Marso, S. P. (2007). Intravascular ultrasound radiofrequency analysis of coronary atherosclerosis: An emerging technology for the assessment of vulnerable plaque. *European Heart Journal, 28*(11), 1283–1288. doi:10.1093/eurheartj/ehm112

Meier, D., Cothren, R., Vince, D., & Cornhill, J. (1997). Automated morphometry of coronary arteries with digital image analysis of intravascular ultrasound. *American Heart Journal, 133*(6), 681–690. doi:10.1016/S0002-8703(97)70170-4

Mejia, J., Ruzzeh, B., Mongrain, R., Leask, R., & Bertrand, O. F. (2009). Evaluation of the effect of stent strut profile on shear stress distribution using statistical moments. *Biomedical Engineering Online, 8,* 8. doi:10.1186/1475-925X-8-8

Mendelson, Y. (1992). Pulse oximetry: Theory and applications for noninvasive monitoring. *Clinical Chemistry, 38,* 1601–1607.

Meredith, I. T., Whitbourn, R., Walters, D., Popma, J., Cutlip, D., & Fitzgerald, P. (2007). The next-generation Endeavor Resolute stent: 4-month clinical and angiographic results from the Endeavor Resolute first-in-man trial. *EuroIntervention, 3,* 50–53.

Meredith, I. T., Worthley, S., Whitbourn, R., Walters, D. L., McClean, D., & Horrigan, M. (2009). Clinical and angiographic results with the next-generation resolute stent system: A prospective, multicenter, first-in-human trial. *JACC: Cardiovascular Interventions, 2*(10), 977–985. doi:10.1016/j.jcin.2009.07.007

Miller, J. M., Rochitte, C. E., Dewey, M., Arbab-Zadeh, A., Niinuma, H., & Gottlieb, I. (2008). Diagnostic performance of coronary angiography by 64-row CT. *The New England Journal of Medicine, 359*(22), 2324–2336. doi:10.1056/NEJMoa0806576

Min, J. K., Shaw, L. J., Devereux, R. B., Okin, P. M., Weinsaft, J. W., & Russo, D. J. (2007). Prognostic value of multidetector coronary computed tomographic angiography for prediction of all-cause mortality. *Journal of the American College of Cardiology, 50*(12), 1161–1170. doi:10.1016/j.jacc.2007.03.067

Mintz, G. S., Kent, K. M., Pichard, A. D., Satler, L. F., Popma, J. J., & Leon, M. B. (1997). Contribution of inadequate arterial remodeling to the development of focal coronary artery stenoses. An intravascular ultrasound study. *Circulation, 95*(7), 1791–1798.

Mintz, G. S., Nissen, S. E., Anderson, W. D., Bailey, S. R., Erbel, R., & Fitzgerald, P. J. (2001). American College of Cardiology clinical expert consensus document on standards for acquisition, measurement and reporting of intravascular ultrasound studies (IVUS). A report of the American College of Cardiology Task Force on Clinical Expert Consensus Documents. *Journal of the American College of Cardiology, 37*(5), 1478–1492. doi:10.1016/S0735-1097(01)01175-5

Mintz, G. S., & Weissman, N. J. (2006). Intravascular ultrasound in the drug-eluting stent era. *Journal of the American College of Cardiology, 48*(3), 421–429. doi:10.1016/j.jacc.2006.04.068

Mintz, G. S., Nissen, S. E., Anderson, W. D., Bailey, S. R., Elber, R., & Fitzgerald, P. J. (2001). American College of Cardiology clinical expert consensus document on standards for acquisition, measurement and reporting of intravascular ultrasound studies: A report of the American College of Cardiology task force on clinical expert consensus documents (committee to develop a clinical expert consensus on standards for acquisition, measurement and reporting of intravascular ultrasound studies [IVUS]). *Journal of the American College of Cardiology*, *37*, 1478–1492. doi:10.1016/S0735-1097(01)01175-5

Mintz, G. S., Painter, J. A., Pichard, A. D., Kent, K. M., Satler, L. F., & Popma, J. J. (1995). Atherosclerosis in angiographically "normal" coronary artery reference segments: An intravascular ultrasound study with clinical correlations. *Journal of the American College of Cardiology*, *25*(7), 1479–1485. doi:10.1016/0735-1097(95)00088-L

Mintz, G. S. (2007). Features and parameters of drug-eluting stent deployment discoverable by intravascular ultrasound. *The American Journal of Cardiology*, *100*, 26M–35M. doi:10.1016/j.amjcard.2007.08.019

Mintz, G. S., Pichard, A. D., Kovach, J. A., Kent, K. M., Satler, L. F., & Javier, S. P. (1994). Impact of preintervention intravascular ultrasound imaging on transcatheter treatment strategies in coronary artery disease. *The American Journal of Cardiology*, *73*(7), 423–430. doi:10.1016/0002-9149(94)90670-X

Mintz, G. S., & Weissman, N. J. (2006). Intravascular ultrasound in the drug-eluting stent era. *Journal of the American College of Cardiology*, *48*(3), 421–429. doi:10.1016/j.jacc.2006.04.068

Mintz, G. S. (2007). Features and parameters of drug-eluting stent deployment discoverable by intravascular ultrasound. *The American Journal of Cardiology*, *100*(8B), 26M–35M. doi:10.1016/j.amjcard.2007.08.019

Mintz, G., & Weissman, N. (2006). Intravascular ultrasound in the drug-eluting stent era. *Journal of the American College of Cardiology*, *48*, 421–429. doi:10.1016/j.jacc.2006.04.068

Missel, E., Mintz, G. S., Carlier, S. G., Qian, J., Shan, S., & Castellanos, C. (2008). In vivo virtual histology intravascular ultrasound correlates of risk factors for sudden coronary death in men: Results from the prospective, multi-centre virtual histology intravascular ultrasound registry. *European Heart Journal*, *29*(17), 2141–2147. doi:10.1093/eurheartj/ehn293

Mitsumori, L. M., Hatsukami, T. S., Ferguson, M. S., Kerwin, W. S., Cai, J., & Yuan, C. (2003). In vivo accuracy of multisequence MR imaging for identifying unstable fibrous caps in advanced human carotid plaques. *Journal of Magnetic Resonance Imaging*, *17*(4), 410–420. doi:10.1002/jmri.10264

Miyagi, M., Ishii, H., Murakami, R., Isobe, S., Hayashi, M., & Amano, T. (2009). Impact of long-term statin treatment on coronary plaque composition at angiographically severe lesions: A nonrandomized study of the history of long-term statin treatment before coronary angioplasty. *Clinical Therapeutics*, *31*(1), 64–73. doi:10.1016/j.clinthera.2009.01.002

Miyazawa, A., Ako, J., Hassan, A., Hasegawa, T., Abizaid, A., & Verheye, S. (2007). Analysis of bifurcation lesions treated with novel drug-eluting dedicated bifurcation stent system: Intravascular ultrasound results of the AXXESS PLUS trial. *Catheterization and Cardiovascular Interventions*, *70*(7), 952–957. doi:10.1002/ccd.21269

Miyazawa, A., Ako, J., Hongo, Y., Hur, S. H., Tsujino, I., & Courtney, B. K. (2008). Comparison of vascular response to zotarolimus-eluting stent versus sirolimus-eluting stent: Intravascular ultrasound results from ENDEAVOR III. *American Heart Journal*, *155*(1), 108–113. doi:10.1016/j.ahj.2007.08.008

Mizushina, S., Shimizu, T., & Sugiura, T. (1992). Noninvasive thermometry with multi-frequency microwave radiometry. *Frontiers of Medical and Biological Engineering*, *4*, 129–133.

Mojsilović, A., Popović, M., Amodaj, N., Babić, R., & Ostojić, M. (1997). Automatic segmentation of intravascular ultrasound images: A texture-based approach. *Annals of Biomedical Engineering*, *25*(6), 1059–1071.

Moore, M. P., Spencer, T., Salter, D. M., Kearney, P. P., Shaw, T. R., & Starkey, I. R. (1998). Characterisation of coronary atherosclerotic morphology by spectral analysis of radiofrequency signal: In vitro intravascular ultrasound study with histological and radiological validation. *Heart (British Cardiac Society)*, *79*(5), 459–467.

Moreno, R., Fernandez, C., Alfonso, F., Hernandez, R., Perez-Vizcayno, M. J., & Escaned, J. (2004). Coronary stenting versus balloon angioplasty in small vessels: A meta-analysis from 11 randomized studies. *Journal of the American College of Cardiology*, *43*(11), 1964–1972. doi:10.1016/j.jacc.2004.01.039

Moreno, P., Lodder, R., Purushothaman, K., Charash, W., O'Connor, W., & Muller, J. (2002). Detection of lipid pool, thin fibrous cap, and inflammatory cells in human aortic atherosclerotic plaques by near-infrared spectroscopy. *Circulation*, *105*, 923–927. doi:10.1161/hc0802.104291

Moreno, P. R., Purushothaman, K. R., Fuster, V., Echeverri, D., Truszczynska, H., & Sharma, S. K. (2004). Plaque neovascularization is increased in ruptured atherosclerotic lesions of human aorta: Implications for plaque vulnerability. *Circulation*, *110*(14), 2032–2038. doi:10.1161/01.CIR.0000143233.87854.23

Moreno, P., Purushothaman, K., Sirol, M., Levy, A., & Fuster, V. (2006). Neovascularization in human atherosclerosis. *Circulation*, *113*, 2245–2252. doi:10.1161/CIRCULATIONAHA.105.578955

Moreno, P., Ryan, S., & Hopkins, D. (2001). Identification of lipid-rich aortic atherosclerotic plaques in living rabbits with a near infrared spectroscopy catheter. *Journal of the American College of Cardiology, Suppl A: 3A*(37).

Morice, M. C., Serruys, P. W., Sousa, J. E., Fajadet, J., Ban Hayashi, E., & Perin, M. (2002). A randomized comparison of a sirolimus-eluting stent with a standard stent for coronary revascularization. *The New England Journal of Medicine*, *346*(23), 1773–1780. doi:10.1056/NEJMoa012843

Morikawa, Y., Uemura, S., & Ishigami, K. (2011). Morphological features of coronary arteries in patients with coronary spastic angina: Assessment with intracoronary optical coherence tomography. *International Journal of Cardiology*, *46*(3).

Moses, J. W., Leon, M. B., Popma, J. J., Fitzgerald, P. J., Holmes, D. R., O'Shaughnessy, C. (2003). Sirolimus-eluting stents versus standard stents in patients with stenosis in a native coronary artery. *N Engl J Med, 349*(14), 1315-1323.4

Motoyama, S., Sarai, M., Harigaya, H., Anno, H., Inoue, K., & Hara, T. (2009). Computed tomographic angiography characteristics of atherosclerotic plaques subsequently resulting in acute coronary syndrome. *Journal of the American College of Cardiology*, *54*(1), 49–57. doi:10.1016/j.jacc.2009.02.068

Motreff, P., Souteyrand, G., & Levesque, S. (2009). Comparative analysis of neointimal coverage with paclitaxel and zotarolimus drug-eluting stents: Using optical coherence tomography 6 months after implantation. *Arch Cardiovasc Dis*, *102*, 617–624. doi:10.1016/j.acvd.2009.05.010

Moussa, I., Di Mario, C., & Reimers, B. (1997). Subacute stent thrombosis in the era of intravascular ultrasound-guided coronary stenting without anticoagulation: Frequency, predictors and clinical outcome. *Journal of the American College of Cardiology*, *29*(1), 6–12. doi:10.1016/S0735-1097(96)00452-4

Mudra, H., Di Mario, C., de Jaegere, P., Figulla, H., Macaya, C., & Zahn, R. (2001). Randomized comparison of coronary stent implantation under ultrasound or angiographic guidance to reduce stent restenosis (OPTICUS study). *Circulation*, *104*, 1343–1349. doi:10.1161/hc3701.096064

Mueller, C., Hodgson, J. M., & Schindler, C. (2003). Cost-effectiveness of intracoronary ultrasound for percutaneous coronary interventions. *The American Journal of Cardiology*, *91*(2), 143–147. doi:10.1016/S0002-9149(02)03099-0

Muller, J., Tawakol, A., Kathiresan, S., & Narula, J. (2006). New opportunities for identification and reduction of coronary risk: Treatment of vulnerable patients, arteries, and plaques. *Journal of the American College of Cardiology*, *C*(47), 2–6. doi:10.1016/j.jacc.2005.12.044

Muller, J. E., Abela, G. S., Nesto, R. W., & Tofler, G. H. (1994). Triggers, acute risk factors and vulnerable plaques: The lexicon of a new frontier. *Journal of the American College of Cardiology, 23*(3), 809–813. doi:10.1016/0735-1097(94)90772-2

Munce, N. R., Yang, V. X., & Standish, B. A. (2007). Ex vivo imaging of chronic total occlusions using forward-looking optical coherence tomography. *Lasers in Surgery and Medicine, 39*(1), 28–35. doi:10.1002/lsm.20449

Munson, B. R., Young, D. F., & Okiishi, T. H. (2002). *Fundamentals of fluid mechanics* (4th ed.). New York, NY: John Wiley & Sons, Inc.

Murashige, A., Hiro, T., Fujii, T., Imoto, K., Murata, T., & Fukumoto, Y. (2005). Detection of lipid-laden atherosclerotic plaque by wavelet analysis of radiofrequency intravascular ultrasound signals: In vitro validation and preliminary in vivo application. *Journal of the American College of Cardiology, 45*(12), 1954–1960. doi:10.1016/j.jacc.2004.10.080

Myers, P., Barrett, A., & Sadowsky, N. (1980). Microwave thermography of normal and cancerous breast tissue. *Annals of the New York Academy of Sciences, 335*, 443–455. doi:10.1111/j.1749-6632.1980.tb50768.x

Nadaud, S., Philippe, M., Arnal, J. F., Michel, J. B., & Soubrier, F. (1996). Sustained increase in aortic endothelial nitric oxide synthase expression in vivo in a model of chronic high blood flow. *Circulation Research, 79*(4), 857–863.

Nadkarni, S. K., Boughner, D., & Fenster, A. (2005). Image-based cardiac gating for three-dimensional intravascular ultrasound imaging. *Ultrasound in Medicine & Biology, 31*(1), 53–63. doi:10.1016/j.ultrasmedbio.2004.08.025

Nadkarni, S., Bouma, B., de Boer, J., & Tearney, G. (2009). Evaluation of collagen in atherosclerotic plaques: the use of two coherent laser-based imaging methods. *Lasers in Medical Science, 24*, 439–445. doi:10.1007/s10103-007-0535-x

Nagai, H., Ishibashi-Ueda, H., & Fujii, K. (2010). Histology of highly echolucent regions in optical coherence tomography images from two patients with sirolimus-eluting stent restenosis. *Catheterization and Cardiovascular Interventions, 75*, 961–963.

Naghavi, M., Libby, P., Falk, E., Casscells, S. W., Litovsky, S., & Rumberger, J. (2003). From vulnerable plaque to vulnerable patient: A call for new definitions and risk assessment strategies: Part I. *Circulation, 108*(14), 1664–1672. doi:10.1161/01.CIR.0000087480.94275.97

Naghavi, M., John, R., Naguib, S., Siadaty, M., Grasu, R., & Kurian, K. (2002). pH heterogeneity of human and rabbit atherosclerotic plaques: A new insight into detection of vulnerable plaque. *Atherosclerosis, 164*, 27–35. doi:10.1016/S0021-9150(02)00018-7

Naghavi, M., Madjid, M., Gul, K., Siadaty, M., Litovsky, S., & Willerson, J. (2003). Thermography basket catheter: in vivo measurement of the temperature of atherosclerotic plaques for detection of vulnerable plaques. *Catheterization and Cardiovascular Interventions, 59*, 52–59. doi:10.1002/ccd.10486

Naghavi, M., John, R., Naguib, S., Siadaty, M., Grasu, R., & Kurian, K. (2002). pH Heterogeneity of human and rabbit atherosclerotic plaques; a new insight into detection of vulnerable plaque. *Atherosclerosis, 164*.

Nahrendorf, M., Zhang, H., Hembrador, S., Panizzi, P., Sosnovik, D. E., & Aikawa, E. (2008). Nanoparticle PET-CT imaging of macrophages in inflammatory atherosclerosis. *Circulation, 117*(3), 379–387. doi:10.1161/CIRCULATIONAHA.107.741181

Nahrendorf, M., Waterman, P., Thurber, G., Groves, K., Rajopadhye, M., & Panizzi, P. (2009). Hybrid in vivo FMT-CT imaging of protease activity in atherosclerosis with customized nanosensors. *Arteriosclerosis, Thrombosis, and Vascular Biology, 29*, 1444–1451. doi:10.1161/ATVBAHA.109.193086

Nahrendorf, M., Zhang, H., Hembrador, S., Panizzi, P., Sosnovik, D., & Aikawa, E. (2008). Nanoparticle PET-CT imaging of macrophages in inflammatory atherosclerosis. *Circulation, 117*, 379–387. doi:10.1161/CIRCULATIONAHA.107.741181

Nair, A., Kuban, B., Tuzcu, E., Schoenhagen, P., Nissen, S., & Vince, D. (2002). Coronary plaque classification with intravascular ultrasound radiofrequency data analysis. *Circulation, 106*, 2200–2206. doi:10.1161/01.CIR.0000035654.18341.5E

Nair, A., Calvetti, D., & Vince, D. G. (2004). Regularized autoregressive analysis of intravascular ultrasound backscatter: Improvement in spatial accuracy of tissue maps. *IEEE Transactions on Ultrasonics, Ferroelectrics, and Frequency Control, 51*(4), 420–431. doi:10.1109/TUFFC.2004.1295427

Nair, A., Kuban, B. D., Obuchowski, N., & Vince, D. G. (2001). Assessing spectral algorithms to predict atherosclerotic plaque composition with normalized and raw intravascular ultrasound data. *Ultrasound in Medicine & Biology, 27*(10), 1319–1331. doi:10.1016/S0301-5629(01)00436-7

Nair, A., Margolis, M. P., Kuban, B. D., & Vince, D. G. (2007). Automated coronary plaque characterisation with intravascular ultrasound backscatter: Ex vivo validation. *EuroIntervention, 3*(1), 113–120.

Najafi, Z., Taki, A., Setarehdan, S. K., Zoroofi, R., Konig, A., & Navab, N. (2007). *A new method for automatic border detection in IVUS images and 3D visualization of segmented frames.* The 4th Visual Information Engineering Conference: VIE 2007, London, July 2007.

Naqvi, T. Z., Zarbatany, D., Molloy, M. D., Logan, J., & Buchbinder, M. (2006). Intracardiac echocardiography for percutaneous mitral valve repair in a swine model. *Journal of the American Society of Echocardiography, 19*(2), 147–153. .doi:10.1016/j.echo.2005.09.008

Nasu, K., Tsuchikane, E., Katoh, O., Tanaka, N., Kimura, M., & Ehara, M. (2009). Effect of fluvastatin on progression of coronary atherosclerotic plaque evaluated by virtual histology intravascular ultrasound. *JACC: Cardiovascular Interventions, 2*(7), 689–696. doi:10.1016/j.jcin.2009.04.016

Nasu, K., Tsuchikane, E., Katoh, O., Vince, D. G., Margolis, P. M., & Virmani, R. (2008). Impact of intramural thrombus in coronary arteries on the accuracy of tissue characterization by in vivo intravascular ultrasound radiofrequency data analysis. *The American Journal of Cardiology, 101*(8), 1079–1083. doi:10.1016/j.amjcard.2007.11.064

Nasu, K., Tsuchikane, E., Katoh, O., Vince, D. G., Virmani, R., & Surmely, J. F. (2006). Accuracy of in vivo coronary plaque morphology assessment: A validation study of in vivo virtual histology compared with in vitro histopathology. *Journal of the American College of Cardiology, 47*(12), 2405–2412. doi:10.1016/j.jacc.2006.02.044

Nazemi, M., Kleinstreuer, C., Archie, J. P., & Sorrell, F. Y. (1989). Fluid-flow and plaque-formation in an aortic bifurcation. *Journal of Biomechanical Engineering-Transactions of the ASME, 111*(4), 316–324. doi:10.1115/1.3168385

Neumeister, V., Scheibe, M., Lattke, P., & Jaross, W. (2002). Determination of the cholesterol-collagen ratio of arterial atherosclerotic plaques using near infrared spectroscopy as a possible measure of plaque stability. *Atherosclerosis, 165*, 251–257. doi:10.1016/S0021-9150(02)00279-4

Nicholls, S. J., Hsu, A., Wolski, K., Hu, B., Bayturan, O., & Lavoie, A. (2010). Intravascular ultrasound-derived measures of coronary atherosclerotic plaque burden and clinical outcome. *Journal of the American College of Cardiology, 55*(21), 2399–2407. doi:10.1016/j.jacc.2010.02.026

Nicholls, S. J., Tuzcu, E. M., Wolski, K., Sipahi, I., Schoenhagen, P., & Crowe, T. (2007). Coronary artery calcification and changes in atheroma burden in response to established medical therapies. *Journal of the American College of Cardiology, 49*(2), 263–270. doi:10.1016/j.jacc.2006.10.038

Nishimura, R., Edwards, W., Warnes, C., Reeder, G., Holmes, D. Jr, & Tajik, A. (1990). Intravascular ultrasound imaging: in vitro validation and pathologic correlation. *Journal of the American College of Cardiology, 16*, 145–154. doi:10.1016/0735-1097(90)90472-2

Nishimura, Y., Fukuchi, K., Katafuchi, T., Sagou, M., Oka, H., & Ishida, Y. (2004). Superimposed display of coronary artery on gated myocardial perfusion scintigraphy. *Journal of Nuclear Medicine, 45*(9), 1444–1449.

Nishioka, T., Amanullah, A. M., Luo, H., Berglund, H., Kim, C. J., & Nagai, T. (1999). Clinical validation of intravascular ultrasound imaging for assessment of coronary stenosis severity: Comparison with stress myocardial perfusion imaging. *Journal of the American College of Cardiology, 33*(7), 1870–1878. doi:10.1016/S0735-1097(99)00100-X

Nishioka, H., Shimada, K., Kataoka, T., Hirose, M., Asawa, K., & Hasegawa, T. (2004). Impact of HMG-CoA reductase inhibitors for non-treated coronary segments. *Osaka City Medical Journal, 50*(2), 61–68.

Nissen, S. E. (2002). Application of intravascular ultrasound to characterize coronary artery disease and assess the progression or regression of atherosclerosis. *The American Journal of Cardiology, 89*(4A), 24B–31B. doi:10.1016/S0002-9149(02)02217-8

Nissen, S. E., Gurley, J. C., Grines, C. L., Booth, D. C., McClure, R., & Berk, M. (1991). Intravascular ultrasound assessment of lumen size and wall morphology in normal subjects and patients with coronary artery disease. *Circulation, 84*(3), 1087–1099.

Nissen, S. E., Nicholls, S. J., Sipahi, I., Libby, P., Raichlen, J. S., & Ballantyne, C. M. (2006). Effect of very high-intensity statin therapy on regression of coronary atherosclerosis: The ASTEROID trial. *Journal of the American Medical Association, 295*(13), 1556–1565. doi:10.1001/jama.295.13.jpc60002

Nissen, S. E., Nicholls, S. J., Wolski, K., Nesto, R., Kupfer, S., & Perez, A. (2008). Comparison of pioglitazone vs glimepiride on progression of coronary atherosclerosis in patients with type 2 diabetes: The PERISCOPE randomized controlled trial. *Journal of the American Medical Association, 299*(13), 1561–1573. doi:10.1001/jama.299.13.1561

Nissen, S. E., Tuzcu, E. M., Schoenhagen, P., Brown, B. G., Ganz, P., & Vogel, R. A. (2004). Effect of intensive compared with moderate lipid-lowering therapy on progression of coronary atherosclerosis: A randomized controlled trial. *Journal of the American Medical Association, 291*(9), 1071–1080. doi:10.1001/jama.291.9.1071

Nissen, S. E., & Yock, P. (2001). Intravascular ultrasound: Novel pathophysiological insights and current clinical applications. *Circulation, 103*(4), 604–616.

Nissen, S. E., Nicholls, S. J., Sipahi, I., Libby, P., Raichlen, J. S., & Ballantyne, C. M. (2006). Effect of very high-intensity statin therapy on regression of coronary atherosclerosis: The ASTEROID trial. *Journal of the American Medical Association, 295*(13), 1556–1565. doi:10.1001/jama.295.13.jpc60002

Nissen, S. E., Nicholls, S. J., Wolski, K., Nesto, R., Kupfer, S., & Perez, A. (2008). Comparison of pioglitazone vs glimepiride on progression of coronary atherosclerosis in patients with type 2 diabetes: The PERISCOPE randomized controlled trial. *Journal of the American Medical Association, 299*(13), 1561–1573. doi:10.1001/jama.299.13.1561

Nissen, S. E., Nicholls, S. J., Wolski, K., Rodes-Cabau, J., Cannon, C. P., & Deanfield, J. E. (2008). Effect of rimonabant on progression of atherosclerosis in patients with abdominal obesity and coronary artery disease: The STRADIVARIUS randomized controlled trial. *Journal of the American Medical Association, 299*(13), 1547–1560. doi:10.1001/jama.299.13.1547

Nissen, S. E., Tardif, J. C., Nicholls, S. J., Revkin, J. H., Shear, C. L., & Duggan, W. T. (2007). Effect of torcetrapib on the progression of coronary atherosclerosis. *The New England Journal of Medicine, 356*(13), 1304–1316. doi:10.1056/NEJMoa070635

Nissen, S. E., Tsunoda, T., Tuzcu, E. M., Schoenhagen, P., Cooper, C. J., & Yasin, M. (2003). Effect of recombinant ApoA-I Milano on coronary atherosclerosis in patients with acute coronary syndromes: A randomized controlled trial. *Journal of the American Medical Association, 290*(17), 2292–2300. doi:10.1001/jama.290.17.2292

Nissen, S. E., Tuzcu, E. M., Brewer, H. B., Sipahi, I., Nicholls, S. J., & Ganz, P. (2006). Effect of ACAT inhibition on the progression of coronary atherosclerosis. *The New England Journal of Medicine, 354*(12), 1253–1263. doi:10.1056/NEJMoa054699

Nissen, S. E., Tuzcu, E. M., Libby, P., Thompson, P. D., Ghali, M., & Garza, D. (2004). Effect of antihypertensive agents on cardiovascular events in patients with coronary disease and normal blood pressure: The CAMELOT study: a randomized controlled trial. *Journal of the American Medical Association, 292*(18), 2217–2225. doi:10.1001/jama.292.18.2217

Nissen, S. E., Tuzcu, E. M., Schoenhagen, P., Brown, B. G., Ganz, P., & Vogel, R. A. (2004). Effect of intensive compared with moderate lipid-lowering therapy on progression of coronary atherosclerosis: a randomized controlled trial. *Journal of the American Medical Association, 291*(9), 1071–1080. doi:10.1001/jama.291.9.1071

Nissen, S., Grines, C., Gurley, J., Sublett, K., Haynie, D., & Diaz, C. (1990). Application of a new phased-array ultrasound imaging catheter in the assessment of vascular dimensions. In vivo comparison to cineangiography. *Circulation, 81*, 660–666. doi:10.1161/01.CIR.81.2.660

Nissen, S. E., Di Mario, C., & Tuzcu, E. M. (1998). Intravascular ultrasound angioscopy, doppler and pressure measurements . In Topol, E. J. (Ed.), *Comprehensive cardiovascular medicine* (pp. 2471–2501). Philadelphia, PA: Lippincott-Raven Publishers.

Ntziachristos, V., Tung, C., Bremer, C., & Weissleder, R. (2002). Fluorescence molecular tomography resolves protease activity in vivo. *Nature Medicine, 8*, 757–760. doi:10.1038/nm729

Ochiai, M., Ogata, N., Araki, H., Ashida, K., Isomura, N., & Mikoshiba, Y. (2006). Intravascular ultrasound guided wiring for chronic total occlusions. *Indian Heart Journal, 58*(1), 15–20.

Oemrawsingh, P. V., Mintz, G. S., & Schalij, M. J. (2003). Intravascular ultrasound guidance improves angiographic and clinical outcome of stent implantation for long coronary artery stenoses: Final results of a randomized comparison with angiographic guidance (TULIP Study). *Circulation, 107*(1), 62–67. doi:10.1161/01. CIR.0000043240.87526.3F

Oh, W., Yun, S., & Vakoc, B. e. (2008). High-speed polarization sensitive optical frequency domain imaging with frequency multiplexing. *Optics Express, 16*, 1096–1103. doi:10.1364/OE.16.001096

Ohayon, J., & Finet, G., & al., G. A. (2008). Necrotic core thickness and positive arterial remodeling index: Emergent biomechanical factors for evaluating the risk of plaque rupture. *American Journal of Physiology. Heart and Circulatory Physiology, 295*, H717–H727. doi:10.1152/ajpheart.00005.2008

Ohlmann, P., Kim, S. W., Mintz, G. S., Pregowski, J., Tyczynski, P., & Maehara, A. (2005). Cardiovascular events in patients with coronary plaque rupture and non-significant stenosis. *The American Journal of Cardiology, 96*(12), 1631–1635. doi:10.1016/j.amjcard.2005.07.087

Okabe, T., Mintz, G., Ashesh, N., Roy, P., Hong, Y., & Smith, K. (2007). Intravascular ultrasound parameters associated with stent thrombosis after drug-eluting stent deployment. *J Am Coll Cardiol Intv, 100*, 615–620.

Okazaki, S., Yokoyama, T., Miyauchi, K., Shimada, K., Kurata, T., & Sato, H. (2004). Early statin treatment in patients with acute coronary syndrome: demonstration of the beneficial effect on atherosclerotic lesions by serial volumetric intravascular ultrasound analysis during half a year after coronary event: The ESTABLISH study. *Circulation, 110*(9), 1061–1068. doi:10.1161/01. CIR.0000140261.58966.A4

Okimoto, T., Imazu, M., Hayashi, Y., Fujiwara, H., Ueda, H., & Kohno, N. (2002). Atherosclerotic plaque characterization by quantitative analysis using intravascular ultrasound: Correlation with histological and immunohistochemical findings. *Circulation Journal, 66*(2), 173–177. doi:10.1253/circj.66.173

Okubo, M., Kawasaki, M., Ishihara, Y., Takeyama, U., Yasuda, S., & Kubota, T. (2008). Tissue characterization of coronary plaques: Comparison of integrated backscatter intravascular ultrasound with virtual histology intravascular ultrasound. *Circulation Journal, 72*(10), 1631–1639. doi:10.1253/circj.CJ-07-0936

Okubo, M., Kawasaki, M., Ishihara, Y., Takeyama, U., Kubota, T., & Yamaki, T. (2008). Development of integrated backscatter intravascular ultrasound for tissue characterization of coronary plaques. *Ultrasound in Medicine & Biology, 34*(4), 655–663. doi:10.1016/j. ultrasmedbio.2007.09.015

Okura, H., Kobayashi, Y., Sumitsuji, S., Terashima, M., Kataoka, T., & Masutani, M. (2009). Effect of culprit-lesion remodeling versus plaque rupture on three-year outcome in patients with acute coronary syndrome. *The American Journal of Cardiology, 103*(6), 791–795. doi:10.1016/j.amjcard.2008.11.030

Okura, H., Morino, Y., Oshima, A., Hayase, M., Ward, M. R., & Popma, J. J. (2001). Preintervention arterial remodeling affects clinical outcome following stenting: an intravascular ultrasound study. *Journal of the American College of Cardiology, 37*(4), 1031–1035. doi:10.1016/ S0735-1097(01)01145-7

Okura, H., Taguchi, H., Kubo, T., Toda, I., Yoshida, K., & Yoshiyama, M. (2007). Atherosclerotic plaque with ultrasonic attenuation affects coronary reflow and infarct size in patients with acute coronary syndrome: An intravascular ultrasound study. *Circulation Journal, 71*(5), 648–653. doi:10.1253/circj.71.648

O'Leary, D. H., Polak, J. F., Kronmal, R. A., Manolio, T. A., Burke, G. L., & Wolfson, S. K. Jr. (1999). Carotid-artery intima and media thickness as a risk factor for myocardial infarction and stroke in older adults. Cardiovascular Health Study Collaborative Research Group. *The New England Journal of Medicine, 340*(1), 14–22. doi:10.1056/NEJM199901073400103

O'Malley, S. M., Carlier, S. G., Naghavi, M., & Kakadiaris, I. A. (2007). Image-based frame gating of IVUS pullbacks: A surrogate for ECG. *IEEE International Conference on Acoustics, Speech and Signal Processing, 1*, (pp. I-433-I-436).

Ophir, J., Cespedes, I., Ponnekanti, H., Yazdi, Y., & Li, X. (1991). Elastography: A quantitative method for imaging the elasticity of biological tissues. *Ultrasonic Imaging, 13*(2), 111–134. doi:10.1016/0161-7346(91)90079-W

Ormiston, J. A., Serruys, P. W., Regar, E., Dudek, D., Thuesen, L., & Webster, M. W. (2008). A bioabsorbable everolimus-eluting coronary stent system for patients with single de-novo coronary artery lesions (ABSORB): A prospective open-label trial. *Lancet, 371*(9616), 899–907. doi:10.1016/S0140-6736(08)60415-8

Ormiston, J., Serruys, P., & Regar, E. (2008). A bioabsorbable everolimus-eluting coronary stent system for patients with single de-novo coronary artery lesions (ABSORB): A prospective open-label trial. *Lancet, 371*, 899–907. doi:10.1016/S0140-6736(08)60415-8

O'Rourke, R. A., Brundage, B. H., Froelicher, V. F., Greenland, P., Grundy, S. M., & Hachamovitch, R. (2000). American College of Cardiology/American Heart Association expert consensus document on electron-beam computed tomography for the diagnosis and prognosis of coronary artery disease. *Journal of the American College of Cardiology, 36*(1), 326–340. doi:10.1016/S0735-1097(00)00831-7

O'Rourke, M., Staessen, J., Vlachopoulos, C., Duprez, D., & Plante, G. (2002). Clinical applications of arterial stiffness: Definitions and reference values. *American Journal of Hypertension, 15*(5), 426–444. doi:10.1016/S0895-7061(01)02319-6

Otake, H., Shite, J., Ako, J., Shinke, T., Tanino, Y., & Ogasawara, D. (2009). Local determinants of thrombus formation following sirolimus-eluting stent implantation assessed by Optical Coherence Tomography. *J Am Coll Cardiol Intv, 2*, 459–466.

Ozaki, Y., Okumura, M., & Ismail, T. (2010). The fate of incomplete stent apposition with drug-eluting stents: an optical coherence tomography-based natural history study. *European Heart Journal, 31*, 1470–1476. doi:10.1093/eurheartj/ehq066

Packard, R. R. S., & Libby, P. (2008). Inflammation in atherosclerosis: From vascular biology to biomarker discovery and risk prediction. *Clinical Chemistry, 54*(1), 24–38. doi:10.1373/clinchem.2007.097360

Packer, D. L., Stevens, C. L., Curley, M. G., Bruce, C. J., Miller, F. A., & Khandheria, B. K. (2002). Intracardiac phased-array imaging: Methods and initial clinical experience with high resolution, under blood visualization: Initial experience with intracardiac phased-array ultrasound. *Journal of the American College of Cardiology, 39*(3), 509–516. doi:10.1016/S0735-1097(01)01764-8

Palmer, N. D., Northridge, D., Lessells, A., McDicken, W. N., & Fox, K. A. (1999). In vitro analysis of coronary atheromatous lesions by intravascular ultrasound; reproducibility and histological correlation of lesion morphology. *European Heart Journal, 20*(23), 1701–1706. doi:10.1053/euhj.1999.1627

Pande, A., Kohler, R., Aikawa, E., Weissleder, R., & Jaffer, F. (2006). Detection of macrophage activity in atherosclerosis in vivo using multichannel, highresolution laser scanning fluorescence microscopy. *Journal of Biomedical Optics, 11*, 021009. doi:10.1117/1.2186337

Pandian, N. G. (1989). Intravascular and intracardiac ultrasound imaging. An old concept, now on the road to reality. *Circulation, 80*(4), 1091. doi:10.1161/01.CIR.80.4.1091

Pant, S., Bressloff, N. W., Forrester, A. I., & Curzen, N. (2010). The influence of strut-connectors in stented vessels: A comparison of pulsatile flow through five coronary stents. *Annals of Biomedical Engineering, 38*(5), 1893–1907. doi:10.1007/s10439-010-9962-0

Papadogiorgaki, M., Mezaris, V., Chatzizisis, Y., Giannoglou, G., & Kompatsiaris, I. (2008). Image analysis techniques for automated IVUS contour detection. *Ultrasound in Medicine & Biology, 34*(9), 1482–1498. doi:10.1016/j.ultrasmedbio.2008.01.022

Papadogiorgaki, M., Mezaris, V., Chatzizisis, Y., Giannoglou, G., & Kompatsiaris, I. (2007). Texture analysis and radial basis function approximation for IVUS image segmentation. *The Open Biomedical Engineering Journal, 1*, 53–59.

Papafaklis, M. I., Bourantas, C. V., Theodorakis, P. E., Katsouras, C. S., Fotiadis, D. I., & Michalis, L. K. (2009). Relationship of shear stress with in-stent restenosis: Bare metal stenting and the effect of brachytherapy. *International Journal of Cardiology, 134*(1), 25–32. doi:10.1016/j.ijcard.2008.02.006

Papafaklis, M. I., Bourantas, C. V., Theodorakis, P. E., Katsouras, C. S., Fotiadis, D. I., & Michalis, L. K. (2007). Association of endothelial shear stress with plaque thickness in a real three-dimensional left main coronary artery bifurcation model. *International Journal of Cardiology, 115*(2), 276–278. doi:10.1016/j.ijcard.2006.04.030

Papafaklis, M. I., Bourantas, C. V., Theodorakis, P. E., Katsouras, C. S., Naka, K. K., & Fotiadis, D. I. (2010). The effect of shear stress on neointimal response following sirolimus- and paclitaxel-eluting stent implantation compared to bare metal stents in humans. *Journal of the American College of Cardiology: Cardiovascular Interventions, 3*(11), 1181–1189.

Papafaklis, M. I., Katsouras, C. S., Theodorakis, P. E., Bourantas, C. V., Fotiadis, D. I., & Michalis, L. K. (2007). Coronary dilatation 10 weeks after paclitaxel-eluting stent implantation. No role of shear stress in lumen enlargement? *Heart and Vessels, 22*(4), 268–273. doi:10.1007/s00380-006-0970-9

Papafaklis, M. I., Koskinas, K. C., Chatzizisis, Y. S., Stone, P. H., & Feldman, C. L. (2010). In-vivo assessment of the natural history of coronary atherosclerosis: Vascular remodeling and endothelial shear stress determine the complexity of atherosclerotic disease progression. *Current Opinion in Cardiology, 25*(6), 627–638. doi:10.1097/HCO.0b013e32833f0236

Papafaklis, M. I. (2008). *Three-dimensional coronary artery reconstruction and blood flow simulation.* Doctoral Dissertation, University of Ioannina, Greece.

Papaioannou, T., Vavuranakis, M., Androulakis, A., Lazaros, G., Kakadiaris, I., & Vlaseros, I. (2009). In-vivo imaging of carotid plaque neoangiogenesis with contrast-enhanced harmonic ultrasound. *International Journal of Cardiology, 134*, e110–e112. doi:10.1016/j.ijcard.2008.01.020

Papaioannou, T. G., Christofidis, C., Mathioulakis, D. S., & Stefanadis, C. I. (2007). A novel design of a noncylindric stent with beneficial effects on flow characteristics: An experimental and numerical flow study in an axisymmetric arterial model with sequential mild stenoses. *Artificial Organs, 31*(8), 627–638. doi:10.1111/j.1525-1594.2007.00431.x

Papaioannou, T. G., Karatzis, E. N., Vavuranakis, M., Lekakis, J. P., & Stefanadis, C. (2006). Assessment of vascular wall shear stress and implications for atherosclerotic disease. *International Journal of Cardiology, 113*(1), 12–18. doi:10.1016/j.ijcard.2006.03.035

Parissi, E., Kompatsiaris, Y., Chatzizisis, Y. S., Koutkias, V., Maglaveras, N., Strintzis, M. G., & Giannoglou, G. D. (2006). An automated model for rapid and reliable segmentation of intravascular ultrasound images. *Proceedings Biological and Medical Data Analysis, 43*(45), 368–377. doi:10.1007/11946465_33

Park, S. J., Kim, Y. H., Park, D. W., Lee, S. W., Kim, W. J., & Suh, J. (2009). Impact of intravascular ultrasound guidance on long-term mortality in stenting for unprotected left main coronary artery stenosis. *Circ Cardiovasc Interv, 2*(3), 167–177. doi:10.1161/CIRCINTERVENTIONS.108.799494

Park, S. J., Kim, Y. H., Park, D. W., Lee, S. W., Kim, W. J., & Suh, J. (2009). MAIN-COMPARE Investigators: Impact of intravascular ultrasound guidance on long-term mortality in stenting for unprotected left main coronary artery stenosis. *Circ Cardiovasc Interv, 2*(3), 167–177. doi:10.1161/CIRCINTERVENTIONS.108.799494

Park, Y., Park, H. S., & Jang, G. L. (2009). Intravascular ultrasound guided recanalization of stumpless chronic total occlusion. *International Journal of Cardiology, 148*(2).

Patel, N., Stamper, D., & Brezinski, M. (2005). Review of the ability of optical coherence tomography to characterize plaque, including a comparison with intravascular ultrasound. *Cardiovascular and Interventional Radiology, 28*, 1–9. doi:10.1007/s00270-003-0021-1

Pawlowski, T., Mintz, G. S., Kulawik, T., & Gil, R. J. (2010). Virtual histology intravascular ultrasound evaluation of the left anterior descending coronary artery in patients with transient left ventricular ballooning syndrome. *Kardiologia Polska, 68*(10), 1093–1098.

Peters, R. J., Kok, W. E., Havenith, M. G., Rijsterborgh, H., van der Wal, A. C., & Visser, C. A. (1994). Histopathologic validation of intracoronary ultrasound imaging. *Journal of the American Society of Echocardiography, 7*(3 Pt 1), 230–241.

Petronio, A. S., Amoroso, G., Limbruno, U., Papini, B., De Carlo, M., & Micheli, A. (2005). Simvastatin does not inhibit intimal hyperplasia and restenosis but promotes plaque regression in normocholesterolemic patients undergoing coronary stenting: A randomized study with intravascular ultrasound. *American Heart Journal, 149*(3), 520–526. doi:10.1016/j.ahj.2004.10.032

Pflederer, T., Marwan, M., Schepis, T., Ropers, D., Seltmann, M., & Muschiol, G.Characterization of culprit lesions in acute coronary syndromes using coronary dual-source CT angiography. *Atherosclerosis, 211*(2), 437–444. doi:10.1016/j.atherosclerosis.2010.02.001

Philipp, S., Bose, D., Wijns, W., Marso, S. P., Schwartz, R. S., & Konig, A. (2010). Do systemic risk factors impact invasive findings from virtual histology? Insights from the international virtual histology registry. *European Heart Journal, 31*(2), 196–202. doi:10.1093/eurheartj/ehp428

Pinto, S. T., Pakala, R., Lovec, R., Tio, F., & Waksman, R. (2007). Optical coherence tomographic imaging of a bioabsorbable magnesium stent lost in a porcine coronary artery. *Cardiovascular Revascularization Medicine; Including Molecular Interventions, 8*, 293–294. doi:10.1016/j.carrev.2007.09.002

Pinto, S. T., Pakala, R., & Waksman, R. (2008). Serial imaging and histology illustrating the degradation of a bioabsorbable magnesium stent in a porcine coronary artery. *European Heart Journal, 29*, 314. doi:10.1093/eurheartj/ehm365

Platt, M., Ankeny, R., Shi, G., Weiss, D., Vega, J., & Taylor, W. J. (2007). Expression of cathepsin K is regulated by shear stress in cultured endothelial cells and is increased in endothelium in human atherosclerosis. *American Journal of Physiology. Heart and Circulatory Physiology, 292*, H1479–H1486. doi:10.1152/ajpheart.00954.2006

Plissiti, M. E., Fotiadis, D. I., Michalis, L. K., & Bozios, G. E. (2004). An automated method for lumen and media-adventitia border detection in a sequence of IVUS frames. *IEEE Transactions on Information Technology in Biomedicine, 8*(2), 131–141. doi:10.1109/TITB.2004.828889

Post, M. J., de Smet, B. J., van der Helm, Y., Borst, C., & Kuntz, R. E. (1997). Arterial remodeling after balloon angioplasty or stenting in an atherosclerotic experimental model. *Circulation, 96*(3), 996–1003.

Potkin, B. N., Bartorelli, A. L., Gessert, J. M., Neville, R. F., Almagor, Y., & Roberts, W. C. (1990). Coronary artery imaging with intravascular high-frequency ultrasound. *Circulation, 81*(5), 1575–1585. doi:10.1161/01.CIR.81.5.1575

Prat-Gonzalez, S., Sanz, J., & Garcia, M. (2008). Cardiac CT: Indications and limitations. *Journal of Nuclear Medicine Technology, 36*(1), 18–24. doi:10.2967/jnmt.107.042424

Prati, F., Arbustini, E., Labellarte, A., Dal Bello, B., Sommariva, L., & Mallus, M. T. (2001). Correlation between high frequency intravascular ultrasound and histomorphology in human coronary arteries. *Heart (British Cardiac Society), 85*(5), 567–570. doi:10.1136/heart.85.5.567

Prati, F., Pawlowski, T., Sommariva, L., Labellarte, A., Manzoli, A., & Boccanelli, A. (2002). Intravascular ultrasound and quantitative coronary angiography assessment of late in-stent restenosis: In vivo human correlation and methodological implications. *Catheterization and Cardiovascular Interventions, 57*(2), 155–160. doi:10.1002/ccd.10298

Prati, F., Arbustini, E., Labellarte, A., Dal Bello, B., Sommariva, L., & Mallus, M. T. (2001). Correlation between high frequency intravascular ultrasound and histomorphology in human coronary arteries. *Heart (British Cardiac Society), 85*(5), 567–570. doi:10.1136/heart.85.5.567

Prati, F., Cera, M., Ramazzotti, V., Imola, F., Giudice, R., & Albertucci, M. (2007). Safety and feasibility of a new non-occlusive technique for facilitated intracoronary optical coherence tomography (OCT) acquisition in various clinical and anatomical scenarios. *EuroIntervention, 3*(3), 365–370. doi:10.4244/EIJV3I3A66

Prati, F., Cera, M., Ramazzotti, V., Imola, F., Giudice, R., & Giudice, M. (2008). From bench to bed side: A novel technique to acquire OCT images. *Ciculation, 72*, 839–843. doi:10.1253/circj.72.839

Prati, F., Regar, E., Mintz, G. S., Arbustini, E., Di Mario, C., & Jang, I. K. (2010). Expert review document on methodology, terminology, and clinical applications of optical coherence tomography: Physical principles, methodology of image acquisition, and clinical application for assessment of coronary arteries and atherosclerosis. *European Heart Journal, 31*(4), 401–415. doi:10.1093/eurheartj/ehp433

Prati, F., Cera, M., Ramazzotti, V., Imola, F., Giudice, R., & Albertucci, M. (2007). Safety and feasibility of a new non-occlusive technique for facilitated intracoronary optical coherence tomography (OCT) acquisition in various clinical and anatomical scenarios. *EuroInterv, 3*, 365–370. doi:10.4244/EIJV3I3A66

Prati, F., Zimarino, M., & Stabile, E. (2008). Does optical coherence tomography identify arterial healing after stenting? An in vivo comparison with histology, in a rabbit carotid model. *Heart (British Cardiac Society), 94*, 217–221. doi:10.1136/hrt.2006.112482

Pujol, O., Radeva, P., Vitria, J., & Mauri, J. (2004). Adaboost to classify plaque appearance in IVUS images. *Lecture Notes in Computer Science, 3287*, 629–636. doi:10.1007/978-3-540-30463-0_79

Pundziute, G., Schuijf, J. D., Jukema, J. W., Decramer, I., Sarno, G., & Vanhoenacker, P. K. (2008). Head-to-head comparison of coronary plaque evaluation between multislice computed tomography and intravascular ultrasound radiofrequency data analysis. *JACC: Cardiovascular Interventions, 1*(2), 176–182. doi:10.1016/j.jcin.2008.01.007

Qi, Y., Qu, M., Long, D., Liu, B., Yao, Q., & Chien, S. (2008). Rho-GDP dissociation inhibitor alpha downregulated by low shear stress promotes vascular smooth muscle cell migration and apoptosis: A proteomic analysis. *Cardiovascular Research, 80*, 114–122. doi:10.1093/cvr/cvn158

Radu, M., Jorgensen, E., Kelbaek, H., Helqvist, S., Skovgaard, L., & Saunamaki, K. (2010). Strut apposition after coronary stent implantation visualised with optical coherence tomography. *EuroIntervention, 6*, 86–93. doi:10.4244/EIJV6I1A13

Raffel, O., Tearney, G., Gauthier, D., Halpern, E., Bouma, B., & Jang, I. (2007). Relationship between a systemic inflammatory marker, plaque inflammation, and plaque characteristics determined by intravascular optical coherence tomography. *Arteriosclerosis, Thrombosis, and Vascular Biology, 27*, 1820–1827. doi:10.1161/ATVBAHA.107.145987

Raghunathan, D., Abdel Karim, A., & DaSilva, M. (2011). (in press). Association between the presence and extent of coronary lipid core plaques detected by near-infrared spectroscopy with post percutaneous coronary intervention myocardial infarction. *The American Journal of Cardiology*. doi:10.1016/j.amjcard.2011.01.044

Ramaswamy, S., Vigmostad, S., Wahle, A., Lai, Y., Olszewski, M., & Braddy, K. (2004). Fluid dynamic analysis in a human left anterior descending coronary artery with arterial motion. *Annals of Biomedical Engineering, 32*(12), 1628–1641. doi:10.1007/s10439-004-7816-3

Ramcharitar, S., Gonzalo, N., van Geuns, R. J., Garcia-Garcia, H. M., Wykrzykowska, J. J., & Ligthart, J. M. (2009). First case of stenting of a vulnerable plaque in the SECRITT I trial-the dawn of a new era? *Nat Rev Cardiol, 6*(5), 374–378. doi:10.1038/nrcardio.2009.34

Ramkumar, P., Mitsouras, D., Feldman, C., Stone, P., & Rybicki, F. (2009). New advances in cardiac computed tomography. *Current Opinion in Cardiology, 24*(6), 596–603. doi:10.1097/HCO.0b013e3283319b84

Rasheed, Q., Dhawale, P. J., Anderson, J., & Hodgson, J. M. (1995). Intracoronary ultrasound-defined plaque composition: Computer-aided plaque characterization and correlation with histologic samples obtained during directional coronary atherectomy. *American Heart Journal, 129*(4), 631–637. doi:10.1016/0002-8703(95)90307-0

Rathore, S., Terashima, M., & Suzuki, T. (2009). Late-acquired stent malapposition after sirolimus-eluting stent implantation following acute coronary syndrome: Angiographic, IVUS, OCT and coronary angioscopic observation. *The Journal of Invasive Cardiology, 21*, 666–667.

Rathore, S., Katoh, O., & Tuschikane, E. (2010). A novel modification of the retrograde approach for the recanalization of chronic total occlusion of the coronary arteries intravascular ultrasound-guided reverse controlled antegrade and retrograde tracking. *JACC: Cardiovascular Interventions, 3*(2), 155–164. doi:10.1016/j.jcin.2009.10.030

Rees, M., Gehani, A., Ashley, S., & Davies, A. (1989). Percutaneous video angioscopy. *Clinical Radiology, 40*, 347–351. doi:10.1016/S0009-9260(89)80116-3

Rees, M., Gehani, A., & Feith, F. (1989). Percutaneous angioscopy. *British Heart Journal, 61*(1), 86.

Rees, M., & Michalis, L. (1995). Activated guidewire technique for treating chronic coronary artery occlusion. *Lancet, 346*, 943–944. doi:10.1016/S0140-6736(95)91560-5

Rees, M., & Richens, D. (1988). Coronary angioscopy. *The British Journal of Radiology, 61*, 728.

Rees, M., Wexler, L., Sivananthan, U., Fishcell, T., & Dake, M. (1993, January). Treatment of peripheral vascular disease with the pullback atherectomy catheter - Assessment by intravascular ultrasound and angioscopy. Endovascular Interventions. *International Congress VI*, Scottsdale, (pp. 27-31).

Regar, E., Prati, F., & Serruys, P. W. (2006). *Intracoronary OCT application: Methodological considerations.* Abingdon, UK: Taylor & Francis.

Regar, E., van Soest, G., Bruining, N., Constantinescu, A. A., van Geuns, R. J., van der Giessen, W., et al. (2010). Optical coherence tomography in patients with acute coronary syndrome. *EuroIntervention, 6 Suppl G*, G154-160.

Ren, J. F., Marchlinski, F. E., Callan, D. J., & Zado, E. S. (2002). Intracardiac doppler echocardiographic quantification of pulmonary vein flow velocity: An effective technique for monitoring pulmonary vein ostia narrowing during focal atrial fibrillation ablation. *Journal of Cardiovascular Electrophysiology, 13*(11), 1076–1081. doi:10.1046/j.1540-8167.2002.01076.x

Renshaw, P. F., Owen, C. S., McLaughlin, A. C., Frey, T. G., & Leigh, J. S. Jr. (1986). Ferromagnetic contrast agents: a new approach. *Magnetic Resonance in Medicine, 3*(2), 217–225. doi:10.1002/mrm.1910030205

Ricciardi, M. J., Meyers, S., & Choi, K. (2003). Angiographically silent left main disease detected by intravascular ultrasound: a marker for future adverse cardiac events. *American Heart Journal, 146*(3), 507–512. doi:10.1016/S0002-8703(03)00239-4

Richardson, P. D., Davies, M. J., & Born, G. V. (1989). Influence of plaque configuration and stress distribution on fissuring of coronary atherosclerotic plaques. *Lancet, 2*(8669), 941–944. doi:10.1016/S0140-6736(89)90953-7

Richens, D., Rees, M., & Watson, D. (1987, September 19). Laser coronary angioplasty under direct vision. *Lancet, 2*(8560), 683. doi:10.1016/S0140-6736(87)92462-7

Richens, D., Renzulli, A., & Hilton, C. (1990, March). Dissection of the left main coronary artery: Diagnosis by angioscopy. *The Annals of Thoracic Surgery, 49*(3), 469–470. doi:10.1016/0003-4975(90)90259-9

Richter, Y., Groothuis, A., Seifert, P., & Edelman, E. R. (2004). Dynamic flow alterations dictate leukocyte adhesion and response to endovascular interventions. *The Journal of Clinical Investigation, 113*(11), 1607–1614.

Rickenbacher, P. R., Pinto, F. J., Chenzbraun, A., Botas, J., Lewis, N. P., & Alderman, E. L. (1995). Incidence and severity of transplant coronary artery disease early and up to 15 years after transplantation as detected by intravascular ultrasound. *Journal of the American College of Cardiology, 25*(1), 171–177. doi:10.1016/0735-1097(94)00323-I

Rieber, J., Meissner, O., & Babaryka, G. (2006). Diagnostic accuracy of optical coherence tomography and intravascular ultrasound for the detection and characterization of atherosclerotic plaque composition in ex-vivo coronary specimens: A comparison with histology. *Coronary Artery Disease, 17*, 425–430. doi:10.1097/00019501-200608000-00005

Riga, M., Toutouzas, K., Tsiamis, E., Karanasos, A., Tsioufis, C., & Stefanadi, E. (2008). Increased local inflammatory activation is associated with thin fibrous caps in culprit lesions of patients with acute myocardial infarction. New insights by optical coherence tomography. *European Heart Journal, 29*, 4825.

Ringqvist, I., Fisher, L. D., Mock, M., Davis, K. B., Wedel, H., & Chaitman, B. R. (1983). Prognostic value of angiographic indices of coronary artery disease from the Coronary Artery Surgery Study (CASS). *The Journal of Clinical Investigation*, *71*(6), 1854–1866. doi:10.1172/JCI110941

Rioufol, G., Finet, G., Ginon, I., Andre-Fouet, X., Rossi, R., & Vialle, E. (2002). Multiple atherosclerotic plaque rupture in acute coronary syndrome: A three-vessel intravascular ultrasound study. *Circulation*, *106*(7), 804–808. doi:10.1161/01.CIR.0000025609.13806.31

Rioufol, G., Gilard, M., Finet, G., Ginon, I., Boschat, J., & Andre-Fouet, X. (2004). Evolution of spontaneous atherosclerotic plaque rupture with medical therapy: Long-term follow-up with intravascular ultrasound. *Circulation*, *110*, 2875–2880. doi:10.1161/01.CIR.0000146337.05073.22

Rispler, S., Keidar, Z., Ghersin, E., Roguin, A., Soil, A., & Dragu, R. (2007). Integrated single-photon emission computed tomography and computed tomography coronary angiography for the assessment of hemodynamically significant coronary artery lesions. *Journal of the American College of Cardiology*, *49*(10), 1059–1067. doi:10.1016/j.jacc.2006.10.069

Roberts, W., Bax, J., & Davies, L. (2008). Cardiac CT and CT coronary angiography: Technology and application. *Heart (British Cardiac Society)*, *94*(6), 781–792. doi:10.1136/hrt.2007.116392

Rodes-Cabau, J., Bertrand, O., & Larose, E. e. (2009). Comparison of plaque sealing with paclitaxel-eluting stents versus medical therapy for the treatment of moderate nonsignificant saphenous vein graft lesions. The moderate vein graft lesion stenting with the taxus stent and intravascular ultrasound (VELETI). *Circulationm*, *120*, 1978–1986. doi:10.1161/CIRCULATIONAHA.109.874057

Rodriguez-Granillo, G. A., Aoki, J., Ong, A. T., Valgimigli, M., Van Mieghem, C. A., & Regar, E. (2005). Methodological considerations and approach to cross-technique comparisons using in vivo coronary plaque characterization based on intravascular ultrasound radiofrequency data analysis: Insights from the Integrated Biomarker and Imaging Study (IBIS). *International Journal of Cardiovascular Interventions*, *7*(1), 52–58.

Rodriguez-Granillo, G. A., Bruining, N., Mc Fadden, E., Ligthart, J. M., Aoki, J., & Regar, E. (2005). Geometrical validation of intravascular ultrasound radiofrequency data analysis (virtual histology) acquired with a 30 MHz Boston Scientific corporation imaging catheter. *Catheterization and Cardiovascular Interventions*, *66*(4), 514–518. doi:10.1002/ccd.20447

Rodriguez-Granillo, G. A., Garcia-Garcia, H. M., Mc Fadden, E. P., Valgimigli, M., Aoki, J., & de Feyter, P. (2005). In vivo intravascular ultrasound-derived thin-cap fibroatheroma detection using ultrasound radiofrequency data analysis. *Journal of the American College of Cardiology*, *46*(11), 2038–2042. doi:10.1016/j.jacc.2005.07.064

Rodriguez-Granillo, G. A., Garcia-Garcia, H. M., Valgimigli, M., Vaina, S., van Mieghem, C., & van Geuns, R. J. (2006). Global characterization of coronary plaque rupture phenotype using three-vessel intravascular ultrasound radiofrequency data analysis. *European Heart Journal*, *27*(16), 1921–1927. doi:10.1093/eurheartj/ehl104

Rodriguez-Granillo, G. A., McFadden, E. P., Valgimigli, M., van Mieghem, C. A., Regar, E., & de Feyter, P. J. (2006). Coronary plaque composition of nonculprit lesions, assessed by in vivo intracoronary ultrasound radio frequency data analysis, is related to clinical presentation. *American Heart Journal*, *151*(5), 1020–1024. doi:10.1016/j.ahj.2005.06.040

Rodriguez-Granillo, G. A., Vos, J., Bruining, N., Garcia-Garcia, H. M., de Winter, S., & Ligthart, J. M. (2007). Long-term effect of perindopril on coronary atherosclerosis progression (from the perindopril's prospective effect on coronary atherosclerosis by angiography and intravascular ultrasound evaluation [PERSPECTIVE] study). *The American Journal of Cardiology*, *100*(2), 159–163. doi:10.1016/j.amjcard.2007.02.073

Rodriguez-Granillo, G. A., Garcia-Garcia, H. M., Valgimigli, M., Schaar, J. A., Pawar, R., van der Giessen, W. J., et al. (2006). In vivo relationship between compositional and mechanical imaging of coronary arteries. Insights from intravascular ultrasound radiofrequency data analysis. *Am Heart J*, *151*(5), 1025 e1021-1026.

Roelandt, J. R., di Mario, C., Pandian, N. G., Wenguang, L., Keane, D., & Slager, C. J. (1994). Three-dimensional reconstruction of intracoronary ultrasound images. Rationale, approaches, problems, and directions. *Circulation*, *90*(2), 1044–1055.

Roelandt, J., di Mario, C., Pandian, N., Wenguang, L., Keane, D., & Slager, C. (1994). Three-dimensional reconstruction of intracoronary ultrasound images. Rationale, approaches, problems, and directions. *Circulation, 90,* 1044–1055.

Rogers, I. S., Nasir, K., Figueroa, A. L., Cury, R. C., Hoffmann, U., & Vermylen, D. A.Feasibility of FDG imaging of the coronary arteries: comparison between acute coronary syndrome and stable angina. *JACC: Cardiovascular Imaging, 3*(4), 388–397. doi:10.1016/j.jcmg.2010.01.004

Rogers, C., & Edelman, E. R. (1995). Endovascular stent design dictates experimental restenosis and thrombosis. *Circulation, 91*(12), 2995–3001.

Rogers J. (2009 June/July). Forward-looking IVUS in chronic total occlusions. A new approach to an old problem. *Cardiac Interventions Today,* (pp. 21-24).

Rogowska, J., Patel, N. A., Fujimoto, J. G., & Brezinski, M. E. (2004). Optical coherence tomographic elastography technique for measuring deformation and strain of atherosclerotic tissues. *Heart (British Cardiac Society), 90*(5), 556–562. doi:10.1136/hrt.2003.016956

Rollins, A. M., & Izatt, J. A. (1999). Optimal interferometer designs for optical coherence tomography. *Optics Letters, 24*(21), 1484–1486. doi:10.1364/OL.24.001484

Rosamond, W., Flegal, K., Furie, K., Go, A., Greenlund, K., & Haase, N. (2008). Heart disease and stroke statistics--2008 update: A report from the American Heart Association Statistics Committee and Stroke Statistics Subcommittee. *Circulation, 117,* e25–e146. doi:10.1161/CIRCULATIONAHA.107.187998

Rosenfield, K., Losordo, D. W., Ramaswamy, K., Pastore, J. O., Langevin, R. E., & Razvi, S. (1991). Three dimensional reconstruction of human coronary and peripheral arteries from images recorded during two-dimensional intravascular ultrasound examination. *Circulation, 84*(5), 1938–1956.

Rosenthal, N., Guagliumi, G., Sirbu, V., & Zocai, G. B. (2009). *Comparing intravascular ultrasound and optical coherence tomography for the evaluation of stent segment malapposition.* Paper presented at the Transcatheter Therapeutics meeting (TCT), San Francisco.

Ross, R. (1999). Atherosclerosis--an inflammatory disease. *The New England Journal of Medicine, 340,* 115–126. doi:10.1056/NEJM199901143400207

Ross, R., & Glomset, J. A. (1976a). The pathogenesis of atherosclerosis (first of two parts). *The New England Journal of Medicine, 295*(7), 369–377. doi:10.1056/NEJM197608122950707

Roy, P., Steinberg, D. H., Sushinsky, S. J., Okabe, T., Pinto Slottow, T. L., & Kaneshige, K. (2008). The potential clinical utility of intravascular ultrasound guidance in patients undergoing percutaneous coronary intervention with drug-eluting stents. *European Heart Journal, 29*(15), 1851–1857. doi:10.1093/eurheartj/ehn249

Rudd, J. H., Narula, J., Strauss, H. W., Virmani, R., Machac, J., & Klimas, M.Imaging atherosclerotic plaque inflammation by fluorodeoxyglucose with positron emission tomography: Ready for prime time? *Journal of the American College of Cardiology, 55*(23), 2527–2535. doi:10.1016/j.jacc.2009.12.061

Ruehm, S. G., Corot, C., Vogt, P., Kolb, S., & Debatin, J. F. (2001). Magnetic resonance imaging of atherosclerotic plaque with ultrasmall superparamagnetic particles of iron oxide in hyperlipidemic rabbits. *Circulation, 103*(3), 415–422.

Rybicki, F. J., Melchionna, S., Mitsouras, D., Coskun, A. U., Whitmore, A. G., & Steigner, M. (2009). Prediction of coronary artery plaque progression and potential rupture from 320-detector row prospectively ECG-gated single heart beat CT angiography: Lattice Boltzmann evaluation of endothelial shear stress. *The International Journal of Cardiovascular Imaging, 25,* 289–299. doi:10.1007/s10554-008-9418-x

Rzeszutko, L., Legutko, J., Kaluza, G., Wizimirski, M., Richter, A., & Chyrchel, M. (2006). Assessment of culprit plaque temperature by intracoronary thermography appears inconclusive in patients with acute coronary syndromes. *Arteriosclerosis, Thrombosis, and Vascular Biology, 26,* 1889–1894. doi:10.1161/01.ATV.0000232500.93340.54

Saad, E. B., Marrouche, N. F., Saad, C. P., Ha, E., Bash, D., & White, R. D. (2003). Pulmonary vein stenosis after catheter ablation of atrial fibrillation: Emergence of a new clinical syndrome. *Annals of Internal Medicine, 138,* 634–638.

Saam, T., Cai, J., Ma, L., Cai, Y. Q., Ferguson, M. S., & Polissar, N. L. (2006). Comparison of symptomatic and asymptomatic atherosclerotic carotid plaque features with in vivo MR imaging. *Radiology, 240*(2), 464–472. doi:10.1148/radiol.2402050390

Sabate, M., Serruys, P. W., van der Giessen, W. J., Ligthart, J. M., Coen, V. L., & Kay, I. P. (1999). Geometric vascular remodeling after balloon angioplasty and beta-radiation therapy: A three-dimensional intravascular ultrasound study. *Circulation, 100*(11), 1182–1188.

Sacks, F., Rudel, L., & Conner, A. (2009). Selective de-lipidation of plasma HDL enhances reverse cholesterol transport in vivo. *Journal of Lipid Research, 50*, 894–907. doi:10.1194/jlr.M800622-JLR200

Saeed, B., Banerjee, S., & Brilakis, E. (2010). Slow flow after stenting of a coronary lesion with a large lipid core plaque detected by near-infrared spectroscopy. *EuroIntervention, 6*, 545. doi:10.4244/EIJ30V6I4A90

Sakurai, R., Hongo, Y., Yamasaki, M., Honda, Y., Bonneau, H. N., & Yock, P. G. (2007). Detailed intravascular ultrasound analysis of Zotarolimus-eluting phosphoryl-choline-coated cobalt-chromium alloy stent in de novo coronary lesions (results from the ENDEAVOR II trial). *The American Journal of Cardiology, 100*(5), 818–823. doi:10.1016/j.amjcard.2007.04.016

Salem, M. I., Makaryus, A. N., Kort, S., Chung, E., Marchant, D., Ong, L., & Mangion, J. (2002). Intracardiac echocardiography using the acunav ultrasound catheter during percutaneous balloon mitral valvuloplasty. *Journal of the American Society of Echocardiography, 15*(12), 1533–1537. doi:10.1067/mje.2002.126771

Sales, F. J., Falcao, B. A., Falcao, J. L., Ribeiro, E. E., Perin, M. A., & Horta, P. E. (2010). Evaluation of plaque composition by intravascular ultrasound "virtual histology": The impact of dense calcium on the measurement of necrotic tissue. *EuroIntervention, 6*(3), 394–399. doi:10.4244/EIJV6I3A65

Sanborn, T., Faxon, D., & Kellett, M. E. (1986). Percutaneous coronary laser thermal angioplasty. *Journal of the American College of Cardiology, 8*, 1437–1440. doi:10.1016/S0735-1097(86)80320-5

Sanidas, E., Vavuranakis, M., Papaioannou, T., Kakadiaris, I., Carlier, S., & Syros, G. (2008). Study of atheromatous plaque using intravascular ultrasound. *Hellenic Journal of Cardiology; HJC = Hellenike Kardiologike Epitheorese, 49*, 415–421.

Sanmartin, M., Goicolea, J., Garcia, C., Garcia, J., Crespo, A., & Rodriguez, J. (2006). [Influence of shear stress on in-stent restenosis: In vivo study using 3D reconstruction and computational fluid dynamics]. *Revista Espanola de Cardiologia, 59*(1), 20–27.

Sano, K., Kawasaki, M., Ishihara, Y., Okubo, M., Tsuchiya, K., & Nishigaki, K. (2006). Assessment of vulnerable plaques causing acute coronary syndrome using integrated backscatter intravascular ultrasound. *Journal of the American College of Cardiology, 47*(4), 734–741. doi:10.1016/j.jacc.2005.09.061

Sano, K., Mintz, G. S., Carlier, S. G., de Ribamar, C., Qian, J., & Missel, E. (2007). Assessing intermediate left main coronary lesions using intravascular ultrasound. *American Heart Journal, 154*(5), 983–988. doi:10.1016/j.ahj.2007.07.001

Santana, C. A., Garcia, E. V., Faber, T. L., Sirineni, G. K. R., Esteves, F. P., & Sanyal, R. (2009). Diagnostic performance of fusion of myocardial perfusion imaging (MPI) and computed tomography coronary angiography. *Journal of Nuclear Cardiology, 16*(2), 201–211. doi:10.1007/s12350-008-9019-z

Sanz-Requena, R., Moratal, D., García-Sánchez, D., Bodí, V., Rieta, J., & Sanchis, J. (2007). Automatic segmentation and 3D reconstruction of intravascular ultrasound images for a fast preliminary evaluation of vessel pathologies. *Computerized Medical Imaging and Graphics, 31*(2), 71–80. doi:10.1016/j.compmedimag.2006.11.004

Sarno, G., Garg, S., Gomez-Lara, J., & Serruys, P. W. (2010). Intravascular ultrasound radiofrequency analysis after optimal coronary stenting with initial quantitative coronary angiography guidance: An ATHEROREMO sub-study. *EuroIntervention* (ahead of print, June 2010).

Sathyanarayana, S., Carlier, S., Li, W., & Thomas, L. (2009). Characterisation of atherosclerotic plaque by spectral similarity of radiofrequency intravascular ultrasound signals. *EuroIntervention, 5*(1), 133–139. doi:10.4244/EIJV5I1A21

Sathyanarayana, S., Carlier, S., Li, W., & Thomas, L. (2009). Characterisation of atherosclerotic plaque by spectral similarity of radiofrequency intravascular ultrasound signals. *EuroIntervention, 5*(1), 133–139. doi:10.4244/EIJV5I1A21

Satoko, T., Bezerra, H. G., & Hiroyuki, S. (in press). Ex vivo comparison of the accuracy of measurements by OCT and IVUS. *EuroIntervention.*

Savonitto, S., Ardissino, D., & Granger, C. (1999). Prognostic value of the admission electrocardiogram in acute coronary syndromes. *Journal of the American Medical Association, 281*, 707–713. doi:10.1001/jama.281.8.707

Sawada, T., Shite, J., Garcia-Garcia, H. M., Shinke, T., Watanabe, S., & Otake, H. (2008). Feasibility of combined use of intravascular ultrasound radiofrequency data analysis and optical coherence tomography for detecting thin-cap fibroatheroma. *European Heart Journal, 29*(9), 1136–1146. doi:10.1093/eurheartj/ehn132

Sawada, T., Shite, J., & Shinke, T. (2009). Low plasma adiponectin levels are associated with presence of thin-cap fibroatheroma in men with stable coronary artery disease. *International Journal of Cardiology, 142*(3).

Scanlon, P., Faxon, D., Audet, A., Carabello, B., Dehmer, G., & Eagle, K. (1999). ACC/AHA guidelines for coronary angiography: Executive summary and recommendations. A report of the American College of Cardiology/American Heart Association Task Force on Practice Guidelines (Committee on Coronary Angiography) developed in collaboration. *Circulation, 99*(17), 2345–2357.

Schaar, J. A., de Korte, C. L., Mastik, F., Baldewsing, R., Regar, E., & de Feyter, P. (2003). Intravascular palpography for high-risk vulnerable plaque assessment. *Herz, 28*(6), 488–495. doi:10.1007/s00059-003-2488-6

Schaar, J. A., De Korte, C. L., Mastik, F., Strijder, C., Pasterkamp, G., & Boersma, E. (2003). Characterizing vulnerable plaque features with intravascular elastography. *Circulation, 108*(21), 2636–2641. doi:10.1161/01.CIR.0000097067.96619.1F

Schaar, J. A., Muller, J. E., Falk, E., Virmani, R., Fuster, V., & Serruys, P. W. (2004). Terminology for high-risk and vulnerable coronary artery plaques. Report of a meeting on the vulnerable plaque, June 17 and 18, 2003, Santorini, Greece. *European Heart Journal, 25*(12), 1077–1082. doi:10.1016/j.ehj.2004.01.002

Schaar, J. A., Regar, E., Mastik, F., McFadden, E. P., Saia, F., & Disco, C. (2004). Incidence of high-strain patterns in human coronary arteries: Assessment with three-dimensional intravascular palpography and correlation with clinical presentation. *Circulation, 109*(22), 2716–2719. doi:10.1161/01.CIR.0000131887.65955.3B

Schaar, J., Mastik, F., & Regar, E. (2007). Current diagnostic modalities for vulnerable plaque detection. *Current Pharmaceutical Design, 13*, 995–1001. doi:10.2174/138161207780487511

Scharf, C., Sneider, M., Case, I., Chugh, A., Lai, S. W. K., & Pelosi, F. Jr (2003). Anatomy of the pulmonary veins in patients with atrial fibrillation and effects of segmental ostial ablation analyzed by computed tomography. *Journal of Cardiovascular Electrophysiology, 14*(2), 150–155. doi:10.1046/j.1540-8167.2003.02444.x

Schartl, M., Bocksch, W., Koschyk, D. H., Voelker, W., Karsch, K. R., & Kreuzer, J. (2001). Use of intravascular ultrasound to compare effects of different strategies of lipid-lowering therapy on plaque volume and composition in patients with coronary artery disease. *Circulation, 104*(4), 387–392. doi:10.1161/hc2901.093188

Schiele, F., Meneveau, N., Gilard, M., Boschat, J., Commeau, P., & Ming, L. P. (2003). Intravascular ultrasound-guided balloon angioplasty compared with stent: immediate and 6-month results of the multicenter, randomized balloon equivalent to stent study (BEST). *Circulation, 107*, 545–551. doi:10.1161/01.CIR.0000047212.94399.7E

Schmermund, A., Rodermann, J., & Erbel, R. (2003). Intracoronary thermography. *Herz, 28*, 505–512. doi:10.1007/s00059-003-2495-7

Schoenhagen, P., DeFranco, A., Nissen, S. E., & Tuzcu, E. M. (2006). *IVUS made easy.* Informa Healthcare.

Schoenhagen, P., Sapp, S. K., Tuzcu, E. M., Magyar, W. A., Popovich, J., & Boumitri, M. (2003). Variability of area measurements obtained with different intravascular ultrasound catheter systems: Impact on clinical trials and a method for accurate calibration. *Journal of the American Society of Echocardiography, 16*(3), 277–284. doi:10.1067/mje.2003.45

Schoenhagen, P., Ziada, K. M., Kapadia, S. R., Crowe, T. D., Nissen, S. E., & Tuzcu, E. M. (2000). Extent and direction of arterial remodeling in stable versus unstable coronary syndromes: An intravascular ultrasound study. *Circulation, 101*(6), 598–603.

Schultz, C., Serruys, P., & van der Ent, M. (2010). Prospective identification of a large lipid core coronary plaque with a novel near-infrared spectroscopy and intravascular ultrasound (NIR-IVUS) catheter: Infarction following stenting possibly due to distal embolization of plaque contents. *Journal of the American College of Cardiology*, *314*, 314. doi:10.1016/j.jacc.2009.10.090

Schultz, C. J., Serruys, P. W., van der Ent, M., Ligthart, J., Mastik, F., & Garg, S. (2010). First-in-man clinical use of combined near-infrared spectroscopy and intravascular ultrasound: A potential key to predict distal embolization and no-reflow? *Journal of the American College of Cardiology*, *56*(4), 314–314. doi:10.1016/j.jacc.2009.10.090

Schwarten, D., Katzen, B., Simpson, J., & Cutcliff, W. (1988, Apr). Simpson catheter for percutaneous transluminal removal of atheroma. *AJR. American Journal of Roentgenology*, *150*(4), 799–801.

Sdringola, S., Assali, A., & Ghani, M. (2001). Risk assessment of slow or no-reflow phenomenon in aortocoronary vein graft percutaneous intervention. *Catheterization and Cardiovascular Interventions*, *54*, 318–324. doi:10.1002/ccd.1290

Segar, D. S., Bourdillon, P. D. V., Elsner, G., Kesler, K., & Feigenbaum, H. (1995). Intracardiac echocardiography-guided biopsy of intracardiac masses. *Journal of the American Society of Echocardiography*, *8*(6), 927–929. doi:10.1016/S0894-7317(05)80018-5

Seimon, T., & Tabas, I. (2009). Mechanisms and consequences of macrophage apoptosis in atherosclerosis. *Journal of Lipid Research*, *50*(Suppl), S382–S387. doi:10.1194/jlr.R800032-JLR200

Serfaty, J. M., Chaabane, L., Tabib, A., Chevallier, J. M., Briguet, A., & Douek, P. C. (2001). Atherosclerotic plaques: classification and characterization with T2-weighted high-spatial-resolution MR imaging-- An in vitro study. *Radiology*, *219*(2), 403–410.

Serruys, P. W., Garcia-Garcia, H. M., Buszman, P., Erne, P., Verheye, S., & Aschermann, M. (2008). Effects of the direct lipoprotein-associated phospholipase A(2) inhibitor darapladib on human coronary atherosclerotic plaque. *Circulation*, *118*(11), 1172–1182. doi:10.1161/CIRCULATIONAHA.108.771899

Serruys, P. W., Ormiston, J. A., Onuma, Y., Regar, E., Gonzalo, N., & Garcia-Garcia, H. M. (2009). A bioabsorbable everolimus-eluting coronary stent system (ABSORB): 2-year outcomes and results from multiple imaging methods. *Lancet*, *373*(9667), 897–910. doi:10.1016/S0140-6736(09)60325-1

Serruys, P. W., Degertekin, M., Tanabe, K., Abizaid, A., Sousa, J. E., & Colombo, A. (2002). Intravascular ultrasound findings in the multicenter, randomized, double-blind RAVEL (RAndomized study with the sirolimus-eluting VElocity balloon-expandable stent in the treatment of patients with de novo native coronary artery Lesions) trial. *Circulation*, *106*(7), 798–803. doi:10.1161/01.CIR.0000025585.63486.59

Serruys, P. W., Garcia-Garcia, H. M., Buszman, P., Erne, P., Verheye, S., & Aschermann, M. (2008). Effects of the direct lipoprotein-associated phospholipase A(2) inhibitor darapladib on human coronary atherosclerotic plaque. *Circulation*, *118*(11), 1172–1182. doi:10.1161/CIRCULATIONAHA.108.771899

Serruys, P. W., Ong, A. T., Piek, J. J., Neumann, F. J., van der Giessen, W. J., & Wiemer, M. (2005). A randomized comparison of a durable polymer Everolimus-eluting stent with a bare metal coronary stent: The SPIRIT first trial. *EuroIntervention*, *1*(1), 58–65.

Serruys, P. W., Ruygrok, P., Neuzner, J., Piek, J. J., Seth, A., & Schofer, J. J. (2006). A randomised comparison of an everolimus-eluting coronary stent with a paclitaxel-eluting coronary stent:the SPIRIT II trial. *EuroIntervention*, *2*(3), 286–294.

Serruys, W., & Di Mario, C. (1995). Who was thrombogenic: The stent or the doctor? *Circulation*, *91*, 1891–1893.

Serruys, P., Ormiston, J., & Onuma, Y. (2009). A bioabsorbable everolimus-eluting coronary stent system (ABSORB): 2-year outcomes and results from multiple imaging methods. *Lancet*, *373*, 897–910. doi:10.1016/S0140-6736(09)60325-1

Shah, P. (2003). Mechanisms of plaque vulnerability and rupture. *Journal of the American College of Cardiology*, *41*, 15S–22S. doi:10.1016/S0735-1097(02)02834-6

Shalganov, T. N., Paprika, D., Borbás, S., Temesvári, A., & Szili-Török, T. (2005). Preventing complicated transseptal puncture with intracardiac echocardiography: Case report. *Cardiovascular Ultrasound*, *3*, 5. .doi:10.1186/1476-7120-3-5

Shekhar, R., Cothern, R. M., Vince, D. G., Chandra, S., Thomas, J. D., & Cornhill, J. F. (1999). Three – dimensional segmentation of luminal and adventitial borders in serial intravascular ultrasound images. *Computerized Medical Imaging and Graphics, 23*, 299–309. doi:10.1016/S0895-6111(99)00029-4

Shin, E. S., Garcia-Garcia, H. M., Garg, S., Park, J., Kim, S. J., & Serruys, P. W. (2010). The assessment of Shin's method for the prediction of creatinine kinase-MB elevation after percutaneous coronary intervention: an intravascular ultrasound study. *The International Journal of Cardiovascular Imaging, 27*(6).

Shin, E. S., Garcia-Garcia, H. M., & Serruys, P. W. (2010). A new method to measure necrotic core and calcium content in coronary plaques using intravascular ultrasound radiofrequency-based analysis. *The International Journal of Cardiovascular Imaging, 26*(4), 387–396. doi:10.1007/s10554-009-9567-6

Shinnar, M., Fallon, J. T., Wehrli, S., Levin, M., Dalmacy, D., & Fayad, Z. A. (1999). The diagnostic accuracy of ex vivo MRI for human atherosclerotic plaque characterization. *Arteriosclerosis, Thrombosis, and Vascular Biology, 19*(11), 2756–2761. doi:10.1161/01.ATV.19.11.2756

Sihan, K., Botha, C., Post, F., de Winter, S., Gonzalo, N., & Regar, E. (2009). Fully automatic three-dimensional quantitative analysis of intracoronary optical coherence tomography: Method and validation. *Catheterization and Cardiovascular Interventions, 74*(7), 1058–1065. doi:10.1002/ccd.22125

Simonton, C. A., Leon, M. B., Baim, D. S., Hinohara, T., Kent, K. M., & Bersin, R. M. (1998). Optimal directional coronary atherectomy: Final results of the Optimal Atherectomy Restenosis Study (OARS). *Circulation, 97*(4), 332–339.

Sinusas, A., Bengel, F., Nahrendorf, M., Epstein, F., Wu, J., & Villanueva, F. (2008). Multimodality cardiovascular molecular imaging: Part I. *Circulation: Cardiovascular Imaging, 1*, 244–256. doi:10.1161/CIRCIMAGING.108.824359

Sirol, M., Moreno, P., Purushothaman, K., Vucic, E., Amirbekian, V., & Weinmann, H. (2009). Increased neovascularization in advanced lipid-rich atherosclerotic lesions detected by gadofluorine-M-enhanced MRI: Implications for plaque vulnerability. *Circulation: Cardiovascular Imaging, 2*(5), 391–396. doi:10.1161/CIRCIMAGING.108.801712

Skinner, M. P., Yuan, C., Mitsumori, L., Hayes, C. E., Raines, E. W., & Nelson, J. A. (1995). Serial magnetic resonance imaging of experimental atherosclerosis detects lesion fine structure, progression and complications in vivo. *Nature Medicine, 1*(1), 69–73. doi:10.1038/nm0195-69

Slager, C., Wentzel, J., Schuurbiers, J., Oomen, J., Kloet, J., & Krams, R. (2000). True 3 – Dimensional reconstruction of coronary arteries in patients by fusion of angiography and IVUS (ANGUS) and its quantitative validation. *Circulation, 102*, 511–516.

Slager, C. J., Wentzel, J. J., Gijsen, F. J., Thury, A., van der Wal, A. C., & Schaar, J. A. (2005). The role of shear stress in the destabilization of vulnerable plaques and related therapeutic implications. *Nature Clinical Practice. Cardiovascular Medicine, 2*(9), 456–464. doi:10.1038/ncpcardio0298

Sluimer, J., Kolodgie, F., & Bijnens, A. (2009). Thin-walled microvessels in human coronary atherosclerotic plaques show incomplete endothelial junctions relevance of compromised structural integrity for intraplaque microvascular leakage. *Journal of the American College of Cardiology, 53*, 1517–1527. doi:10.1016/j.jacc.2008.12.056

Sonka, M., Zhang, X., Siebes, M., Bissing, M., Dejong, S., Collins, S., & McKay, C. R. (1995). Segmentation of intravascular ultrasound images: A knowledge–based approach. *IEEE Transactions on Medical Imaging, 14*(4), 719–732. doi:10.1109/42.476113

Sonoda, S., Morino, Y., Ako, J., Terashima, M., Hassan, A., & Bonneau, H. (2004). Impact of final stent dimensions on long-term results following sirolimus-eluting stent implantation: Serial intravascular ultrasound analysis from the SIRIUS trial. *Journal of the American College of Cardiology, 43*, 1959–1963. doi:10.1016/j.jacc.2004.01.044

Sousa, J. E., Costa, M. A., Abizaid, A., Abizaid, A. S., Feres, F., & Pinto, I. M. (2001). Lack of neointimal proliferation after implantation of sirolimus-coated stents in human coronary arteries: a quantitative coronary angiography and three-dimensional intravascular ultrasound study. *Circulation, 103*(2), 192–195.

Spanos, V., Stankovic, G., Tobis, A., & Colombo, A. (2003). The challenge of in-stent restenosis: Insights from intravascular ultrasound. *European Heart Journal, 24,* 138–150. doi:10.1016/S0195-668X(02)00418-9

Spears, J., Ali, M., Raza, S., Ayer, G., Ravi, S., & Crilly, R. (1994). Quantative angioscopy: A novel method of measurement of luminal dimensions during angioscopy with se of a lightwire. *Cardiovascular and Interventional Radiology, 17,* 197–203. doi:10.1007/BF00571534

Stahr, P. M., Hofflinghaus, T., Voigtlander, T., Courtney, B. K., Victor, A., & Otto, M. (2002). Discrimination of early/intermediate and advanced/complicated coronary plaque types by radiofrequency intravascular ultrasound analysis. *The American Journal of Cardiology, 90*(1), 19–23. doi:10.1016/S0002-9149(02)02379-2

Stary, H. C. (1992). Composition and classification of human atherosclerotic lesions. *Virchows Archiv. A, Pathological Anatomy and Histopathology, 421*(4), 277–290. doi:10.1007/BF01660974

Stary, H. C. (2000). Lipid and macrophage accumulations in arteries of children and the development of atherosclerosis. *The American Journal of Clinical Nutrition, 72*(5Suppl), 1297S–1306S.

Stefanadis, C., Diamantopoulos, L., Dernellis, J., Economou, E., Tsiamis, E., & Toutouzas, K. (2000). Heat production of atherosclerotic plaques and inflammation assessed by the acute phase proteins in acute coronary syndromes. *Journal of Molecular and Cellular Cardiology, 32,* 43–52. doi:10.1006/jmcc.1999.1049

Stefanadis, C., Diamantopoulos, L., Vlachopoulos, C., Tsiamis, E., Dernellis, J., & Toutouzas, K. (1999). Thermal heterogeneity within human atherosclerotic coronary arteries detected in vivo: A new method of detection by application of a special thermography catheter. *Circulation, 99,* 1965–1971.

Stefanadis, C., Toutouzas, K., Tsiamis, E., Mitropoulos, I., Tsioufis, C., & Kallikazaros, I. (2003). Thermal heterogeneity in stable human coronary atherosclerotic plaques is underestimated in vivo: the "cooling effect" of blood flow. *Journal of the American College of Cardiology, 41,* 403–408. doi:10.1016/S0735-1097(02)02817-6

Stefanadis, C., Toutouzas, K., Tsiamis, E., Stratos, C., Vavuranakis, M., & Kallikazaros, I. (2001). Increased local temperature in human coronary atherosclerotic plaques: an independent predictor of clinical outcome in patients undergoing a percutaneous coronary intervention. *Journal of the American College of Cardiology, 37,* 1277–1283. doi:10.1016/S0735-1097(01)01137-8

Stefanadis, C., Toutouzas, K., Tsiamis, E., Vavuranakis, M., Tsioufis, C., & Stefanadi, E. (2007). Relation between local temperature and C-reactive protein levels in patients with coronary artery disease: effects of atorvastatin treatment. *Atherosclerosis, 192,* 396–400. doi:10.1016/j.atherosclerosis.2006.05.038

Stefanadis, C., Toutouzas, K., Vavuranakis, M., Tsiamis, E., Tousoulis, D., & Panagiotakos, D. (2002). Statin treatment is associated with reduced thermal heterogeneity in human atherosclerotic plaques. *European Heart Journal, 23,* 1664–1669.

Stefanadis, C., Toutouzas, K., Vavuranakis, M., Tsiamis, E., Vaina, S., & Toutouzas, P. (2003). New balloon-thermography catheter for in vivo temperature measurements in human coronary atherosclerotic plaques: A novel approach for thermography? *Catheterization and Cardiovascular Interventions, 58,* 344–350. doi:10.1002/ccd.10449

Stefanadis, C., & Toutouzas, P. (1998). In vivo local thermography of coronary artery atherosclerotic plaques in humans. *Annals of Internal Medicine, 129,* 1079–1080.

Stefanadis, C., Tsiamis, E., Vaina, S., Toutouzas, K., Boudoulas, H., & Gialafos, J. (2004). Temperature of blood in the coronary sinus and right atrium in patients with and without coronary artery disease. *The American Journal of Cardiology, 93,* 207–210. doi:10.1016/j.amjcard.2003.09.040

Stefanadis, C., Diamantopoulos, L., Dernellis, J., Economou, E., Tsiamis, E., & Toutouzas, K. (2000). Heat production of atherosclerotic plaques and inflammation assessed by the acute phase proteins in acute coronary syndromes. *Journal of Molecular and Cellular Cardiology, 32*, 43–52. doi:10.1006/jmcc.1999.1049

Stefanadis, C., Diamantopoulos, L., Vlachopoulos, C., Tsiamis, E., Dernellis, J., & Toutouzas, K. (1999). Thermal heterogeneity within human atherosclerotic coronary arteries detected *in vivo*: A new method of detection by application of a special thermography catheter. *Circulation, 99*, 1965–1971.

Stefanadis, C., Toutouzas, K., Tsiamis, E., Mitropoulos, I., Tsioufis, C., & Kallikazaros, I. (2003). Thermal heterogeneity in stable human coronary atherosclerotic plaques is underestimated *in vivo*: The "cooling effect" of blood flow. *Journal of the American College of Cardiology, 41*, 403–408. doi:10.1016/S0735-1097(02)02817-6

Stefanadis, C., Toutouzas, K., Tsiamis, E., Stratos, C., Vavuranakis, M., & Kallikazaros, I. (2001). Increased local temperature in human coronary atherosclerotic plaques: An independent predictor of clinical outcome in patients undergoing a percutaneous coronary intervention. *Journal of the American College of Cardiology, 37*, 1277–1283. doi:10.1016/S0735-1097(01)01137-8

Stefanadis, C., Toutouzas, K., Vavuranakis, M., Tsiamis, E., Vaina, S., & Toutouzas, P. (2003). New balloon-thermography catheter for *in vivo* temperature measurements in human coronary atherosclerotic plaques: A novel approach for thermography? *Catheterization and Cardiovascular Interventions, 58*, 344–350. doi:10.1002/ccd.10449

Stefanadis, C., Toutouzas, K., Stefanadi, E., Lazaris, A., Patsouris, E., & Kipshidze, N. (2007). Inhibition of plaque neovascularization and intimal hyperplasia by specific targeting vascular endothelial growth factor with bevacizumab-eluting stent: An experimental study. *Atherosclerosis, 195*, 269–276. doi:10.1016/j.atherosclerosis.2006.12.034

Stefanadis, C., Toutouzas, K., Tsiamis, E., Vavuranakis, M., Stefanadi, E., & Kipshidze, N. (2008). First-in-man study with bevacizumab-eluting stent: A new approach for the inhibition of atheromatic plaque neovascularisation. *EuroIntervention, 3*, 460–464. doi:10.4244/EIJV3I4A82

Stefanadis, C., & Toutouzas, K. (2009). Paclitaxel versus sirolimus: The battle is still ongoing. *Journal of the American College of Cardiology, 53*(8), 665–666. doi:10.1016/j.jacc.2008.10.048

Steinberg, D., Mintz, G., Mandinov, L., Yu, A., Ellis, S., & Grube, E. (2010). Long-term impact of routinely detected early and late incomplete stent apposition: an integrated intravascular ultrasound analysis of the TAXUS IV, V, and VI and TAXUS ATLAS workhorse, long lesion, and direct stent studies. *JACC: Cardiovascular Interventions, 3*(5), 486–494. doi:10.1016/j.jcin.2010.03.007

Stolzmann, P., Alkadhi, H., Scheffel, H., Hennemuth, A., Kuehnel, C., & Baumueller, S. (2010). Image fusion of coronary CT angiography and cardiac perfusion MRI: A pilot study. *European Radiology, 20*(5), 1174–1179. doi:10.1007/s00330-010-1746-2

Stone, G. W., Maehara, A., Lansky, A. J., de Bruyne, B., Cristea, E., & Mintz, G. S. (2011). A prospective natural-history study of coronary atherosclerosis. *The New England Journal of Medicine, 364*(3), 226–235. doi:10.1056/NEJMoa1002358

Stone, G. W., Hodgson, J. M., St Goar, F. G., Frey, A., Mudra, H., & Sheehan, H. (1997). Improved procedural results of coronary angioplasty with intravascular ultrasound-guided balloon sizing: The CLOUT pilot trial. Clinical outcomes with ultrasound trial (CLOUT) investigators. *Circulation, 95*(8), 2044–2052.

Stone, G. W., Maehara, A., Lansky, A. J., de Bruyne, B., Cristea, E., & Mintz, G. S. (2011). A prospective natural-history study of coronary atherosclerosis. *The New England Journal of Medicine, 364*(3), 226–235. doi:10.1056/NEJMoa1002358

Stone, G. W., Midei, M., Newman, W., Sanz, M., Hermiller, J. B., & Williams, J. (2008). Comparison of an everolimus-eluting stent and a paclitaxel-eluting stent in patients with coronary artery disease: A randomized trial. *Journal of the American Medical Association, 299*(16), 1903–1913. doi:10.1001/jama.299.16.1903

Stone, G. (2009). *First presentation of the baseline features & plaque characteristics from the PROSPECT trial.* TCT.

Stone, P. H., Coskun, A. U., Kinlay, S., Popma, J. J., Sonka, M., & Wahle, A. (2007). Regions of low endothelial shear stress are the sites where coronary plaque progresses and vascular remodelling occurs in humans: an in vivo serial study. *European Heart Journal, 28*(6), 705–710. doi:10.1093/eurheartj/ehl575

Stone, G., Webb, J., & Cox, D. (2005). Distal microcirculatory protection during percutaneous coronary intervention in acute ST-segment elevation myocardial infarction: A randomized controlled trial. *Journal of the American Medical Association, 293*, 1063–1072. doi:10.1001/jama.293.9.1063

Stone, P. H., Coskun, A. U., Kinlay, S., Popma, J. J., Sonka, M., & Wahle, A. (2007). Regions of low endothelial shear stress are the sites where coronary plaque progresses and vascular remodelling occurs in humans: An in vivo serial study. *European Heart Journal, 28*(6), 705–710. doi:10.1093/eurheartj/ehl575

Stone, P. H., Coskun, A. U., Kinlay, S., Clark, M. E., Sonka, M., & Wahle, A. (2003). Effect of endothelial shear stress on the progression of coronary artery disease, vascular remodeling, and in-stent restenosis in humans: In vivo 6-month follow-up study. *Circulation, 108*(4), 438–444. doi:10.1161/01.CIR.0000080882.35274.AD

Stone, P. H., Coskun, A. U., Yeghiazarians, Y., Kinlay, S., Popma, J. J., & Kuntz, R. E. (2003). Prediction of sites of coronary atherosclerosis progression: In vivo profiling of endothelial shear stress, lumen, and outer vessel wall characteristics to predict vascular behavior. *Current Opinion in Cardiology, 18*(6), 458–470. doi:10.1097/00001573-200311000-00007

Stone, G. W., & Mintz, G. S. Letter by Stone and Mintz regarding article, "unreliable assessment of necrotic core by virtual histology intravascular ultrasound in porcine coronary artery disease". *Circ Cardiovasc Imaging, 3*(5), e4; author reply e5.

Subramanian, K. R., Thubrikar, M. J., Fowler, B., Mostafavi, M. T., & Funk, M. W. (2000). Accurate 3D reconstruction of complex blood vessel geometries from intravascular ultrasound images: In vitro study. *Journal of Medical Engineering & Technology, 24*(4), 131–140. doi:10.1080/03091900050163391

Sukhova, G., Schoenbeck, U., Rabkin, E., Schoen, F., Poole, A., & Billinghurst, R. (1999). Evidence of increased collagenolysis by interstitial collagenases-1 and -3 in vulnerable human atheromatous plaques. *Circulation, 99*, 2503–2509.

Sukhova, G., Shi, G., Simon, D., Chapman, H., & Libby, P. (1998). Expression of the elastolytic cathepsins S and K in human atheroma and regulation of their production in smooth muscle cells. *The Journal of Clinical Investigation, 102*, 576–583. doi:10.1172/JCI181

Sum, S., Madden, S., Hendricks, M., Chartier, S., & Muller, J. (2009). Near-infrared spectroscopy for the detection of lipid core coronary plaques. *Current Cardiovascular Imaging Reports, 2*, 307–315. doi:10.1007/s12410-009-0036-3

Sun, F. R., Liu, Z., Li, Y. L., Babyn, P., Yao, G. H., & Zhang, Y. (2009). *Improved T-snake model based edge detection of the coronary arterial walls in intravascular ultrasound images*. iCBBE, Beijing, China, 2009.

Suzuki, N., Kozuma, K., & Maeno, Y. e. (2010). Quantitative coronary optical coherence tomography image analysis for the signal attenuation observed in-stent restenotic tissue. *International Journal of Cardiology, 145*(2). doi:10.1016/j.ijcard.2010.04.020

Suzuki, Y., Ikeno, F., & Koizumi, T. (2008). In vivo comparison between optical coherence tomography and intravascular ultrasound for detecting small degrees of in-stent neointima after stent implantation. *JACC: Cardiovascular Interventions, 1*, 168–173. doi:10.1016/j.jcin.2007.12.007

Suzuki, N., Nanda, H., Angiolillo, D. J., Bezerra, H., Sabate, M., & Jimenez-Quevedo, P. (2008). Assessment of potential relationship between wall shear stress and arterial wall response after bare metal stent and sirolimus-eluting stent implantation in patients with diabetes mellitus. *The International Journal of Cardiovascular Imaging, 24*(4), 357–364. doi:10.1007/s10554-007-9274-0

Swirski, F. K., Pittet, M. J., Kircher, M. F., Aikawa, E., Jaffer, F. A., & Libby, P. (2006). Monocyte accumulation in mouse atherogenesis is progressive and proportional to extent of disease. *Proceedings of the National Academy of Sciences of the United States of America, 103*(27), 10340–10345. doi:10.1073/pnas.0604260103

Synetos, A., Toutouzas, K., & Drakopoulou, M. (2010). *Biodegradable bevacizumab eluting stent effectively inhibits revascularization and intimal hyperplasia: An experimental study. ESC2010.* (abstract)

Szili-Torok, T., Kimman, G. P., Theuns, D., Res, J., Roelandt, J., & Jordaens, L. J. (2001). Transseptal left heart catheterisation guided by intracardiac echocardiography. *Heart (British Cardiac Society), 86*(5), e11. doi:10.1136/heart.86.5.e11

Tahara, N., Kai, H., Ishibashi, M., Nakaura, H., Kaida, H., & Baba, K. (2006). Simvastatin attenuates plaque inflammation: Evaluation by fluorodeoxyglucose positron emission tomography. *Journal of the American College of Cardiology, 48*(9), 1825–1831. doi:10.1016/j.jacc.2006.03.069

Tahara, N., Kai, H., Nakaura, H., Mizoguchi, M., Ishibashi, M., & Kaida, H. (2007). The prevalence of inflammation in carotid atherosclerosis: analysis with fluorodeoxyglucose-positron emission tomography. *European Heart Journal, 28*(18), 2243–2248. doi:10.1093/eurheartj/ehm245

Takagi, A., Tsurumi, Y., Ishii, Y., Suzuki, K., Kawana, M., & Kasanuki, H. (1999). Clinical potential of intravascular ultrasound for physiological assessment of coronary stenosis: Relationship between quantitative ultrasound tomography and pressure-derived fractional flow reserve. *Circulation, 100*(3), 250–255.

Takagi, A., Hibi, K., Zhang, X., Teo, T., Bonneau, H., Yock, P., & Fitzgerald, P. (2000). Automated contour detection for high-frequency intravascular ultrasound imaging: A technique with blood noise reduction for edge enhancement. *Ultrasound in Medicine & Biology, 26*(6), 1033–1041. doi:10.1016/S0301-5629(00)00251-9

Takano, M., Jang, I., & Inami, S. (2008). In vivo comparison of optical coherence tomography and angioscopy for the evaluation of coronary plaque characteristics. *The American Journal of Cardiology, 101*, 471–476. doi:10.1016/j.amjcard.2007.09.106

Takano, M., Yamamoto, M., & Inami, S. (2009). Appearance of lipid-laden intima and neovascularization after implantation of bare-metal stents extended late-phase observation by intracoronary optical coherence tomography. *Journal of the American College of Cardiology, 55*, 26–32. doi:10.1016/j.jacc.2009.08.032

Takarada, S., Imanishi, T., Liu, Y., Ikejima, H., Tsujioka, H., & Kuroi, A. (2010). Advantage of next-generation frequency-domain optical coherence tomography compared with conventional time-domain system in the assessment of coronary lesion. *Catheterization and Cardiovascular Interventions, 75*(2), 202–206. doi:10.1002/ccd.22273

Takarada, S., Imanishi, T., & Kubo, T. (2009). Effect of statin therapy on coronary fibrous-cap thickness in patients with acute coronary syndrome: assessment by optical coherence tomography study. *Atherosclerosis, 202*, 491–497. doi:10.1016/j.atherosclerosis.2008.05.014

Takashima, H., Ozaki, Y., Yasukawa, T., Waseda, K., Asai, K., & Wakita, Y. (2007). Impact of lipid-lowering therapy with pitavastatin, a new HMG-CoA reductase inhibitor, on regression of coronary atherosclerotic plaque. *Circulation Journal, 71*(11), 1678–1684. doi:10.1253/circj.71.1678

Takayama, T., Hiro, T., Yamagishi, M., Daida, H., Hirayama, A., & Saito, S. (2009). Effect of rosuvastatin on coronary atheroma in stable coronary artery disease: multicenter coronary atherosclerosis study measuring effects of rosuvastatin using intravascular ultrasound in Japanese subjects (COSMOS). *Circulation Journal, 73*(11), 2110–2117. doi:10.1253/circj.CJ-09-0358

Takebayashi, H., Mintz, G., Carlier, S., Kobayashi, Y., Fujii, K., & Yasuda, T. (2004). Non-uniform strut distribution correlates with more neointimal hyperplasia after sirolimus-eluting stent implantation. *Circulation, 110*, 3430–3434. doi:10.1161/01.CIR.0000148371.53174.05

Takumi, T., Lee, S., Hamasaki, S., Toyonaga, K., Kanda, D., & Kusumoto, K. (2007). Limitation of angiography to identify the culprit plaque in acute myocardial infarction with coronary total occlusion utility of coronary plaque temperature measurement to identify the culprit plaque. *Journal of the American College of Cardiology, 50*, 2197–2203. doi:10.1016/j.jacc.2007.07.079

Takumi, T., Lee, S., Hamasaki, S., Toyonaga, K., Kanda, D., & Kusumoto, K. (2007). Limitation of angiography to identify the culprit plaque in acute myocardial infarction with coronary total occlusion utility of coronary plaque temperature measurement to identify the culprit plaque. *Journal of the American College of Cardiology, 50*, 2197–2203. doi:10.1016/j.jacc.2007.07.079

Tan, K., & Lip, G. (2008). Imaging of the unstable plaque. *International Journal of Cardiology, 127*, 157–165. doi:10.1016/j.ijcard.2007.11.054

Tanaka, A., Imanishi, T., & Kitabata, H. (2008). Distribution and frequency of thin-capped fibroatheromas and ruptured plaques in the entire culprit coronary artery in patients with acute coronary syndrome as determined by optical coherence tomography. *The American Journal of Cardiology*, *112*, 975–979. doi:10.1016/j.amjcard.2008.05.062

Tanaka, A., Imanishi, T., & Kitabata, H. (2008). Morphology of exertion-triggered plaque rupture in patients with acute coronary syndrome: An optical coherence tomography study. *Circulation*, *118*, 2368–2373. doi:10.1161/CIRCULATIONAHA.108.782540

Tang, T., Howarth, S., Miller, S., Trivedi, R., & Graves, M., U-King-Im, J., *et al.* (2006). Assessment of inflammatory burden contralateral to the symptomatic carotid stenosis using high-resolution ultrasmall, superparamagnetic iron oxide-enhanced MRI. *Stroke*, *37*, 2266–2270. doi:10.1161/01.STR.0000236063.47539.99

Tani, S., Watanabe, I., Anazawa, T., Kawamata, H., Tachibana, E., & Furukawa, K. (2005). Effect of pravastatin on malondialdehyde-modified low-density lipoprotein levels and coronary plaque regression as determined by three-dimensional intravascular ultrasound. *The American Journal of Cardiology*, *96*(8), 1089–1094. doi:10.1016/j.amjcard.2005.05.069

Tanigawa, J., Barlis, P., & Di Mario, C. (2007). Intravascular optical coherence tomography: Optimisation of image acquisition and quantitative assessment of stent strut apposition. *EuroIntervention*, *3*(1), 128–136.

Tanigawa, J., Barlis, P., Dimopoulos, K., Dalby, M., Moore, P., & Di Mario, C. (2009). The influence of strut thickness and cell design on immediate apposition of drug-eluting stents assessed by optical coherence tomography. *International Journal of Cardiology*, *134*, 180–188. doi:10.1016/j.ijcard.2008.05.069

Tanigawa, J., Barlis, P., Dimopoulos, K., & Di Mario, C. (2008). Optical coherence tomography to assess malapposition in overlapping drug-eluting stents. *EuroInterv*, *3*, 580–583. doi:10.4244/EIJV3I5A104

Tanigawa, J., Barlis, P., & Di Mario, C. (2008). Heavily calcified coronary lesions preclude strut apposition despite high pressure balloon dilatation and rotational atherectomy: In-vivo demonstration with optical coherence tomography. *Circulation Journal*, *72*, 157–160. doi:10.1253/circj.72.157

Tanigawa, J., Barlis, P., Dimopoulos, K., Dalby, M., Moore, P., & Di Mario, C. (2009). The influence of strut thickness and cell design on immediate apposition of drug-eluting stents assessed by optical coherence tomography. *International Journal of Cardiology*, *134*, 180–188. doi:10.1016/j.ijcard.2008.05.069

Tanimoto, S., Rodriguez-Granillo, G., Barlis, P., de Winter, S., Bruining, N., & Hamers, R. (2008). A novel approach for quantitative analysis of intracoronary optical coherence tomography: High inter-observer agreement with computer-assisted contour detection. *Catheterization and Cardiovascular Interventions*, *72*(2), 228–235. doi:10.1002/ccd.21482

Tardif, J. C., Gregoire, J., L'Allier, P. L., Anderson, T. J., Bertrand, O., & Reeves, F. (2004). Effects of the acyl coenzyme A:cholesterol acyltransferase inhibitor avasimibe on human atherosclerotic lesions. *Circulation*, *110*(21), 3372–3377. doi:10.1161/01.CIR.0000147777.12010.EF

Tardif, J. C., Gregoire, J., L'Allier, P. L., Ibrahim, R., Anderson, T. J., & Reeves, F. (2008). Effects of the antioxidant succinobucol (AGI-1067) on human atherosclerosis in a randomized clinical trial. *Atherosclerosis*, *197*(1), 480–486. doi:10.1016/j.atherosclerosis.2006.11.039

Tardif, J. C., Gregoire, J., L'Allier, P. L., Ibrahim, R., Lesperance, J., & Heinonen, T. M. (2007). Effects of reconstituted high-density lipoprotein infusions on coronary atherosclerosis: A randomized controlled trial. *Journal of the American Medical Association*, *297*(15), 1675–1682. doi:10.1001/jama.297.15.jpc70004

Tawakol, A., Migrino, R. Q., Hoffmann, U., Abbara, S., Houser, S., & Gewirtz, H. (2005). Noninvasive in vivo measurement of vascular inflammation with F-18 fluorodeoxyglucose positron emission tomography. *Journal of Nuclear Cardiology*, *12*(3), 294–301. doi:10.1016/j.nuclcard.2005.03.002

Tearney, G., Yabushita, H., Houser, S., Aretz, H., Jang, I., & Schlendorf, K. (2006). Quantification of macrophage content in atherosclerotic plaques by optical coherence tomography. *Circulation*, *107*, 113–119. doi:10.1161/01.CIR.0000044384.41037.43

Tearney, G. J., Jang, I. K., Kang, D. H., Aretz, H. T., Houser, S. L., & Brady, T. J. (2000). Porcine coronary imaging in vivo by optical coherence tomography. *Acta Cardiologica*, *55*(4), 233–237. doi:10.2143/AC.55.4.2005745

Tearney, G. J., Waxman, S., Shishkov, M., Vakoc, B. J., Suter, M. J., & Freilich, M. I. (2008). Three-dimensional coronary artery microscopy by intracoronary optical frequency domain imaging. *JACC: Cardiovascular Imaging*, *1*(6), 752–761. doi:10.1016/j.jcmg.2008.06.007

Tearney, G. J., Yabushita, H., Houser, S. L., Aretz, H. T., Jang, I. K., & Schlendorf, K. H. (2003). Quantification of macrophage content in atherosclerotic plaques by optical coherence tomography. *Circulation*, *107*(1), 113–119. doi:10.1161/01.CIR.0000044384.41037.43

Tekabe, Y., Li, Q., Luma, J., Weisenberger, D., Sedlar, M., & Harja, E. Noninvasive monitoring the biology of atherosclerotic plaque development with radiolabeled annexin V and matrix metalloproteinase inhibitor in spontaneous atherosclerotic mice. *Journal of Nuclear Cardiology*, *17*(6), 1073–1081. doi:10.1007/s12350-010-9276-5

ten Have, A., Draaijers, E., Gijsen, F., Wentzel, J., Slager, C., & Serruys, P. (2007). Influence of catheter design on lumen wall temperature distribution in intracoronary thermography. *Journal of Biomechanics*, *40*, 281–288. doi:10.1016/j.jbiomech.2006.01.016

ten Have, A., Gijsen, F., Wentzel, J., Slager, C., Serruys, P., & van der Steen, A. (2006). A numerical study on the influence of vulnerable plaque composition on intravascular thermography measurements. *Physics in Medicine and Biology*, *51*, 5875–5887. doi:10.1088/0031-9155/51/22/010

ten Have, A., Gijsen, F., Wentzel, J., Slager, C., & van der Steen, A. (2004). Temperature distribution in atherosclerotic coronary arteries: Influence of plaque geometry and flow (a numerical study). *Physics in Medicine and Biology*, *49*, 4447–4462. doi:10.1088/0031-9155/49/19/001

Ten Have, A., Gijsen, F., Wentzel, J., Slager, C., Serruys, P., & van der Steen, A. (2005). Intracoronary thermography: heat generation; transfer and detection. *EuroIntervention*, *1*, 105–114.

The_PROSPECT_authors. (2009). *The multicenter, prospective, international providing regional observations to study predictors of events in the coronary tree (PROSPECT) trial.* (ClinicalTrials.gov identifier NCT00180466). TCT. (abstract)

Thim, T., Hagensen, M. K., Wallace-Bradley, D., Granada, J. F., Kaluza, G. L., & Drouet, L. (2010). Unreliable assessment of necrotic core by virtual histology intravascular ultrasound in porcine coronary artery disease. *Circ Cardiovasc Imaging*, *3*(4), 384–391. doi:10.1161/CIRCIMAGING.109.919357

Thury, A., Wentzel, J. J., Vinke, R. V., Gijsen, F. J., Schuurbiers, J. C., & Krams, R. (2002). Images in cardiovascular medicine. Focal in-stent restenosis near step-up: Roles of low and oscillating shear stress? *Circulation*, *105*(23), e185–e187. doi:10.1161/01.CIR.0000018282.32332.13

Timaran, C. H., Rosero, E. B., Martinez, A. E., Ilarraza, A., Modrall, J. G., & Clagett, G. P. (2010). Atherosclerotic plaque composition assessed by virtual histology intravascular ultrasound and cerebral embolization after carotid stenting. *Journal of Vascular Surgery*, *52*(5). doi:10.1016/j.jvs.2010.05.101

Tobis, J. M., Mallery, J., Mahon, D., Lehmann, K., Zalesky, P., & Griffith, J. (1991). Intravascular ultrasound imaging of human coronary arteries in vivo. Analysis of tissue characterizations with comparison to in vitro histological specimens. *Circulation*, *83*(3), 913–926.

Toi, T., Taguchi, I., Yoneda, S., Kageyama, M., Kikuchi, A., & Tokura, M. (2009). Early effect of lipid-lowering therapy with pitavastatin on regression of coronary atherosclerotic plaque. Comparison with atorvastatin. *Circulation Journal*, *73*(8), 1466–1472. doi:10.1253/circj.CJ-08-1051

Tonino, P., De Bruyne, B., & Pijls, N. (2009). Fractional flow reserve versus angiography for guiding percutaneous coronary intervention for the FAME study investigators. *The New England Journal of Medicine*, *360*, 213–224. doi:10.1056/NEJMoa0807611

Topol, E. J., & Nissen, S. E. (1995). Our preoccupation with coronary luminology. The dissociation between clinical and angiographic findings in ischemic heart disease. *Circulation*, *92*(8), 2333–2342.

Topol, E. J., Leya, F., Pinkerton, C. A., Whitlow, P. L., Hofling, B., & Simonton, C. A. (1993). A comparison of directional atherectomy with coronary angioplasty in patients with coronary artery disease. The CAVEAT Study Group. *The New England Journal of Medicine*, *329*(4), 221–227. doi:10.1056/NEJM199307223290401

Topol, E. J., & Nissen, S. E. (1995). Our preoccupation with coronary luminology. The dissociation between clinical and angiographic findings in ischemic heart disease. *Circulation*, *92*(8), 2333–2342.

Tousoulis, D., Antoniades, C., Koumallos, N., & Stefanadis, C. (2006). Pro-inflammatory cytokines in acute coronary syndromes: From bench to bedside. *Cytokine & Growth Factor Reviews*, *17*, 225–233. doi:10.1016/j.cytogfr.2006.04.003

Toussaint, J. F., LaMuraglia, G. M., Southern, J. F., Fuster, V., & Kantor, H. L. (1996). Magnetic resonance images lipid, fibrous, calcified, hemorrhagic, and thrombotic components of human atherosclerosis in vivo. *Circulation*, *94*(5), 932–938.

Toussaint, J. F., Southern, J. F., Fuster, V., & Kantor, H. L. (1995). T2-weighted contrast for NMR characterization of human atherosclerosis. *Arteriosclerosis, Thrombosis, and Vascular Biology*, *15*(10), 1533–1542.

Toutouzas, K., Colombo, A., & Stefanadis, C. (2004). Inflammation and restenosis after percutaneous coronary interventions. *European Heart Journal*, *25*, 1679–1687. doi:10.1016/j.ehj.2004.06.011

Toutouzas, K., Drakopoulou, M., Markou, V., Karabelas, I., Vaina, S., & Vavuranakis, M. (2007). Correlation of systemic inflammation with local inflammatory activity in non-culprit lesions: Beneficial effect of statins. *International Journal of Cardiology*, *119*, 368–373. doi:10.1016/j.ijcard.2006.08.026

Toutouzas, K., Drakopoulou, M., Markou, V., Stougianos, P., Tsiamis, E., & Tousoulis, D. (2006). Increased coronary sinus blood temperature: Correlation with systemic inflammation. *European Journal of Clinical Investigation*, *36*(4). doi:10.1111/j.1365-2362.2006.01625.x

Toutouzas, K., Drakopoulou, M., Mitropoulos, J., Tsiamis, E., Vaina, S., & Vavuranakis, M. (2006). Elevated plaque temperature in non-culprit de novo atheromatous lesions of patients with acute coronary syndromes. *Journal of the American College of Cardiology*, *47*, 301–306. doi:10.1016/j.jacc.2005.07.069

Toutouzas, K., Drakopoulou, M., Stefanadi, E., Siasos, G., & Stefanadis, C. (2005). (485-489). Intracoronary thermography: Does it help us in clinical decision making? *Journal of Interventional Cardiology*, 18.

Toutouzas, K., Markou, V., Drakopoulou, M., Mitropoulos, I., Tsiamis, E., & Stefanadis, C. (2005). Patients with type two diabetes mellitus: increased local inflammatory activation in culprit atheromatous plaques. *Hellenic Journal of Cardiology; HJC = Hellenike Kardiologike Epitheorese*, *46*, 283–288.

Toutouzas, K., Markou, V., Drakopoulou, M., Mitropoulos, I., Tsiamis, E., & Vavuranakis, M. (2005). Increased heat generation from atherosclerotic plaques in patients with type 2 diabetes: An increased local inflammatory activation. *Diabetes Care*, *28*, 1656–1661. doi:10.2337/diacare.28.7.1656

Toutouzas, K., Riga, M., Patsa, C., Synetos, A., Vavuranakis, M., & Tsiamis, E. (2007). Thin fibrous cap and ruptured plaques are associated with increased local inflammatory activation: Insights from optical coherence tomography in patients with acute coronary syndromes. *European Heart Journal*, *28*, 4041.

Toutouzas, K., Riga, M., Synetos, A., Karanasos, A., Tsiamis, E., & Tousoulis, D. (2009). Optical coherence tomography analysis of culprit lesions of patients with acute myocardial infarction in combination with intracoronary thermography: Excessive macrophage infiltration of thin fibrous caps are associated with increased local temperature. *Journal of the American College of Cardiology*, *53*, 2523.

Toutouzas, K., Riga, M., Vaina, S., Patsa, C., Synetos, A., & Vavuranakis, M. (2008). In acute coronary syndromes thin fibrous cap and ruptured plaques are associated with increased local inflammatory activation: A combination of intravascular optical coherence tomography and intracoronary thermography study. *Journal of the American College of Cardiology*, *51*, 1033.

Toutouzas, K., Riga, M., Vaina, S., Patsa, C., Synetos, A., & Vavuranakis, V. (2007). Optical coherence tomography in patients with acute coronary syndromes. Increased local inflammatory activation in ruptured plaques with thin fibrous cap. *Circulation*, *116*, 1989.

Toutouzas, K., Spanos, V., & Ribichini, F. (2003). A correlation of coronary plaque temperature with inflammatory markers obtained from atherectomy specimens in humans. *The American Journal of Cardiology*, *92*, 476.

Toutouzas, K., Stougianos, P., Drakopoulou, M., Mitropoulos, J., Bosinakou, E., & Markou, V. (2006). Coronary sinus thermography in idiopathic dilated cardiomyopathy: Correlation with systemic inflammation and left ventricular contractility. *European Journal of Heart Failure, 9*(2).

Toutouzas, K., Synetos, A., Stefanadi, E., Vaina, S., Markou, V., & Vavuranakis, M. (2007). Correlation between morphologic characteristics and local temperature differences in culprit lesions of patients with symptomatic coronary artery disease. *Journal of the American College of Cardiology, 49*, 2264–2271. doi:10.1016/j.jacc.2007.03.026

Toutouzas, K., Tsiamis, E., Drakopoulou, M., & Stefanadis, C. (2009). Regarding the study in vitro and in vivo studies on thermistor-based intracoronary temperature measurements: Effect of pressure and flow. *Catheterization and Cardiovascular Interventions, 74*, 815–816. doi:10.1002/ccd.22083

Toutouzas, K., Tsiamis, E., Drakopoulou, M., Synetos, A., Karampelas, J., & Riga, M. (2009). Impact of type 2 diabetes mellitus on diffuse inflammatory activation of de novo atheromatous lesions: Implications for systemic inflammation. *Diabetes & Metabolism, 35*, 299–304. doi:10.1016/j.diabet.2009.01.005

Toutouzas, K., Tsiamis, E., & Stefanadis, C. (2007). The Radi PressureWire thermistor for intracoronary thermography. *The Journal of Invasive Cardiology, 19*, 152–154, author reply 152–154.

Toutouzas, K., Vaina, S., Tsiamis, E., Vavuranakis, M., Mitropoulos, J., & Bosinakou, E. (2004). Detection of increased temperature of the culprit lesion after recent myocardial infarction: The favorable effect of statins. *American Heart Journal, 148*, 783–788. doi:10.1016/j.ahj.2004.05.013

Toutouzas, K., Drakopoulou, M., Markou, V., Karabelas, I., Vaina, S., & Vavuranakis, M. (2007). Correlation of systemic inflammation with local inflammatory activity in non-culprit lesions: Beneficial effect of statins. *International Journal of Cardiology, 119*, 368–373. doi:10.1016/j.ijcard.2006.08.026

Toutouzas, K., Drakopoulou, M., Mitropoulos, J., Tsiamis, E., Vaina, S., & Vavuranakis, M. (2006). Elevated plaque temperature in non-culprit de novo atheromatous lesions of patients with acute coronary syndromes. *Journal of the American College of Cardiology, 47*, 301–306. doi:10.1016/j.jacc.2005.07.069

Toutouzas, K., Markou, V., Drakopoulou, M., Mitropoulos, I., Tsiamis, E., & Stefanadis, C. (2005). Patients with type two diabetes mellitus: Increased local inflammatory activation in culprit atheromatous plaques. *Hellenike Kardiologike Epitheoresis. Hellenic Journal of Cardiology, 46*, 283–288.

Toutouzas, K., Markou, V., Drakopoulou, M., Mitropoulos, I., Tsiamis, E., & Vavuranakis, M. (2005). Increased heat generation from atherosclerotic plaques in patients with type 2 diabetes: An increased local inflammatory activation. *Diabetes Care, 28*, 1656–1661. doi:10.2337/diacare.28.7.1656

Toutouzas, K., Riga, M., Synetos, A., Karanasos, A., Tsiamis, E., & Tousoulis, D. (2009). Optical coherence tomography analysis of culprit lesions of patients with acute myocardial infarction in combination with intracoronary thermography: Excessive macrophage infiltration of thin fibrous caps are associated with increased local temperature. *Journal of the American College of Cardiology, 53*, 2523.

Toutouzas, K., Riga, M., Vaina, S., Patsa, C., Synetos, A., & Vavuranakis, M. (2008). In acute coronary syndromes thin fibrous cap and ruptured plaques are associated with increased local inflammatory activation: a combination of intravascular optical coherence tomography and intracoronary thermography study. *Journal of the American College of Cardiology, 51*, 1033.

Toutouzas, K., Spanos, V., & Ribichini, F. (2003). A correlation of coronary plaque temperature with inflammatory markers obtained from atherectomy specimens in humans. *The American Journal of Cardiology, 92*.

Toutouzas, K., Synetos, A., Stefanadi, E., Vaina, S., Markou, V., & Vavuranakis, M. (2007). Correlation between morphologic characteristics and local temperature differences in culprit lesions of patients with symptomatic coronary artery disease. *Journal of the American College of Cardiology, 49*, 2264–2271. doi:10.1016/j.jacc.2007.03.026

Toutouzas, K., Tsiamis, E., Drakopoulou, M., Synetos, A., Karampelas, J., & Riga, M. (2009). Impact of type 2 Diabetes Mellitus on diffuse inflammatory activation of de novo atheromatous lesions: Implications for systemic inflammation. *Diabetes & Metabolism, 35*, 299–304. doi:10.1016/j.diabet.2009.01.005

Toutouzas, K., Vaina, S., Tsiamis, E., Vavuranakis, M., Mitropoulos, J., & Bosinakou, E. (2004). Detection of increased temperature of the culprit lesion after recent myocardial infarction: The favorable effect of statins. *American Heart Journal, 148*, 783–788. doi:10.1016/j.ahj.2004.05.013

Toutouzas, K., Karanasos, A., & Stefanadis, C. (2010). Multiple plaque morphologies assessed by optical coherence tomography in a patient with acute coronary syndrome. *Heart (British Cardiac Society), 96*, 1335–1336. doi:10.1136/hrt.2010.194928

Toutouzas, K., Karanasos, A., & Tsiamis, E. (2011). New insights by optical coherence tomography into the differences and similarities of culprit ruptured plaque morphology in non-ST-elevation myocardial infarction and ST-elevation myocardial infarction. *American Heart Journal, 161*, 1162–1169. doi:10.1016/j.ahj.2011.03.005

Toutouzas, K., Synetos, A., & Stefanadi, E. (2007). Correlation between morphologic characteristics and local temperature differences in culprit lesions of patients with symptomatic coronary artery disease. *Journal of the American College of Cardiology, 49*, 2264–2271. doi:10.1016/j.jacc.2007.03.026

Toutouzas, K., Tsiamis, E., & Karanasos, A. e. (2010). Morphological characteristics of culprit atheromatic plaque are associated with coronary flow after thrombolytic therapy: New implications of optical coherence tomography from a multicenter study. *JACC: Cardiovascular Interventions, 3*, 507–514. doi:10.1016/j.jcin.2010.02.010

Toutouzas, K., Vaina, S., Riga, M., & Stefanadis, C. (2009). Evaluation of dissection after coronary stent implantation by intravascular optical coherence tomography. *Clinical Cardiology, 32*, E47–E48. doi:10.1002/clc.20173

Toutouzas, K., Drakopoulou, M., Markou, V., Stougianos, P., Tsiamis, E., Tousoulis, D., *et al.* (2006). Increased coronary sinus blood temperature: Correlation with systemic inflammation. *Eur J Clin Invest.*

Toutouzas, K., Drakopoulou, M., Synetos, A., Stathogiannis, K., Klonaris, C., Liasis, N., *et al.* (2010). *Noninvasive detection of local inflammatory activation in atherosclerotic carotid arteries: First clinical application of microwave radiometry.* ESC2010.

Toutouzas, K., Riga, M., & Drakopoulou, M. (2009). *Combination of optical coherence tomography and intracoronary thermography for the morphological and functional assessment of the culprit lesion in patients with acute coronary syndromes.* ESC2010. (abstract)

Toutouzas, K., Synetos, A., Drakopoulou, M., Moldovan, C., Siores, E., Grassos, C., *et al.* (n.d.). *A new non-invasive method for detection of local inflammatory activation in atheromatic plaques: Experimental evaluation of microwave thermography.* ESC2010.

Toutouzas, K., Synetos, A., Drakopoulou, M., Moldovan, C., Siores, E., Grassos, C., *et al.* (2010). *A new non-invasive method for detection of local inflammatory activation in atheromatic plaques: Experimental evaluation of microwave thermography.* ESC2010.

Tsiamis, E., Toutouzas, K., & Synetos, A. (2010). Prognostic clinical and angiographic characteristics for the development of a new significant lesion in remote segments after successful percutaneous coronary intervention. *International Journal of Cardiology, 143*, 29–34. doi:10.1016/j.ijcard.2009.01.026

Tsuchida, K., Piek, J. J., Neumann, F. J., van der Giessen, W. J., Wiemer, M., & Zeiher, A. M. (2005). One-year results of a durable polymer everolimus-eluting stent in de novo coronary narrowings (The SPIRIT FIRST Trial). *EuroIntervention, 1*(3), 266–272.

Tu, S., Holm, N. R., Koning, G., Huang, Z., & Reiber, J. H. C. (2011). Fusion of 3D QCA and IVUS/OCT. *The International Journal of Cardiovascular Imaging, 25*.

Tuzcu, E. M., Berkalp, B., De Franco, A. C., Ellis, S. G., Goormastic, M., & Whitlow, P. L. (1996). The dilemma of diagnosing coronary calcification: Angiography versus intravascular ultrasound. *Journal of the American College of Cardiology, 27*(4), 832–838. doi:10.1016/0735-1097(95)00537-4

Tziakas, D., Chalikias, G., Tentes, I., Stakos, D., Chatzikyriakou, S., & Mitrousi, K. (2008). Interleukin-8 is increased in the membrane of circulating erythrocytes in patients with acute coronary syndrome. *European Heart Journal*, 29, 2713–2722. doi:10.1093/eurheartj/ehn382

Tziakas, D., Kaski, J., Chalikias, G., Romero, C., Fredericks, S., & Tentes, I. (2007). Total cholesterol content of erythrocyte membranes is increased in patients with acute coronary syndrome. *Journal of the American College of Cardiology*, 49, 2081–2089. doi:10.1016/j.jacc.2006.08.069

U.S. Food and Drug Administration. (n.d.). *Press annoucements*. Retrieved from http://www.fda.gov/ NewsEvents/ Newsroom/ PressAnnouncements/2008/ ucm116888. html 2008

Ueda, Y., Ohtani, T., Shimizu, M., Hirayama, A., & Kodama, K. (2004, Aug). Assessment of plaque vulnerability by angioscopic classification of plaque color. *American Heart Journal*, 148(2), 333–335. doi:10.1016/j.ahj.2004.03.047

Unal, G., Bucher, S., Carlier, S., Slabaugh, G., Tong, F., & Tanaka, K. (2008). Shape-driven segmentation of the arterial wall in intravascular ultrasound images. *IEEE Transactions on Information Technology in Biomedicine*, 12(3), 335–347. doi:10.1109/TITB.2008.920620

Valgimigli, M., Rodriguez-Granillo, G. A., Garcia-Garcia, H. M., Malagutti, P., Regar, E., & de Jaegere, P. (2006). Distance from the ostium as an independent determinant of coronary plaque composition in vivo: An intravascular ultrasound study based radiofrequency data analysis in humans. *European Heart Journal*, 27(6), 655–663. doi:10.1093/eurheartj/ehi716

van de Pol, S., Romer, T., Puppels, G., & van der Laarse, A. (2002). Imaging of atherosclerosis. Raman spectroscopy of atherosclerosis. *Journal of Cardiovascular Risk*, 9, 255–261. doi:10.1097/00043798-200210000-00005

van der Giessen, A. G., Schaap, M., Gijsen, F. J., Groen, H. C., van Walsum, T., & Mollet, N. R. (2010). 3D fusion of intravascular ultrasound and coronary computed tomography for in-vivo wall shear stress analysis: A feasibility study. *The International Journal of Cardiovascular Imaging*, 26(7), 781–796. doi:10.1007/s10554-009-9546-y

van der Giessen, A. G., Wentzel, J. J., Meijboom, W. B., Mollet, N. R., van der Steen, A. F., & van de Vosse, F. N. (2009). Plaque and shear stress distribution in human coronary bifurcations: A multislice computed tomography study. *EuroIntervention*, 4(5), 654–661. doi:10.4244/EIJV4I5A109

van der Steen, A., de Korte, C., Mastik, F., & Schaar, J. (2003). Three dimensional tissue hardness imaging. *World Patent, WO03*(017845), A1.

Van Herck, J., De Meyer, G., Ennekens, G., Van Herck, P., Herman, A., & Vrints, C. (2009). Validation of in vivo plaque characterisation by virtual histology in a rabbit model of atherosclerosis. *EuroIntervention*, 5(1), 149–156. doi:10.4244/EIJV5I1A23

Van Mieghem, C. A., Bruining, N., Schaar, J. A., McFadden, E., Mollet, N., & Cademartiri, F. (2005). Rationale and methods of the integrated biomarker and imaging study (IBIS): Combining invasive and non-invasive imaging with biomarkers to detect subclinical atherosclerosis and assess coronary lesion biology. *The International Journal of Cardiovascular Imaging*, 21(4), 425–441. doi:10.1007/s10554-004-7986-y

Van Mieghem, C. A., McFadden, E. P., de Feyter, P. J., Bruining, N., Schaar, J. A., & Mollet, N. R. (2006). Noninvasive detection of subclinical coronary atherosclerosis coupled with assessment of changes in plaque characteristics using novel invasive imaging modalities: The integrated biomarker and imaging study (IBIS). *Journal of the American College of Cardiology*, 47(6), 1134–1142. doi:10.1016/j.jacc.2005.09.075

van Soest, G., Goderie, T., & Regar, E. (2010). Atherosclerotic tissue characterization in vivo by optical coherence tomography attenuation imaging. *Journal of Biomedical Optics*, 15, 011105. doi:10.1117/1.3280271

van Soest, G., Mastik, F., de Jong, N., & van der Steen, A. (2007). Robust intravascular optical coherence elastography by line correlations. *Physics in Medicine and Biology*, 52, 2445–2458. doi:10.1088/0031-9155/52/9/008

Varnava, A. M., Mills, P. G., & Davies, M. J. (2002). Relationship between coronary artery remodeling and plaque vulnerability. *Circulation*, 105(8), 939–943. doi:10.1161/hc0802.104327

Vavuranakis, M., Toutouzas, K., Stefanadis, C., Chrisohou, C., Markou, D., & Toutouzas, P. (2001). Stent deployment in calcified lesions: Can we overcome calcific restraint with high-pressure balloon inflations? *Catheterization and Cardiovascular Interventions*, *52*(2), 164–172. doi:10.1002/1522-726X(200102)52:2<164::AID-CCD1041>3.0.CO;2-S

Verheye, S., Agostoni, P., Dawkins, K. D., Dens, J., Rutsch, W., & Carrie, D. (2009). The GENESIS (Randomized, Multicenter Study of the Pimecrolimus-Eluting and Pimecrolimus/Paclitaxel-Eluting Coronary stent system in patients with de novo lesions of the native coronary arteries) trial. *JACC: Cardiovascular Interventions*, *2*(3), 205–214. doi:10.1016/j.jcin.2008.12.011

Verheye, S., De Meyer, G., Krams, R., Kockx, M., Van Damme, L., & Mousavi Gourabi, B. (2004). Intravascular thermography: Immediate functional and morphological vascular findings. *European Heart Journal*, *25*, 158–165. doi:10.1016/j.ehj.2003.10.023

Verheye, S., De Meyer, G., Van Langenhove, G., Knaapen, M., & Kockx, M. (2002). In vivo temperature heterogeneity of atherosclerotic plaques is determined by plaque composition. *Circulation*, *105*, 1596–1601. doi:10.1161/01.CIR.0000012527.94843.BF

Verheye, S., De Meyer, G., Krams, R., Kockx, M., Van Damme, L., & Mousavi, G. B. (2004). Intravascular thermography: Immediate functional and morphological vascular findings. *European Heart Journal*, *25*, 158–165. doi:10.1016/j.ehj.2003.10.023

Verheye, S., De Meyer, G., Van Langenhove, G., Knaapen, M., & Kockx, M. (2002). *In vivo* temperature heterogeneity of atherosclerotic plaques is determined by plaque composition. *Circulation*, *105*, 1596–1601. doi:10.1161/01.CIR.0000012527.94843.BF

Vetshev, P., Chilingaridi, K., Zolkin, A., Vesnin, S., Gabaidze, D., & Bannyi, D. (2006). Radiothermometry in diagnosis of thyroid diseases. *Khirurgiia*, 54–58.

Vince, D. G., Dixon, K. J., Cothren, R. M., & Cornhill, J. F. (2000). Comparison of texture analysis methods for the characterization of coronary plaques in intravascular ultrasound images. *Computerized Medical Imaging and Graphics*, *24*(4), 221–229. doi:10.1016/S0895-6111(00)00011-2

Virmani, R., Burke, A. P., Farb, A., & Kolodgie, F. D. (2006). Pathology of the vulnerable plaque. *Journal of the American College of Cardiology*, *47*(8), 13–18. doi:10.1016/j.jacc.2005.10.065

Virmani, R., Kolodgie, F. D., Burke, A. P., Farb, A., & Schwartz, S. M. (2000). Lessons from sudden coronary death: A comprehensive morphological classification scheme for atherosclerotic lesions. *Arteriosclerosis, Thrombosis, and Vascular Biology*, *20*(5), 1262–1275. doi:10.1161/01.ATV.20.5.1262

Virmani, R., Burke, A. P., Farb, A., & Kolodgie, F. D. (2006). Pathology of the vulnerable plaque. *Journal of the American College of Cardiology*, *47*(8Suppl), C13–C18. doi:10.1016/j.jacc.2005.10.065

Virmani, R., Burke, A. P., Kolodgie, F. D., & Farb, A. (2002). Vulnerable plaque: The pathology of unstable coronary lesions. *Journal of Interventional Cardiology*, *15*(6), 439–446. doi:10.1111/j.1540-8183.2002.tb01087.x

Virmani, R., Burke, A., Farb, A., & Kolodgie, F. (2006). Pathology of the vulnerable plaque. *Journal of the American College of Cardiology*, *47*, C13–C18. doi:10.1016/j.jacc.2005.10.065

Virmani, R., Kolodgie, F., Burke, A., Farb, A., & Schwartz, S. (2000). Lessons from sudden coronary death: A comprehensive morphological classification scheme for atherosclerotic lesions. *Arteriosclerosis, Thrombosis, and Vascular Biology*, *20*, 1262–1275. doi:10.1161/01.ATV.20.5.1262

Virmani, R., Kolodgie, F., Burke, A., Farb, A., & Schwartz, S. (2000). Lessons from sudden coronary death: A comprehensive morphological classification scheme for atherosclerotic lesions. *Arteriosclerosis, Thrombosis, and Vascular Biology*, *20*, 1262–1275. doi:10.1161/01.ATV.20.5.1262

Volcano. (n.d.). *Clinical studies and trials*. Retrieved from http://volcanocorp.com/clinical/clinical-studies-trials.asp

Volcano. (n.d.). *Products: IVUS imaging*. Retrieved from http://volcanocorp.com/products/ivus-imaging/vh-ivus.asp

Vollmar, J., & Storz, L. (n.d.). Vascular endoscopy: Possibilities and limits of its clinical application. *Surgical Clinics of North America*, *54*, 111-112.

Volmink, J., Newton, J., Hicks, N., Sleight, P., Fowler, G., & Neil, H. (1998). Coronary event and case fatality rates in an English population: Results of the Oxford myocardial infarction incidence study. The Oxford Myocardial Infarction Incidence Study Group. *Heart (British Cardiac Society)*, *80*, 40–44.

von Birgelen, C., Hartmann, M., Mintz, G. S., van Houwelingen, K. G., Deppermann, N., & Schmermund, A. (2004). Relationship between cardiovascular risk as predicted by established risk scores versus plaque progression as measured by serial intravascular ultrasound in left main coronary arteries. *Circulation*, *110*(12), 1579–1585. doi:10.1161/01.CIR.0000142048.94084.CA

von Birgelen, C., de Vrey, E., Mintz, G., Nicosia, A., Bruining, N., & Li, W., ... de Feyter, P. (1997). ECG-gated three-dimensional intravascular ultrasound: Feasibility and reproducibility of the automated analysis of coronary lumen and atherosclerotic plaque dimensions in humans. *Circulation*, *96*, 2944–2952.

von zur Muhlen, C., von Elverfeldt, D., Moeller, J. A., Choudhury, R. P., Paul, D., & Hagemeyer, C. E. (2008). Magnetic resonance imaging contrast agent targeted toward activated platelets allows in vivo detection of thrombosis and monitoring of thrombolysis. *Circulation*, *118*(3), 258–267. doi:10.1161/CIRCULATIONAHA.107.753657

Wahle, A., Prause, P. M., DeJong, S. C., & Sonka, M. (1999). Geometrically correct 3-D reconstruction of intravascular ultrasound images by fusion with biplane angiography--Methods and validation. *IEEE Transactions on Medical Imaging*, *18*(8), 686–699. doi:10.1109/42.796282

Wahle, A., Olszewski, M. E., & Sonka, M. (2004). Interactive virtual endoscopy in coronary arteries based on multimodality fusion. *IEEE Transactions on Medical Imaging*, *23*(11), 1391–1403. doi:10.1109/TMI.2004.837109

Wahle, A., Prause, P., DeJong, S., & Sonka, M. (1999). Geometrically correct 3-D reconstruction of intravascular ultrasound images by fusion with biplane angiography-Methods and validation. *IEEE Transactions on Medical Imaging*, *18*, 686–699. doi:10.1109/42.796282

Wainstein, M., Costa, M., Ribeiro, J., Zago, A., & Rogers, C. (2007). Vulnerable plaque detection by temperature heterogeneity measured with a guidewire system: Clinical, intravascular ultrasound and histopathologic correlates. *The Journal of Invasive Cardiology*, *19*, 49–54.

Walimbe, V., Jaber, W. A., Garcia, M. J., & Shekhar, R. (2009). Multimodality cardiac stress testing: Combining real-time 3-dimensional echocardiography and myocardial perfusion SPECT. *Journal of Nuclear Medicine*, *50*(2), 226–230. doi:10.2967/jnumed.108.053025

Walimbe, V., Zagrodsky, V., Raja, S., Jaber, W. A., DiFilippo, F. P., & Garcia, M. J. (2003). Mutual information-based multimodality registration of cardiac ultrasound and SPECT images: A preliminary investigation. *The International Journal of Cardiovascular Imaging*, *19*(6), 483–494. doi:10.1023/B:CAIM.0000004325.48512.5a

Wang, X., Lu, C., Chen, X., Zhao, X., & Xia, D. (2008). A new method to quantify coronary calcification by intravascular ultrasound - The different patterns of calcification of acute myocardial infarction, unstable angina pectoris and stable angina pectoris. *The Journal of Invasive Cardiology*, *20*(11), 587–590.

Wang, J. C., Normand, S. L., Mauri, L., & Kuntz, R. E. (2004). Coronary artery spatial distribution of acute myocardial infarction occlusions. *Circulation*, *110*(3), 278–284. doi:10.1161/01.CIR.0000135468.67850.F4

Wang, H., Fleming, C., & Rollins, A. (2007). Ultrahigh-resolution optical coherence tomography at 1.15 mum using photonic crystal fiber with no zero-dispersion wavelengths. *Optics Express*, *15*, 3085–3092. doi:10.1364/OE.15.003085

Wang, J., Geng, Y., & Guo, B. (2002). Near-infrared spectroscopic characterization of human advanced atherosclerotic plaques. *Journal of the American College of Cardiology*, *39*, 1305–1313. doi:10.1016/S0735-1097(02)01767-9

Wang, Y., Shu, Y., Hu, B., & Chen, J. (2009). *An improved level set method of ultrasound imaging to detect blood vessel walls*. International Conference on Image Analysis and Signal Processing, IASP 2009.

Waseda, K., Miyazawa, A., Ako, J., Hasegawa, T., Tsujino, I., & Sakurai, R. (2009). Intravascular ultrasound results from the ENDEAVOR IV trial: Randomized comparison between zotarolimus- and paclitaxel-eluting stents in patients with coronary artery disease. *JACC: Cardiovascular Interventions*, *2*(8), 779–784. doi:10.1016/j.jcin.2009.05.015

Waxman, S., Dixon, S. R., L'Allier, P., Moses, J. W., Petersen, J. L., & Cutlip, D. (2009). In vivo validation of a catheter-based near-infrared spectroscopy system for detection of lipid core coronary plaques: Initial results of the SPECTACL study. *JACC: Cardiovascular Imaging*, *2*(7), 858–868. doi:10.1016/j.jcmg.2009.05.001

Waxman, S., Ishibashi, F., & Caplan, J. (2007). Rationale and use of near-infrared spectroscopy for detection of lipid-rich and vulnerable plaques. *Journal of Nuclear Cardiology*, *14*, 719–728. doi:10.1016/j.nuclcard.2007.08.001

Waxman, S., Khabbaz, K., & Connolly, R. e. (2008). Intravascular imaging of atherosclerotic human coronaries in a porcine model: A feasibility study. *The International Journal of Cardiovascular Imaging*, *24*, 37–44. doi:10.1007/s10554-007-9227-7

Waxman, S., Tang, J., & Marshik, B. (2004). In vivo detection of a coronary artificial target with a near infrared spectroscopy catheter. *American Journal of Cardiology . Suppl*, *6A*(94), 141E.

Webster, M., Stewart, J., & Ruygrok, P. (2002). Intracoronary thermography with a multiple thermocouple catheter: initial human experience. *The American Journal of Cardiology*, *90*, 24H.

Weichert, F., Müller, H., Quast, U., Kraushaar, A., Spilles, P., & Heintz, M. (2003). Virtual 3D IVUS vessel model for intravascular brachytherapy planning. 3D segmentation, reconstruction and visualization of coronary artery architecture and orientation. *Medical Physics*, *30*(9), 2530–2536. doi:10.1118/1.1603964

Weissman, N. J., Koglin, J., Cox, D. A., Hermiller, J., O'Shaughnessy, C., & Mann, J. T. (2005). Polymer-based paclitaxel-eluting stents reduce in-stent neointimal tissue proliferation: A serial volumetric intravascular ultrasound analysis from the TAXUS-IV trial. *Journal of the American College of Cardiology*, *45*(8), 1201–1205. doi:10.1016/j.jacc.2004.10.078

Weissman, N. J., Ellis, S. G., Grube, E., Dawkins, K. D., Greenberg, J. D., & Mann, T. (2007). Effect of the polymer-based, paclitaxel-eluting TAXUS Express stent on vascular tissue responses: A volumetric intravascular ultrasound integrated analysis from the TAXUS IV, V, and VI trials. *European Heart Journal*, *28*(13), 1574–1582. doi:10.1093/eurheartj/ehm174

Wennogle, M., & Hoff, W. (2009). Three dimensional segmentation of intravascular ultrasound data. *Lecture Notes in Computer Science*, *5627*, 772–781. doi:10.1007/978-3-642-02611-9_76

Wentzel, J. J., van der Giessen, A. G., Garg, S., Schultz, C., Mastik, F., & Gijsen, F. J. H. (2010). In vivo 3D distribution of lipid-core plaque in human coronary artery as assessed by fusion of near infrared spectroscopy-Intravascular ultrasound and multislice computed tomography scan. *Circulation-Cardiovascular Imaging*, *3*(6), E6–E7. doi:10.1161/CIRCIMAGING.110.958850

Wentzel, J. J., Gijsen, F. J., Schuurbiers, J. C., van der Steen, A. F., & Serruys, P. W. (2008). The influence of shear stress on in-stent restenosis and thrombosis. *EuroIntervention*, *4*(Suppl C), C27–C32.

Wentzel, J. J., Janssen, E., Vos, J., Schuurbiers, J. C., Krams, R., & Serruys, P. W. (2003). Extension of increased atherosclerotic wall thickness into high shear stress regions is associated with loss of compensatory remodeling. *Circulation*, *108*(1), 17–23. doi:10.1161/01.CIR.0000078637.21322.D3

Wentzel, J. J., Krams, R., Schuurbiers, J. C., Oomen, J. A., Kloet, J., & van Der Giessen, W. J. (2001). Relationship between neointimal thickness and shear stress after Wallstent implantation in human coronary arteries. *Circulation*, *103*(13), 1740–1745.

Wentzel, J. J., Whelan, D. M., van der Giessen, W. J., van Beusekom, H. M., Andhyiswara, I., & Serruys, P. W. (2000). Coronary stent implantation changes 3-D vessel geometry and 3-D shear stress distribution. *Journal of Biomechanics*, *33*(10), 1287–1295. doi:10.1016/S0021-9290(00)00066-X

Wentzel, J., van der Giessen, A., & Garg, S. e. (2010). In vivo 3D distribution of lipid-core plaque in human coronary artery as assessed by fusion of near infrared spectroscopy-intravascular ultrasound and multislice computed tomography scan. *Circulation: Cardiovascular Imaging*, *e*(3), 6-7.

White, C., Ramee, S., Collins, T., Mesa, J., Jain, A., & Ventur, A. H. (1993, Mar). Percutaneous coronary angioscopy: Applications in interventional cardiology. *Journal of Interventional Cardiology*, *6*(1), 61–67. doi:10.1111/j.1540-8183.1993.tb00442.x

Wijesekera, N., Duncan, M., & Padley, S. (2010). X-ray computed tomography of the heart. *British Medical Bulletin*, *93*, 49–67. doi:10.1093/bmb/ldp043

Wijns, W. (2009). Late stent thrombosis after drug-eluting stent: Seeing is understanding. *Circulation*, *120*, 364–365. doi:10.1161/CIRCULATIONAHA.109.882001

Williams, L., & Springer, E. (1981). Microwave radiation: Environmental impact and medical application. *Minnesota Medicine*, *64*, 593–599.

Williams, P., & Norris, K. (2001). *Near-infrared technology in the agriculture and food industries.* American Association of Cereal Chemists.

Wojtkowski, M., Leitgeb, R., Kowalczyk, A., Bajraszewski, T., & Fercher, A. F. (2002). In vivo human retinal imaging by Fourier domain optical coherence tomography. *Journal of Biomedical Optics*, *7*(3), 457–463. doi:10.1117/1.1482379

Worthley, S., Farouque, M., Worthley, M., Baldi, M., Chew, D., & Meredith, I. (2006). The RADI PressureWire high-sensitivity thermistor and culprit lesion temperature in patients with acute coronary syndromes. *The Journal of Invasive Cardiology*, *18*, 528–531.

Wu, X., Maehara, A., Mintz, G., Kubo, T., Xu, K., & Choi, S. (2010). Virtual histology intravascular ultrasound analysis of non-culprit attenuated plaques detected by grayscale intravascular ultrasound in patients with acute coronary syndromes. *The American Journal of Cardiology*, *105*(1), 48–53. doi:10.1016/j.amjcard.2009.08.649

Wykrzykowska, J., Lehman, S., Williams, G., Parker, J. A., Palmer, M. R., & Varkey, S. (2009). Imaging of inflamed and vulnerable plaque in coronary arteries with F-18-FDG PET/CT in patients with suppression of myocardial uptake using a low-carbohydrate, high-fat preparation. *Journal of Nuclear Medicine*, *50*(4), 563–568. doi:10.2967/jnumed.108.055616

Xie, L., Hu, Y., Nunes, J. C., Bellanger, J. J., Bedossa, M., & Luo, L. (2010). A model-based reconstruction method for 3-D rotational coronary angiography. *Proceedings of the IEEE Engineering Medical Biology Society*, *1*, 3186–3189.

Xu, C., Schmitt, J., Carlier, S., & Virmani, R. (2008). Characterization of atherosclerosis plaques by measuring both backscattering and attenuation coefficients in optical coherence tomography. *Journal of Biomedical Optics*, *13*, 034003. doi:10.1117/1.2927464

Xu, Y., Wang, L., Buttice, G., Sengupta, P., & Smith, B. (2003). Interferon gamma repression of collagen (COL1A2) transcription is mediated by the RFX5 complex. *The Journal of Biological Chemistry*, *278*, 49134–49144. doi:10.1074/jbc.M309003200

Yabushita, H., Bouma, B. E., Houser, S. L., Aretz, H. T., Jang, I. K., & Schlendorf, K. H. (2002). Characterization of human atherosclerosis by optical coherence tomography. *Circulation*, *106*(13), 1640–1645. doi:10.1161/01.CIR.0000029927.92825.F6

Yamagishi, M., Terashima, M., Awano, K., Kijima, M., Nakatani, S., & Daikoku, S. (2000). Morphology of vulnerable coronary plaque: insights from follow-up of patients examined by intravascular ultrasound before an acute coronary syndrome. *Journal of the American College of Cardiology*, *35*(1), 106–111. doi:10.1016/S0735-1097(99)00533-1

Yamaguchi, T., Terashima, M., Akasaka, T., Hayashi, T., Mizuno, K., & Muramatsu, T. (2008). Safety and feasibility of an intravascular optical coherence tomography image wire system in the clinical setting. *The American Journal of Cardiology*, *101*(5), 562–567. doi:10.1016/j.amjcard.2007.09.116

Yasuhiro, H., & Fitzgerald, P. (2008). Frontiers in intravascular imaging technologies. *Circulation*, *117*, 2024–2037. doi:10.1161/CIRCULATIONAHA.105.551804

Yock, P., Linker, D., & Angelsen, B. (1989). Two-dimensional intravascular ultrasound: Technical development and initial clinical experience. *Journal of the American Society of Echocardiography*, *2*, 296–304.

Yokoyama, M., Komiyama, N., Courtney, B. K., Nakayama, T., Namikawa, S., & Kuriyama, N. (2005). Plasma low-density lipoprotein reduction and structural effects on coronary atherosclerotic plaques by atorvastatin as clinically assessed with intravascular ultrasound radio-frequency signal analysis: A randomized prospective study. *American Heart Journal*, *150*(2), 287. doi:10.1016/j.ahj.2005.03.059

Young Joon, H., Myung Ho, J., Yun Ha, C., Eun Hye, M., Jum Suk, K., Min Goo, L., et al. (2009). Plaque components at coronary sites with focal spasm in patients with variant angina: Virtual histology-intravascular ultrasound analysis. *Int J Cardiol.*

Yu, X., Song, S. K., Chen, J., Scott, M. J., Fuhrhop, R. J., & Hall, C. S. (2000). High-resolution MRI characterization of human thrombus using a novel fibrin-targeted paramagnetic nanoparticle contrast agent. *Magnetic Resonance in Medicine*, *44*(6), 867–872. doi:10.1002/1522-2594(200012)44:6<867::AID-MRM7>3.0.CO;2-P

Yu, W., Chuang, S., Lin, Y., & Chen, C. (2008). Brachial-ankle vs carotid-femoral pulse wave velocity as a determinant of cardiovascular structure and function. *Journal of Human Hypertension*, *22*(1), 24–31. doi:10.1038/sj.jhh.1002259

Yuan, C., Kerwin, W. S., Ferguson, M. S., Polissar, N., Zhang, S., & Cai, J. (2002). Contrast-enhanced high resolution MRI for atherosclerotic carotid artery tissue characterization. *Journal of Magnetic Resonance Imaging*, *15*(1), 62–67. doi:10.1002/jmri.10030

Yuan, C., Mitsumori, L. M., Ferguson, M. S., Polissar, N. L., Echelard, D., & Ortiz, G. (2001). In vivo accuracy of multispectral magnetic resonance imaging for identifying lipid-rich necrotic cores and intraplaque hemorrhage in advanced human carotid plaques. *Circulation*, *104*(17), 2051–2056. doi:10.1161/hc4201.097839

Yun, S., Tearney, G., de Boer, J., Iftimia, N., & Bouma, B. (2003). High-speed optical frequency-domain imaging. *Optics Express*, *11*(22), 2953–2963. doi:10.1364/OE.11.002953

Yun, S., Tearney, G., & Vakoc, B. (2006). Comprehensive volumetric optical microscopy in vivo. *Nature Medicine*, *12*, 1429–1433. doi:10.1038/nm1450

Zanchetta, M., Rigatelli, G., Pedon, L., Zennaro, M., Maiolino, A., & Onorato, P. (2003). Role of intracardiac echocardiography in atrial septal abnormalities. *Journal of Interventional Cardiology*, *16*(1), 63–77. doi:10.1046/j.1540-8183.2003.08004.x

Zarins, C. K., Zatina, M. A., Giddens, D. P., Ku, D. N., & Glagov, S. (1987). Shear stress regulation of artery lumen diameter in experimental atherogenesis. *Journal of Vascular Surgery*, *5*(3), 413–420.

Zarrabi, A., Gul, K., Willerson, J., Casscell, W., & Naghavi, M. (2002). Intravascular thermography: A novel approach for detection of vulnerable plaque. *Current Opinion in Cardiology*, *17*, 656–662. doi:10.1097/00001573-200211000-00012

Zhang, Q., Wang, Y., Wang, W., Ma, J., Qian, J., & Ge, J. (2010). Automatic segmentation of calcifications in intravascular ultrasound images using snakes and the contourlet transform. *Ultrasound in Medicine & Biology*, *36*(1), 111–129. doi:10.1016/j.ultrasmedbio.2009.06.1097

Zhang, X., McKay, C. R., & Sonka, M. (1998). Tissue characterization in intravascular ultrasound images. *IEEE Transactions on Medical Imaging*, *17*(6), 889–899. doi:10.1109/42.746622

Zhang, L., Liu, Y., Zhang, P. F., Zhao, Y. X., Ji, X. P., & Lu, X. T. (2010). Peak radial and circumferential strain measured by velocity vector imaging is a novel index for detecting vulnerable plaques in a rabbit model of atherosclerosis. *Atherosclerosis*, *211*(1), 146–152. doi:10.1016/j.atherosclerosis.2010.01.023

Zhao, Y. H., Chen, Z. P., Ding, Z. H., Ren, H. W., & Nelson, J. S. (2002). Real-time phase-resolved functional optical coherence tomography by use of optical Hilbert transformation. *Optics Letters*, *27*(2), 98–100. doi:10.1364/OL.27.000098

Zhu, B., Jaffer, F., Ntziachristos, V., & Weissleder, R. (2005). Development of a near infrared fluorescence catheter: Operating characterisitics and feasibility for atherosclerotic plaque detection. *Journal of Physics. D, Applied Physics*, *38*, 2701–2707. doi:10.1088/0022-3727/38/15/024

Zhu, H., Oakeson, K. D., & Friedman, M. H. (2003). Retrieval of cardiac phase from IVUS sequences. *Proc SPIE Medical Imaging*, *5035*, 135–146.

Zimarino, M., Prati, F., & Stabile, E. (2007). Optical coherence tomography accurately identifies intermediate atherosclerotic lesions--An in vivo evaluation in the rabbit carotid artery. *Atherosclerosis*, *139*, 94–101. doi:10.1016/j.atherosclerosis.2006.08.047

About the Contributors

Vasilios D. Tsakanikas was born on 1st of January of 1983 in Agrinio, Greece. He graduated from the 1st High School of Agrinio in 2000. He received the Diploma Degree in Electrical and Computer Engineering in 2005 from the National Technical University of Athens, Greece. In his thesis, he performed an analysis of the established link between terminal mobile communication devices and users' heads, utilizing the F.D.T.D. (Finite Difference Time Domain) numerical method. He received a M.Sc. in Computer Science from the Athens University of Economics and Business, Department of Informatics, Greece in 2007. Today, he is working as Software Engineer on several biomedical projects.

Dimitrios I. Fotiadis received the Diploma degree in Chemical Engineering from the National Technical University of Athens, Athens, Greece, in 1985, and the Ph.D. degree in Chemical Engineering and Materials Science from the University of Minnesota, Minneapolis, MN, in 1990. He is currently a Professor of Biomedical Engineering in the Department of Materials Science and Engineering and the Director of the Unit of Medical Technology and Intelligent Information Systems, Department of Materials Science and Engineering, University of Ioannina, Ioannina, Greece. He was a Visiting Researcher at the RWTH, Aachen, Germany and the Massachusetts Institute of Technology, Boston, MA. He has authored or coauthored more than 130 papers in scientific journals, 270 papers in peer-reviewed conference proceedings, and more than 25 chapters in books. He is the Editor of 16 books. His research interests include modeling of human tissues and organs, intelligent wearable devices for automated diagnosis, and bioinformatics. He is IEEE senior member, Associate Editor for *IEEE Transactions of Information Technology in Biomedicine*, and participates in the organisation of several international conferences. Prof. Fotiadis coordinates several R&D projects funded by the EC and other bodies.

Lampros K. Michalis was born in Arta, Greece, in 1960. He received the M.D. degree with Distinction from the University of Athens Medical School, Greece in 1984 and in 1989, he was awarded his M.D. Thesis with Distinction also from the University of Athens Medical School. He has been fully trained in clinical and interventional cardiology in the United Kingdom. Since 1995 he has been with the University of Ioannina Medical School, Ioannina, Greece, where he is a Professor of Cardiology. His research interests focus on interventional cardiology, intravascular imaging, percutaneous treatment of peripheral arterial disease, bioengineering, and diagnosis and prevention of preclinical arteriosclerosis.

Katerina K. Naka received the M.D. degree with distinction from the University of Ioannina Medical School, Ioannina, Greece and the Ph.D. degree in Cardiology from the University of Wales College of Medicine, Cardiff, Wales, U.K in 2003. She is fully trained in cardiology and since 2006, she has been with the University of Ioannina Medical School, Ioannina, Greece, where she is currently an Assistant Professor of Cardiology. Her research interests include vascular endothelial function, large arterial mechanics, heart failure, echocardiography, intravascular ultrasound, and bioengineering.

Christos V. Bourantas graduated from the Medical School, University of Ioannina, Greece in 1999, and 6 years later, he was awarded with distinction for his PhD degree in Cardiology from the same Medical School. He completed his training in Cardiology in UK and he is currently working as a Fellow in interventional cardiology in East Yorkshire NHS Trust, UK. His research interests include image processing, 3D modeling, invasive imaging, and cardiac MRI. He is an Honorary Lecturer in the Department of Academic Cardiology Hull University, Kingston upon Hull, UK.

* * *

Farqad M. Alamgir was born in Multan, Pakistan in 1956. He graduated from King Edward Medical College in 1989. He is a Member of the Royal College of Physicians since 1996. In 2003 he was appointed as a Consultant Cardiologist in East Yorkshire NHS Trust. He is currently the Clinical Director in the Department of Cardiology and Honorary Senior Lecturer in the Department of Academic Cardiology, University of Hull. He is actively involved in research and he is the principal investigator of most of the interventional clinical trials taking place in Hull. His research interests include chronic total occlusions, intravascular imaging, and structural interventions.

Lambros S. Athanasiou was born in Ioannina, Greece, in 1985. He received the diploma degree in the Department of Information and Communication Systems Engineering from the University of Aegean, Greece, in 2008. He is currently working toward the Ph.D. degree in the Dept. of Materials Science and Engineering at the University of Ioannina. His research interests include medical image processing, biomedical engineering, decision support, and medical expert systems.

Antonios P. Antoniadis attended Medical School, Aristotle University of Thessaloniki, Greece, completing his MD in 2000, his MSc in Medical Research Methodology in 2005 with distinction, and his PhD in 2011 with distinction. The topic of his PhD thesis is "Three dimensional in-vivo simulation of coronary arterial alterations during cardiac cycle." Currently he works as a Cardiovascular Research Fellow at Brigham and Women's Hospital, Harvard Medical School, Boston, MA, USA. He has authored several peer-reviewed research papers and received four times the first prize for research work in national conferences. During his PhD studies he was awarded a scholarship by the Alexander S. Onassis Public Benefit Foundation, a prize for excellence and innovation by the research committee of the Aristotle University of Thessaloniki, Greece and a prize in the Innovative Ideas in Business regional contest. During his cardiology fellowship, he received the best fellow award for the period from 2008 to 2010 by the institutional scientific committee. He serves as a reviewer in international journals. His research interests focus on the molecular mechanisms of atherosclerosis, 3D modeling and computational fluid dynamics of coronary flow, as well as the pathophysiology of the vulnerable plaque.

Thanjavur K.M. Bragadeesh, MRCP (UK), completed his undergraduate medical school education at the Madras Medical College, Madras, India before coming to the UK for postgraduate training in 1995.

He completed general medicine training in Scotland and moved to England for cardiology training as registrar first at Ipswich and then at Castle Hill hospital in Cottingham. As part of his cardiology training he took time to do research as cardiovascular imaging research fellow at the University of Virginia, USA, and subsequently at the Oregon Health Sciences University as a fellow in Cardiac MR and Cardiac CT. He is currently at Castle Hill hospital as Consultant Cardiologist with expertise in cardiac imaging.

Emmanouil S. Brilakis, MD, PhD, FACC, FAHA, FESC, FSCAI, is Director of the Cardiac Catheterization Laboratories at VA North Texas Healthcare System and an Associate Professor of Medicine at University of Texas Southwestern Medical School. After graduating from Lycee Leonin de Patissia, Dr. Brilakis received his medical degree from the National Kapodistrian University of Athens, Greece. He trained in Internal Medicine, Cardiovascular Diseases and Interventional Cardiology at the Mayo Clinic. He also completed a Master's in Clinical Research at the Mayo Clinic and a PhD in Clinical Research at the National Kapodistrian University of Athens, Greece. Since 2004 he has been an interventional cardiologist at VA North Texas Healthcare System where he leads a very active clinical trial research group. His research interests include the prevention and treatment of saphenous vein graft disease, percutaneous treatment of chronic total occlusions, intracoronary imaging, and antiplatelet treatment optimization post coronary stenting. Dr. Brilakis has authored or co-authored over 130 peer-reviewed articles. His receives funding by the National Institutes of Health and the Department of Veterans Affairs. He is a reviewer for several journals and grant agencies and has lectured at several institutions within the United States and abroad.

Salvatore Brugaletta was born in Ragusa on February 24th 1979. He graduated "cum laude" in Medicine in 2003 at the Catholic University of Rome. In 2007 he gained his cardiology degree "cum laude" at the Catholic University in Rome, under the supervision of Prof. Filippo Crea. In 2008 he won a research grant from EAPCI and he moved to Spain, when he works together with Manel Sabaté as fellow in interventional cardiology. In 2010 he moved as Research Fellow to the Thoraxcenter in Rotterdam, where under the supervision of Prof. Patrick W. Serruys he was involved in the field of new bioresorbable vascular scaffolds and of new intra-coronary imaging techniques, such as Lipiscan. From 2011 he is staff member of the Interventional Cardiology Unit at the "Hospital Clinic i provincial" de Barcelona.

Nico Bruining studied Technical Computer Sciences at the Hogeschool Rotterdam and started his career at the Thoraxcenter (the current department of cardiology of the Erasmus Medical center in Rotterdam, The Netherlands) in 1985 within the heart catherization laboratory, where he was employed as technician. In 1993 he moved to the Department of Clinical and Experimental Informatics, specializing in cardiovascular imaging, invasive as well as non-invasive, with as focus clinical applications. He received his Ph.D. in 1998 at the Erasmus University, in Rotterdam, The Netherlands, on a thesis with as topic: "Quantitative 3-D Echocardiography of The Heart and The Coronary Vessels." During the last decade at the Thoraxcenter, he has focused on the development of new quantitative analysis techniques to evaluate new interventional therapies, including "first in man" trials of the so-called the Cypher stent and, currently, the bioabsorbable stent of Abbott. He works with visiting Master and PhD students on projects and training. He is author of over more than 200 research papers, books chapters, conference proceedings, and abstracts, is a regular reviewer for a dozen scientific medical journals, is the past-chairman of the working group of computers in cardiology of the European Society of Cardiology (ESC) and is a member of the council for cardiovascular imaging of the ESC.

Yiannis S. Chatzizisis, MD, PhD is a clinical fellow in Cardiovascular Medicine at AHEPA University Hospital, Aristotle University Medical School, Thessaloniki, Greece. In 2002 he received the MD degree from Aristotle University Medical School, Thessaloniki, Greece and in 2004, the MSc degree from the same university. In 2005 he completed his residency in Internal Medicine in AHEPA University Hospital, Thessaloniki, Greece. From 2005 to 2008 he has been with the Cardiovascular Division at Brigham and Women's Hospital, Harvard Medical School and with Harvard-MIT Division of Health Sciences and Technology, Massachusetts Institute of Technology as Research Fellow. In 2009 he received his PhD from Aristotle University of Thessaloniki. He has been a Research Scientist in the Cardiovascular Engineering and Atherosclerosis Laboratory of Aristotle University Medical School for the last ten years. He is recipient of many national and international awards including the Young Investigators Award by European Society of Cardiology, the Young Investigators Award by European Atherosclerosis Society, and the Merit Award for Young Investigators by American Heart Association. He has been supported by research grants from national, European, and American funding bodies, such as European Commission, Hellenic Heart Foundation, George D. Behrakis Foundation, Hellenic Harvard Foundation, Propondis Foundation, Alexander S. Onassis Foundation, AG Leventis Foundation, Hellenic Atherosclerosis Society, Greek State Scholarships Foundation, Boston Scientific Inc., and Novartis Pharmaceuticals Inc., among others. He serves as manuscript reviewer for *Circulation, Circulation Research, Circulation Cardiovascular Imaging, Atherosclerosis, Heart, International Journal of Cardiology,* and *American Journal of Cardiology*, among others. His research is focused on the molecular biology of atherosclerosis, cardiovascular fluid dynamics, and cardiovascular imaging.

Alessandro Di Giorgio received the MD degree with distinction from the University of Catania and the Fellowship in Cardiology. He works as Interventional Cardiologist at Ferrarotto Hospital in Catania, Italy. Alessandro Di Giorgio is co-author of several publications on national and international journals (*Heart, Eurointervention, Interv Cardiology,* and others), mainly on interventional cardiology and on the clinical and research application of intravascular imaging techniques.

Roberto Diletti was born on 31st May, 1980, in Rieti, Italy. He graduated in Medicine from University of Perugia in 2006 with *summa cum laude* and completed his training in Cardiology in 2011. He is currently attending a Research Fellowship in the catheterization laboratory of the Thoraxcenter, Erasmus Medical Centre in Rotterdam, under the supervision of Prof. Patrick Serruys. In the field of interventional cardiology, his special areas of interest are intravascular imaging, coronary physiology, and development of the new generation of the Bioresorbable Vascular Scaffolds. He is the author of several articles on international peer-reviewed scientific journals. He is member of the Italian Society of Cardiology (SIC), of the National Association of Hospital Cardiologists (A.N.M.C.O) and of the Italian Resuscitation Council (IRC). He has taken part in various European Interventional Cardiology courses. He is winner of The European Association of Percutaneous Cardiovascular Interventions (EAPCI) Interventional Cardiology Research Grant 2011, with a scientific contribution, entitled "OCT Light Intensity Analysis. A New Tool for the Detection of Bioresorbable Vascular Scaffold Tissue Coverage."

Hector Manuel Garcia-Garcia is an Interventional Cardiologist working at Erasmus Medical Center, Rotterdam, The Netherlands. He is also Supervising Cardiologist of Intravascular Imaging at Cardialysis (an academic research organization) in Rotterdam. In 1997, as a *summa cum laude* graduate of the Medical School of University Autonoma of Guadalajara in Mexico, Dr Garcia-Garcia started his internal medicine training in Medical Center "Siglo XXI" and continued his training in Cardiology in the National Institute of Cardiology "Ignacio Chavez." In 2004, he did 2 years training in Interventional Cardiology. In 2006 the Erasmus University Rotterdam granted the Master in Science degree to him and in 2009 the doctoral degree. He has published ~150 articles in peer-reviewed journals and more than 10 book chapters in renowned cardiology books (i.e. Hurst the Heart). His main research topics are intravascular imaging and coronary atherosclerosis.

Scot Garg is a Consultant Interventional Cardiologist at the Royal Blackburn Hospital, Blackburn, UK. He qualified from the University of Manchester in 1999, and following membership of the Royal College of Physicians in 2002, completed cardiology training in East Yorkshire, UK with a specialist interest in coronary intervention. He worked for 18-months at the Thoraxcenter, Rotterdam between 2008 and 2010, undertaking research in new coronary stents and the risk stratification of patients treated by PCI. His PhD thesis, "Risk Stratification in Patients Undergoing Percutaneous Coronary Revascularization," was awarded *cum laude* at the Erasmus University, Rotterdam in 2011.

George D. Giannoglou, MD, PhD: Professor of Cardiology in AHEPA University General Hospital, Aristotle University Medical School, Thessaloniki, Greece. In 1971 he received the MD degree from Aristotle University Medical School, Thessaloniki, Greece and in 1985 he received his PhD from Aristotle University of Thessaloniki. His scientific course: Lecturer in 1990, Assistant Professor in 1994, Associate Professor in 2002 and Professor in 2007. He is founder of the Cardiovascular Engineering and Atherosclerosis Laboratory in the 1st University Cardiology Department, AHEPA University Hospital. He is involved with research in atherosclerosis, cardiovascular imaging, and cardiology.

Angela Hoye MB ChB, PhD is a Senior Lecturer and practising Interventional Cardiologist in the United Kingdom. She trained initially in the United Kingdom before undertaking two years as a clinical Research Fellow working in Rotterdam under the mentorship of Prof. Patrick Serruys (2002-2004). During this period she gained experience in performing complex coronary intervention with a high proportion of cases undertaken with adjunctive intra-vascular imaging. She currently works in Castle Hill Hospital at the University of Hull, UK.

Fabrizio Imola received the MD degree with distinction from the University of Rome and Fellowship in Cardiology, *summa cum laude* at the University of Rome. He now works in the Interventional Cardiology department of the San Giovanni Hospital in Rome, and is involved in research in coronary atherosclerosis at Center of Rome Heart Research. Fabrizio Imola is author and co-author of over 30 publications on national and international journals (*Circulation, European Heart Journal, American Heart Journal, EuroIntervention, JACC Intv, Heart,* and others), mainly on interventional cardiology and on the clinical and research application of intravascular imaging techniques.

Antonios Karanasos has worked as a Research Fellow in Interventional Cardiology in the 1st Department of Cardiology, University of Athens, Hippokration Hospital since 2007, and his research field includes evaluation of atherosclerosis progression, detection of plaque inflammatory activation, and research of plaque pathophysiology by intravascular imaging with optical coherence tomography. He is currently developing his thesis on the association of plaque morphology with the outcome of thrombolysis.

Sotirios A. Katranas, MD is a Resident Doctor in Cardiology Department, AHEPA University Hospital, Aristotle University Medical School, Thessaloniki, Greece. In 2005 he received the MD degree from Aristotle University Medical School, Thessaloniki, Greece. In 2010 he completed his residency in Internal Medicine in Hospital of Infectious Diseases, Thessaloniki, Greece. From 2009 he has been working on computed tomography angiography, while he is candidate on receiving a PhD title from Aristotle University of Thessaloniki. He has been a Research Scientist in the Cardiovascular Engineering and Atherosclerosis Laboratory of Aristotle University Medical School for the last three years. He has been supported by research grant from Hellenic State Scholarships Foundation and distinction grant from Greek Church. His research is focused on the molecular biology of atherosclerosis, computational fluid dynamics, and cardiovascular imaging.

Ourania Katsarou, MD., is a PhD Candidate with focus: "Interaction between atherosclerotic plaque characteristics and stent apposition in patients undergoing percutaneous coronary intervention." Activities include: participation in 11 abstracts in international and Greek cardiology meetings (2007- today). She contributed in the writing of 4 chapters of the book ' Valvular Heart Disease' (in Greek)(2009). Dr. Katsarou graduated from Medical School of Athens in 2007. She was admitted 1st rank in scholarship examinations and awarded tuitions scholarship for 6 years (2001). Honors include: 3rd Young Scientists' Prize in the 30th National Cardiology Congress of Greece for the paper: "Association of residual platelet activity after clopidogrel loading with intracoronary thrombus and myocardial necrosis in PCI treated patients with AMI" (in Greek) (2008).

Konstantinos C. Koskinas received the M.D. degree in 2002 and the MSc degree in 2006 with distinction from the Aristotle University Medical School, Thessaloniki, Greece. He completed a postdoctoral research fellowship at Brigham and Women's Hospital, Harvard Medical School, Boston, MA, USA. He is currently a Cardiology clinical fellow at Hippocrateion University Hospital, Thessaloniki, Greece. His research interests include coronary hemodynamics, endothelial function, intravascular ultrasound and bioengineering, and mechanism of atherosclerosis.

Dimitris Koutsouris was born in Serres, Greece in 1955. He received his Diploma in Electrical Engineering in 1978 (Greece), DEA in Biomechanics in 1979 (France), Doctorat in Genie Biologie Medicale (France), Doctorat d' Etat in Biomedical Engineering 1984 (France). Since 1986 he was Research Associate on the USC (Los Angeles), Renè Dèscartes (Paris), and Assoc. Professor at the Dept. of Electrical & Computers Engineering of National Technical University of Athens. He is currently Professor and Head of the Biomedical Engineering Laboratory. He has published over 150 research articles and book chapters and more than 350 peer reviewed conference communications. He has been the former elected President of the Hellenic Society of Biomedical Technology, HL7 Hellas and Chairman at the School of Electrical and Computer Engineering. Prof. D. Koutsouris has been principal investigator in more than 100 European and National Research programs, especially in the field of telematics and informatics in healthcare. His work has received more than 1800 citations.

Poay Huan Loh was born in Alor Setar, Malaysia. He graduated from the University College Dublin, Ireland in 1998 and obtained the Membership of the Royal Colleague of Physician (UK) in 2001. He received his basic medical and cardiology training in the United Kingdom. Dr. Loh's subspecialty interest is in the field of interventional cardiology, and he is undergoing fellowship training in trans-catheter structural and valvular heart disease intervention in Copenhagen, Denmark. He has research interest in the treatment of patients with refractory angina and enhanced external counterpulsation (EECP), anaesthetic consideration in patients undergoing trans-catheter aortic valve implantation (TAVI) and risk stratification using multiple biomarkers in patients with left ventricular systolic dysfunction.

Sean P. Madden is currently Principal Scientist of Analytical Instrumentation and Business Development at InfraReDx, Inc. He was a key member of a multifunctional team that devised and validated the technology that led to the FDA approval of the first device to detect lipid core plaques in the coronary arteries. He continues to lead efforts to refine the instrument and algorithm, design clinical trials to demonstrate its efficacy, and cultivate lipid core plaque detection technology as a tool for development of novel cardiovascular therapies. He has worked on utilizing complex data analysis with novel spectroscopic instrumentation to solve important problems for the past fifteen years, in diverse fields including drug discovery, retina characterization, non-invasive glucose measurement, and detection of coronary lipid core plaques.

Maria Teresa Mallus received the MD degree with distinction from the University of Rome and Fellowship in Cardiology, *summa cum laude* at the University of Rome, and PhD degree at the University of Rome. She now works in the Interventional Cardiology of the San Giovanni Hospital in Rome, and is involved in research in coronary atherosclerosis at Center Rome Heart Research. Maria Teresa Mallus is author and co-author of over 35 publications on national and international journals (*Circulation, European Heart Journal, American Heart Journal, EuroIntervention, JACC Intv, Heart,* and others), mainly on interventional cardiology and on the clinical and research application of intravascular imaging techniques.

James E. Muller serves as CEO and Chief Medical Officer of InfraReDx, Inc., the company that developed the LipiScan device that has been approved by the FDA for detection of lipid-core plaque. Dr. Muller formerly served as a Professor of Medicine at the Harvard Medical School where he conducted research for over 25 years on the causes of acute coronary syndromes. In 1989, Dr. Muller, Dr. Stone, and Dr. Tofler introduced the term "vulnerable plaque" to describe those plaques likely to disrupt and cause disease onset. Dr. Muller co-founded InfraReDx in 1998 after a detailed search to find the optimal technology to identify lipid-core containing coronary artery plaques that are suspected to be vulnerable plaques. He is the author of a multiple articles related to technical approaches that are under study for the identification of vulnerable plaque, the leading cause of death in developed countries.

Rajesh Nair studied Medicine in University of Kerala, India and obtained membership from the Royal College of Physicians in Edinburgh, UK. He subsequently did Cardiology training in Leeds University Hospitals NHS Trust and coronary artery intervention at Castle Hill Hospital, England. Dr. Nair did clinical and basic sciences research at the Baker Heart research institute, Melbourne, Australia for 3 years. He did his fellowship in structural heart disease intervention at Rigshosiptalet, Copenhagen. Dr. Nair works as a Consultant Cardiologist at Waikato Hospital, Hamilton, New Zealand.

Michail I. Papafaklis was born in Athens, Greece, in 1978. He graduated from the Medical School, University of Ioannina in 2002, and he was awarded with Distinction his PhD degree in Cardiology from the Medical School, University of Ioannina in 2008. He currently holds an appointment as a Postdoctoral Research Fellow at the Brigham and Women's Hospital, Harvard Medical School in Boston, USA. His research interests focus on hemodynamics, invasive and non-invasive imaging of coronary arteries, biomedical engineering, interventional cardiology, and pathophysiology and molecular mechanisms of atherosclerosis.

Nikolaos D. Papamichael, MD, is currently a Consultant Cardiologist at the General Hospital of Arta (Northwestern Greece) providing clinical service, which includes the responsibility for the prevention, diagnosis, and treatment of wide range of illness. He has a special interest in Cardiac Imaging and Echocardiography. He graduated from the Medical School of the University of Ioannina, Ioannina, Greece receiving his M.D. degree in 2000. He was awarded his Doctorate Diploma (Ph.D. equivalent) in 2009 from the Medical School of the University of Ioannina after extensive research. He is fully and actively involved in most research projects of the Department of Cardiology of the University of Ioannina. His research interests include coagulation and platelets, vascular endothelial function, heart failure, echocardiography, cardiac imaging, and intravascular ultrasound.

Francesco Prati received the MD degree with distinction from the University of Rome and Fellowship in Cardiology, *summa cum laude*, at the University of Bologna. He is now Chief of the Interventional Cardiology of the San Giovanni Hospital in Rome, President of the CLI Foundation, and Scientific Director of the research Center Rome Heart Research. Francesco Prati is author and co-author of over 140 publications on national and international journals (*Circulation, European Heart Journal, American Heart Journal, EuroIntervention, JACC Intv, Heart*, and others), mainly on interventional cardiology and on the clinical and research application of intravascular imaging techniques.

Michael Rees is the Professor of Cardiovascular Studies at Bangor University. He is also a Consultant Cardio-Radiologist and Nuclear Medicine Specialist in the Betsi Cadwalladr University Health Board. He has research interests in cardiovascular imaging and intervention and has published over 100 peer reviewed papers and book chapters in these subjects. He has lectured extensively internationally. He is the current President of the European Society of Cardiac Radiology and co founder of that society. He is Co-Chair of the Medical Academic Staff Committee of the BMA and previously served as Chair of that committee. He is on the editorial Board of the International Journal of Cardiovascular Imaging and Insights into Imaging. He is a member of the UK Health Education Advisory Committee and the Health Education National Strategic Exchange. He has previously held Chairs at the University of Bristol and Keele University and a consulting Chair at Stanford University California. He is a visiting Professor at the University of Ioanina Greece. He founded the School of Medical Sciences at Bangor University and served as the Head of School. He has been involved in clinical academic training in England and Wales and has served on the NIHR faculty development committee and the Clinical Academic Careers Panel UK.

Evelyn Regar is Interventional Cardiologist and Associate Professor at the Thoraxcenter, Erasmus MC, in Rotterdam. Her research interest is in invasive coronary imaging and diagnostics, specifically the application of innovative technologies to improve the understanding of atherosclerotic plaque progression over time and the impact of novel treatment strategies. Regar originates from Munich, Germany. After completing the medical studies at the Technical University in Munich, she worked at the Medizinische Klinik Innenstadt, Ludwig-Maximilians University in Munich in internal medicine and cardiology, where she holds an appointment as associate professor. Regar completed a thesis on "Intravascular ultrasound imaging in patients with coronary artery disease and coronary Stents" at the Technical University, Munich, Germany and holds a PhD title from the Erasmus University, Rotterdam, the Netherlands on "Prevention of restenosis in coronary arteries: Ionic radiation, non-ionic radiation and drug eluting stents." Regar is co-organizer of the "International working group on OCT standardization and validation," director of training courses in intracoronary OCT, organizer and supervising cardiologist for international core laboratory for intracoronary optical coherence tomography (Cardialysis, Rotterdam, The Netherlands; 2007-2010). Regar is Fellow of the European Society of Cardiology (FESC), member of the Dutch Society for Cardiology (NVC), the German Society for Cardiology (DFK), member of women in innovation (WIN) and served as a member of the German Working Group for Health Technology Assessment (1998-2000). Regar authored of more than 150 original articles in peer-reviewed major cardiology journals, more than 30 book chapters, and served as (co-) editor for various books on interventional cardiology.

Antonis I. Sakellarios was born in Kozani, Greece, in 1983. He is now doing his PhD on "Mathematical modeling of atherosclerotic plaque development" at the University of Ioannina, at the Department of Materials Science and Engineering. He studied Biology at the University of Ioannina, Department of Biological Applications and Technology. His research interests focus on atherosclerosis, plaque development, biological and mechanical factors which affect its progress, and computational modeling of these procedures.

Patrick W. Serruys is Professor of Interventional Cardiology at the Interuniversity Cardiological Institute of the Netherlands (1988-1998), and the Erasmus University. Since 1980 he has been Director of the Clinical Research Program of the Catheterization Laboratory, Thoraxcenter, Erasmus University, Rotterdam, The Netherlands and since 1997 the Head of the Interventional Department, Heartcenter Rotterdam. He is a Fellow of the American College of Cardiology and a Fellow of the European Society of Cardiology and scientific council of the International College of Angiology. He is the author or coauthor of over 1600 papers and editor or coeditor of 37 books, and a member of 20 Editorial Boards of Scientific Journals. Dr. Serruys received the M.D. degree (1972) from the Catholic University of Louvain, Louvain, Belgium and his PhD degree (1986) from the Erasmus University, Rotterdam, The Netherlands. He has been associate editor of *Circulation* for Europe for five years and he co-edited the Textbook of Cardiology of the European Society of Cardiology. In 1996 he received the TCT Career Achievement Award and in 1997 he was awarded the Wenkebach Prize of the Dutch Heart Foundation. In 2000 he was awarded the Gruentzig Award of the European Society of Cardiology. In 2001 he held the Paul Dudley White Lecture at the American Heart Association in the USA. In 2004 he received the Andreas Gruentzig Award of the Swiss Society of Cardiology. In 2005 he held the 4th International Lecture at the AHA and Mikamo Lecture at the Japanese Heart Association. In 2006 he received the highest award of the Clinical Council of the American Heart Association: the James Herrick Award. In 2007 he received the Arrigo Recordati International Prize (Italy) and the ICI Achievement Award (bestowed by the President of Israel – Shimon Perez). In 2008 he received the Einthoven Penning (Leiden). In 2009 he became Doctor Honoris Causa from the University of Athens. In 2011 he received the Lifetime Achievement Award, bestowed by the American College of Cardiology, in recognition of many years of service and invaluable contributions to the ACC.

Panagiotis K. Siogkas was born in Athens, Greece, in 1982. He received his diploma in Mechanical and Aeronautical Engineering from the University of Patras Polytechnic School, Greece, in 2009. He is currently a PhD candidate in the field of Biomedical Engineering in the Department of Material Science Engineering in the University of Ioannina. More particularly, his research focuses on blood flow modeling in patient-specific 3-dimensional arterial models with deformable walls.

Lars Søndergaard was born in Denmark in 1961. He graduated from the University of Copenhagen, Denmark in 1988. Dr. Søndergaard completed his basic medical and cardiology training in Denmark, during which period he was also granted a PhD degree for his research in the quantification of flow using magnetic resonance phase mapping at the Danish Centre for Magnetic Resonance, Hvidovre Hospital. He embarked on paediatric cardiology and adult congenital heart disease subspecialty training in the Great Ormond Street Hospital for the Sick Children and Middlesex hospital in 1999. Soon after his return to Denmark, he was appointed as a Consultant Cardiologist for adult congenital heart disease and paediatric cardiology in 2003 with a special interest in structural and valvular intervention in Rigshospitalet University Hospital, Copenhagen. Dr. Søndergaard is well recognised in his field of interest and pioneer to many of the trans-catheter interventional procedures and devices in Denmark. He is the Proctor for many of these procedures and also runs regular training workshops using including intra-cardiac echocardiogram using animal model . He is also active in clinical research and is the principal or co-investigator for multiple single- and multi-centre clinical trials and taking part in the development of some new devices. There are also multiple PhD research fellows working under the auspice of Dr. Søndergaard in the fields of Eisenmanger's Syndrome and uni-ventricle and the use of endothelin receptor antagonists and phosphodiesterase-5 inhibitors in these patients.

Christodoulos Stefanadis is the Professor of Cardiology and Head of the 1st Department of Cardiology of the University of Athens, Athens Medical School at Hippokration Hospital. He has also served as the head of the Medical School of the University of Athens, and as the Chairman of the Hellenic Society of Cardiology and the Hellenic College of Cardiology. His main fields of research are the identification and passivation of the vulnerable atherosclerotic plaque and the retrograde nontransseptal balloon mitral valvuloplasty. He has over 950 publications in peer reviewed journals.

Stephen Sum is a Research Scientist and Director of Biomedical Systems at InfraReDx. He holds undergraduate and graduate degrees in Chemistry, Mathematics and Information and Systems Science, including a Ph.D. in Analytical Chemistry from the University of Delaware where he specialized in Chemometrics. Dr. Sum's work at InfraReDx is centered on the development of coronary lipid core plaque detection algorithms and subsystems for intravascular spectroscopic and ultrasonic devices.

Simon Thackray MD, MRCP, undertook undergraduate training in St George's Hospotal, London before moving to the North on England to pursue specialty training and research in Hull. His Doctoral thesis was British Heart Foundation funded looking at the interaction between ventricular pacing and left ventricular performance - this led to a number of publications. Subsequent research interests branched into intra-coronary imaging after a period spent as a senior fellow at the Ludwig-Maximillion University, Munich. Interventional training was completed at the National Heart Centre in Singapore and in Hull before being appointed as an interventional cardiologist in 2005 in Hull. He has subsequently become clinical lead for the department of cardiology, and is program lead for the renal denervation therapy service in Hull. Current research interests are renal denervation, structural cardiac intervention, and health economics.

Attila Thury is an Associate Professor at the Invasive Cardiology Unit of the Cardiology Center of University of Szeged, Hungary. He has been serving as a Senior Interventional Cardiologist since 2006. After achieving medical diploma (MD) at the University of Szeged, he has been working at the Cardiology Center, where completed internal medicine, then cardiology training. He worked as a research fellow of the Thoraxcenter, Erasmus Medical Center, Rotterdam in 2000 under the supervision of Professor Patrick W. Serruys, then in 2003-2005 he worked as a post-doc with the Biomedical Engineering group of the Thoraxcenter. He defended doctoral thesis at the University of Szeged titled "Restenosis after percutanous coronary intervention: mechanisms and prevention." His research interest is invasive coronary imaging, specifically intravascular ultrasound for diagnosing vulnerable plaque. Also, he carried out research in hemodynamic biomechanical factors in vascular biology, and coronary multislice computed tomography. Thury is Member the European Association of Percutaneous Cardiovascular Intervention since 2006 and the nucleus of the Hungarian Working Group on Interventional Cardiology and secretary of Cardiac CT WG of the Hungarian Society of Cardiology. He authored more than 30 original articles in peer-reviewed cardiology journals, and 4 book chapters.

Konstantinos Toutouzas is an Assistant Professor of Cardiology in the 1st Department of Cardiology, University of Athens, Hippokration Hospital. He has performed research on the fields of percutaneous cononary intervention, evaluation of plaque inflammatory activation by intracoronary thermography, intravascular imaging by optical coherence tomography and intravascular ultrasound, and the development of a new method for non-invasive assessment of thermal heterogeneity in atherosclerosis. He has over 150 publications in peer reviewed journals.

Ann Tweddel, a graduate of Glasgow University trained at Glasgow Royal Infirmary, where she worked as a Junior Doctor and subsequently as a Consultant Transplant Physician. Following a short period working in Professor Kubler's laboratory in the University of Heidelberg on microvascular flow, she was appointed as Director of Nuclear Cardiology at University Hospital of Wales, Cardiff. A short period as visiting Professor at Stanford University allowed for experience in Positron Emmission Tomography Imaging, and subsequent appointment as Consultant Cardiologist at Hull and East Yorkshire NHS Trust and Honorary Senior Lecturer at Hull University. Interests include cardiovascular imaging, microvascular flow, and workflow management.

Manolis Vavouranakis is Assistant Professor of Cardiology in National & Kapodistrian University of Athens Medical School 1st Department of Cardiology, Hippokration Hospital. He has extensive experience in diagnostic and therapeutic Interventional Cardiology. He is in charge of the Biomedical Engineering Unit at Hippokration Hospital. He is a fellow of SCAI, ACC, and ESC. His research and clinical interests are focused in the field of Interventional Cardiology and includes Intravascular Ultrasound, Percutaneous Coronary Interventions, and treatment of structural heart disease. He has more than 100 publications in peer review journals. He has presented his work in international scientific meetings.

Index